Religion and Change in Modern Britain

D0025722

Since 1945 the story of religion in Britain is one of diversity and change. This book offers an unparalleled guide to religion in contemporary Britain. It examines:

- the increasingly important role played by non-Christian communities
- the growth of secularism and the rise of alternative spiritualities
- religion and media, welfare and education, politics and law
- religious change from cultural and social perspectives.

Survey chapters are combined with contemporary case study material to give students a broad framework and a detailed understanding of religion on the ground. The text is accompanied by photographs and a companion website.

Linda Woodhead is Professor of Sociology of Religion at Lancaster University and Director of the AHRC/ESRC Religion and Society Research Programme. She is co-editor of *Religions in the Modern World* (2nd edition, Routledge 2009) and author of several books including *A Sociology of Religious Emotion* (with Ole Riis, 2010) and *The Spiritual Revolution* (with Paul Heelas, 2005).

Rebecca Catto is a Research Associate at Lancaster University, supporting the Religion and Society Programme. Her publications focus on religion and globalization, secularism and non-religious identities.

Religion and Change in Modern Britain

Edited by Linda Woodhead and Rebecca Catto

Routledge
Taylor & Francis Group

LONDON AND NEW YORK

First published in 2012
by Routledge
2 Park Square, Milton Park, Abingdon, Oxon OX14 4RN

Simultaneously published in the USA and Canada
by Routledge
711 Third Avenue, New York, NY 10017

Routledge is an imprint of the Taylor & Francis Group, an informa business

British Library Cataloguing in Publication Data
A catalogue record for this book is available from the British Library

Library of Congress Cataloging in Publication Data
A catalog record for this book has been requested

ISBN: 978-0-415-57580-5 (hbk)
ISBN: 978-0-415-57581-2 (pbk)
ISBN: 978-0-203-13064-3 (ebk)

Typeset in Goudy
by FiSH Books, Enfield

Printed and bound in Great Britain by
CPI Antony Rowe, Chippenham, Wiltshire

Contents

List of figures and tables

Figures

Tables

List of plates

People

Events

Objects, places and spaces

Notes on contributors

Elisabeth Arweck is Senior Research Fellow at the University of Warwick and Editor of the *Journal of Contemporary Religion*. She has conducted research on New Religious Movements, religion and education, alternative educational programmes, mixed-faith families, religious socialization and religious diversity. She is Senior Research Fellow on the AHRC/ESRC Religion and Society funded project 'Young People's Attitudes to Religious Diversity'.

James A. Beckford is Professor Emeritus of Sociology at the University of Warwick. He has conducted research on religious organizations, Jehovah's Witnesses, controversial new religious movements, church–state relations, religion in prisons and theoretical ideas about religion. He has also served as a member of the Commissioning Panel for the AHRC/ESRC Religion and Society Programme.

Robert Bluck (now retired) was Associate Lecturer in Religious Studies at The Open University. His doctoral research on Buddhism in Britain was published as *British Buddhism* (2006) and in several articles and book chapters. He has been a practising Buddhist for 40 years in the Theravada and Zen traditions.

Ralf Brand is Senior Lecturer in Architectural Studies at the University of Manchester's Architecture Research Centre (MARC). He studies the 'co-evolution' of social and material change and applies this angle as Principal Investigator on the AHRC/ESRC Religion and Society funded project 'Multi-Faith Spaces – Symptoms and Agents of Religious and Social Change'.

Callum Brown is Professor of Religious and Cultural History at the University of Dundee. He has published ten books and more than 50 articles and book chapters, including *The Death of Christian Britain* (2nd edn 2009) and *Religion and Society in Twentieth-Century Britain* (2005).

Rebecca Catto is Research Associate for the AHRC/ESRC Religion and Society Programme at Lancaster University. She has published on contemporary non-Western Christian missions to the UK, religion in Britain, and law and the sociology of religion. She has advised the Equality and Human Rights Commission on religion or belief and is currently Principal Investigator on 'The Young Atheists Research Project', funded by the Jacobs Foundation.

Mark Chapman is Vice-Principal of Ripon College Cuddesdon, Oxford, Reader in Modern Theology at the University of Oxford and Visiting Professor at Oxford Brookes University. His most recent books are *Anglican Theology* (2012), *Doing God: Religion and*

Public Policy in Brown's Britain (2008) and *Bishops, Saints and Politics: Anglican Studies* (2007). He has written widely on modern church history and theology. He is also a Church of England priest ministering in a group of parishes near Oxford.

Yuko Chiba studied at Queen's University Belfast, London School of Economics and University of Ulster. Her research interests include the rights of minority belief people and persons with disabilities. She is a former Research Fellow on the AHRC/ESRC Religion and Society funded project 'Opting Out of Religious Education: The Views of Young People from Minority Belief Backgrounds' at the School of Law, Queen's University Belfast.

Douglas J. Davies is now Professor in the Study of Religion at Durham University and before that was a professor at Nottingham University. As an anthropologist and theologian he has published many books on Mormons, Anglicans, Death Studies and on historical-theoretical aspects of religious studies. He holds the higher Oxford Doctor of Letters degree, is an Honorary Doctor of Theology from Uppsala University, and an Academician of the Academy of Social Sciences. He has been Principal Investigator on the AHRC/ESRC Religion and Society funded collaborative studentship 'British Woodland Burial: Its Theological, Ecological and Social Values'.

Adam Dinham is Reader in Religion and Society at Goldsmiths, University of London. He is qualified as a social worker and has practised in Social Work and Community Development in city contexts. He is policy advisor to a number of faith-based agencies and policy bodies, and has advised central government on issues of public faith. He is Director of the Faiths and Civil Society Unit, Goldsmiths, University of London and has published widely on faith in the public realm. He is also Principal Investigator on the AHRC/ESRC Religion and Society funded research network 'FaithXchange'.

Gladys Ganiel is Lecturer in Conflict Resolution and Reconciliation at Trinity College Dublin at Belfast (the Irish School of Ecumenics). She is the author of *Evangelicalism and Conflict in Northern Ireland* (2008) and co-author, with Claire Mitchell, of *Evangelical Journeys: Choice and Change in a Northern Irish Religious Subculture* (2011). She has also published on religion and politics in Zimbabwe and South Africa, charismatic Christianity, the emerging church and the Democratic Unionist Party. She blogs at www.gladysganiel.com.

Sophie Gilliat-Ray is Reader in Religious and Theological Studies at Cardiff University, and Founding Director of the Islam-UK Centre, also at Cardiff University. She is the author of numerous books and journal articles concerned with religion in British public life, and the training and education of religious professionals. Her new book *Understanding Muslim Chaplaincy* is due for publication in 2013, arising from the AHRC/ESRC Religion and Society funded project 'Leadership and Capacity Building in the British Muslim Community' on which she is Principal Investigator.

David J. Graham is Director of Social and Demographic Research at the Institute for Jewish Policy Research, London, and Honorary Research Associate at the Department of Hebrew, Biblical and Jewish Studies, University of Sydney. He is a Board member of the Association of Social Scientific Study of Jewry (ASSJ) and was formerly Senior Researcher at the Board of Deputies of British Jews. He has written widely on demographic, geographic and sociological aspects of Britain's Jewish population and recently (2008) completed his DPhil on this topic at the University of Oxford under the supervision of Professor Ceri Peach. He is currently working on a series of national quantitative surveys of Britain's Jewish community.

Mathew Guest is Senior Lecturer in the Sociology of Religion at Durham University. He has published widely on Christianity in late modern Western cultures, focusing especially on the evangelical movement, and is the author of *Evangelical Identity and Contemporary Culture* (2007) and *Bishops, Wives and Children: Spiritual Capital Across the Generations* (with Douglas Davies, 2007). He is Principal Investigator for 'Christianity and the University Experience in Contemporary England', funded by the AHRC/ESRC Religion and Society Programme.

Graham Harvey is Reader in Religious Studies at The Open University, with research interests in the performance, material cultures and literatures of Jews, Pagans and indigenous peoples. His publications include *Religions in Focus: New Approaches to Tradition and Contemporary Practices* (2009), *Listening People, Speaking Earth: Contemporary Paganism* (2nd edn, 2007), *Animism: Respecting the Living World* (2006), *Researching Paganisms* (co-edited with Jenny Blain and Douglas Ezzy, 2004) and *The A to Z of Shamanism* (co-authored with Robert Wallis, 2010).

Robert Jackson is Professor of Religions and Education at the University of Warwick and Director of the Warwick Religions and Education Research Unit. He is also Professor of Religious Diversity and Education at the European Wergeland Centre, Oslo. His books include *Rethinking Religious Education and Plurality: Issues in Diversity and Pedagogy* (2004). He is Principal Investigator on the AHRC/ESRC Religion and Society project 'Young People's Attitudes to Religious Diversity' and a member of the Programme's Steering Committee.

Sarah Johnsen is Senior Research Fellow at Heriot-Watt University, Edinburgh. Her main research interests include homelessness and street culture (begging, street drinking and street-based sex work), the role of faith-based organizations in the provision of social welfare, and ethical issues in research involving vulnerable groups. She is co-author of *Swept up Lives? Re-envisioning the Homeless City* (with Paul Cloke and Jon May, 2010) and contributed to *Homelessness in the UK: Problems and Solutions* (edited by Suzanne Fitzpatrick, Deborah Quilgars and Nicholas Pleace, 2009). She has been Principal Investigator on AHRC/ESRC Religion and Society funded project 'The Difference that "Faith" Makes'.

Peter Jones is Professor of Political Philosophy at the University of Newcastle. He has written on many different aspects of rights, including human rights, group rights, democratic rights, welfare rights and rights of free expression. His published work has also ranged over a number of other subjects, including toleration, identity, recognition, cultural diversity, democracy, global justice, international society and the nature of liberalism. He has been Principal Investigator on the AHRC/ESRC Religion and Society funded research network 'Religion, Discrimination and Accommodation'.

Kim Knott is Professor of Religious Studies at the University of Leeds, and was Director of AHRC's 'Diasporas, Migration and Identities' Programme from 2005 to 2011. She participated in the AHRC/ESRC Religion and Society Programme, completing a replication of a project (first carried out in the 1980s) on religion and the secular sacred in the British media. A co-authored book is forthcoming. Her previous books include *Diasporas: Concepts, Intersections, Identities* (co-edited with Seán McLoughlin, 2010), *The Location of Religion: A Spatial Analysis* (2005) and *Hinduism: A Very Short Introduction* (2000).

Gordon Lynch is Michael Ramsey Professor of Modern Theology at the University of Kent. He has previously been co-chair of the Media, Religion and Culture Group within the American Academy of Religion, and Chair of the British Sociological Association's Sociology of Religion Study Group. His books include *The Sacred in the Modern World: A Cultural Sociological Approach* (2012). He is Principal Investigator on the Religion and Society funded collaborative studentship 'Negotiating the Secular and the Religious in Higher Education' and the research network 'Belief as Cultural Performance'. He is also a member of the Programme's Steering Committee.

David Martin is Emeritus Professor of Sociology at the London School of Economics and Adjunct Professor at Liverpool Hope University. Before that he worked at the LSE from 1962 to 1986 and then at Southern Methodist University, Dallas and in association with Boston University. He also taught at Lancaster University from 1993 to 2006. His most recent book is *The Future of Christianity: Reflections on Violence and Democracy, Religion and Secularization* (2011). This discusses some of the issues raised in the chapter in this volume, as does his *On Secularization: Towards a Revised General Theory* (2005).

Alison Mawhinney is a lecturer in human rights and public law at the School of Law, Bangor University. She has published on religious discrimination in employment, the human rights obligations of non-state service providers, and the protection of religious liberty in education. She has been Principal Investigator on the AHRC/ESRC Religion and Society funded project 'Opting Out of Religious Education: The Views of Young People from Minority Belief Backgrounds'.

Jolyon Mitchell is Professor of Communications, Arts and Religion, and Director of the Centre for Theology and Public Issues (CTPI) at the University of Edinburgh. A former BBC World Service producer and journalist, his publications include: *Promoting Peace, Inciting Violence: The Role of Religion and Media* (forthcoming, 2011), *Media Violence and Christian Ethics* (2007) and *The Religion and Film Reader* (co-edited with S. Brent Plate, 2007).

Shuruq Naguib is Lecturer in Islamic Studies at the Department of Politics, Philosophy and Religion at Lancaster University. Her research interests include Classical Muslim hermeneutics, Modern Islam and gender, ritual purity and Islamic law. Two of her recent publications are 'Aisha Abd al-Rahman (Bint al-Shati): The Journey of an Egyptian Exegete from Hermeneutics to Humanity', in *Reading the Qur'an: Language, Culture and Interpretation in 20th Century Tafsir* (edited by Suha Taji-Farouki, forthcoming, 2011) and 'Horizons and Limitations of Muslim Feminist Hermeneutics: Reflections on the Verse of Menstruation', in *New Topics in Feminist Philosophy of Religion* (edited by Pamela Sue Anderson, 2010).

Ulrike Niens is Lecturer in the School of Education, Queen's University Belfast. Her research and teaching focuses on peace education and inclusion, identity and citizenship. Ulrike is chair of the School of Education's Ethics Committee and editorial board member of *Compare* and *Peace & Conflict: The Journal of Peace Psychology*. She was a member of the team for the AHRC/ESRC Religion and Society funded project 'Opting Out of Religious Education: The Views of Young People from Minority Belief Backgrounds'.

Malory Nye is Principal of the Al-Maktoum College in Dundee, an independent college of higher education, and is also Professor of Multiculturalism at the college and Honorary

Professor at the University of Aberdeen. He has authored three books, including *Multiculturalism and Minority Religions in Britain* (2001) and *Religion: The Basics* (second edition, 2008), and co-authored the report *Time for Change* (2006), which mapped out the development of the teaching of the study of Islam and Muslims in British universities. He has also edited the journal *Culture and Religion* for a number of years.

Elizabeth Olson is Senior Lecturer of Human Geography at the University of Edinburgh who specializes in geographies of religion, development and ethics. She is the author of numerous book chapters and articles, and editor of several books on development and religion including *Religion and Place* (with Peter Hopkins and Lily Kong, forthcoming). She is Principal Investigator of two research projects funded by the AHRC/ESRC Religion and Society Programme. The first explores the changing perspectives of young Scottish Christians ('Relational Religious Identities'), and the second examines the religiosity of young people living in deprived neighbourhoods of Britain ('Marginalized Spiritualities').

Stephen Orchard is Honorary Associate Professor, School of Education, Brunel University and a retired United Reformed Church minister who, after local ministries, served as Assistant General Secretary (Community Affairs), British Council of Churches, 1982–1986; Director of the Christian Education Movement, 1986–2001; Principal of Westminster College, Cambridge, 2001–2007; and President of the Cambridge Theological Federation from 2005 to 2007. He was Secretary of the Religious Education Council of England and Wales from 1991 and Chairman from 1999 to 2001. In retirement he serves on various educational trust bodies and is currently working on several projects in church history.

Christopher Partridge is Professor of Religious Studies in the Department of Politics, Philosophy and Religion at Lancaster University. His research and writing focuses on alternative spiritualities, counter-cultures and popular music. He is the editor, with Alyn Shipton, of the monograph series 'Studies in Popular Music' (Equinox). His most recent book is *Dub in Babylon: Understanding the Evolution and Significance of Dub Reggae in Jamaica and Britain from King Tubby to Post-punk* (2010). He has also served as a member of the AHRC/ESRC Religion and Society Programme's Commissioning Panel.

Brian Pearce OBE was Director of the Inter Faith Network for the UK for 20 years from its establishment in 1987, and helped over the previous two years in the process which led to this. He stood down as Director in September 2007 and has subsequently worked for the Network on a part-time basis as an Adviser on Faith and Public Life. Before becoming involved full time in interfaith work, he served in the civil service from 1959 to 1986, including posts in the Department of Economic Affairs, Civil Service Department and HM Treasury, where he was an Under Secretary. He is a member of the AHRC/ESRC Religion and Society Programme's Steering Committee.

Norman Richardson lectures in religious studies and intercultural education at Stranmillis University College, Belfast, where most of his current work is with student teachers. He has been involved in promoting inclusive and intercultural approaches to the content and teaching of RE in Northern Ireland's schools and also in processes of community relations and inter-religious encounter, as reflected in his recent co-edited book *Education for Diversity and Mutual Understanding: The Experience of Northern Ireland* (2011). He was a member of the team for the AHRC/ESRC Religion and Society funded project 'Opting Out of Religious Education: The Views of Young People from Minority Belief Backgrounds'.

Gurharpal Singh is Dean of Arts and Humanities at SOAS and Chair in Religions and Development in the Department for the Study of Religion. He was the Deputy Director of the Religions and Development research programme (DFID) and has served as a member of the AHRC/ESRC Religion and Society Programme's Commissioning Panel. His publications include *The Partition of India* (with Ian Talbot, 2009), *Ethnic Conflict in India: A Case Study of Punjab* (2000) and *India's Troubled Democracy* (forthcoming, 2013).

Brendan Stuart is a mature doctoral student in the Department of Politics, Philosophy and Religion, Lancaster University, having started his academic studies following a career in mental health. He is currently undertaking his PhD study into the spiritual dimensions of mainstream contemporary music festivals in Britain, exploring a primary interest in the interface between religion, popular culture and generational dynamics.

Giselle Vincett is a sociologist of religion at the University of Edinburgh where her recent work has focused on studying the religiosity of young people in the UK in two research projects: the first, centred on young Christians, and the second on young people growing up in areas of deprivation, both led by Elizabeth Olson and funded by the AHRC/ESRC Religion and Society Programme. Previously, her work has focused on alternative spiritualities and religious feminism. She is currently working on a co-edited book on contemporary forms of Christianity.

Paul Weller is Professor of Inter-Religious Relations at the University of Derby and Visiting Fellow at the Oxford Centre for Christianity and Culture, Regent's Park College, Oxford. He is Principal Investigator on the AHRC/ESRC Religion and Society Programme project 'Religion and Belief, Discrimination and Equality in England and Wales: Theory, Policy, and Practice, 2000–2010' (see www.derby.ac.uk/religion-and-society). His published works include *Time for a Change: Reconfiguring Religion, State and Society* (2005) and *Religions in the UK: Directory 2007–10* as editor (2007).

John Wolffe is Professor of Religious History at The Open University. He is the author of *The Protestant Crusade in Great Britain 1829–1860* (1991), *God and Greater Britain: Religion and National Life in Britain and Ireland 1843–1945* (1994), *Great Deaths: Grieving, Religion and Nationhood in Victorian and Edwardian Britain* (2000) and *The Expansion of Evangelicalism: The Age of Wilberforce, More, Chalmers and Finney* (2006) as well as numerous journal articles and book chapters. He is currently working on a project on Protestant–Catholic conflict and *A Short History of Evangelicalism*. He has also been Principal Investigator on the AHRC/ESRC Religion and Society funded collaborative studentship 'From Sunday Schools to Christian Education' and served as a member of the Programme's Commissioning Panel.

Linda Woodhead is Professor of Sociology of Religion at Lancaster University, Director of the AHRC/ESRC Religion and Society Programme, and Visiting Professor at Aarhus University. Her research considers religion in late modern societies. Her books include *A Sociology of Religious Emotion* (with Ole Riis, 2010), *The Spiritual Revolution: Why Religion is Giving Way to Spirituality* (with Paul Heelas, 2005) and *An Introduction to Christianity* (2010). She is currently editing a book on *Innovative Methods in the Study of Religion*, and preparing a book on *Religion in Public: Realignments in State, Society and Market*, based on the Wilde Lectures delivered at the University of Oxford in 2011.

John Zavos is Lecturer in South Asian Studies at the University of Manchester. His recent publications include *Religious Traditions in Modern South Asia* (co-authored with Jacqueline Suthren Hirst, 2011), and several articles on Hinduism and Hindu organizations in the UK. He is also principal editor of *Public Hinduisms* (2012). He has worked extensively on the Hindu nationalist movement and is the author of *The Emergence of Hindu Nationalism in India* (2000). Since 2008 he has been editor of the journal *Contemporary South Asia*.

Introduction

Linda Woodhead

This extended introduction pulls together some of the main themes arising from the chapters which follow. In doing so, it offers a framework for thinking about religion in post-war Britain, and relates what has been happening to wider social changes. It suggests that religion in the first part of the period was chiefly shaped by its relation to the state, but that the relation with the market became increasingly important after the 1970s. A crucial development for the whole period is the formation of the welfare state, which became a focus of unity and national hope in Britain, and an object of faith in its own right. Although many forms of Christianity allied themselves with this project, 'welfare utopianism' also developed secular forms and commitments which sowed the seeds of later secular–religious controversy. Although religion seemed to many people to have gone away in the 1960s–1990s, and though narratives of secularization were prevalent, the analysis shows that the religious field was in fact transforming outside the control of state and church and in relation to new opportunities of market and media. This time of 'deregulation' allowed new religious actors to emerge – both ethnic minorities and women – so that when religion came to public notice again after the late 1980s, it was more varied and multifaceted than before. The result was growing controversy, some significant misunderstandings, and urgent attempts by state and law in the twenty-first century to 'reregulate' religion and bring it under control. But new forms of religious organization and identity, new religious actors, new uses of media, and transnational rather than national religious linkages had changed the terms of engagement.

> We [had] thought we were living in a stable secular age.
> Marina Warner, commenting on the Rushdie Affair[1]

Religion in Britain is not what it used to be. Within living memory significant changes have taken place. In television comedy the figure of the benign but bumbling clergyman of *Dad's Army* or *All Gas and Gaiters* has given way to the female 'Vicar of Dibley', and in tabloid newspapers tales about kinky vicars have been overtaken by stories of murderous Muslim terrorists. These same tabloids bemoan the decline of Christian values, yet Christians can now be prosecuted for expressing their belief in public. Churches are being turned into commercial spaces, dwellings, temples and mosques; multi-faith prayer rooms have become the most distinctive form of recent religious construction. Whereas once politicians at the Palace of Westminster enjoyed easy relations with senior Anglican clergy around the corner in Church House, now religion has become something to be dealt with by consultations, legislation and policy. A sharp line is drawn between socially useful 'faith' initiatives, and dangerous forms of 'religion' which put the claims of God above those of citizenship. Britain is now regularly spoken of as a secular country with a secular state, yet it still has an established church, and the majority of Britons still call themselves 'Christian'.

This book analyses and explains these and other changes and apparent contradictions in the post-Second World War period. In order to do so it adopts an approach which considers religion not in isolation, but in relation to the wider social, political, economic and global changes in which it has been immersed. This means that it is implicitly critical of a characteristic assumption of the post-war period: that religion has become a purely private matter with no public or political significance. So long as this idea prevailed, both in scholarship and in society, it was possible to treat religions as discrete entities which could be analysed solely in terms of their inner logics and characteristic texts, beliefs, rituals and symbols.[2] The alternative, integrated, approach developed in this volume views religion not only as affected by wider changes in the global economy, politics, media, the law and other arenas, but as integral to them. In other words, it takes the idea of strong social differentiation – which assumes that modern societies like Britain are made up of separate 'spheres' or 'domains' of which religion is one – as a loaded claim which should be the subject of empirical enquiry rather than its starting point.

The challenge for such an integrated approach is the breadth of knowledge and expertise it demands. From the start, it was clear that this book would have to be a collaborative and interdisciplinary venture.[3] It has been carefully designed as such – not as an edited collection of discrete reflections, but as a common creation. The authors met together in a residential setting in Lancaster on two separate occasions: first to plan the shape of the book, and then to read and comment on one another's draft chapters.[4] We worked, talked, ate, socialized and argued together. Bernice Martin and Hugh McLeod gave sociological and historical feedback on individual chapters and the book as a whole; Emily Laycock, Kjersti Loken and Brendan Stuart commented from the point of view of student readers; Lesley Riddle, Amy Grant and Katherine Ong offered the publisher's point of view. Most of the chapters are themselves collaborative, often between authors who had not previously worked together, but who have complementary expertise. The editors were closely involved at every step of the way, not only in planning the volume and commissioning chapters, but in reading, commenting upon, rereading and reworking the volume as a whole, in order to ensure an appropriate degree of coherence in structure, coverage, expression and argument. This does not mean that differences of approach and interpretation have been eliminated, but that they have been woven into a fabric – or pasted into a collage – in which coherent outlines can be discerned.

This undertaking was only possible because of the generosity of the Arts and Humanities Research Council and the Economic and Social Research Council (the AHRC and ESRC). Both councils had come together at the start of the new millennium to develop a 'strategic initiative' which would stimulate UK research on religion, and encourage collaboration across the arts, humanities and social sciences. The ensuing 'Religion and Society Programme' was launched in 2007 as a six-year initiative, with a budget of £12 million. This was used to fund 75 separate research projects, which were commissioned competitively.[5] Linda Woodhead has served as Director of the Programme, Peta Ainsworth as Administrator and Rebecca Catto as Research Associate. This book flows directly from the Programme, and has drawn on its resources. It is not a 'book of the Programme', because the Programme's research goes beyond the topics – and geography – covered here, and because several contributing authors are not involved in the Programme. But nearly all chapters have at least one author whose research has been funded by 'Religion and Society', and new data, findings and analysis arising from this research inform the entire project. The Programme also sponsored the residential meetings at which the book was shaped, and provided the impetus and framework within which such an ambitious project could be realized.[6]

Secularization and desecularization

Part of the challenge of a book on religion in post-war Britain is that the changes it seeks to illuminate are so recent and so extensive that it is difficult to gain a proper perspective on them. For most of this period reflection has been shaped by the dominant framework of 'secularization', and, more recently, the competing idea of 'desecularization' – not only in the social sciences, but in the arts and humanities, as well as in wider discourse, debate and policy-making.[7] According to secularization theories, societies inevitably secularize as they modernize: the post-war period is read as one of continuing decline and privatization of religion; not only does religion in Britain become less important to individuals, it diminishes in significance within society as a whole (Wilson 1969, 1976, 1982; Bruce 1995). According to desecularization theories, on the other hand, predictions of inexorable secularization have now been undermined: far from being a declining force in society, religion has staged a revival and a public comeback – a 'desecularization' and 'deprivatization'.[8]

Taken together, the contributions to this book endorse neither perspective. The statistical evidence they present, briefly summarized in the next section, is ambiguous: it supports both positions – and neither. Instead, post-war Britain emerges as religious *and* secular. This only seems puzzling if existing frameworks are retained, because they assume not only that 'religion' and 'secularity' are clear and distinct entities, but that they are elements in a zero-sum equation, such that modern history can only be told as a simple evolutionary tale: either from the religious to the secular, or from the secular to the religious.

It is possible to favour a different approach without abandoning the secularization framework completely – even if such abandonment were possible. Secularization is now so established that it has shaped the entire field: how agendas are set, research questions asked, survey questions framed, data collected and analysed. Even theories of desecularization are framed in its image. Many of the chapters which follow review this achievement, and some endorse at least part of what it represents. Something similar can be said for theories of desecularization, though their contribution is far less extensive.

Although it moves beyond both theories, this book is therefore open to their insights. What is more, it draws upon them in an additional way: by treating them not as lenses to look through, but as important evidence to consider – not just as *explicans* but as *explicandum*. For, far from being neutral voices speaking on the post-war religious condition, these theories are integral to it. And, as such, they offer an important route into some of its deepest presuppositions.

An important clue lies in the sheer incompatibility of the accounts of secularization and desecularization, and the energy with which each is defended by its supporters. This suggests that we are dealing with something more fundamental than a dispute over evidence: fundamental commitments are at stake as well. That there is more to secularization theory than a desire to explain 'the facts' with scientific dispassion is evident in the way that many of its advocates dismiss counter-evidence and defend their theory with great tenacity. Whilst it is fairly obvious why religious people might want to defend religion against those who proclaim not only its imminent demise but its incompatibility with modern society and enlightened values (for secularization theory maintains that it is contradictory to be modern *and* religious), it is not immediately obvious why defenders of secularization should be hostile to the continued existence of religion. The answer must be that very often secularization theory is not merely describing the decline of religion, but endorsing belief in an evolutionary progress from pre-modern superstition to modern enlightenment. As such, the secular is not merely the subtraction of religion – the secular bedrock left behind when the tide of religion recedes – but a counter-ideology which needs to be defended and institutionalized just as religion does (Taylor 2007). Like religion, it makes alliances with power. And like religion it has its charismatic figures, prophets, elites, holy books, and heretics. So theories of secularization, bound up with secular commitments, may be just as value-laden and passionately held as theories of de-secularization.

This is the part of what the final chapter in this book on 'The religious and the secular' shows. It is an argument which David Martin has developed since the 1960s, when it cut against the grain of consensus (Martin 1965). Through his early work on peace movements, Martin had realized that the secular parties and ideologies of modern times had Christian analogues, and that the former could best be understood in terms of the latter (Martin 2010). As he argued in later books (Martin 1969, 1978, 2005, 2011), the 'secular' gains substance in relation to the kind of 'religion' it rejects. This is why secularism varies so widely across different national and political contexts: French *laïcité*, for example, is very different from northern European 'moderate' secularism, which is different again from the USA's brand of secular separationism (between religion and state).

This also explains why secular critiques of 'religion' are in fact critiques of one very particular type – or construction – of religion, which serves as the perfect foil for the alternative 'secular' position proposed. In the work of the prominent post-war British atheist Richard Dawkins, for example, 'religion' has the contours of a form of modern conservative evangelical Protestantism which consists of a series of (false) empirical propositions about the way the world is. This is the opposite of the set of (true) propositions which modern science delivers, which are yielded by human reason and scientific method rather than blind faith in revelation, and which show that human beings – or at least rational ones like scientists – can figure things out for themselves without the need for priests or a Bible, and that there is therefore no need to believe in any (other) higher being (Dawkins 2006). By contrast, secular socialists are more likely to stress the oppressive and alienating nature of religion, secular feminists its patriarchal quality, secular advocates of free expression its repressive features – and so on. The inverse can also be observed in relation to modern forms of religion which develop in relation to secularism. Christian creationism, for example, makes the Bible literally and 'scientifically' true and scriptural stories 'as tangible as test tubes' (Toumey 1994: 261). Similarly, the Christian churches' post-war fixation on issues of sex and gender can be explained, in part, by the fact that this was a period in which sexuality was liberalized and gender equalized, with both becoming symbols of secular progress (Woodhead 2007).

The consequence for this book is that it cannot afford to ignore the secular. That is also a key part of an integrated approach. To try to understand what has been happening to religion without understanding the secular part of the picture is like trying to explain the development of masculinity without femininity, or Labour politics without Conservative. In the process the meanings of 'secular' and 'religious' are destabilized. Neither makes sense without the other, and their shifting meanings must be analysed in relation to their changing linkages, configurations, commitments and mutual hostilities. Therefore it is important to be more discriminating about the dominant forms of secularism in post-war Britain, rather than speaking of 'the secular' as something timeless and singular. It is necessary to analyse the sacred values, rituals, 'priesthoods', symbols and communities affirmed by 'secular' groups as well as religious ones. And it is essential to take seriously the politics which lie behind the construction and retention of these categories, not least by asking whose interests are served by attacking 'religion' or 'secularism'.

These themes and approaches are developed below. Before that, it is helpful to review briefly some of the statistical evidence to which both advocates of secularization and desecularization have traditionally appealed – in order to see both what these frameworks can still tell us about the post-war situation, and why they need to be transcended. There is a danger in this exercise, because in order to undertake it, it is necessary to accept the terms and data of the existing debate. That means not only proceeding as if the 'religious' and 'the secular' are stable, ahistorical categories, but treating them in isolation from wider society and politics in a way which goes against the grain of the integrated approach being advocated. But by framing the debate in the terms which prevailed for so much of the post-war period – that is, by asking whether post-war Britain secularized or desecularized – it is possible to see what that debate achieved, why the form it took in the post-war period is integral to the era, and how it now points beyond itself to a new approach.

Post-war Britain: religious or secular?

The reason this evidence can be dealt with summarily is because it is presented in detail elsewhere in the book, particularly in Chapters 2 ('Christianity') and 10 ('Cultural perspectives').

Starting with secularization, the strongest evidence which proponents of religious decline have produced is that of church decline. Figures presented throughout indicate decline across a wide range of indicators including: churchgoing, church membership, Sunday School attendance, and rites of baptism, confirmation and marriage. For churchgoing, for example, Peter Brierley's reliable censuses of church attendance carried out approximately every ten years since 1979 show a pattern of decline which has seen numbers nearly halve over a quarter of a century, as indicated in Table 0.1.

Table 0.1 Churchgoing in England

Years	1979	1989	1998	2005
per cent attending on Sunday	11.7	9.9	7.5	6.3

Source: Brierley 2006: 12.2.1

Other chapters present evidence of decline in Christian belief, Christian knowledge and possibly in Christian values. With regard to the first, there is statistical evidence of a fall in belief in a 'personal God', Jesus Christ and the Bible (see Chapter 5 on 'God-change'). With regard to an abandonment of Christian values, Callum Brown (2001 and in this volume), relying on sources like oral history and popular magazines, makes a forceful case that a Christian ethic focused around values like duty, chastity, modesty and respectability collapsed in the 1960s, particularly as a result of the sexual revolution.

As well as a decline in personal belief and practice, it has been argued that there was a shrinkage of the churches' role in society and in political life in the post-war period. This is much harder to measure or quantify, but was documented in the 1970s and 1980s by Bryan Wilson (e.g. 1969, 1976, 1982). In this volume Elisabeth Arweck, James Beckford, Gladys Ganiel and Peter Jones present additional, and more recent, evidence. Since the 1990s this apparent decline must also be viewed in relation to the increasingly public role of 'other' religions in the UK, which has been institutionalized in various ways, including in interfaith bodies (see Chapter 3 and Case study 2 on the growth of the Inter Faith Network). Overall, it may be that this growth in the public visibility of 'minority faiths' has served to accentuate the relative decline in public significance of the churches – seen now as just one among several world religions.

However, a simple story of secularization is complicated by a number of factors – even in the terms of the existing debate. One is that the picture is not uniform across the UK. The most important exception is Northern Ireland, in which Christianity has remained highly visible, powerful, politically relevant and personally significant to most citizens – as discussed in Chapter 9. Another is that even in relation to Christianity, the decline has not been uniform. Brierley's surveys of England and Wales reveal that the churches which have historically been most powerful have also been those which have declined the most, with the Church of England now accounting for only about a third of church attendance. In 2005, 28 per cent of churchgoers in Britain were Anglican, 28 per cent Roman Catholic, and 44 per cent belonged to a range of smaller, often voluntaristic churches, including Baptist, independent and Charismatic churches (Brierley 2006: 12.2.2). Chapter 2 discusses these issues in more detail, highlighting areas of vitality as well as decline – such as the recent expansion of black and ethnic minority churches.

The level of self-declared Christian adherence also remains high in Britain, with 72 per cent of the population identifying as Christian in the 2001 Census.[9] Overall 76.8 per cent identified as religious, and 23.2 per cent as 'no religion' or 'not stated'.[10] As for what people meant by ticking 'Christian', Abby Day (2011), using follow-up interviews, finds a range of meanings tied to interwoven commitments and belongings – including to family, class, history, values, ethnicity and nation.

Advocates of desecularization point to evidence like this to support their case that Britain is no longer secular. They can also cite the growing number of people who are committed to minority religions, the high salience which religion has for these communities and their growing public significance – all documented in Chapter 3. In addition, there is evidence that even if Britain has been getting less religious, or at least less Christian, it has also been getting more spiritual. More people now believe in 'God as Spirit or Lifeforce' than in a 'personal God' (see Chapter 5). In 2000 when an ORB survey commissioned by the BBC asked 'Which of these would you say you are?' (not exclusive options) the following percentages replied:

A spiritual person	31%
A religious person	27%
An agnostic person	10%
Not a spiritual person	7%
Not a religious person	21%
A convinced atheist	8%
Don't know	5%.[11]

A small proportion of those who identify as 'spiritual' belong to committed groups, and a study of such activists in 2000–2002 estimated that they made up 1.6 per cent of the British population (Heelas and Woodhead 2005). But there are many more who pursue their own versions of spirituality and reject 'packages' of beliefs and practices offered by organized religions. Even those who call themselves Christian may think of themselves as 'Christian in my own way', and not accept the whole church 'package'.[12]

Nor did post-war Britain lose connection with Christian culture and history – as is evident in the calendar, festivals, the built environment, common language and some continuing forms of ritual practice (see Douglas J. Davies in this volume, Chapter 6). It is certainly true that the post-war period saw a decline in the importance of Christian sub-cultures, both Protestant and Catholic, which before the war and immediately after it could still structure a good deal of personal life, family life, work life, education and consumption (McLeod 2007). But although such sub-cultures remain in Northern Ireland and parts of Scotland and the north of England, especially where there are large Catholic communities, this has become the exception rather than the norm. Nevertheless, around half of the population still attends church at least annually for an 'occasional office' like a wedding or funeral, and around a third for a religious festival, particularly Christmas.[13] Belief in paranormal experience, answer to prayer, an afterlife, ghosts, angels and contact with the dead has also remained fairly steady in the post-war period – as Case study 3 on religion among young people growing up in poverty shows (though this is no longer well described as 'folk religion', but contains elements from a wide range of sources, including popular culture).

As for the continuing role of religion in public life, much of this book is dedicated to exploring that topic and presenting new data and analysis – and the evidence pushes against the existing terms of the debate about secularization. Until now, most attention has been paid to changing relations between the state and religion. When this is at issue, the evidence of the declining influence of the churches and growing power and independence of the state relative to them is strong – and supports arguments for secularization. Despite the fact that there is still a 'state church' in England – the Church of England – and something rather like a state church in Scotland – the Church of Scotland – the volume as a whole shows how the post-war period has seen the state take over many of the functions and resources of churches and religious voluntary bodies, as well as exercise a growing control over all forms of religion through new legislation, charities regulation and other means. However, it also shows that when 'public life' is defined more broadly to take account not just of state government (legislature, executive and judiciary), but also of education, politics, welfare, the media, the workplace and market, and the voluntary, charitable or 'third' sector, a rather different picture emerges – one in which religion has played a significant role throughout the post-war period, and continues to do so.

Does all this amount to desecularization? The answer is no. For there is not enough evidence to support what is implied: that a period of secularization has now gone into reverse. It is true that minority religions have become much more prominent since the 1980s, as symbolized by the Rushdie Affair (1988–1989) in particular (see Nye and Weller in this volume, Chapter 1, and Weller 2009). It is true that forms of alternative spirituality have also been growing in the same period. It is true that religion has been an element in terrorism. And it is true that religion has been much more on the agenda since the late 1990s in government policy, legislation and legal cases, in the media (see the new data presented in Chapter 7), and for many public bodies. But the evidence gathered here also shows that religion never really went away, so that talk of its 're-emergence' or 'return', or of 'post-secularity' is misleading. There have certainly been significant changes in the nature of religious life in Britain, in the characteristic forms of religion, in civil religion and in religion's influence in different social arenas – but these are not such that they can be quantified, measured and weighed in the debate about religion versus secularity.

Is the corollary that the evidence does not support secularization either? The answer is yes. There is not enough to support the idea that religion has been inexorably or catastrophically declining in post-war Britain at the level of personal adherence or public life. Britain has not become a secular country. But there are some important qualifications. First, there has been dramatic decline in church Christianity – particularly in those churches which have closest historical relations to the state. Second, the state has become a more powerful force in society at the expense of religion, and now positions itself not so much as a partner with the churches as a parent. And third, secularism has been growing in terms of number of followers, public visibility, stridency – and possibly power and influence in certain elite circles. The emergence of new atheism in the twenty-first century is one sign. And although the number of atheists in Britain remains fairly small – Bruce (2002) puts the number of 'convinced atheists' at 8 per cent and 'agnostics' at 10 per cent – the number claiming 'no religion' is growing: up from 24 per cent in 1979 to 39 per cent in 1999 according to Gallup and Lindsay (1999: 121). Moreover, the self-identified secular are influential: white, clustered in higher occupational categories, slightly more men than women, and slightly on the left of a left–right political scale (Voas and Day 2007; O'Beirne 2004: tables 2.3, 2.4).

Turning points in secular–religious relations

Existing evidence, chiefly from surveys, clearly has a bearing on claims of secularization and desecularization. But although each makes sense of some parts of it, neither is able to account for the whole picture. Once findings yielded by a broader range of methods are added, the failure becomes more obvious. Increasingly, the existing frameworks seem inadequate to the situation they attempt to explain. But looking at the theories of secularization (and desecularization) as *part* of the picture of the post-war situation we are trying to understand can help in a number of ways, not least in providing important clues about the timing of religious change and, above all, the changing phases and articulations of secular–religious relations.

Talk of desecularization first started to appear in 1999 (Berger 1999),[14] and more militant and angry versions of secularism a few years after that (e.g. Dawkins 2006; Hitchens 2007). Anger and defensiveness often flow from a threatened loss of status. This prompts the question not only how and why secularization had remained privileged for so long, but what shook that status so dramatically around the turn of the century. The answer which the theories themselves offer is that religion, having gone away, suddenly reappeared in Western societies like Banquo's ghost. Many commentators point to the attacks of 9/11 and subsequent atrocities in the name of Islam as the turning point. Others invoke the growing impact of post-war immigration into Europe, particularly the growing visibility of Muslims and Islam. It is these factors, it is argued, which suddenly put religion back on the agenda.

Although there is some truth in these claims, the answer is too simple. It was not just religion which brought about the change. After all, secularization theory had managed to explain away the resurgence of religion in public and political life which had been evident around the world since the late 1970s as dissatisfaction with secular regimes mounted in various places, not only on the part of Muslims, but also Hindus, Sikhs, Christians, Buddhists and forms of embodied spiritual cultivation like Falun Gong in China. Closer to home, religiously inflected terrorism by the IRA had also been a much more serious threat in Britain for much longer than anything done in the name of Islam – yet this did not shake secular certainties.[15] And immigration and the rising profile of religious minorities had been a feature of life in Britain since at least the 1960s, with Sikh, Jewish and other groups making significant claims on the state, and controversy raging over turbans and *kirpans* (Sikh daggers) – the former just as visible and the latter much more dangerous than veils.

Secularization could deal with all this because it had built into it the belief that Western societies were at the cutting edge of progress – they were the societies which defined modernity, and modernity was an evolutionary stage which supplanted a pre-modernity characterized by religious backwardness. Consequently, all signs of continued religious vitality outside the West could be explained away in terms of less 'advanced' countries lagging behind in their 'development'. Give them time and they would catch up. The same could be said about the 'immigration' of religion into Europe from other parts of the world. Religion was bound to persist for immigrant groups for a while, and perhaps even intensify as a form of 'cultural defence'. But in time they would grow up. The 'cultural defence' argument was also mobilized to explain the situation in Northern Ireland; alternatively it was said that the conflict there was 'communal' and 'ethnic' rather than religious. And when religion did appear in Britain before the late 1980s, it was often categorized as 'race' rather than religion (Modood 2005).

But if developments in religion did not unsettle secular confidence, what did? It could be argued that it was the sheer weight of accumulating counter-evidence which eventually led to a shift, but the more credible answer is that it was only when this was combined with pressures external to religion that something changed.

One was the diminishing prestige of science. Modern secularism is historically bound up with belief in the epistemological priority of science and its ability to deliver reliable knowledge which trumps all other forms. In the position maintained by many positivists, science holds the key to *all* knowledge, and what cannot be known by scientific means must be dismissed as nonsense. This epistemological position is supported by metaphysical commitments which depend on alternative narratives to those offered by religion – not least evolutionary biological schemes which invoke Darwin but go further in attempting to explain all facets of human personal and social life (Midgley 2002). Socio-biological explanations now purport to explain everything, from why religion exists to why women prefer pink and men don't like shopping. But above all, the power of science, especially the natural sciences, is supported by money and politics: by massive research investment and other forms of state legitimation. In many ways, the 1950s and 1960s were the high point for 'big' science: the moon landing of 1968 seemed to prove its almost supernatural abilities, scientific medicine under the guise of the National Health Service (NHS) took over from more traditional forms of healing and care, and governments of all kinds, both capitalist and communist, rested their hopes on the ability of scientific planning and policy to deliver the perfect society.

Much of this power and prestige remains, but public confidence in the ability of science and technology to deliver all that is needed for a good life in good societies on a sustainable planet has diminished. Greater prosperity and health were delivered, but not for all. Continuing poverty, the AIDS disaster and the growth of alternative forms of 'holistic medicine' revealed both the power and the limitations of social policy and bio-medicine. A series of environmental disasters, culminating in damage to the ozone layer and convincing evidence of global warming, have convinced more people that science does not have all the answers – and may even be part of the problem when it overreaches its limitations.

Alliances between science and big business have undermined the idea that science is always value-free or benign. The idea, still widely current in the 1950s and 1960s, that scientists 'know better' and can be trusted to have the answers no longer has the same wide acceptance.

This took place in relation to an even greater cause of waning secular confidence: loss of faith in the secular socialist solutions and – in Britain – in the welfare state. Much of the period considered in this book was dominated by the ideal of the welfare state. More than an idea or a policy, this was an ideology, a belief, an ethic, a form of economic arrangement, a type of politics, a cultural mood and a restoration of national pride. It affected every person, and it effected significant change at personal level, local level and state level. Just like religion – but in place of it – it promised to look after every individual 'from cradle to grave' (Kynaston 2007, 2009). Throughout the 1950s and into the 1970s, this utopian project was at its height. It seemed to deliver employment, prosperity, renewed national confidence and pride. But after the oil crisis of 1973 things started to go wrong: growth faltered, unemployment rose, trade union power seemed out of control, and basic services faltered as a result of industrial action and other pressures (Fraser 2003; Clarke 2004). By the time the Conservative government under Margaret Thatcher came to power in 1979 – under the slogan 'Labour isn't Working' – many people wanted a change, and the Thatcher government was ready to deliver it.

The welfare ideal, though fed and supported by Christian as well as non-religious inspiration and resources, grew increasingly secular over time. It strengthened its relationships with various forms of secularism: with socialism and its commitment to bringing about a just, equal and unified society through central planning and the nationalization of economic production; with a modernist aesthetic which believed in the power of good design to engineer a new society; with a revitalized feminist movement which sought an end to all patriarchal structures including those of religion; with faith in the power of science and 'the white heat of technology' to conquer all the fears and wants which had previously troubled humankind; with an ethic of humanitarianism institutionalized in new human rights instruments and international agreements; with a youth counter-culture which believed that destruction of existing forms of hierarchy and power – the tearing down of 'the establishment' – would deliver perfect human equality, solidarity, love and peace (see Case study 5). It also had a relation, albeit a controversial one, with the wider post-war project of a united Europe, bound by a common prosperity which would make war and division a thing of the past. On the whole the welfare project was a national – and often a nationalistic – one. It enabled Britons to retain some pride despite their diminished status in the world. It was largely forgetful of Empire – so recently and still not completely shed – and only fitfully committed to a greater equality of races, even within the umbrella of the 'New Commonwealth'.

Thus the welfare ideal was optimistic, progressivist and utopian. It had many features of a religion – but a secular, civil religion (in Quebec it was even called *l'État-providence*). Hope and faith were invested, and a New Jerusalem was to be built in Britain's green and pleasant land. It would be a secure and civilized haven in an insecure world, caught as it was between the great superpowers in the Cold War. It would be characterized not by unbridled American-style capitalism, nor by what Harold Macmillan (1957) called the 'doctrinaire nightmare' of communism, but by a one-nation solution in which government, industry and the public would achieve harmonious consensus. It would be brought about by peaceful co-operation and rational planning, not by divine intervention or coercive measures.

The gradual loss of faith in this welfare ideal, signalled by the three successive election victories of Margaret Thatcher in 1979, 1983 and 1987, was therefore a blow to secular confidence. It was not just that welfare utopianism was chastened, but that a new global ideology had arisen to challenge it: neoliberalism. Becoming politically influential at the same point in the late 1970s across the globe – Washington, London, Beijing – this rival post-war ideology sought salvation not in society but in the market, and exalted the value of freedom rather than equality (Harvey 2005). The consequences for religion were different. Whereas welfare utopianism sought to confine religion to a private sphere of diminished significance and expected its imminent demise, neoliberalism was much more willing to make alliance with it – most notably in the growing neoconservative movement in the USA. Thatcher was also open to the intermeshing of her Christian and political credos, as discussed below.

This shift developed in relation to much wider events, most importantly the collapse of communism in Eastern Europe and the Union of Soviet Socialist Republics (USSR) after 1989. This had serious repercussions for secularism – because the revolutions in the East constituted a genuine example of desecularization as well as a symbolic blow to secularism. Part of the 'war' in 'Cold War' had always been that between religion and secularism, with the USA standing for religious freedom, and the communist bloc for the abolition of all forms of outdated and oppressive 'superstition'. For the more religious USA, the collapse of communism was therefore a straightforward victory for religious freedom. In Europe, however, the fall of communism had a rather different and more melancholy resonance, particularly for those who retained a hope of state-led reform towards a more just and equal society based on secular faith.

Thus turn-of-the-millennium talk of desecularization and a resurgence of religion, together with a loss of faith in secularization theory – as well as more strident reassertions of secularism – can be explained not just in terms of 9/11 or immigration, but in terms of a crisis of confidence in secularism itself, bound up with challenges to the prestige of science and a loss of faith in utopian post-war secular projects. Given that secularism had packaged religion as a force of pre-modern violence and atavism, it was, however, easier to focus anxiety and blame on religion, veiled women and Islamic terrorism.

So the waxing and waning of theories of secularization and desecularization reveal important phases in the changing relationship between the secular and the religious in post-war Britain (and more widely), and suggest a periodization which is borne out by the chapters which follow: above all, a long period of growing secular confidence from the late 1950s to the 1980s, preceded by a more religious phase in the immediate post-war years, and followed by a more mixed economy as confidence in secularization faltered from the late 1980s, and religion – though always present – started to be become visible once more.

Post-war Christian restoration

Adapting a classificatory scheme from Weller (2008 and in this volume, Chapter 1), this post-war periodization can be characterized in terms of a move from Christian to secular to multi-faith, but with a number of important provisos: that this is not a smooth evolutionary process; that each phase persists into the next; that 'multi-faith' embraces both religious and secular commitments; that there is contestation and jostling for position between them; that they may co-exist at different social scales and in different social arenas – for example, secularism being dominant at state level, and multi-faith at local or regional level. Each phase is associated with the ascendancy of particular elites and power interests, and what secularization theory presented as an impersonal, inexorable progress from the religious to the secular is, in reality, better understood as a complex set of ongoing competitions for power between different groups in society associated with different ideologies, interests and employments. At different phases in the post-war period, a different set of interests attains heightened visibility and power.

Starting with the first of these three phases, several chapters in this book document the Christian 'revival' of the immediate post-war years. They agree that its apogee was the coronation of Queen Elizabeth II in 1953 (see Plate 2.1), an occasion later described by the Bishop of Durham, David Jenkins, as 'the most universally impressive ceremonial event in history'.[16] In religious terms, the 1950s were, as Grace Davie puts it: 'an Anglican decade, in which the social role of the church was confirmatory rather than confrontational. The sacred... synchronized nicely with the secular in this predominantly Conservative period' (1994: 31). To recall a comment made by David Martin (1989: 339) which lays bare the interests which were served, it was a time when the average Anglican expected 'God, the Queen, the Church, and Oxford University, to act together in reasonable harmony'. This was a period of rejuvenated civil religion – when a national church found itself able to carry and symbolize the hopes of a nation, and when state and religion could act in harmony. At the local level, particularly in more rural areas, a Christian order could still be upheld by the intermeshing authority of clergyman, schoolmaster, policeman and parents.

This Christian 'revival' is actually better understood as a nostalgic 'restoration' (Hastings 1991: 444). It is best comprehended in relation to the upheavals and dislocations of the Second World War which preceded it and the Cold War which was closing in around it. In Britain, as in the USA, the result was a strong desire to return to a safe, homely space – both domestic and national – in which order reigned, family values were reinstated, men took the helm of the nuclear household and women became the homemakers (marked in fashion by the ultra-feminine 'New Look' with cinched-in waists and exaggerated breasts and hips). This 'restoration' of gender roles was a reaction not only to the upheaval of sexual mores in wartime (and the first wave of feminism at the start of the century), but an attempt to return to 'normal' after a period in which women had taken over male jobs, with childcare provided by the state. To many women's lasting grief and anger, these options were closed down immediately when the war ended, with trade unions and politicians making sure the paid jobs were returned to men, and the new welfare system organized to enshrine the model of a breadwinning male and domestic female (Summerfield 1989). The churches were largely supportive, whilst also providing women with an outlet for some of their energies and an important social arena outside the home. 'For the children of the 1950s,' says David Kynaston, 'there would be – for better or worse – no escape from the tough, tender, purifying embrace of family Britain' (2007: 633).

The apparent unity of this period, however, should not be taken too much at face value. The sheer amount of energy poured into the attempt to celebrate national unity – as in the 1953 coronation and the Festival of Britain of 1951 – was in many ways a sign of the fragility of the project. A sense of 'Britishness' (as opposed to Englishness, Welshness, Scottishness, Irishness and other more local or complex identities) which had been forged in relation to Empire (Colley 2003), had quickly to reinvent itself in relation to a much-diminished status in Europe and in the world. The idea of a new Commonwealth of nations, with Britain as the mother country, failed as a popular rallying point – though paternalistic attitudes to 'other races' lived on. These attitudes shaped the experience of the large number of immigrants who came to Britain from Commonwealth countries in order to assist with post-war reconstruction. An implicit sense of Britain as a white, Christian society did not allow the idea of it becoming a multi-racial one to take hold (Gilroy 1987). Moreover, although Britain's long history of Empire may have lived on in a sense of national importance, the realities of the imperial past and Britain's entanglements with the rest of the world quickly gave way to a renewed sense of British 'island' nationhood (one reason why membership of the new European Economic Community took so long and was so controversial, eventually realized in 1973).

In religion as well, the apparent unity of an Anglican-dominated new Elizabethan age was another lid placed over a cauldron of differences which had been bubbling away long before the war. Despite a show of unity at the coronation, Anglican domination was often resented by the other British churches, both Protestant and Catholic, which outnumbered the Church of England in terms of Sunday attendances. The Catholic Church was continuing to grow in confidence and social influence, and Protestant nonconformity was also working to strengthen its position, including through mergers and alliances (see Case study 1). New ecumenical movements and configurations at a global scale, including the formation of the World Council of Churches in 1948, offered fresh opportunities to Protestant churches. In many ways, the idea of Britain and its constituent nations as *Protestant* gave way to the idea of Britain as a *Christian* nation (Green 2010), though the realities of inter- and intra-ecclesiastical politics at local as well as national level meant that the ideal of Christian unity was never realized. Even the unifying force of Anglicanism was actually divided between rival 'churchmanships', focused around liturgical and doctrinal differences on a spectrum from the 'low' and more Protestant, to the 'high' and more Catholic, which were also bound up with complex political and class differences. Most important of all in terms of intra-Protestant tension and difference was the growing strength of the evangelical tendency.

As Chapter 2 shows, evangelicalism differed from more traditional Anglicanism in many ways, not least in its emphasis on the importance of the relationship of the individual more than the nation or church to God. As Chapter 5 shows, the God of evangelicalism showed a very different face from the high God of the coronation: known directly in Jesus Christ, this was a God who cared for each and every individual – a very present help in times of trouble. As the post-war era continued, this more friendly and accessible God would eclipse the sterner God of civic tradition. Adept at using new modes of mass communication, and part of a worldwide movement, evangelicalism was thoroughly at home in the post-war era, and ready to present itself as a modern faith for modern times – albeit one which chimed with the conservative mood in terms of ethics, gender roles and the nuclear family. In Britain, Billy Graham's rallies attracted huge numbers of spectators and participants, and fitted with a mood of national revival and Christian confidence (Chapters 2, 5 and 10).

Given this mood, the interesting question is why it gave way after the 1950s to a more secular one. This volume explores some different answers. For Callum Brown and Gordon Lynch the answer lies in a rebellion – particularly on the part of women – against the stultifying repressions the churches had placed around their lives, particularly their sexual lives. These authors suggest that the dreary, puritanical and paternalistic vapours of Christian 'respectability' were blown away by the fresh air of the 1960s counter-culture. For Hugh McLeod (2007) and other contributors to this volume, however, the shift was more gradual than that, and was one in which the churches were willing partners rather than reactionary critics. What took place, in other words, was a liberalization of Christianity which amounted to an internal secularization. Whilst some more conservative forms of Christian and Christian-derived religion (for example, Mormons and Jehovah's Witnesses) remained aloof, much of mainstream Protestantism and, to some extent, Catholicism, embraced the need for 'modernization' and 'demythologization'. These explanations are not necessarily incompatible. But both are best considered in relation to the growth of the welfare state.

Religion in relation to welfare

Despite being a Conservative era, the immediate post-war period was the one in which the welfare state was inaugurated. From the start, this was a Christian as well as a secular vision, and one which owed a great deal to churches, religious charitable organizations and voluntary groups which, from the nineteenth century onwards, had contributed to the diverse activities and reforms which lay behind its creation (Fraser 2003). Clerical radicals had campaigned against unemployment and bad housing for decades, and many Christians accepted the rising critique of existing forms of charity and voluntary action as insufficiently co-ordinated and funded. A significant number of the early architects of the welfare state – like Harold Macmillan – were themselves Christians, whilst other Christians, including William Temple, William Beveridge and Richard Tawney, provided inspiration for religious and secular politicians alike. The Christian contribution was not only cultural: had religious bodies not been willing to surrender control of schools, hospitals, philanthropic institutions, buildings, personnel and expertise, the welfare state would have lacked necessary resources and infrastructure (Prochaska 2006).[17]

Many co-operated because they believed that the welfare ideal was an extension of Christian aims. It expressed the humanitarian, fraternal and nationalistic values which were increasingly widely shared – as well as being a way of keeping more extreme socialist demands at bay. In the words of the Anglican Bishop J. W. C. Ward, the welfare state was: 'an expression at the national level of the humanitarian work of the Church'.[18] Welfare utopianism can be seen as a sacralization of political ideals, as well as a secularization of the Godly nation. Like a secular clergy, a new body of political 'fathers' arose to serve the nation, care for its children and take responsibility for its welfare – in temporal rather than spiritual matters. It is no coincidence that the icon of this venture – displayed on a good deal of literature of the time – was the 'family doctor'. Grey-haired, male, kindly, wise and wearing a stethoscope, the local doctor was the latter-day vicar: but with a professional qualification behind him and science on his side.

There were nevertheless some tricky negotiations to be had with religious bodies before the various elements of the welfare project – especially health, education and welfare – could be co-ordinated under state control. The sphere of education, discussed by Adam Dinham and Robert Jackson in Chapter 8, serves as a good example. Historically the churches had, of course, preceded the state in the field of education by many centuries. That started to change in the modern era, as the state grew in size and reach. By 1940, if fee-paying schools are excluded, around half the schools in Britain were church schools (most Church of England and about a fifth Catholic). The idea of reforming and rationalizing the system was in motion even before the Second World War had ended: the President of the Board of Education, R. A. Butler, wanted to create a more uniform system and improve the entire standard of education. Butler was an Anglican, and negotiated directly with the churches; he used to ask the Archbishop of Canterbury to close their joint meetings with prayer (Hastings 1991: 418). Without too much difficulty, he persuaded the Anglicans not only to relinquish control over most of their schools, but to agree the introduction of non-denominational 'agreed syllabuses' of religious instruction in all schools – in return for greater state funding. It was a sort of gentleman's compromise. Some Anglicans were horrified, but most went along with it, were glad that it respected the importance of a broadly Christian formation and considered it best for the country as a whole. The Roman Catholic Church was more resistant. Conscious of the importance of nurture in the faith, it was unwilling to give up confessional religious instruction for non-denominational religious or merely 'Christian' education, and insisted on keeping greater control. Again, a compromise was eventually reached, but one which conceded more to the Catholics. Overall, most church schools in Britain were nudged into national state control within the emerging 'secular' welfare state – where they remain to this day (only after the 1980s did 'faith schools' become a matter of wide notice and contention).

Through the 1960s, church and welfare state continued to develop in a largely symbiotic relationship – albeit with the state as the increasingly powerful and independent partner. As several chapters in this book remind us, far from being a reactionary force, the Church of England was in fact deeply involved in initiating and supporting a raft of social reforms, including relaxation of laws relating to abortion, homosexual activity and divorce (see also McLeod 2007). Theology was undergoing a liberalization as well, and some of its radical ideas were conveyed to the public in John Robinson's bestselling book *Honest to God* (1963), which rejected the old idea of a God 'in the skies' in favour of one imagined as the 'ground of being'. Even for liberals who were not willing to go this far, the image of God softened considerably, with the stern and judgemental God of the coronation giving way to a more fatherly and benevolent image of a 'welfare God' (Chapter 5 and Nicholls 1989). Modernization extended to the Catholic Church, with the Second Vatican Council (1962–1965) initiating some quite radical changes, including a secularization of religious orders and clergy which was intended to break down barriers with lay people and bring both into co-operative relation in a new, less hierarchical church. The liturgy was reformed, with Latin giving way to English, and formal ritual to a more informal style of worship (Hornsby-Smith 1989). As Chapter 8 reminds us, in both Catholic and Protestant circles many clergy and lay people were also turning their attention from traditional religious and parish-based activities to welfare and 'community' projects often indistinguishable from other secular, left-wing initiatives of the time.

Once the churches had thrown in their lot with the welfare state and with secular priorities, however, their distinctiveness was in danger. They became part of the social fabric and the reigning moral and cultural ethos. This was one reason why religion became increasingly invisible in the welfare era. Another was that, once the churches had surrendered control to the state, the partnership could easily be forgotten, particularly by the political left. There was, in addition, a wilful determination to turn a blind eye to religion on the part of its increasingly confident opponents among the baby boom generation. Some of the welfare state's greatest beneficiaries neither saw nor cared how it had been brought about, and believed that it represented secular enlightenment throwing off the shackles of the past. For some groups, such as feminists, it seemed essential to clear a secular space in order to imagine different priorities and different ways of organizing social relations. There was no need for religion once the promises of heaven had been translated to earth. For a brief period it seemed to some that the dark ages of ideological and religious conflict really had been banished, and a new era of peace and social harmony had dawned. For Richard Titmuss, the pioneering professor of social policy who helped to define many characteristics of British welfare, the institution of voluntary blood donation represented a secular sacrament of communion (Titmuss 1972). And it was precisely because welfare utopianism took on the contours of a this-worldly faith, absorbing much of the state church, that it became increasingly difficult for it to share the same space with *other* faiths – that is to say, with what it came to oppose as 'religion'.

This was not just an ideological eclipse of religion, for there were important takeovers of resources as well. As well as the religious resources which went into the making of the welfare state, there was also a takeover of forms of employment once carried out by religious people, both clerical and lay. In some cases Christian workers simply swapped one paymaster for another – or were made redundant. But there were also struggles to remove clerical and Christian privileges in relation to certain roles. The justification was that professional standards must banish amateurism, 'care' and 'aid' must cast out 'charity' and 'mission', and a universal system of centrally controlled welfare must replace an army of volunteers co-ordinated by a plethora of independent bodies. As the baby boomers came of age, often equipped with qualifications from the growing number of state-funded further and higher education institutions, many found employment within the welfare state. In the process higher-paid professionals such as professors and doctors (mainly but not exclusively male) took over functions from the clergy (mainly male); and (mainly female) nurses, health visitors, social workers and ancillaries took over from church volunteers, nuns and other Christian workers (also mainly female).

These changes were part of the shifting class structure of British society at the time. The generation which remained in power until – and including – Margaret Thatcher was rigidly stratified, with the ruling classes drawn from an extremely narrow pool: male, upper-class, public-school and Oxbridge educated (Annan 1990; Thatcher was an extraordinary exception). The institutions which formed them all had church connections. Partly because of the success of the welfare state in enhancing equality of opportunity and lowering barriers of class and gender, the next generation had a broader power elite, with some grammar-school boys being especially successful. The middle class expanded considerably. More people entered higher education, and there were more jobs in state-related employment and the service sector for them to enter. For the first time, a majority of women entered into paid employment, albeit on less favourable terms than men. A new class of 'cultural creatives' began to grow which included those working in media, education, advertising, marketing and the creative industries. The new cultural workers broke the old cultural monopoly enjoyed by clergy and dons, just as many of the new professionalizing groups adopted secular, 'rational' standards and turned their backs on the Christian ethic which had often inspired their predecessors – in law, teaching and nursing, for example.

It is in relation to these shifts that the growing plausibility of secularization theory makes sense. An important voice in articulating this perspective was that of the burgeoning social sciences, often appealed to by new professionalizing groups as they sought to bring new 'standards' and status to existing occupations (from teaching to social work). It was from the social sciences, of course, that the narrative of secularization was drawn. From the perspective of many of the baby boom generation, religion (historic church religion) was not only declining before their eyes in terms of church attendance and levels of belief, it was also being pushed to the margins of public life – in order to clear the way for a better, freer, more equal welfare society. Even where this 'privatization' was in fact patchy, the churches' embrace of liberal welfare ideals could render their contribution invisible. The state was taking more and more control over religion, with churches and other religious bodies increasingly subject to state regulation (see later), and starting to be viewed as legitimate only when they acted as faithful agents of state and welfare priorities and values.

There was also a growing tide of active antagonism to 'religion' of all kinds. Not that anti-clericalism was ever a powerful force in Britain: on the whole, the Dad's Army image of the clergy as dippy but harmless prevailed. But interviews with baby boomers reveal that some harboured significant hostility towards church and churchgoers, characterizing them as 'do-gooders' at best and 'hypocrites' at worst.[19] Many have personal stories of how clergy or churchgoers exemplified these attitudes in practice (Richter and Francis 1998; Francis and Richter 2007). For others, this is a cultural stereotype, which public figures like Mary

Whitehouse seemed to confirm (see Plate 1.1). The publication of *Humanae Vitae* by Pope Paul VI in 1968 condemning artificial forms of birth control strengthened this impression, and started to roll back the liberalizing potential of Vatican II. Later battles against the ordination of women, homosexual practice and 'gay marriage' only reinforced the perception that Christians wanted to return to 'Victorian values' (or perhaps, more accurately, 1950s values).

On the whole, however, religion posed no real threat to the welfare consensus or to its secular beneficiaries. Even where it retained a counter-cultural impetus, secularization narratives were effective at recoding this as something else. The growth of alternative forms of spirituality was dismissed as flaky, feminized, self-indulgent and lacking in salience. Thus, as Chapter 1 shows, controversies over religion were not as significant in the 1960s, 1970s and earlier 1980s as they became thereafter. Where new forms of religion did arise which flouted the secular consensus and could not easily be coded as something else, they were lumped together as 'cults' or 'sects' and treated with great hostility. The fact that people were attracted to them had to be explained in terms of 'brainwashing' – a notion which had no scientific basis, but nevertheless spawned an industry of experts (Barker 1984; Beckford 1985). (Very similar ideas would later be revived to explain Islamic 'radicalization' and 'extremism', and to justify state surveillance and intervention on a much larger scale.) In the context of a greatly expanded state, and taken-for-granted secular premises, the continued existence of forms of religion 'doing their own thing' and calling for an allegiance to principles which transcended national loyalty had already become a threat.

Religion in relation to the market

It would be wrong to suggest that everyone had faith in the welfare project, or embraced its secular hopes. There is evidence of considerable scepticism from its very inception (Kynaston 2007: 42–49). In the Mass Observation archives, the diaries of Nella Last, housewife from Barrow-in-Furness, give a flavour. Writing in January 1950 just prior to a general election in which Labour were briefly returned to power, she reflects: 'I've had a little cynical feeling as I listened to J. B. Priestley and Maurice Webb that for many waverers and Pollyanna-minded ones the last speaker, provided he or she insists that "Everything is ALRIGHT, the worst is over"... will win.' She describes a speech by Webb as 'a triumph of wishful thinking mixed with sincere conviction. If things *could* be as rosy and serene as some of the Labour speakers make out.' Unconvinced that the NHS and other welfare reforms have actually made life better than before the war, she reflects: 'We've got a Health Scheme, and less time for doctors to find out what's wrong with you' (Malcolmson and Malcolmson 2010: 16, 17).

It was another woman and 'housewife', Margaret Thatcher, who offered a credible political alternative. As sceptical as Nella Last about the ability of state planning to solve social problems, Thatcher believed that it was only the industry and enterprise of individuals, working within the framework of a free market, that would promote personal freedom and national prosperity. She shared with her Labour predecessors a powerful nationalist sentiment – a belief in making Britain 'Great' again – but differed widely on how to achieve it. She was deeply suspicious of the 'grandees' and their grammar-school successors who had engineered the welfare state and made themselves comfortable as its clients. She was equally hostile to the cosy relations which had developed between politicians and trade unions, resulting in special privileges and subsidies for declining industries and their male manual labourers. During her period as Prime Minister between 1979 and 1990, Thatcher effected a decisive ideological and structural shift away from social democratic priorities towards those of neoliberalism. The achievement of the 'New Labour' government which eventually unseated the Tories in 1997 and held power until 2010 was not to deviate from this neoliberal trajectory, but to attempt to combine it with a better-functioning welfare state which was itself reformed around free-market principles including improved consumer choice. In the process, post-war concern with social equality and national greatness became additional to a concern with individual freedom and prosperity.

Religion was deeply implicated in these changes. Not surprisingly, given how fully they had embraced the welfare ideal, the mainline churches were deeply hostile to the Thatcherite revolution. This hostility received public expression in the publication of the 1985 report *Faith in the City: A Call for Action by Church and Nation* published by the Archbishop of Canterbury's Commission on Urban Priority Areas (see Plate 2.4, Church of England 1985). *Faith in the City* criticized the government for not living up to the ideals of welfare utopianism, particularly in relation to the urban poor. The immediate background was the second term of the Thatcher government, and its continuing application of a 'supply-side' economics which involved cutting subsidies to traditional industries and tolerating the ensuing rise in unemployment and associated dislocation of working-class communities. *Faith in the City* also turned its criticism on the Church of England itself: for failing to 'get alongside' the poor, for not maintaining an adequate presence in the urban priority areas and for having congregations which did not play a leading role in 'community life'.

Mrs Thatcher was not pleased. Three years later, she may still have had the report in mind when she was invited to attend the opening of the 1988 General Assembly of the Church of Scotland and to give an address which later became known by critics as the 'Sermon on the Mound' (see Plate 2.5). She began by saying that she would speak 'personally as a Christian, as well as a politician, about the way I see things. Reading recently, I came across the starkly simple phrase: "Christianity is about spiritual redemption, not social reform."' Although this became the most quoted phrase of the speech, what followed showed that she did not mean that she was against the churches' social work: far from it. However, she notes that all sorts of people do such work, and it is not what makes Christians distinctive. In an almost Augustinian account of church–state relations, she quotes the popular hymn, 'I vow to thee my country all earthly things above; entire, whole and perfect the service of my love,' and says:

> [the hymn] goes on to speak of 'another country I heard of long ago' whose King can't be seen and whose armies can't be counted, but 'soul by soul and silently her shining bounds increase'. Not group by group, or party by party, or even church by church – but soul by soul – and each one counts.
>
> That, members of the Assembly, is the country which you chiefly serve. You fight your cause under the banner of an historic Church. Your success matters greatly – as much to the temporal as to the spiritual welfare of the nation. I leave you with that earnest hope that may we all come nearer to that other country whose 'ways are ways of gentleness and all her paths are peace'.[20]

With its emphasis on personal responsibility, personal piety, wealth creation and the danger of an overly active state, this address met with a frosty reception in church circles. Immediately after she had completed it, the Moderator of the General Assembly, Dr James Whyte, pointedly presented her with some books as a memento of her visit. As he handed over recent church reports on poverty, housing and a fair social benefit system, the Assembly broke into laughter and applause.

What is so interesting about these exchanges is that the Church of England and Church of Scotland present themselves as guardians of a welfare utopianism often considered secular, whilst the 'secular' Prime Minister appears as the preacher of Christian virtue and distinctiveness. Rather than a clash between the religious and the secular, this was really a clash between two different sets of sacred commitments, two different faiths, one welfare-inflected and the other market-oriented. Thatcher had many advisors and friends who supported her interpretation, including her policy advisor Brian Griffith, the Chief Rabbi Immanuel Jakobovits, plus a number of evangelicals. Rooted in her Methodist background, her version of the gospel fitted with an evangelical Protestant emphasis on the importance of personal virtue and salvation, and sat less easily with the state church's concern with the 'common good' of the nation as a whole.

So as well as marking a turning point in politics, the Thatcher era marked a shift in religion. The two were closely connected. One obvious sign was the growing power of the evangelical wing of the Protestant churches, including the Church of England – a shift marked by the selection of George Carey as Archbishop of Canterbury (1991–2002). Another was the way in which the state church was becoming less central to national life. Bishops' ties with an old power elite were weakened, the national media turned their attention elsewhere, numbers of churchgoers fell and the prominence of other religions grew. These were symptoms of a deeper shift, whereby religion in Britain started to float free of existing social locations and anchoring points (Beckford 1989). Before, church-inflected religion had its most important linkages with the state. Clergy and politicians – often linked by gender, class and ethnicity – were the key actors. Now a much more varied religious field had emerged which was integrally bound up with the market, consumer capitalism and a proliferation of new media. Religion had become increasingly diverse, its ties to the nation state and the welfare project were loosening, the power of the clergy was diminishing and new religious actors were establishing themselves.

These changes looked different depending on your vantage point. Compared with the 1950s when church and state were implementing a shared moral and political vision from above, it looked like decline. But from a perspective less concerned with state–religion relations than with developments on the ground it looked like reconfiguration and renewal, albeit within a society in which secularism was now powerfully embedded.

The forms of religion which were growing fastest in the Thatcher era were Christian evangelicalism and Pentecostalism (in which a growing number of black majority churches, including African-initiated churches, had an important place), alternative spirituality, and the non-Christian 'world' religions associated with post-war immigration. Usually these religious developments are considered in isolation from one another, but looking at them together as this book does in Part 1, it is easier to see the common threads. All are characteristically entrepreneurial, democratized, and individualized or autonomized. That is to say, they take for granted the importance of the individual – albeit the individual within close social networks of kith and kin – and place higher value on consumer choices than on central planning by experts, elites or even representative bodies. Their forms of organization tend to be thin, and they move away from bureaucratic modes of operation. They are characterized by a plethora of different 'grass-roots' groups, movements, networks and organizations, some of which may join in loose federations (e.g. the Evangelical Alliance, the Pagan Federation or the Foundation for Holistic Spirituality), but many of which operate autonomously. The whole range of media, but particularly the internet and new social media, provides means by which not only wealthy religious collectives but also a host of new religious actors can promote themselves, gather support, offer resources and forge new alliances. There is no central oversight, and no undisputed national leadership. When the government calls for the latter, bodies which claim to be representative may emerge (e.g. the Muslim Council of Britain or the Sikh Federation), but are inevitably contested by many of those they claim to represent, and make no real attempt at leadership of their 'communities'.

A market logic is also evident in the entrepreneurial spirit of these forms of religion. Churches which grew up with nation states tend to organize in a similar manner: new initiatives are debated by central leaderships and implemented from above by bureaucratic means. The newer market-oriented forms of religion operate quite differently. They are composed of the constant and unco-ordinated activities of the myriad groups and individuals which make them up. So long as they remain outside the overseeing authority of clergy and 'religious professionals' any individual is free – within the cultural logic of their own broad form of religion – not only to decide upon a distinctive form of piety and practice, but to 'set up stall' and offer spiritual goods to others, or simply join with like-minded people for mutual support and inspiration. Even where more formal structures of authority develop, as in some forms of Islam, Hinduism and evangelical Christianity, the entrepreneurial spirit tends to remain, with new initiatives designed to promote, market, recruit and brand the form of religion in question being encouraged and supported – even when this places pressures on the preservation of tradition and 'orthodoxy' (Warner 2007). As Kim Knott and Jolyon Mitchell show in Chapter 7, these new forms of religion are both marketized and 'mediatized'. This is not to say that they are necessarily right-wing, or uncritical of the market, or neoliberal, or individualized. Some are, and some are not. But in contrast to the forms of church Christianity dominant in the religious field in the 1950s–1970s, their characteristic logics are those of consumer capitalism not national state bureaucracy. It is only when they seek to enter into dialogue with the state that the latter logic prevails – as when they operate in prisons, or in the structures of interfaith bodies.

Many of these forms of religion choose not to engage with the state at all – if they can help it. They prefer to cultivate personal piety and oversee their own initiatives and forms of direct social action. Many also foster transnational links which render national boundaries less salient for their operation. But there remains a pressure on religious groups to engage with the state if they wish to establish permanent premises and receive funding to expand their charitable initiatives. In the post-Thatcher era that pressure has increased, as successive governments, including New Labour (1997–2010) and the Conservative–Liberal coalition which followed, have embraced the idea of a 'mixed economy' of welfare providers, which includes 'faith-based organizations' alongside secular agencies. As described in Chapter 8, this approach also embraces the neoliberal idea of contract-based work. By this, the state tenders for services, enters into contractual obligations with the successful providers, and maintains close supervision and regulation thereby, whilst divesting itself of the actual task of carrying out the social activity in question. The consequences for religion are mixed. On the one hand this represents an opening up of economic possibilities for 'faith', and a renewed role in state-related public life. On the other, it comes with many strings attached, and makes many difficult demands on religion – including that religious bodies leave their particular faith commitments at the door, and offer universal services rather than catering for their own communities (Dinham et al. 2009). Case study 6 on faith-based and secular provision of services for homeless people gives a concrete example of what this can mean in practice.

Religion, healing and healthcare

An interesting illustration of all the transitions for religion covered above, including the shift from state-inflected to market-oriented religion, is provided by the changing role of religion in healthcare in the post-war period. Prior to the advent of the modern state, healing was, of course, offered chiefly by religious providers: churches, religious orders, individual men and women known for their healing powers (Porter 1999). With the rise of modern science and the growth of the enlarged state comes a partial and patchy takeover of these services by 'scientific' medicine and its providers. Right up to the formation of the National Health Service (NHS) in 1948, however, such providers were supplemented, and indeed outnumbered, by armies of voluntary providers, many of them Christian. The nineteenth century and first half of the twentieth century witnessed an expansion of more rationalized forms of voluntary and paid community provision, often run and staffed by women (Digby 1996). As well as midwives and women guardians in poorhouses, there were female sanitary inspectors, health visitors and women 'counsellors' whose work was focused on infant and maternal health. The interwar period saw the consolidation of municipal health boards, and maternity and child welfare clinics, and women and religious groups were active in the campaigning which led to the formation of the NHS. But the latter, when it came into existence, did not only absorb this contribution: it also erased a good deal. In many ways the NHS represented the triumph of scientific medicine over a wider programme of social healthcare and preventative medicine; of the national over the local; of the male medical profession over voluntaryism; and of secular medicine over religious, or mixed, provision of health and healing.

Interestingly, however, the eclipse was short-lived. From the 1970s onwards there was an explosion of provision by complementary and alternative forms of healing and healthcare, such that, by the turn of the millennium, the yearly use of the most established forms of complementary and alternative health practices (CAM) was estimated to involve around a third of the adult population of the UK (Thomas *et al.* 2001). Many of these have an explicitly religious, or more precisely 'spiritual', dimension (Heelas and Woodhead 2005; Sointu and Woodhead 2008). Their philosophy is explicitly 'holistic'. Against a bio-medical view of the human person as an organism subject to disease, they treat the 'whole person' understood as a unity of 'body, mind and spirit'. This ties to an underlying metaphysic which views all forms of life as manifestations of an underlying energy, spirit or '*chi*'. Disease is a symptom of a blockage of energy, and the multifarious techniques of alternative healing seek to uncover the physical, spiritual or mental causes of this, and to free 'the spirit'.

Thus religion returns to healthcare under the market regime – but in a new form. Whereas before it had been Christianity and the churches which had dominated the religious contribution, and then secular medicine, now individual practitioners set up stall in a marketplace which allows them free entry, and they use new media like the internet to attract clients. It is not simply a case of religion taking up where it left off before the NHS, because it is significantly changed under the new conditions in which it arises. Not only does it display a market logic, it arises in reaction to forms of scientific medicine which are said to neglect the whole person and dwell only on physical symptoms. A significant number of practitioners are ex-nurses, refugees not only from the churches, but also from the NHS and its bureaucratic structures, rationalized target cultures and unsympathetic doctors or managers.[21] Even though such practical spirituality may preserve, or recapitulate, traditional elements of healing and the preservation of health, including charms, amulets, laying on of hands, herbalism and various forms of magical practice, this is no 'folk religion'. It is a form of religion which is as inseparable from advanced consumer capitalism, popular culture and the media as the Church of England is from the nation state.

The interesting twist to this tale lies in the way in which holistic healing then creeps back into the state-run health system. From the 1990s onwards, some doctors started refer-ring patients to alternative practitioners; some practices and hospitals employed holistic practitioners on their staff; nursing training started to incorporate spiritual care; and the NHS set up an official directory of CAM providers.[22] This is not simply because some of these treatments are effective, but because 'customers' demand them, and because the NHS has itself been reformed according to market logics and in a way which takes patient choice increasingly seriously (Klein 2006). Not surprisingly, there is controversy over these changes, particularly from the scientific professionals who want to defend the integrity of 'scientific medicine'. One result is a clinical testing and ranking of holistic healthcare prac-tices, in which some are endorsed and others rejected.[23] Another is an ongoing controversy over the value of CAM, which intensified in the twenty-first century, and in which home-opathy has become a particular focus of debate (because the dilution of its 'medicines' makes it seem an obvious placebo-based practice or, in the words of its critics, 'mumbo-jumbo' and 'quackery'). In many ways this has become Britain's version of the battles between evolu-tion and creationism in the USA: a rallying point for mutual excoriations between defenders of secularism and of spirituality. But the more important point is that this illustrates not just the religious coming back to challenge the secular, but coming back in a market-inflected form to challenge 'older' welfare-inflected scientific and secular formations.

Deregulation and reregulation of religion

The growing desire by health professionals and scientists to regulate and license alternative health provision illustrates a final key theme to emerge from this volume: the deregulation and reregulation of religion in post-war Britain. The attempt to regulate CAM is only one of a raft of measures which were put in place in the first decades of the twenty-first century in an attempt to extend greater state control over religion. One of the most high-profile was the 'securitization' of Islam in Britain, whereby – especially after the 7 July 2005 London bombings – serious attempts were made to monitor, control and re-engineer the practice and teachings of Islam and associated activities. As well as more direct anti-terrorist measures, the 'Prevent' initiative, introduced by New Labour, was intended to change the hearts and minds of British Muslims, and to make 'moderate' forms of Islam more attractive than 'extremist' forms. Such direct intervention in religious belief was a radical new move for a modern state, which in theory keeps out of religious 'doctrine' and opinion as a matter of principle (on the grounds that this is a private concern). It was effected not only by meas-ures of control, such as banning certain 'radical' groups, but by offering considerable amounts of funding and other incentives to groups and projects which promised to promote acceptable forms of Islamic teaching, especially to young people. A whole new section of government resource and policy was dedicated to dealing with this problem, a problem which was treated as unprecedented and therefore calling for special measures. This policy area developed a new language to make sense of 'radical' Islam, which spoke of 'vulnerable' Muslims susceptible to being 'radicalized', and the importance of 'deradicalization' programmes – in an approach which unconsciously recapitulated a great deal of the anti-cult movement of the 1960s–1980s. The Coalition government endorsed a similar strategy in 2011, launching a revised Prevent strategy and calling for an approach which would be less apologetic about defending 'fundamental British values' and more robust in tackling religious extremism.[24]

Even more far-reaching in terms of religious regulation were the legal measures put in place in a raft of equalities legislation rolled out in the early twenty-first century in response to European directives. The details are covered in Chapter 9. Part of the rationale was to extend the protection which had previously been enshrined in law against discrimination on the basis of race and gender to a wider range of 'grounds' including religion and sexual orientation. The Equality and Human Rights Commission, an independent statutory body, was established by the integrated Equality Act in 2006 and came into being in 2007; its purpose was to promote and enforce the new legislation. An unintended consequence, however, was a series of legal judgements which were widely perceived to disadvantage religion and religious people, and to prevent rather than protect them from expressing sincerely held beliefs. Some of the most controversial cases and *causes célèbres*, including those concerning the wearing of Christian crucifixes, a silver chastity ring and the Muslim face-veil, praying with patients and refusing to celebrate civil partnerships for gay couples, are discussed in Chapters 1 and 9 (see also Case study 7 on the application of human rights in relation to religious education in Northern Ireland).

Less commented upon, but also important in extending greater state control over religion, were other changes in regulation, including changes in charity law, which imposed much stricter rules on religious bodies seeking charitable status (which means most of them), and the extension of the 'contractual' approach to 'faith-based organizations' receiving government funding described above (see Chapter 11). Also significant in this regard was the state's growing concern from the late 1990s onwards to enter into more regularized forms of consultation with a range of 'faith communities', rather than simply relying on historical forms of relationship with the major churches and with the long-established Jewish community in Britain. As Case study 2 documents, this was effected through the growth of interfaith bodies, most notably the Inter Faith Network for the UK. As Chapter 3 shows, it also led to a growth of various bodies claiming to be representative of all the minority faiths in Britain. The circle which these developments tried to square was to make the various proliferating forms of non-Christian religion in Britain act more like a state church – that is, with national leaders and centralized representative bodies with which the state could 'do business'.

But these attempts to control and regulate religion – and to improve state–religion relationships – were premised on eras which were passing: on the close state–church relations of the early days of the welfare state, and on the expanded state secularism which pertained until the 1990s. For those who believed that religion had simply 'reappeared' it was easy to assume that the state should simply attempt to re-enter into relations with it and try to regulate it as if it was a church, but with more faces (the so-called 'world religions'). Given this expectation, many religious communities made efforts to do as they were asked. But below the surface of national consultations, religion had changed dramatically – in a more market- and media-inflected way, and in relation to transnational rather than national connections and concerns.

Ironically, it was the long era of post-war secular sentiment and faith in secularization which had contributed to this shift. For an effect of marginalizing religion, of rendering it less visible, and of taking power, resources and prestige away from the churches and male religious professionals, was to open up the religious arena to new religious ideas, organizations and agents, and to allow them to flourish without state control or regulation. The mechanisms were complex. One was that, as religion lost prestige, barriers to entry were lowered, and women and other minorities could take up positions of leadership formerly more restricted in terms of gender, class and race. Another was that the market opened new opportunities, allowing new religious providers to set up stall, advertise their wares on the internet and charge for their services. The new neoliberal contractual approach to 'buying' faith-based services also encouraged new entrants, as well as favouring some – like the Salvation Army – which were able to mobilize effectively to take advantage. And, above all, these changes were allowed to take place unchecked and largely unnoticed because religion was widely believed to be a dying force: even the Church of England enjoyed an unprece- dented relaxation of state control over its affairs because it was considered harmless (Green 1996). Thus a de facto deregulation of religion led to a growth in many new forms of reli- gion – from holistic spirituality to Muslim 'radicalism' – which, when they eventually came to secular attention, called forth a panicked reregulation as state bodies struggled to take control of something which had become much harder for them to get a grip on – either intellectually or legislatively. In relation to the market and the media, and on a global stage, however, these newer forms of religion were quite at home.

Conclusion

This volume consolidates a new interpretation of religious change in the post-war period, an interpretation which has been emerging for some time in the work of scholars from many different disciplines, including those gathered here. It is not one which discards all that went before or repudiates every insight offered by the once-dominant secularization frame- work. Although it makes significant criticisms of the latter, it is equally critical of recent talk of 'desecularization', talk which recognizes the need for change but clings too tightly to the existing terms of debate to effect it.

   The approach offered here rejects the starting point that the terms 'religion' and 'the secular' are neutral concepts which can serve as unproblematic building blocks of data- collection and analysis. It treats them instead as an integral part of the milieu to be analysed rather than as detached standpoints from which it can be viewed. As we will see, their meaning is constantly constructed, reconstructed and disputed throughout the post-war period, and bound up with particular political struggles, interests and social shifts. Secularization theories went awry when they failed to appreciate the contingent nature of their own currency. In trying to demonstrate that religion was declining by citing only data related to declining churchgoing and church influence on national government, for exam- ple, they confused a very particular historical manifestation of religion (post-Reformation churches with links to the nation state) with a universal process to do with the 'religion' in 'secular modernity'. They also failed in critical self-awareness of the ways in which such a point of view supported the interests and struggles of particular social groups in the post-war period – including many academics. By remaining alert to the emergence of new forms of reverence, ritualization and excoriation during the post-war period, the approach advocated here is better able to take account of shifting constructions of the sacred and profane, whether these are labelled as 'religion', 'secularity', 'spirituality', or simply regarded as what is 'natural' and 'normal'. It is also more willing to scan all domains of society, and to be crit- ically aware of its own situated standpoint.

   From this perspective, what emerges as the single most important sacred commitment of post-war Britain is 'welfare utopianism'. The volume shows how a sense of British national pride, which had previously rested on Empire, settled after the Second World War on victory over the Nazis and the creation of a welfare state – above all a National Health Service – which would be the envy of the world. At first a religious as well as a secular dream, by the 1960s this was increasingly represented by powerful groups as a secular achievement, and the contributions of religion were eclipsed. Now the gains of a secular society were set against those of religion: equality, enlightenment, liberation and progress against patriarchy, repression, superstition – and just plain dullness. Integral to this development was a takeover of power by more self-consciously secular classes: a new political elite, an expanded class of cultural producers (including academics and media professionals), scientists and those whose jobs had been created by the vast expansion of welfare. Though this dream was soon beset by economic and social problems and the rise of an alternative neoliberal vision, a great deal remains – not least a powerful political class, an extensive state apparatus, and residual forms of secularism and national pride.

In the process 'religion' in post-war Britain has changed its position from majority to minority, in a number of different senses. All had to do with the very particular construction of religion and secularity which emerged at this time, and in which the 'secular' gained increasingly powerful representation. In the first place, the actively religious (in the old sense of members of designated church-like institutions) became a numerical minority, and the open expression of religion in many public arenas – particularly governmental and state-controlled – became highly contentious. 'God' becomes the great taboo – far more than sex or violence.[25] This is true even though the majority of the population continue to identify as Christian and to believe in some kind of God. Second, the fastest-growing forms of religion cease to be those which are most closely allied with political power and social prestige. Rather than being 'the Tory party at prayer', religion becomes more closely associated with minorities, including the women active in many forms of alternative spirituality and healthcare, and the Muslims, Sikhs, Hindus and others forging new forms of identity and representation in British society. Third, religion becomes the place where some of the tasks which are not being carried out by other social actors are attended to: caring for the chronically ill and dying; providing for the homeless and asylum seekers; dignifying life and death through ritual action; sacralizing beliefs, values and commitments; dealing with emotions of anger, shame, guilt and grief; forging identities and objects of shared symbolic significance for minority groups. Throughout, religion is positioned, represented and actively constructed as a minority interest by secular lobbies in politics, the media, state services, science, education and professional bodies – the effect being to maintain religion's minority status by regulation, opposition, exclusion and silencing.

Thus one of the most important turning points for post-war religion in Britain has to do with the shifting balance of power between the secular and the religious in the context of a welfare-state society. In the 1960s secular interests gain power in relation to welfare nationalism; from the late 1980s confidence in this secular settlement begins to be seriously shaken – though not entirely abandoned – and religion becomes visible again. A second turning point has to do with a shift of location from state to market which takes place gradually from the late 1970s onwards. State churches suffer the most dramatic decline in power and influence, and civil religion fragments. Conversely, the most vibrant and fastest growing forms of religion are those which embrace the opportunities of the market and new media and the imperative of personal decision: from charismatic forms of Christianity to alternative forms of spirituality. It is not that the state does not remain important for religion: we have noted how a period of 'deregulation' under 'secularism' is replaced in the new millennium with increasing state 'reregulation' of religion. However, insofar as religious groups wish to relate to the state, they have to resort to anachronistic church-like forms of national organization, membership and representation. And the state's new interest in religion becomes increasingly imbued with a market logic, as in the way that 'faith-based organizations' come to be used as means to achieve a 'mixed economy' of welfare which is more responsive to consumer 'choice'. This is not to say that religion ceases to be political, but that activist forms of religiosity take new forms outside traditional politics, becoming rooted in electronically mediated sources of knowledge and campaigning, direct political action, international gatherings and transnational communities of interest. The 'minoritization' of religion gives it a natural opportunity to serve as a natural support for a wide variety of identities and claims-making, whilst a majority retains a residual loyalty to a diffused sense of being Christian and/or secular.

This leaves a situation in the new millennium which is diverse, complex, multi-layered and contradictory. In the concluding chapter, David Martin points out that revolutions in Britain have never been followed through to their conclusion. A corollary is that little is ever completely destroyed or discarded. The forms and impress of past forms of religious faith live on, alongside the latest offerings of new ones. On different occasions, among different classes, and in relation to different circumstances and imperatives, the old can be revitalized and reformed, and the new may become recessive. There are few genuinely novel elements in the picture presented by this volume – what is new are their modes of reconfiguration. Britain now finds itself in a situation in which old and new forms of commitment, power and organization co-exist and compete with one another. After the 1980s no one social formation was powerful enough to control the others (as the state had been in the immediate post-war period). Nor was there a common ideology with enough support to suppress dissident voices – whether religious or secular. This helps explain why the conflicts and contradictions with which this Introduction began abound: why Britain can be religious and secular; why we think of religion in terms of the Vicar of Dibley (see Plate 1.8) and Muslim terrorists; why the majority of the population call themselves Christian but are hostile or indifferent to many aspects of religion; why governments embrace 'faith' but are suspicious of 'religion'; why public debate swings between 'multiculturalism' and 'integration'; why religion is viewed as both radical and conservative; why we build multi-faith spaces (see Case study 4 and Plate 3.9) but can no longer speak of God in public.

This multi-layered, sedimented situation explains why secularization theory continues to be able to explain some, but not all, of the present situation. More importantly, it makes sense of how it gained such plausibility for much of the post-war period, but lost conviction after the 1990s when talk of 'desecularization' began to gain ground. For the geopolitical conditions which made it possible to view the world in a teleological fashion have been passing away in the period under discussion. The idea that an increasingly 'secular' Europe was beating a path which the rest of the world would one day follow is part of the faith that has dissolved. Britain is no longer a great world power, and the West in general is rapidly being decentred by growing wealth and power elsewhere. 'Civilization' no longer appears as the exclusive preserve of secular nations. And nation states are in any case no longer the main containers of society or of religion: new forms and flows of power and ideas cross their boundaries with speed and ease. For the past five centuries, it has been the nation state with which Western forms of religion have been chiefly entangled, and both state and church have shaped one another's distinctive forms. The real significance of the post-war period lies in the fact that this ceased to be true. In that sense, it was the start of a remarkable new phase for religion, in which the relationship with state and nation ceased to be decisive, even though it remained important, and the relation with consumer capitalism – whether opportunistic or critical – became increasingly salient.

There is no question of a 'return' of religion. For one thing, it never really went away, and for another, it emerged after the 1980s in significantly different forms. The kinds of Christianity which supported a sense of national greatness are not dead, but are diminished. The new entrants to the spiritual marketplace are more focused on supporting individuals in their everyday lives, fostering new kinds of identity and lifestyle, and linking the like-minded and like-hearted to one another in a vast plurality of different forms of religious alliance. There is a weakening of linkages with the state and a strengthening of those with consumer capitalism and a wide range of media. Centralized, state-like, religious bureaucracies and hierarchies of leadership have lost influence relative to much looser forms of association including small groups, occasional gatherings and festivals, and real and virtual networks.

This is a situation which supports intellectual investigation and tentativeness rather than the certainties and predictions of grand theory. It cannot support a sovereign line of analysis, but it allows new interpretations to emerge, quieter voices to be heard, everyday lives and struggles to count, and conflicts and unintended consequences to be taken more seriously. Its focus on a single national situation is 'of its time', but may become less and less defensible as that unit diminishes in salience relative to transnational formations. No framework ever truly transcends the conditions it tries to explain, and this volume is no exception. It bears witness to an era in which certainties were lost, pride was chastened and utopian projects lost conviction. For religion, there was both loss and gain: as a small number of old gods lost authority, a vast number of new ones arose to take their place. As existing religious actors failed to hold onto power, the way was cleared for new entrants. And as the secular ceased to seem like the inevitable destination on a journey all must take, horizons of present vision and future possibility opened up in interesting, but more modest, ways.

The book's design

This book was deliberately designed so that it could be read either as a whole, to gain a full picture of religion and change in Britain since the Second World War, or by selecting contributions which are of particular interest to the reader. The chapters have therefore been presented as self-standing units with integral bibliographies, notes, etc.

The chapters are interspersed with short case studies. The latter supplement the former, and offer concrete examples and illustrations of issues dealt with in a more abstract or general way in the chapters. The Plates are grouped to represent the 'People', 'Events' and 'Objects and places' which contributors selected as particularly key to religion in the post-war period.

The first chapter of the book sets the scene by using controversies as a lens on change. The chapters in Part 1 focus on changing forms of religion. Part 2 examines religion's relations with different aspects of social life. Part 3 offers theoretical perspectives on religion and change in the post-war period. The book as a whole draws on a variety of approaches and disciplines in order to capture different facets of religion, to present it from several perspectives and to view it in relation to other aspects of society rather than in isolation.

Key terms

Baby boom generation: Refers to those born, roughly, between the end of the Second World War and the mid-1960s when there was a marked increase in the birth rate in Britain and other Western societies.

Creationism: Belief that God created the world according to the 'seven day' account in the book of Genesis in the Bible, and not by evolution.

Deprivatization: A process whereby religion, which had been confined to the private sphere, returns to civil society and/or public life.

Desecularization: A process whereby religious decline is reversed and religion 're-emerges', giving rise to a 'post-secular' era.

Differentiation: A process, often thought to be coterminous with modernization, whereby social functions are distributed to autonomous spheres with their own logics and resources – for example, education, law, politics, religion.

Ecumenism: A movement towards Christian unity, or unity among those believing in Jesus Christ.

Established church: A church which has an established, constitutional relationship with the state, also called a 'state church' and sometimes a 'national church'.

Evangelicalism: A pan-denominational movement within Protestantism which emphasizes the authority of the Bible, a commitment to personal conversion and sharing the gospel.

Fundamentalism: The rigorous maintenance of perceived religious teaching, which in the Christian case means particular conviction of the inerrancy of the Bible.

New Commonwealth: A post-imperial 'family of nations' which had once been under British control. The Queen is the ceremonial head of the Commonwealth.

Privatization: The process whereby religion is removed from public life into a sphere of private life.

Secularization: The process whereby religion declines in personal and social significance. Secularization theories offer different descriptions and explanations of the process.

Securitization: The process by which, and the mechanisms whereby, certain groups, individuals, discourses, etc. are framed as security risks.

Further reading

Bruce, Steve (1995). *Religion in Modern Britain*. Oxford: Oxford University Press. Analyses the history of post-war Britain through the prism of secularization.

Clarke, Peter (2004). *Hope and Glory: Britain 1900–2000*. 2nd edition. London: Penguin Books. An informative one-volume general history of twentieth-century Britain.

Davie, Grace (1994). *Religion in Britain since 1945: Believing without Belonging*. Oxford: Blackwell. Takes a different approach from Steve Bruce's *Religion in Modern Britain* and is usefully read alongside it.

Hastings, Adrian (1991). *A History of English Christianity 1920–1990*. 3rd edition. London: SCM. A well-informed account of the recent history of the churches in England.

Kynaston, David (2007). *Austerity Britain 1945–51*. London, Berlin and New York, NY: Bloomsbury, and David Kynaston (2009). *Family Britain 1951–57*. London, Berlin and New York, NY: Bloomsbury. The first two books of an authoritative history of post-war Britain (religion is downplayed).

McLeod, Hugh (2007). *The Religious Crisis of the 1960s*. Oxford: Oxford University Press. A balanced analysis of religious change in the 1960s.

References

Annan, Noel (1990). *Our Age: The Generation that Made Post-war Britain*. London: Weidenfeld and Nicholson.

Bäckström, Anders and Grace Davie (2011). 'Welfare and Religion in Europe: Themes, Theories and Tensions', in Anders Bäckström, Grace Davie, Ninna Edgardh and Per Pettersson (eds), *Welfare and Religion in 21st Century Europe. Volume 2: Gendered, Religious and Social Change*. Aldershot: Ashgate, 151–171.

Barker, Eileen (1984). *The Making of a Moonie: Choice or Brainwashing?* Oxford and New York, NY: Basil Blackwell.

Barley, Lynda (2003). 'Believing without Belonging'. Research and Statistics Department, Archbishop's Council. Unpublished lecture handout.

Beckford, James A. (1985). *Cult Controversies: The Societal Response to New Religious Movements*. London and New York, NY: Tavistock Publications.

Beckford, James A. (1989). *Religion and Advanced Industrial Society*. London: Unwin Hyman.

Berger, Peter (ed.) (1999). *The Desecularization of the World: Resurgent Religion and World Politics*. Grand Rapids, MI: Eerdmans.

Brierley, Peter (ed.) (2006). *UK Christian Handbook: Religious Trends 6, 2006/7, Pulling out of the Nosedive*. London: Christian Research.

Brown, Callum G. (2001). *The Death of Christian Britain: Understanding Secularisation, 1800–2000*. London and New York, NY: Routledge.

Brown, Callum G. and Michael Snape (eds) (2010). *Secularisation in the Christian World: A Festschrift for Hugh McLeod*. Aldershot: Ashgate.

Bruce, Steve (1995). *Religion in Modern Britain*. Oxford: Oxford University Press.

Bruce, Steve (2002). *God is Dead: Secularization in the West*. Oxford and Malden, MA: Blackwell.

Casanova, José (1994). *Public Religions in the Modern World*. Chicago, IL: University of Chicago Press.

Church of England. Commission on Urban Priority Areas (1985). *Faith in the City: A Call for Action by Church and Nation*. London: Church House.

Clarke, Peter (2004). *Hope and Glory: Britain 1900–2000*. 2nd edition. London: Penguin Books.

Colley, Linda (2003). *Britons: Forging the Nation 1701–1837*. London: Pimlico.

Davie, Grace (1994). *Religion in Britain since 1945: Believing without Belonging*. Oxford: Blackwell.

Dawkins, Richard (2006). *The God Delusion*. London: Bantam Press.

Day, Abby (2011). *Believing in Belonging: Belief and Social Identity in the Modern World*. Oxford: Oxford University Press.

Digby, Ann (1996). 'Medicine and the English State, 1901–1948', in S. J. D. Green and R. C. Whiting (eds), The Boundaries of the State in Modern Britain. Cambridge: Cambridge University Press, 213–230.

Dinham, Adam, Robert Furbey and Vivien Lowndes (2009). *Faith in the Public Realm: Controversies, Policies and Practices*. Bristol: The Policy Press.

Eccles, Janet (2010). 'How Have Preboomer and Boomer Women Raised in Christianity who Have Lived Through the "Sixties Revolution" Been Affected in Terms of Their Religious and Value Commitments? An Interview-Based Study with Informants from South Cumbria', unpublished PhD thesis, University of Lancaster.

Fane, R. S. (1999). 'Is Self-assigned Religious Affiliation Socially Significant?', in Leslie J. Francis (ed.), *Sociology, Theology and the Curriculum*. London: Cassell, 113–123.

Francis, Leslie J. (2008). 'The Social Significance of Self-assigned Religious Affiliation: A Study Among Adolescents in England and Wales', in Basia Spalek and Alia Imtoual (eds), *Religion, Spirituality and Social Science Research*. Bristol: Policy Press, 149–162.

Francis, Leslie and Philip Richter (2007). *Gone for Good? Church-Leaving and Returning in the Twenty-First Century*. Peterborough: Epworth.

Fraser, Derek (2003). *The Evolution of the British Welfare State: A History of Social Policy since the Industrial Revolution*. 3rd edition. Basingstoke: Palgrave Macmillan.

Gallup, George and Michael Lindsay (1999). *Surveying the Religious Landscape*. Harrisburg, PA: Morehouse.

Garnett, Jane, Matthew Grimley, Alana Harris, William Whyte and Sarah Williams (eds) (2007). *Redefining Christian Britain: Post 1945 Perspectives*. London: SCM.

Gilroy, Paul (1987). *There Ain't No Black in the Union Jack: The Cultural Politics of Race and Nation*. London: Hutchinson.

Green, S. J. D. (1996). 'Survival and Autonomy: On the Strange Fortunes and Peculiar Legacy of Ecclesiastical Establishment in the Modern British State, c.1920 to the Present Day', in S. J. D. Green and R. C. Whiting (eds), *The Boundaries of the State in Modern Britain*. Cambridge: Cambridge University Press, 299–324.

Green, S. J. D. (2010). *The Passing of Protestant England: Secularisation and Social Change c.1920–1960*. Cambridge: Cambridge University Press.

Hamberg, Eva (2003). 'Christendom in Decline: The Swedish Case', in Hugh McLeod and Werner Ustorf (eds), *The Decline of Christendom in Western Europe, 1750–2000*. Cambridge and New York: Cambridge University Press, 47–62.

Harvey, David (2005). *A Brief History of Neoliberalism*. Oxford: Oxford University Press.

Hastings, Adrian (1991). *A History of English Christianity 1920–1990*. 3rd edition. London: SCM.

Heald, Gordon (2000). 'The Soul of Britain', *The Tablet*, 3 June: 770.

Heelas, Paul and Linda Woodhead (2005). *The Spiritual Revolution: Why Religion is Giving Way to Spirituality*. Oxford: Blackwell.

Hitchens, Christopher (2007). *God is Not Great: The Case Against Religion*. London: Atlantic Books.

Hornsby-Smith, Michael (1989). *The Changing Parish: A Study of Parishes, Priests and Parishioners after Vatican II*. London and New York, NY: Routledge.

Klein, Rudolph (2006). *The New Politics of the NHS: From Creation to Reinvention*. 5th edition. Oxford and Seattle: Radcliffe Publishing.

Kynaston, David (2007). *Austerity Britain 1945–51*. London, Berlin and New York, NY: Bloomsbury.

Kynaston, David (2009). *Family Britain 1951–57*. London, Berlin and New York, NY: Bloomsbury.

McLeod, Hugh (2007). *The Religious Crisis of the 1960s*. Oxford: Oxford University Press.

Macmillan, Harold (1957) 'Most of our People Have Never Had it so Good'. Speech delivered in Bedford, 20 July. http://news.bbc.co.uk/onthisday/hi/dates/stories/july/20/newsid_3728000/3728225.stm (accessed 1 October 2010).

Malcolmson, Patricia and Robert Malcolmson (2010). *Nella Last in the 1950s: Further Diaries of 'Housewife, 49'*. London: Profile Books.

Martin, David (1965). 'Towards Eliminating the Concept of Secularisation', in Julius Gould (ed.), *Penguin Survey of the Social Sciences*. Harmondsworth: Penguin, 185–197.

Martin, David (1969). *The Religious and the Secular*. London: Routledge and Kegan Paul.

Martin, David (1978). *A General Theory of Secularization*. London: Blackwell.

Martin, David (1989). 'The Churches, Pink Bishops and the Iron Lady', in Dennis Kavanagh and Anthony Seldon (eds), *The Thatcher Effect: A Decade of Change*. Oxford: Clarendon Press, 330–341.

Martin, David (2005). *On Secularization: Towards a Revised General Theory*. Aldershot: Ashgate.

Martin, David (2010). Lecture presented at 'Workshop on the Work of David Martin' at the Excellence-Cluster, University of Munster, November.

Martin, David (2011). *The Future of Christianity: Reflections on Violence and Democracy, Religion and Secularization*. Aldershot: Ashgate.

Micklethwait, John and Adrian Wooldridge (2009). *God is Back: How the Global Rise of Faith is Changing the World*. London: Penguin.

Midgley, Mary (2002). *Evolution as a Religion: Strange Hopes and Stranger Fears*. London and New York, NY: Routledge.

Modood, Tariq (2005). *Multicultural Politics: Racism, Ethnicity and Muslims in Britain*. Edinburgh: University of Edinburgh Press.

Nicholls, David (1989). *Deity and Domination: Images of God in the Nineteenth and Twentieth Centuries*. London and New York, NY: Routledge.

O'Beirne, Maria (2004). *Religion in England and Wales: Findings from the 2001 Home Office Citizenship Survey.* Home Office Research Study 274. London: Her Majesty's Stationery Office.

Porter, Roy (1999). *The Greatest Benefit to Mankind: A Medical History of Humanity from Antiquity to the Present.* London: Fontana.

Prochaska, Frank (2006). *Christianity and Social Service in Modern Britain: The Disinherited Spirit.* New York, NY: Oxford University Press.

Richter, Philip and Leslie Francis (1998). *Gone but not Forgotten: Church Leaving and Returning.* London: Darton, Longman and Todd.

Robinson, John (1963). *Honest to God.* London: SCM.

Sointu, Eeva and Linda Woodhead (2008). 'Holistic Spirituality, Gender, and Expressive Selfhood', *Journal for the Scientific Study of Religion*, 47/2: 259–276.

Summerfield, Penny (1989). *Women Workers in the Second World War: Production and Patriarchy in Conflict.* London and New York, NY: Routledge.

Taylor, Charles (2007). *A Secular Age.* Cambridge, MA: Harvard University Press.

Thomas, K. J., J. P. Nicholl and P. Coleman (2001). 'Use and Expenditure on Complementary Medicine in England: A Population Based Survey', *Complementary Therapies in Medicine*, 9/1: 2–11.

Titmuss, Richard (1972). *The Gift Relationship: From Human Blood to Social Policy.* New York, NY: Vintage Books.

Toumey, Christopher P. (1994). *God's Own Scientists: Creationists in a Secular World.* New Brunswick, NJ: Rutgers University Press.

Voas, David (2003). 'Is Britain a Christian Country?', in Paul Avis (ed.), *Public Faith? The State of Religious Belief and Practice in Britain.* London: SPCK, 92–105.

Voas, David and Abby Day (2007). 'Secularity in Great Britain', in Barry A. Kosmin and Ariela Keysar (eds), *Secularism and Secularity: Contemporary International Perspectives.* Hartford: Institute for the Study of Secularism in Society and Culture, 95–110.

Warner, Rob (2007). *Re-inventing English Evangelicalism, 1966–2001.* Milton Keynes: Paternoster.

Warner, Rob (2010). *Secularization and its Discontents.* London: Continuum.

Weller, Paul (2008). *Religious Diversity in the UK: Contours and Issues.* London: Continuum.

Weller, Paul (2009). *A Mirror for our Times: 'The Rushdie Affair' and the Future of Multiculturalism.* London: Continuum.

Wilson, Bryan (1969). *Religion in Secular Society.* Harmondsworth: Penguin.

Wilson, Bryan (1976). *Contemporary Transformations of Religion.* London and New York, NY: Oxford University Press.

Wilson, Bryan (1982). *Religion in Sociological Perspective.* Oxford: Oxford University Press.

Woodhead, Linda (2007). 'Sex and Secularisation', in Gerard Loughlin (ed.), *Queer Theology: Rethinking the Western Body.* Oxford and Malden, MA: Blackwell, 230–244.

Woodhead, Linda (2011). 'Five Concepts of Religion', *International Review of Sociology*, 21/1: 121–143.

Notes

1   Marina Warner (writer, literary critic and cultural commentator): 'In their Own Words: British Novelists 1970–1990', Programme Three, BBC 4, broadcast in 2010.

2   This approach has been widely criticized in academic circles, but remains widespread, including in religious education in schools. For discussion of some of the main critiques see Woodhead (2011). For discussion of how this approach entered into education and took over from 'religious instruction', see Chapter 8.

3   Thanks to Lesley Riddle at Routledge for helping originate the idea of an edited collection on religion in Britain.

4   Thanks are also due to Kaye Haw, Peter Hopkins and Basia Spalek who took part in these meetings, and provided a valuable perspective on issues of religion and identity, and religion and securitization.

5 For more details see the Programme website www.religionandsociety.org.uk

6 Acknowledgements are due to the staff at the AHRC and ESRC who directly assisted the Programme, including Lou Matter, Katherine Warren and Chris Wyatt, and to the Steering Committee chaired by Ivon Asquith which supported the idea of this volume. Thank you also to Dave Perfect from the Equality and Human Rights Commission for his careful proof reading of this volume.

7 In the academy, the sway of secularization theory is clearest in the social sciences. British historians have generally been more cautious about embracing a secularization framework without qualification, as the influential work of Hugh McLeod demonstrates. There have also been exceptions, most recently the work of Callum Brown (2001 and in this volume), which defends secularization. A vocal rejection of secularization theory became common in recent historical research, and is exemplified by the edited collection by Garnett *et al.* (2007). The collection of essays edited by Brown and Snape (2010) in honour of Hugh McLeod gives a good sense of the current balance of debate among historians. For a useful survey of the state of sociological debate about secularization see Warner (2010).

8 Steve Bruce's book on *Religion in Modern Britain* (1995) adopted a secularization framework, whereas Grace Davie's *Religion in Britain since 1945: Believing without Belonging* (1994) took a more qualified approach. The first major book to argue the deprivatization thesis was José Casanova's *Public Religions in the Modern World* (1994), and the first to argue the desecularization thesis was Peter Berger's edited collection *The Desecularization of the World* (1999). Although both authors were based in the USA, their books address resurgence in Europe as well (Davie has a chapter in the latter). A desecularization perspective was given popular expression by the *Economist* journalists John Micklethwait and Adrian Wooldridge in their book *God is Back* (2009), which took a global view. Their title is a neat counterpoint to the opposite point of view expressed in Steve Bruce's *God is Dead* (2002).

9 Voas (2003) and Voas and Day (2007) argue that the 'Christian' figure is inflated, especially in the Census for England and Wales. They suggest that the form and placement of the religion question may have implied to people that it was asking about cultural background rather than present religious affiliation. The 2004 British Social Attitudes survey finds only a bare majority belonging to a Christian denomination, with 43 per cent of people saying they belong to no religion. On the other side of the debate, others point out that self-reported affiliation and belonging at the very least gives a useful indication of the cultural background and general orientating values of a person, and of their self-identification and dis-identification, belonging and difference (Fane 1999; Francis 2008).

10 National Statistics Online. Online. Available HTTP: www.statistics.gov.uk/cci/nugget_print.asp?ID=293 (accessed May 2009). The total figure for no religion/not stated includes cases in N. Ireland where data is only available as a combined category.

11 The Opinion Research Business BBC Soul of Britain Questionnaire Results (unpublished data). Key findings are presented in Heald (2000).

12 As yet this has not been researched by survey in the UK, but Eva Hamberg's research in Sweden found that 9 per cent reported being 'a practising Christian', 26 per cent 'I'm not a Christian' and 63 per cent 'I'm a Christian in my own personal way' (Hamberg 2003). See also Day (2011).

13 Barley (2003) found over half the British population had attended a funeral connected to a church over the past year, 39 per cent a wedding and 29 per cent a baptism.

14 See note 8 above.

15 The leaders of the IRA were not necessarily devout; some were secular, including secular Marxist. But they represented the nationalism of a Roman Catholic population, while also 'terrorizing' that population into conformity.

16 Quoted by Grace Davie (1994: 31).

17 See also Bäckström and Davie (2011) on the continuing contribution of religion, especially the churches, to welfare in Europe.

18 J. W. C. Ward, *God and Goodness* (1954). Quoted by Green (1996: 310).

19 Based on a number of sources, including interviews carried out by the author in Kendal and Lancaster, and interviews carried out by Eccles in south Cumbria (Eccles 2010). This was not unprecedented. A Mass Observation survey in the late 1940s picked up comments about religion like: 'A lot of bloody hypocrisy, if you ask me' (quoted by Kynaston 2007: 126).

20 Speech to the General Assembly of the Church of Scotland, 21 May 1988. Online. Available HTTP: www.margaretthatcher.org/document/107246 (accessed 13 June 2011).

21 This was a finding from research carried out in Kendal by Paul Heelas, Bronislaw Szerszynski, Karin Tusting and Linda Woodhead. Further details in Heelas and Woodhead (2005).

22 The NHS Directory of Complementary and Alternative Practitioners. Online. Available HTTP: www.nhstadirectory.org/default.aspx (accessed 14 June 2011).

23 'NHS Evidence – Complementary and Alternative Medicine'. Online. Available HTTP: www.uclh.nhs.uk/ourservices/ourhospitals/rlhim/pages/nhsevidence-complementaryandalternativemedicine.aspx (accessed 14 June 2011).

24 The main difference was that it would be more targeted on universities, prisons and particular localities which were perceived breeding grounds of radicalization (rather than on Muslim communities in general), and more rigorous in not funding any groups which even attempted to engage with 'radical' religious ideas. Online. Available HTTP: www.homeoffice.gov.uk/media-centre/news/prevent-strategy (accessed 13 June 2011).

25 Not that God and religion cannot be discussed, but that in public debates – especially in the public sector – it is taboo to invoke God. 'We don't do God,' as Tony Blair's advisor Alastair Campbell famously said. In other words, religious discourse can be spoken *about* but cannot be *used* in many public settings like universities, parliamentary debate, doctors' surgeries and so on.

1 Controversies as a lens on change

Malory Nye and Paul Weller

Conflicts and controversies over religion offer a useful lens onto wider developments in the post-war period. This chapter charts the development of such controversies over time, showing how they have intensified in recent decades, and analysing them by considering their changing nature and the issues and parties involved. It shows that 'cults' or 'New Religious Movements' were the focus of public controversies in the 1960s and 1970s, but that from the 1980s, especially with the Rushdie Affair, attention shifted to Islam, issues of free speech, the question of how far religion could be publicly manifest, and what privileges and exemptions it could claim. Terrorism associated with religion, both Irish nationalist and Islamist, endures as a public and political concern. The chapter sets this in broader context, showing how in a society which is now Christian, secular and religiously plural the place and 'rights' of religion become complex and contested. Although there is a tendency to see religious conflict as something new, the chapter also mentions earlier historical examples – like the Gunpowder Plot – to show that violent conflict is hardly novel in British history. As in the Introduction and Chapter 12, it is noted that the tendency to see religion as uniquely violent – and to ignore the more common non-religious forms of violence, whether domestic/gender-based or political – is itself a viewpoint which grows out of secular–religious conflict.

Introduction

There are multiple strands that make up the landscape of religion in contemporary Britain, and there are a number of quite distinct trajectories of change (secularization, consumerism, migration/settlement and globalization, to name just a few) that have influenced this current process. Within this, the role played by controversies relating to religion and diversity is itself of significance – controversies have helped to create change and have also reflected the changes that have been occurring.

Therefore the aims of this chapter are largely directed in two ways. First, the controversies that we discuss have all been significant in their own right. They have been events that have shaped the public domain in some way, and have impacted in most cases directly on religious and cultural groups and communities in Britain (as well as on how others have viewed such groups). Second, controversies are very often a means by which we can understand the values of the wider society, in particular the ways in which we can see discourses of controversy being manifest around particular ideas, religious groups and activities (see Beckford 1985). On an historical level, the changing subjects of controversy can be indicators of changes in the wider social issues – which of course may relate to specific issues discussed elsewhere in this book, such as secularism and the change in organized (majority and minority) religions.

An important issue to note at this stage is that there is nothing new about controversy. Religion and religious differences have been controversial in Britain for centuries, and are very likely to continue to be. Indeed, even the dynamics of particular controversies tend to share some discernible characteristics, since much of what becomes controversial revolves around what are taken as the 'normative' or majority values of the larger group, and how minorities and dissidents from the 'norm' may and do express themselves. To put this simply, there have been moral panics in British history for centuries, likewise minorities have been demonized, and differences between the religious majority and minorities (both religious and non-religious) have always been involved in conflict. This chapter will consider what, if anything, is new about recent controversies.

The chapter will take account of controversies across Britain, including, for example, those that relate to sectarian conflict (between Protestants and Catholics) as, for example, in Northern Ireland and Scotland. To understand these, and also the broader context of controversies in Britain, we need to take account of a long history of religion and difference.

The themes of this chapter interact with a number of the other chapters of this volume. In order to understand some of the particular events we need to have in mind the background materials of both Christianity (Chapter 2) and other religious groups in Britain (Chapters 3 and 4), together with the changing nature of religion and faith in the current time (Chapter 5), the influence of the media and media audiences on conflict and controversy (Chapter 7), and the legal framework through which much controversy is mediated (Chapter 9).

TEXT BOX 1

Setting the scene

In July 2009 an exhibition at the Glasgow Museum of Modern Art took an unconventional approach to engaging the viewer with the text of the Christian Bible. At the centre of an exhibition was an open Bible, together with a box of pens and a notice saying: 'If you feel you have been excluded from the Bible, please write your way back into it.' Alongside this was a video installation of a young woman ripping pages out of a Bible and stuffing them into her knickers, bra and mouth (Wade 2009). The stated aims of the artists, Anthony Schrag and David Malone, were to encourage the reclamation of the Bible as a sacred text by those who felt excluded, particularly lesbians and gays. However, a number of Christian churches and organizations expressed concern and disdain for the way the exhibition had encouraged a desecration of the sacred text in the name of art. The exhibition was picketed by various Christian protestors, and the story of the exhibition and its opposition was widely reported in the local and national media.

On 5 February 2011, the UK Prime Minister, David Cameron, gave a speech at the Munich Security Conference in Germany. In the speech, he argued that what he called 'the doctrine of state multiculturalism' in Britain had 'encouraged different cultures to live separate lives, apart from each other and the mainstream' (Cameron 2011). This led the media to headline his speech 'Failure of multiculturalism' (although in fact Cameron did not himself use this phrase). What he went on to say, though, was that 'we' had 'failed to provide a vision of society to which [the different cultures]...feel they want to belong. We've even tolerated these segregated communities behaving in ways that run completely counter to our values' (Cameron 2011). Very pointedly, the remainder of the speech was an outline by Cameron of his vision for the more successful integration, specifically, of Muslims and Islam in Britain, through a combination of what he called 'muscular liberalism', 'active participation in society' and a side-lining of extremism. The speech echoed comments made by the German Chancellor Angela Merkel a few months before about the 'utter failure of multiculturalism' in Germany.

Religious controversy from the Reformation to the 1970s

A key historical element underpinning much controversy over religion in Britain is the close historical relationship between Protestantism and 'Britishness'. This developed in the post-Reformation period, and one of its by-products was a powerful current of anti-Catholicism (Marrotti 2005). For hundreds of years Catholics as a group (as distinct from individual Catholics) were seen as potentially disloyal 'fifth columnists' with religio-political allegiances to the Papacy and other predominantly Catholic foreign powers beyond the boundaries of the national community.

Such tropes continued to have strong resonance in England and Wales until reforming legislation in the nineteenth century removed from Catholics (and others, such as Jews and Free Church Christians) the majority of the civil and legal disabilities with which they had lived for centuries (see Larsen 1999; Salbstein 1982). Nevertheless, in what is still a powerful symbol of the relationship between Britishness and Protestantism, under the Act of Succession anyone wishing to retain their succession to the throne is still prevented from embracing Roman Catholicism, while the Royal Marriages Act 1772 prevents the succession of anyone who marries a Roman Catholic.

In Northern Ireland such tropes continued to have resonance into the twentieth century and, indeed, continue down to the present. This has been through an intertwining of various religious, political and ideological currents in the struggle for Irish independence by Irish Nationalists and Republicans and resistance to it on the part of Unionists and Loyalists (Bruce 1986). These struggles first resulted in the establishment of the Irish Free State (1922–1937) and then the Republic of Ireland. Violent conflict re-emerged in the late 1960s during the decades-long 'Troubles' (McSweeney 1989) that followed the violence meted out to the Civil Rights Movement of the 1960s. There followed a period of armed conflict involving Republican and Loyalist paramilitary forces, the forces of the British state and of the Northern Ireland province, during which over 3,000 people were killed until a political settlement with the principal parties to the conflict was reached in the Belfast/Good Friday Agreement of 1998 (see Chapter 9 for more information).

The potent admixture of religion and national identity that has come to be known as 'sectarianism' (Liechty and Clegg 2001) can also be found in Scotland, although its extent is hotly debated (see Walls and Williams 2003, 2005; and Bruce *et al.* 2005 for differing interpretations). In England and Wales, generally speaking, the 'temperature' around religion had 'cooled' for much of the twentieth century. When, in the 1960s, the notion and phenomenon of secularization came into public, political and religious consciousness it was often assumed that, with the exception of Northern Ireland, the continued privatization of religion would mean that big religious controversies would increasingly become something of the past. But in Scotland, the significance of conflicting religious identities, particularly in the west (around Glasgow), has continued to belie this perspective – to the extent that even as recently as 2003 the Scottish government added a clause to the Criminal Justice (Scotland) Act 2003 creating a defence for individuals and groups from aggravation based on religious prejudice (which was largely targeted at sectarian Protestant–Catholic issues, see Scottish Executive 2006). Such sectarianism is strongly linked to the footballing rivalry between the Glasgow teams of Celtic and Rangers, and in April 2011 parcel bombs were sent to the Celtic manager Neil Lennon, along with two other high-profile Celtic supporters.

Even in the so-called secular 1960s and 1970s, controversies over religion did occasionally flare up, including in England and Wales. When this happened it was usually in relation to the actual and perceived beliefs and practices of religious groups described variously in academic, popular and religious literature as 'sects' or 'cults', which in academic discourse later became generally referred to as New Religious Movements or 'NRMs' (Barker 1982, 1995). When 'sects' were spoken of, this often referred to groups with nineteenth- and/or early twentieth-century origins which had some contested relationship with the broader Christian tradition – such as Jehovah's Witnesses, Mormons and Christian Scientists. Controversies from time to time emerged around the refusal of Jehovah's Witnesses to accept blood transfusions and Christian Scientists' preference for using what they understand to be Divine Healing as compared with medical science. Since, in some cases, individuals (and especially legal minors) have died when their lives might have been saved by the use of blood transfusion or other medical means, the competing moral values involved have given rise to controversy and debate in the media and among health professionals.

With the 'turn to the East' among the youth of the late 1960s and the 1970s (Leech 1973), controversies also started to emerge around groups that were less culturally familiar and/or linked to Christianity. These are the 'cults' of popular imagination, and included the group ISKCON (the International Society for Krishna Consciousness), popularly known as the 'Hare Krishnas' (Knott 1986; Dwyer and Cole 2007), whose devotees emerged into public consciousness dancing and chanting in the high streets of major British cities, and through association with George Harrison and the Beatles. In time ISKCON has become less noticed on the public level, largely through its establishment in Britain as a specific group within the broader (ethnically Indian) Hindu population (see Nye 2001). A number of other more 'quietist' (that is, resembling the Christian movement advocating withdrawal into contemplation of God) Hindu and Buddhist associated groups and traditions have slowly become established in Britain since the 1960s, often without any significant controversy (see Chapter 3).

More serious concerns developed in the 1970s about other groups that, as traced by Robert Zaehner in books such as *Drugs, Mysticism and Make-Believe* (Zaehner 1972) and *Our Savage God* (Zaehner 1974), appeared to mix a 'pop' understanding of Eastern mysticism with an emergent drug culture, and who were attracted to the idea of being able to go beyond conventional understandings of good and evil. Of these, the most prominent was probably the Bhagwan Shree Rajneesh Movement (later renamed the Osho Movement), based around its charismatic founder Rajneesh. This movement achieved a certain notoriety, largely due to its combination of forms of Hindu mysticism with counter-cultural values, including liberal and liberating attitudes to sexuality.

During the same period, other Christian-related groups – such as the Children of God (now known as The Family International) and the Unification Church (Chryssides 1991) popularly known as the 'Moonies' (and now formally known as the Family Federation for World Peace and Unification) – became a focus for controversies over religion. In both cases, issues about religious freedom came to the fore as discussed in James Beckford's classic study *Cult Controversies* (1985).

The international dimensions of these 'cultic' movements made them more controversial. Events like the mass suicides and murders among the largely Pentecostalist Christian followers of the Reverend Jim Jones (the Peoples Temple) in Jonestown, Guyana in November 1978 (see Maaga 1998), and the deaths of David Koresh and the Branch Davidian Seventh Day Adventists at their ranch outside Waco in April 1993 (Tabor and Gallagher 1997), and the poison gas attacks by the Aum Shinrikyo group in Tokyo in March 1995 (Reader 1996), gave considerable notoriety to the whole area of alternative religiosity. In Britain (as elsewhere), they created public and media conceptions of stereotypical 'cultish' attributes and behaviour. Although scientifically discredited, the idea spread that impressionable people could be 'brainwashed', and a minor industry of 'deprogramming' developed, which could entail the forcible mental and physical isolation of individuals from their former group membership (see Barker 1995). The 'cult controversies' also involved debate around the limits of freedom of religion in social and legal systems, as when the British Member of the European Parliament Richard Cotterell (1984) attempted unsuccessfully to bring in European legislation specifically to limit the activities of New Religious Movements.

Controversies since the 1980s over free speech

By the end of the twentieth century, these New Religious Movement controversies had largely receded in Britain (though not in many parts of mainland Europe). They have been largely replaced by controversies around Muslims and Islam and other forms of so-called religious 'radicalism' and/or 'extremism'. Academic study has shifted accordingly. One way of understanding this shift could be in terms of changes in the way that the phenomena referred to as the 'secular' and 'secularization' are playing out in social debate and academic understanding (see Chapter 12). At a time when 'secularization' was generally thought to be in the ascendant, political and academic focus and controversy cohered around relatively small groups which could be seen as socially marginal.

Following the fall of the Berlin Wall in 1989 and the associated collapse of a Marxist vision which imposed severe constraints upon religion, there was a rebirth both of religion and of a concern to understand it. In part, this represented a return of that which had been repressed. But with the apparent death of Marxism as an alternative to an increasingly globalized capitalism and its impact on local cultures throughout the world, religion increasingly became linked with an identity politics in which on the global level Islam, with its universal vision and its religious concern for justice and peace, came to the fore as a force of challenge and for change.

In the UK one of the emblematic markers of this shift towards a politics of identity in which religion has a key place was what became known as 'the Rushdie Affair' or '*The Satanic Verses* Controversy'. This erupted in the wake of the publication, on 26 September 1988, of Salman Rushdie's novel *The Satanic Verses* (Rushdie 1988). After a peak of intensity in 1988–1990, the controversy rumbled on for over a decade. It has been argued that the controversy was a 'lightning rod', a 'catalyst' and a 'magnifying mirror' (Weller 2009: 1) for a range of issues that are still with us today. These include issues: 'of religion and public policy; of believing and belonging; of religion, art and values in contention; legal rights and constraints; and of political representation and participation in a plural society' (Weller 2009: 1). The Rushdie Affair also marked a watershed in which religious identity ceased to be submerged with a previous emphasis on 'race' and 'ethnicity'.

TEXT BOX 2

What are the 'satanic verses'?

The title of Salman Rushdie's book, *The Satanic Verses*, comes from a story that was recounted by two early Muslim commentators, al-Tabari and Ibn Sa'd. In al-Tabari's version (see Guillaume 1987: 165f. for English translation) the Prophet Muhammad wanted to help the pre-Islamic people of the city of Mecca more easily to accept his teaching of monotheism.

According to the story, the so-called 'satanic verses' were apparent revelations that permitted the Meccans to seek intercession from their female tribal deities. Because of this 'concession', it was said that the Meccans joined Muhammad in prostration. However, the Angel Jibreel showed Muhammad that this was an error. Because of this, the original so-called 'satanic verses' were replaced by the current text of the Qur'anic Sura known in English by the name of 'The Star' (Surat al-Najm, Qur'an 53: 19–30) which condemns the worship of these deities and also of the female infanticide illogically associated with their worship.

In Islam, traditions are recognized partly through having a strong 'chain of transmission'. But in this case, the veracity of the story was dismissed by a number of early Muslim scholars and it was not included in any of the six authoritative collections of authentic narrations on the Prophet Muhammad's life (the Hadith) that were put together in the centuries following the Prophet's death. But especially because of the history of Christian polemic against Islam that attacked Muhammad's integrity and charged him with being a 'liar' and 'imposter', many Muslims have seen the story as a weapon that has been used against Islam. Erikson (1998) has argued that it is likely that Rushdie's interest in these contested ('satanic') verses derived from the influence of the orientalist scholar Montgomery Watt, who was one of Rushdie's tutors when he was an undergraduate at Cambridge University.

In many ways, the novel itself became lost in the controversy generated around it (see Appignanesi and Maitland 1989; Ahsan and Kidwai 1991). At face value, the novel dealt with a story of migration and of exile, exploring its themes through what are basically fantasies, but which also utilize historical elements in a style of writing known as 'magical realism'. The average Western reader is not likely to have the cultural capital for locating the novel's allusion to the story of the 'satanic verses' or to other themes. But they were full of resonance and meanings for those within a Muslim cultural and linguistic universe – and many of these meanings were offensive. For example, Rushdie's use of the name 'Mahound', which is a corruption of the name Muhammad, was used historically in Christian attacks on Islam. Particularly offensive for many Muslims was one of the scenes of the book that takes place in a brothel called 'The Curtain' in which prostitutes act out the parts of Mahound's wives. The brothel's clients are said to go round a so-called 'Fountain of Love' in its inner courtyard 'much as the pilgrims rotated for other reasons around the ancient Black Stone'

(Rushdie 1988: 381) in a reference to the Ka'ba in Mecca, which lies at the heart of the Muslim ritual universe.

In the early phase of the controversy, a number of concerned Muslims had been calling, not for the banning of the book, but for the publishers to include an historical and factual erratum note in it. But the controversy as it developed became inextricably linked in the public mind with the 14 January 1989 burning of a copy of *The Satanic Verses*, organized as a media event in Bradford. And it then deepened and became highly internationalized and politicized when the supreme leader of Iran, the Ayatollah Khomeini, on 14 February 1989 pronounced Rushdie to be an apostate, and an Iranian foundation put a bounty upon his death. With that the controversy was propelled into a global context.

In the UK, Muslims tried, unsuccessfully, to invoke the common laws of blasphemy against the author, Salman Rushdie, and his publishers, Viking Penguin. In invoking these laws there was an echo of how, just over a decade previously, Mary Whitehouse (see Plate 1.1) and the National Viewers' and Listeners' Association had, in the case of *R v. Lemon* and *R v. Gay News* in 1976 successfully brought a private prosecution for blasphemous libel against the publication and its publishers for publishing James Kirkup's poem 'The Love that Dares to Speak its Name'. This referred to the Roman centurion in attendance at Jesus' crucifixion as having homosexual fantasies about sexual relations with Jesus following his crucifixion.

In a subsequent echo of that case, at the beginning of 2005 the musical *Jerry Springer the Opera* faced opposition led by the campaigning group Christian Voice against BBC 2's plans to broadcast it. As with *The Satanic Verses* controversy, this controversy was noteworthy for the intersection between revered figures of religion and lewd sexuality. Thus, when Jesus was introduced, he bore a great similarity to a previous character who had a nappy fetish. In addition, in other echoes of *The Satanic Verses* there was a confusion or reversal of good and evil, with the figures of Jesus and of Satan being made to indulge in a battle of wits in which Eve is called as a witness and ends up attacking Jesus. Although legal action against the BBC was unsuccessful, many Christians were left feeling that the play's depiction of what they held sacred had been a gratuitous attack upon them and their faith.

Just prior to the conflict over *Jerry Springer the Opera* there had also been conflict around a play called *Behzti* that was written by Gurpreet Kaur Bhatti, a British-born woman of Sikh background, and opened on 4 December 2004 at the Birmingham Repertory Theatre. The play's title means 'dishonour'. The writer intended through it to expose hypocrisies that can be found, including among the religious, and so it was set in the precincts of a Sikh gurdwara (temple). It explored issues to do with social status, mixed-race relationships, corruption, drug-taking, domestic violence, rape, paedophilia and murder. The theatre management decided to undertake proactive consultations with the local Sikh community because they realized the play involved a potentially explosive cocktail of topics. However, when the community representatives requested that the play should be set in a community centre rather than a gurdwara, the consultations broke down. After opening, the play faced daily protests by Sikhs. These were at first peaceful, but on 19 December around 400 Sikhs attempted to storm the theatre, resulting in some damage to property and injury to security guards, the police and protestors. After this, the play was cancelled for an indefinite period on the basis of the theatre's duty of care to its audiences, staff and performers. As with *The Satanic Verses* controversy, the issues involved went global. And like Rushdie, Bhatti felt forced to go into hiding following receipt of hate mail, including some death threats.

Religious rights and other rights

The controversies narrated above are a reminder that in the UK, outside of Northern Ireland, there was very little legislation relating to religious rights. It was only after the passage of the Human Rights Act 1998 (implemented from 2000 onwards) that, in domestic law, the grounds of religion or belief began to take a more central place within legal, policy and practice considerations, with duties relating to these being placed on 'public bodies'.

Prior to that, it had been necessary to go to the European Court of Human Rights in order to pursue a case under the European Convention on Human Rights Article 9 guaranteeing freedom of 'thought, conscience and religion' (see Nye 2001). Under earlier race relations legislation, protection had been accorded to 'racial' or 'ethnic' groups, but not to religious ones unless they were deemed to be of an ethno-religious character by having a long shared history of which religion had been a key part. This applied only to Sikhs and Jews. As a consequence Muslims, especially, started to campaign for a law specifically on religious discrimination (UK Action Committee on Islamic Affairs 1993), and eventually the government commissioned research into the nature and extent of religious discrimination – albeit in England and Wales only.

TEXT BOX 3

Islamophobia and perceptions of Muslims

In 1997 the Runnymede Trust produced a report entitled *Islamophobia: A Challenge for Us All* (Runnymede Trust 1997). The report outlined the rising levels of prejudice and stereotyping against Muslims in Britain, and defined the then neologism of 'Islamophobia' as referring to 'to unfounded hostility towards Islam' along with 'the practical consequences of such hostility in unfair discrimination against Muslim individuals and communities, and to the exclusion of Muslims from mainstream political and social affairs'. The timeliness of this report became clear several years later, following the 9/11 tragedies in the USA and the exponential rise of public discourses on Islam and Muslims. Chris Allen (2010) has published a comprehensive review of the role of the concept of Islamophobia since the publication of the Runnymede Trust report, and many of the issues in the report criticizing the stereotyping of *all* Muslims in Britain (and elsewhere) as 'monolithic', 'other' and 'extremist' later became clearly visible in media coverage (see Chapter 7).

The term Islamophobia also draws our attention to another issue – that is, the way in which Islam is generally seen as a problem. But such problematizing can itself be problematized. Islamophobia-related issues are in fact a key feature of the nexus of religion and non-religion, diversity and controversy in contemporary Britain. That is, a number (although certainly not all) of the controversies in the past 25 years have involved Islam and Muslims. This should not be taken as an accident, and certainly should not imply that the 'problem' of Muslims in Britain is the problem that it is often publicly taken to be. Rather, it can be argued that the problem is due to a number of historical factors and processes, including in particular the centuries-long negative perceptions of Islam within Christianity, a geopolitical construction of Islam as being at the boundary of Europe (and therefore outside European/Christian civilization, see Asad 2003) and of course the impact of international events, including both the political violence by extremists claiming Islam as their rationale and the counter-war on terror.

Research commissioned by the government on religious discrimination (Weller *et al.* 2001) showed that unfair treatment on the basis of religion – especially in the fields of employment, education and media – was, in comparison with other religious groups, reported especially by Muslims as being both more frequent and more serious. At the same time Hindus and Sikhs also reported this comparatively more than other groups, while Pagans and members of New Religious Movements reported considerable experience of religious hatred. Under the Amsterdam Treaty of the European Union – which was signed in 1997 and came into force in 1999 – the government was in any case obliged to legislate on religious discrimination in employment, and the Employment Equality (Religion or Belief) Regulations 2003 represented a qualitative development in addressing discrimination and harassment on grounds of religion and belief in employment and vocational training. Following this, the Religious and Racial Hatred Act 2006 addressed incitement to religious hatred.

The legal territory relating to discrimination on grounds of religion or belief was developed further by the Equality Act 2006, which extended these grounds also into the provision of goods and services. As this has happened, new questions have emerged about how far pluralist societies can and should go in accommodating difference and to what degree (Ahdar and Leigh 2005). And as early as 1994, in an essay significantly entitled 'Deciding How Far You Can Go', Gerald Parsons (1994: 19) helpfully highlighted the issues that have increasingly arisen, when he argued that there is a need constantly to ask questions about:

> how far any of us can go in any particular direction without throwing out something vital to the preservation of a viable balance in British society between the interests of a variety of particular religious groups, the interests of dissenting groups and individuals within them, the concerns of those who stand outside and claim the right to criticize all religions, and the well-being, coherence and creative co-existence of the community of communities that is Britain at the end of the twentieth century.

Especially because of the legal developments that have taken place over the past decade, that complexity is even more the case at the beginning of the twenty-first century (Ghanea *et al.* 2007) than it was when Parsons first posed these questions. All along there has been the tension between the rights of the 'religious' and the 'non-religious' which was reflected in many of the debates that took place around the issue of whether straightforward humour – and sometimes necessary debunking of religious people – would be put at risk by legislation on incitement to religious hatred. Within the overall human rights and equality framework there have been issues on the relationship between 'religion' and 'belief', and especially with regard to the scope of the latter (see Woodhead with Catto 2009). And, finally, there has been a growing sense of unease expressed by organizations such as the National Secular Society and the British Humanist Association (brap 2009) that religious rights may be being privileged relative to other rights – especially when a number of legislative developments have allowed for 'exemptions' on the grounds of religion.

Two distinct cases illustrate the sharp juxtaposition between the expectations of minority groups for their religious needs to be met and the strain such demands may put on the majority's perceived 'limits' of tolerance for diversity. The first predates the recent legislation of the Human Rights Act and the Equality Acts. This was the long-running conflict over the use of Bhaktivedanta Manor, a small country house in Letchmore Heath, rural Hertfordshire, which is the centre for the 'Hare Krishnas' (ISKCON) in England (for full details of this see Nye 2001). A fairly small room in this house was dedicated as a temple by ISKCON, and during the 1970s this became very well used by the local (ethnically Indian) Hindu residents of north-west London. This use of the place as a public temple caused two distinct but related problems – the planning permission granted by the local Hertsmere council to the site did not include authorization for public worship, and the actual use of the building in this way by the visiting worshippers caused very severe traffic congestion each weekend in the small country village and lanes around the Manor.

Therefore, for nearly 20 years ISKCON and their supporters in the Indian community were in conflict with the local council and residents in the village. This conflict was mediated and worked through at various levels – both in negotiation between ISKCON and the local residents, and through legal action brought by the council. At a broader level there was a large media interest in the issues brought forward by the case, especially as the organizations representing the Hindu worshippers argued that they were expressing their rights for freedom of religious practice, while also establishing their religion as having a place within British society. This right, however, needed to be considered in law in balance against the rights of the local residents to enjoy the amenity of their properties. This was eventually resolved in 1996 through an extended legal process, when planning permission was given by the council to use Bhaktivedanta Manor as a place of public worship, alongside permission for the construction of a new road which bypassed the village and therefore allowed large numbers to visit without causing disturbance to the local residents.

Such conflicts and controversies over the use of buildings for religious worship have been quite common in Britain, and organizations of various religious affiliations have been unable to develop public worship projects because of a lack of planning consent from their local council. This has not been limited to non-Christian groups, however. For example, a Roman Catholic Church in Cambridgeshire was refused planning permission in 1986 partly on the basis that it would be particularly busy 'at times when the residents could reasonably expect maximum peace and quiet' – that is, on Sunday mornings (Edge 1998).

In quite a different context, a recent issue considered under the Equality Act 2006 has again challenged the grounds of what the majority might consider to be reasonable. This involved the application by Bushra Noah, a woman of Muslim background, to be employed at a trendy hairdressing salon in King's Cross, London. Ms Noah appeared at the interview wearing a hijab, a Muslim covering of her hair, which prompted the reaction by the salon owner, Sarah Desrosiers, to decline to employ her – on the basis that an employee in the salon with her hair covered could not show the 'funky, urban' image of the business. At an employment tribunal case in June 2008, Ms Noah's claim for direct religious discrimination was not upheld. However, the tribunal panel did find that the refusal to employ was a matter of indirect discrimination, since they could see no specific evidence of 'the actual [negative] impact of [Ms Noah] working in [the] salon with her head covered at all times'. The discrimination by the salon owner was not directly religious, since it was based on the covering of the hair rather than on Ms Noah's actual religious identity, but this finding of discrimination led to an order by the tribunal panel for the owner to pay Ms Noah £4,000 in compensation for the 'injury to [her] feelings' caused by the indirect discrimination (BBC News 2008a; see also Woodhead with Catto 2009: 21; Sandberg 2011a).

In parallel to the development of legislation around religion or belief, there has also been the further (in the case of gender, ethnicity and disability) and new (in the case of age and sexual orientation) development of legislation in relation to what the Equality Act 2010 calls 'protected characteristics'. Both developments most recently culminated in the Equality Act 2010, which integrated previously diverse legal provision across the range of equalities and human rights 'strands' which the government has an obligation to address under European Union law. While the interface between any combination of these equality strands can give rise to controversy, the most controversial cases have been those at the interface between religion and belief and sexual orientation. Thus the development and initial implementation of the Sexual Orientation Regulations 2007 and their incorporation now into the Equality Acts, with positive duties relating to sexual orientation, have led to considerable contestation around whether one right or duty (to prevent discrimination on the basis of religion or sexual orientation) 'trumps' another; or, if not, to the question of how at least apparently conflicting duties might both be realized.

The introduction of civil partnerships between homosexual couples in 2005 has provided a state recognition of relationships which, in most practical ways, is largely equivalent to (but not the same as) heterosexual marriage (see Hill 2008; Pearce 2008). This has had an impact on the duties of government-employed registrars – the people who have the authority to conduct both weddings and now civil partnerships. Therefore for those registrars who have religious convictions which do not, on grounds of religion, recognize an equivalence between homosexual partnerships and heterosexual ones, a conflict of rights has arisen.

The controversial case of Lillian Ladele illustrates this. As a registrar in Islington, London, she refused to conduct civil partnerships for homosexual couples because of her Christian beliefs. Because of this she was put under pressure both by her employer, Islington Council, and by some of her work colleagues. In 2007 the council took disciplinary action against her, as it felt she was not performing the duties of her employment. In challenge to this she took her employer to tribunal with the support of an evangelical Christian lobbying group called the Christian Institute. Ms Ladele claimed the pressure and action by the council to conduct the civil partnerships was a form of both direct and indirect discrimination. The tribunal found in her favour in July 2008, finding that there was discrimination (see BBC News 2008b), but the council appealed the decision and Ms Ladele lost this appeal in December 2008 and the case was dismissed. The Employment Appeal Tribunal considered that the Sexual Orientation Regulations placed a requirement on the registrar to conduct the ceremony without discrimination on the basis of sexuality, and there was therefore no discrimination in this requirement towards Ms Ladele's religious beliefs. This left Ms Ladele with no alternative other than to resign from her post, as she considered her Christian beliefs were in conflict with the requirement for her to conduct the civil ceremonies (BBC News 2009; Sandberg 2010, 2011a, 2011b: 171–2).

A similarly sharp example of the tensions and conflicts between these intersecting rights and duties has occurred in relation to the work of religiously based (and especially Catholic Christian) adoption agencies. Since public funding would no longer be able to go to agencies that would not act in accordance with the Sexual Orientation Regulations, it appeared that if they did not consider the placing of adoptees with gay and lesbian applicants, Catholic adoption agencies would need to close down. In the end, the majority of Catholic agencies either ended their adoption services or severed their formal ties with the Catholic Church. The charity Catholic Care, which has maintained its links with the church, requested exemption from this legislation because of its religious/moral view on the issue, but this request was rejected in 2010 by the English Charity Commission on the grounds that the charity's religious views 'did not justify its continuing discrimination' (BBC News 2010a). An appeal against this decision was then dismissed by the Charity Tribunal in 2011 (BBC News 2011a).

In a similar vein, a couple, Eunice and Owen Johns, who had previously fostered children in the 1990s, found that they were no longer allowed to do so by their local authority Derby

City Council, because they felt unable, because of their traditional Pentecostal Christian views, to tell children in their care that homosexual relationships were acceptable. This case has so far been heard up to the level of the High Court, with the court taking the view that, in such circumstances, fostering is impermissible. Indeed, in the judgment given on this case, Lord Justice Munby and Mr Justice Beatson ruled that 'the laws protecting people from discrimination because of their sexual orientation "should take precedence" over the right not to be discriminated against on religious grounds' (BBC News 2011b).

The perception is growing among many Christians and others that the rights on sexual orientation are a trump card over religious rights – a point that will most likely be further contested in the courts and in public debates. This relates to a growing concern among Christian groups that the rights of Christians are not being taken seriously enough (Boucher 2010) and that Christians are experiencing increasing marginalization (Christian Institute 2009) as compared with both secular people and people of other, minority, religious traditions in Britain.

Religion and terror, loyalty and disloyalty

Terrorism, and the controversies that have arisen both from the phenomenon itself (see Furedi 2007) and from a range of government, legal and religious responses to it, is another 'hot topic' which involves religion (see Knott *et al.* 2006). Acts of terror have been carried out in Britain by individuals acting in the name of Islam, as in the 7 July 2005 attacks on the London Transport system which left 52 people dead and over 700 wounded, and the failed Glasgow Airport attack on 30 June 2007. Prior to the signing of the Good Friday Agreement, as well as in Northern Ireland itself, the Provisional Irish Republican Army also used acts of terror in 'mainland' Britain for political reasons as part of its campaign to try to force British withdrawal from the Province of Northern Ireland. This campaign was widely perceived in Britain as being supported by the Catholic/Irish minority in Northern Ireland and Britain.

Religiously inflected violence in Britain is nothing new. Thus the annual 5 November event of Bonfire Night or Guy Fawkes Day is a reminder of the complex relationships that can exist between attempted and actual violent events with intended symbolic meanings; national and transnational identities of various kinds; governance, loyalty and disloyalty; and violence by the state. For contemporary understanding and analysis, it is important to ask how far some of the dynamics involved across the centuries may or may not be similar. Albeit, these have been played out through different social actors in the past (Catholics) and in the present (Muslims), and in the setting of a changed political (previously monarchical government and now parliamentary democracy), and social (previously pre-modern and now modern) contexts.

TEXT BOX 4

The Gunpowder conspiracy: an historical mirror?

How far do the similarities and differences illuminate current controversies?

Guy or Guido Fawkes (1507–1606) had, in 1593 or 1594, fought in a Spanish army in Belgium and France under the command of Archduke Albert of Austria who became Governor of the Netherlands. In 1603 he left that army and went to visit King Philip of Spain to provide him with information on the position of 'Romanists' in England, where, together with Anthony Dutton, they sought Spanish support for an invasion of England to follow the death of Queen Elizabeth I.

In 1604, together with other co-conspirators (led by Sir Robert Catesby), Fawkes took an oath to take part in the 'Gunpowder Plot' (Fraser 1996). Mass was celebrated for the men by the Jesuit priest John Gerard, although Fraser states that Gerard was unaware of the nature of their discussions. The conspirators first tried to dig a mine and subsequently to pack a cellar under Parliament with explosives. Guy Fawkes, who had been given care of the explosives – it would seem because of his military experience – was captured when the plot was uncovered on 5 November 1605.

Torture was not allowed under English common law unless authorized by the monarch or Privy Council. But when Guy Fawkes refused to give more than a minimum of information, King James authorized the use of 'graduated torture' to elicit information from him. In his confession he stated that he had been motivated by a wish to spread the Catholic faith which, in this instance, although obtained under torture, would seem to be consistent with other information about him. In January 1606, the other conspirators were tried and found guilty. On 31 January Guy Fawkes and three of his co-conspirators were hanged, drawn and quartered. Five others had already been executed on 30 January, while Robert Catesby had already been killed under attack from government forces at Holbeach House where the conspirators had made a last stand.

At the beginning of the twenty-first century it could in many ways be said that just as Catholics were once often seen by the majority and the powerful as potentially disloyal 'fifth columnists', this is the position of Muslims today. Like Catholics, Muslims have a transnational vision of religion. And like those Catholics who planned to or used violence to advance their cause, so also those who have invoked the name of Islam to carry out contemporary acts of terror have acquired their military training abroad.

In responding to this today, there would seem to be increasing evidence that in the use of measures such as 'rendition' to countries where torture could be practised, and the normalization of practices such as 'waterboarding' (see Gude 2010), the forces of the contemporary state have, as in the time of Guy Fawkes, not baulked at either suspending, changing or going outside the normal boundaries of the law. In the UK, under the Prevention of Terrorism Act 2005, the Labour government brought in one of the longest periods (up to 28 days) of possible detention without charge of any jurisdiction in the world. It also brought in so-called Control Orders which can be imposed by decision of the Home Secretary and restrict an individual's liberty for the purpose of 'protecting members of the public from a risk of terrorism'.

As a consequence of this, the position of many ordinary Muslims has become 'securitized' under a cloak of suspicion just as the position of loyal Catholics once was. Just as Catholics such as the Appellants (a group of Catholic priests who tried to combine continued Catholic devotion in the 1590s and 1600s with overt loyalty to the Crown) sought to demonstrate that they were more loyal than others, so also in the past decade have Muslims been under pressure to dissociate themselves from anything that might be thought to be connected with what is called 'radicalization'. Thus Muslims in the UK found themselves targeted at the heart of the Labour government's Prevent programme (see Her Majesty's

Government 2008a – at the time of writing under review by the Coalition government, see the Introduction to this volume). In the face of this, some Muslims have themselves sought to develop their own strategies to challenge 'extremism', an example being from a Muslim-inspired organization, the Dialogue Society (2009), and its document *Deradicalisation by Default*.

Muslims have been subject to particular surveillance measures. At the same time, there have also been national and local government policy and funding interventions (see Her Majesty's Government 2008b) to encourage the development of what are seen as more liberal forms of Islam and to marginalize other Muslim groups. Within this there has some-times been a failure to distinguish between very traditionalist Muslim groups and Muslims of 'jihadist' tendencies. There is controversy over whether the government should exercise control over ideas (rather than actions), and the overall policy of 'deradicalization' has been subject to significant critique (Kundnani 2009).

Moral panics, health and social welfare

Religion has been a focus of certain moral panics in recent decades. Although many media-derived panics have been over health issues – such as fears of bird-flu and swine-flu in the 2000s, or the link between childhood immunization and the risks of developing autism – religion has also figured.

In February 1991 nine children in Orkney, north Scotland, were removed by social work-ers from their families and placed into social care. This was on the basis of fears by the social workers that the children were being subject to a particular form of child abuse which had sinister ritualistic and 'satanic' elements. Following further investigation the issue came to court in April that year, when custody of the children was considered. At this point the case based on allegations of ritual abuse collapsed, and the children were returned home. One of the social workers dealing with the case, Liz McLean, had previously been involved with a similar issue in Rochdale in England in 1990, when 20 children had been taken into care on the basis of the allegation of ritual abuse by adult carers. As with the later Orkney case, no such abuse was proven, and the children were returned to their families (BBC News 1991). Before these two cases, there had been similar action taken by social workers in the Nottingham area, in 1987 and 1989 (Nathan and Snedeker 1995).

A clear link between all of these cases was the salacious controversy based on the idea of adults molesting children through satanic rituals. Although the media soon took a strong interest in such possibilities, no evidence could be produced – either through interviews with the children at the centre of these cases, or in the wider communities and the adults alleged to be the perpetrators. A UK government-commissioned report by the anthropolo-gist Professor Jean La Fontaine eventually concluded in 1994 that although there were clearly many instances of physical, mental and sexual abuse, there was no strong evidence for any of this being organized ritual abuse (La Fontaine 1994). A more subtle link, however, emerged when it came to light that largely Christian evangelical fears about organized ritu-alistic abuse of children by Satanists (enemies of Christ and Christians) might have prompted social care professionals to take action to protect vulnerable children.

In contrast to these cases of over-intervention by social workers, the death of Victoria Climbié in London in February 2000 was largely attributed to a very serious failure to inter-vene by social workers in the borough of Haringey (Laming 2003). However, the sustained abuse of the eight-year-old girl from the Ivory Coast, with over 128 separate injuries inflicted on her by her aunt, has been largely interpreted as being derived (at least in part) from religious factors. Following her death, it became apparent that Victoria had been regularly beaten by her aunt and the aunt's boyfriend, and one possible explanation for the frequency and severity of these beatings was that they were attempting to exorcize demons from her body.

There was certainly evidence that the aunt had visited some African churches in London, in particular the Mission Ensemble Pour Christ in Borough and the Universal Church of the Kingdom of God in Finsbury Park. The pastors of both these churches had suggested to Victoria's aunt that the girl's behavioural problems (such as regular bed-wetting) could be caused by demonic possession. The advice given by the churches had been regular prayer, but following the subsequent death of Victoria it is widely assumed that the aunt had regularly tried to beat the devil out of her.

In the year after Victoria's death a child's torso was discovered floating in the River Thames in central London. The boy, labelled 'Adam', was identified as being originally from Nigeria. It was largely speculated that the dismemberment of his body had been part of a dark ritualistic practice, with the severed limbs and head being used for medicinal/magical purposes (BBC News 2003). This interpretation could never be substantiated, but it has been widely used in the media – together with the exorcism beatings of Victoria Climbié – as a general stereotyping and demonization of African (particularly West African) Christianity in Britain.

Global dimensions of religious controversy

Both Victoria Climbié and the child 'Adam' were migrants to Britain before their violent deaths. A common theme in much of the above discussion has been the global dimension impacting on events and controversies in this country.

Two other international events threatened to have significant impact in Britain in 2010 (as well as across the globe). Following some threats made to the artists of the US TV cartoon *South Park* in April 2010 over the possible broadcast of a pictorial representation of the Prophet Muhammad (and in the wake of the 'Danish Cartoons' controversy of 2006, with the publication of drawings of the Prophet in the *Jyllands Posten*), an internet campaign built up very quickly to support the principles of free speech. In fact, the makers of *South Park*, the network Comedy Central, deleted the references to Muhammad in the broadcast show, after a potential death threat against the artists was posted on the internet by a known 'Islamist' group. From this developed a movement that sought to challenge the threat to individuals. This was on the basis that if 'everybody' drew Muhammad then not everybody could be killed by the extremists. This vague idea quickly spread to become a page on the social networking site Facebook, leading up to an 'Everyone Draw Muhammad Day' in May 2010. This movement created protest and resentment in various Muslim-majority countries across the world, and in Pakistan the government imposed internet restrictions, including preventing access to the Facebook and YouTube sites (BBC News 2010b).

Later in the year a different type of event was proposed by a US Christian preacher, Pastor Terry Jones. This was for a 'Burn the Koran' day, on 11 September – to mark the anniversary of the 9/11 tragedy and to protest about the creation of a Muslim centre near to the Ground Zero site. The idea of this day was itself inflammatory – it was clearly intended to cause a reaction in the Muslim world. In fact, Pastor Jones called off the event two days before, on 9 September, under the gaze of the world media (BBC News 2010c). However, a few months later he did publicly burn a Qur'an, in March 2011 – an act which was followed soon after by protests in Afghanistan leading to the deaths of ten people, including international UN staff (BBC News 2011c).

In both cases the provocative challenges from within the US to Muslims have had resonances internationally, and have had wide-ranging potential implications in Britain. In
echo of the Pastor Jones Qur'an burning, claims have been made about a far-right British
National Party Welsh Assembly candidate, who was alleged to have been filmed burning a
Qur'an – although subsequently the charges were dropped (BBC News 2011d). Neither
case, however, had a profound impact as controversies – although the reporting of both in
the broadcast media, and the engagement of many people with them through social
networking sites, has meant they had some impact on the religious landscape of Britain. In
both cases what has been notable is the interaction between high-profile international
events and the localization of these events in the particularities of religions in contemporary Britain through the potentially instantaneous nature of the media. It is quite likely that
future controversies stemming from Britain could be similarly internationalized, and issues
emerging elsewhere will become controversies in Britain due to their localization here
through the media.

Controversy, multiculturalism and co-creating the future

The controversies explored in this chapter stem from changes in British society, especially
those which are felt to threaten the 'mainstream/majority' of the society. The causes of
controversy are broadly threefold.

First, there are differing and changing perceptions about the value of religion and its
proper role (if any) in society. This is clearly different from British society pre-1945, where
religion – and in particular Christianity – was largely taken for granted as part of the fabric
of society.

Second, there are various and divergent evaluations of religious diversity, pluralism and
multiculturalism. Again there is considerable contestation over whether such diversity is
good or bad, whether there is any alternative and how such diversity should be managed.
Some changes, like new 'equalities' and 'rights' frameworks, seem designed to protect diversity (in principle at least), whilst proclamations of the dangers of diversity and the 'death of
multiculturalism' continue. Religious diversity (particularly between Muslims and non-
Muslims), and diversity between secularism and religion are both at issue.

Third, there are conflicting and unresolved ideas about what constitutes British identity.
This comes back to whether contemporary Britishness is made up of either a Christian religious or post-Christian secular majority, and in what ways layers of difference fit into such
identities. And within such debates also lie dimensions relating to the distinctive national
identities within the 'four-nations-state' (Weller 2005: 73) that constitutes the UK.

The chapter has noted many historical precedents, but in discussing what is new about
the controversies analysed here, the following has been highlighted.

First, that the principal focus of controversy related to religion has shifted from Catholics
to New Religious Movements and then to Islam and Muslims. In the future it may change
again from Muslims to another group. What appears to have been quite resonant over a long
period of time is the perceived relationship between religious minorities and the state. As
Beckford argued (Beckford 1985: 273), in earlier parts of the twentieth century groups such
as Jehovah's Witnesses and Mormons were often seen as defying the state and the rule of
law. Since 2000, such charges have also been raised against Muslims in a similar way, for
allegedly prioritizing international over national allegiances.

Second, recent controversies in contemporary Britain are strongly 'mediatized'. Indeed
there can even sometimes be a sense in which the controversy might not exist – or at least

not in the same way – without the very significant role of the media in instant transmission of messages and images that themselves often appear pre-set to identifying and highlighting controversy. Such media is by definition without clear national boundaries, and at least from the time of the Rushdie Affair in 1988 the events in one particular distant locality can be the spark of major issues and controversy in Britain and vice versa.

Third, that controversies are linked with the end of longstanding 'religious monopolies'. The religious landscape of Britain has been changing so that it is now (Weller 2005: 117) a 'three-dimensional' (Christian, secular and religiously plural) religious landscape in a 'four-nations-state'. At stake is the future shape and content of the relationship between Britain's Christian and secular heritages, in kaleidoscopic interplay with the country's increasing religious plurality and the implications arising from this.

As a last word, it is worth noting that controversies are not always negative. Religious actors, the media and 'the powers that be' tend to see controversies as negative. But, arguably, if there is to be change towards greater justice and equity, then 'disruptions' and 'disturbances' are a 'normal' way for developments to occur within a democracy (see Hesse 2000). Controversies are often necessary to effect the kind of paradigm shifts necessary for religious, social, legal and political change to occur.

Key terms

Controversy: An event and debate which has reached public attention, particularly in the media, usually with negative reactions. What is of particular interest here is why certain events are taken as controversial, and what such controversies tell us about the wider social values – such as about religion and specific religious groups.

Multiculturalism: A very widely used word, often taken to mean many different ideas and processes (both negative and positive). Broadly used here not to describe any particular social programme or ideology, but rather to describe social contexts of, and responses to, cultural diversity, and, with that, responses to religious diversity.

New religiosity: A term that refers to a range of different types of religious groups and practices. Broadly it means any form of religion that has emerged in recent decades, particularly through innovation and/or conversion. It is usually distinguished from other forms of religion that are new to Britain, such as religions that are established through groups migrating and settling, and also the extant forms of Christianity that have adapted to changes in contemporary society. In practice, however, the boundaries between these three areas are hard to distinguish.

Religious monopolies: The context of how within contemporary Britain certain religious groups (particular the Christian churches) have a key and socially defining role – not only in terms of numbers of supporters, but more importantly in dominating the values and debates about religion in society.

Sectarianism: Literally this refers to the conflicts between different religious groups (or sects) within a particular society. However, in contemporary Britain – particularly Scotland – it refers specifically to social tensions between Catholics and Protestants, not only on religious grounds but also with reference to other markers of group identity (such as allegiance to certain football teams).

Further reading

Dinham, Adam, Robert Furbey and Vivienne Lowndes (eds) (2009). *Faith in the Public Realm: Controversies, Policies and Practices*. Bristol: Policy Press. A collection of essays exploring 'faith' within the public realm in relation to issues of public policy and practice.

Nye, Malory (2001). *Multiculturalism and Minority Religions in Britain: Krishna Consciousness, Religious Freedom, and the Politics of Location*. Richmond: Curzon. Explores concepts of religions, minorities and power in political and legal discourse through the Bhaktivedanta Manor controversy.

Parekh, Bhikhu (2005). *Rethinking Multiculturalism: Cultural Diversity and Political Theory*. Second edition. London: Palgrave Macmillan. Develops a theory of multiculturalism applied to a number of key policy issues for a plural society.

Weller, Paul (2008). *Religious Diversity in the UK: Contours and Issues*. London: Continuum. Presents a 'critical incident' and 'case study' approach to religious diversity in the UK and the debates associated with it.

Weller, Paul (2009). *A Mirror for our Times: 'The Rushdie Affair' and the Future of Multiculturalism*. London: Continuum. Takes the *Satanic Verses* controversy as a mirror in which a range of social, political, legal and religious issues for a plural society are highlighted.

References

Ahdar, Rex and Ian Leigh (2005). *Religious Freedom in the Liberal State*. Oxford: Oxford University Press.

Ahsan, Muhammad and Abdul Raheem Kidwai (eds) (1991). *Sacrilege Versus Civility: Muslim Perspectives on The Satanic Verses Affair*. Leicester: The Islamic Foundation.

Allen, Chris (2010). *Islamophobia*. Farnham: Ashgate.

Appignanesi, Lisa and Sarah Maitland (eds) (1989). *The Rushdie File*. London: Fourth Estate.

Asad, Talal (2003). *Formations of the Secular*. Stanford, CA: Stanford University Press.

Barker, Eileen (1982). *New Religious Movements: A Perspective for Understanding Society*. Lampeter: Edwin Mellen Press.

Barker, Eileen (1995). *New Religious Movements: A Practical Introduction*. London: Home Office.

BBC News (1991). 'Orkney "abuse" Children Go Home', *BBC News Online: on this day*, 4 April. Online. Available HTTP: http://news.bbc.co.uk/onthisday/hi/dates/stories/april/4/newsid_2521000/2521067.stm (accessed 29 May 2011).

BBC News (2003). 'Breakthrough in Torso Murder Inquiry', *BBC News Online*. Online. Available HTTP: http://news.bbc.co.uk/1/hi/england/2713927.stm (accessed 29 May 2011).

BBC News (2008a). 'Muslim Stylist Wins £4,000 Payout', *BBC News Online*. Online. Available HTTP: http://news.bbc.co.uk/1/hi/england/london/7457794.stm (accessed 29 May 2011).

BBC News (2008b). 'Registrar Wins Same-Sex Tribunal', *BBC News Online*. Online. Available HTTP: http://news.bbc.co.uk/1/hi/7499248.stm (accessed 29 May 2011).

BBC News (2009). 'Christian Registrar Loses Same-Sex Partnership Case', *BBC News Online*. Online. Available HTTP: http://news.bbc.co.uk/1/hi/england/london/8413196.stm (accessed 29 May 2011).

BBC News (2010a). 'Catholic Charity's Appeal over Gay Adoption Fails', *BBC News Online*. Online. Available HTTP: www.bbc.co.uk/news/uk-11019895 (accessed 30 August 2011).

BBC News (2010b). 'US Cartoonist Apologises over Facebook Muhammad Row', *BBC News Online*. Online. Available HTTP: www.bbc.co.uk/news/10136576 (accessed 29 May 2011).

BBC News (2010c). 'Pastor Terry Jones: "God is Telling us to Stop"', *BBC News Online*. Online. Available HTTP: www.bbc.co.uk/news/world-us-canada-11273678 (accessed 29 May 2011).

BBC News (2011a). 'Tribunal Rejects Catholic Care's Gay Adoption Appeal', *BBC News Online*. Online. Available HTTP: www.bbc.co.uk/news/uk-england-leeds-13205558 (accessed 30 August 2011).

BBC News (2011b). 'Christian Foster Couple Lose "Homosexuality Views" Case', *BBC News Online*.

Online. Available HTTP: www.bbc.co.uk/news/uk-england-derbyshire-12598896 (accessed 29 May 2011).

BBC News (2011c).'Afghanistan: Koran Protests in Kandahar and Jalalabad', *BBC News Online*. Online. Available HTTP: www.bbc.co.uk/news/world-south-asia-12949975 (accessed 29 May 2011).

BBC News (2011d). '"Koran burning" Inquiry Continues after Case Withdrawn', *BBC News Online*. Online. Available HTTP: www.bbc.co.uk/news/uk-wales-13098246 (accessed 29 May 2011).

Beckford, James (1985). *Cult Controversies: The Societal Response to the New Religious Movements*. London and New York, NY: Tavistock Publications.

Boucher, Dan (2010). *A Little Bit Against Discrimination: Reflection on the Opportunities and Challenges Presented by the Equality Bill 2009–2010*, Care Research Paper, Equalities Series: Paper 2. London: CARE (Christian Action Research and Education).

brap (2009). *The 'Religion or Belief' Equality Strand in Law and Policy: Current Implications for Equalities and Human Rights*. A 'State of the Nation' Report Researched and Written by brap for the British Humanist Association. London: British Humanist Association.

Bruce, Steve (1986). *God Save Ulster!: The Religion and Politics of Paisleyism*. Clarendon University Press.

Bruce, Steve, Tony Glendinning, Iain Paterson and Michael Rosie (2005). 'Religious Discrimination in Scotland: Fact or Myth?', *Ethnic and Racial Studies*, 28/1: 151–168.

Cameron, David (2011). 'PM's Speech at Munich Security Conference', 5 February 2011, *Number10.gov.uk: the official website of the Prime Minister's Office*. Online. Available HTTP: www.number10.gov.uk/news/speeches-and-transcripts/2011/02/pms-speech-at-munich-security-conference-60293 (accessed 29 May 2011).

Christian Institute (2009). *Marginalising Christians: Instances of Christians Being Sidelined in Modern Britain*. Newcastle-upon-Tyne: Christian Institute.

Chryssides, George (1991). *The Advent of Sun Myung Moon: The Origins, Beliefs and Practices of the Unification Church*. Basingstoke: Macmillan.

Cotterell, Richard (1984). 'Interview: Richard Cotterell, MEP', *Update: A Quarterly Journal on New Religious Movements*, 8/3–4: 30–34.

Dialogue Society (2009). *Deradicalisation by Default: The Dialogue Approach to Rooting out Violent Extremism*. London: Dialogue Society.

Dwyer, Graham and Richard J. Cole (2007). *The Hare Krishna Movement: Forty Years of Chant and Change*. London: I. B. Tauris.

Edge, Peter W. (1998). 'Sacred Spaces: Planning Law and Religion', paper presented to the Department of Legal Studies, University of Central Lancashire, May.

Erikson, John (1998). *Islam and Postcolonial Narrative*. Cambridge: Cambridge University Press.

Fraser, Antonia (1996). *The Gunpowder Plot: Terror and Faith in 1605*. London: Weidenfeld and Nicholson.

Furedi, Frank (2007). *Invitation to Terror: The Expanding Empire of the Unknown*. London: Continuum.

Ghanea, Nazila, Alan Stephens and Raphael Walden (eds) (2007). *Does God Believe in Human Rights? Essays on Religion and Human Rights*. Leiden: Martinus Nijhoff Publishers.

Gude, Ken (2010). 'The Necessary Reckoning on Rendition and Waterboarding', *Guardian.co.uk*, 16 November. Online. Available HTTP: www.guardian.co.uk/commentisfree/cifamerica/2010/nov/16/torture-human-rights (accessed 29 May 2011).

Guillaume, Alfred (1987). *The Life of Muhammad: A Translation of Ishaq's Sirat Rasul Allah*. Oxford: Oxford University Press.

Her Majesty's Government (2008a). *Preventing Violent Extremism: A Strategy for Delivery*. London: Her Majesty's Government.

Her Majesty's Government (2008b). *The Prevent Strategy: A Guide for Local Partners in England Stopping People Becoming or Supporting Terrorists and Violent Extremists*. London: Her Majesty's Government.

Hesse, Barnor (2000). *Un/settled Multiculturalisms: Diasporas, Entanglements, Transruptions*. London: Zed Books.

Hill, Mark (2008). 'Civil Partnerships and Religious Organisations', paper presented to the Centre for Law and Religion, Cardiff University, June.

Knott, Kim (1986). *My Sweet Lord: The Hare Krishna Movement.* Wellingborough: Aquarian Press.

Knott, Kim, Alistair McFadyen, Seán McLoughlin and Matthew Francis (2006). *The Roots, Practices and Consequences of Terrorism: A Literature Review of Research in the Arts and Humanities. Final Report for the Home Office.* Leeds: Department of Theology and Religious Studies, University of Leeds.

Kundnani, Arun (2009). *Spooked: How Not to Prevent Violent Extremism.* London: Institute of Race Relations. Online. Available HTTP: www.irr.org.uk/pdf2/spooked.pdf (accessed 29 May 2011).

La Fontaine, Jean (1994). *Extent and Nature of Organised and Ritual Abuse.* London: Her Majesty's Stationery Office.

Laming, Lord (2003). *The Victoria Climbié Inquiry: Report of an Inquiry.* London: Her Majesty's Stationery Office.

Larsen, Timothy (1999). *Friends of Religious Equality: Nonconformist Politics in Mid-Victorian England.* Woodbridge: The Boydell Press.

Leech, Ken (1973). *Youthquake: Spirituality and the Growth of a Counter-Culture.* London: Sheldon.

Liechty, Joseph and Cecilia Clegg (2001). *Moving Beyond Sectarianism: Religion, Conflict and Reconciliation in Northern Ireland.* Dublin: The Columba Press.

Maaga, Mary McCormick (1998). *Hearing the Voices of Jonestown.* New York, NY: Syracuse University Press.

Marrotti, Arthur (2005). *Religious Ideology and Cultural Fantasy: Catholic and Anti-Catholic Discourses in Early Modern England.* Notre Dame, IN: University of Notre Dame Press.

McSweeney, Bill (1989). 'The Religious Dimension of the "Troubles" in Northern Ireland', in Paul Badham (ed.), *Religion, State and Society in Modern Britain.* Lampeter: Edwin Mellen Press, 68–83.

Nathan, Debbie and Mike Snedeker (1995). *Satan's Silence: Ritual Abuse and the Making of a Modern American Witch Hunt.* New York, NY: Basic Books.

Nye, Malory (2001). *Multiculturalism and Minority Religions in Britain: Krishna Consciousness, Religious Freedom, and the Politics of Location.* Richmond: Curzon.

Parsons, Gerald (1994). 'Introduction: Deciding How Far You Can Go', in Gerald Parsons (ed.), *The Growth of Religious Diversity: Britain from 1945. Volume II: Controversies.* London: Routledge, 5–22.

Pearce, Augur (2008). 'Coupledom: The Meaning of Civil Partnership', *New Law Journal*, 158/7328: 951–953.

Reader, Ian (1996). *A Poisonous Cocktail?: Aum Shinrikyo's Path to Violence.* Copenhagen: NIAS Press.

Runnymede Trust (1997). *Islamophobia: A Challenge for Us All.* London: Runnymede Trust.

Rushdie, Salman (1988). *The Satanic Verses.* London: Viking Penguin.

Salbstein, Michael (1982). *The Emancipation of the Jews in Britain: The Question of the Admission of the Jews to Parliament, 1828–1860.* East Brunswick, NJ and London: Associated University Presses.

Sandberg, Russell (2010). 'The Implications of the Court of Appeal Decision in Ladele and other Case Law Developments', paper presented to the Centre for Law and Religion, Cardiff University.

Sandberg, Russell (2011a). *Law and Religion.* Cambridge: Cambridge University Press.

Sandberg, Russell (2011b). 'The Right to Discriminate', *Ecclesiastical Law Journal*, 13/2: 157–181.

Scottish Executive (2006). *Sectarianism: Action Plan on Tackling Sectarianism in Scotland.* Edinburgh: Scottish Executive. Online. Available HTTP: www.scotland.gov.uk/Resource/Doc/90629/0021809.pdf (accessed 29 May 2011).

Tabor, James D. and Eugene Gallagher (1997). *Why Waco?: Cults and the Battle for Religious Freedom in America.* Berkeley, CA: University of California Press.

UK Action Committee on Islamic Affairs (1993). *Muslims and the Law in Multi-Faith Britain: The Need for Reform.* London: UK Action Committee on Islamic Affairs.

Wade, Mike (2009). 'Gallery's Invitation to Deface the Bible Brings Obscene Response', *Times Newspapers*, 23 July. Online. Available HTTP: www.timesonline.co.uk/tol/comment/faith/article6723980.ece (accessed 29 May 2011).

Walls, Patricia and Rory Williams (2003). 'Sectarianism at Work: Accounts of Employment Discrimination Against Irish Catholics in Scotland', *Ethnic and Racial Studies*, 26/4: 632–662.

Walls, Patricia and Rory Williams (2005). 'Religious Discrimination in Scotland: A Rebuttal of Bruce *et al.*'s Claim that Sectarianism is a Myth', *Ethnic and Racial Studies*, 28/4: 759–767.

Weller, Paul (2005). *Time for a Change: Reconfiguring Religion, State and Society*. London: T & Clark.

Weller, Paul (2009). *A Mirror for our Times: 'The Rushdie Affair' and the Future of Multiculturalism*. London: Continuum.

Weller, Paul, Alice Feldman and Kingsley Purdam, with contributions from Ahmed Andrews, Anna Doswell, John Hinnells, Marie Parker-Jenkins, Sima Parmar and Michele Wolfe (2001). *Religious Discrimination in England and Wales*. London: Home Office.

Woodhead, Linda with Rebecca Catto (2009). *'Religion or Belief': Identifying Issues and Priorities*. Equality and Human Rights Commission Research Report 48. Manchester: Equality and Human Rights Commission.

Zaehner, Robert (1972). *Drugs, Mysticism and Make-Believe*. London: Collins.

Zaehner, Robert (1974). *Our Savage God*. London: Collins.

Part 1
Changing religious forms

2 Christianity

Loss of monopoly

Mathew Guest, Elizabeth Olson and John Wolffe

In looking at controversies over religion, the previous chapter gave an indication of how 'religion' looks from the perspective of majorities in post-war Britain, and showed how politicians, media and cultural elites have dealt with religious change. Part 1 of the book takes a different perspective: that of the religions themselves and those who live by them. It is interested in tactical as well as strategic religion, and in examining how everyday religion has changed in post-war Britain, for majorities as well as minorities.

This chapter traces the way in which Christianity in Britain has undergone a major shift in its national status and role since 1945. It shows that there has been a sharp decline in traditional Christian practices, including regular church attendance, recruitment to ordained ministry and participation in rites of passage. Nevertheless, it also documents how historical and institutional peculiarities ensure Christianity retains influence over the cultural life of Britain, particularly in terms of language, art, music, landscape, literature and some everyday practices. Moreover, it discusses areas of resurgence and innovation which reflect Christianity's continuing significance, not least as a powerful marker of ethnic and social class difference, in relation to both old identities and new and emerging ones related to Britain's new position in a post-colonial and increasingly connected global order.

Two snapshots

On 2 June 1953 Elizabeth II was crowned Queen in Westminster Abbey in an elaborate Christian ritual with origins dating back nearly a millennium to the coronation of King Edgar in 973, but now for the first time watched live on television by an audience of many millions across the country (see Plate 2.1). During the ceremony the Queen took an oath to 'maintain in the United Kingdom the Protestant Reformed religion established by law'. The Moderator of the General Assembly of the Church of Scotland presented her with a Bible, and laying her hand upon it, she said, 'The things which I have here before promised, I will perform and keep. So help me God.' Seated in the historic coronation chair, she was anointed with consecrated oil, and presented with symbols – including the orb, sceptre and ring – that highlighted the spiritual nature and context of kingship. The Archbishop of Canterbury placed St Edward's Crown on her head, the packed congregation in the Abbey and the great crowds in the streets outside shouted 'God save the Queen', and the Archbishop pronounced a benediction over her. The Queen and her husband, the Duke of Edinburgh, then received Holy Communion. (For a full account of the ritual see Carr 2002.)

That same evening the Queen broadcast to her people. She reminded them that she had previously asked them to pray for her on her coronation day, 'that God would give me wisdom and strength to carry out the promises I should then be making', and said that she had been 'uplifted and sustained by the knowledge that your thoughts and prayers were with me'. She asserted that:

> My Coronation is not the symbol of a power and splendour that are gone, but a declaration of our hopes for the future and for the years I may, by God's grace and mercy, be given to reign and serve you as your Queen.
>
> (*The Times*, 3 June 1953)

The sense that the coronation reflected a deep reality of underlying national Christian spiritual cohesion was the view not only of its organizers and central protagonist, but also was reflected in comment at the time. Even an irreligious diarist, who was distracted by caring for young children during the television broadcast, did his utmost to watch the ceremonial and found it 'magnificent' (Harrison 1961: 248). The *Times* leader writer (2 June 1953) saw it as 'a reminder, at once simple and direct, that the British people still profess and call themselves Christian'. The eminent sociologists Edward Shils and Michael Young published an article in which they argued that the coronation was a reaffirmation of the fundamental moral and religious values of society, concluding that it 'provided ... such an intensive contact with the sacred that we believe that we are justified in interpreting it ... as a great act of national communion' (Shils and Young 1953: 80).

The coronation did indeed seem to come at a time of modest Christian resurgence after the disruption of the Second World War: Church of England Easter Day communicant numbers had risen from 1.73 million in 1947 to 1.94 million in 1953, and were to increase further to 2.17 million in 1956 (Currie *et al.* 1977: 129). Catholic numbers were also increasing, and the membership of other denominations was in general holding steady. Around 80 per cent of the population professed belief in God and over 70 per cent held to a distinctively Christian belief in Jesus as the Son of God (Wolffe 2007: 326). Overt secularism was unusual and religions other than Christianity and Judaism remained tiny minorities – in influence and visibility as well as numbers.

The profound changes which have taken place in British religious life during Elizabeth II's long reign, and which are the subject of this volume, mean that such an exclusively Christian and almost exclusively Anglican major national ceremonial now seems inconceivable. Moreover, even in 1953 the reality was a more complex one than was suggested by the official ritual. The organizers had recognized that the ceremonial was in significant respects already anachronistic, but had opted to affirm tradition rather than initiate potentially divisive debate by proposing substantial changes. The televising of the coronation service also had double-edged implications. On the one hand it facilitated a kind of mass participation in the Abbey service through the clustering of extended family groups around the small flickering black and white screens (in exactly the sort of setting described in Chapter 7's reflections on religion and media). On the other, it diminished a sense of mystery and sacredness, and by offering a more immediately compelling attraction, deprived local churches of the opportunity to hold the widespread simultaneous local services that had characterized such major national events in the pre-television era. The reality of grassroots popular behaviour suggests that the kind of 'national communion' that took place was usually more secular than Christian, characterized by numerous street parties and other festivities, but limited religious observance. As the Abbey service was relayed over loudspeakers to the crowd in the Mall, there was hush for a time, but also irreverent and irrelevant comments at the most sacred moments of the ritual (Harrison 1961: 242–243). Shils and Young were criticized at the time for supposing that the archaic language of the service accurately reflected contemporary popular beliefs. More recent analysis has suggested that the media, both broadcasts and newspapers, tended to construct a stronger image of national consensus than was consistent with the reality on the ground (Örnebring 2004).

As the previous chapter has mentioned, in 2005 a very different televised event brought religion into the media limelight, one surrounded by controversy and disharmony rather than the national unity supposedly underpinning the coronation over 50 years before. *Jerry Springer the Opera* had been shown at theatres across Britain from April 2003 and had attracted notoriety for its extensive use of strong swear words and irreverent treatment of Judaeo-Christian themes. A musical scored by Richard Thomas and penned by stand-up comedian Stewart Lee, it took its inspiration from the well-known American TV show hosted by the charismatic former Mayor of Cincinnati, Jerry Springer. The TV show, broadcast on US networks since 1991, had made its name for its shocking and sometimes bizarre content, covering topics like incest, zoophilia and pornography, hence its reputation as tabloid TV. Its format was no less sensationalist, the host often adjudicating between invited guests from the general public whose vocal disagreements would be played out in front of a live audience. Guests would often come to blows, necessitating the frequent intervention of security guards waiting in the wings.

Thomas and Lee composed their opera as a pastiche of the TV show, but added extra poignancy by making Jesus, Satan and even God major characters in the drama. During the second Act, Springer is taken down to Hell, depicted as a version of his own TV studio, where he is compelled to mediate an attempt by Satan to get an apology from Jesus, Mary and then God, portrayed by a vastly overweight actor in a silver suit. It is Springer who saves the day with his own platitudes – at once both acquiescent to life's pathos while also advocating a vague inclusivism and understanding between warring parties. Then we are back in the real studio, for the Hell episode turns out to be a dream, and Jerry is fighting for his life after an assassination attempt. Softly calling for his safe deliverance, the chorus sing 'Jerry eleison', an unapologetic lift from Christian liturgy that hints at who the real saviour of the day is in our TV age.

Jerry Springer the Opera understandably attracted some controversy as a theatre production, but registered only mild discomfort in the print media, and commentaries in the British broadsheets focused on Thomas and Lee's attempt to parody both opera and reality TV as much as Christianity. However, in January 2005 the BBC announced its intention to broadcast a production of the opera on BBC 2, provoking a chorus of disapproval from moral traditionalists and some evangelicals. Ofcom, the media regulator, received a record 5,500 complaints before the broadcast, three times as many as it received before the showing of Martin Scorsese's film *The Last Temptation of Christ* (released in 1988), and on the day before the broadcast, the BBC announced that it had received 47,000 complaints, the most ever received for a single broadcast (BBC News 2005). Senior BBC executives received telephone calls from outraged Christians calling for the broadcast to be cancelled, and when it was not, and they received death threats, security firms were employed for their personal protection. Much of the protest emanated from the conservative evangelical campaign group Christian Voice, although the ensuing public debate also featured MediaWatch UK, the Evangelical Alliance, the pro-life pressure group UK Life League and several Anglican bishops. Their complaints focused on accusations of blasphemy, excessive profanity (the opera features 300 uses of the 'f' and 'c' words, amplified by opponents to a figure of 8,000 because of the 40-strong chorus singing them), and the demeaning depiction of biblical characters, including Jesus as a pathetic figure wearing a baby's nappy.

Voicing the opposing argument, the BBC defended its decision to broadcast the opera on the grounds of its mission to cover a breadth of viewpoints (Thompson 2005), and the National Secular Society weighed in by supporting the BBC's defence of free speech and calling for it to resist the bullying of religious 'extremists'. Following Christian Voice's picketing of numerous theatres and its threat of a religious boycott of a cancer charity which was offered a £3,000 donation from *Jerry Springer the Opera*, the campaign group was widely condemned and Revd Sheila Maxey, Moderator of the United Reformed Church, called them a 'disgrace'. The controversy thus unmasked divisions within the Christian community.

Hence while the opera exposed the sensitivities of some Christian parties, it also highlighted the status of Christianity at the beginning of the twenty-first century as a contested tradition. The relatively stable reverence affirmed across society during the 1950s had given way to a more uncertain, fragmented culture, in which Christianity appears as a minority pursuit, no longer at the heart of civic unity, instead a media curiosity, inspiring fierce defence among some, open mockery among others.

Analytical framework

The vignettes rehearsed above illustrate the significant changes that have occurred to the status of Christianity in Britain in the post-war period. By the beginning of the twenty-first century, Christianity and its institutions were no longer secure in their status as the dominant religious tradition, let alone as a monopoly, and the orientation of Christian groups to the British context has correspondingly been adjusted in light of this, although not always in ways expected by commentators writing at the time of the 1953 coronation. In acknowledgement of the emerging multi-layered picture, this chapter maps the complex ways in which British Christianity has changed and adapted to shifting circumstances according to three trajectories: the decline and dissolution of formal association; the relative continuity of Christianity's role informing patterns of ethnic and cultural identification; and the emergence and resurgence of a variety of changing forms of Christian commitment and religious engagement. This framework suggests neither inexorable decline on the one hand, nor naïve optimism about Christian vitality and influence on the other. The picture which emerges is one in which Christianity continues to enjoy cultural and religious significance within the British context, but a significance which is complicated and transformed by the social and cultural changes discussed in the Introduction to this volume. Before tracing these trajectories, a fundamental question needs to be addressed.

What is a Christian?

Any attempt to define a religious identity inevitably imposes an artificial boundary around a contested community. Christianity is no exception, and while it has had a significant presence in Britain since the fourth century CE, its characterization as an identity marker remains problematic. Theologically, at its centre is the figure of Jesus, worshipped as the Son of God and saviour of all humankind, whose life and teachings are mediated by the New Testament scriptures. These are conjoined with the Jewish scriptures, redefined as the Old Testament, reflecting the belief that Jesus as the Messiah came to fulfil the Jewish prophecies.

Christianity is internally diverse, with different elements and groups emerging throughout Christian history, and extending recognition to each other to varying degrees. Each has its own understanding of what constitutes Christian faith, as well as its own expectations of religious practice. The denominational spectrum in modern Britain – spanning Roman Catholic and Protestant churches, with the latter subdivided into Anglican (Church of England), Presbyterian, Methodist, etc. – is complicated by the established Church of England. Unlike the other major Protestant churches in Europe, the Church of England understands itself as both Catholic *and* Reformed (its Anglo-Catholic wing celebrates a more highly ritualized form of worship than many of the Roman Catholic churches it aspires to emulate). There are also subdivisions defined by 'churchmanship' (theological and ritual orientation) which cut across denominational boundaries. This is most evident among evangelicals, whose Bible-centred, mission-oriented brand of Christianity can be found among Anglicans, Baptists and many churches which consider themselves 'independent'. Similarly, Charismatics – often defined by their emphasis on the importance of spiritual gifts such as speaking in tongues – include some Roman Catholics as well as many evangelicals.

It is also worth noting how cultural and ethnic factors influence the way such Christian labels are ascribed and embodied. For example, Roman Catholicism assumes a different form and function in the lives of Polish immigrants to Britain, compared with its role among Catholics in Northern Ireland. While relations between these various denominations are mostly mutually respectful (and generally became more so in the post-war period; see Case study 1 on the United Reformed Church and ecumenism), there remain a number of Christian groups which are commonly viewed as illegitimate or deviant, often on account of their rejection of the Trinity – the belief that God is three in one – or a belief in divine revelation beyond the Bible. In this latter category can be included Jehovah's Witnesses, Mormons and Christadelphians.

In addition to these boundaries, the label 'Christian' has acquired a life of its own as a preferred identity for those wishing to distance themselves from the trappings of denominational church structures, and as a symbolic marker for a constellation of ethnic, cultural and moral, rather than religious, values. As the Introduction shows, according to 2001 Census figures for Great Britain, 71.8 per cent of the population would describe themselves as 'Christian' (Perfect 2011), and yet figures for weekly church attendance are less than 10 per cent (Brierley 2006b), hence the importance of distinguishing Christian identity on a number of levels: at the very least as church membership, active church involvement and self-designation or identity.

TEXT BOX 5

Counting Christians

The task of ascertaining the number of Christians in modern Britain is a difficult one. British Christianity has a long history relative to other faiths that arrived here much later, and retains associations with the state and social elites, so that Christians have not felt the need to erect tight boundaries around themselves in the way Jews, Muslims and Sikhs often have. Such sociological factors are compounded by differences internal to the Christian community concerning what constitutes Christian commitment – who is 'in' and who is 'out' – and these shape attempts by Christian organizations to take stock of their number. Secularization has destabilized traditional understandings of the Christian life and has also influenced the perspectives of government, so that the very issue of measuring religious identities is seen as of questionable importance.

However, in the 2001 and 2011 national Censuses – following a period of determined campaigning by religious communities, academics and secular groups – a question on religion was introduced. The question was optional, but most chose to answer it, generating a 2001 figure of 71.8 per cent for the proportion of self-identifying Christians among the population of Great Britain. This sits awkwardly alongside contemporaneous figures on church practice generated by Peter Brierley's Church Censuses which, to take England for example, put regular church attendance at 7.5 per cent in 1998, decreasing to 6.3 per cent in 2005 (Brierley 2006b). Hence popular understandings do not appear to associate being a Christian necessarily with regular churchgoing. The British Social Attitudes Survey, which gauges the values of the population annually by interviewing a sample of around 3,000 respondents, includes slightly differently worded questions on religion every few years. In 2008, the results suggested that Christians made up 50 per cent of the population of England, Scotland and Wales, with those affiliating to the Church of England making up almost half this number (Voas and Ling 2010). The inconsistency with the Census figures from 2001 well illustrates how problematic such statistics can be. The absence of Northern Ireland is not significant in accounting for this difference, as Census figures for Scotland, England and Wales were also all around the 70 per cent mark. However, it is important to note how the situation in Ulster further complicates the issue, given the high levels of religious engagement there – 86 per cent self-identifying as Christian according to the 2001 Census (almost half of these Roman Catholic, compared to 9 per cent elsewhere in the UK), with regular churchgoing at 45 per cent according to a 2007 survey (Ashworth and Farthing 2007).

The decline of church association

Turning to the first trajectory to be discussed, the predominant long-term trend in British Christianity over the second half of the twentieth century was the major decline in the extent of formal association with the churches, as measured by Sunday attendances and denominational memberships. This broad generalization needs to be nuanced in significant ways, and also only addresses one aspect of the wider question of the more diffuse and informal role of Christianity in British society. Nevertheless, the overall picture is unmistakable. Membership of the Church of England stood at 2.96 million (6.7 per cent of the population of England and Wales) in 1950, but declined to 1.82 million (3.7 per cent of the population) by 1980 and to 1.34 million (2.5 per cent of population) in 2000. At the same dates the membership of the Church of Scotland stood respectively at 24.9 per cent, 18.7 per cent and 11.9 per cent of the population of Scotland. Roman Catholic Mass attendances are estimated at 4.8 per cent of the population of the United Kingdom in 1950, and probably even rose significantly in the 1950s, but by 1980 they too had fallen back to 4.3 per cent, and dropped steeply to 2.8 per cent in 2000 (Wolffe 2007: 324). Reliable figures for Sunday attendances are not generally available for dates before the last quarter of the century, but they too show very marked decline over that period. Total Christian attendances in England on a 'typical' Sunday were 5.4 million (11.7 per cent of the population) in 1979 but fell to 3.7 million (7.4 per cent of the population) in 1998 (Robbins 2008: 469) and to 3.17 million (6.3 per cent of the population) in 2005 (Brierley 2008: 2.24). If these trends were continued, the organized Christian church would come close to extinction in England within little more than another generation.

Moreover, the average age of remaining congregations has been steadily increasing (Brierley 2008: 2.14–2.17), reflecting a failure to recruit younger people, or even to retain the children of churchgoers beyond the early teenage years. Earlier in the twentieth century the majority of Britons had attended Sunday School at some point in their childhood, and in 1953 around a third of 14-year-olds were still enrolled in them. However, in the 1960s participation began to decline catastrophically, and by the turn of the millennium Sunday Schools in the traditional sense had largely ceased to exist (Brierley 1999: 2.15).[1] In the past, churches had struggled to translate Sunday School attendance into teenage and adult commitment, but the virtual collapse of the movement meant that the pool of potential recruits with at least a sense of past connection was drastically reduced. Among samples of students at Sheffield University, the proportion claiming to have had a religious upbringing declined from 94 per cent in 1961 to 51 per cent in 1985, while those claiming to be active church members dropped from 36 per cent in 1961 to 9 per cent in 1985 (Bebbington 1992: 268). As the class of 1985 began to bring up their own children in the 1990s and 2000s, they were much less likely than their parents (represented by the class of 1961) to pass on any sense of connection to organized Christianity (see Chapter 10 on cultural change for more information and discussion about these trends).

The changes are easier to describe than to explain. But it is clear that the 1960s and 1970s were the pivotal decades, and the cultural shifts that then took place, and their significance for Christianity, were profound. However differently scholars may interpret them, they agree that this was a turning point – one which is interpreted as leading to 'the death of Christian Britain' by Callum Brown (Brown 2009 and in this volume, Chapter 10), to 'the passing of Protestant England' by Simon Green (Green 2010) and as amounting to a 'religious crisis of the 1960s' by Hugh McLeod (McLeod 2007).

As noted above, in the 1950s, most indicators of church association were stable, or even slightly increasing. The large-scale Billy Graham missions of 1954 and 1955 appeared at the time to be strikingly successful, although their longer-term impact on churchgoing is much more debatable. Quite steep decline set in within the space of a few years in the early to mid-1960s. In looking for explanations it is important not to assume that contemporaneous events were necessarily causes. The 1960s certainly saw significant shifts in other long-established cultural and social patterns, especially in relation to the situation of women and sexual mores, transformed by the availability of the contraceptive pill (Brown 2009). There was also a general climate of youth revolt against established institutions, to which the churches were particularly vulnerable. Nevertheless the indications are that people who ceased to attend church did so not as a result of any conscious rejection of Christianity, but more from a sense of boredom, gradual drift away from a habit of regular involvement or a sense that their lifestyle was no longer consistent with perceived Christian standards. A subjective feeling that their sexual behaviour was 'sinful' or would be disapproved of by the clergy was probably far more widespread than any explicit condemnation by the church. However, in 1968, the publication of the papal encyclical *Humanae Vitae*, disallowing artificial means of contraception, provoked a particular sense of crisis among Roman Catholics, and undoubtedly alienated many people, including married couples, who were thereby faced with an inconsistency between their private practice and the authoritative statements of the Catholic Church. David Lodge's novel *How Far Can You Go?* effectively evokes the impact of *Humanae Vitae* on a group of previously conscientious Catholics (Lodge 1980: 113–127).

It was not that the churches did not try to adapt to changing times. The Second Vatican Council, which met from 1962 to 1965, initiated wide-ranging reforms intended to make the Roman Catholic Church more responsive to the conditions of the later twentieth century. The Protestant churches pursued liturgical change and ecumenism, explored radical theological ideas as epitomized in Bishop John Robinson's *Honest to God* (1963; see Chapter 5 on 'God-change') and sought to engage actively with social welfare and the needs of a changing and increasingly multi-racial society. None of this, however, enabled them to halt the haemorrhage of congregations. They may even have made things worse by alarming and alienating conservatives, raising expectations among more progressive Christians that could not in the end be fulfilled, and conveying a general sense of crisis and loss of direction.

There were, however, significant variations in the pattern of decline across the United Kingdom. Initially attendances appear to have been somewhat higher in Wales than in England, but by 2005 there was minimal difference (Brierley 2008: 2.24). Scotland, meanwhile, retained markedly higher levels of church attendance, at 17.1 per cent of the population in 1980 and 11.2 per cent in 2002, but still showed a steep decline (Brierley 2004: 12.3). Northern Ireland has up to the present retained significantly higher levels of attendance than in England: in 2003, 60 per cent of Catholics and 34 per cent of Protestants still claimed to attend one or more times a week. Nevertheless, in 1968, 95 per cent of Catholics and 46 per cent of Protestants attended church each week, and substantial decline since then shows that the province has not been immune to a wider secularization (Mitchell 2006: 24–25). These variations support the generalization that congregations are more loyal where churches are perceived as central to a strong national, regional or community identity. In Scotland and Wales, the earlier importance of the churches – especially Welsh nonconformist 'chapels' and the Church of Scotland – as focal points for the expression of national identity declined with the emergence of secular nationalist political parties in the late twentieth century. As Chapter 9 shows, the Northern Ireland situation reflects the continuing role of religion in defining polarized community identities during the three decades of the Troubles between 1969 and the 1990s.

There has also been significant regional variation. In Scotland in 2002 attendance rates ranged from 6.8 per cent in Angus and West Lothian to 39.2 per cent in the Western Isles, Skye and Lochalsh (Brierley 2003: 12.6, 12.22, 12.29); in England in 2005 they varied from 3.9 per cent in South Yorkshire to 8.3 per cent in Greater London and 8.7 per cent in Merseyside (Brierley 2006a: 12.46, 12.70, 12.90). While the persistence of the church-going in the far north-west of Scotland might be seen as a function of its remoteness, it is striking that English Christianity was at its strongest in two of the nation's largest urban conurbations.

At a local level too, the trajectories of individual churches have differed substantially. While some went into terminal decline, other nearby churches could be thriving and growing. This was hardly coincidental in that the increased mobility brought by general ownership of motor cars meant that it was easy for congregations to desert a depressing declining church in favour of a more flourishing and slightly more distant neighbour. For the less adaptable and mobile, however, closures and mergers of churches could lead to a withdrawal from such unfamiliar and less convenient new places of worship. For example, in the 1970s, in the small North Yorkshire village of Staithes, the local congregations fiercely resisted denominational attempts to amalgamate the Wesleyan and Primitive Methodist chapels, to the extent that the two churches appeared more viable apart than together (Clark 1982: 81–88). Ill-considered attempts to make a church more attractive to newcomers could antagonize an existing congregation, causing a rapid vicious circle of localized decline, as in the case of an Anglican church in a major Welsh seaport in the 1980s (Chambers 2004: 64–66).

In general the churches that succeeded in bucking the overall trend of decline were those that combined a clear and often a conservative theological and moral message with the capacity to make effective adaptations to a rapidly changing social and cultural environment. Such adaptation was particularly facilitated by the Charismatic Movement which, cultivating a greater immediacy of the Holy Spirit in worship and devotion, gathered momentum from the later 1960s onwards. In denominational terms the groups that most effectively resisted decline were evangelical Anglicans and Baptists, both characterized by conservative Protestant theologies. Meanwhile the 'house' or 'new' churches, so-called because of their small beginnings and rejection of the formal structures of traditional churches, expanded rapidly. They combined organizational radicalism – for example in their openness to lay leadership from both men and women – with theological conservatism, and usually placed a particular emphasis on charismatic manifestations of God. Their informality and dynamism appealed both to those dissatisfied with more traditional forms of Christianity, and, to some extent at least, to the previously unchurched.

The post-war period also saw important organizational innovations in Christianity, including the annual Spring Harvest gatherings at Butlin's holiday parks which were attracting up to 80,000 in the 1990s, and the Alpha course, which was very widely adopted as a means of initiating or strengthening adult enquirers into basic Christian teachings (Warner 2007).

A further significant force in mitigating the extent of Christian decline was the immigration of African and Caribbean Christians to Britain from the 1950s onwards. Many of these immigrant Christians gradually integrated into existing churches thus boosting their numbers, but others formed new ones of their own. The progress of black people within the Church of England was symbolized by the appointment of the Ugandan-born John Sentamu as Archbishop of York in 2005. The size and significance of black majority churches outside the 'old' denominations continue to grow, and are seen very clearly in the establishment of a number of megachurches in urban conurbations.

In light of such developments there are some, still limited, grounds for viewing the decline of the institutional Christian churches in the late twentieth century not as terminal, but as curved and limited, with the slope bottoming out and perhaps even in some contexts reversing around 2000. For example, the Church of England diocese of London, in contrast to national trends, saw a substantial increase in membership from 45,000 to over 70,000 between 1990 and 2010 (Jackson and Pigott 2011; Brierley 2008: 2.20). Whether or not such short-lived local trends prove to be a forerunner of wider national developments, it is certain that the future fabric of institutional Christianity in Britain will be very different from the situation in 1953.

Continuity, culture and identification

Turning to the second trajectory, it is an indication of the enormous influence of the secularization thesis (see the Introduction and Chapters 11 and 12) that treatments of religion in Britain during the post-1945 period have tended to emphasize decline and dissolution at the expense of continuity or growth. There are some important trends suggestive of a continuing cultural significance for Christianity that are all too often papered over or missed.

One of these counter-indications has to do with a discourse of national identity and with how Christianity continues to inform popular perceptions of 'Britishness'. One reading of the 2001 Census finding that 71.8 per cent of the population of Great Britain, when asked about their religion, opt for 'Christian', relates this trend to anxieties about national or 'ethnic' identity, enlivened in an age of heightened multiculturalism, religious plurality and radical Islam (Voas and Bruce 2004). Here, 'Christian' is said to be a synonym for 'British' and hence a cultural rather than religious self-ascription, and this evokes historical arguments that link religious vitality to periods when national or cultural identity is in question (McLeod 2007: 39–40).

However, some commentators suggest that this is a declining association, as 'Christian' becomes increasingly associated with the customs of churchgoing, and hence an elective identity opted into by personal volition, rather than something seamlessly tied to the conventions of being British. Callum Brown develops this argument by suggesting that this declining association was triggered by the changing role of women within the family in the 1960s; as the guardian of Christian virtue relinquishes her role, so such virtues lose their embodied resonance in British culture (Brown 2009). Nevertheless, recent research into undergraduate students at English universities suggests that Christianity may retain significant cultural importance for younger generations. A 2010/2011 survey of over 4,000 students funded by the AHRC/ESRC Religion and Society Programme reveals that over 50 per cent self-identify as 'Christian', while well under half of these express their Christianity in regular churchgoing, suggesting a sizeable 'periphery' for whom Christianity is still culturally important, in ways which may be more complex than Brown's argument might suggest (Guest *et al.* forthcoming).

There is even less doubt about the continuing importance of cultural associations with Christianity at the 'Celtic fringes' of the UK, where Christian affiliation remains important as an identity marker for those outside the dominant, English-centred national discourse (even when this is couched in terms of 'Britishness'). In Scotland, where the state church is Presbyterian and many Roman Catholics trace their ancestry to Irish immigrants, identities reflect religious, cultural and nationalistic legacies, and religious language is still important in a 'sectarianism' which is manifest in various ways, not least in the behaviour and chants of supporters of Rangers (Protestant) and Celtic (Catholic) football clubs (Bruce *et al.* 2004; Devine 2000). Wales is more characterized by religious decline and indifference, but chiefly because religio-cultural bonds – in this case bound up in the history of the Liberal Party and Methodism as carriers of Welsh identity – unravelled in the latter half of the twentieth century in parallel with traditional industries and gender roles (Chambers 2005: 72–73).

As Chapter 9 shows, Northern Ireland is different again, as 'civic religion' remains important and religion supports competing nationalist discourses – of a Unionist and Nationalist stripe. Claire Mitchell's work on Northern Ireland demonstrates that polarized political allegiances are not positively related to conventional indicators of Christian commitment such as church attendance and clear-cut religious beliefs, illustrating how Christian traditions of meaning have evolved into powerful identity markers among those who in some cases have only minimal connection to the churches (Mitchell 2006: 33–35). A sense of cultural opposition is also germane to this pattern. For example, the Unionist cause has been marked by a particularly strong expression of British identity, coloured in some quarters by a form of Protestantism that owes as much to its opposition to Roman Catholicism as it does to its Reformed theology (Brewer with Higgins 1998). Thus Christianity remains caught up in expressions of political and cultural struggle in the UK, with more recent variations found among immigrants from Africa, Eastern Europe and the West Indies, for whom Christianity functions as an identity resource in affirmations of ethnic and cultural difference (see below).

A more subtle set of associations has to do with language, not least the significance of the King James Bible and the 1662 Anglican *Book of Common Prayer* (BCP) in furnishing the British with an enduring stock of common phrases and turns of expression. Five hundred and forty-nine of the BCP's phrases appear in the *Oxford Dictionary of Quotations*; expressions like 'movable feasts', to 'be at death's door', to 'give up for lost' remain in common parlance, while many would not be aware when they use phrases like 'salt of the earth', 'bite the dust' or 'by the skin of my teeth' that they are citing the King James Bible. In this sense, two of the key literary influences over everyday language are Christian devotional documents, in spite of their diminishing function as liturgical sources. *The Book of Common Prayer*, while still used in some Anglican churches, has been gradually superseded by the *Alternative Service Book* in 1980 and then by *Common Worship* in 2000, both of which prioritize accessibility and choice over the nurturing of a common language rooted in British history. Both also coincide with a parallel liturgical shift in the Church of England from worship facing east, to worshipping 'in the round' (see Chapter 6 on ritual change). The Prayer Book Society, which championed the BCP against the forces of liturgical reform in the 1970s and 1980s, now exists more as a focus for nostalgia and enthusiasm for the English language, issuing the Cranmer Awards which are given to children for skills in oration on the basis of readings they give from the Prayer Book. Nostalgia and a sense of British history sit alongside an increasing disconnection from regular church practice, suggesting ecclesiastical media have the ability to retain cultural resonance even when abandoned by their stewards in the churches.

Sociologist David Martin, a key contributor to the debates surrounding the 'Prayer Book Controversy' (see Chapter 12 for his contribution to this volume), has also drawn attention to the spatial dimensions of Christian continuities, repeatedly demonstrating how religion is embedded in territory, leaving strong resonances within the natural landscape of Britain and, especially, in the built environment (Martin 2002). Fewer people may now have the vocabulary and knowledge to 'read' the iconographic references that adorn parish church, town hall and cemetery (though a number of popular books and TV programmes offering such knowledge have recently appeared), but these emblems of Christian tradition nevertheless remain as ambient identity markers. It is questionable whether crooked steeples and neglected graveyards are culturally significant only as village wallpaper or novelties for passing tourists, and although many a town has witnessed the conversion of redundant churches into carpet salesrooms, cafés, pubs and even nightclubs, there are also frequent examples of devotion to and popular defence of church buildings, perhaps especially in rural areas.

The material culture of Christianity is not immune to social change, and examples of disuse or neglect ought not to overshadow cases of adaptation or reinvigoration. Cathedrals also continue to be treasured as sites of historical and cultural significance; apparently, Coventry Cathedral, bombed in the Second World War and reconsecrated in 1962 to Benjamin Britten's *War Requiem* (see Plate 3.1), was the 'last modern building in Britain *of any type* that ordinary people have queued to see inside' (cited in Whyte 2007: 192). Peter Brierley's 2005 English Church Census revealed a 21 per cent rise in attendance at Anglican cathedral services between 2000 and 2004, suggesting that the continued significance of cathedrals as historical and architectural landmarks has some relation to a renewed interest in them as sites of religious activity, whether for loyal locals or passing visitors (Brierley 2006b: 198).

It must not be forgotten that Britain also lays claim to a rich seam of artistic, musical and literary work that derives much of its inspiration from the Christian tradition. True, the boundaries between ecclesiastical and popular song have been increasingly blurred, but this has been a persistent pattern throughout the modern period, traceable at least to Wesley's hymns and their use of tavern tunes. Identifiably Christian themes continue to inform classical and popular music, from John Tavener to U2, Faithless to Judas Priest (see Case study 5 for more discussion of religion and popular music). On the literary front, C. S. Lewis remains highly popular, even if the allegorical message of his Narnia novels might be lost on the iPod generation (see Chapters 5 and 7 for more on Lewis). There seems to be more to these trends than a colonization of religious language for the purposes of entertainment. As Bernice Martin (2007) has shown in an essay on Philip Pullman's *His Dark Materials* trilogy, Christian sources continue to furnish popular volumes with narrative structure and a sense of what constitutes moral virtue. Ostensibly a children's fantasy story with a thinly veiled critique of established, institutional Christianity, Pullman's best-selling books are notable for how they treat theological matters with 'the deepest seriousness in what is to all appearances a "secular" culture' (Martin 2007: 187). While 'new atheists' like Richard Dawkins and Christopher Hitchens publish rationalist polemics against religion, over in the fiction section of the bookstore popular novels affirm a persistent engagement with Christian themes in a much more subtle and concerted manner. This can also be seen in movie watching, with adaptations of Pullman's *Northern Lights*, Dan Brown's *The Da Vinci Code* and *Angels and Demons*, and even in Mel Gibson's *The Passion of the Christ*. However, the last of these was also an example of how conservative Christians use the culture industries in advancing their cause, reflecting a pragmatic entrepreneurialism that is as old as evangelicalism itself.

More tangible carriers of cultural Christianity can be found among church-sponsored educational institutions, as documented in Chapter 8. While controversial faith academies have attracted media attention in recent years, it is the numerous Church of England and Roman Catholic primary and secondary schools within the state system that exert more influence. Despite controversy over 'faith schools', and growing opposition from secular quarters, such schools remain oversubscribed and attract numbers disproportionate to the levels of participation in Sunday church services held by their ecclesiastical sponsors.

The Church of England continues to enjoy more institutional opportunities than other religious bodies to shape the cultural landscape of the nation, even in secularized times. Schools are a striking example; another is the House of Lords. Today, the Archbishops of Canterbury and York, the Bishops of London, Durham and Winchester, together with 21 of the most senior remaining diocesan bishops, sit in the House of Lords outside the party political system as an independent voice of 'spiritual insight' (Church of England Online). As a consequence they enjoy a unique status as religious officials at the heart of the political establishment. As Chapter 9 explains in more detail, this institution – and other aspects of church 'establishment' – has its detractors, and the semblance of privilege based on religion receives short shrift in a society increasingly governed by the language of equal opportunities. Evidence from a study of bishops in office during the 1980s and 1990s confirms that Church of England bishops increasingly see their role as defenders of 'faiths' in the plural, rather than just the Anglican Church, with 85 per cent claiming that they viewed their episcopal role at least in part as one of service to 'all those of religious conscience' (Davies and Guest 2007: 63). This leads to the paradoxical situation in which religious tolerance may be advanced via a religio-political institution that owes its traction to traditions of Christian privilege.

The Church of England continues to have a strong link to many elite institutions, including the public schools (that is, the most exclusive fee-paying schools), the law, Oxbridge colleges, Parliament, the royal family and institutions of the armed services. Indeed, the importance of religion, particularly Anglicanism, in supporting class and 'establishment' interests, is another continuing aspect of the wider cultural significance of Christianity in the UK. While the foremost pews may no longer be reserved for the local squire, there remains a subtle but profound set of cultural correlations between the Anglican Church and the middle and upper middle classes. This can be complicated further in identifying cultural similarities and differences among parties within the state church, so that the high liturgies of Anglo-Catholicism and the doctrinal severity of Conservative Evangelicalism each emerge as different vehicles for upper-middle-class identity, both equally alien to the lives of many working-class people. Both have long histories, the latter traceable to the 'Bash' student camps of the early twentieth century, evangelical events aimed at the elite public schools, which in turn equipped the Intervarsity Fellowship with the next generation of evangelical leaders, many of them shaped by Oxford and Cambridge universities. Continuities are found in a close cross-fertilization of identities, whereby Christianity becomes a vehicle for social class and class cultures become potent indicators of Christian propriety. This is most apparent in popular understandings of respectability, authority and proper conduct, all keenly endorsed by many church communities – and maintained by older generations – while owing more to British class culture than to anything peculiar to the church as such (Jenkins 1999).

Christianity also informs a persistent strand of what used to be called 'popular' or 'folk' religion, and which is now being studied as 'everyday' or 'lived' religion, but which often evades conventional methods of data collection, as the Introduction to this volume explains. Here we refer to the forms of religiosity which more elite opinion has commonly associated with notions of 'superstition', local 'folklore' and 'heterodox' tradition, but which is nevertheless rooted in a peculiarly British experience. While historians have noted how such religion has often co-existed with – indeed, has formed relationships with – Christian piety (e.g. Hempton 1988 and Williams 1999), other commentators have tended to emphasize disjuncture, perhaps in light of the recent prominence of the New Age, paganism and other 'alternative spiritualities' (see Chapter 4). However, the influence of Christian symbols, practices and beliefs remains often shaped by variations of social class, generation and local context.

David Clark's study of the North Yorkshire fishing village of Staithes revealed that conventional religious ideas of church and chapel sat comfortably alongside a loose collection of non-orthodox customs and cyclical rituals mostly forged around the dangers of the fishing industry (Clark 1982). In a recent volume that brings together a variety of ethnographic accounts from across Britain, Martin Stringer (2008) builds a cumulative picture of 'ordinary religion' in terms of human experiences that appeal to the non-empirical within the context of an everyday need to address ordinary problems that face ordinary people. 'Religion' here is pragmatic, everyday and immediate, and while the analysis unmasks some heterodox understandings, the examples largely remain enmeshed within the traditional contexts of Christian devotion: the church, chapel and graveyard (Stringer 2008). The recent Religion and Society Programme study by Peter Hopkins, Elizabeth Olson, Rachel Pain and Giselle Vincett of religion among young people growing up in deprived parts of Glasgow and Manchester also shows the continuing importance of a range of traditional and new religious symbols, rites and beliefs, including Christian ones – see Case study 3 by Vincett and Olson in this volume. Such practices may now be transmitted by new media, rather than handed down the generations.

Changing commitments

Turning to a third trajectory, post-war Britain has also seen the rise of new forms of organized Christian expression, often in opposition to what are perceived to be the 'secular' values of the majority society. Some of these developments are closely linked to Britain's changing place in a postcolonial world.

Though it is possible to tell a story of Christian Britain as grounded in the distinctive character and culture of a nation, it would be incomplete without acknowledgement of the dramatic changes in the place of the United Kingdom in a postcolonial world order, and the new geographies of global Christianity. By 1973, just 20 years after the coronation of Elizabeth II, the majority of UK colonies throughout Africa, South America and Asia had gained independence. Also during this time, Christian affiliation began shifting southward towards Africa, Asia and Latin America, such that cities like Kinshasa and Buenos Aires could replace Rome and London as centres of Christianity during the first decades of the twenty-first century (Jenkins 2002). In Britain, the character of a postcolonial world has become knitted into new patterns of migration, racism and multiculturalism, and changes in attitudes towards gender, sex and sexuality. Though the rejection of tradition, the sexual revolution of the 1960s and 1970s and changing gender roles in that period have been associated with Christian decline (Brown 2009), this period has also witnessed profound reinvention and change as commitment and practice are shaped by new influences in Christian faith and new structures of transnational ecumenism and confessional alliance.

As described above, the beliefs and commitments embraced by self-identified Christians are more diverse now than they were in the 1950s. In the 1950s, there was a restoration of an ecclesiastically informed and culturally conservative formality, echoed in the coronation ceremony and lived through a communion in which belief in God and belief in the church were reassuringly compatible (Hastings 1986). By the 1980s, however, those who considered themselves Christian might believe in a Christian God and engage in active prayer, but without feeling the need to be part of a church community, or perhaps only attending a church for major rites of passage. Grace Davie (1994) suggests that this 'believing without belonging' is characteristic of the British religious landscape, in which individuals eschew more traditional forms of religious membership.

These unchurched, self-identified Christians are at the heart of British secularization theories, but their approach towards religiosity is in stark contrast to the major growth areas of Christianity in the form of Charismatic, born again or fundamentalist churches. These churches are not homogeneous, ranging from large, well-networked Baptist and Pentecostal congregations to intimate house churches that might consist of just a few families. There are also theological variations, such as the emphasis on the Holy Spirit as found in Charismatic Christianity (including 'Pentecostal' churches), or the centrality of charismatic leadership in some planted African churches (fellowships established through deliberate missionary activity). However, their general embrace of conservative social and theological values, and their shared success in the face of wider Christian decline, has led them to be categorized generically by some commentators under one umbrella of 'conservative' or 'evangelical' or even 'fundamentalist' Christianity. Despite their variation – and very significant differences between fundamentalist and evangelical Christianity – these different forms do share a search for an authentic form of Christianity which rejects the apparent confines of the historic churches for what is felt to be a more personal and meaningful relationship with God. This sometimes leads to a critique of 'Sunday' Christians who are seen to favour association and community and 'empty ritual' over a living faith.

The growth in Pentecostal and other Charismatic forms of Christianity in Britain is in part an outcome of historical processes of transnationalism, or the flow of ideas and processes between and across national boundaries, including religious ideas and institutions (Olson and Silvey 2006). The flourishing of Pentecostalism is intimately linked to histories of displacement and settlement, and phases of immigration of Afro-Caribbean, Western African and, most recently, Korean communities. The rapid growth of black Pentecostalism at the end of the twentieth century is one example of this process, for it is largely due to the migration of a new contingent of West Africans, mostly Nigerians, to British cities. In contrast to the Pentecostalism associated with Jamaican economic migrants in the 1950s, the 'new' Black Pentecostal churches of the 1980s grew out of a wave of immigration triggered by the political unrest and economic turmoil of post-independence Nigeria (Burgess 2008). The theological underpinnings of churches such as the Redeemed Christian Church of God embody the hardships experienced by many Nigerian migrants, including those of movement and displacement, and of resettling and community building (Hunt and Lightly 2001). Many black majority churches remain embedded in black ethnic communities, and they are often the most important network for new immigrants to Britain, providing for practical arrangements such as the sending of remittances to families living in Africa and information related to all aspects of living in Britain. For Zimbabwean migrants who have also established mainline churches and joined existing Methodist or Catholic churches, the church is an important space for retaining culture and for political mobilization (McGregor 2009).

TEXT BOX 6

Immigration and the Christian church

The labels 'black church', 'black majority church' and 'black-led church' obscure important differences in the conditions encountered by immigrant communities. Gilroy (1991) explains how Jamaicans moving into British cities in the 1950s were surprised that, rather than 'coming home' to a colonial motherland, everyday life was punctuated with structural racism in housing, labour and even religious practice. In Jamaica, church membership and attendance was an important marker of status and belonging, but experiences of racism within some parishes in England encouraged Dr Oliver Lyseight to found the New Testament Church of God in 1953. In addition to providing a respite from a loss of status due to ethnicity and race (Hill 1971), Pentecostalism also provided an ethical framework of hard work and individual conscience that could help Jamaicans (Toulis 1997). Nigerian migrants arriving in the 1980s also encountered racism and economic hardship, yet their arrival in Britain coincided with an emerging state agenda focused on multiculturalism as a mechanism for growing racial and ethnic diversity. By 2010, Pentecostal churches were viewed as an important political constituency and a key network for the state to communicate with the broader African community (Burgess *et al.* 2010). These churches also consider themselves to be part of 'reverse mission', an evangelization of northern secularizing countries by those who were previously the recipients of mission activities (Asamoah-Gyadu 2005). Though black Pentecostal leaders admit that reverse mission in Britain has not extended fully to white communities, churches like the Redeemed Christian Church of God embrace their public role nationally and internationally (Adogame 2004).

It is impossible to provide an accurate count of these churches since some of the smaller movements are guarded about their practices and choose to remain isolated from the broader Christian community, sometimes because of concerns that greater integration might mean greater exposure and, subsequently, inquiries over illegal immigration (Harris 2006). Additionally, some of the practices and theology of these churches sit uncomfortably with traditional British churches, resulting in dissociation. Indeed, it was not until 1978 that the first black-led church obtained full membership of the British Council of Churches. Other temporary migrant ethnic groups from continental Europe, such as Roma people from Slovakia and Romania, are also establishing new Christian traditions in Britain, but very little is known about these due to the often isolating conditions of their settlement.

The flow of new forms of Christianity onto British soil is only one illustration of the ways that transnationalism shapes religious practice. Postcolonial Christianity is also marked by new debates between those who embrace liberal expressions of Christianity, and those who favour traditionalism and social conservatism. Conflicts over the place of women, gays and lesbians in Christian leadership are particularly poignant examples of how these tensions are simultaneously global and local in their character. The Roman Catholic rejection of the ordination of women into the priesthood and unequivocal condemnation of homosexuality was articulated in 2004 in the *Letter to the Bishops of the Catholic Church on the Collaboration of Men and Women in the Church and in the World* (Ratzinger and Amato 2004), which emphasized the gendered differentiation of work and worship based on 'natural law' (God-given biological structures).

In contrast to the Catholic Church, Protestant positions towards female clergy have changed dramatically since the 1960s, when women were ordained in Anglican ('Episcopal') churches in the former British colonies of Hong Kong and the United States, and in Japan (Nason-Clark 1987; Raming *et al.* 2004). In 1967, five women successfully argued in an open letter to the General Assembly of the Church of Scotland for formal recognition of 'the reality of God's call of a woman to the ministry', and the first female minister was ordained two years later. Two decades later, the Church of Ireland voted for the ordination of female priests in 1990, followed by the Church of England in 1992. The first female priests in the Church of England (see Plate 1.8) were ordained in Bristol in 1994, but the decision was not universally accepted, and a potential fracture of the church was avoided by allowing conservative parishes to bypass any formal recognition of ordained women and to follow a 'separate integrity' with bishops who would not ordain women. In 2010, this fragile solution faced another challenge as the General Synod engaged in protracted debates over the progression of women to the status of bishop, a move which has not yet been approved, but which could help in overcoming the discrimination still experienced by women clergy (e.g. Lummis and Nesbitt 2000). Following the General Synod that put in place the motion towards female bishops, the Roman Catholic Church offered an Apostolic Constitution laying the groundwork for the acceptance into the Catholic Church of Church of England congregations and priests who might wish to move, with the first parishes accepting this offer in 2010.

The debate regarding the ordination of openly gay bishops follows similar patterns in the twenty-first century, reinforcing mildly conservative and liberal alliances, but with an even more visible role for the conservative churches of Asia, Africa and Latin America. The first openly gay bishop was elected to the New Hampshire diocese of the Protestant Episcopal Church of the United States in 2003, with the Archbishop of Canterbury endorsing the appointment of a gay bishop in England in the same year, although, following protests from conservatives, the candidate was subsequently pressured to withdraw his acceptance

(Keenan 2008). Alliances between conservative or traditionalist Anglican communities in Asia, Africa and Latin America were formalized during this time through the formation of organizations such as the Fellowship of Confessing Anglicans, a movement orientated towards a unified traditionalist voice across the Anglican Communion, but driven largely by the initiatives of an African understanding of Christian orthodoxy (and the money of Americans). Though there is no resolution to these debates at the time of writing, or what effect these debates will have on future Christian affiliation in the UK, they demonstrate how global ecumenism influences the everyday practices and commitments of British Christians. Transnational links can therefore serve to give a stronger voice to groups which might otherwise remain marginal.

The dramatic visibility of these debates can obscure other important changes in Christian commitment, many of which have as significant an impact but attract less attention from the global media. Shifts in economic organization and social class since the 1950s have required adaptation by Christian communities in a range of ways. Christian commitment in the later twentieth century was marked by the continued influence of faith organizations as social actors, often central to the provision of basic services for a society facing growing economic inequality. The neoliberal economic policies of the 1980s and the withdrawal of the state left some areas of social service without sufficient support, and Christian communities and charities mobilized to provide for the needs of the homeless, immigrants and the poor (see Cloke *et al.* 2005 and Chapter 8 in this volume).

Yet at the same time that Christian charities were reaching out with various forms of support, older churches in economically deprived neighbourhoods throughout Britain were often closing or reducing their service provision. The Church of Scotland has responded to this class division by establishing a ministry committee dedicated to 'priority areas', the 58 poorest communities in the church. These efforts echo a longer historical project to engage the working class as congregants, even going to the lengths of implementing industry-based chaplaincy in the 1960s and 1970s throughout Scotland (Johnston and McFarland 2010), with similar efforts in England. The earlier attempts failed to win sustained congregations among the working class when many industries of the North suffered fatal economic blows in the 1980s. Today's ministry faces very different challenges, ranging from the general distrust that ageing congregants often feel towards young people in these areas, to the recognition that, in some urban areas, Christianity is a minority religion among other vibrant traditions. While middle-class young people may go on a Christian work trip abroad during their gap year, these opportunities are rarely viewed as options among young people living in deprivation. In their communities, many of the historical churches might be abandoned or, if still occupied, mounted with CCTV surveillance cameras. Here, the vibrancy of Christian faith is more likely to be found in the dedication of individual ministers who open their halls to a mother and toddlers group, or in the house churches of African immigrants, or through the doors of a Pentecostal youth club. It is also interesting to note the way in which newer evangelical churches are, in some cases, starting to move into social outreach activities.

The future of Christianity: death, resurrection and reincarnation

Callum Brown (2009) and Steve Bruce (2002), among others, make stark predictions of the 'death of Christian Britain', even if churches 'continue to exist in some skeletal form' (Brown 2009: 232). Their arguments are supported by an impressive array of statistical evidence, some of it marshalled above, and more in Chapter 10, showing a steep decline in conventional Christian observance and affiliation since the 1950s. Nevertheless, in this chapter, we have also presented some additional and rather different perspectives. These may be aptly characterized in conclusion by applying both the Christian concept of resurrection, and the Asian one of reincarnation. Both resurrection and reincarnation are of course denials not of the physical reality of death, but of its spiritual finality.

According to St Paul (I Corinthians 15:35–54) the 'spiritual body' with which the dead in Christ are raised is very different from their former 'physical body'. A parallel distinction can be drawn between the decline of the 'physical' Christianity of regular participation in Sunday worship and the persistence of the 'spiritual' (or cultural) Christianity of loose identification, artistic reference, education and constitutional formality. The latter, like the risen Jesus on the road to Emmaus, can at times seem very tangible, and at others vanish out of sight (Luke 24:13–31). Nevertheless there have been cogent scholarly arguments for its enduring existence and influence (e.g. Davie 2000; Garnett *et al.* 2007). Those convinced of the finality of the 'death of Christian Britain' readily dismiss such evidence as insubstantial and probably transient (Brown 2009: 231), but others would want to distinguish between the trajectory of the organized churches and that of wider Christian ideas and values, asserting that the latter continue to be formative influences in British culture and society. As in the debate over the resurrection itself, theological presuppositions and deep value commitments play a part in shaping both interpretations of the empirical evidence.

Meanwhile the concept of reincarnation suggests a third approach, one that still acknowledges the reality of the decline – even death – of traditional Christianity, but points to its rebirth in new and sometimes vigorous forms. The apparent incongruity of applying an alien theological concept to Christianity points in particular to the inescapable reality for Christians in later twentieth- and early twenty-first-century Britain of the loss of their erstwhile religious monopoly and ongoing existence in a pluralist environment alongside Buddhist, Hindu, Jewish, Muslim, Sikh and other minorities (see Chapter 3). From the mid-1940s to the mid-1970s, however, there had been very little awareness of the importance of religious diversity for the situation of Christianity at home, as opposed to the context of overseas missions. Only in 1977 did the General Synod of the Church of England formally acknowledge a plural society and embrace, as suggested by the Bishop of Winchester, 'enrichment through a greater openness in our discourse with other faiths here in this nation' (Wolffe 1994: 40). By the early 1980s, Christian leaders were making attempts to meet with Muslim communities to establish interfaith dialogue, but others still viewed non-Christian communities as targets for evangelism. Others came out in vocal opposition to interfaith prayer and worship. In 2008, however, Dr Rowan Williams, the Archbishop of Canterbury, proposed that Muslim communities in Britain should be allowed to continue to implement some elements of Islamic *shari'a* law among their own members (Williams 2008). His views reflected a growing recognition that faith communities would have to align themselves as allies in a battle against some of the more damaging effects of secular modernity, and were symbolic of an increasing acceptance by most mainline Christian churches that religious pluralism had become a fixture of the British religious landscape. For some Christian leaders indeed, interfaith alliances had the potential to deflect a much more menacing future represented by secularism and evangelistic atheism (see Case study 2 on the growth of the Inter Faith Network).

A reincarnated Christianity thus appears in a British context shorn of its traditional numerical ascendancy, and transformed into the largest and historically most deeply rooted of a wide range of committed religious minorities in a predominantly secular society. Like those other minorities, it has strong ties with other parts of the world, including the United

States of America, but most especially with the global South, from where many British Christians have migrated, and where Christianity remains a vibrant and growing social and political force. Viewed in this light it becomes possible to see a very viable future for Christianity in a multicultural globalized society in which there remain numerous avenues for religious innovation and resurgence.

Key terms

Anglicanism: A Protestant movement that split from the Roman Catholic Church in the sixteenth century, for which the Archbishop of Canterbury is regarded as the symbolic head; some Anglicans consider themselves Anglo-Catholics and continue to value links with Roman Catholicism.

Charismatic: An expression of Christian belief which places particular emphasis on the gifts of the Holy Spirit. Commonly associated with Pentecostalism, but increasingly found in other Christian traditions (where it is often called Charismatic renewal or neo-Pentecostalism).

Ecumenism: A movement towards Christian unity, or unity among those believing in Jesus Christ.

Evangelicalism: A pan-denominational movement within Protestantism which emphasizes the authority of the Bible, a commitment to personal conversion and sharing the gospel.

Fundamentalism: The rigorous maintenance of perceived traditional religious teaching, which in the Christian case means particularly conviction of the inerrancy of the Bible.

Liturgy: Public or communal worship carried out according to particular rituals, such as a Mass.

Pentecostalism: A Christian movement based around the present-day reality of 'spiritual gifts', such as healing, prophecy and speaking in tongues, which traces its history to US-based revivals around the turn of the twentieth century.

Presbyterianism: A form of Protestantism associated with Calvinist theology, articulated in Scotland by John Knox through the Scottish Reformation. See also p.316.

Further reading

Brown, Callum G. (2006). *Religion and Society in Twentieth-Century Britain*. London: Longman Pearson. This book provides an overview of religious change in the period, and can be read alongside his co-authored chapter in this volume.

Davie, Grace (1994). *Religion in Britain since 1945: Believing without Belonging*. Oxford: Blackwell. A sociological study, exploring particularly the persistence of Christian influence despite the decline of the institutional churches.

Collins-Mayo, Sylvia, Bob Mayo and Sally Nash (2010). *The Faith of Generation Y*. London: Church House. A study of the attitudes of young people to Christianity and hence of likely futures.

Garnett, Jane, Matthew Grimley, Alana Harris, William Whyte and Sarah Williams (eds) (2007). *Redefining Christian Britain: Post 1945 Perspectives*. London: SCM. This multi-authored volume offers an important alternative, less 'pessimistic', perspective than Brown.

McLeod, Hugh (2007). *The Religious Crisis of the 1960s*. Oxford: Oxford University Press. An authoritative and balanced overview of a critical period.

References

Adogame, Afe (2004). 'Contesting the Ambivalences of Modernity in a Global Context: The Redeemed Christian Church of God, North America', *Studies in World Christianity*, 10/1: 25–48.

Asamoah-Gyadu, J. Kwabena (2005). 'An African Pentecostal on Mission in Eastern Europe: The Church of the "Embassy of God" in the Ukraine', *Pneuma: The Journal for the Society for Pentecostal Studies*, 27/2: 297–321.

Ashworth, Jacinta and Ian Farthing (2007). *Churchgoing in the UK: A Research Report from Tearfund on Church Attendance in the UK*. Teddington: Tearfund.

BBC News (2005). 'Protests as BBC Screens Springer', *BBC News Online*. Online. Available HTTP: http://news.bbc.co.uk/1/hi/entertainment/tv_and_radio/4154071.stm (accessed 18 August 2010).

Bebbington, David W. (1992). 'The Secularization of British Universities since the Mid-Nineteenth Century', in George M. Marsden and Bradley J. Longfield (eds), *The Secularization of the Academy*. New York: Oxford University Press, 259–277.

Brewer, John D. with Gareth Higgins (1998). *Anti-Catholicism in Northern Ireland 1600–1998: The Mote and the Beam*. London: Palgrave Macmillan.

Brierley, Peter (ed.) (1999, 2003, 2004, 2006a, 2008). *UK Christian Handbook: Religious Trends Nos. 2, 4, 6, 7*. London: Christian Research.

Brierley, Peter (2006b). *Pulling Out of the Nosedive: A Contemporary Picture of Churchgoing*. London: Christian Research.

Brown, Callum G. (2009). *The Death of Christian Britain*. 2nd edition. London: Routledge.

Bruce, Steve (2002). *God is Dead: Secularization in the West*. Oxford and Malden, MA: Blackwell.

Bruce, Steve, Tony Glendinning, Iain Paterson and Michael Rosie (2004). *Sectarianism in Scotland*. Edinburgh: Edinburgh University Press.

Burgess, Richard (2008). *Nigeria's Christian Revolution. The Civil War Revival and its Pentecostal Progeny (1967–2004)*. Carlisle: Regnum/Paternoster.

Burgess, Richard, Kim Knibbe and Anna Quaas (2010). 'Nigerian-Initiated Pentecostal Churches as a Social Force in Europe: The Case of the Redeemed Christian Church of God', *PentecoStudies*, 9/1: 97–121.

Carr, Wesley (2002). 'This Intimate Ritual: The Coronation Service', *Political Theology*, 4/1: 11–24.

Chambers, Paul (2004). 'The Effects of Evangelical Renewal on Mainstream Congregational Identities', in Mathew Guest, Karin Tusting and Linda Woodhead (eds), *Congregational Studies in the UK*. Aldershot: Ashgate, 57–69.

Chambers, Paul (2005). *Religion, Secularization and Social Change in Wales: Congregational Studies in a Post-Christian Society*. Cardiff: University of Wales Press.

Church of England. Online. Available HTTP: www.cofe.anglican.org/about/bishopsinlords/#1 (accessed 18 August 2010).

Clark, David (1982). *Between Pulpit and Pew: Folk Religion in a North Yorkshire Fishing Village*. Cambridge: Cambridge University Press.

Cloke, Paul, Sarah Johnsen and John May (2005). 'Exploring Ethos? Discourses of "Charity" in the Provision of Emergency Services for Homeless People', *Environment and Planning A*, 37/3: 385–402.

Currie, Robert, Alan Gilbert and Lee Horsley (1977). *Churches and Churchgoers: Patterns of Church Growth in the British Isles since 1700*. Oxford: Clarendon Press.

Davie, Grace (1994). *Religion in Britain since 1945: Believing without Belonging*. Oxford: Blackwell.

Davie, Grace (2000). *Religion in Modern Europe: A Memory Mutates*. Oxford: Oxford University Press.

Davies, Douglas and Mathew Guest (2007). *Bishops, Wives and Children: Spiritual Capital Across the Generations*. Aldershot: Ashgate.

Devine, Thomas M. (2000). *Scotland's Shame?: Bigotry and Sectarianism in Modern Scotland*. Edinburgh: Mainstream Press.

Garnett, Jane, Matthew Grimley, Alana Harris, William Whyte and Sarah Williams (eds) (2007). *Redefining Christian Britain: Post 1945 Perspectives*. London: SCM.

Gilroy, Paul (1991). *There Ain't No Black in the Union Jack: The Cultural Politics of Race and Nation*. Chicago, IL: University of Chicago Press.

Green, S. J. D. (2010). *The Passing of Protestant England: Secularisation and Social Change, c.1920–1960*. Cambridge: Cambridge University Press.

Guest, Mathew, Sonya Sharma, Kristin Aune and Rob Warner (forthcoming). 'Challenging "Belief" and the Evangelical Bias: Evidence from English Universities', *Journal of Contemporary Religion*.

Harris, Hermione (2006). *Yoruba in Diaspora: An African Church in London*. New York: Palgrave Macmillan.

Harrison, Tom (1961). *Britain Revisited*. London: Victor Gollancz.

Hastings, Adrian (1986). *A History of English Christianity 1920–1985*. London: SCM Press.

Hempton, David (1988). 'Popular Religion, 1800–1986', in Terence Thomas (ed.), *The British: Their Religious Beliefs and Practices 1800–1986*. London and New York: Routledge, 181–210.

Hill, Clifford (1971). 'Pentecostalist Growth-Result of Racialism?' *Race Today* 3/3: 187–190.

Hunt, Stephen and Nicola Lightly (2001). 'The British Black Pentecostal "Revival": Identity and Belief in the "New" Nigerian Churches', *Ethnic and Racial Studies*, 24/1: 104–124.

Jackson, Robert and Alan Pigott (2011). 'Another Capital Idea: Church Growth in the Diocese of London 2003–2010'. Online. Available HTTP: www.london.anglican.org (accessed 6 September 2011).

Jenkins, Philip (2002). *The Next Christendom: The Coming of Global Christianity*. Oxford: Oxford University Press.

Jenkins, Timothy (1999). *Religion in English Everyday Life*. New York, NY and Oxford: Berghahn Books.

Johnston, Ronald and Elaine McFarland (2010). 'Out in the Open in a Threatening World: The Scottish Churches' Industrial Mission 1960–1980', *International Review of Social History*, 55/1: 1–27.

Keenan, Michael (2008). 'Freedom in Chains: Religion as Enabler and Constraint in the Lives of Gay Male Anglican Clergy', in Abby Day (ed.), *Religion and the Individual: Belief, Practice, Identity*. Aldershot: Ashgate, 169–181.

Lodge, David (1980). *How Far Can You Go?* London: Secker and Warburg.

Lummis, Adair T. and Paula D. Nesbitt (2000). 'Women Clergy Research and the Sociology of Religion', *Sociology of Religion*, 61/4: 443–453.

McGregor, Joann (2009). 'Associational Links with Home among Zimbabweans in the UK: Reflections on Long-Distance Nationalisms', *Global Networks*, 9/2: 185–208.

McLeod, Hugh (2007). *The Religious Crisis of the 1960s*. Oxford: Oxford University Press.

Martin, Bernice (2007). 'Dark Materials? Philip Pullman and Children's Literature', in Jane Garnett, Matthew Grimley, Alana Harris, William Whyte and Sarah Williams (eds), *Redefining Christian Britain: Post 1945 Perspectives*. London: SCM, 178–189.

Martin, David (2002). *Christian Language and its Mutations*. Aldershot: Ashgate.

Mitchell, Claire (2006). *Religion, Identity and Politics in Northern Ireland*. Aldershot: Ashgate.

Nason-Clark, Nancy (1987). 'Ordaining Women as Priests: Religious vs. Sexist Explanations for Clerical Attitudes', *Sociological Analysis*, 48/3: 259–273.

Olson, Elizabeth and Rachel Silvey (2006). 'Transnational Geographies: Rescaling Development, Migration, and Religion', *Environment and Planning A*, 38/5: 805–808.

Örnebring, Henrik (2004). 'Revisiting the Coronation', *Nordicom Review*, 25/1–2: 175–195.

Perfect, David (2011). *Religion or Belief*. Equality and Human Rights Commission Briefing Paper 1. Manchester: Equality and Human Rights Commission.

Raming, Ida, Gary Macy and Bernard Cooke (2004). *A History of Women and Ordination. Volume 2: The Priestly Office of Women: God's Gift to a Renewed Church*. 2nd edition. Lanham, MD: The Scarecrow Press.

Ratzinger, Joseph and Angelo Amato (2004). *Letter to the Bishops of the Catholic Church on the Collaboration of Men and Women in the Church and in the World*. Online. Available HTTP: www.vatican.va/roman_curia/congregations/cfaith/documents/rc_con_cfaith_doc_20040731_collaboration_en.html (accessed 7 September 2011).

Robbins, Keith (2008). *England, Ireland, Scotland, Wales: The Christian Church 1900–2000*. Oxford: Oxford University Press.

Robinson, John (1963). *Honest to God*. London: SCM.

Shils, Edward and Michael Young (1953). 'The Meaning of the Coronation', *Sociological Review*, new series, 1/2: 63–81.

Stringer, Martin (2008). *Contemporary Western Ethnography and the Definition of Religion*. London: Continuum.

Thompson, Mark (2005). 'Why I Stand by my Decision to Broadcast Jerry Springer – the Opera', *The Times*, 8 March: 18.

Toulis, Nicole R. (1997). *Believing Identity: Pentecostalism and the Mediation of Jamaican Ethnicity and Gender in England*. Oxford and New York: Berg.

Voas, David and Steve Bruce (2004). 'Research Note: The 2001 Census and Christian Identification in Britain', *Journal of Contemporary Religion*, 19/1: 23–28.

Voas, David and Rodney Ling (2010). 'Religion in Britain and the United States', in Alison Park *et al.* (eds), *British Social Attitudes: The 26th Report*. London: Sage, 65–86.

Warner, Rob (2007). *Reinventing English Evangelicalism, 1966–2001: A Theological and Sociological Study*. Milton Keynes: Paternoster.

Whyte, William (2007). 'The Architecture of Belief', in Jane Garnett, Matthew Grimley, Alana Harris, William Whyte and Sarah Williams (eds), *Redefining Christian Britain: Post 1945 Perspectives*. London: SCM, 190–196.

Williams, Rowan (2008). 'Civil and Religious Law in England: A Religious Perspective', unpublished lecture. Online. Available HTTP: www.archbishopofcanterbury.org (accessed 31 March 2008).

Williams, Sarah C. (1999). *Religious Belief and Popular Culture in Southwark, c. 1880–1939*. Oxford: Oxford University Press.

Wolffe, John (1994). 'How Many Ways to God? Christians and Religious Pluralism', in Gerald Parsons (ed.), *The Growth of Religious Diversity: Britain from 1945. Volume II: Controversies*. London: Routledge, 23–53.

Wolffe, John (2007). 'Religion and "Secularization"', in Francesca Carnevali and Julie-Marie Strange (eds), *20th Century Britain: Economic, Cultural and Social Change*. Harlow: Pearson, 323–338.

Note

1   John Wolffe has been supervising Naomi Stanton's PhD in collaboration with Christian Education into the decline of Sunday Schools and contemporary Christian youth work in Britain, funded by the AHRC/ESRC Religion and Society Programme.

Case study 1

The formation of the United Reformed Church

Stephen Orchard

A central theme of discussion and aspiration in Christian circles in the 1950s–1970s was ecumenism: the attempt to unify Christian churches, especially Protestant denominations. Its most important result in Britain was the creation of the United Reformed Church in 1972 by a union of a number of previously separated historical Protestant churches. This case study discusses the background of this union, its history and significance. As well as reflecting on the fate of the ecumenical ideal, it illustrates a number of other wider issues, including the process by which what were once (Christian) religious minorities in Britain move closer to the 'majority', with new, non-Christian 'minorities' taking their place; and the dilemma which faces churches in a 'religious marketplace' over whether to continue the pursuit of unity, or to emphasize difference and distinctiveness. The aspiration to unity fits with the period in which state–church relations and linkages were particularly important; that for diversity fits more closely with the imperatives of the market.

To many observers the formation of the United Reformed Church (URC) seemed to be the only tangible fruit of the modern ecumenical movement. It came into being in 1972 through the union of the Presbyterian Church of England and the majority of churches in the Congregational Church in England and Wales. It was subsequently joined by the Reformed Association of the Churches of Christ in 1981 and the Congregational Union of Scotland in 2000. The ecumenical ideal was much older: dating back to the nineteenth century, it was consolidated by the Edinburgh Missionary Conference of 1910 which embedded the hope for church unity in new conciliar structures, leading to the formation of the World Council of Churches in 1948. It is important to note the mission context of this enthusiasm for ecumenical activity. Many of the English church leaders of the 1950s had formed their ecumenical convictions while working together in the missions of the Student Christian Movement at university. They always saw church union as promoting more effective mission and evangelism, rather than simply as an ideal, though it was that as well. Hopes ran high: in England an ecumenical conference at Nottingham in 1964 expressed a hope that visible unity might be achieved by Easter Day 1980. The 1972 union was seen as a step towards this objective, but as it turned out it did not precipitate further unions.

To understand the significance of the United Reformed Church, it is necessary to summarize the history of its separate denominations, since tradition is a powerful force in ecclesiastical matters. So far as England is concerned, the origins of Presbyterianism and Congregationalism lie not only in the Protestant Reformation of the sixteenth century, but in the failure to reach a comprehensive settlement of the Church of England after the restoration of the monarchy in 1660. During the Commonwealth period, Parliament abolished bishops and the Prayer Book (the Anglican *Book of Common Prayer*, see Chapter 6 for more details) from the Church of England. Presbyterians and Congregationalists (the latter were normally known as 'Independents') both supported this legislation. Presbyterians, as in Scotland today, were happy to support a national church controlled by national and local councils; Independents, who included Baptists, argued for ultimate power to rest with the local congregation, though they believed such congregations should recognize each other and even take common decisions, but only by consensus. At various times after 1662, when about 2,000 ministers who could not conform to the church settlement left the Church of England, the two groups considered union, especially when their views secured formal legal toleration in 1689.

English Presbyterians became increasingly heterodox in their views in the eighteenth century, developing what we would now term Unitarian congregations. Some Congregationalists took the same route but on the whole they were more conservative theologically. Their culture is best represented by the hymns of Isaac Watts, who was an Independent, and the intellectual life of their academies, both Presbyterian and Independent, which were developed as alternatives to Oxford and Cambridge universities, which were effectively closed to non-Anglicans. Through the eighteenth century the numbers of nonconformists and meeting houses declined. What changed the situation dramatically was the rise of Methodism.

While most contemporary views of Methodism are focused on the heritage of the Wesleys, a careful reading reveals the significant contribution of George Whitefield and his followers, including the Countess of Huntingdon. Although both the Wesleys and Whitefield professed their loyalty to the Church of England, they represented different theological strains within it. Their point of agreement was on the need for the Church of England to engage in mission to the indifferent part of the population and, in particular, to promote the personal spiritual awakening known as 'conversion'. Both parts of Methodism eventually came up against the reluctance of bishops to ordain their candidates for ministry. Faced with this impasse they resorted to non-episcopal[1] ordination by a group of other ministers – which brought them, effectively, to a Presbyterian position. In addition, to secure their chapels, Methodists utilized legislation for the registration of nonconformist meeting houses.

In the opening years of the nineteenth century, there were growing numbers of congregations formed in the broad tradition of Whitefield, generally identifying with a Calvinist theology, and appropriating the earlier history of Independents to themselves. There were instances of enthusiasts taking over moribund meeting houses with a seventeenth-century history. The historians and theologians of what came to be known exclusively as Congregationalism wrote a new narrative built on the stories of Independents from the sixteenth century onwards. This narrative stressed individual freedom, especially in religious belief, and marched with the Whig[2] view of history. The executions of Elizabethan Separatists and the hardships of the Pilgrim Fathers were invoked to support the cause of equal rights for Protestants who were not Anglicans. Specific campaigns were launched to amend the law so that nonconformists could take a full part in civic life, attend university, marry in their own places of worship and be exempted from church rates. A similar flowering of Independent congregations in Scotland led to Congregationalism growing there, though opposition to the established Church of Scotland was subsequently taken up by those who left it to form the Free Church in the 1840s. The Churches of Christ, which flourished more in the United States than in Britain, also arose from discontent with the

Scottish establishment, but were distinct from Congregationalism in the practice of (adult) believer's baptism and weekly celebration of the Lord's Supper.

Once their civil liberties were attained, Congregationalists flourished throughout the nineteenth century. The remaining orthodox English Presbyterian congregations, mostly in the north of England, were soon supplemented by those formed by migrant Scots, from both the Church of Scotland and the Free Church. The twentieth century saw a gradual decline in membership, masked at first by population growth. Congregationalists and Presbyterians gave serious consideration to union after the end of the Second World War, but were unable to agree a scheme. By the 1960s enthusiasm for church unity in England had reached a peak and numerical decline continued remorselessly. In those circumstances Presbyterian and Congregational talks reopened, with the encouragement of unity enthusiasts in other denominations. It was hoped that if two very similar denominations could be united it would begin a process of union for others, like the fall of dominoes. Negotiations were opened, culminating in the union of 1972, which required a parliamentary bill to secure the trust property of the two denominations. A minority of local Congregational churches remained outside this union, largely on grounds that the autonomy of local churches could be overridden by the church as a whole and that individual rights of conscience were not sufficiently secured. The largest number of these constituted themselves as the Congregational Federation, others formed an evangelical federation and a few remained purely independent.

The union was celebrated in 1972 with a service in Westminster Abbey at which the then Archbishop of Canterbury and Cardinal Archbishop of Westminster pledged themselves to continue the search for wider unity. Dr John Huxtable, the former General Secretary of the Congregational Church in England and Wales, went on to head up the Churches Commission for Unity, which prepared proposals for a more general union of the main Protestant denominations in England. The latter fell when the Church of England failed to reach sufficient agreement, frustrating the hopes of the Nottingham Conference of 1964. Meanwhile, in 1981, the United Reformed Church united with the Re-formed Association of the Churches of Christ, including its Scottish congregations. In spite of their distinctive views on baptism, the Churches of Christ held doctrines and practised a church order which was broadly compatible with Congregationalism. The United Reformed Church resolved the major issue by declaring its belief in baptism as a once in a lifetime event for church members but offered the possibility of either infant or believer's baptism. It also embraced the concept of a non-stipendiary ministry, which was common in the Churches of Christ and beginning to be introduced in other denominations. Further changes to the structure of the denomination followed the union with Scottish Congregationalists. Probably the most significant was the declaration that in Scotland and Wales national synods could negotiate church union on the assurance that it could not be blocked by the English majority.

The United Reformed Church which has finally emerged from these unions is a British representative of the worldwide communion of Reformed churches, which is second only to that of Roman Catholics in its total membership. The church sets a high value on the individual conscience and the ability of its members to reach common understanding. The church is governed by a General Assembly, representative of its members, which makes decisions after consultation and debate. There are 13 synods, the national synods of Scotland and Wales and 11 regional synods for England, providing pastoral and legal support in their own areas, in which all local congregations are represented. Originally, in 1972, a second tier of District Councils, which were subsets of the synod and discharged some of its responsibilities, was established, but with the numerical decline of the church these councils were abandoned in 2007. Local congregations hold church meetings to govern their affairs, with a group of elders to take day-to-day responsibility. All these meetings are held in the belief that the Holy Spirit guides members of the church in their decision-making. The Bible is taken to be the supreme authority for the church, together with the classic creeds held by most major Christian churches and particular historic statements of the constituent denominations of the United Reformed Church. However, given the respect for individual belief and a conviction that majorities are not always right, the church is not dogmatic and includes a wide variety of opinions.

The formal leadership of the General Assembly is provided by two Moderators, who serve alongside one another for two years, in an honorary capacity. They are elected by the members of the Assembly. One of the Moderators is a layperson and the other a minister. A permanent staff, led by the General Secretary, services the Assembly and its committees. The synods employ their own Moderators and staff to support the work of local churches. Local churches are usually grouped together under the pastoral care of a paid minister, although the church continues to ordain unpaid ministers. Ministers may be men or women. All churches contribute to a central fund from which ministers are paid a stipend to cover their living costs. The church pursues equal opportunities policies, including provisions to secure the representation of its black and minority ethnic members in its councils. Other policies address the need to keep a balance of men and women, lay and ordained people, and young people in the representative meetings of the United Reformed Church.

The continuing postponement of the union of denominations in Britain has posed the United Reformed Church with a particular dilemma. Recognizing that its position was rather like a bride standing at the altar awaiting a reluctant groom, the denomination has had some heart-searching about its identity and purpose. The current stance is to promote itself as a denomination which sets store on open-mindedness, while remaining willing to submerge its identity in a greater whole if that should become a realistic option. It has structures which enable it to ride out differences. A very tiny minority of its congregations resist women's ministry, and such local wishes are respected even when they are contested. Like all mainstream British churches it found itself in conflict over different views of human sexuality. Unlike others, it chose to adopt a moratorium on national decision-making in respect to matters such as the ordination of avowed homosexuals to ministry. This seven-year pause has been followed by renewed dialogue and agreement to respect differences of opinion until wider unanimity emerges. Whatever the views of individuals and congregations, there is a reluctance to allow a central decision-making body to impose its majority decisions on all. In recent years the adoption of a consensus-building approach to decision-making has reinforced this view. Consequently there remain painful tensions within the denomination between those whose principles place them on one side or the other of debates on such matters as human sexuality, but only those who regard such ambiguity as culpable have left the denomination. Others have remained to defend their convictions. It is sometimes alleged that the denomination has no firm principles on anything, because it accommodates so many views. This overlooks the more subtle position it adopts, which is to be prepared to tolerate a range of difference in the belief that truth is complex and may take time to emerge.

The public statements of the church are rarely reported in the media, since they tend to be uncontroversial or un-newsworthy. It subscribes to the ideas of a generous overseas development budget and the promotion of green technology. It has made no pronouncements on abortion but declared itself opposed to assisted dying. It has encouraged its members to see the church as multicultural and has received representatives of major world faiths at its General Assembly. It has condemned the policies of the British National Party. The church has left the judgement on whether to conduct the blessing of same-sex unions to local congregations but has issued a form of words to be used on such occasions. In its early years the church also supported the growth of modern hymn-writing, notably in the cases of Brian Wren, Fred Kaan and Alan Gaunt. Although it is generally seen as tolerant rather than dogmatic, it retains significant numbers of conservative believers who would not be comfortable in episcopal or centrally directed denominations. It shares with other denominations the phenomenon of localism, that is to say, isolated worshipping units which have little awareness of denominational positions and politics unless they impinge dramatically on local life. As in other denominations, withholding contributions to central funds is the ultimate sanction a local congregation may adopt.

At the time of writing, something approaching a third of all local churches in the United Reformed Church are actually shared with other denominations and all its ministerial training is in ecumenical settings. There are particularly strong links with English Methodism and the possibility of union of the denominations is canvassed from time to time. The position is complicated by the ongoing attempts to draw the Church of England and Methodists into closer union, based on their existing covenant relationship. The suspicion is that a substantial number of church members, across denominations, take a pragmatic view of church union, based on the need to respond to church decline by combining strengths in mission. For instance, as the United Reformed Church moved into new housing areas in the late twentieth century, this activity increasingly took place jointly with the Church of England, the Methodist Church and the Baptist Union. Against this pragmatic view is the objection that church unity rests in historic continuities represented by the succession of bishops and that resolving the differences between episcopal churches precedes unity. The non-episcopal denominations would, on this analysis, have to be prepared to take episcopacy into their systems to make unity possible. Some of the pragmatists would be prepared to make this step for the greater good, but a sufficient minority of those opposed to this view would join forces to block this avenue. The position is complicated by the fact that Reformed and Methodist churches in other parts of the world have bishops, though they do not invest them with the same significance as the Orthodox and Roman Catholic churches. To the outsider, and to many lay members of the United Reformed Church, much of this argument is arcane. However, these are the road blocks which have brought its ecumenical ambitions to a halt.

While hoping that its ecumenical commitment may yet lead to further church unity, the United Reformed Church has determined to promote its own strengths in a campaign addressed to those who have no church commitment. It wishes to take its history of being a radical religious group, with freedom to change and develop, and promote itself as a socially aware denomination, not controlled by a tradition-bound hierarchy. This is ambitious, since it would be easier, so far as publicity is concerned, to draw a line in the sand and defend it. Drawing on the experience of one of its partners in the United States, the Church of Christ, the United Reformed Church hopes to increase public awareness of its ethos, in the belief that it is appropriate to Britain today. If it succeeds, this will have a wider significance for all churches and may displace the ecumenical priority. However, unless the United Reformed Church can discover a distinctive role, then the historic trajectory leads to further local unions and eventual absorption into one of the other Christian denominations.

Notes

1 The term 'episcopacy' denotes governance by bishops in a hierarchical church structure.
2 The Whigs were a British political party found in the seventeenth which opposed Catholic monarchs, absolute rule and the Tories and enjoyed non-conformist support. It was eventually absorbed into the Liberal Party in the nineteenth century.

3 Judaism, Sikhism, Islam, Hinduism and Buddhism

Post-war settlements

Robert Bluck, Sophie Gilliat-Ray, David J. Graham,
Gurharpal Singh and John Zavos
Edited by Linda Woodhead

Having considered the 'majority' faith of Christianity in the last chapter, this chapter deals with what are sometimes called 'minority' religions. Although most had a presence in Britain long before the Second World War, their numbers and visibility increased dramatically in the post-war period. This is particularly the case for religions associated with territories which had been part of the British Empire, and whose followers came to Britain after the Second World War from Commonwealth countries, often as British citizens. Despite their differences, the traditions considered here have in common a categorization as 'world religions', which gives them a status denied to other forms of religion, like those forms of 'spirituality' discussed in the next chapter.

As well as supplying basic facts and figures about the different religious communities, the chapter explores how they have gone about achieving 'settlements' in Britain – how they 'make space' for themselves in a society and culture which has not been shaped around them. It begins with Judaism, which has not only had the longest presence in Britain (since medieval times), but which has been most successful in becoming 'established' in British society – so much so that some members of the community now worry that it has been too fully assimilated. It then considers Sikhism, which effected a settlement in the post-war period by political action, and was classified as a 'racial' or 'ethnic' group rather than a religious group. Turning to Islam, the chapter shows how and why its settlement has been more controversial (especially since the 1980s), but also how, away from headlines and national debates, it has been established in many arenas of British society, like hospital and prison chaplaincies. The stories of Hinduism and Buddhism are different again, partly because both traditions have been selectively absorbed into the wider culture for over a century (see the next chapter), and partly because of other factors, including their different global political linkages. Buddhism is considered last because it has been the least active in making political claims, and has not shaped itself according to state demands. In that sense, it remains the least like a 'religion', and in some of its manifestations more like the 'spirituality' discussed in the next chapter. But all the contributions pay attention to everyday religion as well as more strategic forms of religious activity at national level, and show how being Jewish, Sikh, Muslim, Hindu or Buddhist makes a difference to life in Britain.

Introduction

Linda Woodhead

In keeping with an integrated approach to the study of religion, this chapter considers Judaism, Sikhism, Islam, Hinduism and Buddhism not as bounded, autonomous and time-less entities, but as internally varied and related in complex ways both to other religions and to wider social, economic and political developments – in the UK and elsewhere. The central question it addresses is how they have achieved 'settlements' in the UK. Here 'settle-ment' is used in a broad and metaphorical way to refer not just to a place or location, but to the ways in which religious communities 'make space' for themselves in a country where they are not part of the majority – in the built landscape, the culture, the educational system, the law, political process and everyday life.

This question is important because when religions move, it is not merely a case of trans-porting a fixed body of beliefs and practices unchanged from a place of origin to a new location (Tweed 2006). Religions change as they travel, and so do those who live by them. Indeed, it is as they are lived, and help people make sense of their lives in the face of new challenges, that religions change. This chapter shows how religions can be resources which people use to survive in hostile as well as hospitable settings. They are actively employed to make political claims, establish personal and collective identities, define and refine value commitments, consolidate social bonds, and deal with practical as well as spiritual problems and necessities. They enable people to maintain and establish connection with others of similar mind or commitment, often across geographical and ethnic boundaries; those who are a minority in the UK may be a much more important force when supported by those with the same religious commitment elsewhere in the world.

When looking at these religions in terms of their wider relationships, an obvious place to start is by viewing them as 'minority' religions. This expresses their relative position within the religious field in the UK, in which they exist in relation to a majority religion – which is also the religion of the white British majority – namely Christianity. As the previous chapter shows, Christianity retains this majority status, even though it has lost its cultural and religious monopoly. It is not only a numerical majority, it is also a majority in the sense that it is historically entrenched in many British institutions (like schools, universities, Parliament, the law) and, as such, enjoys a higher status and more power than other reli-gions, especially in 'established' forms like the Church of England. (Newer forms of Christianity, and black and ethnic minority forms, both discussed in the previous chapter, do not enjoy the same privileges.) Relative to the religious majority, minority religions have to struggle for recognition and privileges. One way of doing so is to claim the same levels of state support and recognition on the grounds of fairness, equity and non-discrimination. As this chapter documents, all the minority religions have done this in the post-war period, with varying degrees of success. Sometimes the majority religion will support them in their claims, as the Archbishop of Canterbury, Rowan Williams, did when he supported the (limited) use of *shari'a* in Britain (discussed in the previous chapter). There is also pressure on minority religions to conform more closely to the form of majority religion – which in Britain means becoming more church-like, and even more state church-like. Thus Judaism in Britain, for example, has generated a Chief Rabbi, a Board of Deputies and – more recently – a Jewish Leadership Committee. Similarly, mosques start to serve more of the functions of a church, and 'clergy' start to appear in religions which do not traditionally have priests. Likewise, there is a pressure on religions to produce a 'sacred scripture' even when they have not historically had one. Table 3.1 lists some of the many 'representative bodies' which have emerged under these pressures and claim to speak for the religion in question at national, state level. Not surprisingly, their legitimacy is often questioned, not least by their own communities.

Table 3.1 Main bodies claiming to represent Jews, Sikhs, Muslims, Hindus and Buddhists in Britain (2011)

Jews	Board of Deputies of British Jews Office of the Chief Rabbi Jewish Leadership Council (JLC)
Sikhs	Network of Sikh Organizations Sikh Human Rights Group Sikh Federation (UK) Guru Nanak Nishkam Sewak Jatha (GNNSJ) Sri Guru Singh Sabha Gurdwara, Southall
Muslims	Various bodies have emerged since the 1970s claiming to speak for British Muslims, of which the most enduringly significant have been the Union of Muslim Organisations (UMO) and the Muslim Council of Britain (MCB); but there are many others, and state approval has shifted between them over time. See Chapter 1 and the section below on Islam for more information
Hindus	National Council of Hindu Temples Hindu Council UK Hindu Forum of Britain
Buddhists	The Buddhist Society Network of Buddhist Organizations

Also important for minority religions are the relations they have with one another. In different circumstances these may be comparative, co-operative, hostile or accommodating. Sometimes they can be competitive. For example, when one religion is perceived to be getting better treatment from government than others. This was sometimes the case in the wake of the 7/7 bombings when central government initiatives to prevent Islamic 'radicalization' and promote community cohesion led to grants, funding and other special treatment for Muslim communities (though many Muslims did not regard this as a 'privilege'). There are also instances of co-operation, like the hundreds of interfaith and multi-faith groups which have developed in the UK, and which are discussed in Chapter 1 and Case study 2. As noted in the Introduction, the growth of interfaith activity has also led to a downgrading of the majority religion's status relative to the minority faiths, as all become more equal voices in the setting of interfaith consultative bodies.

Another way these religions are placed, defined and contained is in relation to secularism and secular interests. As the Introduction and Chapter 2 and 12 in the book show, the 'religious' only makes sense in relation to 'the secular', and vice versa. Religions are, in part, constructed by secular interests, which try to contain them, define them and keep them out of public life. So the existence of 'world religions' in Britain is simultaneously a co-production with modern secularity, and one which secular interests attempt to control. Secularism also exerts pressure on religion not to be political, not to take up public space and sometimes even on what not to wear. In some of its provocations to religion, the secular also shapes religion through reaction – as when support for Salman Rushdie and 'free speech' provoked Muslims to make a stand *against* free speech. This then confirmed secular opinion that Islam was oppressive – and led to a spiral of reinforcement (see Chapter 1 and Plate 1.6). As this chapter shows, the reality of these 'religions' is in fact a good deal messier and less neatly bounded than talk of the five – or eight or nine – world religions would have us think. Not only are there many groups which fall between the boundaries (e.g. those who are both Hindu and Sikh, or Buddhist and Christian), there are also porous boundaries with ethnic groups and caste groups, and huge internal variation within all of these 'religions'. Some are mentioned here – like *Ravidasis, Valmikis, Namdharis, Nirankaris* and *Radhasoamis* – others are not discussed at all. Despite being subject to what David Graham below calls a 'myth of homogeneity', for minority groups, factionalism and fragmentation and loose and shifting boundaries are the norm not the exception.

Despite secular attempts to ensure the privatization of religion, however, this chapter shows just how entangled these religions continue to be with the political process, with law, with economic activity and with majority culture – albeit in postures and through mechanisms which are not necessarily their own. There are different paths. Some, like Buddhism, maintain a mainly 'private' presence, and are content with a widespread cultural and spiritual influence (though this is different in relation to different groups, e.g. forms of Tibetan Buddhism). Others, like Sikhism, are for various reasons skilled in employing political and legal action, and have been successful in making claims and winning privileges and legal exemptions. Issues of race and class and gender are important too. The minority religions which suffer the highest levels of discrimination and achieve the least equal settlements in Britain are those which are different from the majority in terms of skin colour, ethnicity and often class as well – and within those communities women fare worst of all. Islam from the Indian subcontinent is the main example (Khattab 2009).

Finally, the chapter shows how historic context and relations also matter. The legacy of Empire is a theme which pervades this chapter, as it does so much of the book. With the partial exception of Judaism, these are religions whose main connection to Britain is through the Empire and its aftermath. It is therefore misleading to think of them as 'new' religions, or as foreign incomers to the UK in the post-war period. In fact there is a relationship which stretches back across several generations. These religious communities are tightly woven into Britain's political, economic, cultural and religious past as well as its present. There are bonds of exploitation and anger, service and loyalty, melancholy and disappointment, longing and hope. From this perspective, the history of minority religions in post-war Britain appears as the latest instalment in an ongoing narrative, rather than as an unprecedented episode.

None of these relations are one-way; majorities are shaped and altered by minorities as well as vice versa – albeit from a position of dominance. Although the influence of Hinduism and Buddhism on the development of alternative spirituality is the most obvious example of influence within the religious field (see next chapter), Christianity is also affected by its relation with minority religions, and new alignments and alliances in the religious field are developing all the time, often in relation to wider, transnational religious bodies as well as national settlements. As for the growing impact of minority religions on other aspects of state, society and culture, that is documented throughout the volume as a whole, particularly Parts 2 and 3.

Judaism

David J. Graham

Of all minority religious traditions, Judaism has had the longest presence in Britain – from medieval times onwards. It has suffered intermittent persecution and forms of disadvantage and intolerance, but today members of the Jewish community are prominent at all levels of British social, economic and political life, and Jewish institutions have become an integral part of British society. At the start of the twenty-first century, Britain's 295,000 Jews made up 0.5 per cent of the general British population. Two-thirds live in London and the south-east, and almost a quarter live in just two London boroughs. British Judaism is far from homogeneous. There are six main denominational strands ranging from Liberal through strictly Orthodox as well as a large subsection that does not affiliate to any synagogue. There has always been a pressure on Judaism to become more like a (state) church in order to gain privileges, but this has also been resisted. Although there is a Chief Rabbi, there is no overall rabbinical leadership recognized by all. The main bodies that claim to speak on behalf of Jews in Britain are the Board of Deputies of British Jews, Office of the Chief Rabbi and the Jewish Leadership Council; they are as much a reaction to the state as a desire by the community to speak with a unified voice. Jewish identity is a complex mixture of ethnic, cultural and religious allegiance. One need not have any Jewish 'confession' or 'faith' to be considered Jewish by the most Orthodox of Jewish authorities. Over half of Jews in Britain describe themselves as 'secular' or 'somewhat secular', and the community has assimilated into British society so effectively that some worry that Jewish continuity and identity are being eroded.

Introduction

Jewish presence in Britain was well established by the early Middle Ages, but the contemporary period of Jewish settlement arguably dates from 1656. Though historians dispute the exact details, it was around this time, under the Protectorate of Oliver Cromwell, that Jews were 'readmitted' to England following their expulsion in 1290 by Edward I (Roth 1978: Ch. 7). Thus, 2006 marked the 350th anniversary since the 'readmission' and among the many commemorative events organized that year was a special reception at St James's Palace in which the Queen was presented with a *hannukiah* (ritual candelabra) by the Chief Rabbi. This highly symbolic act presented a picture of Jewish unity in the arena of the state that disguised a great deal of complexity about the actual make-up of this community in Britain, and the nature of Jewish identity itself.

Demography and geography

Jewish population change in Britain

By the nineteenth century there were about 20,000 Jews in Britain, increasing to 60,000 by 1881. It was during this period that Jews finally received full, political emancipation with the election of the first Jewish MP, Baron Lionel de Rothschild, in 1858. Towards the end of the nineteenth century the community underwent rapid and radical change as a result of the large-scale immigration of Jewish refugees fleeing Tsarist persecution in Russia. As a result, by the beginning of the twentieth century the Jewish population numbered about 240,000 people, ranging from noble Victorian gentlemen to hapless and penniless immigrants (Rosenbaum 1905: 541, 554). Following the arrival in the 1930s of yet more refugees, this time fleeing Nazi oppression in Europe, Britain's Jewish population reached its zenith at around the middle of the twentieth century, numbering some 410,000 souls (Prais and Schmool 1968: 19).

Today, most Jews in this country are third- and fourth-generation Britons. They are fully integrated into British society, so much so that one of the community's major concerns in recent times has been assimilation (Kahn-Harris and Gidley 2010). From the peak of over 400,000 people, the community has experienced considerable demographic contraction as a result of ageing, low birth rates, assimilation and secularization. By the time of the 2001 Census the enumerated size of the Jewish population had apparently contracted to 270,000 people; however, as Graham and Waterman (2007) have explained, there are several reasons to believe this figure is an undercount, not least because the religion question is the only voluntary question in the Census. A more accurate figure inferred using alternative Jewish community data sources would have put the population at nearer 300,000 but even at this size Jews still only account for 0.5 per cent of the national population – that is, just 1 in 500 people is Jewish. But in recent years there has been increasing evidence that this downward spiral may be gradually changing. Since the late 1980s a noticeable demographic shift has been observed due to the extraordinary rate of growth of the strictly Orthodox (*haredi*) segment of the Jewish population, due mostly to very high birth rates (Vulkan and Graham 2008).

Another source of population change, migration, has probably been of relatively minor importance in the post-Second World War period. Israel is the key source and destination of would-be migrants, and a recent survey found that one in five respondents had previously lived in Israel at some point in the past, that 7 per cent currently have a second home there and that 3 per cent are Israeli by birth (Graham and Boyd 2010: 18).[1] This is indicative of the strong links which exist between Jews in Britain and Israel, the historic homeland of the Jewish people, re-established as a Jewish state in 1948. It also suggests that although there is a relatively high level of Jewish migration to Israel, it tends to be transitory, not permanent. Over time it is not clear that migration *to* Israel from Britain has been significantly greater than the return movement of migrants *from* Israel to Britain.

The sum effect of these recent demographic processes is surprising, if not remarkable. It is that unlike most other large Jewish populations outside Israel, Britain's has stemmed the tide of demographic decline and may, very soon, start to grow again.

Jewish geography

Prior to the 2001 Census it was well known that, spatially, Jews were a highly concentrated group, and the Census confirmed this in considerable detail. Geographically the Jewish population is one of Britain's most concentrated (Dorling and Thomas 2004: 56–57). And yet, even in the areas of highest concentration, Jews do not form overall majorities. Waterman and Kosmin (1988) once described this pattern of Jewish residential concentration as one of 'congregation not segregation', pointing out that only at the very smallest scales did Jews form local majorities, and even then only very rarely.

The 2001 Census revealed the presence of Jewish people in all local authority districts (LADs) in Britain (the Isles of Scilly being the sole exception). But it also showed that the population distribution was highly skewed: almost a quarter of the whole Jewish population lived in just two out of 408 LADs, the London Boroughs of Barnet and Redbridge; and just ten LADs accounted for over half (52 per cent) of Britain's entire Jewish population. Something similar was found at ward level: just 80 of the more than 8,800 wards in England and Wales accounted for half (50 per cent) the Jewish population. Yet, as Waterman and Kosmin's (1988) work had already predicted, the Jewish residential pattern was one of congregation not segregation – Jews did not even come close to forming a majority in a single one of these 80 wards (the highest proportion being Garden Suburb ward in the London Borough of Barnet of which 37 per cent reported being Jewish). Only at the smallest scales – Output Areas equivalent to about 300 residential units – did Jews form majorities (that is, more than 50 per cent), and even here it was only in 108 out of 218,040 Output Areas (Graham 2008: 221).

A fragmented population: the myth of homogeneity

The discussion until now has treated the Jewish population as a homogeneous group, but the Census and other generalized approaches dramatically oversimplify the 'Jewish community's' true complexity, reinforcing a 'myth of homogeneity'. Like other 'minority' groups, factionalism and fragmentation are the norm not the exception. A simple way of understanding the make-up of the Jewish population in Britain is to examine synagogue membership data. About 83,000 Jewish households belonged to a synagogue in 2010, and just over a quarter of all Jewish households did not belong to a synagogue (Graham and Vulkan 2010).

Of those that do belong, there are a number of subgroups that vary considerably in their attitudes, identities and approaches to Judaism. They tend to affiliate with synagogue movements or 'strands' of Judaism according to levels of religiosity. There are six main strands which themselves constitute two groups: the Orthodox and non-Orthodox. Table 3.2 summarizes the overall picture, including the proportionate size of each group. Each of the synagogue strands shown in the table have their own rabbinical leadership (the Chief Rabbi, for example, is formally the head of the Central Orthodox strand), and each has its own system of administration and organization, as well as offering very different approaches to Judaism (an issue that was central to the court case discussed in Text box 7).

Figure 3.1 shows the relative size of each affiliated denomination over time based on household synagogue membership. It should be noted that during this 20-year period, that is, less than one generation, overall synagogue membership declined by 17 per cent from 100,000 in 1990 to 83,000 in 2010. But this decline disguises a shift in the underlying make-up of the Jewish population. The graph reveals that relative denominational shifts have been taking place over this period. Whilst contracting overall, synagogue membership has also become less Orthodox. However, in each of the three surveys from 2001, the Orthodox proportion has nevertheless remained steady at two-thirds of the overall picture. But within this Orthodox group it is quite clear that one strand in particular is experiencing considerable growth: the haredi strand, which has almost tripled its proportion over the period. As a result the Orthodox strand is gradually becoming more intensely Orthodox, or 'ultra-Orthodox'.

Table 3.2 Synagogue membership and non-membership by household in Britain, by denomination (data for 2001)

	Type	Strand	Movement(s)	Per cent
Affiliated	Orthodox	Strictly Orthodox/*haredi*	Many are aligned with the *Union of Orthodox Hebrew Congregations*, others have a similar ethos	7
		Central Orthodox	The *United Synagogue* (which is the largest synagogal body in Britain), the *Federation of Synagogues* and various independent Orthodox synagogues	42
		Sephardi	N/A	3
	Non-Orthodox	Masorti	*Assembly of Masorti Synagogues*	1
		Reform	*Movement for Reform Judaism*	15
		Liberal	*Liberal Judaism*	5
Unaffiliated		No synagogue membership	N/A	28

Source: Graham and Vulkan 2010: 14

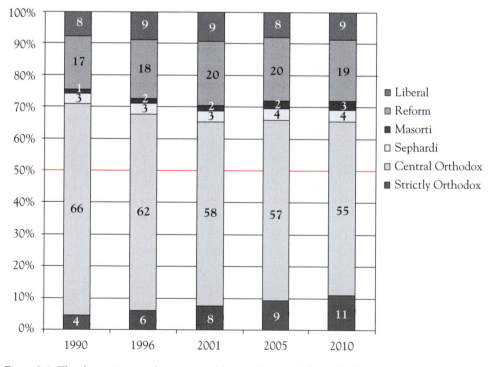

Figure 3.1 The denominational structure of Jews in Britain by household synagogue membership*

Source: Graham and Vulkan 2010: 13
* not including the unaffiliated

The haredi demographic surge

Though still amounting to only 11 per cent of overall synagogue membership, there are several important differences between the haredim and the majority of other Jews in Britain, whether affiliated or unaffiliated, especially in terms of religious practice. Haredim number about 30,000 overall, and are the most visible of all Britain's Jews. Haredi men wear traditional black coats and hats, and women dress modestly and cover their hair with scarves or *sheitals* (wigs). Very substantial differences also exist between the haredim and the rest of the Jewish population socio-economically, geographically and demographically. The 2001 Census showed that, compared with other Jews, haredim are more likely to live in social rented accommodation, in overcrowded conditions, exhibit lower levels of (secular) educational attainment and experience higher levels of unemployment (Graham *et al.* 2007).

There are also significant demographic differences. The average Jewish household size in Britain is 2.3 persons per household (PPH), about the same as the general population. However, in areas where haredim live (such as the London Borough of Hackney), household sizes are far larger at about 3.5 PPH, and one survey has suggested even this was a considerable underestimate, calculating average haredi household sizes to be as high as 5.9 PPH (Holman and Holman 2002; Graham *et al.* 2007: 56–57). Haredim marry early and have many more children than most other Jews in Britain, and because of this, though they make up about 11 per cent of the adult Jewish population, they comprise one-third (33 per cent) of all Jewish children under 18 in Britain. It has been estimated that since the 1990s the haredi population has been growing at a rate of about 4 per cent per year compared with a contraction of about 1.8 per cent per year for the rest of the Jewish population (Vulkan and Graham 2008).

These trends constitute a surprising and remarkable structural shift within Britain's Jewish population, and the implications can only be speculated upon. But the lessons of centuries of Jewish assimilation in Britain have taught us that it should not be assumed that children being born to haredi families now will themselves follow that tradition in adulthood. Nevertheless it is clear that this rapid growth has dampened the rate of Jewish demographic decline experienced in Britain since the 1960s, and has the potential to shift the centre of gravity of the Jewish community in the direction of the ultra-Orthodox.

Who speaks for the Jews of Britain? Institutions and representation

Given this socio-economic and religious diversity, it is perhaps unsurprising that no single institution, let alone individual, can genuinely claim to speak for all Jews in Britain. That said, Jewish institutional make-up does have a clear structure and a long and venerable history, not least because the British state prefers to have a central point of focus when 'Jewish matters' arise, as was demonstrated during the 350th anniversary celebrations referred to at the start of this section.

The institution with the oldest and strongest claim to be 'the voice of the Jewish community' is the Board of Deputies of British Jews. Tracing its history back to 1760, the Board celebrated its 250th anniversary in 2010 (see Plate 2.11). Describing itself as, 'the only democratically elected and national representative body of the British Jewish Community, whose welfare it exists to protect and promote',[2] it is as much a reaction to the state as it is an expression of a desire by the community to speak with one voice. As such, the Board plays an important role in many of the public activities the community is involved with. For example, it is prominent in promoting interfaith activities (with groups such as the Council of Christians and Jews, the Three Faiths Forum and the Inter Faith Network). It defines its role as both a 'defender' of 'the British Jewish community', and also as an educator of the general public about Jews and Judaism. Although nominally representative – the Board has 250 elected representatives – it is generally not recognized as such by haredi Jews nor by many unaffiliated Jews who have very little say, or indeed interest, in the activities of 'the chief voice of British Jewry'.

In addition to the Board, there are other voices and faces that represent Britain's Jewish community. The most famous is probably the Office of the Chief Rabbi (currently Jonathan Sacks) but, as discussed, this office can only claim to speak on behalf of Central Orthodox affiliated Jews who make up less than half of the overall Jewish population.

In recent years another organization has emerged that also claims to speak on behalf of Jews in Britain. Set up in 2003, the Jewish Leadership Council (JLC) aims to 'Enhance the effectiveness of communal political representation, advocacy and relations with Government' and 'influence communal strategic priorities'.[3] Made up of the senior lay leaders of the major Jewish organizations in Britain, including the Board of Deputies, the JLC is an unelected body which is influential within the community. For example, in 2008 it set up a commission to look into the future of Jewish schooling in Britain (JLC 2008).

Jewish identity in Britain

Who is a Jew?

A perennial question that both Jews and non-Jews often ask is, 'Who is a Jew?' This question is deceptively simple. Indeed, in a recent judgment of the Supreme Court of the United Kingdom, Lord Justice Mance, who himself is not Jewish, stated that 'The difficulty … is that the word "Jewish" may refer to a people, race or ethnic group and/or to membership of a religion' (Supreme Court 2009a: S76: 25). Lord Mance's 'difficulty' was the need to square the multi-dimensional nature of Jewish identity with the circle of the state's rather mono-dimensional approach to minority groups.

Jewish identity differs from other 'religious' identities in many more ways than the texts its adherents follow. Unlike other 'monotheistic faiths' such as Islam and Christianity, there is no tradition in Judaism for proselytizing, and non-Jews cannot become Jewish simply by declaring themselves to be so. Though it is possible to convert to Judaism this is not generally encouraged; all Jewish denominations exhibit a distinct lack of proselytizing fervour. And unlike Christianity, a Jew need not practise his or her religion, believe in its tenets or at any point in his or her life be baptized or declare allegiance to God in order to be considered Jewish, even in Orthodox Jewish eyes. In this sense, being Jewish is more akin to race and ethnicity than to religion, a fact that is recognized in the legal system of England and Wales (see Chapter 9).

Generally, a person is considered Jewish if their mother is Jewish (according to Orthodox traditions based on Jewish legal precedent (*halakhah*)). The Orthodox approach is, however, only one approach to defining Jews. During the nineteenth and twentieth centuries, modernity increasingly challenged Jewish people to choose what kind of Jew they wished to be. By the second half of the twentieth century, the definition of who is Jewish had become further complicated by the issue of Jews defining themselves not so much in terms of belonging to a religion, but according to cultural and ethnic criteria. From this sprang various strands of non-Orthodox Judaism which each take a less rigid view of who is and is not Jewish. These placed the notion of conscious choice at the centre of their definitions – the 'chosen people' became the 'choosing people' – with all the complexities of hyphenated, hybrid and fluid identities this entailed. Now, for example, some non-Orthodox Jewish traditions such as Liberal Judaism recognize having a Jewish father as sufficient for a person to be considered Jewish.

This is not just a matter of academic interest; the ethno-religious nature of Jewish identity has important ramifications because it differs substantially from the way the British political and legal establishment defines 'religious' and 'ethnic' groups. The implications have, in some cases, been profound. Jews have been somewhat marginalized in the debates about multiculturalism in Britain (see later). And, as Text box 7 explains, the issue led to an extraordinary dispute between JFS, the largest and oldest Jewish faith school in Britain which traces its history back to 1732, and a child who was denied a place at the school on the grounds of his Jewishness being inauthentic. This dispute was ultimately heard by the Supreme Court in December 2009, and its outcome has had direct implications for the admissions criteria for Jewish faith schools in Britain subsequently.

TEXT BOX 7

Who is a Jew? The JFS case (2009)

JFS (originally Jewish Free School) is a large, voluntary-aided school in London with a 'Jewish religious character'. Like all voluntary-aided schools it is mostly publicly funded, and the school's governors are responsible for setting the school's admissions policy based on Jewish religious affiliation (see Chapter 8 on types of faith schools). Since 1957 the religious body in charge of setting JFS's entry criteria has been the Office of the Chief Rabbi of the United Hebrew Congregations of the Commonwealth (OCR). JFS is therefore a (Central) Orthodox Jewish day school and, should the school be oversubscribed, which is usually the case, the School Admissions Code allows the OCR to base entry criteria on Orthodox Jewish law (*halakhah*). The entry criteria for JFS require applicants to either have a Jewish mother (who herself is recognized as Jewish by the OCR) or have undergone, or to be undergoing, conversion to Judaism (again in accordance with OCR – that is, Orthodox – criteria).

In April 2007 the Governing Body of JFS refused to offer a place to an 11-year-old boy on the grounds that he had not fulfilled these entry criteria. Although the child's father was Jewish under the OCR's own definition, and both of his parents belonged to a Masorti synagogue, his mother was a convert to Judaism and her conversion was not recognized by the OCR since it had not been carried out under Orthodox auspices. The extent of the child's and the family's Jewish practice and faith was of no relevance to their application.

As a result of this rejection, the child, through his father, lodged an appeal against JFS's decision on the grounds that it contravened the Race Relations Act 1976 (see Chapter 9). Faith schools are exempt from certain provisions of this Act because their purpose is to educate children in the religious beliefs of their parents and to maintain the 'religious character' of the school. But that exemption only extends to discrimination made on religious grounds not on racial grounds, and Section 1 of the Act states that discrimination based on 'racial grounds' also refers to discrimination on the grounds of colour, race, nationality, ethnic or national origins. Under the Race Relations Act, both Jews and Sikhs are protected as ethnic groups. Now the JFS itself stood accused of operating an admissions policy that had 'directly discriminated' against the child on the grounds of his 'ethnic origins'.

In June 2008 the High Court ruled in favour of JFS, with Lord Justice Munby (2008) arguing, in a 73-page judgment, that the Governors' decision did not constitute racial discrimination since it was based on Orthodox Jewish legal precedent. This, however, was far from the end of the affair and the child was granted leave to appeal this decision. In June 2009, three judges in the Court of Appeal heard that in contrast to other faith schools, which admit applicants based on the faith of the child's parents, JFS's admissions policy was not technically faith-based, despite the court's acceptance of the theological origin and character of the OCR's definition of Jewishness. The case therefore depended on proving whether the alleged discrimination had been racial/ethnic in nature. On this occasion the Court of Appeal ruled against JFS, arguing that the child had indeed been rejected on the grounds of his ethnic, not his religious, origins. This ruling prompted the Chief Rabbi Jonathan Sacks to claim that the English courts had branded Judaism 'racist' (Rocker 2009).

The seeds of the Court of Appeal's decision were planted some 26 years earlier in the case of *Mandla v Dowell-Lee, [1983]* (see Chapter 8), in which a Sikh child had also claimed racial discrimination against his school. In that case the House of Lords defined 'ethnic' with a broad brush rejecting the notion that the Race Relations Act 1976 referred solely to racial or biological characteristics. Thus, group characteristics such as a long shared history, a shared cultural tradition, a common literature and a common religion were noted as being sufficient criteria for a group to fall within the Act's jurisdiction. Therefore, in the eyes of the law, Jews and Sikhs constitute a racial group. It is ironic that JFS fell foul of legislation that protects its own pupils.

JFS was granted leave to appeal and, this time, nine judges from the newly created Supreme Court (formerly the House of Lords) heard the case. In a 91-page judgment issued on 16 December 2009 the Supreme Court upheld the Court of Appeal's ruling: JFS's admissions policy did 'directly discriminate' against the child on the grounds of his ethnic origins, in contravention of the Race Relations Act 1976.

The judges stressed that this judgment in no way suggested that the policies of JFS or of Jewish faith schools in general were morally wrong, let alone '"racist" as that word is generally understood' (Supreme Court 2009a: 4). However, they concluded that 'one thing is clear about the matrilineal test; it is a test of ethnic origin. By definition, discrimination that is based upon that test is discrimination on racial grounds under the [1976 Race Relations] Act' (Supreme Court 2009a: 17). One of the reasons their Lordships reached this conclusion was their feeling that conversion to Orthodox Judaism constituted a 'significant and onerous burden that is not applicable to those born with the requisite ethnic origins' (Supreme Court 2009b). It would also have required the child to adhere to a set of beliefs that are materially different from those of his (Masorti) parents (Supreme Court 2009a: 82).

As a result of these rulings, voluntary-aided Jewish 'faith' schools in Britain were forced to adopt radically new entry criteria. The Supreme Court ruled that 'Jewish schools in future, if oversubscribed, must decide on preference by reference only to *outward manifestations of religious practice. The Court of Appeal's judgment insists on a non-Jewish definition of who is Jewish*' (Supreme Court 2009a: 89, author's emphasis). Writing in the *Jewish Chronicle*, one observer stated that this is arguably a 'Christian definition of who is Jewish', the outcome of a case that the Supreme Court would 'clearly rather not have heard' (Rosenberg 2009).

A final ironic twist to this case is that the new entry criteria, based as they are on points scored for observing Jewish practices, are antithetical to Orthodox Jewish custom, and could mean that children from families that the OCR recognizes as being Jewish, but who do not 'practise' their religion, no longer automatically qualify for a place at JFS.

Being Jewish in Britain today

Despite the strong demographic growth of the haredi population, the majority of Jews in Britain do not describe themselves as being 'religious'. But that is not to say that they do not observe at least some aspects of ritual Jewish practice.

The most commonly celebrated Jewish festival is *Pesach* (Passover), which generally coincides with Easter in the Christian calendar. A commemoration of the biblical story of the Exodus of the children of Israel from Egypt, the theme of *Pesach* is therefore one of freedom, and has particular resonance among contemporary Jews in Britain regardless of their beliefs. But for the majority of Jews, *Pesach* is less about the religious themes nor even the messages modern-day interpretations draw out of it; rather, it is about families coming together to share a symbolic meal (*seder*). Over 83 per cent of Jews in Britain attend a *seder* 'most years or every year'.[4] In that sense *Pesach* is similar to Christmas both in its power to bring people together and in its overtly religious underpinnings being of somewhat secondary importance to many.

Modern Jewish practice, as the above example suggests, is family focused, and two other aspects of commonly lived Judaism in Britain today also relate to the home. *Shabbat*, the weekly 'day of rest' is, for a majority of Jews, also notable for bringing families together on Friday nights for a meal often accompanied by plaited loaves (*challa*) and the lighting of candles in the home. This highly ritualized practice is carried out 'most weeks' by 60 per cent of Jewish households in Britain.[5] Many of those who light candles on Friday nights or attend a family meal at *Pesach* would not consider these activities, or themselves, to be 'religious'. Indeed, only a small minority of Jews are what might technically be described as 'religious'. But other Jewish practices are generally considered to be 'religious', especially those whose observance demands greater personal sacrifice. The clearest example of this is *Shabbat*, strict Orthodox observance of which is considered onerous by many. Orthodox Judaism requires that on *Shabbat* Jews refrain from activities associated with the other days of the week. This includes driving a car, writing, and using any electrical appliances – even switching on lights. Regular observance of such behaviours is generally considered to define a 'religious' Jew. Surveys have found that between only 15 per cent and 20 per cent of the Jewish population in Britain can be considered 'religious' on this *shomer Shabbat* (keep the Sabbath) criteria.[6]

When asked to self-describe their outlook based on a continuum from secular to religious, a slight majority of Jews in Britain (52 per cent) describe themselves as 'secular' or 'somewhat secular'. As a result, sociologists often observe seeming contradictions between on the one hand Jewish behaviour, and on the other, belief (Lazar *et al.* 2002). For example, a third of Jews who claim to be 'secular' or 'somewhat secular' will eat only kosher meat at home, and fully 80 per cent of these 'secular' Jews attend a *Pesach* meal most years or every year.

Another crucial aspect of British Jewish identity is linkage to Israel. Despite its politically contentious nature, Israel is one of the strongest uniting causes in the community, and its significance requires comment. In their recent survey, Graham and Boyd (2010: 18) found that eight out of ten respondents said that Israel plays a 'central' or 'important but not central' role in their Jewish identity. They also found that 95 per cent of Jews in Britain have visited Israel. The strongest narrative by which Jews connect to Israel, however, is again not a religious one; less than half (48 per cent) of the survey respondents agreed that 'The Land of Israel was given to the Jewish people by God.' Far more important was the finding that the vast majority (90 per cent) agreed that 'Israel is the ancestral homeland of the Jewish people'. Given that very few Jews in Britain were born there, and still fewer had parents or grandparents who were born there, this finding indicates that the strong attachment Jews in Britain feel towards Israel is mostly grounded in cultural terms rather than religious, ethnic or nationalist terms (Graham and Boyd 2010: 15–16). Nevertheless, 72 per cent described themselves as Zionists (see Key terms).

Living in a changing world – assimilation and multiculturalism

In the post-war period, the Jewish community in Britain has, according to Kahn-Harris and Gidley (2010: 26), experienced a shift in internal political priorities. From the beginning of the twentieth century the 'Jewish leadership' adopted a policy of 'differential anglicization'. A conscious effort was made to ensure the Jewish community culturally assimilated into the British mainstream and did not stand out from British society. By 1967 this policy had largely succeeded: the majority of Jews in Britain felt secure in their whiteness and their Britishness. But in June 1967 this suddenly changed. It was the dawn of the Six-Day War between Israel and its Arab neighbours, and as Kahn-Harris and Gidley note: 'The war was seen as underlining threats to Jews … It deepened a perception of the common fate of Jewish people.' From this point on, a clear shift occurred in community politics – from a strategy of security (emphasizing the importance of assimilation and sameness) to a strategy of insecurity (of instead emphasizing vulnerability and difference). A focus on 'Jewish continuity' developed, centring on a crisis discourse: how could Jews and Jewish identity be preserved in the face of intermarriage and secularization? The panic in this discourse was heard loud and clear in Jonathan Sacks's 1995 book *Will We Have Jewish Grandchildren?*

This shift was paradoxical. Having secured their place in British society, long before most other minority groups had even arrived in Britain, the price many Jews felt they had paid for this acceptability suddenly appeared to be too high. Meanwhile, Britain itself had entered a period of reflection about the nature of its 'multicultural' society, as other minority groups began to assert their rights to both Britishness and otherness. But ironically, as Kahn-Harris and Gidley (2010: 7) note, the Jewish community ultimately 'failed to get a place at the table of multiculturalism; the communal leadership's stress on secure British belonging meant it has often been seen by other minorities as simply part of the white mainstream'. Multiculturalism's focus on skin colour as a proxy for ethnicity and 'cultural' diversity effectively excluded Jews from the debate, and nowhere is this clearer than in the rigid confines of the Census. In 2001 the category 'Jewish' appears, but it is located in the question on religion. The question on ethnicity and 'cultural background' has no space for Jews at all.[7] As a result, Jews are missing in many discussions about social integration and diversity in Britain (Graham 2008).

Key terms

Fragmented leadership: No single institution or person can claim to speak for all Jews in Britain.

Halakhah: Jewish religious law.

Haredi (plural: haredim): Strictly Orthodox Jews.

Haredi demographic growth: A reference to the dramatic changes occurring as a result of very high birth rates among haredi Jews.

Holocaust (shoah): The attempt by the Nazis during the Second World War to wipe out European Jewry which resulted in the systematic murder of an estimated 6 million Jews.

Jewish continuity: The success which Jews have had at assimilating into British society has prompted concerns about whether a Jewish population will exist here in the future.

Matrilineal descent: Part of the complex definition of the term 'Jewish'. A person is Jewish if their mother is Jewish.

Myth of homogeneity: The illusion that there is a single 'Jewish community' in Britain; it actually consists of many denominations and unaffiliated Jewish subgroups.

Pesach: The Jewish festival of Passover, celebrating Israel's freedom.

Proselytizing: Actively trying to bring about conversion, for example through preaching.

Shabbat: The Sabbath or day of rest (Saturday).

Zionist: Adherence to Zionism, the political doctrine proclaiming the right of Jews to self-determination in their own national homeland.

Further reading

Graham, David J., Marlena Schmool and Stanley Waterman (2007). *Jews in Britain: A Snapshot from the 2001 Census*, Report No. 1. London: Institute for Jewish Policy Research. A summary of the major findings to come out of Britain's 2001 Census, the first to include a question on religion, is presented in this book-length study.

Kahn-Harris, Keith and Ben Gidley (2010). *Turbulent Times: The British Jewish Community Today*. London: Continuum. This book examines the key contemporary developments which have taken place in Britain's Jewish community in the age of multiculturalism.

Scholefield, Lynne (2004). 'Bagels, Schnitzel and McDonald's – "Fuzzy Frontiers" of Jewish Identity in an English Jewish Secondary School', *British Journal of Religious Education*, 26/3: 237–248. This article presents an interesting assessment of 'the indeterminate boundaries of Jewish identity' from a qualitative perspective.

Waterman, Stanley and Barry A. Kosmin (1988). 'Residential Patterns and Processes: A Study of Jews in Three London Boroughs', *Transactions of the Institute of British Geographers*, 13/1: 75–91. This important article examines the relatively high-density spatial clustering of Jews in Britain and concludes that the pattern of settlement is one of congregation rather than segregation.

The Institute for Jewish Policy Research (JPR) offers the most comprehensive collection of contemporary studies of Britain's Jewish community, most of which can be freely downloaded from JPR's publications page: www.jpr.org.uk/publications/index.php.

Sikhism

Gurharpal Singh

Sikhs in Britain represent a remarkable case of a small and visible minority of South Asian origin which has partly succeeded in establishing a distinctive position in British society and governance in the post-war period. Often described as the 'pioneers' of British multiculturalism, British Sikhs have overcome formidable challenges to build a vibrant and prosperous community in an often hostile and unfriendly environment. At the same time, the experience of living in Britain has had a profound effect on Sikh religious institutions, values and traditions, and in shaping the emergence of a vocal and activist Sikh diaspora (Tatla 1999). This dual process – of settlement and emergence as a self-conscious community – provides a fascinating example of how a minority, non-European religious tradition has been able to make a lasting impact on post-war Britain.

Sikh settlement in Britain

Sikh settlement in Britain dates from after the annexation of Punjab in 1849 by the East India Company. This was followed by the exile of the last Sikh Maharaja, Duleep Singh, to Britain, where he lived, for the most part, as a country gentleman in Norfolk before revolting against the raj towards the end of his life in the late 1880s. Small pockets of Sikh students, princes, soldiers and itinerant workers were to be found in most large cities, but the earliest Sikhs to lay down permanent roots were the *Bhatras*, who established colonies in Glasgow, Cardiff, Manchester, Birmingham and Peterborough during the interwar years. The *Bhatras* were followed by labourers from the *Doaba* (central districts of Punjab) who settled in the West Midlands and founded the Indian Workers' Association (1938), which would become the lead organization of Punjabi migrants after the Second World War (DeWitt 1969). During the war years some Sikhs enlisted in the armed services or worked on the domestic front, but most lived isolated lives with little semblance of communal organization, apart from occasional religious gatherings at the Shepherd's Bush gurdwara (founded 1911) (Bance 2007).

The main growth in Sikh settlement occurred after 1945. The post-war economic recovery in Britain was accompanied by demand for industrial labour that was met by migrants from the New Commonwealth countries (India, Pakistan and the West Indies). In the 1960s, as immigration controls were imposed to restrict this flow, family reunions further bolstered the community's numbers, and these flows were further augmented by the arrival of Sikhs from East Africa (Kenya, Uganda and Tanzania) who sought to escape Africanization. In subsequent decades there were fresh waves of inward migration, notably in the 1970s and 1980s (as well as since 2000), but the major growth in the population was the result of births in the United Kingdom. Thus the Sikh population has increased from about 7,000 in 1951 to 336,179 in 2001, with perhaps the initial primary migration (of the first generation) being around 150,000 by 1981. Since 1981 the decennial percentage rate of increase had declined to 43.0 per cent by 1991, and further to 38.7 per cent by 2001 (Singh and Tatla 2006: 59).

Despite these official statistics, however, community narratives insist that the number of Sikhs is much greater, with some suggesting that the total could be around 700,000. As

Singh and Tatla (2006) have pointed out, it is necessary to take into account illegal settlers, those at the margins of Sikhism who often identify with other traditions (Hinduism, Buddhism, Ravidasis and Punjabi Christians) and the new arrivals during the 'decade of immigration' (2000–2010) – though the figure of 700,000 is probably an exaggeration. The 2011 Census might provide a more accurate picture, but it is unlikely to assuage the community's activists who generally insist on a more expansive definition of a Sikh, and often extrapolate national figures from the representation of Sikhs in particular localities (e.g. Southall, Slough) where they are heavily concentrated.

A socio-economic community profile

One of the distinguishing features of Sikh settlement is that the community is heavily concentrated in Greater London, the South-East and the West Midlands, which together account for 73.1 per cent of its total population. This concentration is even greater in particular localities: Slough, Hounslow, Ealing (Southall), Wolverhampton, Sandwell, Gravesham (Gravesend), Redbridge, Coventry, Hillingdon, Leicester and Birmingham are home to 47 per cent of Sikhs. Additionally, there is a significant Sikh presence in the East Midlands (Derby and Nottingham) and Yorkshire and Humberside (Leeds and Bradford). In the rest of the country, in contrast, Sikhs rarely exceed 5.5 per cent of the population; in large swathes of Britain their presence is as low as 0.5 per cent.

Like other religious communities from South Asia, Sikhs are differentiated by place of birth, ethnicity, and caste. According to the 2001 Census, 56.1 per cent of all Sikhs were British born, 34.9 per cent born in India and 7 per cent recorded their birth in Africa.[8] Nearly 60 per cent of the community was below the age of 35, highlighting the fact that its age profile is very young with a birth rate higher than the national average. Ethnically, on the other hand, 90.4 per cent of Sikhs identified themselves as 'Indian' and 4.3 per cent opted for 'Asian or British Asian'. Sikhs in general have high rates of private home owner-ship and increasingly resemble, with some major qualifications, the national profile for employment; and though they are not Britain's 'ethnic high flyers', neither are they its significant 'under achievers'.

These general statistics do not, of course, adequately capture the variations *within* these categories: there are, for instance, major differences in the education and employment profile of the Indian and British born, a concentration of Sikh females in the traditional low-paid manufacturing sector and high rates of unemployment among those over 49, where the economic inactivity rate among Sikh men and women between 50 and 64 is much higher than the national average. Such differences have led some to suggest that there are in fact two separate Sikh communities: the British and non-British born, who have different life chances and distinct mindsets. It is to these internal differences and contestations that we must now turn (see also Singh and Tatla 2006 and the Conclusion to this chapter).

Sikhism in Britain: devotion, identity and community

Sikhism is a major world religion founded by Guru Nanak in the fifteenth century. It has almost 20 million followers, most of whom live in the Indian province of Punjab, but are also to be found in large numbers in northern India (Delhi and Haryana), plus a significant diaspora of 1–2 million in Europe, North America, the Middle East, Australia and South-East Asia. Sikhism welcomes converts but is not a proselytizing religion.

Table 3.3 Social profile of Sikhs in Britain (2001)

	Per cent of the Sikh population	Per cent of the national average	Per cent +/–
1. Ethnic group:			
White	2.09	91.31	N/A
Mixed	0.84	1.27	–0.43
Asian or Asian British	96.18	4.37	N/A
Black or Black British	0.19	2.19	–2.00
Chinese or Other Ethnic Group	0.71	0.86	–0.15
2. Sex:			
Male	50.20	48.61	+1.59
Female	49.48	51.39	–1.49
3. Age structure:			
0–15	24.53	20.07	+4.46
16–34	34.91	25.15	+9.76
35–64	34.39	38.81	–4.42
Over 65	6.17	15.97	–9.80
4. Households with dependent children:			
No dependent children	45.07	70.62	–25.55
1 dependent child	19.46	12.40	+7.06
2 dependent children	21.97	11.21	+10.76
With 3 or more dependent children	13.51	5.21	+8.30
5. Household tenure:			
Social rented	8.00	19.92	–11.92
Private rented	8.24	9.59	–1.35
Owned	81.97	68.29	+13.68
Rent free	1.80	2.19	–0.39
6. Employment: (2004)			
Public admin, education, health	19.5	27.3	–7.80
Banking, finance and industry	11.7	15.6	–3.90
Transport and communications	12.9	6.9	+6.00
Distribution, hotels and restaurants	26.4	20.0	+6.40
Construction	6.4	7.7	–1.30
Manufacturing	18.7	14.1	+4.60
Energy and water	1.6	1.0	+0.60
Agriculture and fishing	0.0	1.2	–1.20
Other	3.0	6.2	–3.20

Source: Census 2001, and Labour Force Survey 2003/4, Office for National Statistics

The essence of Sikh theology is to be found in the opening hymn of the *Guru Granth Sahib* (the Sikhs' sacred text):

> There is one supreme eternal reality; the truth; immanent in all things; creator of all things; immanent in creation. Without fear and without hatred; not subject to time; beyond birth and death; self-revealing. Known by the Guru's grace.

Sikhs believe that God (*Waheguru*), who created the universe and everything in it, is all-knowing, pervasive as well as supreme, and has unlimited power. Because God is formless, inscrutable and beyond the reach of human intellect, a relationship with the Creator can be established only by recognizing divine self-expression and truth. This relationship is possible through meditation on God's Name (*nam*) and Word (*shabad*) which are the revelation of the divine instructor (the Guru). Without the Guru's grace an individual is doomed to the perpetual cycle of death and rebirth.

The message of Guru Nanak, the founder of Sikhism, went beyond personal reflection and meditation to incorporate a new social vision. This was evident in his strong emphasis on social equality, the rejection of all forms of caste distinction,[9] the collective welfare of all and the centrality of the concept of *seva* (service) to the community. The mundane and the divine in Nanak's social vision are linked together in three simple injunctions to his followers: to adore the divine name; to work hard; and to share the rewards of one's labour with others.

The *Rehat Maryada* (Sikh code of discipline) prescribes the daily routine for adherents. They should rise early (3 am to 6 am) and, having bathed, observe *nam japana* (meditation on the divine name) and read or recite the order known as *nit nem* (the daily rule). This is followed by the reciting of the following scriptures: early morning (3 am to 6 am), *Japji Sahib*, *Jap Sahib* and the ten *Swayyas*; in the evening and sunset, *Sodar Rahiras*; and at night before retiring, *Kirtan Sohila*. At the conclusion of each selection the *Ardas* (prayer) must be recited.

As the influence of the Guru's word is best experienced in the gurdwara, Sikhs are required to join a daily *sangat* (congregation) where, as well as listening to scriptures, they must undertake and perform *seva*. A gurdwara is entered by removing one's shoes and covering one's hair. Sikhs and non-Sikhs bow before the *Guru Granth Sahib* by touching their foreheads to the ground. The *sangat* are served with *Karah Prashad* (sacramental food) at the close of the session. Each gurdwara has a *langar* (common kitchen) where the *sangat* are enjoined to share a meal.

The *Rehat Maryada* also imposes further injunctions: Sikhs are not allowed to eat meat killed in accordance with Muslim custom; the use of all intoxicants is forbidden; they must not cut their hair; and they must be loyal to their marriage partners. For most Sikhs and their families, Sikhism plays a central role in their life cycle. There is a distinctive ceremony for naming the newborn and for baptism into the *Khalsa* (see below); the learning of Punjabi is seen as essential to understanding the scriptures; the marriage ceremony is specifically defined; and, at death, there are prescribed scriptures to be read and procedures to be followed.

Most Sikh children are considered to be born Sikh. All Sikhs who follow elements of the code of discipline and are mature enough to appreciate the commitment can also undergo baptism into the sacred order of the *Khalsa* ('the pure') established by Guru Gobind Singh at *Baisakhi* in 1699. Initiation into the *Khalsa* follows the ceremony known as *khande di pahul* ('tempered with steel') performed by the *Panj Piare* (the symbolic representation of the five beloved ones who were first baptized, and who subsequently, in turn, baptized Guru Gobind Singh). The *Khalsa* are required to keep the five Ks: *kesh* (unshorn hair), *kacha* (short drawers), *kirpan* (steel dagger), *kara* (iron bangle), and *kanga* (comb). In addition they must strictly adhere to all aspects of the *Rehat Maryada*. Baptized *Khalsa* males are renamed as *Singh* and females as *Kaur*. While the majority of Sikhs follow aspects of the *Rehat Maryada* and keep the five Ks, those who follow the strict discipline of the *Khalsa* are in a minority.

It is now generally agreed that the evolution of modern Sikhism was strongly influenced by the reformist Singh Sabha Movement at the end of the nineteenth century (Oberoi 1994). Responding to the colonial encounter and revival and reformist movements among Hindus and Muslims in Punjab, the Singh Sabha Movement succeeded in foregrounding *Khalsa* identity – to the exclusion of other Sikh identities – and began the process of differentiating Sikhism from Hinduism. This culminated in the establishment of separate life rituals and the creation of new institutions such as the Shiromani Gurdwara Prabandhak Committee (SGPC) for the control and management of gurdwaras (sometimes referred to as the Sikh parliament). These activities of the reformers laid the basis of modern 'mainstream Sikhism' that is further codified in the new *Rehat Maryada* issued in 1950.

Although Sikhism is an egalitarian tradition, most of the Sikhs who migrated to Britain after the Second World War were *Jats* (middle to poor peasant) from the *Doaba*. Traditionally *Jats* make up nearly two-thirds of Sikh society and are identified with the Sikh 'mainstream'. It was therefore natural that they would seek to reproduce their religious and cultural institutions in their new homes. However, along with *Jats* came a significant proportion of Punjabi Dalits,[10] who in some of the migrating districts made up nearly 30 per cent of the total population. These groups were always at the margin of the Sikh universe and were further differentiated from *Jats* by experience of caste discrimination, often because they were engaged in providing service to upper castes. Over time, as we shall see later, they too established their own institutions, though their relationship with mainstream Sikhism remains problematic. In between these two categories are those who arrived from East Africa. Often referred to as 'twice migrants', this group is mainly comprised of the *Ramgarhias* caste who traditionally occupied an intermediate position in the rural social structure between *Jats* and Dalits. However, because *Ramgarhia* Sikhs identify closely with mainstream Sikhism, their differentiation from Sikh institutions over time has been not on the basis of a separate *identity* but *caste*. Like the *Ramgarhias*, the *Bhatras* also adhere to mainstream Sikh identity but have their own gurdwaras which are exclusive rather than inclusive.

Gurdwaras are the Sikhs' principal religious institutions. First and foremost, as places of worship, they are the foundations of community building, act as guardians of its core values, and provide a forum for collective worship by the *sangat*. Yet as institutions they are much more, because historically community leadership has only emerged from *within* gurdwaras, and as the popular adage goes, 'those who control the gurdwaras control the Sikh community'.

Diversity and change within British Sikhism

In the past century the growth of the Sikh population in Britain has been accompanied by the increase in the number of gurdwaras. Table 3.4 provides an overview of these institutions from the first decade of the twentieth century when the first gurdwara was established in Shepherd's Bush.

The overwhelming majority of gurdwaras in Britain, 83.3 per cent, belong to what might be called the Sikh 'mainstream'; that is, they do not identify along caste lines. Since the mainstream is associated with *Jats*, who make up most of the community, it might reasonably be argued that these in fact are de facto *Jat* caste gurdwaras. Such an interpretation, however, would be misleading because these institutions do not restrict membership or participation in the management committee to particular caste groups, and their *sangat* can be, and often is, caste plural. Interestingly, Sikh urban castes (*Khatris, Aroras*) in Britain

Table 3.4 Gurdwaras in Britain (1910–2001)

	1910–51	1972	1975	1980	1985	1990	1995	1999	2001
England and Wales	1	40	59	90	129	149	174	180	202*
Scotland		2	3	5	9	11	11	11	11
Northern Ireland								1	1
Total	1	42	62	95	138	160	185	192	214

*Includes 5 for Wales.
Source: Weller (2001)

have eschewed the model of the former rural non-*Jat* caste in setting up their own separate establishments. In any case 'mainstream' gurdwaras are anything but uniform: they range from *sant-* (a religious leader/preacher) managed institutions to locally run institutions that would be more appropriately described as a religious cooperative. Nonetheless, what separates these bodies from the rest is the latter's *explicit* distinction of caste.

Beyond the 'mainstream', the second major cluster of gurdwaras is provided by *Ramgarhias* who combine a social identity that draws on a caste heritage with a narrative of Sikh history that underscores their distinctive contribution to the development of the *panth* (Sikh community). This consciousness of a separate identity has been further consolidated by migration to East Africa in the nineteenth century and, following Africanization, settlement in Britain as 'twice migrants'. Upwardly mobile with significant skills, the *Ramgarhia* migrants soon began to establish their own places of worship both as a mark of separate identity and as a way of distancing themselves from what many saw as lapsed Punjabi 'rustics'. This drive, in many ways, was underpinned by a perception that *Ramgarhias* were more committed Sikhs than the early settlers by virtue of their adherence to the male mark of identity, the turban and unshorn hair. Bhachu (1985) asserts that in the late 1960s the *Ramgarhias* led the return to the familiar Sikh dress code that triggered a religious revival within the community in locations like Southall, Birmingham and Leeds. And precisely because of this attachment to the Sikh tradition, the main divide between 'mainstream' Sikhs and *Ramgarhias* occurs not along the fault lines of doctrine or theology but caste/social class.

Bhatras, the oldest Sikh sub-communities in Britain, are not strictly part of the rural Punjabi caste hierarchy from where most of the migration has taken place. Originating from Sialkot, West Punjab, they are generally viewed by other Sikhs as a low-caste group, but despite this have remained steadfastly loyal towards *Khalsa* ideals, preserving a form of religious and social conservatism that is atypical of 'mainstream' British Sikhism. Outwardly sharing the symbols of the Sikh tradition, *Bhatras* prefer to maintain their autonomy both from fellow Sikhs and from wider British society (Bance 2007).

The complexity of setting clear boundaries around Sikh identity is illustrated by a number of lower-caste groups and sects. Whereas *Ramgarhias* (and *Bhatras*), despite their caste distinction, share the common dominant *Khalsa* discourse familiar in the 'mainstream', the same cannot be said of sects and movements at the boundaries of Sikhism. Among those which are represented in Britain are *Ravidasis*, *Valmikis*, *Namdharis*, *Nirankaris* and *Radhasoamis*. All five have established centres in Britain, asserting their distinction through institutions, lifestyles and ritual practices. Table 3.5 shows the number and location of their places of worship.

Table 3.5 Sikh sects' places of worship (2003)

Region	Ravidasis	Namdharis	Nirankaris	Radhasoamis	Valmikis
England	13	6	12	4	9
Scotland	1	1			
Total	14	7	12	4	9

Sources: Weller (2001), websites, interviews and personal communications

Of these groups, the largest are the *Ravidasis*, who are sometimes viewed as Sikhs. Although such a designation might be justified with reference to ritual practices, there is also sufficient evidence to argue that *Ravidasi* identity is far more heterodox and reflective of their emerging desire to be at some distance from conventional Sikhism, even if they remain 'within the Sikh universe'. As former untouchables outside the caste hierarchy, *Ravidasis* suffered the double indignity of caste and religious discrimination in rural Punjab, though most had been influenced to some degree by Sikhism. In the 1920s this community's leadership began a movement to establish an alternative social vision for itself in response to the general mobilization led by the Indian National Congress. This movement received a further stimulus with the independence of India, which was followed by affirmative action in government employment for the former 'untouchables' (designated as Scheduled Castes), and the rise of the Dalit movement. In contrast, in Britain the assertion of *Ravidasi* identity has taken the form of separate places of worship that are often called bhavans, the innovation of new practice and rituals, and a desire to be recognized as equals in a new society where egalitarianism is valued. Hence although the community retains some adherence to gurdwara rituals and Punjabi identity, in terms of its subject identification it seems to have settled at some distance from the Sikh faith (Singh *et al.* 2011).

The position of *Valmikis*, also of former untouchable/Dalit background and the next largest group, is far more ambiguous. Smaller in number, they straddle between several Punjabi folk traditions which also combine elements of Sikhism and Hinduism. As Nesbitt (1994: 130–131) has observed, '*Valmiki* religious identity has largely been forged as a means of resistance to higher-caste Sikh and Hindu exclusionism, so it is hardly surprising that contemporary *Valmiki* practice draws freely on both those traditions, while adding something distinctive of its own.' While the behavioural conventions in the *Valmiki* temple in Coventry were found to be 'indistinguishable from the gurdwara', the dominant idiom was 'reinterpreted to create their own distinctive variations'. The largest concentrations of *Valmikis* are in Birmingham, Bedford, Bradford, Southall, Coventry, Oxford, Wolverhampton, Glasgow, Derby, Gravesend, Huddersfield and Hounslow – all areas of Sikh settlement.

If *Ravidasis* and *Valmikis* can be understood as caste-based sects, then the *Namdharis*, *Nirankaris* and *Radhasoamis* are distinguished by their veneration for the 'living guru', which fundamentally challenges the basic tenets of Sikh orthodoxy. The *Namdharis*, however, have evolved a relatively benign image within the *panth* through their intense religiosity that draws on an historical narrative that emphasizes the tradition of revolt against colonial rule. They have seven gurdwaras, and are currently trying to develop a resource centre and a library in order to build a 'worthy' historical lineage.

Finally, the *Radhasoami* sect has considerable appeal among Sikhs of all castes. The movement emerged in the early twentieth century but now thrives in Punjab by promoting orthopraxy and the veneration of a living guru. *Radhasoami* is one of the fastest growing sects in contemporary Punjab, with an extensive social network system that has all the attributes of a comprehensive social welfare system. Many of its opponents have accused the movement of emulating the worst methods of modern franchising, such that all its *Bhawans* (centres) in Punjab's major towns are planned uniformly with white-washed exteriors. In Britain *Radhasoamis*, like *Nirankaris*, tend to keep a low public profile, but have an extensive network of mutual support and collaboration.

Sikhism in twenty-first century Britain

The success of the gurdwara movement has led to a high degree of institutionalization among British Sikhs that is reflected in an ability to protect vital Sikh interests when these appear to be threatened.

Since the late 1960s, gurdwaras have provided the resources for Sikhs to mobilize for the right to wear the Sikh dress code (turbans, *kirpans* and beards). Perhaps much more significantly, however, these campaigns succeeded in establishing the dominant *Khalsa* discourse of Sikh identity within English law. A key step was the *Mandla v. Lee Dowell* [1983] judgment of the House of Lords that approved the right of a Sikh pupil to wear a turban in school (see the discussion of Judaism above, and Chapters 1 and 9). As such, it also brought the Sikhs, like the Jews, under the protection of the Race Relations Act 1976 by recognizing them as deserving of protection as an 'ethnic group'. Yet interestingly, this judgment coincided with a major turning point in the community's history in Britain following the entry of the Indian Army into the Golden Temple (June 1984). This led to a decade of militant insurgency in Punjab for an independent Sikh homeland, cost over 30,000 lives and catapulted British Sikhs into the leadership role of the Sikh diaspora (Tatla 1999). Inevitably this turbulent period has left a deep psychological scar on the community and continues, in some measure, to influence its institutions and outlook today.

Although the diversity and divisions within British Sikhism highlighted above have remained more or less constant, the tradition as a whole faces a number of serious challenges today. Foremost among these is the increasing disjunction between the neo-orthodoxy which is practised in most gurdwaras and the sensibilities of the growing population of British-born Sikhs who share little of the culture or heritage of Indian-born Sikhs. Nowhere is the disjuncture more apparent than in the assertion of gender equality by young British Sikh women in the home and Sikh public spaces. It is also ever present in the theological bias towards pro-life issues, and the negative pronouncements of Sikh religious leaders on sexualities discrimination legislation. Neo-orthodoxy still controls the commanding heights of the community's power structures, but it seems to be increasingly disengaged from the lives of most Sikhs (see Singh and Tatla 2006).

One outcome of this dissonance is the rise of new spiritualities centred on *sants, deras* (gatherings) and *babas* (revered old men) who stand outside the mainstream tradition and offer new modes of worship and personal communion. In the past these innovations were tolerated as long as they did not pose a serious threat to established official Sikhism. In recent years, however, the increasing assertion of some groups in Punjab associated with unconventional practices has led to violent confrontations between their followers and mainstream Sikhism, a pattern that has only been partly mirrored in Britain. Whether these new spiritualities will be able to provide a sustained challenge to the hegemony of traditional Sikhism remains to be seen because they, too, have to overcome the not inconsiderable hurdles of language, culture and relevance for the British-born Sikhs. Amongst the current generation of young Sikhs ('Generation Y') there is a continuing reverence for the *Guru Granth Sahib* (and hence respect for the gurdwara), but this is often combined with dissatisfaction with 'elders'. Many in this generation also learn about Sikhism from the internet, peers, and in festivals and camps organized for young Sikhs.

A differentiation from mainstream Sikhism is beginning to emerge among Dalit Sikhs. In Punjab and among British Sikhs, the Dalit assertion has resulted in building a new religious identity; and this process has been hastened among *Ravidasi* Sikhs following the attempt on the life of two of their leaders by militant Sikhs in Vienna in May 2009. This incident led to *Ravidasi* Sikhs removing the *Guru Granth Sahib* from their places of worship and replacing it with one compiled from the writings of their own saint. To what extent these changes will be welcomed in Britain, again, remains to be seen, but if they do take hold, they would mark a major departure from the existing diversity within Sikhism (Singh *et al.* 2011).

Overall, it would be reasonable to say that mainstream Sikhism in Britain today is adapting unwillingly to the rapid social change that is occurring within Sikh and wider society around it. Whereas Sikh society in Britain is increasingly plural, British-centred and consists of a very young population, its principal institutions are still controlled by the first or second generation who remain intimately integrated with the structures of religious and political authority in Punjab and other parts of India. To some extent this is perhaps to be expected, because, as the events of 1984 demonstrated, the community's fortunes are always open to being reshaped by a 'critical event', a periodic tsunami that restructures its political and social outlook. At the same time, it needs to be recognized that diaspora Sikh communities like the British Sikhs are far more able to deal with such potential 'waves' than ever before, because through their own struggles they have made the British state far more sensitive to their transnational needs.

Despite the group's small size, British Sikhs retain a prominent public profile that is often demonstrated by formal representations to government, lobbying and court cases. The recent judgment in the High Court in *HH Sant Baba Jeet Singh Ji Maharaj* v. *Eastern Media Group & Anor* [2010], which reasserted the principle that the courts will not interfere in the regulation and governance of religious groups, has been seen as a definitive blow to religious groups and sects that seek to use the law of defamation and libel to silence their critics. But given the history of the community thus far, there is every indication that in the future it will continue to set legal precedents in the area of religious freedom and human rights.

Almost a century and half after Duleep Singh first appeared at Queen Victoria's court, a British Sikh community has come into being, though it is a community that has been made self-consciously by the choices of Sikh migrants and their interactions with the British state and society, especially since the Second World War. Despite being so long at the heart of the 'motherland', this community has taken time to mature and to establish a distinctive autonomy from its 'colonized' self. Of all the Sikhs in the diaspora, it is the British who have gone through the most intense process of self discovery as postcolonial people. Today they are faced with a stark choice between neo-orthodoxy or a more cosmopolitan future. The choice they will make will have profound consequences for Sikhs all over the globe.

Key terms

Ardas: Prayer.

Aroras: Caste of urban Sikhs.

Babas: Revered old men.

Bhatras: A small subgroup among Sikhs linked together by kinship networks.

Biasakhi: Sikh new year.

Caste: A system of social hierarchy based on birth, religion and culture.

Dalits: Members of Indian lower-caste groups. Formerly 'untouchables' or 'Scheduled castes'; term in common use in India to describe the rise of subaltern caste groups.

Deras: Gatherings; centres.

Diaspora: A people spread out beyond their homeland; the Sikh diaspora is found in Europe, North America, the Middle East, Australia and South-East Asia.

Gurdwara: Sikh place of worship.

Guru Granth Sahib: Sikh holy book.

Japji Sahib: Sikh morning prayer.

Jats: Agriculturalists caste group.

Kacha: Short drawers.

Kahnde di pahul: Tempered with steel.

Kanga: Comb.

Kara: Steel bangle.

Kara Parshad: Sacramental food given at a gurdwara.

Kesh: Unshorn hair.

Khalsa: The Sikh brotherhood.

Khatris: Caste of urban Sikhs.

Kirpan: Steel dagger.

Kirtan Sohila: A section of the *Guru Granth Sahib* recited in the evening.

Langar: Communal kitchen.

Nam: God's name.

Namdhari: Follower of the *Namdhari* sect.

Nam Japana: Meditation on the divine name.

Nit Nem: Daily rule.

Panj Piare: The five disciples.

Panth: The Sikh community.

Radhasoami: Follower of the *Radhasoami* sect.

Ramgarhia: Member of the *Ramgarhia* caste.

Ravidasi: A follower of guru Ravidas.

Rehat Maryada: Sikh code of conduct.

Sangat: Gurdwara congregation.

Sants: Preachers/holy men.

Seva: Service.

Shabad: Word of god; hymns.

Sodar Rahiras: Sunset liturgy.

Further reading

Bance, Peter (2007). *The Sikhs in Britain: 150 Years of Photographs*. Stroud: The History Press. A history of the community in Britain as seen through old photographs.

Hall, Kathleen D. (2002). *Lives in Translation: Sikh Youth as British Citizens*. Philadelphia, PA: University of Pennsylvania Press. A detailed study of Sikh pupils in secondary education in north England.

Jhutti-Johal, Jagbir (2011). *Sikhism Today*. London: Continuum International Publishing. Examines some of the ethical issues facing Sikhs in Britain and other Western societies.

Nesbitt, Eleanor (2005). *Sikhism: A Very Short History*. Oxford: Oxford University Press. A short and concise introduction to Sikhism, including Sikh practices in Britain.

Tatla, Darshan Singh (1999). *The Sikh Diaspora: The Search for Statehood*. Seattle, WA: University of Washington Press. This volume provides a detailed coverage of the post-1984 events in the Sikh diaspora, especially Britain.

Islam

Sophie Gilliat-Ray

> The past and present of Islam in Britain are bound up with Britain's colonial past and postcolonial present. After showing how this history brought about distinctive patterns of settlement in the UK, this section explores the ensuing diversity of British Muslims in terms of socio-economic status, ethnicity, language and adherence to a particular school of thought. Such diversity has often been an obstacle to the formation of organizations that might represent Muslim interests to politicians and civil society. However, as noted in Chapter 1, the impact of the Rushdie Affair in the early 1990s was an important catalyst for the formation of more effective bodies, such as the Muslim Council of Britain and the British Muslim Forum. The deepening involvement of British Muslims in the religious, economic, political and cultural life of the UK is explored, including examples such as involvement in chaplaincy departments in hospitals. The changing role of Islam in British Muslim lives is also considered, and generational shifts towards more international, individualized, 'media-ted' and in some ways more conservative forms of Islamic identity are discussed (see also Chapter 5, for more on British Muslim thought and 'God-change').

It is often assumed that the presence of Muslims in Britain is a relatively new phenomenon, confined almost entirely to the post-Second World War period. It is more accurate to view this presence, and Britain's modern encounter with Islam, in relation to Britain's history as a colonial power, and the aftermath of this history.

Although the decades after 1945 were certainly distinctive in terms of the *scale* of Muslim settlement in Britain, historical records indicate that Muslims have been coming to the British Isles as traders, students, seafarers and explorers from as early as the ninth century (Ansari 2004; Gilliat-Ray 2010). However, many of these early Muslims coming to Britain were transient settlers, and they were usually unaccompanied single men who eventually returned to their countries of origin. It is questionable as to whether they would have regarded themselves as 'Muslims in Britain' in any meaningful sense, such was the temporary character of their residence in most cases.

From the late nineteenth century however, a distinct Anglo-Muslim community began to evolve in Britain, stimulated by Britain's colonial links, and especially those with the Indian subcontinent. The first registered mosque was established in Liverpool in 1887, and later, the first purpose-built mosque was founded in 1889 in Woking, Surrey. The maritime port cities of South Shields, Cardiff and Liverpool were especially important at the turn of the twentieth century. Muslim seafarers, especially from Yemen, Somalia and India, were recruited to work on colonial shipping routes. Having completed their passage on one ship, they would reside in dockland boarding houses, awaiting work on the next outbound vessel. But some of these seafarers became permanent residents in Britain, and the first embryonic 'British Muslim' communities were established in or near these port cities.

If the availability of employment was a determining factor influencing where these early Muslims settled in Britain in the nineteenth century, much the same can be said about the post-Second World War period also. As noted in the Introduction to the volume, with the need to redevelop towns and cities damaged by the war, and the expansion of manufacturing industries in the 1950s and 1960s, there was a demand for unskilled and semi-skilled factory workers. Britain looked to those countries with which it had colonial ties in order to meet the labour shortages. As a consequence, many relatively poor, uneducated migrant labourers came to Britain, especially from the Indian subcontinental countries of Pakistan, Bangladesh and India. They were once again mainly single men, and, like many of their earlier seafaring counterparts, they envisaged a time when they would return to their countries of origin. Being a Muslim in Britain at this time was therefore primarily a matter of belonging to a particular ethnic group or kinship network. Referring to this generation of South Asians, Anshuman Mondal has noted:

> for many Muslims of the older generation, the observance of Islam was less about piety and more to do with participation in communal life. Whether sincerely undertaken or not, the performance of rituals, the attendance at mosques and the undertaking of fasting during Ramadan were aspects of a social life which established a semblance of community for the older generation of South Asian migrants, and the dense network of relationships that such activities helped to sustain would provide them the stability and support they needed in an unfamiliar environment. It seems that this *collective* observance is what motivated the older generations in their adherence to Islam rather than any particular sense of personal religiosity.
>
> (Mondal 2008: 4–5)

Without diminishing the significance of collective identification with Islam, one of the distinctive changes that has perhaps taken place over the past two to three decades – and a theme of what follows – is the gradual adoption of a more personal, proactive and individual relationship to Islam, especially among younger, British-born Muslims (see also Chapter 5 on 'God-change' in this volume).

The beginnings of a permanent settlement

Early South Asian migrants to Britain in the post-war period used their social networks and kinship ties to find work and boarding-house accommodation. The demand for unskilled and semi-skilled workers for factories and textile mills in the Yorkshire and Lancashire conurbations, the Midlands and London has meant that Muslims were (and remain today) unevenly distributed around the UK. This reliance on kinship networks sometimes resulted in a somewhat insular orientation to life in Britain, and a consequent reluctance to participate in civil society or politics. Over the past 30 years, this worldview has changed considerably.

Important legislative changes in the 1960s and 1970s had a dramatic impact on the nature of Muslim settlement in Britain. The new legislation was designed to place strict limits on further large-scale immigration to Britain. This meant that among those Muslims already in the UK, the new policies were seen as obstacles to any possible reunification of families. In order to 'beat the ban' of the new immigration laws, many South Asian men in Britain sent for their wives and children from their villages and towns in the Indian sub-continent to join them in the UK.

Although permanent family settlement was not intended as a result of the arrival of women and children, it was an inevitable consequence. As children were born and educated in Britain, more time, energy and resources were invested in the development of community facilities, especially those that would support the religious identity and wellbeing of the new British-born generation. Some of the first institutions established by Muslims in the 1960s and 1970s were therefore independent schools and mosques that incorporated religious instruction for children. With their construction came the 'myth of return' to homelands (Anwar 1979), which meant that any serious intention actually to return became illusory. However, transnational links back to extended family members in countries of origin remained important for many British Muslims (and often remain so today), and these ties are sustained through the continued practice of contracting marriages with relatives from 'back home', sending financial remittances, going on holidays, and receiving visiting relatives and friends.

Demographics and growing visibility after the 1980s

Alongside South Asian Muslim settlement in Britain, Muslims from other parts of the world have also made Britain their home. During the 1980s and 1990s, economic and political unrest in some parts of the world meant that Britain was an attractive destination for educated and professional Iranians, Arabs, Kurds, Turks, and those fleeing situations of persecution in Bosnia, Somalia, Uganda and other African states. So during the later decades of the twentieth century, the ethnic composition of British Muslims diversified considerably, and towns and cities with existing Muslim communities, especially London, provided obvious places to settle and to build new lives. These patterns of migration have influenced, and continue to influence today, the demography, the internal diversity and the socio-economic circumstances of Muslim communities in Britain.

Conversion to Islam by those of many different ethnic backgrounds (but mainly white British and Afro-Caribbean) is significant, not from a numerical perspective, but more because of the 'disproportionate contribution [they] can make to the indigenization of Islamic practice, thought and discourse in the West' (Zebiri 2008: 1). Converts account for about 1 per cent of the British Muslim population, so this means that there are likely to be about 21,000 converts in Britain today (Gilliat-Ray 2010). The reasons for their conversion continue to fascinate journalists, research students and to some extent 'born' Muslims themselves, who often take particular pride and delight in a new Muslim joining the worldwide Muslim community (the *umma*).

During the latter decades of the twentieth century, information about the number, ethnicity or employment of Muslims in Britain was based on speculation and intelligent guesswork. But in 2001 a question about 'religion' was included in the Census for the first time since 1851. The mere inclusion of this question was largely a consequence of lobbying by British Muslim organizations, concerned that their religious identity should be regarded as a defining characteristic of their self-understanding and a meaningful category of difference affecting their socio-economic situation. As soon as the Census data was analysed and made public, it became clear that many British Muslims were seriously affected by a range of socio-economic disadvantages, each compounding the others. Compared to all other faith communities in Britain, the Census data revealed the vulnerable position of Muslims in relation to housing, education, employment, health and so on. The cumulative effect of these difficulties means that today, many British Muslims tend to reside in the most deprived areas of the UK, live in overcrowded homes of poor quality and experience higher levels of ill-health compared to other faith communities (Khattab 2009). However, the basic statistical information gathered through the Census and subsequent government surveys has provided policy-makers with evidence that might provide strategies for alleviating this urban poverty in the longer term.

According to Labour Force Survey data gathered in 2009, there are approximately 2.4 million Muslims in Britain, and about two-thirds are of South Asian (Pakistani, Bangladeshi, Indian) origin. Muslims now constitute 4 per cent of the UK population. However, what is notable is the relative youth of British Muslims. Approximately half are under the age of 25, and by now, about half have been born in the UK itself. In contrast, only 5 per cent of Muslims in Britain are over the age of 60, compared to 20 per cent of the rest of the population. Because of the migration patterns outlined above, Muslims have tended to be located in particular cities and neighbourhoods, and in some places they may constitute up to 36 per cent of the local population (for example, in Tower Hamlets, East London). The average household size for Muslims in 2001 was 3.8, compared to the national average of 2.4, and about a third of Muslim homes contain five or more people. This reflects the higher birth rate among British Muslims, relative to the general population.

TEXT BOX 8

Unity in diversity: a Cardiff case study

The historic port city of Cardiff has been attracting Muslim settlement for well over 100 years. During the late nineteenth century, Muslim seafarers from Yemen, Somalia and the Indian subcontinent formed part of a transient, mostly male, seafaring community in the city. They pioneered the establishment of boarding houses, mosques and other community facilities, as well as contributing to the First World War and Second World War effort. The legacy of their hard work is apparent in Cardiff today, where there are now some 13 mosques, a number of Muslim schools, several Islamic charities (Muslim Aid, Islamic Relief), and strong ties between Muslim organizations and the Welsh Assembly Government. The 15,000 or so Muslims in Cardiff today are still predominantly of Somali, Yemeni or South Asian origin, and most of the major schools of Islamic thought are represented in the city (Gilliat-Ray and Mellor 2010).

Socio-economic status

Many of the South Asian Muslims who came to Britain for work in the post-war period were from poor, rural areas and they had rarely received any formal education. Although this generalization masks important variations and exceptions, on the whole they arrived in Britain with relatively little social or material capital beyond their kinship networks. All this has had consequences for later generations. While some families have actively encouraged educational achievement as a means for improving their prosperity and social status, it remains the case that not all families have had the knowledge or resources to enable this process to happen effectively. Therefore, educational underachievement remains a challenge within Muslim communities, and rates of economic inactivity remain higher compared to all other faith groups (Hussain 2008, and see the discussion of Sikh levels of employment earlier in this chapter).

To some extent, however, higher levels of economic inactivity are due to the fact that, compared to other faith groups, Muslim women are less likely to be in paid employment. This partly reflects the decision that many British Muslim women make that their primary role and responsibility is motherhood. Islam accords a high degree of respect to the status of mothers and numerous Qur'anic verses and Hadith (sayings of the Prophet Muhammad) allude to the important role that mothers have as those who nurture and educate future generations. This does not mean that Muslim women who are mothers are confined to this role alone however. Muslim communities in Britain still need female doctors and teachers, for example, and those who fulfil such roles are often doing so alongside their other domestic responsibilities. It is also important to take into account the fact that the way data is collected about employment and economic activity in quantitative surveys is such that a good deal of work done by Muslim women is probably invisible to statisticians. As part of a report on women and society conducted by the BBC, Heidi Safia Mirza noted that current figures 'don't record home-working, time spent on family-run businesses, and unpaid work, so the idea that they do not participate is not very helpful' (Mirza 2002).

At least some of the unpaid work that Muslim women are engaged in relates to religious activity both within and outside mosques. Over the past three decades, they have developed their own formal and informal networks, and religious study circles, and they have lobbied for their religious needs to be taken into account in many dimensions of public life (such as the Metropolitan Police adapting its uniforms to enable female Muslim officers to wear the hijab). The various ways by which Muslim women in Britain have sought to empower themselves and their communities reflect an organic and important process of change in British Muslim communities, as we shall see below.

Diversity of thought and practice

Although it is important to look at the socio-economic situation of British Muslims through the lens of large-scale qualitative datasets such as the Census, these studies mask significant aspects of diversity within and between Muslim communities. In particular, it becomes more difficult to appreciate the many different Islamic 'schools of thought' that are now present in Britain. Not all Muslims actively identify with a distinctive strand of religious thought and practice, but many do, and this has been well documented by some of the leading scholars of Islam in Britain in recent decades (Geaves 1996; Lewis 1994). Inevitably, the various Islamic traditions now present in Britain have their origins in those South Asian and Arab countries from which British Muslims have largely been drawn.

Islamic teaching has been interpreted and practised in various ways since the time of the Prophet Muhammad in the seventh century. This means that in cities such as Birmingham, Bradford, London or Cardiff, there are Muslims not only from very different ethnic and linguistic backgrounds, but also from very different schools of religious interpretation. As a consequence of travel and migration, these different religious ideas, once separated by large geographical distances in the Muslim world, are now found on adjacent streets. As a consequence, there is debate and sometimes tension within Muslim communities about the most authoritative and correct way of interpreting Islamic texts and living as a Muslim in Britain today. So, far from being a monolithic community, Muslims in Britain are in fact from many different schools of thought, and it is unfortunate that many contemporary discussions about Islam in Britain, especially in the media, tend to present British Muslims as a single homogeneous community. This is far from the reality.

The different Islamic movements present in Britain share, however, some common characteristics, irrespective of their geographic or historical origins. For example, they nearly all regard the era of the Prophet Muhammad and his early companions as providing a template for authentic Islamic practice and belief. They are seeking to approximate that assumed 'pristine' time in the modern world. The variation between them essentially arises from different understandings about *how* and in what ways Muslims should actually implement the social mores of the Prophetic time. Fundamentally, the various schools of thought differ in their *methodology* for trying to *interpret and practice* this religious reality, and the place of the Prophetic tradition (*sunna*) within this process. So, some of these traditions look for answers to contemporary religious questions and issues via the scholarly study of religious texts and the accumulated knowledge to be found in legal commentaries written over the centuries. Others rely instead on fresh interpretation of original Islamic sources. Amid these different approaches to religious knowledge and authority, some British Muslims also emphasize their connection to a spiritual lineage of scholars and saints, and it is the relationship they have with their spiritual teacher that provides the basis for day-to-day religious life and practice.

To some extent, the way in which the various religious reform movements in Britain today relate to one another and wider society as a whole is a reflection of the ideological and political stances that they adopted during the period of their formation, especially vis-à-vis the former colonial power. For example, many of the South Asian reform movements that flourish in Britain today were founded during the height of British imperial rule in India, or during its immediate aftermath. As Muslims found themselves living under the authority of a foreign power and in an atmosphere of religious competition, they adopted different religious and political responses to this situation. Although contemporary Britain is very different from colonial/postcolonial India, it is still nevertheless marked by religious diversity, and poses challenges to religious communities about how to live according to religious laws in a society largely shaped by secularism and a non-Muslim majority. In many ways, therefore, the migration of South Asian Muslims to Britain in the 1960s and 1970s has provided a new opportunity to interpret and implement historical reformist ideas afresh. The outcome of this transmission of religious ideologies, from one social context to another, is that some Muslims in Britain are engaged in the challenging process of establishing 'what counts' as the most authentic way of living as a Muslim in the modern world. However, they do so in such a way that both past tradition and contemporary context are taken into account. It is the new geographic proximity of religious ideas and their associated social structures that often makes this process of debate and negotiation particularly contested.

Mobilizing causes

Despite inevitable divisions, there have been occasions over the past two to three decades when British Muslims have come together to express concerns on matters that unify, rather than divide them. At the local level, this was especially evident in the 1970s and 1980s, when parents of the new generation of British-born Muslims were concerned about their children's schooling. They were especially keen to establish ways whereby school environments might adapt to enable Muslim children to maintain religious norms and expectations with regard to such things as modest dress, maintenance of a *halal* diet and the scope to celebrate the Eid festivals. Organizing campaigns on these matters, alongside the development of local welfare associations orientated towards practical support for members of particular ethnic groups, gave rise to the emergence of local 'community leaders'. These 'leaders' were rarely religious specialists or imams. Rather, they were usually educated professionals with a good command of English, and some familiarity with the structures of local government. Over time they became recognized as semi-official 'spokesmen' (and they were nearly all men) on matters affecting Muslims in the locality. The dynamics of this local community leadership remain contested, and the degree to which the individuals involved are truly 'representative' is debatable (Kundnani 2007). However, community leadership has also become both more diverse and 'professionalized' in recent decades, and this reflects another important dimension of change within British Muslim communities, as we shall see below.

At a national level, the ability of British Muslims to unite in a common cause was most evident in 1989, following the publication of Salman Rushdie's novel *The Satanic Verses* (see the discussion of this controversy in Chapter 1 and Plate 1.6). The long-term significance of the book's publication for Muslims in Britain cannot be overstated. First, due to a common sense of hurt and anger about the way in which the Prophet Muhammad had been portrayed in the book, Muslims became aware of a specific and collective threat to their *religious* identity for the first time. The so-called 'Rushdie Affair' brought a latent sense of being Muslim to the fore, and to some extent the identity 'British Muslim' came into being as a consequence of the unity engendered by the book's publication. Second, the demonstrations organized around the UK to protest against the novel brought British Muslims, as members of a distinctive religious minority, to public attention at a national level in a new way. Arguably, the increased visibility of Muslims in the public sphere in Britain began at this time as journalists, politicians and academics started to debate the social, religious, and political consequences of Muslim activism. To some extent, this event was the beginning of a process which has led to the intense politicization of Islam and Muslims in Britain, and this represents another significant dimension of change affecting British Muslims over recent decades. Third, if *The Satanic Verses* was a turning point in wider public perceptions of Muslims in Britain, it was also an important catalyst for the formation of a national body to represent Muslim interests to the government in Westminster. The UK Action Committee on Islamic Affairs (UKACIA), formed in the immediate aftermath of the book's publication, brought a number of leading British Muslims together in a formal way for the first time. The success of this body is evident from the fact that it evolved and became the Muslim Council of Britain (MCB) in 1997. The MCB continues to provide a forum for British Muslim consultation with government and with civil society more generally (e.g. interfaith organizations, see Case study 2).

Disputes and contests that sometimes characterize local Muslim community representation are equally evident at the national level. Over the past 13 years, the reputation and status of the MCB have fluctuated according to social and political circumstances both in Britain and abroad. So while some British Muslims have come to regard the MCB as 'remote and elitist' (Radcliffe 2004), at times it has also been accused by government of not doing enough to 'prevent' religious extremism. Against the background of these kinds of accusations, the government has in recent years sought to promote other so-called 'representative'

British Muslim bodies, such as the British Muslim Forum (BMF), established in 2005, and the Sufi Muslim Council (SMC), established in 2006. By starting to provide political support for a range of organizations, it is arguable that the government is perpetuating colonial models of alliance, and perhaps deliberately creating the conditions whereby Muslims from one school of thought are placed in opposition to, or competition with, others. Regardless of intentions, it remains the case that the MCB continues to provide one of the few platforms that enables British Muslims from a range of different ideological positions to lobby and to work together at national level, despite the largely decentralized character of Islam in Britain.

Changing identities, maturing settlement

In this brief survey of the history of Muslims in Britain, the circumstances that underpin a number of aspects of religious change have been identified and contextualized. However, it is the changes themselves that form the focus for the last part of this section, which will consider the gradual adoption of a more self-confident sense of religious identity among Muslims (especially those born in the UK), the growing involvement and prominence of Muslim women in public life, the changing and developing role of religious professionals, and the increasing politicization of Islam in this country. These are all indicative of the fact that a distinctive Muslim presence in British society in a fully involved, if not fully evolved, way is an established fact. As a consequence, social and political structures, public institutions, and British Muslims themselves (both individually and corporately), have sought to find ways of accommodating the implications of this reality.

The increasing involvement of Muslims (and especially women) in publicly funded chaplaincies in Britain provides a lens through which many of these dynamic changes seem to become especially clear, and particularly as they manifest in the context of real life situations (see Plate 1.7, and Beckford and Gilliat 1998; Gilliat-Ray 2008). It is within the setting of chaplaincy departments that many issues can be seen in microcosm, and the context of a hospital provides a particularly useful example. For instance, the relatively high birth rate among Muslim women in Britain today means that they have particular needs in relation to healthcare and maternity services. These needs often require the support of a religiously knowledgeable Muslim (preferably a woman), who can advise both the hospital and the patient (and her family) with regard to such things as: facilities for prayer within the hospital (especially for visiting male relatives), ways of accommodating medication regimes with requests to observe Ramadan fasts, or religious support following the loss of a baby or foetus (and the need to dispose of these losses according to Islamic law through burial, rather than cremation). Managing these kinds of very real issues and needs requires hospital managers to make complex judgements about facilities, personnel and other resources, informed by budgetary constraints and legal requirements. Likewise, Muslim chaplains themselves have to find ways of making the fulfilment of the *shari'a* possible within the frameworks and norms of a public institution, and this often requires an ability to make contextually appropriate, flexible and sometimes very rapid interpretations of Islamic legal principles.

The decisions that hospital managers make are not made in a socio-political vacuum, however. They are shaped by such things as local politics, the lobbying power of local 'community leaders' and the possible anxieties of hospital staff or chaplains of other faiths, who may be concerned by what they might regard as the undue attention to, or accommodation of, Muslim needs. Where these anxieties exist, they are of course a reflection of the increasing public visibility and 'politicization' of Islam in Britain which in many ways started during the Rushdie Affair. However, as the Introduction and Chapter 1 in this volume show, subsequent events (such as the London bombings in July 2005) have only served to increase concerns in some quarters about the multicultural, multi-faith character of British society, largely regarded as a consequence of an increasing Muslim population in particular. But by the same token, the agency and capacity of Muslims in Britain to respond to the challenges of living as a religious minority in the UK, so clearly evident in the concrete reality of engagement with public institutions like hospitals, reflects internal and organic processes of change that have been taking place in recent decades.

The place of chaplaincy in public institutions indicates that the religious framework of British society has provided both the opportunity, and the necessity, for Muslim religious professionals to expand their role beyond the confines of mosques and Islamic centres.[11] Although there is a long history of what might be called 'pastoral care' in Islam, this has never been especially formal, and it has certainly never been institutionalized. However, there is a strong tradition of formal chaplaincy in Christianity, and many British public institutions have been employing a Christian chaplain for centuries. The context of contemporary Britain has therefore resulted in the growing incorporation of Muslims into chaplaincy work, and with it the development of an entirely new role within the Islamic tradition.

This development is not merely a consequence of the synergy between Islamic traditions and the religious framework of British society, however. It is also a reflection of a valued and self-confident religious identity among many (young) British Muslims themselves. Many of them are concerned to protect and maintain that identity in daily life, especially in their dealings with public institutions. Consequently, the observance of appropriate Islamic gender roles has become increasingly important, and, in relation to health and childbirth, a Muslim woman with appropriate religious knowledge is often best placed to provide pastoral care to her 'sisters'. As an outcome of the efforts that British Muslim women have been making to support and empower one another (for example, through local religious study circles), there are now a growing number of women able to take up the newly created opportunities that exist for them as 'Muslim chaplains' in Britain.

The example of chaplaincy also illuminates another important reality about the growth and development of Muslim communities in Britain, and that is the disjuncture between lived reality and mainstream media portrayal (see Chapter 7 for further discussion of Islam in the British media). The actual reality of life as a Muslim in Britain today is typically concerned with issues surrounding birth and death, the acquisition of knowledge both in mainstream and religious institutions, supporting family life and young children, and finding employment in a difficult economic climate. However, the preoccupations of politicians and the mainstream media in relation to Muslims are typically centred around 'terrorism', 'violent extremism' or the supposed 'oppression' of Muslim women who are presumed to be lacking in freedoms relating to dress, movement or sexuality. Without denying the reality of religious extremism among a minority of British Muslims, or the lack of freedom that some Muslim women may suffer, what political assumptions and media stereotypes fail to recognize are the structural and economic issues that affect British Muslims (and especially women) far more, such as poor-quality overcrowded accommodation, educational underachievement or access to equitable healthcare.

British Muslims have, unwillingly, seen themselves become the subject of public debate and a focus for social and security policy in British society as a result of local, national and global events. The decisions they make on a whole range of issues are public, in a way that is far less evident in other faith communities in Britain. British Muslims are 'increasingly subject to a forced telling of the self in UK public life' (Archer 2009: 88). However uncomfortable this may be, the 'spotlight' does also provide opportunities to inhabit a wider canvas and influence an emerging social agenda in Britain. The new and growing involvement of Muslim women in publicly funded chaplaincy provides a good example of ways in which this is now starting to happen in towns and cities across the country. It is also an example of how the presence of Muslims in Britain, far from diminishing existing traditions (such as chaplaincy), often serves to bring to them new dimensions and possibilities.

The gradual involvement of Muslims in publicly funded chaplaincy in Britain is also an indicator of an increasingly outward-facing, proactive involvement in civil society and public institutions more generally. The way in which Muslims are now part of multi-faith chaplaincy teams (and in some cases the most senior chaplain in the institution) is also reflected in the degree to which they contribute to and lead the business, economic, political, cultural, sporting and religious life of the country. There is now greater capacity for engagement in civil society, in multi-faith and interfaith initiatives, and a willingness to see that, to some extent, faith communities will flourish or decline together in a society widely termed 'secular'.

However, it is important to note that for many British Muslims, the supposedly binary categories 'religious' and 'secular' are not especially meaningful in relation to their own religious practice. Given the degree to which Islam provides guiding principles and teachings in relation to so many aspects of life (from how to pray, to how to distribute inheritance), even the most apparently mundane daily activities (such as preparing food, or going on a journey) can be transformed into opportunities for worship and spiritual reflection. However, many Muslims in Britain, like members of other faiths, share an awareness of the degree to which a religious worldview and an awareness of the Divine can be undermined by aggressive consumerism, materialism and selfish individualism.

Looking to the future

As will be clear from the discussions thus far, the character of Muslim communities in Britain has been shaped by numerous different socio-economic and political factors, including the legacies of British colonialism. Migration histories and settlement patterns have often had a determining influence upon the relative strength of different Muslim communities and various 'schools of thought' in particular parts of the UK. An awareness of this is important for considering possible future trends and developments. For example, the consequence of large numbers of Gujaratis settling in Leicester in the 1970s (as a result of their expulsion from Uganda by Idi Amin), means that the Deobandi school of thought is particularly strong in this city. This contrasts with the predominance of Pakistanis (especially from rural Mirpur) in northern towns and cities such as Bradford or Oldham. As a result, those schools of thought that might be regarded as especially sympathetic to Sufi traditions have a strong presence in these northern areas. Large numbers of Muslims from the Middle East, Africa and the Far East (e.g. Malaysia) give the Muslim population of London a particularly multicultural, cosmopolitan character and, consequently, Muslims who are sympathetic to the international 'Islamic Movement' (e.g. the Muslim Brotherhood, or the Jamaat-i-Islami) are well represented here. As a result of these important regional variations, the findings of research conducted with British Muslims in one city cannot necessarily be generalized further afield, because of the distinctiveness of Muslim communities in particular places in the UK. So far, no research has been conducted which might indicate the relative strength of different Islamic schools of thought in Britain, but an evaluation of the size and school of thought for different mosques in various cities would provide an indication.

Having stressed the significance of regional variation in the character of Muslim communities in Britain, it is clear that today many young British-born Muslims share the quest for Islamic knowledge beyond their immediate locality. Networks of international Islamic scholars whose teachings are accessible via online resources (e.g. IslamiCity.com), TV channels (e.g. the Islam Channel) and blogs are democratizing knowledge, and making Islamic teaching widely available globally. The means by which these sources are accessed are distinctly individualized and personalized (from iPhone to Facebook), but, at the same time, their content is often conservative, textual and 'traditional' in many ways. It is the pursuit of relatively conservative, scriptural Islamic teaching via new forms of internationally available information technology that perhaps makes the religious orientation of many young British Muslims distinctive. This contrasts with their parents and grandparents who often relied almost entirely upon the religious authority of local teachers and scholars associated with their kinship networks rooted in particular places (mostly the Indian subcontinent).

There is today a greater awareness among young British Muslims about the diversity that exists within Islamic communities, both in Britain and further afield. The exact consequences of this awareness are difficult to predict. But it seems likely that, in future, the most successful trends and traditions within Muslim communities in Britain will be those that have the human, economic and technological capital to provide 'authentic' Islamic teachings in ways that chime with the spirit of personal choice that characterizes the religious worldview of many young British Muslims.

Key terms

Deobandi: A conservative Islamic reform movement established in India in the nineteenth century in the context of British colonial rule.

Hadith: The sayings of the Prophet Muhammad.

Halal: Means 'lawful' or 'permitted' – often used to refer to meat or foods that are 'lawful' for Muslims to consume.

Jamaat-i Islami: A South Asian Islamic reform movement established by Maulana Mawdudi in 1941 in India.

Shari'a: Literally means 'way to water' but refers to the Divine laws and principles that guide all aspects of human life and flourishing.

Sunna: The actions or example of the Prophet Muhammad.

Umma: Means 'community' or 'nation' and refers to the worldwide community of Muslims.

Further reading

Gilliat-Ray, Sophie (2010). *Muslims in Britain: An Introduction*. Cambridge: Cambridge University Press. This textbook about Muslims in Britain covers history, migration patterns, institutions and contemporary issues, and offers a comprehensive introduction (and bibliography).

Halliday, Fred (2010). *Britain's First Muslims: Portrait of an Arab Community*. London: I. B. Tauris. Based on empirical research conducted from the 1970s onwards, this book tells the story of early Yemeni Muslim seafaring communities in Cardiff, South Shields and Liverpool, and explores the lives of industrial workers in Sheffield, Birmingham and Manchester.

Hopkins, Peter and Richard Gale (eds) (2009). *Muslims in Britain: Race, Place and Identities.* Edinburgh: Edinburgh University Press. The essays by geographers of religion in this collection explore how Muslims negotiate their daily experiences within homes and localities, and how religious identities are shaped by gender, class and ethnicity as well as transnational connections and mobilities.

Hussain, Serena (2008). *Muslims on the Map: A National Survey of Social Trends in Britain.* London: I. B. Tauris. Based on analysis of 2001 Census data in relation to the socio-economic situation of British Muslims, this was the first study to examine in detail the demography of Muslim communities, and their housing, educational and employment circumstances.

Mondal, Anshuman (2008). *Young British Muslim Voices.* Oxford: Greenwood World Publishing. Examines the views of a number of young male and female British Muslims from different ethnic and cultural backgrounds and from different social classes, and gives a valuable insight into the concerns, opinions and fears of those interviewed.

Hinduism

John Zavos

British colonial domination of South Asia provides an important historical context not only for understanding Sikhism and Islam in Britain, but also Hinduism. British Hindus are diverse in terms of region of origin (although Gujaratis form the majority), pattern of migration and settlement, caste status, language use and religious practice. Data from the 2001 Census demonstrates that the Hindu population is generally economically secure and well qualified. The development of temples and other community institutions has occurred both through local community organization and through the intervention of transnational devotional organizations. A broad ecumenical profile is developing in British Hinduism, but eclectic devotional practices are sustained in both home and temple environments, with women playing a prominent role. The twenty-first century has witnessed the development of a more assertive Hindu identity in Britain, associated with emerging representative groups that claim to encompass internal diversity and the establishment of a range of spectacular purpose-built temples (see Plate 3.3).

As with most of the other traditions and communities covered in this chapter, Hinduism and Hindus in Britain are deeply implicated in the historical development of the region of the world known as South Asia: that which is today constituted by the independent states of India, Pakistan, Bangladesh, Nepal, Sri Lanka, Bhutan and the Maldives. What we today recognize as Hindu traditions have developed as an integral feature of the socio-cultural landscape of this region over the past three millennia at least. This South Asian context is one of the principal reasons why Hinduism is now part of the narrative of growing religious diversity in Britain, as this is a part of the world which was profoundly affected by British colonial control.

For about two centuries leading up to the late 1940s, various manifestations of British economic and political power were highly influential in the transitional processes which produced South Asian modernity. Increased mobilities – of capital, goods, ideas and of course people – were a major feature of these processes. The colonial period provided the catalyst for major flows of people across the network of the British Empire, in the first

instance through systems of indentured labour and through engagement in the infrastructures which held this vast network together, such as the armed forces and merchant
fleets. As processes of decolonization were effected in the post-war era, this form of mobility was augmented by increasingly voluntaristic migration, as Commonwealth citizens
sought to engage in capital accumulation practices via sojourns in Britain and elsewhere.
For many, this gradually translated into permanent residence (as above, in relation to
Sikhism and Islam). These deep historical connections, then, provide a backdrop and
framework for understanding the presence of Hindus and Hinduism in contemporary
Britain.

Colonial ramifications

During the colonial period, Hinduism was commonly recognized as the 'default' religion of
the Indian subcontinent, increasingly known through the work of powerful agents – orien-
talist scholars, Christian missionaries, Census enumerators – engaged in the business of
Empire. Some authors even argue that the ideological and institutional structures of what
we understand as Hinduism in the modern era were produced by the collusion of particular
British and Indian social groups (Frykenberg 1993). It is certainly the case that modern
Hinduism emerged in a highly competitive atmosphere, fuelled by the critical approach of
Christian missionaries who frequently characterized Hinduism as idolatrous, polytheistic
and socially oppressive (see Oddie 2006). Although such depictions were countered by
scholars and practitioners (and even some missionaries) from the nineteenth century
onwards, they nevertheless maintained a degree of resonance in Britain. Robert Jackson
(also a contributor to this volume, see Chapter 8) has noted, for example, that Hinduism
was described in a secondary school religious education syllabus adopted in a variety of UK
local authorities in the 1940s as a 'gross polytheism with crude conceptions of its gods and
a rigid caste system' (Jackson 1987: 205). Of course, representations have changed a good
deal since then, but the residue of such colonial caricatures has impacted on the ways that
Hindus themselves seek to represent their religion in Britain.

The competitive atmosphere of the colonial period also encouraged a kind of self-
conscious 'opening out' of Hindu ideas to the world, on the basis that values such as
tolerance, universalism and spirituality are specifically Hindu, but have a global significance, and are globally applicable, regardless of the constraints of *dharma* with which they
may be traditionally associated in India (Halbfass 1992: 51–55). This opening out is sometimes characterized as 'neo-Hinduism', and during the late colonial and postcolonial periods
a number of organizations emerged along these lines. The classic example is provided by
Swami Vivekananda's Ramakrishna Mission, established in 1897 with the twin objectives
of offering spiritual succour and social service in a modern, spiritually impoverished world.
This was a well-managed organization with a vision of global expansion. It became the first
Hindu organization to have an active presence in Britain, a mission centre being established
in London in 1935 (Burghart 1987: 6).

Although the Ramakrishna Mission has remained relatively marginal in Britain,
modern expansionist organizations on the Ramakrishna Mission model have become a
feature of the religious landscape. Significantly, the activities of some of these organizations were, in the first instance, directed primarily at the white population, rather than
the South Asian migrant population. In particular, they met with some success in the
context of the wave of counter-cultural ideas and practices which characterized youth
culture in the late 1960s (see Chapter 10 on 'Cultural perspectives'). Prominent in this

success was the International Society for Krishna Consciousness (ISKCON – also known as the 'Hare Krishnas'), a form of Vaishnavite devotionalism focused on Krishna and developed out of the ideas of the sixteenth-century Bengali *sant* Chaitanya. Having first established a presence in New York, the organization's guru Swami Prabhupada established a small temple in London's Soho in 1969, which became the focal point for the public-chanting and bookselling activities of its devotees or *bhaktas* (Nye 2001: 11). Association with media icons such as the Beatles augmented the organization's public profile. At the same time, because of its sudden emergence, and its initial emphasis on the recruitment of full-time devotees, ISKCON was often categorized – along with a whole series of organizations which emerged during this period, based on a range of religious traditions – as a New Religious Movement or even a worrisome 'cult'. Again, this projection has impacted on the cultural meanings of Hinduism in Britain, and so on the ways in which Hindus emerged as a self-conscious, publicly recognizable group of religious practitioners in the country.

Demography and socio-economic profile

The 2001 Census data records the Hindu population of Britain as 558,342, about 1 per cent of the total population and just over 18 per cent of the non-Christian religious population.[12] Hindus are overwhelmingly of South Asian heritage,[13] although this statement disguises a high degree of diversity. In terms of place of birth, 37 per cent of Hindus recorded that they had been born in the UK – a much lower figure than, for example, the Muslim population (46 per cent). Thirty per cent were born in India, and, of the remainder, 21 per cent were born in East Africa, 6 per cent in Sri Lanka and about 3 per cent in areas such as Pakistan and the Caribbean. The influence of colonial history in these figures is clear. Many East African and Caribbean Hindus are descendants of that earlier wave of migration associated with colonialism, the indentured labour system. Many others had settled as traders in these places when they were part of the British Empire. Those born in Pakistan may well have seen their families disrupted by the partition of India which accompanied the transition to Independence in 1947 (see Raj 2003: 53–75). Most Sri Lankan-born Hindus are Tamil refugees, fleeing the Sri Lankan civil war, and this group offers a counterpoint to the major cultural identities associated with UK Hinduism, identities linked primarily to the two regions of Punjab and Gujarat.[14] It is estimated that in 1991 some 70 per cent of Hindus in Britain were Gujarati speaking, as against 15 per cent Punjabi speaking (Vertovec 2000: 88).

In addition to these regional variations, there is also a high degree of social differentiation among Hindus in Britain based around caste identities. Amongst Gujaratis in particular, these identities remain influential in various aspects of social networking, especially marriage.[15] Caste groups among Gujarati Hindus in Britain tend to be trading castes (*Banias*), which have a relatively high social status in Gujarat. These groups have become influential forces in the development of institutional Hinduism in the UK, as they seek to demonstrate ritual purity through investment in temples and sect-specific organizations (Dwyer 1994). In addition, there are a significant number of low-caste groups in the UK, largely from either Gujarat or Punjab again.[16] For some of these groups, the epithet 'Hindu' is not always appropriate, as their practices and identities sometimes cut across normative religious boundaries (Leslie 2003: 64–74).

TEXT BOX 9

Unity and diversity of Hinduism in Britain

It is very difficult to encapsulate the internal diversity of Hinduism, even among the relatively small population in Britain. Part of this difficulty derives from the many varied traditions associated with different teachers (*sampradayas* and *guru* traditions), the interweaving of ritual practice with caste identity, the strength of regional modes of devotional worship and language-based traditions, and the tendency for individuals to explore and develop their own approaches. As these variables suggest, the difficulty also arises partly out of the conceptual issue of identifying what, exactly, is outside and what is inside such a diverse set of traditions. The work of Eleanor Nesbitt (e.g. Nesbitt 2004) on Sikhs, Hindus and low castes in the Midlands exemplifies this point.

In general terms, we can point to the idea of 'sanatana dharma' as significant in identifying a mainstream or composite form of British Hinduism. This idea is invoked in the name of many British Hindu temples. It is often translated as 'eternal religion', and in the UK is used to refer to a general devotional Hinduism, in which major deities such as Krishna, Radha, Ganesh, Ram and Sita are propitiated, alongside a philosophical emphasis on Vedanta. This general ecumenical approach, however, can often exist alongside more clearly sectarian and regionally specific traditions. It is apparent, for example, at the famous Neasden temple in north London, even though this temple is the UK headquarters of a very particular Gujarati organization, the Bochasanwasi Shri Akshar Purushottam Swaminarayan Sanstha, which views Bhagwan Swaminarayan as the supreme divine Lord.

Like most South Asian migrants, Hindus are an overwhelmingly urban population, and more than 50 per cent live in London itself. On the figures of the 2001 Census, the three London boroughs of Brent, Harrow and Ealing are home to approximately 110,000 Hindus, more than one-fifth of the overall Hindu population. Other major centres of Hindu population are Leicester in the East Midlands (41,000), Barnet in East London (21,000) and Birmingham in the West Midlands (19,000). In comparison to Sikh and Muslim groups, a high proportion of Hindu males are employed in professional or managerial positions, and a very low proportion are unemployed (Office for National Statistics 2004: 13). Similarly, a comparatively high number of Hindus between the ages of 16 and 30 hold a degree, and nearly three-quarters of households own their own home. In short, this is a population which is comparatively well off, and as a significant report on the status of British Hindus proclaimed, 'the contribution of Hindu individuals to business and wealth creation in the UK has never been quantified but it is clear that there are many industrialists and business-men and -women from Hindu communities that have made a significant contribution … Similarly in other professions such as medicine, accountancy and the law there are many members of Hindu communities making a significant contribution' (Runnymede Trust 2006: 19).

The Organization of Hindu Britain

In a similar way to Sikhs and Muslims, early communities of predominantly male Hindu migrants clustered in areas close to employment opportunities, and institutional developments within the community were more likely to have a regional than religious or caste focus (see, for example, Bowen 1987; Josephides 1991). In the 1970s and 1980s, more culturally defined organizations began to emerge. Two factors were important. First, chain migration led to many family and kinship groups being gradually reconstituted in Britain, resulting in the development of what Roger Ballard calls 'ethnic colonies' or 'desh pardesh', that is, 'homes away from home' (Ballard 1994: 15–16). As these family-based communities were established, cultural practices were increasingly perceived as an affirmative feature of their presence in the new locality. Second, the influx of 'twice migrants' from East Africa in the late 1960s and early 1970s was significant, as they were already skilled urban operators, with a strong sense of cultural distinctiveness honed in the minority context of East Africa (as with Sikh migrants from the same area, see earlier). One way in which this manifested itself was in strong traditions of caste identification and temple attendance, especially among the large number of Gujarati Hindus in this group.

These factors, then, encouraged the establishment of organizations which consolidated and projected specific identities. Low-caste *Valmiki* organizations in areas such as Southall, Wolverhampton and Coventry were established fairly early, perhaps reflecting the 'double exclusion' experienced by these communities in the UK (Nesbitt 1994: 127, and see the discussion of Sikhism above). Another, very different example of this kind of caste-based initiative was the Federation of Patidar Associations, which brought together six smaller-scale Patidar associations in north London in 1976. Just two years after this, the National Council of Hindu Temples (NCHT) was established. The NCHT is the first of several explicitly Hindu 'umbrella'-style organizations to be set up in Britain. From its inception, it operated primarily as a resource for, and a means of, representing the burgeoning number of small temples being established in localities across urban Britain. These temples, which during this period were almost exclusively housed in existing public buildings such as deconsecrated churches and ex-primary schools, were of two main kinds. First, temples where regionalized practices were brought together in a kind of compromise arrangement, incorporating deities and temple practices associated with different traditions. Kim Knott's study of the Hindu Charitable Trust temple in Leeds is a key example of this type of development. She describes how Gujaratis of a variety of castes (including low-caste *Mochis*) and Punjabis came together to establish the Trust, and traces the way in which 'Temple religion … changed to suit its new social and geographical location' through 'a process of standardization, selecting key "national" festivals and daily and weekly rituals, serving major deities and acknowledging the early texts' (Knott 1986: 231). Second, sect-specific temples continued to develop. In particular, neo-Hindu organizations such as ISKCON, and the Gujarat-based Swaminarayan *sampradaya*, which had an established presence in East Africa, expanded in key urban areas.

The NCHT provided an institutional forum for both these types of temple, and some mutually beneficial collaborations resulted. This is illustrated in the NCHT introductory booklet on Hinduism, which claims the authority of 'those who know it best – not the scholars or the mystics, but the people who practise it as a daily way of life' (National Council of Hindu Temples 1983). The booklet, then, projects the power and significance of 'ordinary' Hindus associated with localized 'composite temples', where forms of worship and other aspects of temple life are negotiated by locally prominent members of different communities. At the same time, the pamphlet projects a *bhakti*-orientated, Vaishnavite Hinduism, in which the influence of ISKCON is quite evident; in fact, it quotes directly from Swami Prabhupada's *Bhagavad-Gita As It Is*, the key ISKCON text. This reflects the influence of ISKCON on the NCHT, as the relatively sophisticated, transnational infrastructure of the former was able to provide institutional and other material resources to assist the NCHT in its development. In turn, the NCHT provided ISKCON – still struggling to shed its post-sixties 'cultish' image – with legitimacy as a recognizable form of Hinduism, the Hinduism, as it were, of the 'ordinary' Hindu.

Practising Hinduism in Britain

What then constitutes the ordinary practice of Hinduism in Britain? Temples certainly play a significant role. As well as being a place to offer *puja* (see Key terms below), they act as 'a social and political space used to meet other people, to meet friends, to educate children and in some cases to meet prospective marriage partners' (Raj 2003: 91). Practising Hinduism, then, is often a process which combines ritual and spiritual practice with other aspects of community identity. Indeed, it may also connect Hindus with other religions. This can be seen in some temple situations, particularly low-caste ones (Nesbitt 1994), and also in the everyday, informal practices of Hindus in the UK. For example, Raj observes that Hindus frequently attend and donate to local gurdwaras, and also that in the home shrines/altars are often marked by a syncretic collection of symbols and images, such as the Christian cross and Guru Nanak (see earlier, section on Sikhism). Such approaches reflect an eclectic approach to religiosity in the home environment, as demonstrated in Raj's ethnographic account:

> In many of the houses I visited, people kept their *mandir* in the kitchen cupboard ... The door to this cupboard stays slightly ajar, or may be made of glass. More recently, as their children leave their parental homes, some families are dedicating entire rooms to a home temple ... All deities are present ... pictures of gurus that the family currently follows or has followed in the past are represented as well ... Day-to-day activities at home vary. Some women told me that they performed a variety of rituals. The form and duration of these depended on whether the woman was working and the age of her children ... There are other forms of domestic devotion ... Watching religious videos, such as the Mahabharat or Ramayan, or Bollywood films with a religious theme, falls into this category, as does listening to religious tapes of *bhajans*, *kirtan* or lectures either at home or in the car ... Increasingly, religious symbolism is incorporated into more general patterns of personal consumption.
>
> (Raj 2003: 96–97)

One notable aspect of this evolving, adaptive practice is the prominent role that women play. Where Raj notes this in the home environment, it is also evident in small, less visible temple environments. For example, Ann David examines practices in the East Ham Sakthi Peetham, a small temple in a converted house dedicated to Goddess Adhiparasakthi. This Tamil devotional tradition has been vigorously pursued by Sri Lankan Tamil women in London, and, as the tradition is established, 'the female devotees no longer remain simply participants, but are transformed into religious specialists and leaders of ritual' (David 2009: 337). David suggests that this capacity to innovate is in some ways a result of the extension of the home environment in the temple, fashioned in the particular social conditions of the diaspora. 'Temples,' she says, 'are providing an extension of the domestic sphere for diasporic groups, offering a committed community of worshipers and ritual practice in a situation where the extended family is not physically present to take care of essential life rituals' (David 2009: 343).

Thus religion in the diaspora can challenge established understandings of religion mentioned in the Introduction to this book; both the idea that there are discrete religious traditions, and that there is a clear division between the public and the private. Although in the context of East London we may note the relative invisibility of the Sakthi Peetham in an undistinguished converted house, in another sense this is a very broad kind of public space. As David notes, it connects with Tamil communities in Tamil Nadu (location of the 'parent' temple from which this tradition originates, in the village of Melmuravathur) in Sri Lanka, and in other areas of Europe where Tamil refugees are based. Hindu practices in Britain are frequently part of complex transnational networks, developing a sense of Hindu consciousness which transgresses the idea of a 'settled' UK Hinduism.

One interesting resource for examining these dynamics is social networking sites such as YouTube. Transnationalism is of course a key feature here. For example, one prominent way in which Hinduism in the UK manifests itself on YouTube is in the recording of small-scale *puja* practices among students and other sojourner groups, seeking a connection with a sense of 'home'. These videos are often accompanied by approving comment on the way in which the participants have maintained their tradition, or critical comment on practices, which may be strongly rebuffed. Such material reminds us of the ways in which different South Asian religious identities are negotiated in the complex webs of transnational networks.

Being British Hindus

Puja practices which make their way on to YouTube are often related to festival occasions such as Diwali. Indeed, a search for UK Diwali *puja* on YouTube brings up not just the home and small-scale celebrations noted above, but also large, spectacular Diwali celebrations held each year on the Belgrave Road in Leicester, and the celebrations held at the Houses of Parliament, organized by the Hindu Forum of Britain. These latter are indicative of an emerging sense of British Hinduism, a dominant, composite identity marked by certain major symbols, festivals, buildings and organizations. The idea is perhaps most consciously projected by the major umbrella organizations which seek to represent Hindus and Hinduism in relation to national discourses. We have already referred to the National Council of Hindu Temples. The Hindu Council UK, established in 1994, and the Hindu Forum of Britain, established in 2004, are two more recent organizations which enthusiastically project this image (see also Zavos 2009).

How has this distinctive sense of British Hindu-ness emerged? Various factors have been involved since the late 1980s. Principal among these have been the dynamics of community formation among Hindus themselves, the role of the state and the role of powerful transnational organizations. We have already noted the development of temple worship and the emergence of caste-based organizations in the 1970s and 1980s. Such organizations were frequently courted by local authorities as they sought to demonstrate a commitment to multiculturalism (Baumann 1998). We have also noted the role that ISKCON in particular played during the 1980s in encouraging a certain degree of organization, and indeed theological coherence, through its influence in the NCHT. ISKCON remains a major force. Indeed, during the late 1980s and early 1990s, it fashioned a position very much at the centre of emerging ideas of British Hindu-ness, through a developing campaign to preserve communal worship at its major UK site, Bhaktivedanta Manor, in Hertfordshire, north of London.

The rural location and quality of worship at this site meant that it became a popular destination for Hindus living in north London, particularly during festival occasions. This

popularity, however, led ISKCON into a protracted planning dispute with the local authority over the use of the site for public worship. Malory Nye's work on this dispute
demonstrates how it was an instrumental factor in the development of Hindu identity in
Britain (Nye 2001 and in this volume). In particular, he charts the public campaign which
developed a national profile in the early 1990s. Direct action campaigns aimed at mobilizing Hindus in support of ISKCON's position were complemented by political and media
campaigns – that is, strategies focused on lobbying political and other prominent national
figures, and on explaining the case for the Manor in a range of media outlets. ISKCON
argued that preventing public worship at the Manor was against the spirit of tolerance associated with a multicultural society, and that minorities had a right to practise their religion
in such a context. This carefully managed campaign raised the profile of Hindus as a recognizable community within the logic of multicultural Britain, a community with 'rights'
based on their religious practices which were legitimately defendable in public contexts.

This significant development was supported by other Hindu organizations, including the
Hindu nationalist Vishwa Hindu Parishad (VHP). This organization had in fact been established in the UK as far back as 1969, but worked very much in local contexts until the late
1980s/early 1990s. The VHP is part of a much larger network of organizations in India
known as the Sangh Parivar, the 'family of organizations' all linked in one way or another
to the assertively Hindu Rashtriya Swayamsevak Sangh (RSS).[17] The links between the
Indian Sangh Parivar and the UK VHP network are indicated by the fact that the latter
came more to national prominence in response to the political concerns of the Indian
movement. In particular, 1989 witnessed the organization of the so-called Virat Hindu
Sammelan, a major gathering of Hindus at Milton Keynes Bowl over a two-day period. The
agenda at this gathering was very much geared towards gaining support for the developing
campaign in India around a mosque site in the pilgrimage town of Ayodhya in Uttar
Pradesh, claimed by the Sangh as the birthplace of the Hindu god-king Ram.

As this suggests, the VHP's ability to galvanize support in Britain has often been tied to
a particular, antagonistic approach towards Muslims. This point was again demonstrated in
the wake of the intense communal violence which took place in Gujarat in 2002, when
many UK Hindus rallied to support the VHP in the face of extreme criticism of the Sangh
Parivar and its culpability for the violence. As these examples show, Indian politics has in
recent years been one spur to the development of Hindu identity in the UK. Wider politics
have also played their part. Antagonistic attitudes towards Muslims in Britain have risen in
the context of the Rushdie Affair, 9/11, and international military campaigns in Iraq and
Afghanistan. This antagonism has played itself out among Indians as much as among other
parts of the UK population, particularly since many UK families of Indian heritage have
well-hewn memories of the partition of India and the subsequent wars between India and
Pakistan.

One associated development here has been an emerging semi-formal campaign against
the established identity marker 'Asian'. This marker has been a means of identifying those
of South Asian descent in the UK since the 1970s influx of South Asians from East Africa.
From the late 1990s, the VHP and related organizations in the UK have argued strongly that
this way of identifying South Asians should be replaced by more particular markers, especially markers of religious identity. Into the twenty-first century, this approach has
undoubtedly spread wider than the Sangh.[18] Indeed, a tendency to reject the term 'Asian'
was noted in a government-sponsored report prepared by the Runnymede Trust in collaboration with the Hindu Forum of Britain, *Connecting British Hindus* (Runnymede Trust 2006).
This report presented a number of findings about Hindus in Britain, on the basis of an

online survey and focus groups run by the Forum. The rejection of the term 'Asian' in favour of 'Hindu' was recorded as running at about 75 per cent in the online survey. At the same time, there was a high degree of ambivalence recorded in the focus groups about the suitability of the term Hindu as marking a distinct community in Britain, and a lower figure (66 per cent) was recorded among the 20–24 age group. This lower figure reflects a familiar concern among minority groups – highlighted above in relation to Judaism – that their distinct identity is being eroded through the generations. The report goes on to reiterate this concern, noting that a shift to smaller, more nuclear patterns of family organization impacts on the development of Hinduism, as transmission of ideas and practices in the home are particularly important in this tradition. Vigorous community action is recommended to counter the effects of this trend. Similar conclusions are drawn in a survey of Hindu youth conducted in 2001.[19] The survey reports positive attitudes towards practising their religion among this group, alongside concern about the transmission of knowledge. As the survey authors report, 'although Hindu youth feel a strong personal sense of community, they also feel Hindus need to work together more in order to gain greater recognition in British society and better resources for their own community'.

The call for community action reflects a new assertive tendency, as demonstrated by a series of campaigns over the past ten years or so to protect the image of Hinduism in various media contexts. Again, ISKCON has played a significant role, suing the House of Fraser chain of department stores in 2002 after it published an advertisement for a clothes range which implied that members of the *sampradaya* were 'chanting, cymbal-banging, easily-led nutcase(s)' (see Zavos 2008: 330). A light-hearted reference to the familiar sight of Hare Krishna devotees dancing and singing their way through the shopping mecca of Oxford Street in central London may have worked in the early 1970s, when ISKCON was viewed primarily as a cultish new religious movement (see Chapter 1). However, by the early twenty-first century ISKCON had been thoroughly 'Hinduised' (Nye 2001) and professionalized through its experience of the campaign to save public worship at Bhaktivedanta Manor. Its defamation claim was upheld, and House of Fraser was forced to pay heavy damages.

This campaign, celebrated at the time by the President of NCHT as 'the first time the British Hindu community have won a legal case against ridicule' (see Zavos 2008: 330), was followed by a whole series of campaigns to protect the image of Hinduism against, for example, pictures of deities on tissues, shoes and women's underwear; against a *Guardian* newspaper columnist's light-hearted approach to Hindu asceticism; and against the use of a statue of Ganesh, the elephant-headed god, in a threatening manner in the long-running soap opera *Coronation Street*. In each of these cases, the treatment of Hinduism was objected to by one or more representative groups on the basis that it hurt the corporate feelings or sentiments of 'the Hindu community' in Britain (Zavos 2008). Most of these campaigns have achieved some measure of success in terms of the withdrawal of products and/or the issue of an apology. More generally, they have served to concretize the notion of a British Hindu community, even though the parameters of that community remain nebulous and contested.

The state has also been a major factor in the promotion of the idea of a British Hindu community. *Connecting British Hindus*, which was commissioned by the Department for Communities and Local Government, is evidence of that commitment. The report reflects the government's more general concern to accommodate religious identities as mediators of ethnic plurality in Britain, particularly in association with the general policy commitment to community and social cohesion (see Chapter 9 in this volume). The Hindu Forum has been a major beneficiary of this concern, as it has provided Hindu representation on key government initiatives such as the Commission on Integration and Cohesion (2006–2007), and the 'Faith Advisers' appointed by Communities and Local Government Secretary John Denham in January 2010. The Forum provides a confident and assertive British Hindu voice in these government arenas, speaking the language of community cohesion and navigating the possibilities provided by the newly emerging 'faith relations industry' (see Case study 2 on the Inter Faith Network).

This confidence is also reflected in the emergence of some major new temples in Britain in recent years. The BAPS Swaminarayan temple in Neasden was opened in 1995, and proclaims on its website that it is recognized by *Guinness World Records* as the 'largest traditionally built Hindu stone Mandir in the Western hemisphere'. The Shri Venkateshwara Temple in Birmingham, opened in 2006, has also been proclaimed the 'largest Hindu temple in Europe' by the BBC. The most recent addition to the ranks of major British Hindu temples is the Shree Sanatan Mandir in Wembley, opened by the Shri Vallabh Nidhi UK Charitable Trust in the summer of 2010. Like the Neasden temple, the Shree Sanatan Mandir is associated with the Gujarati community in the UK, and its impressive façade represents the influence of this community in the representation of British Hinduism. Despite this particularity, its profile is as an 'all-inclusive' temple, housing images not just of 'all saints from our faith', but also 'saints from other faiths', such as Guru Nanak and Mother Theresa,[20] reflecting the move towards ecumenism which has been a consistent feature of British Hinduism since the 1980s. A further major recent development has been the opening in 2009 of the first voluntary-aided Hindu faith school in Harrow, north London, the Krishna Avanti primary school. This school presents itself as based on 'Vaishnava values', Vaishnavism being articulated as 'one of four main strands within Hinduism'.[21] The 'faith partner' for this venture is ISKCON, reflecting again the leading role that this distinctive, theistic *sampradaya* has played in the fashioning of British Hinduism.

Together these two recent developments – the Shree Sanatan Mandir in Wembley and the Krishna Avanti primary school – demonstrate key influences in the development of a modern British Hinduism. It is projected as a distinct British religion, representative both of diasporic theological developments and of the particular communities which have dominated the emergence of the UK Hindu community. Although there are certainly other vigorous developments in the emerging idea of British Hinduism, these symbols of twenty-first-century British Hinduism reflect a process of continuous development in the post-war era.

Key terms

Bhakti: Devotion (*bhakta* = devotee).

Dharma: Order – ritual, cosmic, social; duties, correct social behaviour.

Diwali: Festival of Lights, occurring each autumn; variously associated with gods Rama and Krishna and goddess Lakshmi.

Mandir: Shrine or temple.

Puja: Worship, either at home or in a temple.

Sampradaya: Literally something which is handed down; the teaching of a particular tradition; the teaching tradition itself.

'*Sant*': 'saint'; especially of those in various north Indian traditions which emphasized devotion to a Lord without qualities (*nirgun bhakti*); grouped together as 'the Sant tradition'.

Further reading

Ballard, Roger (ed.) (1994). *Desh Pardesh: The South Asian Experience in Britain.* London: Hurst. Includes a useful introduction on patterns of settlement and a range of articles by anthropologists and religious studies scholars, several focused on different Hindu groups.

Nye, Malory (2001). *Multiculturalism and Minority Religions in Britain.* Richmond: Curzon. A detailed analysis of ISKCON's campaign to preserve public worship at Bhaktivedanta Manor and its significance.

Raj, Dhooleka (2003). *Where Are You From? Middle-class Migrants in the Modern World.* Berkeley, CA: University of California Press. An ethnographic account of the lives, ideas and attitudes of Hindu Punjabis in north London.

Runnymede Trust (2006). *Connecting British Hindus: An Enquiry into the Identity and Public Engagement of Hindus in Britain.* London: Runnymede Trust/Hindu Forum of Britain. Based on focus group research and an online survey as well as 2001 Census data, this report provides some interesting primary data on Hindus in twenty-first-century Britain.

Vertovec, Steven (2000). *The Hindu Diaspora: Comparative Patterns.* London: Routledge. Placing British Hindus in a broader diasporic perspective, this book nevertheless has plenty of material on Hindus in Britain.

Buddhism

Robert Bluck

There are a number of significant differences between Buddhism and the religions discussed so far in this chapter, and it exemplifies a different – and often much closer – majority–minority relationship. Buddhism did not come to Britain primarily through migration. The first Buddhists in London were white converts rather than the Asian Buddhist immigrants who began to arrive some decades later. 'Convert' and 'ethnic' Buddhists tend to practise their religion in rather different ways (the continuing influence of Buddhism on alternative spirituality in Britain is discussed in the chapter which follows). The process of adaptation has included the growing influence of lay (as opposed to monastic) Buddhists. As this section shows, there is a great deal of additional diversity in British Buddhism, including the differences between Theravada, Tibetan, Zen and other Buddhist traditions. There are also both traditional forms of monasticism and new Buddhist movements. In many ways Buddhism does not fit neatly into the category of 'religion' at all: as well as being highly diverse, it is mainly non-theistic, with teachings to be explored and practised rather than beliefs to be accepted. All this, together with the fact that Buddhism has also tended to be less concerned than other minority traditions in Britain in engaging with the state, means that descriptions of Buddhism as a 'faith community' are problematic. In general Buddhists in Britain focus on spiritual practice rather than on seeking public recognition or making political claims. Although some Buddhists accept being treated as a 'world religion', take part in interfaith bodies and accept the inclusion of Buddhism on religious syllabuses in schools, the discussion shows why the Buddhist 'settlement' in Britain remains importantly different from other examples discussed in this chapter (see also Chapter 4 on alternative spiritualities).

Historical development

Nineteenth-century missionaries and scholars fostered a gradual awareness of Buddhism in the West, sometimes as a romantic oriental tradition whose noble founder and moral precepts had parallels in the New Testament. However, there was little understanding of Buddhist teaching and deep suspicion of its monastic rituals. Victorian conventions also meant there were very few converts in Britain. The early twentieth century saw a gradual move from academic interest towards personal involvement, sponsored by the Buddhist Society in London, with a mainly ethical or intellectual focus on the Buddha's life and teachings, as presented by the Theravada school. The first meditation group was not formed until 1930 and numbers grew slowly. Even by the Second World War, English Buddhists were usually seen as heathens or eccentrics.

In the 1950s there was increasing interest in Zen and Tibetan Buddhism, and the Buddhist Society's journal *The Middle Way* began to discuss the possibility of a 'Western Buddhism'. There were plans to ordain Westerners, though the London Buddhist Vihara opened in 1954 with only Singhalese monks. The first Buddhist Summer Schools took place, and influential books by the scholar and translator Edward Conze and the Society's formidable president Christmas Humphreys encouraged new interest in London and beyond. In 1958 Humphreys claimed that Theravada practitioners, Tibetan ritual and the popularity of Zen had made Buddhism 'an integral part of Western thought' (quoted in Bluck 2006: 10). With only a dozen Buddhist groups in Britain, this seems exaggerated, but it highlights the new emphasis on different schools which developed during the 1960s. Buddhism grew more rapidly as part of Britain's increasing religious pluralism, influenced by both Asian immigration and growth of interest in alternative spirituality – one supporting traditional values and the other promoting innovation (see next chapter on the growth of alternative spirituality). As young people encountered Buddhism on the hippy trail to Asia or at new centres in London and Scotland, the Buddhist Society appeared increasingly conservative.

Following the Chinese occupation of Tibet in 1959, many Tibetans fled to India and beyond, and monks and teachers began to arrive in Britain. The first Tibetan Buddhist centre in Europe was established at Samye Ling in Dumfriesshire in 1967 by two young Tibetan Buddhist teachers, Akong Rinpoche and the controversial Chogyam Trungpa. Their Karma Kagyu school has sought to preserve traditional Tibetan teaching, practice and culture, passing on meditation and devotional practices in a monastic context with ethnic Tibetan teachers.

New Theravada temples opened in London for the Sri Lankan and Thai communities, and the English Theravada monk Sangharakshita returned from India to lead the Hampstead Buddhist Vihara, the first intended for Western monks. However, trustees became alarmed by his unconventional approach and behaviour, and in 1966 he was dismissed. Sangharakshita's response in 1967 was to start his own movement, the Friends of the Western Buddhist Order (FWBO), a conscious attempt to promote teachings and practices appropriate for modern Britain. Sangharakshita selected elements from Theravada and Tibetan traditions and presented them as an essential Western Buddhism shorn of Asian cultural accretions. He ordained core members into a new order which was seen as neither monastic nor lay, emphasizing personal commitment rather than a celibate lifestyle.

During the 1970s the number of lay groups grew to over 100 and four significant new traditions emerged. In 1972 Throssel Hole monastery in Northumberland was founded by Roshi Kennett, an Englishwoman who trained in Japan. This tradition is firmly rooted in

Japanese Soto Zen monasticism and emphasizes *zazen* meditation, moral and compassionate behaviour, and the Buddha nature of all beings. In 1973 the Samatha Trust was formed, following retreats led by a Thai meditation teacher. Local groups of this lay Theravada organization practise structured *samatha* (calmness) meditation (see Text box 10) with individual guidance from teachers, as well as Pali chanting, textual study and discussion. In 1975 Richard Causton became leader of Soka Gakkai International UK, and the movement started to grow rapidly as a lay branch of Japanese Nichiren Shoshu Buddhism, partly through enthusiastic proselytizing. Their central practice is the repeated chanting of *Nammyoho-renge-kyo*, honouring the name of the Lotus Sutra, rather than silent meditation. In 1978 a Western Theravada sangha was finally established at the Hampstead Vihara with the arrival from Thailand of American-born Ajahn Sumedho and three other Western monks. Soon the trustees were able to purchase Chithurst House in Sussex to develop a larger monastery. This Forest Sangha tradition first appeared as a conservative Theravada monasticism, emphasizing both *samatha* and *vipassana* (insight) meditation (see Text box 10), as well as mindfulness and devotional practice, within a social structure little adapted to modern urban Britain.

New Tibetan centres also opened, most significantly in 1976 the Manjushri Institute in Cumbria, a Gelug centre soon led by Geshe Kelsang. He began to operate increasingly independently, resulting in conflict with the international founding organization. The FWBO opened the London Buddhist Centre in Bethnal Green, and began to establish a distinctive pattern of urban centres, right livelihood businesses and single-sex communities.

The 1980s witnessed further expansion. The number of Buddhist groups trebled to around 300, partly due to the growth of Soka Gakkai, which established an impressive national headquarters at Taplow Court in Berkshire. New Theravada temples were opened by Thai and Sri Lankan communities with their own Asian monks; and in 1984 the Forest Sangha established a large monastery at Amaravati in Hertfordshire for Western monks and nuns, with an adjoining lay retreat centre. The FWBO opened further centres and by 1986 there were 300 Order members. In Tibetan Buddhism, Kagyu and Gelug schools were prominent, with a growing community of monastics and lay members at Samye Ling (where a magnificent Tibetan temple was inaugurated in 1988), and a similar expansion at Manjushri.

The fastest growth yet was seen in the 1990s, again linked to continued development within Soka Gakkai. In 1991 the Japanese Nichiren Shoshu priesthood expelled the worldwide lay membership after a dispute, but even this disruption did not slow expansion, and British membership grew to 6,000. Geshe Kelsang returned to Manjushri after a three-year retreat and introduced a more structured teaching regime. In 1991 he founded the New Kadampa tradition, independent of the Gelug school, and the new movement spread rapidly from the Manjushri centre, establishing almost 200 groups in ten years. The New Kadampa emphasizes an unbroken Gelug lineage, yet has no Tibetan followers and sees itself as outside Tibetan Buddhism. It emphasizes the importance of Geshe Kelsang as a spiritual guide, and the development of strong faith, inner peace and compassion through detailed study programmes based on his books. Elsewhere in Tibetan Buddhism, Geshe Tashi arrived at the Jamyang Centre in London, which became the new focus for traditional Gelug teaching. Kagyu Samye Ling had some 30,000 visitors a year, and purchased Holy Island off Arran to develop as an international retreat centre. With new Nyingma and Sakya groups, all four schools of Tibetan Buddhism were represented in Britain.

Other traditions also continued to grow. There was controversy in 1998 with anonymous allegations of abuse within the FWBO; but the number of Order members rose to 500. The Samatha Trust opened a new national centre at Greenestreete in Powys; and 30 Soto Zen groups were affiliated to Throssel Hole. By 2000 there were 16 Theravada viharas in London, Birmingham and other cities, with Asian communities supporting Thai, Sri Lankan or Burmese monks. At Amaravati, the largest of four rural Forest Sangha monasteries, an elegant new temple was opened in 1999, combining Thai and British vernacular architecture.

By the turn of the twenty-first century there were about 1,000 Buddhist groups in almost 30 different sub-traditions, with many independent practitioners as well. The 2001 Census figures suggested there were 152,000 Buddhists in Britain, though the picture given in Table 3.6 may obscure the full picture. As well as the 14,600 'Asian or Asian British' Buddhists there were many Thai, Sri Lankan and Burmese (and some Koreans, Vietnamese and Tibetans) who described themselves as 'Other Ethnic Groups'. There appear to have been about 60,000 white convert Buddhists and over 85,000 with a mainly Asian background (Bluck 2006: 14–16), though the numbers may now be roughly equal. There are also those who include Buddhism within multiple spiritual identities, including both ethnic Chinese and those Quakers, Catholics and adherents of alternative spiritualities who see Buddhist meditation as part of their personal practice.

Table 3.6 Ethnicity of Buddhists in the UK

Ethnicity	Percentage	Numbers
White	38.79	59,000
Mixed	3.22	4,900
Asian or Asian British	9.64	14,600
Black or Black British	1.04	1,600
Chinese	23.75	36,100
Other Ethnic Groups	23.56	35,800
All Buddhists	*100.00*	*152,000*

Source: 2001 Census, numbers rounded to the nearest hundred

Current patterns of diversity

Since 2000 the complex pattern of traditions and sub-traditions catering for converts and/or Asian Buddhists in Britain has continued to develop, with Theravada, Tibetan, Zen and FWBO groups now found in most cities and large towns. All four traditions are present from Cornwall to Northumberland, from Edinburgh to the Highlands, and in various parts of Wales and Ireland. Table 3.7 lists the main organizations in each tradition. Reliable numbers are often unavailable, but Soka Gakkai, New Kadampa and the FWBO are clearly the largest, with the Forest Sangha, Samatha Trust, Karma Kagyu, Gelug, Soto Zen and the Community of Interbeing all with substantial support. Though the other organizations are smaller, in aggregate they may nevertheless represent the majority of Asian Buddhists in Britain.

In the Theravada tradition the monastic Forest Sangha (www.forestsangha.org.uk) is supported by 40 local groups and remains part of the Thai Theravada tradition. Senior monks and nuns lead week-long retreats at Amaravati, though lay people lead their own weekend events. Smaller monastic centres cater mainly for Asian Buddhists. The Samatha Trust offers meditation courses at Greenestreete and 28 local groups, describing *samatha*

Table 3.7 Internal diversity in UK Buddhism

Theravada:	Forest Sangha (Amaravati Buddhist Monastery) Samatha Trust (Greenestreete) Vipassana centres Sri Lankan, Thai and Burmese temples (London and Birmingham)
Tibetan	New Kadampa Tradition (Manjushri Centre) Karma Kagyu (Samye Ling) Gelug (Jamyang Centre) Smaller Sakya and Nyingma centres
East Asian	Soka Gakkai International (Taplow Court) Soto Zen (Throssel Hole Abbey) Community of Interbeing Smaller Zen and Chan groups Chinese, Vietnamese and Korean temples (London)
Western	Friends of the Western Buddhist Order (FWBO) Buddhist Society (London), Network of Buddhist Organizations Educational, social and charitable organizations

Source: *Buddhist Directory* 2007

meditation as 'training the mind to develop inner strength and freedom from turmoil, leading on to clarity and understanding' (www.samatha.org); and there are several lay centres teaching *vipassana* meditation.

In Tibetan Buddhism, practitioners are predominantly converts rather than ethnic Tibetans. Samye Ling (www.samyeling.org) encourages 'people of all faiths or none' for day visits and weekend courses which include meditation, mindfulness and yoga; while retreats range from a week to a full year, with a four-year retreat for experienced practitioners. The New Kadampa (www.kadampa.org) is now an international organization with 1,100 centres and branches, 300 of them in Britain, often with a resident monk or nun; and the Manjushri Centre offers a programme of meditation classes, courses and retreats aimed at applying Buddhist teachings to daily life. There are also smaller groups following each of the four traditional Tibetan schools or combining elements from them.

In East Asian Buddhism (a convenient term for traditions originating in China or Japan), Soka Gakkai (www.sgi-uk.org) has 450 local groups and remains part of the Japanese-based international humanistic movement, though individual members may focus more directly on changing their own lives through chanting. Throssel Hole (www.throssel.org.uk) remains a substantial Soto Zen monastic community supported by lay groups and offering a programme of retreats and other events. The Community of Interbeing (www.interbeing.org.uk) is an international movement led by the Vietnamese Zen Master Thich Nhat Hanh, which only came to Britain in 1996 but already has 50 local groups, several UK teachers and a programme of retreats and training. Smaller Zen and Chan groups cater mainly for converts, while there are Chinese, Vietnamese and Korean temples in London for their respective ethnic communities.

Turning to what might be described as Western Buddhism, the FWBO (www.fwbo.org) remains very much the largest organization, with over 600 Order members in Britain and 90 groups, centres and businesses. Their activities include meditation, yoga, arts and health centres, wholefood cafés, and Buddhist publications and films. Sangharakshita stood down as head of the order in 2000 and became a less dominant figure. There are many other Western organizations, from the Buddhist Society to Buddhist charities, some of which will be mentioned later. Finally there are unknown numbers of 'lone Buddhists' who practise outside formal organizations, perhaps attending groups or centres occasionally.

Personal Buddhist practice

With both Asians and converts practising in one of many traditions or independently, there is no 'typical British Buddhist' whose experience may be conveniently described. However, there are three elements which are widely practised. First, Buddhists have a formal ethical code, based on the Five Precepts of avoiding harming living beings, stealing, sexual misconduct, lying and intoxication. They are also encouraged to develop the opposite qualities of compassion, generosity, faithfulness, truthfulness and mindfulness. This does not mean all British Buddhists are teetotal vegetarian pacifists; though they would respect rather than ridicule those who are. Second, many British Buddhists practise daily meditation (see Text box 10), perhaps supplemented by weekly group meetings, visits to monasteries or other centres, and more intensive weekend or week-long meditation retreats. Meditation affects people differently: one person finds mental calm, another is deeply energized by the practice. Third, there are devotional activities which may include formally offering food and other necessities to a monastic community, or bowing to a Buddha image, offering candlelight and incense, and chanting scripture verses in English or Asian languages. The aim here is usually to develop and express reverence for the Buddha or other enlightened beings rather than to worship them as gods.

As with other religions, there is a wide range of commitment, from nominal Buddhists to ordained monks and nuns. Converts often begin by reading about Buddhism and then visiting a group or centre to receive meditation instruction. Most remain as regular meditators and group members, though a few eventually become leaders or even lay teachers. Less than 1 per cent will make the full-time commitment of ordination, about half of them as Theravada, Tibetan or Zen monks and nuns (with New Kadampa as the largest group), and half as Western Buddhist Order members.

There are various reasons why people in Britain convert to Buddhism, often as a reaction to the Christian churches' (real or perceived) emphasis on the central importance of correct doctrine and belief reinforced by hierarchical authority structures. Some are attracted by a spiritual path of morality and meditation which encourages self-reliance and offers an end to human suffering without the need for divine intervention. Others may seek a new sense of spiritual community and mutual support. Some are drawn to Buddhist organizations which can explain methods of practice and offer 'personal spiritual guidance from experienced practitioners, in a context where neither theistic belief nor creedal assent are expected' (Bluck 2006: 190). There is even an attraction to the 'differentness' of Buddhism as an oriental mysticism, a colourful Tibetan spiritual iconography, or a philosophical system which both eludes Western categories and challenges Western values (see the next chapter on the enduring appeal of 'alternative' spiritualities in Britain).

The popular appeal of books by the Dalai Lama and other Buddhist authors, encouraging the development of compassionate attitudes and behaviour, is one of several examples of Buddhism's wider influence in Britain. Whether they follow a spiritual path or not, many people have experienced the therapeutic value of Buddhist-style meditation in reducing stress or coping with personal problems. Buddhism's First Precept (to avoid harming living beings) may strike a chord with non-Buddhists inclined to vegetarianism or pacifism, which feature little in the Christian tradition. This Buddhist concept of the preciousness of human life has also been cited in wider debates on abortion, suicide and euthanasia, as well as armed conflict and terrorism. However, it is not always clear whether Buddhist teaching and practice are actually influencing British social attitudes and behaviour or merely reflecting them.

TEXT BOX 10

Buddhist meditation

The central practice of mental training is familiar to most Buddhists but notoriously hard to describe. This list indicates the main forms used throughout Buddhism. Underlying them all is the concept of 'mindfulness', mental alertness or awareness of the present moment.

Samatha (calming meditation) usually involves observing the breathing to help develop mental tranquillity. It may also include meditating on loving-kindness to encourage compassionate attitudes and behaviour towards all beings (including oneself). *Samatha* methods are sometimes seen as introductory and are not confined to Buddhism.

Vipassana (insight meditation) uses this calmed mind to observe, in turn: the body and physical sensations; feelings (pleasant, unpleasant or neutral); mental states (emotions and moods); and mental concepts or thoughts. This practice is said to develop direct understanding of Buddhist teachings about the nature of reality.

Samatha and *vipassana* methods are often used together and meditators may not always distinguish between them. Tibetan Buddhists will also visualize spiritual beings in order to focus on the purified mind; and Zen trainees either wrestle with *koans* (puzzling questions which lead beyond logical responses), or practise *zazen*, enigmatically described as 'just sitting'.

Representation and relationships

Buddhism is usually seen as a peaceable and tolerant religion. Compared with other minority religious voices in Britain, Buddhists have appeared remarkably quiet, rarely seeking public recognition or campaigning for state-funded schools. This is partly due to their smaller numbers and the ethnic and denominational diversity described above. The largest single group (Soka Gakkai) represents only about 5 per cent of British Buddhists; and convert Buddhists may well see their identity as already established within mainstream British society.

However, some organizations have consciously sought publicity. The FWBO has sometimes portrayed itself as the new British Buddhism, though its earlier emphasis on creating an ideal Buddhist society which could influence and change Britain has now faded into a more accommodating approach. Other organizations tend to focus on private practice rather than public influence, though the media may view this in different ways. The Forest Sangha has been regarded as the quiet face of traditional Buddhism, or the monastic centre of official Buddhism in Britain. The New Kadampa by contrast has been criticized as inward-looking and secretive; and early press coverage of Soka Gakkai described it as a cult rather than genuine Buddhism. Both organizations remain wary of media contacts, with their public relations somewhat strained.

The Buddhist Society still sometimes sees itself as the official voice of Buddhism in meetings with government departments and religious leaders, though very few British Buddhists are members. Since its formation in 1994 the Network of Buddhist Organizations has supported dialogue between the various traditions in Britain, and has become 'the primary inter-Buddhist organization in the UK' (Waterhouse 2001: 154). However, neither organization can provide the single authoritative voice on current issues which public bodies wish for: the question of who speaks for British Buddhists – as for many of the other religions discussed in this chapter – remains unresolved.

There is considerable variety in both internal relationships between Buddhist traditions and their attitudes to society as a whole. The Forest Sangha has established links with other Buddhists and some Christian groups, supported interfaith conferences and peace vigils, and invited local people to see the new Amaravati temple. Samye Ling and Throssel Hole have also engaged with other Buddhist and Christian traditions, and overcome the initial wariness of their local communities. However, the FWBO has sometimes had awkward relationships with other Buddhist groups and has shown hostility towards Christianity, though these attitudes have softened in recent years. New Kadampa followers are not always convinced of the benefits of contact with other Buddhists: they and Soka Gakkai members may still see their own movement as the true Buddhism, prompting a rather more exclusive approach.

Political and social roles in a secularized Britain

Despite internal disagreements and criticism, there has been little overt political activity associated with Buddhist communities in Britain. There were noisy protests against the Dalai Lama's 1996 visit by New Kadampa members who felt he was restricting their freedom of worship; and in 2009 the Kingsbury Buddhist Temple was firebombed by suspected Tamil militants, probably targeting ethnic Singhalese rather than Buddhism. But these were both exceptional events.

Since Buddhism's ethical and social teachings are firmly opposed to what is often portrayed as Western materialism and individualism, we might expect a robust political response from the Buddhist community. This has very rarely been the case, partly because of the lack of a central Buddhist voice, but also due to a feeling that such activities generate more heat than light and are less important than personal spiritual practice. During the Vietnam War, for example, Christmas Humphreys proclaimed that Buddhist organizations should ignore the fighting, the arguments and 'politics of any kind' (quoted in Bluck 2006: 10); and the Buddhist Society is prevented by its constitution from supporting 'any activity of a political nature' (www.thebuddhistsociety.org). The Forest Sangha is sometimes criticized for ignoring social problems, though monastics would argue that their engagement with the inner life provides a beneficial example in a materialistic society. Ajahn Sumedho has encouraged lay people to reflect on the causes of third world problems, but would not involve the monastic community in active campaigning.

However, individuals and some groups have become involved with various forms of social action – ranging from simple kindness to political activism – which are collectively described as 'engaged Buddhism'. Activities include educational projects, psychotherapy, prison chaplaincy, and support for the homeless and the terminally ill. The Rokpa movement based at Samye Ling, founded to help Tibetan refugees in Nepal, has expanded into other countries including Britain: Rokpa Glasgow runs both a soup kitchen and yoga, psychotherapy and meditation classes. The Network of Engaged Buddhists, started in 1982 by peace activists and environmentalists, describes itself as 'both affinity group and pressure group, attempting both personal and social transformation' (*Buddhist Directory* 2007: 18). Bell (2000: 418) concluded that the willingness of many British Buddhists to engage with 'social and political realities' shows increasing confidence among those working 'to integrate Buddhism further into the mainstream of British society'.

As regards internal social roles, there is comparatively little gender bias in British Buddhism, with both men and women becoming teachers in several traditions. Soto Zen rules even emphasize that gender equality is part of Buddhist teaching. However, most senior teachers are still men, and there has been a sense of discrimination in some traditions. Western lay women are sometimes uncomfortable with the Forest Sangha's patriarchal rules, and despite the nuns' more flexible regime, some tension remains between traditional practice and gender equality. The initial impetus for FWBO single-sex communities came from men whose attitudes seemed to ignore or exclude women, though this has faded as more women become ordained.

Convert British Buddhists still tend to be middle class and well educated, often employed in teaching, medical or other caring professions; though there is wider social representation within Asian communities, and movements with large urban centres also attract a broader membership. It is worth remembering that young people who joined Buddhist organizations in the early years are now entering retirement. Some of the founders have died, and those who remain are elderly, so that these traditions are entering a crucial period where the leadership passes to a younger generation with more tenuous links to the Asian parent tradition.

Buddhism seems to have been largely unaffected by the secularizing and assimilatory pressures which have sometimes caused problems for other religions in Britain. It is, for example, inherently sympathetic to scientific rationalism. However, the First Precept of not harming living beings challenges prevailing views on abortion, euthanasia and militarism. Buddhism has historically been responsible for education and social welfare in some Asian countries, but never in Britain, where state control of these functions poses no problem for Buddhists. Although Buddhism is unsympathetic to Western materialism, its teaching that the problem is the *desire* for things (rather than things themselves) may strike a chord in a society obsessed with individual consumption. Attacks on religion by the New Atheists tend to forget that one of the world's great religions is non-theistic.

Transnational links

Asian Buddhists in Britain often maintain strong links with their individual countries, whose own Buddhist communities support British temples financially or by sponsoring monks from Sri Lanka, Burma and Thailand, and occasionally Vietnam or Korea. The traditional iconography in such temples may be funded by wealthy Buddhists in Colombo or Bangkok rather than London or Birmingham. This flow of money and monastics is sometimes interrupted by political problems in Asian countries. In Tibet the process works almost in reverse, with British organizations dedicated to supporting refugees and preserving Tibetan spiritual and cultural life.

Most of the organizations catering for convert Buddhists in Britain retain links with Asian Buddhism, though in different ways. The Forest Sangha's position as a Western branch of Thai Theravada monasticism has sometimes limited its adaptation in Britain.

Soka Gakkai has received significant funding from its Japanese parent organization, though the influence of Japanese leaders in Britain is not welcomed by all members. The mainstream Tibetan schools in Britain trace their lineages through ethnic Tibetan teachers who continue to support and inspire their British followers.

Other organizations have more tenuous links through their founders. Roshi Kennett was authorized by her Japanese Zen master to teach in the West, but the Soto Zen tradition is fully independent of Japanese support. Thich Nhat Hanh was exiled from his native Vietnam for many years. Sangharakshita is the only connection between the FWBO and Asian Buddhist teachers, though the movement is now also active in India, in an unusual re-exporting of Westernized Buddhism. In 2010 the FWBO changed its name to the Triratna Buddhist Community to reflect its development as an international rather than a Western movement, and to emphasize its commitment to the Three Jewels (*triratna*) of the Buddha, Dharma and Sangha.

Change and adaptation

The process of change in British Buddhist organizations is more complex than a simple 'spectrum of adaptation' from a thoroughly traditional Forest Sangha to a wholly innovative FWBO. Although the Forest Sangha is a conservative Thai tradition following ancient monastic rules, there have been significant adaptations in Britain, including a new nuns' order, chanting in English as well as Pali, and enhanced roles for committed lay people. While the FWBO's selection and adaptation of elements from different schools is innovative, the elements themselves remain traditional.

In Tibetan Buddhism, Samye Ling has introduced temporary ordination for up to three years, full ordination for nuns, and various humanitarian, therapeutic and environmental activities. Presenting teaching in forms acceptable to Westerners reflects an individualized approach traditional in Tibet. Similarly, in the New Kadampa, simplified teachings and practices with English translations are seen as a skilful re-presentation of traditional elements rather than adaptation.

Throssel Hole combines traditional Soto Zen ceremonial with adapted English language and music, in an attempt to establish a British Buddhist identity. Further adaptations from Japanese practice include a return to celibate monasticism, gender equality and equal emphasis on monastic and lay training. Soka Gakkai may appear markedly different from most Buddhist movements in Britain, but is relatively little changed from its Japanese parent movement.

The FWBO, Soka Gakkai and New Kadampa have sometimes been labelled as 'new Buddhist movements', and regarded with suspicion by some British Buddhists who see them as controversial. Each of them has experienced a crucial separation from their Asian roots, through Sangharakshita leaving Theravada monasticism, Soka Gakkai's expulsion from Nichiren Shoshu, and Geshe Kelsang's rejection of mainstream Gelug Buddhism. They have used various methods of proselytizing, growing rapidly into the three largest Buddhist organizations in Britain, though together they only account for about one-tenth of British Buddhists. All have attracted criticism from the media and from within British Buddhism, and are variously described as evangelistic, dogmatic, exclusive and intolerant. However, such attacks are often inaccurate or exaggerated or motivated by ill-will. All three movements could equally well be described as enthusiastic, committed and confident, usually with charismatic leadership. Such characteristics are commonly seen in new religious movements, often changing as they grow and mature. There is no clear dividing line between these three movements and more conventional Buddhist organizations in Britain.

Perhaps the most important overall change has been the participation of lay people, who form over 99 per cent of British Buddhists. The Samatha Trust and Soka Gakkai are completely lay movements, and some monastic traditions are increasingly involving lay people as teachers or community members, sometimes in liminal roles where they can develop their own practice, support the monastic sangha and perhaps prepare for ordination. Most local groups are run entirely by lay people, and many independent Buddhists practise with no contact with monastic communities.

Asian and convert forms of Buddhism

Lay participation introduces the question of differences between convert and Asian forms of Buddhism in Britain. Asians often perceive the religion as a monastic core with support from the lay community, while converts tend to seek a new balance between monastic and lay practice which values both lifestyles equally. There are also more obvious differences here. Visitors to the Buddhapadipa Temple in London will see traditional Thai architecture and iconography and hear Thai monks chanting in Pali (see Plate 3.4); while in the FWBO London Buddhist Centre they will see statues and paintings by Western artists and usually hear only English.

This is more than a cultural preference for Asian or Western decoration and language. Asian Buddhists in Britain, whether Thai or Sri Lankan or Chinese, may look for and expect the Buddhism they, or their parents or even grandparents, remember from their country of origin, where making offerings to the monastic community or the Buddha is often their central devotional practice. They usually see Buddhism as part of their cultural as well as religious identity, and while there are many committed practitioners, many others (particularly in the Chinese community) are perhaps comparable to those Christians whose church attendance centres on Christmas and Easter.

Even in organizations which cater for both Asian and convert Buddhists, the two communities sometimes relate to the tradition in different ways. At Amaravati, for example, Thai supporters may come to offer a formal meal, bowing frequently while paying their respects to Ajahn Sumedho; while Westerners may attend for meditation or to hear Sumedho speak, perhaps chatting informally with him afterwards.

Converts who have chosen rather than inherited Buddhist practice are sometimes bewildered or irritated by Asian Buddhist symbolism and monastic ritual, which has no cultural value for them. Instead they expect monastics to be dharma teachers and meditation instructors (and sometimes priests, social workers and psychotherapists too). While Asian Buddhists may make offerings to gain merit, and convert Buddhists may willingly support monastics, there is a grain of truth in the notion that Asians ask what they can give and Westerners ask what they can get. This suggests an underlying contrast between communal and individual approaches. Asian Buddhists value continuity with their religious and cultural roots, while converts are drawn by Buddhism's emphasis on personal responsibility.

Conclusion: British Buddhists and British Buddhism

This discussion has shown how Buddhism in post-war Britain has grown from a small group in London into substantial communities of both Asians and converts practising throughout the country in 30 different Theravada, Tibetan, Zen and other sub-traditions, either at national or at regional monastic and lay centres, in 1,000 local Buddhist groups, or largely on their own. Internal adaptations are taking place within a complex pattern which is beginning to blend Asian and Western cultural forms, and which includes conservative monastic traditions and dynamic lay movements. There are also significant differences in the spiritual practice, motivation and expectations of Asian and convert Buddhists in Britain.

Despite this multi-layered diversity, there are important common features. Almost all traditions teach silent meditation as their central practice, apart from Soka Gakkai, whose main practice of chanting is also used in most traditions, together with other devotional activities. All organizations use traditional teachings drawn directly from their parent tradition, though the FWBO has combined Theravada and Tibetan elements. There is widespread emphasis on studying sacred texts and the writings of contemporary teachers. Most traditions offer courses and retreats, from introductory meditation weekends to longer retreats for committed members. All value the Buddha's life story and other important narratives concerning historical and contemporary figures; and Soka Gakkai, New Kadampa and the FWBO have developed further narratives to explain or reinterpret their Asian roots. Each tradition except Soka Gakkai has a formal ethical code, usually based on the Five Precepts. All include some form of teacher–pupil relationship, varying from personal supervision to reading the leader's books for guidance. Apart from the mainstream Tibetan traditions, Western teachers are now the norm. Finally there is increasing lay participation within monastic traditions, as well as lay movements and independent practitioners.

With few statistics available, it is difficult to be sure which traditions are expanding or contracting. In the Theravada tradition, numbers appear to have stabilized after steady growth. Tibetan Buddhism is still growing, partly though not wholly due to enthusiastic expansion in the New Kadampa tradition. East Asian Buddhism shows a more complex pattern of growth and stability, with continued expansion in Soka Gakkai and the much smaller Community of Interbeing. Numbers of 'Western' Buddhists are impossible to determine, partly because of the fluidity of the term itself, but the FWBO (now Triratna) is still flourishing. New religious movements often grow quickly at first and then more slowly as they mature; but even this simple pattern does not cover all the Buddhist traditions in Britain.

Prebish and Keown (2010: 207) confidently predict that 'in the twenty-first century independent Western forms and schools of Buddhism will develop and prosper on a much larger scale'. How and when this might happen in Britain is still far from clear. It implies a common English vocabulary for Buddhist teaching and practice, a group of wholly Western teachers, full independence from Asian Buddhist organizations, a co-operative spirit which seeks to evolve together rather than separately, and a truly representative Buddhist voice. Even in a period of such rapid change, these elements seem many years away. The diversity of Buddhist traditions in Britain, the differences between Asian and convert practitioners, and the frequent emphasis on personal transformation rather than social or political action, all suggest that there will continue to be many British Buddhists but no single form of uniquely British Buddhism.

Key terms

Ajahn: Senior Theravada Buddhist monk.
Dharma: In relation to Buddhism, the teaching of the Buddha.
Gelug: School of Tibetan Buddhism.*

Geshe: Senior teacher in the Gelug school.

Kagyu: School of Tibetan Buddhism.*

Karma Kagyu: Main branch of the Kagyu school.*

Koan: Puzzling questions which lead beyond logical responses.

Mindfulness: Mental alertness, awareness of the present moment.**

Nyingma: School of Tibetan Buddhism.*

Pali: The language of Theravada Buddhist texts.

Rinpoche: Senior teacher in Tibetan Buddhism.

Roshi: Senior Zen teacher.

Sakya: School of Tibetan Buddhism.*

Samatha: (calming) Buddhism meditation practice used to quieten the mind.**

Sangha: Community of Buddhist monks.

Soto: Zen Buddhist school emphasizing sitting meditation.

Theravada: Oldest surviving school of Buddhism.

Vihara: A Buddhist monastery.

Vipassana: (insight) Buddhist meditation practice used to reach greater understanding.**

Zazen: Sitting meditation in Zen Buddhism.**

Zen: Japanese school of Buddhism based on meditation.

* See also Table 3.7: Internal diversity in UK Buddhism
** See also Text box 10: Buddhist meditation

Further reading

Bell, Sandra (2000). 'A Survey of Engaged Buddhism in Britain', in Christopher Queen (ed.), *Engaged Buddhism in the West*. Boston, MA: Wisdom Publications, 397–422. Sets therapeutic, social and environmental projects within the context of Buddhism's relation to British society.

Bluck, Robert (2006). *British Buddhism: Teachings, Practice and Development*. London: Routledge. A comprehensive survey of the seven largest traditions, including new movements, with an historical overview and statistical information. Extensive bibliography.

Buddhist Directory (2007) 10th edition. London: Buddhist Society. Details 650 national and local centres and groups, with sections on related organizations and resources.

Prebish, Charles and Damien Keown (2010). *Introducing Buddhism*. 2nd edition. London: Routledge. Clear explanation of key teachings, historical development and contemporary social and ethical issues. Substantial glossary of Buddhist terms and teachers.

Waterhouse, Helen (2001). 'Representing Western Buddhism: A United Kingdom Focus', in Gwilym Beckerlegge (ed.), *From Sacred Text to Internet*. Aldershot: Ashgate, 117–160. Sets three British case studies within the context of a developing Western Buddhism.

Conclusion

Linda Woodhead

If we employ the metaphor of a force field to think about the religious 'field', we can imagine the minority religions discussed in this chapter as subject to constant pulls and pushes of energy, as they come into the orbit of other forces. A major one is Christianity, not only as a cultural force, but also in the form of established churches which still enjoy some priv-ileged access to social and political power in Britain. Even more important are the legal and political constraints and opportunities which these religions have to negotiate, at local as well as national and transnational levels. Some of the cultural and political forces they encounter have a strongly secular hue, and seek to confine them to a very marginal place in the wider field of social power; others are more moderate and 'multicultural', and offer greater opportunities of influence and accommodation. These religions do not merely oper-ate in a national field, they are also part of much larger transnational communities, and that creates an interference in the play of energies, in their relation both to one another and to majority religion and society. When Jews and Muslims meet at the local level – in a univer-sity or town council – they carry with them wider histories and connections which affect their encounter; the Israeli–Palestinian conflict may, for example, shape an encounter in the student union just as much as a shared birthplace in Manchester.

As this chapter has also shown, one of the ways in which the modern British force field exercises a pressure on these religions is precisely to make them appear as 'world religions': as distinct from (secular) politics and culture, as well as from one another, and as having clear boundaries and distinct markers (sacred scriptures, institutions, rituals and so on). This pressure is not merely imposed from outside, it is also internalized and operationalized by 'followers' of the religions themselves, particularly those who take positions of leadership and seek national and sometimes international leadership. The institutions, representative bodies, consultative councils and leaders which emerge in this process all have a strategic importance. But on the ground, the importance of these religions for those who live by them, and for whom they are part of the everyday business of 'making do' and making the best of life (and death), may be distant or detached from these strategic uses. At this every-day level, individuals and groups are much more likely to employ a whole variety of religious and non-religious resources and fail to comply with the neat definitions of a Sikh, a Hindu or a Muslim which teachers, academics, lawyers, politicians and social workers would like them to display. This mixing and making the best of things leads to new religious adapta-tions and creative developments in the post-war British context, and to a rapidly changing religious field which refuses to be pinned down. The categories used to frame this chapter – Judaism, Sikhism and so on – are shifting tokens in this field, with their own history of use, and their own power and limitations.

Reading this chapter together with the previous ones, the overall picture which emerges is of the tight spot in which both majority and minority religions have found themselves in later post-war Britain. In the context of secular welfarism, they had little or no place *qua* religion, and were rendered invisible for a time – even though they were highly active on the ground. After the 1980s their activities became more visible, not least because many minorities rejected imposed labels of race and ethnicity ('Asian', 'Pakistani' and so on) and sought greater agency in their own self-definition by way of their religious commitments. This 'resurgence' led to flashpoints, controversies and oppositions, not least with some majority interests, which are continuing into the twenty-first century, and reshaping the religious field yet again. Away from the more visible conflicts, however, all the religions discussed here made considerable progress in the post-war period in effecting a whole range of settlements within British society, which have rooted them in the fabric of the country in ways which have been indicated. Although the secular settlement which was thought to prevail in the welfare years has been undermined, and the shape of new settlement is still a matter of struggle and contestation, the idea that religion can be controlled, contained and excluded is less plausible than before.

Further reading

Paul Weller (ed.) (2007). *Religions in the UK. Directory 2007–2010*. Derby: Multi-Faith Centre at the University of Derby. A reference work which provides detailed and practical information about nine major religious communities in Britain, plus information on several smaller groups, listings of organizations and places of worship, and an opening overview.

References

Ansari, Humayun (2004). *The Infidel Within: Muslims in Britain since 1800*. London: Hurst.

Anwar, Muhammad (1979). *The Myth of Return*. London: Heinemann Educational Books.

Archer, Louise (2009). 'Race, "Face" and Masculinity: The Identities and Local Geographies of Muslim Boys', in Peter Hopkins and Richard Gale (eds), *Muslims in Britain: Race, Place and Identities*. Edinburgh: Edinburgh University Press, 74–91.

Ballard, Roger (1994). 'Introduction: The Emergence of Desh Pardesh', in Roger Ballard (ed.), *Desh Pardesh: The South Asian Experience in Britain*. London: Hurst, 1–34.

Bance, Peter (2007). *The Sikhs in Britain: 150 Years of Photographs*. Stroud: The History Press.

Baumann, Gerd (1998). 'Body Politic or Bodies of Culture? How Nation-State Practices Turn Citizens into Religious Minorities', *Cultural Dynamics*, 10/3: 263–280.

Becher, Harriet, Stanley Waterman, Barry Kosmin and Katarina Thomson (2002). *A Portrait of Jews in London and the South-east: A Community Study*, Report No. 4. London: The Institute for Jewish Policy Research/National Centre for Social Research.

Beckford, James and Sophie Gilliat (1998). *Religion in Prison: Equal Rites in a Multi-Faith Society*. Cambridge: Cambridge University Press.

Bell, Sandra (2000). 'A Survey of Engaged Buddhism in Britain', in Christopher Queen (ed.), *Engaged Buddhism in the West*. Boston, MA: Wisdom Publications, 397–422.

Bhachu, Parminder (1985). *Twice Migrants: East African Sikh Settlers in Britain*. London: Tavistock Publications.

Bluck, Robert (2006). *British Buddhism: Teachings, Practice and Development*. London: Routledge.

Borbas, Gina, David Haslam and Balram Sampla (2006). *No Escape: Caste Discrimination in the UK*. London: Dalit Solidarity Network UK.

Bowen, David (1987). 'The Evolution of Gujarati Hindu Organizations in Bradford', in Richard Burghart (ed.), *Hinduism in Great Britain*. London: Tavistock, 15–31.

Buddhist Directory (2007). 10th edition. London: Buddhist Society.

Burghart, Richard (1987). 'Introduction: The Diffusion of Hinduism to Great Britain', in Richard Burghart (ed.), *Hinduism in Great Britain*. London: Tavistock, 1–14.

David, Ann (2009). 'Gendering the Divine: New Forms of Feminine Hindu Worship', *International Journal of Hindu Studies*, 13/3: 337–355.

DeWitt, John (1969). *Indian Workers' Associations in Britain*. London: Oxford University Press.

Dorling, Daniel and Bethan Thomas (2004). *People and Place: A 2001 Census Atlas of the UK*. Bristol: The Policy Press.

Dwyer, Rachel (1994). 'Caste, Religion and Sect in Gujarat: Followers of Vallabhacharya and Swaminarayan', in Roger Ballard (ed.), *Desh Pardesh: The South Asian Experience in Britain*. London: Hurst, 165–190.

Frykenberg, Robert E. (1993). 'Constructions of Hinduism at the Nexus of History and Religion', *Journal of Inter-disciplinary History*, 23/3: 523–550.

Geaves, Ron (1996). *Sectarian Influences within Islam in Britain with Reference to the Concepts of 'Ummah' and 'Community'*. Leeds: Community Religions Project.

Gilliat-Ray, Sophie (2008). 'From "Visiting Minister" to "Muslim Chaplain": The Growth of Muslim Chaplaincy in Britain, 1970–2007', in Eileen Barker (ed.), *The Centrality of Religion in Social Life: Essays in Honour of James A. Beckford*. Aldershot: Ashgate, 145–160.

Gilliat-Ray, Sophie (2010). *Muslims in Britain: An Introduction*. Cambridge: Cambridge University Press.

Gilliat-Ray, Sophie and Jody Mellor (2010). '*Bilad al-Welsh* (Land of the Welsh): Muslims in Cardiff, South Wales: Past, Present and Future', *The Muslim World*, 100/4: 452–475.

Graham, David J. (2008). 'The Socio-Spatial Boundaries of an "Invisible" Minority: A Quantitative (Re)Appraisal of Britain's Jewish Population', unpublished DPhil thesis, University of Oxford. Online. Available HTTP: http://ora.ouls.ox.ac.uk/objects/uuid per cent3A9bdbd348-b50c-4090-9e2d-e86ffe198601 (accessed 1 June 2011).

Graham, David J. and Jonathan Boyd (2010). *Committed, Concerned and Conciliatory: The Attitudes of Jews in Britain towards Israel, Initial Findings from the 2010 Israel Survey*. London: Institute for Jewish Policy Research.

Graham, David J., Marlena Schmool and Stanley Waterman (2007). *Jews in Britain: A Snapshot from the 2001 Census*, Report No. 1. London: Institute for Jewish Policy Research.

Graham, David J. and Daniel Vulkan (2010). *Synagogue Membership in the United Kingdom in 2010*. London: The Board of Deputies of British Jews and Institute for Jewish Policy Research.

Graham, David J. and Stanley Waterman (2007). 'Locating Jews by Ethnicity: A Reply to D. Voas (2007), Estimating the Jewish Undercount in the 2001 Census: A Comment on Graham and Waterman (2005) Underenumeration of the Jewish Population in the UK 2001 Census', *Population, Space and Place*, 13/5: 409–414.

Halbfass, Wilhelm (1992). *On Being and What There is: Classical Vaiśesika and the History of Indian Ontology*. New York, NY: State University of New York Press.

Holman, Christine and Naomi Holman (2002). *Torah, Worship and Acts of Loving Kindness: Baseline Indicators for the Charedi Community in Stamford Hill*. Leicester: De Montfort University.

Hussain, Serena (2008). *Muslims on the Map: A National Survey of Social Trends in Britain*. London: I. B. Tauris.

Jackson, Robert (1987). 'Changing Conceptions of Hinduism in a Timetabled Religion', in Richard Burghart (ed.), *Hinduism in Great Britain*. London: Tavistock, 201–223.

Jewish Leadership Council (JLC) (2008). *The Future of Jewish Schools: The Commission on Jewish Schools*. London: The Jewish Leadership Council.

Josephides, Sasha (1991). 'Organizational Splits and Political Ideology in the Indian Workers Associations', in Pnina Werbner and Muhammad Anwar (eds), *Black and Ethnic Leaderships in Britain: The Cultural Dimensions of Political Action*. London: Routledge, 253–276.

Kahn-Harris, Keith and Ben Gidley (2010). *Turbulent Times: The British Jewish Community Today*. London: Continuum.

Khattab, Nabil (2009). 'Ethno-Religious Background as a Determinant of Educational and Occupational Attainment in Britain', *Sociology*, 43/2: 304–322.

Knott, Kim (1986). *Hinduism in Leeds: A Study of Religious Practice in the Indian Hindu Community and in Hindu-related Groups*. Leeds: Community Religions Project, University of Leeds.

Kundnani, Arun (2007). *The End of Tolerance: Racism in 21st Century Britain*. London: Pluto Press.

Lazar, Aryeh, Shlomo Kravetz and Peri Frederich-Kedem (2002). 'The Multidimensionality of Motivation for Jewish Religious Behavior: Content, Structure, and Relationship to Religious Identity', *Journal for the Scientific Study of Religion*, 41/3: 509–519.

Leslie, Julia (2003). *Authority and Meaning in Indian Religions: Hinduism and the Case of Valmiki*. Aldershot: Ashgate.

Lewis, Philip (1994). *Islamic Britain: Religion, Politics and Identity among British Muslims*. London: I. B. Tauris.

Mirza, Heidi Safia (2002). 'Women and Society', BBC News Online. Online. Available HTTP: http://news.bbc.co.uk/hi/english/static/in_depth/uk/2002/race/women_and_society.stm (accessed 19 May 2006).

Mondal, Anshuman (2008). *Young British Muslim Voices*. Oxford: Greenwood World Publishing.

Munby, Lord Justice (2008). 'High Court Judgement Neutral Citation Number: [2008] EWHC 1535/1536 (Admin) Case No: CO/7896/2007'.

National Council of Hindu Temples (NCHT) (1983). *Hinduism: An Introduction to the World's Oldest Living Religion*. Leicester: National Council of Hindu Temples.

Nesbitt, Eleanor (1994). 'Valmikis in Coventry: The Revival and Reconstruction of a Community', in Roger Ballard (ed.), *Desh Pardesh: The South Asian Presence in Britain*. London: Hurst, 117–141.

Nesbitt, Eleanor (2004). 'I'm a Gujarati Lohana and a Vaishnav as Well: Religious Identity Formation among Young Coventrian Punjabis and Gujaratis', in Simon Coleman and Peter Collins (eds), *Religion Identity and Change*. Aldershot: Ashgate, 174–190.

Nye, Malory (2001). *Multiculturalism and Minority Religions in Britain*. Richmond: Curzon.

Oberoi, Harjot (1994). *The Construction of Religious Boundaries: Culture, Identity and Diversity in the Sikh Tradition*. New Delhi: Oxford University Press/University of Chicago Press.

Oddie, Geoffrey (2006). *Imagined Hinduism: British Protestant Missionary Constructions of Hinduism, 1793–1900*. New Delhi: Sage.

Office for National Statistics (2004). 'Focus on Religion'. London: Her Majesty's Stationery Office.

Prais, S. J. and Marlena Schmool (1968). 'The Size and Structure of the Anglo-Jewish Population, 1960–65', *Jewish Journal of Sociology*, 10: 5–34.

Prebish, Charles and Damien Keown (2010). *Introducing Buddhism*. 2nd edition. London: Routledge.

Radcliffe, Liat (2004). 'A Muslim Lobby at Whitehall? Examining the Role of the Muslim Minority in British Foreign Policy Making', *Islam and Christian–Muslim Relations*, 15/3: 365–386.

Raj, Dhooleka S. (2003). *Where Are You From? Middle-class Migrants in the Modern World*. Berkeley, CA: University of California Press.

Rocker, Simon (2009). 'JFS: What Next?', *The Jewish Chronicle*, 3 July: 1.

Rosenbaum, Simon (1905). 'A Contribution to the Study of the Vital and Other Statistics of the Jews in the United Kingdom', *Journal of the Royal Statistical Society*, 68/3: 526–562.

Rosenberg, Joshua (2009). 'This Ruling Creates More Problems than it Resolves', *The Jewish Chronicle*, 18 December: 4.

Roth, Cecil (1978). *A History of the Jews of England*. 3rd edition. Oxford: Clarendon Press.

Runnymede Trust (2006). *Connecting British Hindus: An Enquiry into the Identity and Public Engagement of Hindus in Britain*. London: Runnymede Trust/Hindu Forum of Britain.

Sacks, Jonathan (1995). *Will We Have Jewish Grandchildren? Jewish Continuity and How to Achieve It*. London: Vallentine Mitchell and Co.

Singh, Gurharpal, Charlene Simon and Darshan Singh Tatla (2011). 'New Forms of Religious Transnationalism and Development Initiatives: A Case Study of Dera Sant Sarwan Dass, Ballan, Punjab, India', *Religion and Development Research Programme, University of Birmingham, Working Paper 52*: 1–108.

Singh, Gurharpal and Darshan Singh Tatla (2006). *The Sikhs in Britain: The Making of a Community*. London: Zed Press.

Supreme Court (2009a). 'Judgement: R (on the application of E) (Respondent) v. The Governing Body of JFS and the Admissions Appeal Panel of JFS and others (Appellants) [2009] UKSC 15, On appeal from the Court of Appeal (Civil Division) [2009] EWCA Civ 626', 16 December.

Supreme Court (2009b). 'Press Summary: R (on the application of E) (Respondent) v The Governing Body of JFS and the Admissions Appeal Panel of JFS and others (Appellants) [2009] UKSC 15 On appeal from the Court of Appeal (Civil Division) [2009] EWCA Civ 626', 16 December.

Tatla, Darshan Singh (1999). *The Sikh Diaspora: The Search for Statehood*. Seattle, WA: University of Washington Press.

Tweed, Thomas (2006). *Crossing and Dwelling: A Theory of Religion*. Cambridge: Cambridge University Press.

Vertovec, Steven (2000). *The Hindu Diaspora: Comparative Patterns*. London: Routledge.

Vulkan, Daniel and David J. Graham (2008). *Population Trends among Britain's Strictly Orthodox Jews*. London: Board of Deputies of British Jews.

Waterhouse, Helen (2001). 'Representing Western Buddhism: A United Kingdom Focus', in Gwilym Beckerlegge (ed.), *From Sacred Text to Internet*. Aldershot: Ashgate, 117–160.

Waterman, Stanley and Barry A. Kosmin (1988). 'Residential Patterns and Processes: A Study of Jews in Three London Boroughs', *Transactions of the Institute of British Geographers*, 13/1: 75–91.

Weller, Paul (ed.) (2001). *Religions in the UK: A Multi-faith Directory*. Derby: University of Derby.

Zavos, John (2008). 'Stamp it out! Disciplining the Image of Hinduism in a Multicultural Milieu', *Contemporary South Asia*, 16/3: 323–337.

Zavos, John (2009). 'Negotiating Multiculturalism: The Organization of Hindu Identity in Contemporary Britain', *Journal of Ethnic and Migration Studies*, 35/6: 881–900.

Zebiri, Kate (2008). *British Muslim Converts: Choosing Alternative Lives*. Oxford: Oneworld.

Notes

1 The data is taken from the Israel Survey which was carried out in January 2010 in order to explore the attitudes of Jews in Britain towards Israel in terms of both Jewish identity and political opinion. The sample contained over 4,000 respondents, representing the single largest national survey of Jews ever undertaken in Britain.

2 Online. Available HTTP: www.boardofdeputies.org.uk/page.php/Deputy/109/2/1 (accessed 22 July 2010).

3 Online. Available HTTP: www.thejlc.org/ (accessed 23 July 2010).

4 Author's calculations using data from the Institute for Jewish Policy Research's 2002 London survey (Becher *et al.* 2002) and the 2010 Israel survey (Graham and Boyd 2010).

5 Author's calculations using data cited in note 3.

6 Author's calculations using data cited in note 3.

7 The Canadian Census includes 'Jewish' as a category in its ancestry question and this actually receives a higher 'Jewish' response than the religion question.

8 East African Sikhs are the descendants of emigrants who settled on the east coast of Africa from the late nineteenth century onward. In the 1960s they moved to the United Kingdom in large numbers as the newly independent African states followed policies of Africanization.

9 Caste is a system of endogamous social hierarchy sanctioned by religious practices and rituals that is commonly associated with Hinduism. Non-Hindu traditions in South Asia – Islam, Christianity and Sikhism – continue to be influenced by caste identities. Those at the bottom or outside the caste hierarchy, formerly called 'untouchables', are often referred to as Dalits ('the broken ones').

10 In India the term Dalit has become synonymous for the struggle of subaltern groups. In the United Kingdom while it provides an overall distinction between higher and lower castes, some groups object to the use of the term because of its political overtones. Most Dalits are of Punjabi origin and are keen to assert their own sub-identities, for example *Ravidasi* or *Valmiki*.

11 Sophie Gilliat-Ray has been Principal Investigator on the AHRC/ESRC Religion and Society funded large grant 'Leadership and Capacity Building in the British Muslim Community: The Case of Muslim Chaplains'.

12 The 'religious population' being those who responded to the – non-compulsory – religion question in the Census.

13 Although not entirely – there are some Hindus who are ethnically classed as white in the Census. That is, those who have come to the religion largely through neo-Hindu organizations such as ISKCON. These make up less than 1 per cent of the Hindu population of the UK, but because of their role in these organizations, they nevertheless have a disproportionate influence over the representation of Hinduism as a British religion.

14 Either directly from these areas of the Indian subcontinent, or via earlier settlement in East Africa.

15 There are at least 30 distinct Gujarati castes in Britain – dominant caste groups include Patidars and Lohanas (Vertovec 2000: 92).

16 These groups may number as many as 50,000 (Borbas *et al.* 2006: 21).

17 The RSS itself has a set of branch organizations in the UK, known here as the Hindu Swayamsevak Sangh (HSS).

18 The *Asian Voice* newspaper, for example, ran an editorial called 'We're British Indians and Hindus' (15 July 2006). BBC Radio ran a programme in October 2006 entitled 'Don't Call Me

Asian' in which a number of Hindu and Sikh organizations featured. Online. Available HTTP: www.bbc.co.uk/radio/aod/genres/religion/aod.shtml?asiannet/asiandoc_dontcallmeasian (accessed 14 June 2011).

19 The survey is available online. Available HTTP: http://ochs.org.uk/research/hindu-youth-research-project (accessed 14 June 2011).

20 These statements are made by Raj Pandit Sharma of Shri Vallabh Nidhi UK on an introductory video. Online. Available HTTP: www.svnuk.org/our_temples.php (accessed 14 June 2011).

21 See online. Available HTTP: www.krishna-avanti.org.uk/vaishnava-values.html (accessed 14 June 2011).

Case study 2

The Inter Faith Network and the development of inter faith relations in Britain

Brian Pearce

This case study traces the formation and growth of the Inter Faith Network for the UK, which came into being in 1987. One of the interesting features of this story is the way in which this national body which encourages good relations between different faiths has found itself, as part of this, engaging a great deal with government and other public bodies. The story of the Network provides an interesting window onto an important aspect of the development of 'multi-faith' Britain, and the organizational forms which have been created for government to liaise with religion, in a period when older forms of church–state relation ceased to be sufficient.

The formation of the Inter Faith Network

On 3 January 2000, as part of the official Millennium Celebrations, a 'Shared Act of Reflection and Commitment by the Faith Communities of the United Kingdom' took place in the Royal Gallery in the Houses of Parliament, broadcast live by BBC television. Hosted on behalf of the government by the Department for Culture, Media and Sport, it was held in the presence of Their Royal Highnesses the Duke and Duchess of Gloucester and attended by then Prime Minister Tony Blair, together with other distinguished guests. The event ended with faith community leaders from across the UK inviting all those present to join them in an Act of Commitment, expressing their commitment to working together for the common good on the basis of shared values and ideals.[1]

This was a watershed event, giving recognition to the contribution which the British faith communities make to national life. Writing in *The Times* a few days later, Sir Jonathan Sacks (now Lord Sacks), Chief Rabbi of the United Hebrew Congregations of the Commonwealth, said:

> Far away from the crowds, the fireworks and the razzamatazz of the Millennium celebrations was an event that, in its quiet way, was one of the most remarkable of recent times ... It could not have happened in any previous era, nor even now in many other parts of the world ... In that conversation of many voices in the Royal Gallery I sensed a rare epiphany of hope.
>
> (Letter to *The Times*, 21 January 2000)

This Millennium event was organized jointly by the government and the Inter Faith Network for the UK, which had developed its content with the participating faith communities. The Network had been established in 1987, bringing together as member bodies a wide range of organizations with an interest in inter faith relations in Britain.[2] Its origins go back to September 1984 when the author, Brian Pearce, took a leave of absence from the civil service to launch an informal exploration of ways to enhance the profile of inter faith activity and to strengthen the links between those involved in it. There was, at the time, a growing sense among those members of faith communities which were involved in this work that this was needed. He carried out visits across the country to consult many people, without there initially being any intention of creating a new organization. However, by the end of 1985, the idea was emerging of setting up a new networking body, not just to link existing inter faith initiatives but also to draw the major faith communities into closer engagement with one another and with inter faith work.

After three consultative gatherings in 1986 and 1987, it was agreed in March 1987 that the Inter Faith Network for the UK should be formed, bringing together 60 founder member organizations: national faith community representative bodies; national inter faith organizations; local inter faith bodies; and educational and academic bodies with an interest in multi-faith and inter faith issues. The same broad pattern of membership continues today. The consultation meetings had been chaired by the late Rabbi Hugo Gryn (then Senior Rabbi of the West London Synagogue and involved in a range of inter faith organizations) and the late Bishop Jim Thompson (at that time Bishop of Stepney and Chair of the Committee on Relations with People of Other Faiths of the British Council of Churches). They became the first co-chairs of the new organization. Brian Pearce became its first Director and served in this capacity, on a voluntary basis, until 2007.

The Network's stated aims were, and are: 'to advance public knowledge and mutual understanding of the teachings, traditions and practices of the different faith communities in Britain, including an awareness both of their distinctive features and their common ground and to promote good relations between persons of different faiths'. The founding resolution said:

> We meet today as children of many traditions, inheritors of shared wisdom and of tragic misunderstandings. We recognise our shared humanity and we respect each other's integrity in our differences. With the agreed purpose and hope of promoting greater understanding between the members of the different faith communities to which we belong and of encouraging the growth of our relationships of respect and trust and mutual enrichment in our life together, we hereby jointly resolve: The Inter Faith Network for the United Kingdom should now be established.
>
> (Inter Faith Network for the UK 2007: 12)

With the creation of the Network, national representative bodies of the major faith communities came together within a single framework for the first time: the Baha'i, Buddhist, Christian, Hindu, Jain, Jewish, Muslim and Sikh communities and, two years later, the Zoroastrian community, which had taken part in the preliminary consultations. The question of who can claim to represent whom and which faiths should be included is, of course, a vexed one. The attempt was made to ensure that those organizations coming into Network membership were broadly representative of their communities, with more than one in the case of the larger communities, focusing on 'umbrella' bodies but supplementing these as necessary to achieve a broad-based representation. In the case of the longer established faith communities, representative structures had been in place for some time. They were also emerging in other communities newer to Britain, and over the life of the Network the membership has evolved to take account of subsequent organizational developments within communities.

The growing number of inter faith organizations

Prior to 1987, inter faith activity in Britain had been developing for some time. The London Society of Jews and Christians had been set up in 1927 on the initiative of the Liberal Jewish synagogue in St John's Wood. The World Congress of Faiths had been founded in 1936 on the initiative of Sir Francis Younghusband who, in July of that year, convened a 'congress' in London of people of different religious traditions from Britain and from overseas. This led to the creation of a continuing organization to take its work forward. The Council of Christians and Jews (CCJ) was set up in 1942, partly as a response to the situation of Jews in Nazi Europe, and secured significant political support within the religious and political establishment of the UK.

Over the past few decades, there has been a substantial increase in the number of inter faith organizations (Inter Faith Network for the UK 2009). These include additional bilateral organizations, such as the Christian–Muslim Forum, the Hindu–Christian Forum and the Joseph Inter faith Foundation (which focuses on dialogue between Jews and Muslims).The Three Faiths Forum is a trilateral body bringing together Jews, Christians and Muslims, sometimes described collectively as the 'Abrahamic faiths'. There are also branches/chapters of inter faith organizations which work internationally, including the International Association for Religious Freedom, which has its origins back in 1900; Religions for Peace, set up in 1970; the United Religions Initiative, dating from 1996; and, most recently, the Tony Blair Faith Foundation, established in 2008. Additionally, there are centres for promoting and resourcing inter faith activity, such as St Ethelburga's Centre for Reconciliation and Peace in London, and St Philip's Centre for Study and Engagement in a Multi-faith Society in Leicester. The existence of the Inter Faith Network, linking these different kinds of organizations, facilitates discussion of their plans and issues, and has helped to encourage the development of distinctive areas of activity and programmes of work on their part.

Inter faith activity at local level has a particular importance in developing 'grass roots' dialogue. Some of the early organizers of local inter faith groups were individuals who had participated in events organized by national inter faith organizations and wanted to encourage inter faith engagement in their own home town or city. When the Inter Faith Network was set up in 1987 there were around 30 local inter faith organizations across the UK operating on a multi-faith basis. Nearly all became founding member bodies of the Network. While the Network has helped to promote the development of additional local inter faith activities, through advice and guidance and resources such as *The Local Inter Faith Guide* (2005), these local inter faith organizations are not branches of the Network, but independent bodies in their own right. From its early days, the Network arranged 'link' meetings to bring their organizers together from time to time.

The growth in local inter faith activity in recent years has been very rapid. From around 30 in 1987, the number of local inter faith bodies rose to just under 100 in 2000 and in 2010 reached around 240. Responses to the disturbances in northern towns in the summer of 2001 and the terrorist attacks in the US in September of that year and in London in 2005 have been factors in this growth, alongside the more positive recognition of the mutual enrichment and widening of vision which inter faith engagement can bring.

Some local inter faith groups bring together individuals who wish to learn more about one another's religious traditions and to engage in more informal activity, while others have set out to represent more formally the multi-faith character of their localities and engage on this basis with the local authority and other public bodies. There are also local inter faith bodies which combine a more formal representative role with the facilitation of personal encounter in pursuit of mutual understanding.

Over the past few years, 'Regional Faith Forums' have been established in the different English regions and the regional 'link' meetings for local inter faith organizers are now arranged jointly by the Inter Faith Network and the relevant regional forum. The Forums have met together regularly within the English Regional Faith Forums Network, which is facilitated by the Inter Faith Network and the Faith-based Regeneration Network, a national body with a focus on faith and social action. These independent Forums came into being initially as a response to the need for faith communities to engage with governmental structures at regional level: the Regional Assemblies, Regional Development Agencies and Government Regional Offices and, particularly in recent years, to support local inter faith activity in their regions. Some, at least, of the Forums are continuing despite the recent dismantling of regional governmental structures and the discontinuation of government financial support for the Forums.

There are also separate bodies for other parts of the UK: the Northern Ireland Inter Faith Forum, the Scottish Inter Faith Council and the Inter Faith Council for Wales, all of which, together with the English Regional Faith Forums, are member bodies of the Inter Faith Network.

From the outset there has been a category of Network membership for educational and academic bodies with an interest in multi-faith and inter faith issues. The conversations prior to the setting up of the Network made clear how significant a contribution was being made to the development of an understanding of different faiths and relations between them through the development of multi-faith religious education in schools, and by work being undertaken in a variety of academic institutions. The involvement in the work of the Network of organizations such as the Religious Education Council for England and Wales and the National Association of Standing Advisory Councils for Religious Education (in England) and the parallel body in Wales has been very important. The IFN office was involved alongside them in securing the active encouragement in a variety of curriculum documents for schools to tackle learning about inter faith issues and not just about different faiths. It has also helped to encourage good working relationships between Standing Advisory Councils for Religious Education (SACREs)[3] and local inter faith organizations.

The influence of the Inter Faith Network

The initial impetus for setting up the Network was the desire to promote good inter faith relations, but it was recognized early on that an important aspect of this was to facilitate the active engagement in the 'public square' of faith communities newer to Britain. In consequence, the Network has had a significant engagement with public policy-making. Work on identifying the values which the distinct historic faiths hold in common and which can contribute to building a strong shared society has been a continuing theme (Inter Faith Network for the UK 1996).

One of the IFN's first tasks was to ensure that its member bodies were fully briefed on the developments taking place which led to the Education Reform Act of 1988, with substantial new provisions relating to religious education and collective worship in schools. The controversy over *The Satanic Verses* by Salman Rushdie (see Chapter 1) led to two joint seminars in 1989 and 1990 with the Commission for Racial Equality on issues relating to the law on blasphemy, respect for religious identity in a multi-faith society, and the role of the media (Commission for Racial Equality 1990).

In 1991 the Network office was consulted by the then Department of the Environment on plans to establish an Inner Cities Religious Council (which was set up the following year), to discuss issues of mutual concern to government and faith communities in relation to urban policy, and was represented at the Council's meetings. It also played a major role in the work of the so-called 'Lambeth Group' set up in 1997 to bring together government, the Royal Household, the New Millennium Experience Company and faith community representatives to discuss plans for the forthcoming Millennium celebrations, including the development of what became the 'Faith Zone' at the Greenwich Dome (see Plate 3.8). The Network was represented on the Group by Dr Harriet Crabtree, then its Deputy Director, who became its Director in 2007.

The 'Lambeth Group', co-chaired by the Archbishop of Canterbury's chaplain and by a senior civil servant from the Department for Culture, Media and Sport, demonstrated the potential for fruitful engagement between government and different faith communities. This led to the involvement of the Network in helping with the faith community dimensions of the Golden Jubilee events in 2002. These included a Golden Jubilee Young People's Faith Forum at St James's Palace, reflecting the Network's concern for encouraging inter faith engagement among young people, and a major reception at Buckingham Palace for faith community representatives (Golden Jubilee Office 2002; Inter Faith Network for the UK 2004). It also led, indirectly, to a Home Office review, *Working Together: Co-operation between Government and Faith Communities* (Home Office Faith Communities Unit 2004), and the creation some while later of a Faith Communities Consultative Council.[4] By that time the Network already had in place a Faith Communities Forum, bringing together its member faith communities at national level to discuss issues of common concern, as part of the development by the Network of more formal frameworks for engagement between organizations within the different categories of Network membership.

Over the past decade, the Network has also been heavily involved in work with government departments, local authorities and other public bodies in developing material relating to community cohesion. It contributed significantly to the development of the Labour government's inter faith strategy, *Face to Face and Side by Side: A Framework for Partnership in our Multi Faith Society* (Department for Communities and Local Government 2008). There has also been significant engagement by the Network with developments in the field of equalities legislation.

The Network does not just work with government and other public bodies. It is under the direction of a trustee body reflecting its membership, and seeks to reflect the changing needs of faith communities and inter faith bodies as they work together to promote good inter faith relations in the UK.

Conclusion

The development of inter faith activity across the UK has been the outcome of work by many different organizations. The existence of a national linking and enabling body sharing good practice, holding regular meetings and seminars on inter faith issues, producing resource materials and facilitating engagement with government and other public bodies has been an important factor in giving this work momentum and cohesion.[5] It is a significant fact that the development of frameworks for structured inter faith engagement and dialogue are further advanced in the UK than in most other countries.

References

Commission for Racial Equality (1990). *Law, Blasphemy and the Multi-Faith Society.* London: Commission for Racial Equality.

Department for Communities and Local Government (2008). *Face to Face and Side by Side: A Framework for Partnership in our Multi Faith Society.* London: Department for Communities and Local Government.

Golden Jubilee Office (2002). *Golden Jubilee Young People's Faith Forum 10 June 2002 Report.* London: Department for Culture, Media and Sport.

Home Office Faith Communities Unit (2004). *Working Together: Co-operation between Government and Faith Communities.* London: Department for Communities and Local Government.

Inter Faith Network for the UK (1996). *The Quest for Common Values.* London: Inter Faith Network for the UK.

Inter Faith Network for the UK (2004). *Connect: Different Faiths, Shared Values.* London: Inter Faith Network for the UK.

Inter Faith Network for the UK (2005). *The Local Inter Faith Guide.* London: Inter Faith Network for the UK.

Inter Faith Network for the UK (2007). *20 Years: Milestones on the Journey Together Towards Greater Inter Faith Understanding and Co-operation.* London: Inter Faith Network for the UK.

Inter Faith Network for the UK (2009). *Inter Faith Organisations in the UK.* 5th edition. London: Inter Faith Network for the UK

Notes

1 For more information see website. Available HTTP: www.interfaith.org.uk/rcommit.htm (accessed 14 June 2011).

2 In accordance with the Inter Faith Network's own practice, in this particular case study 'inter faith' is used rather than 'interfaith'. Reflecting faith community conversations at the time it was founded, the Network uses 'inter faith' to signal that inter faith engagement is between different, distinct faith traditions each with their own integrity and that these are not merged or subsumed in a new entity characterized as 'interfaith'.

3 There are Standing Advisory Councils on Religious Education in every local authority in England and Wales. Their responsibilities are to advise the local authority on issues relating to the teaching of religious education and on collective acts of worship in schools. For more information see Chapter 8.

4 The Faith Communities Consultative Council did not meet after the formation in May 2010 of the Coalition government and was disbanded in the summer of 2011. This reflected the government's expressed preference for *ad hoc* meetings on a bilateral or multilateral basis, rather than the use of a standing body of this kind.

5 For a further account of its work up to 2007 see *20 Years: Milestones on the Journey Together Towards Greater Inter Faith Understanding and Co-operation* (Inter Faith Network for the UK 2007).

4 Alternative spiritualities
Marginal *and* mainstream

Graham Harvey and Giselle Vincett

For most of the post-war period, it was the historical relation between state and church, and the distinctive and mutually shaping organizational forms of national churches and nation state, which dominated the imagination about 'religion' – whether that was a secular or a religious perspective. As the Introduction has argued, however, one effect of the secular orientation of the 1960s–1980s was to turn a blind eye to religious change, and – in effect – to deregulate the religious field. In the context of the market, new actors and new forms of religiosity were free to develop and flourish. One of the most significant was the multifaceted phenomenon called 'alternative spirituality'. This chapter explains the various forms and streams of such spirituality, and reveals their historical roots, which often go back to the nineteenth century. It shows how such spirituality inhabits a different space in society, and has a different status, from the forms of religion reviewed in the two preceding chapters (the 'world religions'). In some ways it is truly 'alternative' to majority religion and culture, and it is very important in supporting various minority identities. Women are prominent. It is not included in some of the most important interfaith bodies, such as the Inter Faith Network for the UK, is rarely taken seriously at government level and is sometimes ridiculed. But in other ways it is part of the majority, not least in terms of the class and ethnicity of those who are involved, and the pervasiveness of elements of spirituality in the wider culture – including complementary and alternative medicine (CAM). This chapter assesses its significance, and discusses some of its distinctively British origins and linkages (see also Chapter 5 on God-change and alternative spirituality, and the Introduction on CAM in healthcare).

On 21 September 2010 the Charity Commission for England and Wales granted the Druid Network charitable status after a four-year application process. Under UK charity law, a religious organization may be granted charitable status if it offers public benefit, such as 'the promotion of moral or spiritual welfare or improvement for the benefit of the community' (Charity Commission for England and Wales 2010: 3). To be considered a 'religion' under charity law any religious organization must fit four criteria:

1   belief in a god (or gods) or goddess (or goddesses), or supreme being, or divine or transcendental being or entity or spiritual principle, which is the object or focus of the religion (referred to … as 'supreme being or entity')
2   a relationship between the believer and the supreme being or entity by showing worship of, reverence for, or veneration of the supreme being or entity

3   a degree of cogency, cohesion, seriousness and importance
4   an identifiable positive, beneficial, moral or ethical framework.

(Charity Commission for England and Wales 2010: 4)

It was argued that Druidry, which is polytheistic, answered the first two conditions because 'nature' is considered the 'supreme being' and because both spirits of nature and multiple deities are worshipped. The board accepted that the Druid Network was not only 'based upon a concern for the physical environment but based upon a sacred and honourable relationship with nature' (Charity Commission for England and Wales 2010: 5). It admitted that Druidry, 'was not simply a way of life or philosophy but that it had a spiritual reverence, veneration and recognition of a divine being or entity or spiritual principle and therefore a religious perspective' (Charity Commission for England and Wales 2010: 6). It accepted that in its facilitation and encouragement of worship, reverence and veneration 'of the supreme being or entity', and through its organization of public celebrations and rituals, the Druid Network fulfilled the third point. The diversity of belief within Druidry was recognized by the Commission, but it affirmed that the Network had satisfactorily demonstrated 'a core system of conduct or practice in the form of doctrines and practices' and accepted that this 'could arise by custom and practice, as opposed to a written tradition' (Charity Commission for England and Wales 2010: 9). The morals and ethics of Druidry were also acknowledged as positive and beneficial (Charity Commission for England and Wales 2010: 11). The board concluded that the Druid Network had demonstrated sufficient evidence of positive benefit to the public at large, through such activities as facilitating worship, 'contributing to the preservation of ancient monuments and artefacts', involvement in and financial support for environmental projects, 'raising awareness and developing understanding of ethical and environmental issues', and involvement in interfaith activities (Charity Commission for England and Wales 2010: 13).

The release of this judgement, as well as a public statement by the Druid Network announcing their new charitable status, provoked a flurry of mainstream news stories and comments on the blogosphere ranging from factual reports to bemused commentary. Melanie Phillips in the *Daily Mail* opined, 'Will someone please tell me this is all a joke?' (Phillips 2010). Her objection appeared to be less that the Druid Network had been given charitable status and more that Druidry is not a 'proper' religion according to her personal criteria which were both theistic and transcendent (and would exclude, for example, much of Buddhism and many indigenous religions). She not only treats Druids as figures of fun, but calls the decision of the Charity Commission 'malevolent'. The articles and comments to be found on the blogosphere similarly range from elation by Pagans and Druids (who saw the decision as vindication of their religions) to outrage on the part of religious conservatives. To the critics, Druidry was just about acceptable, so long as it remained, in the words of Phillips, a 'bunch of eccentrics who annually dress up in strange robes at Stonehenge to celebrate the summer solstice' (Phillips 2010). The idea that it might be considered a serious religion was ridiculed and considered nonsensical.

This vignette shows a number of things. First, it demonstrates that controversy is generated whenever alternative spiritualities are mentioned or given serious consideration (even the placement of this chapter in this book was a controversial decision). Second, the Charity Commission's decision is one instance of how alternative spiritualities are rapidly becoming 'mainstreamed' *at the same time* that they continue to be marginalized by some. Alternative spiritualities now have recognition and acceptance in – and growing influence upon – the media and popular culture, healthcare, institutions such as the military or

hospitals (in the provision of time off or chaplains, for example), and, increasingly, in education. Third, Druidry is itself a good exemplar of the way in which many alternative
spiritualities are peculiarly British and have shifted in character and influences over time,
especially during the timeframe of interest in this book. And lastly, the arguments with
which the Druid Network sought to convince the Charity Commission of their status as a
religion would apply to many other alternative spiritualities, especially Paganisms.

This chapter does not provide exhaustive accounts of the history of alternative spiritualities in the UK, or detail all the beliefs, differences and overlaps between groups. These
topics have been well researched and written upon already, as the reading list at the end of
the chapter indicates. Rather, the chapter will show how alternative spiritualities are rooted
in Britain (the place and landscape) and in British culture, how they are so important for
understanding religion in modern Britain, especially since 1945, and why they have come
to have some similarities with 'minority' religions (like those in the previous chapter),
whilst also being in some ways part of the 'majority' and the mainstream (more like the
Christian churches considered in Chapter 1).

Alternative spiritualities in the British context: moving from the periphery to the centre

'Alternative spiritualities' is an umbrella term that includes many different spiritualities or religions, and which highlights several key elements in the forms of spirituality discussed here. As
the name suggests, alternative spiritualities consciously contrast themselves with mainstream,
traditional forms of Christianity and with what they consider to be 'institutionalized religion'
in general. They present themselves as an 'alternative' which an individual may choose. As
Vincett and Woodhead explain, many members of alternative spiritualities draw:

> a contrast between 'religion', understood as having to do with external, dogmatic
> authority set over the individual, and 'spirituality', understood as having to do with the
> deepest experiences of the individual as he or she comes in touch with that which is
> most sacred, or of ultimate concern.
>
> (Vincett and Woodhead 2009: 320)

The plural 'spiritualities' indicates that a wide range of groups, practices and beliefs cluster
under this umbrella. New Age, Paganisms and Mind-Body-Spirit or Wellbeing cultures are
related spiritualities which are often practically different (that is, in what practitioners do),
but very often have similar beliefs or value systems. While some observers would group all
of these together under New Age (Heelas 1996; Houtman and Aupers 2008), we take the
position that they are sufficiently different to warrant separate subcategories. Indeed, diversity between traditions has increased as each tradition has matured and splinter groups have
formed. Within alternative spiritualities, 'diversity' itself has come to be a discourse which
is increasingly emphasized and celebrated, often with reference to diversity in the natural
world. Diversity also arises because alternative spiritualities generally hold that individual
practitioners have the ultimate authority over their own spiritual journey, overriding other
authorities such as the community, its leaders or texts. Paradoxically, however, noting other
potential sources of authority is one way of distinguishing between alternative spiritualities.
For example, some seek to learn from 'nature', others from particular deities, ancestors,
angels and spirits. That is, there are sources of revelation but (as in Protestant Christianity)
the individual must determine his or her own response.

This is not to say that even the most individualistic of alternative spiritualities are necessarily self-centred or narcissistic or that those involved with alternative spiritualities recognize no other authority than the self. Even those who practise individually often come together at large festivals or in informal networks, such as at Mind-Body-Spirit fairs or via magazines and internet networks. Indeed, alternative spiritualities have long interrogated the notion of 'community' and sought to create new (or alternative) forms of community. Hanegraaf (2009) points out that the early New Age, particularly as it formed in the UK, strongly emphasized community-orientated values, and that influence is still found in the New Age of British utopian intentional communities – most famously, Findhorn in Scotland. Similarly, many involved in alternative spiritualities (New Age spiritual teachers or Mind-Body-Spirit massage therapists, for example) see their activities as forging bonds between individuals and reaching out to those isolated by what are seen as the alienating effects of late modernity. In fact, a common way of thinking about 'community' across alternative spiritualities is the metaphor of the 'web'. We refer here to a sense among practitioners that every being in the world is linked in a complex and comprehensive web. The web includes spirits, deities, ancestors and elements of the natural world such as trees or rivers, or even the internet as far as it promotes communication and community. A common value or ethic, then, across traditions, is the necessity of 'nurturing the web'. When New Age practitioners build relationships with spirit guides, Druids celebrate in sacred groves or ancient stone circles, Mind-Body-Spirit therapists offer yoga lessons, or Reiki masters promote world peace by placing crystals in significant locations, each has a sense of reaching out to the web and strengthening the links and pathways upon it. In these ways and more, alternative spiritualities hold together concerns about the individual and the communal (see Text box 11).

Because alternative spiritualities have no official church or religious leaders whose authority is recognized by all (even by all of those within a single tradition), we must look to other ways in which they may influence, co-operate with or subvert political (state) power. Below we will discuss the use and widespread influence of alternative spiritualities on the media and popular cultures, but its members may also more consciously attempt to influence policy by involvement in various 'progressive' causes such as feminism, environmentalism, the peace movement or social justice campaigns. Further, those involved in alternative spiritualities often use public space in innovative and challenging ways. These range from the leading of rituals by Pagans during anti-globalization demonstrations to the increasing adoption of language and practices associated with alternative spiritualities within healthcare. As the Introduction to this volume discusses, 'wellbeing', for example, has almost become a catchphrase in much healthcare literature, especially nursing, pointing to a holistic approach to the person borrowed at least in part from those involved in Mind-Body-Spirit. Similarly, although religion is often 'the elephant in the room' in the workplace, acknowledged or challenged through dress and holidays but rarely openly discussed, certain alternative spirituality practices (and hence their ethos and values) increasingly influence management training and corporate bonding exercises (Aupers and Houtman 2006).

This book takes as its starting point religion in post-Second World War Britain. Although the origins of spirituality in Britain go back to the nineteenth century, and there was a flourishing around the start of the twentieth century (partly as a result of the influence of Asian religions like Buddhism and Hinduism, transmitted within a colonial context – see Chapter 3), there was a lull in the interwar period. In the 1940s people could, in theory, still be prosecuted for practising witchcraft, and alternative spiritualities were highly controversial:

swinging from sensationalist popular fascination (e.g. the popularity of fiction about witches in the first half of the twentieth century) to scaremongering about black magic and Satanism, to acceptability in esoteric ritual societies such as the Freemasons (Heelas 1996; Hutton 1999). The 1951 repeal of the Witchcraft Act 1736 and the Vagrancy Act 1824 (which had made it illegal to accuse others of witchcraft but also to claim to be able to 'work magic') marked changing attitudes towards alternative spiritualities. The publication of ritual guides proliferated and took self-identified Witches 'out of the broom closet' and into public consciousness. The intersection of changing values and beliefs (e.g. towards the body) with changing social roles (e.g. for women) and changing social structures (e.g. with immigration, or the increasing power of the state over education) was generative of or consciously addressed in the development of alternative spiritual traditions (see Chapter 10 on cultural change for more discussion of these shifts and their importance for religion).

A variety of other intersections between alternative spiritualities and trends in popular culture have emerged and evolved since the 1960s. It is not always possible to determine whether alternative spiritualities or popular cultural trends take the lead. The point is that there is a confluence or a dynamic resonance of shared interests (see Lynch 2007; Partridge 2005, and Case study 5 in this volume co-authored by Partridge). To illustrate this, two broad trends might be identified: a therapeutic turn and a pervasive re-enchantment. A visit to any standard supermarket will reveal the extent to which 'alternative' therapies, especially holistic ones and those that might have had esoteric roots (e.g. homeopathy), are now mainstream. This provides a broad context in which more focused spiritual services can be offered. People are taking care of their own wellbeing – physical, mental and spiritual – in ways that blend 'alternative' with 'popular'. The re-enchantment that contests secularizing trends is indicated, for example, by the rise, beginning in the 1990s, of performance cultures both in alternative spiritualities and in popular culture. Colourful dramatic rituals are a frequent part of public protests, and storytelling and live music venues have proliferated. In contrast with the suggestion that 'spirituality' involves thoroughly individualized experiences, many alternative spirituality practitioners are involved in creative and performing arts in ways that establish interesting social experiments. Not every story or musical performance is explicitly 'religious', but even in the Druid-originated 'Bardic Chair' competitions that now take place annually in many British cities and towns the simple fact that people will gather to hear enchanting stories or play music together is celebrated.

TEXT BOX 11

Terry Pratchett's Discworld

Terry Pratchett's Discworld series of novels are popular among many alternative spirituality practitioners because the characters often espouse a worldview which resonates with pagans and others. Here, for example, the character Granny Weatherwax muses about the forest in much the same way that many alternative spirituality practitioners think about the 'other-than-human' or 'more-than-human':

> There was a way in which those brooding forests could have a mind …
>   Of course, it'd be a mind made up of all the other little minds inside it; plant minds, bird minds, even the great slow minds of the trees themselves … She'd often thought of the forest as a sprawling creature … drowsy and purring with

> bumblebees in the summer, roaring and raging in autumn gales, curled in on itself and sleeping in the winter. It occurred to her that in addition to being a collection of other things, a forest was a thing alive in itself.
>
> (Pratchett 1989: 113)

Like other religions, alternative spiritualities hold a mirror up to the societies in which they are practised. As such, it may be argued that alternative spiritualities are representative of some of the biggest and most profound social changes in British society over the past 65 years: secularization and resacralization (see Chapter 11 for discussion of these trends), individualization versus the communal, changing gender relations, challenges to ideas about the body and science, and the various movements which have motivated different generations (peace/anti-war, environmentalism, anti-capitalism). Additionally, the existence and popularity of alternative spiritualities immediately demonstrates the diversity of religion in late modern Britain. As Chapter 1 shows, not only has Christianity changed in 'flavour' over the past half-century (it is at once more liberal and progressive *and* more Pentecostal and evangelistic), but the profile of a 'typical' Christian has also changed. As the chapter also documents, the typical Christian of British heritage is likely to be older now and there are more Christians with different ethnic heritages (Chinese, Korean, Indian and African to name a few) in the pews today. However, the large-scale departure from the churches by white British people since the 1960s does not necessarily mean that those who left the churches abandoned religion. As the Introduction shows, religious identities in post-war Britain are no longer simple. Most of these 'unchurched' people continue to identify themselves as 'Christian', but both they and even some who tick 'no religion' on the Census, also engage with or absorb beliefs from alternative spiritualities, and in some cases they relate to other religions as well, such as Buddhism (see Chapter 3 and Vincett 2007, 2008, 2009).

The small number of people who now publicly declare a clear 'alternative' religious identity (e.g. Holistic, New Age, Pagan, Wiccan, Heathen and so forth) is clearly only part of the story. Vincett and Woodhead (2009: 323), drawing upon different research results from Europe and North America, give the following estimates for those involved in some way with alternative spiritualities:

1 the number of active, highly committed, regular participants stands at around 2–5 per cent of the population
2 the level of adherence/affiliation (indicated by those claiming to be 'spiritual but not religious') stands at around 10–20 per cent
3 agreement with beliefs characteristic of spirituality – such as belief in 'some sort of spirit or life force' or 'God as something within each person rather than something out there' – lies somewhere between 20 per cent and 40 per cent.

Whilst those who would agree with numbers two and three on this list are less likely to be involved in traditional forms of religion, agreement does not exclude Christians or members of other faiths. However, the rise of such beliefs does point to a religious shift among the general population: it indicates that people are 'doing' religion differently – the frequent popular interpretation of 'spirituality' as something personal and interior suggests a privatization and 'personalization' of religion, for example. As we have mentioned, the preference for the word 'spiritual' over 'religious' often indicates an understanding of traditional religion as dogmatic and severe, with 'spirituality' seen as the opposite to that. Further, it suggests that traditional language about the divine is changing, and that the divine is frequently now seen as immanent and life affirming. All of these religious attitudes and beliefs have been hallmarks of alternative spiritualities, which is what makes their assertion by a large percentage of the general population remarkable.

In their book *The Spiritual Revolution* (2005), Heelas and Woodhead investigated what they term 'the holistic milieu', a term roughly synonymous with 'alternative spiritualities' (though Paganism fits less comfortably within Heelas and Woodhead's term than New Age and Mind-Body-Spirit). Extrapolating from their local data, they estimate that 'slightly over 900,000 inhabitants of Great Britain are active on a weekly basis in the holistic milieu of the nation' (Heelas and Woodhead 2005: 53). Based upon these numbers, they refute the claim of Steve Bruce that 'the number of people [in Britain] who have shown any interest in alternative religions is minute' (Bruce 1996: 273). The research thus suggests that the numbers involved in alternative spirituality need to be interpreted along a continuum of participation and belief. On one end of such a continuum we may place those who are regularly active in a religious group. At the other end of the scale are those who have adopted ideas or practices characteristic of alternative spiritualities from various media.

Cole Moreton, writing in the UK national newspaper *The Guardian*, goes so far as to claim that 'at its loosest, Paganism is beginning to look like our new national faith'. Moreton cites BBC programming as being inspired by ideas drawn from alternative spiritualities for use in programmes ranging from 'children's shows such as *Raven* and *Merlin*, or Saturday tea-time blockbusters *Robin Hood* and *Doctor Who*' (Moreton 2009). Even when alternative spiritualities are represented as 'alternative' or unconventional in the media (or simply ignored in some mass-media newspapers and national broadcasts – as Chapter 7 shows), that very alterity is sometimes represented as carrying cultural capital. For example, when a group of Wiccans appeared on the US television show *The Simpsons* in 2009, the character Lisa (herself the most unconventional of her family) viewed them as impossibly cool. Television programmes such as the BBC's drama *Being Human* and books and films such as the *Twilight* series, the *Goddess Summoning* series, and *Avatar* all explore themes which might be thought of as part of alternative spiritualities. As Puttick has noted, books dealing with alternative spiritualities are now published by the 'large conglomerate – i.e. mainstream – publishers' in what is not simply a major category, but an 'uber-category' (2005: 131, 136). Whilst this does not necessarily mean that fans of such programmes, books and films are alternative spirituality practitioners, they are examples of some ways in which popular culture and religious belief interact. To give a concrete example, one young man Vincett interviewed about his religious beliefs and practices (see Case study 3 for details of this research) at first claimed he believed in 'nothing', but later, whilst discussing *Avatar*, confessed he believed in a world populated by 'spirits' which exist in both the human and non-human world, including in nature.[1] Though this young man would not identify himself as an adherent of any religion, his beliefs are similar to many alternative spirituality beliefs. Similarly, it is not uncommon for researchers working with young people to find that even those that loosely identify as Christian incorporate beliefs that are not traditionally part of mainstream Christianity (e.g. Francis and Robbins 2005: 161).

Alternative spiritualities as British religions

Cole Moreton (2009) was correct when he linked environmentalism and a turn to 'nature' as a driving force behind the rise in alternative spirituality beliefs. Though not all forms of alternative spiritualities venerate the natural world, many do and many of those active in alternative spiritualities are also active in environmental causes. Indeed, as we discussed above, the holistic concern of alternative spirituality practitioners with the wellbeing of, and interconnections between, self, place and community is a major counter-argument to those who see alternative spiritualities as being primarily concerned with the self (e.g. Heelas 1996). It should also be noted that along with a tendency to 'absorb' ideas and practices from other cultures within alternative spiritualities, there has been a long-term trend towards rediscoveries of local place and belonging, perhaps starting with the festival and back-to-the-earth movements of the 1960s and 1970s. Thus, for example, New Age therapeutic repertoires may include Easternized practices such as yoga, but also increasingly seek understanding of regional or local 'earth energies' available for spiritual or therapeutic practices. They may have a 'global' feel but frequently make a great deal of their location in specific towns or in proximity to particular hills, springs or ancient monuments.

This increasing concern with place within alternative spiritualities points us to the way that many alternative spiritualities are uniquely British. Wicca has been called the only religion that Britain has given the world (Hutton 1999), and indeed many alternative spiritualities have their origins in late nineteenth- and early twentieth-century occultism practised in Britain and Europe. Perhaps more importantly, many alternative spiritualities nurture a sense of connection with early Europeans or Britons through deities, spirits, ancestors and stories of place. Celebrations in specific locations (such as Stonehenge, the New Forest, Greenham Common, as in Plate 2.3, or the Chalice Well Gardens in Glastonbury) have been formative influences on the evolution of these spiritualities. Such rooting of religion in place has occasionally opened some alternative spiritualities to charges of ethnocentrism or racism. However, most practitioners make no claim that any one tradition is superior, or indeed claim that they alone have access to the truth, and most individuals involved in alternative spiritualities tend to be left-leaning, inclusive and progressive (Berger *et al.* 2003; Lynch 2007).

Along with a growing popular knowledge of sacred places, various popular festivals have appropriated the language and sacred spectacle of alternative spiritualities; Edinburgh's Beltane Festival, held annually on the night of 30 April, is perhaps the largest and most overtly Pagan-inspired of these. It attracts about 12,000 people every year according to the website of the organizing society, which also explains that it originates in the Scottish and Irish-Gaelic pre-Christian festival of the same name (www.beltane.org). Such festivals and celebrations take beliefs, myths and feast times associated with alternative spiritualities to the streets. The festival is almost certainly influenced by the ubiquity of performance culture within alternative spirituality events (live music, dancing, storytelling, poetry and theatre), and the tendency of such events to live spectacle (costumed ritualizing, for example). Although the organizers and participants in Edinburgh's Beltane may not be part of any religious community, they contribute to the popular sense that pre-Christian Paganisms (which are associated with current forms of alternative spiritualities) are part of the history of the UK and are an acceptable form of (ethnic) religion to celebrate in public today. Indeed, there are few other annual religious festivals so loudly and colourfully celebrated by so many people on the streets in the UK.

Such events are a reminder that the festival calendar of alternative spiritualities is largely centred round earth, solar and lunar cycles, which help to root participants in the places where they live. These feasts take participants through the cycles of the seasons and make plain the relationships of the earth with the sun and moon. But they also point to one of the most important and (almost) universal characteristics of alternative spiritualities, which is a belief that the ordinary and the worldly are not divorced from the sacred. Even the most esoteric New Ager or Pagan is apt to acknowledge the sacred 'elements' of earth, air, fire and water, those involved in Mind-Body-Spirit practices consciously strive to unite, rather than divorce, mind-body-spirit, and complementary and alternative medicine (CAM) therapies, which frequently cross into alternative spiritualities, are often based upon natural essences viewed as distillations of the healing powers of the earth. The increasing popularity of celebrations (not simply observations) of solar and lunar eclipses and their broadcasting by mainstream media internationally suggest another intersection between alternative spiritualities and the wider culture, and again raise, somewhat provocatively, the question of whether the 'alternative' is now 'popular'.

In a trend that parallels Paul C. Johnson's (2005) insight into a common tension between globalization and indigenization among indigenous religionists, the refrain common in alternative celebrations that 'all the earth is sacred' is in tension with almost partisan affection for specific locations. There are, for instance, Druid organizations that name themselves in relation to the places in which they most frequently gather (e.g. The Cotswold Order of Druids, and the Anderida Grove – named after a pre-Christian tribal location). Ancient megalithic monuments across the UK may attract religiously motivated visitors (pilgrims perhaps) from around the world, but many are also the sites of regular veneration by locally based practitioners of alternative spiritualities. Avebury in Wiltshire attracts Pagans of many kinds, New Agers, earth mystics, healers, psychonauts, those anticipating visitation by space aliens, alongside tourists with more historical, heritage or archaeological interests. A survey in 1998 showed that nearly 20 per cent of visitors claimed 'spiritual' motivations (cited in Wallis and Blain 2007: 2) – and it is likely this percentage has grown in the past decade.

Even more dramatically, Glastonbury is the venue for multiple and sometimes conflicting demonstrations of devotion. Goddess Feminists, Anglican and Catholic Christians, Druids, reincarnated knights of Arthur's Round Table, New Age entrepreneurs and others are catered for by various events, accommodation and catering establishments, religious locations (built or 'natural') and publications. Two annual Christian pilgrimages (one Catholic, one Anglican) along the High Street and into the Abbey, as well as that in which participants in the Glastonbury Goddess Conference process up the multivalent Tor, make it difficult to decide what exactly is 'alternative' (and what is mundane or normative) here. The 'feminine divine' and the 'once and future' King Arthur are just two of the characters shared (and sometimes, but surprisingly rarely, contested) by people who also offer varying interpretations of the hills and springs of the town. While Glastonbury and Avebury may be the most obvious ancient sacred sites in which multiple communities and stories and experiences of the sacred come together, they are by no means the only such places and most areas in the UK can boast similar sites close by.

Between Christianity and 'other' religions

It is appropriate that alternative spiritualities follow the chapters on Christianity and other 'world religions' in the UK in this book as alternative spiritualities owe much to both and have, at times, been a bridge between both with crossings in both directions. Some forms of alternative spiritualities may be viewed as a reflection and blend of the cultures and religions which now make up the UK. A quick glance at the website of the Mind-Body-Spirit festival (the largest of such festivals in the UK) shows images of Hindu dancers, a woman doing yoga and advertisements for lectures on angels and 'the resurrection' aimed at 'liberating'

Jesus 'from the confines of an organized religious domain'.[2] Such eclectic borrowing and blending, rooted though it is in an increased awareness of diverse religious communities within the UK and globally, has been criticized by some as shallow pick 'n' mix religiosity and as religious colonialism. This eclecticism also reveals an often held viewpoint of alternative spiritualities which states that no one religion contains all of the truth and that all religions are built upon common insights and can enable profound experiences of the sacred. At the most extreme end of this viewpoint, practitioners might avow that all religions are, at base, 'the same', but the celebration of diversity within alternative spiritualities appears to be pushing aside such perennialist philosophies. Without denying that it can be problematic, eclecticism in alternative spiritualities does demonstrate another way in which these contemporary religions fit the era: at a time when everything else can be purchased and mixed, with or without reference to originating cultural contexts and guiding cultural and religious elites and authorities, it would be remarkable if religious resources were treated differently. However, it must also be noted, against the critics, that people rarely blend elements in an entirely random way any more than they shop in supermarkets in entirely random ways. Most commonly, people seek things that will enhance existing predispositions and enrich desired experiences.

The postcolonial movements to the UK of diverse religious communities discussed in Chapter 3, especially from former colonies in Asia, made intimate experience of Eastern religious traditions and rituals increasingly possible for non-Asians in the UK. The involvement of high-profile media figures (e.g. the travels and experimentation of the Beatles in the 1960s) brought Asian ideas, stories, sacred figures and rituals to popular culture, and the growth of home-grown British Asian literature, cinema and music continues this influence. There can be no denying that this 'Easternization' was influenced by a colonialist, romanticizing and exoticizing legacy in the UK 'of stereotypical forms' which enabled 'domestication and control' (King 1999: 92) of both postcolonial immigrants and their religious traditions. However, as the discussion of Buddhism and Hinduism in Chapter 3 also shows, it has allowed for the efflorescence of religion, and the creation of peculiarly British forms of such religions (e.g. the Buddhist Society).

The modern formation of alternative spiritualities in the West, especially since the late eighteenth and nineteenth centuries, meant that they were created by people who had a firm cultural grounding in Christianity. Druids, and others, of the time were Christian and would not have seen that dual identity as incompatible (Hutton 2009). However, because alternative spiritualities have been at pains to emphasize their alterity to Christianity, practitioners have rarely acknowledged what their religions 'borrow' from Christianity. One exception has been the acceptance by Pagans of the ways in which the traditions and histories of (originally pre-Christian) deities and (originally Christian) saints mingle together. Jo Pearson (2007) has traced influences from Christianity on the practices of ritual magicians and Wiccans and indicates a growing acceptance of it among at least some Pagans. Similarly, Hanegraaf (2009) notes that the influence of Christianity was 'pronounced' in the millenarianism and utopianism of early and second stage New Age (up to and including the 1960s), and Woodhead (2011) traces the tangled interconnections of Christianity and spirituality for well over a century. The popularity of angels as spirit guides within New Age and Mind-Body-Spirit is an obvious influence from Christianity. Indeed, it is hard to locate any underlying source other than Christianity for some New Age ideas about angels (e.g. Bollinger 2010).

Alternative spiritualities have also drawn upon other religions, both ancient and modern, especially 'Eastern' religions. Pagans will sometimes include deities such as Kwan Yin or Kali among their personal pantheon (although this is rarer as the trend towards indigenization grows); similarly some practitioners drawn to mysticism may borrow mystical techniques from various Eastern traditions, including Sufism. Within New Age and Mind-Body-Spirit, however, the influence of Eastern traditions is much more pronounced: early spiritual teachers from colonized parts of Asia who came to the West were especially influential and continue to be so. The strong focus on alternative healing methods in Mind-Body-Spirit has meant that Asian healing systems have been significantly influential, especially where it is combined with a poetic spirituality, such as in the person of Deepak Chopra or the modern Japanese therapy Reiki, which originated with the mystical experience of its founder, Mikao Usui. Similarly, the practices of yoga and meditation and spiritualities associated with them (some more traditionally Hindu, others Westernized, including occasionally Christian contemplational forms) are widespread in Mind-Body-Spirit.

Much of this can be illustrated by even a brief overview of common features of the ritual patterns of many (though by no means all) alternative spiritualities. The temporary circular ritual spaces and invocations of 'elemental guardians' in the cardinal directions during many Pagan and New Age celebrations are recognizable as inheritances from nineteenth-century esotericism. They evidence experimentation between a Protestant and Enlightenment rationalism, romanticism and interiorization of spirituality and a more Catholic or High Anglican ritualism. The regular insistence in alternative spiritualities that each individual must find a practice and lifestyle that is suitable to them resonates significantly with a particularly Protestant and nonconformist Christian emphasis on each person's right and need to hear God speaking personally through scripture and spirit. Similarly, the 'priesthood of all believers' is evident in a reluctance in most alternative spiritualities to permit sacerdotal hierarchies to evolve from the more facilitating styles of ritual and group leadership. Nonetheless, these groups evolved in distinctive ways once information about more animistic indigenous practices became more widely known. Increasingly in the later twentieth century, the 'elements' came to be spoken of more as authoritative personal beings, worthy of respect, than as forces or archetypes to be controlled or manipulated. Ritual gestures learnt from migrant religious communities (such as those of Hindu *arti*) could be incorporated into the opening and closing phases of rituals as a means of honouring not only light but also particular powerful beings. Alternative spiritualities thus sought to draw on the riches of an increasingly diverse British religious scene as they evolved in relation to the concerns that most strongly motivated practitioners.

Women and spirituality

Women have long had a prominent role in alternative spiritualities (e.g. Helena Blavatsky in the Theosophical movement, the early British Wiccan priestess Doreen Valiente and the Japanese-American Reiki teacher Hawayo Takata). Although nineteenth- and early twentieth-century female leaders in alternative spiritualities may have had sympathies with the causes of first-wave feminism, it is second-wave feminism that has had the most direct influence on alternative spiritualities. As women in the 1960s and early 1970s began to question their roles and the social construction of 'femininity' (see Chapter 10), a perspective that 'began by asking why little girls had to wear pink ... segued naturally into one that asked why God was a man and women's religious experiences went unnoticed' (Eller 1993: 42). Eller details how women's Consciousness Raising groups, especially in the United States, played a key role in the spiritual questioning of women of this period. At the same time, Christian feminist theologians were asking searching questions of their own, perhaps most vividly encapsulated by Mary Daly staging a walk-out of the Harvard University Chapel where she had been invited to be the first woman to deliver a sermon in 1971. Many of these disaffected Christian women felt the need to explore new spiritualities which would allow for 'female sacrality' (Raphael 1996). Meanwhile, the radical feminist hereditary witch Z. Budapest stamped her mark on the early formation of one of the most influential witches of the late twentieth century, Starhawk, whose first book *The Spiral Dance* (1979) was not only a detailed DIY kit for aspiring egalitarian witches, but was influential in the proliferation of a feminist revisioning of history and myth. Although this revisioning was often romantic and inaccurate, it was nevertheless intensely empowering for many women and fuelled much good later scholarship.

Spiritual feminists continue to be influenced by secular feminist writing and scholarship, and the importance of both French feminism and the 'performance' feminism of Judith Butler can be seen in Goddess Feminist groups. Less obviously, perhaps, the remarkable appeal of Mind-Body-Spirit to women – Heelas and Woodhead (2005: 94) put the percentage of women involved in holistic spiritualities as high as 80 per cent – clearly indicates that such spiritualities offer something special to women. Woodhead's thesis is that alternative spiritualities, and especially Mind-Body-Spirit spiritualities, offer women a way of balancing and coping with their often contradictory roles and gender performances in late modernity (Woodhead 2007, 2008).

Who is an alternative spirituality practitioner?

As the opening example of the reaction to the decision taken by the Charity Commission to the case of the Druid Network showed, practitioners of alternative spiritualities are often portrayed by others as eccentric at best and risible and narcissistic at worst (in the contemporary UK alternative spirituality practitioners are rarely portrayed as dangerous). It is certainly true that the costumes and rituals of some alternative spirituality practitioners may seem to justify this assessment. It is also true that alternative spiritualities often attract those marginalized by society in some way, but this is also true of other religions and has been particularly important in the history of Christianity. However, the assumption that alternative spirituality practitioners are all eccentric misfits does not fit the reality. Research undertaken by Berger *et al.* (2003) in the US shows that the typical Pagan is white (90.8 per cent of their sample), middle-class (defined by income level only) and often well educated (with at least one post-secondary degree). As in the 'holistic milieu' observed by Heelas and Woodhead (2005), Berger *et al.* point to the predominance of women involved in Paganism (64.8 per cent), and the UK Office for National Statistics reports that in the 2001 Census, 67 per cent of Wiccans were female (Office for National Statistics 2004). Berger *et al.* are at pains to point out that while Pagans in America tend to lean towards the left politically, they are nowhere close to the culturally and sexually experimental stereotype: over half are in stable relationships (married or co-habiting), 41.2 per cent have children, many work within the computer industry or are students, writers, teachers or stay-at-home mothers (Berger *et al.* 2003: 18, 33). They conclude that Pagans may belong to an alternative religion, but practitioners 'are demographically mainstream' (Berger *et al.* 2003: 34).

The same can be said of those who participate in the New Age or Mind-Body-Spirit. Although Hanegraaf traces the New Age from its roots in the counter-culture, he claims that there is now a tendency towards 'adaption and assimilation', so that the New Age can now be seen as a 'professionalized "spiritual" wing within the cultural mainstream' (2009: 345). Heelas and Woodhead (2005: 93) state that of those involved in what they call the holistic milieu 'the great majority' were (or had been) teachers, nurses or social workers. Given that most of the groups and activities that Heelas and Woodhead surveyed had to do with Mind-Body-Spirit, perhaps it is unsurprising that most of the careers cited are caring and expressive. However, this would also reflect the sorts of careers that women were traditionally encouraged to enter (the majority of Heelas and Woodhead's informants were women of late middle-age). It is noteworthy, however, that more than half had a university or college degree (Heelas and Woodhead 2005: 93). We may conclude, then, that aside from being well educated and white, there is nothing in any of the evidence to suggest anything other than that the overwhelming majority of those involved with alternative spiritualities are fairly ordinary citizens. However, the recent study by Olson and Vincett of young people in deprived, working-class areas, mentioned above, suggests that elements of spirituality may be more important among working-class people than has previously been documented.[3]

The tension in alternative spiritualities between a discourse of alterity and the reality of fairly mainstream participants may be explained by the fact that many participants feel themselves marginalized in some way. This has perhaps best been explored in the case of women, as we have shown above with feminist women and those involved with Mind-Body-Spirit (see Vincett 2007; Woodhead 2007, 2008). Goldenberg (2004) has bemoaned what she perceives as the 'domestication' and 'routinization' of words and figures such as 'witch', claiming that the mainstreaming of witchcraft weakens the traditional idea of a witch as a woman on the margins who is nevertheless powerful enough to critique or challenge oppressive political and religious systems. Similarly, when one Pagan informant claimed that 'all the really interesting stuff happens at the margins [of society]', he expressed the belief of many (Vincett 2007: 169–170). Heelas early observed that one of the key tenets of New Age is 'your lives do not work', or in other words, 'the mores of the established order – its materialism, competitiveness, together with the importance it attaches to playing roles – are held to disrupt what it is to be authentically human' (1996: 18). There is thus an *ideal* of alterity within alternative spiritualities which is a critique not just of traditional religions, but of mainstream society, borne out by the fact that many alternative spirituality participants are politically liberal (there are, however, political conservatives within alternative spiritualities, most notably in prosperity New Age movements and within Heathenism or High Magick). There is also, as we have noted, a common ethical imperative within alternative spiritualities to be involved with progressive causes – the UK group the Dragon Environmental Network, which uses 'eco-magic' to protest against environmental destruction, is a good example of this. The importance of both the counter-culture and protest movements (such as the peace camp at Greenham Common during the 1980s, see Plate 2.3) to alternative spiritualities has meant that a large store of stories and foundational myths within alternative spiritualities have their base in this discourse of alterity.

Conclusions

While practitioners of alternative spiritualities are numerically a minority, their ideas, practices and products (e.g. health remedies and festivals) have come to have a significant presence in the larger culture. They are now familiar to a wider population in ways that would not have been the case even a few decades ago. There are alternative ways of being religious or spiritual that are increasingly familiar. Alternative spiritualities are part of the diversification of contemporary culture, and even provide bridges between putatively distinct identities and practices. It is increasingly possible to openly identify as a Christian or Jew or Buddhist and, at the same time, participate in alternative spiritualities events, seek benefit from alternative spiritualities therapies or hold alternative spiritualities ideas. Those with hybrid identities ('Fusers' as Vincett 2008 labels them) and consumers (of religion as much as of other 'goods') seem more indicative of the flavour of the contemporary moment than those whose religiosity is constrained within clear normative, dogmatic and institutional boundaries (see the Introduction to this volume). This is one sense in which alternative spiritualities have become more like the larger culture than its alternative in the post-war period.

At the same time, the perception of alterity is what makes alternative spiritualities attractive to some people, and these religions retain strong tendencies to speak from the margins and empower more marginalized identities and causes. They provide another way (alongside other religions) of contesting the perceived male domination, scientism, materialism, consumerism and shallowness of contemporary culture. They promote ideas that can either contest the dominance of scientism or assert the possibility of fusing spirituality with rationality, for example by fusing thoroughly naturalistic understandings of the world with seemingly metaphysical ones. Alternative spiritualities also continue to be 'alternative' in their relationship to other religions. Some have managed to gain acceptance in some interfaith dialogue groups or events, others have not – often on the grounds that they are too new, too strange or too disturbing to the often fragile social processes involved. Thus, while the Druid Network has gained charitable status, not all Druids or Pagans, let alone other alternative spiritualities members, find a welcome in events that are otherwise inclusive and sometimes pluralist (for example, alternative spiritualities are not included in the Inter Faith Network described in Case study 2). Nor do government bodies tend to consult with them or count them as 'proper' religions.

However, the ambiguous position of alternative spiritualities is also indicated by the willingness, for example, of private companies to employ 'alternative' trainers for personnel development, of educationalists to encourage 'spirituality' in primary schools, and of healthcare providers (whether National Health or private) to advocate complementary and alternative medicines (see the Introduction to this volume and Chapter 6 on ritual change). In these and other public arenas it has become noticeably easier for officials to speak or write about 'spirituality' than about 'religion'. That this term continues to be nebulous is, perhaps, part of its virtue: seeming to be attractively inclusive and neither hierarchical nor dogmatic. It might not always refer to specific groups within the alternative spiritualities, but it may provide an entry point into inclusion.

Alternative spiritualities are, then, alternative in various ways but are now a significant element of the popular and mainstream culture of post-war Britain, and beyond. Indeed, it is perhaps this very feature of alternative spiritualities: the attempt to balance and hold together tradition and innovation, diversity with commonalities, pluralism and individualism, rationality with spirituality, which makes them, perhaps even more than other religions in the UK, religions which are 'at home' in the social and cultural conditions of contemporary Britain.

Key terms

Animism: Sometimes interpreted as 'believing in spirits', but more usefully refers to 'treating the world as a community of persons most of whom are not human'.

Esotericism: Tradition using religious practices for self-knowledge and improvement, emphasizing imagination, correspondence between seemingly different things (e.g. stars and humans), a living cosmos and the possibility of change.

Fusers: People who fuse putatively distinct religious traditions, such as Quaker-Pagans, Buddhist-Christians or Jewish-Witches. Such people have hybrid religious identities.

Indigenization: Coined by Paul Johnson to identify a process among contemporary indigenous people in which groups, practices and events are made relevant to what is perceived to be local, traditional and specific, rather than global, general and open to all, the term can be applied to some alternative spiritualities when they emphasize particular places, specific times and received traditions.

Mind-Body-Spirit: A complex of holistic traditions blending interests in physical, spiritual, mental and other kinds of wellbeing.

New Age: Sometimes used as if it were a synonym of all alternative spiritualities, sometimes specifically of Mind-Body-Spirit traditions, and only sometimes used by people as the correct name for what interests them. It implies a specific belief in a change of eras or the anticipating of an 'Aquarian' age of harmony to replace the current, more dualistic and divided age.

Paganism: A new religion, drawing on ancient religions, focused on the celebration of nature (understood in various ways) rather than on transcendence.

Further reading

Bloom, William (ed.) (2000). *The Holistic Revolution*. London: Allen Lane/Penguin. A collection of essential readings about alternative spiritualities, emphasizing holistic interests. It includes work by leading exponents of so-called New Age, neoshamanic, self-therapeutic and 'new science' movements, and argues that these amount to an important revolution in thought and life.

Harvey, Graham (2009). 'Paganism', in Linda Woodhead, Hiroko Kawanami and Chris Partridge (eds), *Religions in the Modern World: Traditions and Transformations*. London and New York, NY: Routledge, 357–378. A survey of key features, practices and scholarly debates about Paganism. In addition to vignettes of specific practices, it discusses the meanings of 'nature' and the relationship between Pagans and modernity, or the wider contemporary culture.

Hutton, Ronald (1991). *The Pagan Religions of the Ancient British Isles*. London: Blackwell. An exhaustive survey of what historical evidence can reveal about contemporary Paganism, especially witchcraft, in relation to ancient paganism, medieval witches, early modern esotericists and Romantics. It places Paganism and, by implication, related alternative spiritualities in their proper historical context.

Lewis, James R. and Murphy Pizza (eds) (2009). *A Handbook of Contemporary Paganism*. Leiden: Brill. A collection of essays that showcase recent and emerging debates among Pagans and among scholars interested in Paganism. It includes sections on history, sociology, magic and ritual, theology, traditions, family, youth, popular culture and racial-ethnic issues.

Sutcliffe, Steven and Marion Bowman (eds) (2000). *Beyond New Age: Exploring Alternative Spirituality*. Edinburgh: Edinburgh University Press. An exploration of many of the forms taken by alternative spiritualities. Divided into sections on people, places and practices, it offers important understandings of the contemporary role of these movements in relation to their precursors and context.

References

Aupers, Stef and Dick Houtman (2006). 'Beyond the Spiritual Supermarket: The Social and Public Significance of New Age Spirituality', *Journal of Contemporary Religion* 21/2: 201–222.

Berger, Helen A., Evan A. Leach and Leigh S. Shaffer (2003). *Voices from the Pagan Census: A National Survey of Witches and Neo-Pagans in the United States*. Columbia, SC: University of South Carolina Press.

Bollinger, Beth (2010). 'Angel Invitation', *Accidental Rabbit Trails* Blog. Online. Available HTTP: http://accidental-rabbit-trails.blogspot.com/2010/11/angel-invitation.html (accessed 23 November 2010).

Bruce, Steve (1996). *Religion in the Modern World: From Cathedrals to Cults*. Oxford: Oxford University Press.

Charity Commission for England and Wales (2010). *The Druid Network: Decision Made On 21 September 2010*. London: Charity Commission.

Eller, Cynthia (1993). *Living in the Lap of the Goddess: The Feminist Spirituality Movement in America*. Boston, MA: Beacon Press.

Francis, Leslie J. and Mandy Robbins (2005). *Urban Hope and Spiritual Health: The Adolescent Voice*. Peterborough: Epworth.

Goldenberg, Naomi (2004). 'Witches and Words', *Embodying Feminist Liberation Theologies: a Special Edition of Feminist Theology*, 12/2: 203–211.

Hanegraaf, Wouter (2009). 'New Age Religion', in Linda Woodhead, Hiroko Kawanami and Chris Partridge (eds), *Religions in the Modern World: Traditions and Transformations*. London and New York, NY: Routledge, 339–356.

Heelas, Paul (1996). *The New Age Movement: The Celebration of the Self and the Sacralization of Modernity*. Oxford: Blackwell.

Heelas, Paul and Linda Woodhead (2005). *The Spiritual Revolution: Why Religion is Giving Way to Spirituality*. Oxford: Blackwell.

Houtman, Dick and Stef Aupers (2008). 'The Spiritual Revolution and the New Age Gender Puzzle: The Sacralisation of the Self in Late Modernity (1980–2000)', in Kristin Aune, Sonya Sharma and Giselle Vincett (eds), *Women and Religion in the West: Challenging Secularization*. Aldershot: Ashgate, 99–118.

Hutton, Ronald (1999). *The Triumph of the Moon*. Oxford: Oxford University Press.

Hutton, Ronald (2009). *Blood and Mistletoe*. New Haven, CT: Yale University Press.

Johnson, Paul C. (2005). 'Migrating Bodies, Circulating Signs: Brazilian Candomblé and the Garifuna of the Caribbean and the Category of Indigenous Religions', in Graham Harvey and Charles D. Thomson (eds), *Indigenous Diasporas and Dislocations*. Aldershot: Ashgate, 37–51.

King, Richard (1999). *Orientalism and Religion: Postcolonial Theory, India and 'the Mystic East'*. London and New York, NY: Routledge.

Lynch, Gordon (2007). *The New Spirituality: An Introduction to Progressive Belief in the Twenty-first Century*. London: I. B. Tauris.

Moreton, Cole (2009). 'Everyone's a Pagan Now', *Guardian.co.uk*. Online. Available HTTP: www.guardian.co.uk/world/2009/jun/22/paganism-stonehenge-environmentalism-witchcraft (accessed 22 June 2009).

Office for National Statistics (2004). 'Focus on Religion: Age and Sex Distribution'. Online. Available HTTP: www.statistics.gov.uk/cci/nugget.asp?id=955 (accessed 1 June 2011).

Partridge, Christopher (2005). *The Re-enchantment of the West*, 2 vols. London: Continuum.

Pearson, Joanne (2007). *Wicca and the Christian Heritage: Ritual Sex and Magic*. London: Routledge.

Phillips, Melanie (2010). 'Druids as an Official Religion? Stones of Praise Here We Come', *Daily Mail Online*. Online. Available HTTP: www.dailymail.co.uk/debate/article-1317490/Druids-official-religion-Stones-Praise-come.html (accessed 4 October 2010).

Pratchett, Terry (1989). *Wyrd Sisters*. London: Corgi.

Puttick, Elisabeth (2005). 'The Rise of Mind-Body-Spirit Publishing: Reflecting or Creating Spiritual Trends?', *Journal of Alternative Spiritualities and New Age Studies*, 1: 129–149.

Raphael, Melissa (1996). *Theology and Embodiment: The Post-Patriarchal Reconstruction of Female Sacrality*. Sheffield: Sheffield Academic Press.

Starhawk (1999). *The Spiral Dance*. 3rd edition. First published in 1979. San Francisco, CA: Harper San Francisco.

Vincett, Giselle (2007). 'Feminism and Religion: A Study of Christian Feminists and Goddess Feminists in the UK', unpublished PhD thesis, University of Lancaster.

Vincett, Giselle (2008). 'The Fusers: New Forms of Spiritualized Christianity', in Kristin Aune, Sonya Sharma and Giselle Vincett (eds), *Women and Religion in the West: Challenging Secularization*. Aldershot: Ashgate, 133–146.

Vincett, Giselle (2009). 'Quagans: Fusing Quakerism with Contemporary Paganism', *Quaker Studies*, 13/2: 220–237.

Vincett, Giselle and Linda Woodhead (2009). 'Spirituality', in Linda Woodhead, Hiroko Kawanami and Chris Partridge (eds), *Religions in the Modern World: Traditions and Transformations*. London and New York, NY: Routledge, 319–338.

Wallis, Robert J., and Jenny Blain (2007). 'A Live Issue: Ancestors, Pagan Identity and the "Reburial Issue" in Britain', in Nick Petrov (ed.), *Security of Archaeological Heritage*. Newcastle: Cambridge Scholars Publishing, 1–22.

Woodhead, Linda (2007). 'Gender Differences in Religious Practice and Significance', in James Beckford and N. J. Demerath III (eds), *The SAGE Handbook of the Sociology of Religion*. London: Sage, 566–586.

Woodhead, Linda (2008). '"Because I'm Worth It": Religion and Women's Changing Lives in the West', in Kristin Aune, Sonya Sharma and Giselle Vincett (eds), *Women and Religion in the West: Challenging Secularization*. Aldershot: Ashgate, 147–164.

Woodhead, Linda (2011). 'Spirituality and Christianity: The Unfolding of a Tangled Relationship', in Giuseppe Giordan and William H. Swatos Jr. (eds), *Religion, Spirituality and Everyday Practice*. New York, NY: Springer, 3–21.

Notes

1   This interview was part of the AHRC/ESRC Religion and Society funded large grant 'Marginalized Spiritualities' undertaken by Elizabeth Olson, Peter Hopkins, Rachel Pain and Giselle Vincett. See Case study 3 for more details.

2   Online. Available HTTP: www.mindbodyspirit.co.uk/events.php?eventID=24 (accessed 25 May 2011).

3   See note 1.

5 God-change

Mark Chapman, Shuruq Naguib and Linda Woodhead

The Introduction suggests that 'God' became taboo in post-war Britain in many public settings: it was possible to talk about God, but not to invoke God or imply that God mattered. Yet surveys show that a majority of people continued to believe in God, even though numbers believing in a 'personal God' declined. This chapter looks more closely at how God changed in the post-war period, not only for Christians but also for British Muslims and for those involved in alternative spirituality. It illustrates the growing variety of Gods of the British, and considers not just personal relationships with God, but political Gods and Gods of civic ritual. Although it finds that there was a tendency for God to become softer, friendlier and more immediately concerned with the individual during this period, it also notes counter-tendencies including the politicization of God, and the invocation of God for purposes of minority as well as majority cultural and ethnic defence.

Introduction

How have understandings and representations of the divine changed in post-war Britain? In addressing this question the main interest of this chapter is not in doctrines of God in academic theology, but in God(s) of lived religion. 'God-change' is a topic about which little has been written, either by social scientists or by theologians. Part of the explanation for this lies in the observation made in the Introduction to this book that 'God' has become the great taboo of the post-war period. Yet social relations with supernatural beings continue to be of interest and importance, and they can be studied because they are mediated by words, symbols, actions and other things which we can investigate, whether or not their referents are 'real'.[1]

Given the taboo about speaking of God in public – other than in explicitly devotional settings – it is surprising that belief in a divine being remains so widespread. The European Values Surveys find that 70 per cent of Britons believe in God, which is average for Europe as a whole (Davie 2000: 10). The 2008 British Social Attitudes (BSA) survey finds that 62 per cent of the population believes in God or in 'a higher power of some kind', 18 per cent are atheist and 19 per cent agnostic.[2] Belief in paranormal experience, answer to prayer and an afterlife have also remained fairly steady in the post-war period: in the Scottish Social Attitudes survey, for example, 50 per cent reported that they felt 'life had a pattern', 47 per cent that there is another existence after death, 35 per cent have had an answer to prayer and 25 per cent have had contact with someone who died (Bruce and Glendinning 2003).[3] Nevertheless, surveys suggest that there has been a change in the *kind* of God most people believe in. The greatest decline is in traditional Christian doctrines of God. Gill *et al.* (1998) analyse over 100 surveys going back to the 1920s, and find that there has been a decline in belief in God, Jesus as the Son of God, the afterlife and the Bible. For example, those believing in a 'personal God' fell from 43 per cent of the population in the 1940s and 1950s to 31 per cent in the 1990s. By contrast belief in 'God as Spirit or Life Force' grew a little: from 39 per cent in the 1960s to 40 per cent in the 1990s (Gill *et al.* 1998).[4] By the year 2000 belief in a 'personal God' had fallen to 26 per cent and belief in a 'spirit or life-force' had climbed to 44 per cent (with 15 per cent believing in 'no God', 12 per cent 'unsure' and 3 per cent 'don't know'.[5]

This chapter analyses additional sources to try to find out more about God-change in post-war Britain.[6] Unlike the polls, it is interested not only in how personal attitudes towards God have changed, but also how collective symbols and representations have altered. It also goes further than the surveys by asking about God-change not only in the British (particularly English) majority, but also in the British Muslim minority.[7]

The question of God-change is complex, given that there is no single 'God of the British', and never has been. But whereas once Christianity provided a common stock of images, narratives and ideas in terms of which God could be represented and approached – albeit in different ways by different Christian groups – there are now many more resources on which to draw, and fewer restrictions in doing so (see the Introduction to this volume and Chapter 7). As this book shows, clergy, theologians and other religious authorities have lost their ability to control sacred symbols and what can be done and thought with them. Nevertheless, far from there now being a free market in Britain in which people 'pick and mix' their gods without let or hindrance, this chapter suggests that membership of particular religio-ethnic communities is still important in shaping practice and belief. Christians, for example, do not select attributes of Rama to mix with those of a pagan goddess. For this reason, the chapter considers separately God-change in Christianity (particularly Anglicanism), alternative spirituality and Islam.

There are also important differences between Gods of everyday life, of formal ritual celebration, of the media, of civic life and so on. Locations and contexts matter. There is variation in register depending on whether the divine is being invoked at a hieratic civic occasion or in some situation of personal epiphany or distress. Civic occasions are usually marked by greater formality, often involving recourse to 'special' and historic religious language, such as that of the *Book of Common Prayer* or the King James Bible. In such settings God is likely to appear in forms which are more impersonal and stern than when called on in intimate settings. This chapter focuses in particular on Gods of everyday devotion, Gods of 'civil religion', and Gods of political mobilization and ethnic defence. Part of its argument is that God has drawn closer to the individual in the post-war period and become less stern and distant in the process; but it is also clear that variation occurs as the divine is invoked by different groups in different contexts and for different purposes.

God-change in Christianity

The 1953 coronation, discussed at length in Chapter 2 (see Plate 2.1), is significant for what it reveals about the 'high' God of the time. It symbolizes the continued relevance of traditional Christian expressions of a God who promotes order and embraces the whole nation: 'Much like Christmas, the Coronation was the ceremonial occasion for the affirmation of the moral values by which society lives' (Shils and Young 1953: 56, 67). It marked a high point of Anglican inclusivity at the end of Empire and before the real onset of the secularization of the welfare period and the more multicultural temper of what followed. It is telling that the Archbishop of Canterbury at the time, Geoffrey Fisher (1887–1972), was a practising Mason, which demonstrated the compatibility of the distant and benevolent deism of Freemasonary (from which women were excluded) with the God of Anglican Christianity. This high God was distant, stern and presiding; a Judge or Monarch. He supported virtues of duty, obligation and obedience. He was not expected to intervene in the affairs of the world, although, like the stern headmastership of Fisher's earlier career, he was undeniably in charge.

At this time theology in Britain was for the most part historical in orientation (Bible, church history and patristics), with few skirmishes into more systematic areas. Represented in the Anglican hierarchy by Michael Ramsey (1904–1988), who succeeded Fisher as Archbishop of Canterbury, theology's main focus remained ecclesiology and church order. God was predominantly expressed and understood through the history of the Christian tradition rather than through experience and personal reflection. With few exceptions, worship was structured according to set patterns, even where these were contested: in the Church of England moderate sacramental ritualism began to replace choral and preaching services. Both, however, remained orderly and were conducted within the framework of traditional forms. Despite demands for renewal, liturgical practice in the Church of England was still shaped by the *Book of Common Prayer* with its stress on God as Father and Judge and on the human need for repentance: as the head of a hierarchical order, God promoted the stability of society. There was little space either for emotions or for the spontaneity of the Holy Spirit. As Chapter 10 shows, religion was still a matter of duty and social position rather than free choice.

Insofar as this high, sovereign God still makes an appearance in Britain, it is largely in the most formal of civil rituals – in state openings of Parliament, Remembrance services at the Cenotaph, coronations and memorial services. He is supported by high ritual, ancient and magnificent architecture, and an austere dignity. But in the everyday life of Christian congregations, and in personal devotion, he was displaced in the post-war period by two main trends in 'God-change', one associated with evangelical and Charismatic forms of Christianity, and one with mainstream and liberal forms, both Protestant and Catholic.

The first shift is bound up with the increasingly dominant position of evangelicalism in British Christianity, as well as with a change in the nature of evangelical belief (see Chapter 2 and Warner 2007). Because of its traditionally more separatist mentality and its greater suspicion of worldliness, evangelicalism was able to provide an alternative to mainstream and liberal versions of Christianity which consciously sought compromises with the wider culture after the 1950s. As it has developed since then, evangelicalism has sat increasingly light to its earlier doctrinal rigidity: in everyday practice dogmatic confessions have largely given way to emotional expressions. The changes can be dated to 1954 and the highly successful visit of Billy Graham during his Crusade to London (Chapters 2 and 10; Chapman 2008). This had the effect of pushing evangelicalism into the mainstream of church life. Drawing on the apocalyptic pessimism of the Cold War, Graham offered the comfort of a religious worldview underpinned by the idea of personal salvation and authenticity against the perceived collapse of the social order. Religion offered a support in difficult times. Graham admitted in an interview given soon after the Crusade: 'the human mind cannot cope with the problems that we are wrestling with today … Some will turn to alcohol. Others will turn to religion in the want of security and peace – something to hold onto' (US News and World Report 1954: 87). Preaching a straightforward message of repentance, Graham stressed not judgement, but the warmth that came with accepting Jesus into the heart: there was no doctrinal complexity but the simple religion of Jesus. Enquirers were asked to make the declaration: 'I take Christ as my personal saviour.'

The acceptance of this style of religion outside the traditionally narrow enclaves of evangelicalism ensured that emotional and experiential versions of Christianity became increasingly dominant. The notion that God was principally at work in the heart meant that academic theology was largely perceived as a threat or an irrelevance: many church leaders recognized the obscurity of theological language, and few theologians were prepared to enter the popular arena (with notable exceptions such as William Barclay). The most popular 'theologian' among many evangelicals was the Oxford amateur apologist C. S. Lewis. By the 1960s – and especially after the 1967 Keele Conference of Anglican Evangelicals – there was a growing evangelical presence in parishes and leadership of many Protestant churches, including the Church of England. Traditional hymnody, with its strong doctrinal emphasis, was gradually supplemented by more contemporary language with simple, catchy tunes. *Hymns for Today's Church* (1982) updated the language of traditional hymns while adding many new ones, including a version of Psalm 46 to Eric Coates's 'Dambusters' March'. What the Jubilate group who produced the hymn book represented, however, was largely in continuity with the older evangelical tradition: God was the God of Abraham and Isaac and Jesus Christ who spoke through the words of scripture rather than directly in the heart of the individual.

An alternative strand in evangelicalism was Charismatic renewal, which affected most British churches in the 1970s (see Chapter 2). Here the doctrinal emphasis of earlier forms of evangelicalism was moderated through exuberant and often highly embodied forms of worship: God has mutated from distant judge into an intimate friend, even a lover. This was demonstrated by a large number of the new songs in the bestselling *Songs of Fellowship* (1981), produced by leading Charismatics, which included 'Abba Father, let me be / Yours and Yours alone' (1977). There was also an emphasis on the awesomeness of God, as with Scott Palazzo's 'I will magnify Thy name / Above all the earth.' Sometimes the language could be extremely intimate, as with Danny Daniels's 'I'm in love with you / For you have called me child' (1987) and Graham Kendrick's 'Lord, you are precious to me … and I love you.' While often this intimacy was associated with Jesus, as in 'My Jesus, My Saviour' (1993), it was also frequently attached to the Father (Percy 1997). Despite the emphasis on the gifts of the Spirit in Charismatic worship, there are surprisingly few references to the Holy Spirit in hymnody. There is more emphasis on the power and majesty of God as the counterpart to the evils of the world: this was particularly influential on the widely used *Mission Praise*, which was produced for the Billy Graham mission in 1983. The best examples are Jack Hayford's 'Majesty' of 1977, and Kendrick's 'Shine, Jesus, Shine' (1987) which combines the themes of awesomeness and conversion.

Key to forging evangelical and Charismatic Christian identities are residential rallies in bounded, isolated communities. For example, Spring Harvest, which takes place in a number of Butlin's holiday camps. Here Christianity becomes an escape from the world in the company of the like-minded, an 'experiential religion of difference' (Woodhead and Heelas 2000: 494). While this is a development from earlier rallies, most obviously the Keswick Convention, a residential Bible Conference established in 1875, it allows for identities to be reaffirmed and reforged, as well as new songs and personalities to emerge, in a safe environment. *Worship Today*, the song book that has grown out of Spring Harvest, contains remarkably few hymns from the broader Christian tradition: the new is celebrated and the old is seen as redundant. The latest edition contains only three hymns by Charles Wesley. To be in the vanguard of Charismatic worship is to be focused on the new, on the future, on joy and hope. The approach to God, to tradition, liturgy and doctrine is in general far less rigid, and it is personal rather than congregational or national relations with God which count.

Alongside these large rallies, there has been a 'commodification' and 'branding' of religion led by religious entrepreneurs and influenced by secular forms of marketing and advertising. This has resulted in franchised versions of Christianity which offer different amalgams of selected traditional evangelical doctrinal emphases and Charismatic enthusiasm, as with the successful Alpha Course. This combines a standardized basic catechetical programme based on talks and DVDs with an emphasis on fellowship through a shared meal, and an experiential weekend to receive the gifts of the Spirit. Earlier conflicts over church practice which had hitherto functioned to instil a sense of evangelical identity are now apparently irrelevant and doctrinal norms as standards of faith have been replaced by a wider variety of more 'niche' evangelical identities, together with some residual common standards focusing more on worship styles. There is also ethical opposition to prevailing moral standards in wider 'secular' society (most importantly homosexual practice).

The second trend in post-war Christian God-change has to do with change in the liberal, mainstream strands of British Christianity, which turned in the post-war period towards social action and welfare in a kind of internal secularization. There was an associated loss of authority and credibility for the guardians of traditional theological and doctrinal reflection, both theologians and clergy. Despite the continuing popularity of 'faith schools' in Britain, discussed in Chapter 8, elementary Christian pedagogy virtually collapsed beyond the committed. The collapse of Sunday School is documented by Callum Brown (2001: 168 and in Chapter 10 of this volume). From the 1960s there was also a serious decline in the numbers of those wishing to be ordained to the ministry, and a virtual absence of theology in the new universities of the 1960s. Many Christians, both Catholic and Protestant, thought that 'speculation' about God had become dusty and irrelevant; God had to become more relevant to society in a secular 'world come of age'. The Second Vatican Council of the Roman Catholic Church (1962–1965) encouraged some Catholics to think that a revolutionary 'modernization' was underway.

A key event in Britain was the publication of John Robinson's *Honest to God* in 1963, which popularized existing theological ideas to make available a secularized and 'unreligious' understanding of a God whose primary locus was outside the churches. As the *Daily Herald* (19 March 1963) headline put it: 'God is not a big daddy in the sky.' For Robinson, God was no longer 'above' but 'below', the ground and substance of our being, the inner depth of experience, the 'ultimate commitment'. 'God' was now spoken of in gender-neutral and humanistic language, which sat uncomfortably with the traditional symbolic language of the churches in which God is personal and male (Chapman 2007). In both Protestant and Catholic Churches, church ritual was also subjected to vigorous critique from within. This had the effect of emphasizing the importance of the 'non-religious' and deflecting resources away from the maintenance of the institution. The otherness of Christianity (and God), together with its traditional doctrinal norms, was deliberately played down in an effort at relevance. Liturgical language was modernized and simplified, church buildings were reordered in less hierarchical ways, and efforts were made at creating new forms of activity for the churches in welfare and charitable work. Traditional language about God was seen as outmoded and in need of 'demythologization'. The perceived inadequacies of the leading hymn books in addressing the needs of the 1960s led to the publication of supplements, the most popular of which in Protestant churches was *100 Hymns for Today* (1969), which included Richard Jones's 'God of Concrete, God of Steel' and Stewart Cross's 'Father, Lord of all Creation / Ground of Being, Life and Love' and which called Jesus Christ 'the Man for Others'. To a modest extent, God was depersonalized, and human beings were seen to be 'by social forces swept along' (Brian Wren) rather than subject to the power of sin.

By the 1980s there were increasing calls for the ordination of women in the Church of England (see Plate 1.8), something which had already been accepted in some other denominations. While the justification was often based on rights language rather than theology, there were some who saw the ministry of women as reflecting the feminine aspect of God. Feminist theology flourished in the 1970s and 1980s, and although it was never made central to liturgical revision, gender-inclusive language was increasingly used in relation to human beings. Feminine language and imagery for God were, however, largely resisted in the churches, and the God of both liberals and evangelicals remains a Father, a Son and a Holy Spirit, even if occasionally He embraces Anglicans like a mother (*Common Worship*, Eucharistic Prayer G). In 2010, when the Scottish Episcopal Church produced a liturgy where masculine imagery for God had been removed, it provoked widespread criticism from the popular press.

In the liberal Christianity of the welfare era, God, at times, functioned as little more than a spur to social action: again this found its way into hymnody, most impressively in Fred Kaan's 'Sing we a song of high revolt'. God calls 'us to revolt and fight / with him for what is just and right / to sing and live Magnificat / in crowded street and council flat'. Doctrine became secondary to the more central task of the church's work in rebuilding communities. This secularizing movement continued into the 1970s and 1980s with the publication of *Faith in the City* (Church of England 1985, see Plate 2.4). This was one of several reports (beginning with Leslie Paul's 1963 Report on *The Deployment and Payment of the Clergy*) which sought structural solutions to the problems facing the Church of England, but which represented a last assertion of the idea of the Church of England as the focus of a 'one nation' ethos, with the church as the somewhat paternalistic moral centre of a benevolent welfare state. Its influence remains. At the Eucharist, for example, Anglicans are still enjoined to build up the 'common good', with God as a distant ethical spur rather than a present, personal reality.

The impact of this detraditionalizing, secularizing movement was enormous. Ministry was redefined in more secular terms: clergy were religious 'professionals', or co-operative agents working collaboratively with laity in specialized teams. What little theological reflection there was seldom rose above suggestions that God was some sort of community (a social Trinity), which probably had implications for how ministers and laity should relate. Similarly, denominational identity was dismissed as perpetuating the doctrinal disputes of the past. Ecumenism was preferred (Anglican–Methodist discussions, and nonconformist unions), and even reunion (as with the United Reformed Church, formed in 1972, discussed in Case study 1). This encouraged an 'inclusive' picture of God, with no sharp characteristics. The importance of theology in the churches and the wider culture declined still further. After the 1970s there was nothing that remotely matched the extraordinary popularity of *Honest to God*, and there were few theologians whose names were known even in the churches or who could communicate beyond the academy. The loss of control of the few remaining university theological departments by the churches, and the closure of others in the 1980s, as well as the decline of theological expertise among church leaders, meant that there was often a huge gulf separating academic theologians from those ministering in parishes. This is evidenced by the controversies over *The Myth of God Incarnate* in the 1970s and over David Jenkins and Don Cupitt in the 1980s, controversies in which academic and popular ideas about God increasingly came into conflict (Clements 1988: Ch. 8).

Thus, when we consider God-change in British Christianity as a whole, the picture which emerges is one in which a distant, judge-like God who maintains order and holds the nation together – the God of the coronation – gives way in mainstream, liberal forms of Christianity to a more diffuse, benevolent, social 'welfare' God. Although this God has a social and a congregational role, he is not one with whom the individual can have an intense personal relationship; He is more a distant ideal than a present friend. In evangelicalism and Charismatic Christianity, however, a very different process of change occurs as God grows closer to the individual, and becomes an intimate friend who loves and cares for the individual, and supports their personal journey through life and the finding of their unique purpose. The 'social' God of the liberal churches made sense in the welfare era; He inspired humanitarian action and the creation of a perfect society on earth. The intimate, intervening evangelical God makes more sense of the demands and opportunities faced by middle-class Britons of the post-Thatcher era, and for black and other ethnic minority Christians making their way within it.

God-change and alternative spirituality

Another major aspect of God-change in post-war Britain, especially for the dominant white, Christian and post-Christian majority, has been the increasing popularity and influence of the alternative spiritualities reviewed in Chapter 4. When the polls show that belief in the 'personal God' of Christianity has declined whilst that in a 'God within', a 'Spirit' or a 'life force' has grown, they suggest that such spirituality has had an increasing influence on the way many British people have come to think about God.

By the end of the Second World War, spirituality as a self-conscious focus of commitment was almost a century old (Woodhead 2001; Schmidt 2005). During that time it had spawned many different schools, teachers, forms and manifestations, and many different conceptions of the divine. Despite tremendous variation in the latter, most forms of spirituality were united in their rejection of the personal God of Christianity and, above all, of conceptions of God as a stern and distant (male) Ruler and Judge. In *Mysticism* (1914), for example, the leading British Theosophist Annie Besant (1847–1933) had fiercely repudiated the idea of an anthropomorphic God who sends men and women to hell and everlasting torment. Like most advocates of an 'alternative' spirituality, she rejected the idea of an unbridgeable chasm between God and humanity, and suggested instead that women and men must enter into an unmediated relationship with a divine Spirit who is known in the depths of personal experience. The Christian 'dogmas', she says, 'must be broken into pieces … they are outgrown when the unfolding Spirit of man begins to know for himself, and no longer needs testimony from outside' (Besant 1914: 21).

Similar sentiments were still being expressed a generation later, not least by one of the leading British advocates of spirituality of the interwar and post-war period, Alan Watts (1915–1973). Raised in the Church of England, Watts realized – in his own words – that he had to: 'get out from under the monstrously oppressive God the Father – nothing like my own father, who never used violence against me' (1972: 69). In his revealingly titled autobiography, *In My Own Way* (1972), Watts says that an alternative was held before him by his mother who, despite a 'wretched fundamentalist Protestant upbringing', lived in 'a world of magic beyond that religion … inhabited not by domineering prophets and sentimental angels … but by sweet peas, scarlet-runner beans, rose trees, crisp apples, speckled thrushes … the South Downs, dew-ponds and wells of chalk-cool water' (1972: 8). Influenced by Theosophy and later by Zen Buddhism, Watts emigrated to the USA where he became a teacher and a guru figure. In his numerous writings he taught that the only way to find God was in complete immersion in the present moment. 'God', he said, 'is what there is and all that there is,' the 'happening' of life, 'beyond all possible conception', to be found by 'getting with it and going with it' and abolishing a sense of a separate 'I' (Watts 1972: 223–224, 451).

With its spirit of Christian revival, national unity and moral conservatism symbolized by the coronation, the immediate post-war years proved inhospitable to such beliefs. Yet this period would prove key in the development of alternative spirituality and its conceptions of the divine for at least two reasons. First, it was in the 1940s and 1950s that Gerald Gardner (1884–1964), working with a number of women, staged a reconstruction and revival of Wicca (the ancient name for witchcraft). Gardner's *Witchcraft Today* was published in 1954, and *The Meaning of Witchcraft* in 1959. A creative amalgam of esoteric and occult traditions (some derived from Aleister Crowley), folklore, Anglo-Catholic ritual and sacramentalism (Pearson 2007), Wicca was important not only as a distinctively British form of religion (Hutton 1999: vii), but because it spurred a subsequent Pagan revival. Wicca inspired many of its characteristic features, including leadership by women, sacralization of the natural world, indigenization and sacralization of place, a feminization of the divine and a recovery of what monotheistic faiths reject as 'polytheism', namely the belief that the sacred is embodied and manifest in many different forms (which may be human or non-human; male, female or neither). Second, the church-infused conservatism of the immediate post-war period would be important for subsequent God-change precisely because it provoked such a hostile reaction in so many of the 'baby boom' generation who were raised within it. The stern 'Father' God offered a rebellious generation of young people a clear symbol of the oppressive, patriarchal, sexually repressive 'establishment' they wished to reject (see Chapter 10), and in doing so gave a boost to the quest for alternatives.

From these immediate post-war and earlier roots, a number of alternative conceptions of the divine gained ground in Britain from the 1960s to the 1980s. They can be separated out into three 'ideal types', though in reality aspects of all of them are often combined in personal devotion and group practices and teachings.

First, a mystical and ineffable 'One', the focus of a formless mysticism. Repudiating an anthropomorphic God as too limited, particular and exclusive, such spirituality looks to a reality which lies beyond, behind and within the phenomenal world. The mystic goes beyond the differences which divide worldly religions to experience the One who unites them all.

This monist tendency had been present in alternative spirituality from its very origins, and is closely linked to movements within Christianity, including late eighteenth- and nineteenth- century Quakerism and Unitarianism, and the revival of interest in mysticism in the Edwardian period.[8] It gained fresh impetus in the later twentieth century for a number of reasons. Importantly, such mysticism is inherently inclusive. It allows its proponents to lay claim to a form of spirituality which embraces all existing forms of religion, but points beyond them: all paths lead to Truth, but it is formless mysticism which points this out. Such inclusiveness was attractive to many: to non-Westerners whose religions had been criticized by missionaries and colonials, and who could now present them as equal or superior to Christianity; to feminists trying to move beyond a male, gendered God; to Christian theologians like John Robinson advocating a 'ground of being' beyond traditional Christian divisions;[9] to humanitarians and peace-activists advocating a point of unity beyond inter- and intra-national divisions; to advocates of interfaith dialogue. Moreover, formless mysticism gained ground because it dispensed with the need to defer to religious experts and clerical guides. If God is known in the depth of one's own life and in an experience of inef-fable unity, then each person is his or her own priest. Such radical egalitarianism appealed to the spirit of the 1960s and since.

A second focus in post-war alternative spirituality was the Divine Feminine. Gerald Gardner, working with Margaret Murray, Doreen Valiente and others, had laid the grounds for more feminized forms of spiritual practice and belief. In Gardnerian Wicca, the divine has a male aspect (the horned God), and an equal and opposite female aspect (the Great Mother and triple goddess – maiden, mother and crone). Although Gardner also spoke of a higher, unknowable God, it is the 'Lady and Lord' who are important in practice, and who make themselves manifest in various ways, not least by taking possession of those who invoke them in ritual settings.

These esoteric ideas and practices spread into the mainstream under the influence of second-wave feminism. Some feminists viewed the male God and saviour of Christianity, mediated by a male priesthood, as central to the 'patriarchy' they were trying to overthrow. Many embraced a thoroughgoing secularism, some turned to formless mysticism and a 'God' beyond gender and tried to reform existing religions, and others sought empowerment through a feminine divine. The most radical rejected even the duality of the Gardnerian God, and sought refuge in the Goddess – in her many manifestations. By the 1970s, Goddess spirituality had become a transnational movement, and there were particularly close links between American and British goddess feminists. Both found inspiration in books like Margot Adler's *Drawing Down the Moon* (1986) and Starhawk's *The Spiral Dance* (1999), both first published in 1979, which did not simply offer historical and theological reflections on feminist spirituality, magic and witchcraft, but offered inspiring symbols, images, rituals, spells and practical wisdom which could be put to use. In Britain the political potential of such spirituality was realized at Greenham Common, in the women's peace camp and protests which took place against nuclear weapons sited there between 1982 and 1991 (see Plate 2.3). Goddess feminists were prominent in the camp, and their songs and reflections entered into its lore; Starhawk was one of many visitors and supporters.

Third, some forms of alternative spirituality have found the divine in Nature itself (Szerszynksi 2005). This tendency can be traced back as far as the English Romantics of the late eighteenth and early nineteenth centuries, and was present in many later forms of spir-ituality – from the neo-Zen of Alan Watts to the Wicca of Gerald Gardner. But it entered into the cultural and political mainstream after the 1970s as a result of a plethora of influ-ences, including a growing concern about ecological disaster, and a succession of popular cartoons, novels, films and nature documentaries (charted by Bron Taylor in *Dark Green Religion* 2009). Some versions of 'eco-spirituality' and 'eco-paganism' have also been inspired by James Lovelock's 'Gaia hypothesis', in which the Goddess functions as a secular metaphor for the ecosystem as a self-regulating living being, but in a way which can easily be turned to spiritual ends.

As Chapter 4 shows, pagan streams of alternative spirituality have become increasingly prominent since the 1980s, and have generally turned in an ecological direction. Eco-paganism offers a very practical faith: with an ethic of reverence of life, a puritanical lifestyle centred around the daily rituals of sustainable living, national and international networks, devotional sites and gatherings, and very effective means of political mobilization and protest (Taylor 2009). For some Pagans the God of Christianity is definitely part of the prob-lem which needs to be overcome. In place of its anthropocentrism they propose a reverence for natural order of which human beings are merely a small part. In place of its commandment to 'subdue' the creation they advocate living in harmony with life, and instead of worshipping a supreme God, they open themselves to the Spirit which flows through all life and is manifest in many different places, landscapes, groves, streams, beings and deities.

TEXT BOX 12

The goddess in alternative spirituality

Queen of the Moon, Queen of the Sun,
Queen of the Heavens, Queen of the Stars,
Queen of the Waters, Queen of the Earth
Bring to us the child of promise!

It is the great mother who giveth birth to him,
It is the Lord of Life who is born again.
Darkness and tears are set aside
When the Sun shall come up early.

Golden Sun of the Mountains,
Illumine the Land, Light up the World,
Illumine the sea and the rivers,
Sorrows be laid, Joy to the World.

Blessed be the Great Goddess,
Without beginning, without end,
Everlasting to eternity.
I.O.EVO.HE Blessed Be.
        Chant at the Dance of the Wheel (Yule) (reproduced in Gardner 1954)

We see the Goddess as immanent in the earth's cycles of birth, growth, death, decay and regeneration. Our practice arises from a deep spiritual commitment to the earth, to healing, and to the linking of magic with political action.
        Manifesto of the Reclaiming collective (Starhawk 1999: 6)

The Goddess does not rule the world; she is the world ... In the Craft we do not believe in the Goddess – we connect with Her; through the moon, the stars, the ocean, the earth, through trees, animals and other human beings, through ourselves.

        (Starhawk 1999: 33, 103)

Between them, these three trajectories in alternative God-change from the 1960s onwards were able to appeal to a wide range of the majority British population, particularly those who felt no reverence for the God of either evangelical or mainstream Christianity. In structural terms, however, all three have something in common with Christianity in that they are highly textual (ideas about the divine are communicated through an ever-growing corpus of writings), and have a corresponding appeal to well-educated and relatively affluent people who have the leisure and the means to pursue a quest for meaning. Although the number of such people expanded fast in the post-war period, there will always be more whose main concern is with practical issues of life and death, health and illness, success and failure, wealth and insecurity, and personal relationships. Alternative spirituality had Gods to offer them too, and they appeared in two rather different guises in the post-war period: in 'New Age', and in 'holistic' or 'Mind-Body-Spirit' spirituality.

New Age came first. It seems to have been growing rapidly in the 1970s and to have reached a peak in the 1980s. The continuities between the New Age God and the divine of formless mysticism are clear: they share an inclusive monism which views the divine as the inner, unifying principle of reality. Some New Age retains a fondness for cosmological speculation about different spheres and eras, angels and higher beings, eras and evolution (as its name suggests, New Age maintains that the human race is entering a new era of spiritual unity and harmony). However, New Age also has a much more practical orientation, and a particular concern with the self, and with realizing individual potential. The ultimate goal is to free oneself from artificial limitations and realize the 'God within' – a goal which, like realizing one's 'purpose' in evangelical Christianity, fits well with aspirations engendered by consumer capitalism. Not surprisingly, New Age teachings about how to realize one's full potential have been readily adapted to training programmes in business settings, and to a plethora of self-help classes and literature.

Holistic spirituality shares a practical emphasis with New Age, and a concern with how to improve your life and your relationships and manage your emotions. It has become an increasingly familiar face of alternative spirituality since the early 1990s, and it continues to spawn a plethora of different 'mind, body, spirit' practices, including forms of Yoga, Reiki, Tai Chi and mindfulness meditation. As with New Age, intellectual reflections on God are less popular than 'how to' and practical manuals – like *How to Know God* (2000) by Deepak Chopra, *Mindfulness for Beginners* (2006) by Jon Kabat-Zinn, *Living Yoga* (2002) by Christy Turlington, *You Can Heal Your Life* (2004) by Louise Hay – and autobiographical accounts of encounters with the divine like Dorothy Chitty's *An Angel Set Me Free* (2009). Like New Age, holistic spirituality also speaks of God as Energy or 'Chi', but, unlike much New Age, it makes the 'whole person', especially the body, central to its scheme. Its therapies offer many techniques for 'unblocking' energy, revitalizing the 'whole person' and opening up a proper connection with the Energy of the Universe. As a Rebirthing practitioner puts it, 'It's very much based in the body, it's not going off somewhere. So although there's the spiritual element, it's not going off into the clouds. It is a wonderful sense people get, they're filling their bodies' (Sointu and Woodhead 2008: 266). Holistic practices also differ from New Age by regarding the Self (the true, sacred self) as a self-in-connection, not only with other people, but also with nature. The divine, and sacred practices, are more explicitly feminized, both in terms of women's involvement and leadership, and in terms of a sacralization of care, healing, touch, relationship and connectedness. Such spirituality represents, in many ways, the re-enchantment of everyday (female) life, and it adapts itself to working-class as well as middle-class settings, and to older elements of spiritualism, belief in angels, charms and Christian prayers and sacraments (see Case study 3).

The post-war period has thus been a richly creative one for Gods of alternative spirituality. Arising, as they do, from the activities of innumerable men and women acting for the most part outside overarching structures of religious authority and bureaucracy, alternative spirituality gave rise not only to a greater profusion of Gods, but to Gods who remain closer to the needs and aspirations of a wide variety of groups, and their everyday lives, than the Christian Gods. They are testimony to the deregulation of religion spoken of in the

Introduction to the book – and, to their high-cultural critics, of the degradation of religion which results.

Despite this proliferation and diversification of alternative conceptions of God in the post-war period, some common threads are evident. One is a turn away from more theological, speculative and intellectual approaches to the divine (symbolized by writing long books about God), to more practical, immediate, embodied and emotional approaches (symbolized by 'How to' books of practical guidance, increased interest in ritual, greater attention to bodily practice). There is a clear parallel with the 'dedogmatization' of Christianity traced above. Another is an immanentism and a rejection of the idea that the sacred is, as it were, sucked out from the world by a high God (or Gods) in whom all divinity resides. This is often bound up with a feminization of God, whereby women's concerns are resacralized: maintenance of relationships, preparation of food, caring and healing activities, and emotional cultivation. Yet the result is not necessarily a privatization or even a domestication of religion and of the divine. On the contrary, as noted above, both eco-spirituality and goddess paganism have demonstrated their ability to mobilize followers in political action, both in the UK and on a global scale.

Although the origins of alternative spirituality lie in a rejection of the Christian God, the success of alternative conceptions of the divine in the post-war period led to a reversal whereby Christianity began to borrow from (and define itself over against) ideas and practices from alternative spirituality (see Chapter 4). The main Protestant and Catholic Churches have rejected both the feminization of God and the re-enchantment of everyday life. But the idea that God is closer to believers than their own breath, integral to their everyday concerns, and able to inspire, possess and heal the embodied person, has become central to Charismatic as well as alternative circles – despite important differences. And mainstream, particularly more Catholic and mystical, strands of Christianity have sometimes literally found shared ground with the sacred in alternative spirituality: shared sites (like Iona, St Brigid's well and fire pit, Kildare or Glastonbury), shared symbols and rituals (like labyrinths and labyrinth walking, plus elements of 'Celtic' Christianity), and shared practices (like silent prayer and meditation).

God-change in British Islam

The history of God in Islam is dominated by the theme of God's absolute oneness and unity (*tawhid*), a theme which also constitutes the leitmotif of Islam's self-differentiation from Trinitarianism and polytheism. This conception of God as comparable to none (Qur'an 112: 3) renders any representation of Him in language or images fraught with risks. Early Islamic theology was largely driven by efforts to 'purify' the divine (*tanzih*), through allegorical interpretation, from anthropomorphic doctrines which were justified by certain Qur'anic references. God's absolute transcendence was strongly asserted even in the face of the Qur'an's notion of his immanence (such as evident in Qur'an 50: 16 'We [God] are nearer to him [man] than his jugular vein'). The emergent orthodoxy of classical Islam, however, did not encourage such theological pursuits, the outcome of which was further alienation of God from His creation, and it eventually suspended enquiry into the Qur'an's anthropomorphic descriptions of God, accepting them 'without asking how'.

This gave way to a doctrinal stability that evolved from a consensus on the oneness and transcendence of God, His creativity and involvement in history, and the possibility of knowing God through His creation and revelation (Netton 1989). These notions constitute the fundamental components of Islam's understanding of God and continue to be re-expressed in intellectual and popular terms by Muslims everywhere (compare, for example, Tariq Ramadan's 'Encounter with the Universal' in *Western Muslims and the Future of Islam*, 2005 and Hassan le Gai-Eaton's awareness booklet *The Concept of God in Islam*, 2008, both published in Britain). The early Muslim resistance to enclosing God in theological discourse has left the conception of God not fully realizable through dogmatic definition, thus allowing the faithful a certain degree of freedom to develop a personal grasp of the divine through their practice. This reflects the idea of faith in Islam as embodied in an act, that is, the act of submission to God which is the very meaning of the word *islam*. Muslim theology was in the end overtaken by enquiry into practice and not dogma, giving rise to two different but traditionally complementary frameworks that inform the way in which the faithful relate to God: the path of *shari'a*, that is the ethico-legal relationship with God which emphasizes responsibility and duty, and the mystical path of Sufism which seeks communion with a beloved God. In Britain, Muslim ideas about the relation to God can be primarily located within these basic frameworks of *shari'a* and Sufism (see also the discussion of British Islam in Chapter 3). And while these remain significant for configurations of Muslim religious practice along a trajectory moving from close adherence to a more loosely defined allegiance, other expressions of this relation have also emerged in the British context, often in connection with transnational developments within Islam.

As Chapter 3 documents, although Islam has existed in Britain since medieval times, Britain's Muslim community has been largely formed by South Asian post-war immigration. The religious lineage of most South Asian Muslim immigrants is traceable to nineteenth-century Islamic reform movements of the Indian subcontinent, most notably the Deobandis who adopt an exclusively *shari'a*-based type of reform, loyal to a scholarly class ('*ulama*); and the Barelwis who extended the revival to Sufi practice centred around a spiritual teacher (*pir*) and Prophet Muhammad as the primary and ever-present guide on the path to God. The Barelwi idea of the Prophet's agency as unbound by time or place is a point of religious contention between the two groups that has caused communal tensions in Britain (Geaves 1996, 2000; Werbner 2002). In addition to ethnic background, this contention over the right path to God marked the lines along which Muslims organized themselves as communities in Britain in the 1960s and 1970s.

During that period of settlement, communal religious activities were focused on preserving and supporting traditional modes of religious practice through religious education and the building of mosques. Deobandis, in particular, devoted substantial efforts to establishing institutions which provided younger generations with a rigorous *shari'a*-based education. Such activities remain important aspects of Muslim religious life in Britain. The number of mosques, for example, has increased from nine in the 1960s (Geaves 1996) to an estimated 850 to 1,500 in the early twenty-first century (Gilliat-Ray 2010). Muslim schools, colleges and other less structured forms of supplementary religious education have also flourished over the past few decades (Mukadam *et al.* 2010). The 1980s, however, saw a transformation in how Muslims in Britain perceived and expressed the path to God in a non-Muslim Western society.

Following decades of religious practice devoted to worship and education, the publication of Salman Rushdie's novel *The Satanic Verses* in 1988, and the ensuing mobilization of disparate Muslim groups in public protestations against the book's unorthodox representation of God and the Prophet Muhammad, forcefully brought Muslims, their doctrines and their religious attitudes to the fore of public discourses in British society (see Chapter 1). Ethnicity was soon superseded by religion as the main marker of identity among Muslims and other immigrant groups (Abbas 2009; Nielsen 2004). This religio-communal mobilization of British Muslims coincided with the Islamic revival triggered by the rise of Islamism in different parts of the Muslim world during the 1970s and 1980s (Haddad and Esposito 1997; Metcalfe 2005). It is thus not insignificant that Ayatollah Khomeini, the leading figure of the Iranian revolution, issued a *fatwa* (ruling) in response to Muslim protests, sentencing Rushdie to death. This was, after all, the revolution which harnessed an idea of the conflict between God and Satan to political struggle.

The *fatwa* seemed to validate at that time the growing sense among British Muslims of belonging to a larger Muslim community whose God and Prophet were under attack. Of course, ethnic and religious loyalties beyond Britain were already existent through transnational connections with countries of origin or with other Muslim countries which supported the building of mosques, schools and Islamic centres (Baxter 2007). Moreover, reference to all Muslims as one community (*umma*) serving God, enjoining good and forbidding evil, is not new in Islamic thought and jurisprudence, for *shari'a* is understood to be concerned, first and foremost, with the communal duty to establish justice (Hallaq 2009). However, the Islamic revival of the late twentieth century politicized the idea of *umma*, whose primary responsibility towards God became perceived as a struggle against political injustice and Western hegemony in a postcolonial secular world. This necessitated restoring the place of God in politics and reviving the role and ascendancy of the *umma*. This was the 'Islamist' idea which became potent for many Muslims in Britain at that time: an *umma* serving and defending God represented a sense of moral victory as well as a source of solace and solidarity, particularly in the face of defeat and marginalization (Roy 2004) – such as that experienced in the failed campaign during the Rushdie Affair to persuade the British legal system to extend its law of blasphemy to protect Islam (Baxter 2007).

There had been earlier instances when British Muslims invoked an *umma* beyond the immediate ethno-religious community, from the 1950s onwards.[10] From the 1970s the Islamic Foundation in Leicester, which derived its ideas from the twentieth-century pan-Islamic movement of Jamaat-i-Islami in South Asia, played an important role (Ansari 2004; Roald 2004). Khurram Murad (d. 1996), its second Director General, conceived of the movement as a struggle to bring about an authentic Islamic society based on God's rule through the Qur'an and prophetic tradition (*sunna*) – a society where Islam's ethico-legal framework is 'supreme and dominant, especially in the socio-political spheres' (Murad cited in Newbigin *et al.* 1998: 110). This politicized concept of God's rule constituted a strong rejection of what was widely viewed by Muslims as the British 'secular' model of a private faith based around devotion to a personal God. In contrast to this model, God and his Prophet were advocated as core to configuring and strengthening Islam's public presence in Britain.

By the 1990s, such ideas had gained wide currency among British Muslims of different persuasions. They were particularly appealing, according to Pnina Werbner, to second- and third-generation British Muslims who saw in belonging to a larger community a way of transcending ethnic culture, parental control and marginality in British society (Werbner 1996, 2002). A politicized religious identity became a catalyst for greater exercise of individual agency and choice. This, no doubt, contributed to the growth of a broad spectrum of British Muslim activism that was anchored in religion. Returning to and reviving Islam constituted a point of convergence within Muslim activism and prompted its publicly visible expressions of religious devotion, most markedly through the spread of the Muslim female dress code which has become the ultimate signifier of Islam's public presence in Britain and Europe.

During the early 1990s, the puritanical reform movement of Salafism also began to gain ground in Britain through Jamiyyat Ihya' Minhaj As-Sunna (JIMAS), a society which reflected a politically orientated Salafism following the Afghan and Gulf wars in the 1980s and early 1990s (Meijer 2010). Salafis perceive themselves as the 'saved community' due to their adherence to the practice of the first pious generations of Islam (*salaf*). They affirm, above all, a strict understanding of the oneness of God which exclusively defines religious practice on the basis of a literal and unequivocal reading of Islam's central texts. Reliance on other sources, including the polyvalent historical tradition of interpretations, is considered a form of associating partners with God (*shirk*) (Wiktorowicz 2006). Salafism appealed during the late 1980s and early 1990s to British Muslims seeking an authentic and unmediated form of Islam that, potentially, permitted the construction of a religious authority beyond its ethnic expressions.

This dehistoricized, 'purified' Salafi version of Islam competed in Britain, at the time, against Hizb al-Tahrir, a revolutionary Arab political party which had successfully re-established itself outside the Arab world. Hizb al-Tahrir advocated a caliphate, a pre-modern form of Muslim rule, as the only means for the revival of the *umma* and the liberation of Palestine (Taji-Farouki 1996). Both movements shared an agenda of struggle against Western politics, and legitimized their approaches on the basis of pre-modern models of Muslim political practice. By the mid-1990s, a growing rapprochement between Hizb al-Tahrir and the radicalized Salafis gave birth to the British offshoot group al-Muhajiroun. This group supported the militant jihad of al-Qaida as a divinely ordained means for redressing the political injustices heaped on the Muslim *umma* by the West (Akhtar 2005). In the wider context of British Muslim activism, Hizb al-Tahrir and al-Muhajiroun were marginal groups, particularly in the aftermath of 9/11 and 7/7. Salafism, in contrast, continues to thrive as a religious movement.

The greater part of Muslim activism in the 1990s, however, was marked by the proliferation of British Muslim organizations and networks which competed to represent Islam in Britain (Silvestri 2007, and Chapter 3 in this volume). These shared with other forms of Muslim activism a perspective of Islam's all-comprehensiveness: God is sovereign in all spheres; hence, the responsibility towards God underlies private and public action. This, in contrast to the Salafis, was an inclusive and dynamic approach that attempted to strike a balance between modern realities and the Islamic tradition. Such organizations were also being formed out of expediency. Their primary aim was wider and more powerful representation of Islam and Muslims in British society. Islam never had a church, and, traditionally, it has been represented by schools of jurists who were independent of, though sometimes coopted by, the Muslim state. The mosque, being a designated functional space and not an institution, could not play the role of a church in representing religion in relation to state and society. And although, theoretically, the mosque is not bound by denominational commitment, it has been controlled in Britain by older generations who remained within the boundaries of the ethnic community.

While they continue to be driven by a concern for the public life of British Muslims, many of these organizations have shied away since 9/11 from the politicized religious discourses of the 1980s and 1990s. As Islam became increasingly prey to security concerns and negative representations (Geaves *et al.* 2004; Ramadan 2005), much of their effort has been reorientated towards revising their missions to salvage the identity of Islam and Muslims from association with extremism and terrorism. There has been a noticeable shift in Muslim public discourses from dissent to accommodation and from political to civic aims, even in politically orientated Salafi sectors (Hamid 2009) and overtly Islamist organizations (Silvestri 2007, 2010). The currently available literature of these organizations deliberately steers clear of the 1990s political rhetoric which posited the larger Muslim community (*umma*) as an ethically superior agent of a God opposed to the West (for first-hand accounts of this rhetoric, see McLoughlin 1996). Instead, commitment to Britain and Europe, and to values of citizenship, social justice and 'the common good' – the current motto of both the Muslim Council of Britain and the Muslim Association of Britain – is now strongly and more widely affirmed (Abbas 2005, 2009).[11]

The prioritization of women's participation in Muslim activism is another shift signalling the move of British Muslim approaches towards an activism which draws upon modern notions of equality and citizenship. It signals the increasing promotion of a softer version of Islam in Britain to counter dominant stereotypes and prevalent suspicion. The communal role and the public presence of Muslims are still reinforced, but there is a notable reference to a repertoire of ideas and terms (e.g. wellbeing, living, loving and humanity) that cut across wider religious and spiritual discourses in Britain. Thus notions of wellbeing pervade the promotional website of the 2011 Living Islam event: 'Be part of this collective remembrance of God … with over 5,000 Muslims. Praying for one another and praying with one another. "Living Islam" will, insha'Allah, strengthen your faith, your hope, your confidence and your will.'[12] Similarly, references to Islamic spirituality and wellbeing are powerfully promoted by the recent UK-based religious coalition the 'Radical Middle Way' (RMW). This was formed after the 7/7 London bombings by a diverse group of charismatic traditional scholars, modern Muslim academics, religious media figures, and young Muslim activists from Britain and other European and Muslim countries. RMW's internet gateway, supported by government funding, is a resource for literature and audiovisual material including podcasts of *khutbas* (sermons) and talks, some of which feature female religious scholars boldly introduced as *sheikhas* (religious scholars), as well as up-to-date commentary connecting Muslims in Britain to the Muslim world. The recurrent message is one of public service and not of political struggle. Peace, compassion and an *umma* in service of humanity are all pivotal keywords for RMW. Radical Middle Way spiritualizes Muslim activism by embracing a Sufi outlook without adopting traditional structures of Sufi practice. It captures the growing sense of loose allegiance to Sufism among Muslims disillusioned with ideologies associated with violence and terrorism.

These neo-Sufi expressions are still bound to Islam and its texts, unlike a universal neo-Sufism which transcends Islam altogether and is part of a global New Age mediated through Sufi sources. The latter type of Sufism is still largely suspect and has hardly evoked any interest among second- and third-generation Muslims in Britain (Geaves 2000; Taji-Farouki 2010). The reluctance to move beyond Islam to an individual and personal form of religion, or beyond religion altogether, cannot be solely attributed to doctrinal commitment and conservatism. The realities of Muslim life in Britain today reinforce the experience of the Muslim community as a threatened and misrepresented minority that faces discrimination and reduced opportunities (Hopkins 2009). 'Are you British or are you Muslim?' is a question that many Muslims have been more and more pressured to answer since 7/7. Radical political groups like Hizb al-Tahrir which, in 2003, hosted a conference attended by 7,000 participants with the above question as its title, endorsed the rejection of British identity in favour of loyalty to the *umma* (Akhtar 2005). Although faith and ethnicity are two different categories, the question – and the proposed answer of Hizb al-Tahrir – suggests another trend, namely the ethnicization of Muslim identity.

This ethnicized identity involves identification with the Muslim community in circles considerably distant from the Muslim faith. However, this conflation has been increasingly problematized by British Muslim intellectuals like Tim Winter (Abdul Hakim Murad) who express unease about commitment to Islam as a community and not as a faith. Winter argues that identity politics have displaced faith by masquerading as religion and transposing 'the vocabulary of faith into the vocabulary of identity' (cited in Hellyer 2010: 25). In his critique of some forms of Muslim activism, Winter alludes to the hidden association of partners with God (*shirk*), the very antithesis of God's Oneness in Islam, and points out a tendency to 'enlist God' as partner in seeking self-promotion and public recognition. Even where a strong commitment to faith is evident in groups like Hizb al-Tahrir and al-Muhajiroun, the militant insistence on the *umma*'s political and moral superiority can be interpreted as undermining the core of the Islamic faith by displacing the centrality of God with supremacist self-idolatory (Abou el-Fadl 2007).

Thus political and jihadi Salafism have been overtaken in Britain and Europe in the twenty-first century by a more apolitical trend focused on the perfection of worship, religious learning and civic service (Hamid 2009; Meijer 2010). The problem with Salafis, according to their Muslim critics, lies not in the form of their activism but in their very perception of *islam* as submission to a distant God whose vengeance and retribution must be feared. Of the many voices competing to be heard in Islam after 9/11 and 7/7, those which have gained momentum in Britain are the voices of neo-Sufi intellectuals and movements which discredit the politicization of God and *umma* and challenge the Salafi perception by embracing the Sufi aspiration to a state of submission to God motivated by pure love for Him. Neo-Sufi movements and intellectuals are likely to have a greater global impact in the years to come. An interesting direction towards which they seem to be heading is the reconciliation of *shari'a* and Sufism, which would undo the separation between Islam's ethic of duty and ethic of love brought about, coercively in some cases, by reformist Muslim movements favouring the former since the nineteenth century.

There are a number of linked developments. One is the emergence of Muslim women from conservative backgrounds as active contributors to evolving British expressions of Islam. Traditionally trained British '*alima*'s (female scholars) are drawing upon their experiences as British Muslim women in transmitting their understanding of South Asian religious texts (Bokhari 2009), and exhibiting a high degree of flexibility in their practice of face veiling to ensure their continued public engagement in roles such as prison chaplains (Mukadam *et al.* 2010). Another is the emergence of an academic Muslim theology which has established itself in British universities and is associated with figures such as Tim Winter and Tariq Ramadan who are simultaneously rooted in the Islamic and Western academic traditions. Given that the study of the Arabic language and Islamic religious texts is attracting young Muslim men and women, some with traditional training, to the modern study of Islam (Siddiqui 2007), there is potentially a new generation of academic theologians in the making. This is only one manifestation of a larger endeavour to retrieve Islamic religious scholarship and rearticulate it in the British context. British faith-based education has also produced home-grown religious scholars who have achieved recognition within the British Muslim community (Gilliat-Ray 2010). In addition, the virtual media in Britain are playing an integral part in God-change (see Chapter 7). They have facilitated an unprecedented level of access to religious texts and learning (Bunt 2003, 2009), have allowed for greater and more autonomous participation, and for the formation of movements which would have otherwise been dispersed, like RMW. At the same time, they have also reinforced the reproduction of existing structures of authority by strengthening global connections with traditional and reformist Islamic institutions and movements.

Thus British Muslim experiences, facilitated by direct or virtual encounters in Britain, are stimulating complex and hybrid expressions of Islam which reflect intersections of contexts, identities and religious perspectives. Given the diverse reconfigurations of Muslim religious thought and practice, these evolving expressions cannot yet be all subsumed under a distinct category of a 'EuroIslam'. What is evident, however, is that Muslims' engagement with religion in Britain, more so than in continental Europe, is vibrantly evolving and largely public, and continues to press the question of the place of God in the public life of Britain.

Conclusion

What emerges most clearly from this discussion of the Gods of post-war Britain is their sheer diversity. That impression would be even stronger had the chapter been able to discuss the Gods of the many other minority religions in the UK. If the 1953 coronation truly embodied a national unity focused around a high God of British civil religion, then it seems remarkable that He disappeared so quickly. It is more plausible to suggest that the coronation marked not so much the end of an era, but a brief and nostalgic return to one which was already a memory. The Gods of the British had been multiplying for a long time before the coronation, and continued to do so even more rapidly afterwards.

Yet the post-war story is not simply one of 'old Gods' being discarded. Conceptions of God tend to live on, but to become confined to certain areas of life, certain niches, certain groups, certain times and certain rituals. The God of the coronation has not disappeared; He can still be invoked in high Anglicanism, Catholicism and Calvinism, and at times of civic ritual solemnity – at the Cenotaph, in cathedrals, abbeys and openings of Parliament – but His sphere of credibility has diminished. His former guardians – priests, theologians and elders – have lost some of their power. And He has largely lost the ability to serve as a focus of national unity. The widely reported claim that Prince Charles intends to substitute the title 'Defender of Faith' for 'Defender of *the* Faith' at his coronation indicates this loss, the loss of a single dogmatic version of Christianity and its replacement by a sense of general religiousness, endorsed even by a future Supreme Governor of the Church of England.

This does not mean that British Gods have become depoliticized, only that their politics has changed. They no longer support a sacred Nation and Empire (Wolffe 1994). Few of the Gods discussed here are wholly apolitical. Even the personal God of evangelicalism has political implications, including an embrace of consumer capitalism – and hence an openness to neoliberalism. The welfare God is a more friendly declension of the civic God of the coronation, who supported the welfare project of building a just social order, and still came trailing clouds of national pride. The Gods of alternative spirituality can be political too, but their focus is local, global and planetary rather than national. The conceptions of God of British Islam may appear more political – and dangerous – just because they are of the minority rather than majority. But there was also a phase of intense politicization after the 1970s when God became a support for national and transnational projects of religio-political assertion against perceived Western injustice and oppression. For some young Muslim men in Britain, this culminated in the invocation of an Islamic God to justify acts of terrorism. Ironically, the genesis of this God lies in a reformist Islam created under conditions of British colonial rule in India and Egypt, and reworked in the context of a perceived ongoing Western (and Zionist) crusade against Islam. The turn towards a 'softer', more feminized, and more personally sustaining piety in the wake of the 7/7 bombings and other atrocities has some interesting parallels with the 'humanizing' of the Christian God into the welfare God, and the feminizing of God in alternative spirituality. This should not necessarily be read as a depoliticizing of God, but as a dissociation of God from projects of state-related political assertion, in favour of projects of moral reform, personal authenticity and relational purification.

Where this leaves God in public life is – in short – in a muddle. In its forms, structures, names and spaces, British public life remains infused with historical reminders of the Christian Gods, saints and festivals, and there is growing popular outcry at any attempt to erase them. Yet some Christians in the early twenty-first century were being censured for wearing crucifixes or talking about God in the workplace (Chapter 1). The growth of spirituality is also increasingly public, yet most of its Gods and Goddesses fail to gain admittance to the circles of religious leaders and politicians. Much more acceptable is a 'formless' divine, who, being more inclusive of all beliefs and traditions, is now favoured over the Christian God in public settings like hospitals, state schools, airports and shopping malls where 'God' is deemed too divisive, but has followers who still need to be catered for (see Case study 4 and Plate 3.9). Meanwhile, most people continue to 'do God' in their own, increasingly diverse ways, but in so doing are more likely to build solidarity with like-minded devotees at home or abroad, rather than with their neighbours, or the British nation.

Key terms

Catechesis: Education in the faith, usually of young people.

Charismatic: An expression of Christian belief which places particular emphasis on the gifts of the Holy Spirit.

Civil religion: When a society becomes sacred, or a religion infuses a society to such an extent that the religion inheres in the 'civil unit' itself; a people, group, nation or state imbued with a semi-sacred quality; a 'chosen people' (see Chapter 9 for further use of the concept).

Crowley, Aleister: An influential and controversial British occultist and magician (1875–1947).

Deism: Religion focused upon a distant God who oversees the world but does not intervene in it.

Ecumenism: A movement towards Christian unity, or unity among those believing in Jesus Christ.

Evangelicalism: A pan-denominational movement within Protestantism which emphasizes the authority of the Bible, a commitment to personal conversion and sharing the gospel.

Jihad: The struggle in the way of God; in Islamic jurisprudence it has come to mean war that fulfils legal requirements of *shari'a*.

Monism: A philosophical position which holds that all reality is ultimately one.

Second-wave feminism: Feminism of the 1960s–1980s which is contrasted with a first wave in the late nineteenth century and a third wave from the 1990s.

Umma: The global Muslim community.

Wesley, Charles: A key figure and hymn writer in early Methodism.

Further reading

Ansari, Humayun (2004). *The Infidel Within: Muslims in Britain since 1800*. London and New York, NY: Hurst and Columbia University Press. This book provides an in-depth account of Muslim presence and identity formation in Britain.

Clements, Keith (1988). *Lovers of Discord*. London: SPCK. A lively discussion of theological controversies through the twentieth century including the major conflicts of the 1960s and 1970s.

Hellyer, H. A. (2010). *Muslims of Europe: The 'Other' Europeans*. Edinburgh: Edinburgh University Press. Explores arising religious discourses for Muslims in Europe with a focus on the United Kingdom as a case study.

Hutton, Ronald (1999). *The Triumph of the Moon: A History of Modern Pagan Witchcraft*. Oxford: Oxford Paperbacks. An historical account of the ideas, practices and development of modern paganism in its many forms.

Nicholls, David (1989). *Deity and Domination: Images of God and the State in the Nineteenth and Twentieth Centuries*. London: Routledge. An exploration of the relationship between changing images of (the Christian) God and shifts in political power in modern Britain.

Warner, Rob (2007). *Re-inventing English Evangelicalism, 1966–2001*. Milton Keynes: Paternoster. A comprehensive and incisive account of the changes in English evangelicalism which discusses all aspects of the movement from both a theological and sociological perspective.

References

Abbas, Tahir (ed.) (2005). *Muslims in Britain: Communities under Pressure*. London: Zed Books.

Abbas, Tahir (2009). *British Islam: The Road to Radicalism*. Cambridge: Cambridge University Press.

Abou el-Fadl, Khalid M. (2007). *The Great Theft: Wrestling Islam from the Extremists*. San Francisco, CA: Harper.

Adler, Margot (1986). *Drawing Down the Moon: Witches, Druids, Goddess-Worshippers and other Pagans in America Today*. Revised and expanded edition. London: Penguin.

Akhtar, Parveen (2005). '(Re)turn to Religion and Radical Islam', in Tahir Abbas (ed.), *Muslims in Britain: Communities under Pressure*. London: Zed Books, 164–178.

Ansari, Humayun (2004). *The Infidel Within: Muslims in Britain since 1800*. London and New York, NY: Hurst and Columbia University Press.

Baxter, Kylie (2007). *British Muslims and the Call to Global Jihad*, Islam and Muslim Affairs vol. 1. Clayton, Victoria: Monash University Press.

Besant, Annie (1914). *Mysticism*. London: The Theosophical Publishing Society.

Bokhari, Raana (2009). 'Places and Perspectives: Gujaratai Muslim Women in Leicester', in Wanda Krause (ed.), *Citizenship, Security and Democracy: Muslim Engagement with the West*. Richmond: Association of Muslim Social Scientists, 155–176.

Brown, Callum G. (2001). *The Death of Christian Britain*. London and New York, NY: Routledge.

Bruce, Steve and Tony Glendinning (2003). 'Religious Beliefs and Differences', in Catherine Bromley, John Curtice, Kerstin Hinds and Alison Park (eds), *Devolution – Scottish Answers to Scottish Questions*. Edinburgh: Edinburgh University Press.

Bunt, Gary (2003). *Islam in the Digital Age: E-jihad, Online Fatwas and Cyber Islamic Environments*. London and Sterling, VA: Pluto Press.

Bunt, Gary (2009). *iMuslims: Re-wiring the House of Islam*. Chapel Hill, NC: University of North Carolina Press.

Chapman, Mark (2007). 'Theology in the Public Arena: The Case of English Bonhoefferism' in Jane Garnett, Matthew Grimley, Alana Harris, William Whyte and Sarah Williams (eds), *Redefining Christian Britain: Post 1945 Perspectives*. London: SCM.

Chapman, Mark (2008). 'Billy Graham in a Secular Society: The Greater London Crusade of 1954', in Michael G. Long (ed.), *Was Billy Graham Right? Progressives in Dissent*. Louisville, KY: Westminster John Knox, 125–140.

Chitty, Dorothy (2009). *An Angel Set Me Free*. London: Harper Element.

Chopra, Deepak (2000). *How to Know God: The Soul's Journey into the Mystery of Mysteries*. London: Rider.

Church of England. Commission on Urban Priority Areas (1985). *Faith in the City: A Call for Action by Church and Nation*. London: Church House.

Clements, Keith (1988). *Lovers of Discord*. London: SPCK.

Davie, Grace (2000). *Religion in Modern Europe: A Memory Mutates*. Oxford: Oxford University Press.

Gai-Eaton, Hassan le (2008). *The Concept of God in Islam*. Birmingham: Islamic Dawah Centre International.

Gardner, Gerald (1954). *Witchcraft Today*. With an Introduction by Margaret Murray. London: Rider and Company.

Geaves, Ron (1996). *Sectarian Influences within Islam in Britain: With Reference to the Concepts of 'Ummah' and Community'*, Community religions project monograph series vol. 5. Leeds: Leeds University Press.

Geaves, Ron (2000). *The Sufis of Britain: An Exploration of Muslim Identity*. Cardiff: Cardiff University Press.

Geaves, Ron, Theodore Gabriel, Yvonne Haddad and Jane Idleman Smith (2004). *Islam and the West Post 9/11*. Aldershot: Ashgate.

Gill, Robin, C. Kirk Hadaway and Penny Long Marler (1998). 'Is Religious Belief Declining in Britain?', *Journal for the Scientific Study of Religion*, 37/3: 507–516.

Gilliat-Ray, Sophie (2010). *Muslims in Britain: An Introduction*. Cambridge: Cambridge University Press.

Haddad, Yvonne Yazbeck and John L. Esposito (1997). *The Islamic Revival since 1988: A Critical Survey and Bibliography*. New York, NY: Greenwood Press.

Hallaq, Wael (2009). *An Introduction to Islamic Law*. Cambridge: Cambridge University Press.

Halliday, Fred (2010). *Britain's First Muslims: Portrait of an Arab Community*. London: I. B. Tauris.

Hamid, Sadek (2009). 'The Attraction of "Authentic" Islam: Salafism and the British Muslim Youth', in Roel Meijer (ed.), *Global Salafism: Islam's New Religious Movement*. London and New York, NY: Hurst and Columbia University Press, 384–403.

Hay, Louise (2004). *You Can Heal Your Life*. Twentieth Anniversary edition. London: Hay House.

Hellyer, H. A. (2010). *Muslims of Europe: The 'Other' Europeans*. Edinburgh: Edinburgh University Press.

Hopkins, Peter (ed.) (2009). *Muslims in Britain: Race, Place and Identities*. Edinburgh: Edinburgh University Press.

Hutton, Ronald (1999). *The Triumph of the Moon: A History of Modern Pagan Witchcraft*. Oxford: Oxford Paperbacks.

James, William (1981). *The Varieties of Religious Experience: A Study in Human Nature*. First published in 1902. Glasgow: Collins, Fontana.

Kabat-Zinn, Jon (2006). *Mindfulness for Beginners*. Audiobook. Louisville, CO: Sounds True Inc.

McLoughlin, Sean (1996). 'In the Name of the *Umma*: Globalisation, Race Relations and Muslim Identity Politics in Bradford', in W. A. R. Shadid and P. Sj. van Koningsveld (eds), *Political Participation and Identities of Muslims in Non-Muslim States*. Kampen: Kok Pharos, 206–228.

Meijer, Roel (2010). 'Salafism: Doctrine, Diversity and Practice', in Khaled Hroub (ed.), *Political Islam: Context versus Ideology*. London: Saqi, 37–60.

Metcalfe, Barbara D. (2005). *Islamic Revival in British India: Deoband, 1860–1900*. Oxford: Oxford University Press.

Mukadam, Mohamed, Alison Scott-Baumann, with Ashfaque Chowdhary and Sariya Contractor (2010). *The Training and Development of Muslim Faith Leaders: Current Practice and Future Possibilities*. London: Department for Communities and Local Government.

Netton, Ian (1989). *Allah Transcendent: Studies in the Structure and Semiotics of Islamic Philosophy, Theology and Cosmology*. London and New York, NY: Routledge.

Newbigin, Lesslie, Lamin Sanneh and Jenny Taylor (1998). *Faith and Power: Christianity and Islam in 'Secular' Britain*. London: SPCK.

Nielsen, Jørgen S. (2004). *Muslims in Western Europe*. Edinburgh: Edinburgh University Press.

Paul, Leslie (1963). *The Deployment and Payment of the Clergy*. London: Church Information Office.

Pearson, Joanne (2007). *Wicca and the Christian Heritage: Ritual, Sex and Magic*. London and New York, NY: Routledge.

Percy, Martyn (1997). 'Sweet Rapture: Subliminal Eroticism in Contemporary Charismatic Worship', *Theology and Sexuality*, 3/6: 71–106.

Ramadan, Tariq (2005). *Western Muslims and the Future of Islam*. 3rd edition. Oxford: Oxford University Press.

Roald, Anne Sofie (2004). *New Muslims in the European Context: The Experience of Scandinavian Converts*. Leiden: Brill.

Robinson, John (1963). *Honest to God*. London: SCM.

Roy, Olivier (2004). *Globalised Islam: The Search for a New Ummah*. London and New York, NY: Hurst and Columbia University Press.

Schmidt, Leigh (2005). *Restless Souls. The Making of American Spirituality*. San Francisco, CA: HarperSanFrancisco.

Shils, Edward and Michael Young (1953). 'The Meaning of the Coronation', *Sociological Review*, new series, 1/2: 63–81.

Siddiqui, Ataullah (2007). *Islam at Universities in England: Meeting the Needs and Investing in the Future*, Report submitted to Bill Brammell (Minister of State for Lifelong Learning, Further and Higher Education). Online. Available HTTP: www.bis.gov.uk/assets/biscore/corporate/migratedd/ publications/d/drsiddiquireport.pdf (accessed 2 June 2011).

Silvestri, Sara (2007). 'Muslim Institutions and Political Mobilisation', in Samir Amghar, Amel Boubekeur and Michael Emerson (eds), *European Islam: Challenges for Public Policy and Society*. Brussels: Centre for European Policy Studies, 169–182.

Silvestri, Sara (2010). 'Moderate Islamist Groups in Europe: The Muslim Brothers', in Khaled Hroub (ed.), *Political Islam: Context versus Ideology*. London: Saqi, 265–286.

Sointu, Eeva and Linda Woodhead (2008). 'Holistic Spirituality, Gender, and Expressive Selfhood', *Journal for the Scientific Study of Religion*, 47/2: 259–276.

Starhawk (1999). *The Spiral Dance: A Rebirth of the Ancient Religion of the Great Goddess*. Twentieth Anniversary Edition. San Francisco, CA: HarperSanFrancisco.

Szerszynski, Bronislaw (2005). *Nature, Technology and the Sacred*. Oxford: Blackwell.

Taji-Farouki, Suha (1996). *A Fundamental Quest: Hizb al-Tahrir and the Search for the Islamic Caliphate*. London: Grey Seal.

Taji-Farouki, Suha (2010). *Beshara and Ibn 'Arabi: A Movement of Sufi Spirituality in the Modern World*. Oxford: Anqa Publishing.

Taylor, Bron (2009). *Dark Green Religion*. Berkeley and Los Angeles, CA: University of California Press.

Turlington, Christy (2002). *Living Yoga: Creating a Life Practice*. London: Penguin Books.

US News and World Report (1954) 'New Crusade in Europe', 27 August: 83–91.

Warner, Rob (2007). *Re-inventing English Evangelicalism, 1966–2001*. Milton Keynes: Paternoster.

Watts, Alan (1972). *In My Own Way: An Autobiography*. New York, NY: Vintage Books.

Werbner, Pnina (1996). 'Allegories of Sacred Imperfection: Magic, Hermeneutics and Passion in The Satanic Verses', *Current Anthropology (Supplementary Issue)*, 37/1: S55–S86.

Werbner, Pnina (2002). *Imagined Diasporas among Manchester Muslims: The Public Performance of Pakistani Transnational Identity Politics*. Oxford: James Currey.

Wiktorowicz, Quintan (2006). 'Anatomy of the Salafi Movement', *Studies in Conflict and Terrorism*, 29/3: 207–239.

Wolffe, John (1994). *God and Greater Britain: Religion and National Life in Britain and Ireland, 1843–1945*. London and New York, NY: Routledge.

Woodhead, Linda (2001). 'The New Spirituality and the World's Parliament of Religions', in Linda Woodhead (ed.), *Reinventing Christianity: Nineteenth-Century Contexts*. Aldershot: Ashgate, 81–96.

Woodhead, Linda (2011a). 'Five Concepts of Religion', *International Review of Sociology*, 21/1: 121–143.

Woodhead, Linda (2011b). 'Spirituality and Christianity: The Unfolding of a Tangled Relationship', in Bill Swatos and Giuseppe Giordan (eds), *Religion, Spirituality and Everyday Practice*. New York: Springer.

Woodhead, Linda and Paul Heelas (2000) *Religion in Modern Times: An Interpretive Anthology*. Oxford: Wiley Blackwell.

Notes

1   See Woodhead (2011a, especially 131–132) for further discussion of this issue.
2   When this question was first put by BSA, in 1991, 74 per cent believed. The number fell to 72 per cent in 1998 and 62 per cent by 2008. Source: British Religion in Numbers. Online. Available HTTP: www.brin.ac.uk/news/?tag=british-social-attitudes-surveys (accessed 28 May 2011).
3   See also Gill *et al.* (1998) who find that 'nontraditional' beliefs – including belief in the paranormal – have remained stable, with levels of belief in reincarnation (26 per cent), foretelling the future (47 per cent) and ghosts (31 per cent) having barely changed in over half a century.
4   The number of definite atheists has also grown: those who 'don't believe in God' show an increase from 10 per cent to 27 per cent over the same period (Gill *et al.* 1998).
5   Online. Available HTTP: www.brin.ac.uk/figures/documents/godpersonal.xls (accessed 31 August 2011).
6   Our primary sources are popular books, internet sites, hymns and choruses, sermons and talks, visual symbols and images, participant observation of prayer meetings, scripture classes, worship meetings, festivals and gatherings.
7   It would also have been interesting to consider God-change in other religious communities and traditions. The rationale for selection was to look at (1) God-change in the ethno-religious majority (ethnically white, religiously Christian), (2) God-change in the largest ethnic majority, religious minority tradition: alternative spirituality and (3) God-change in the largest ethno-religious minority in Britain, Islam (ethnically diverse but largely non-white).
8   In Britain this revival had many sources, including neo-Romanticism, philosophical idealism and vitalism, evolutionary science, the theology of Catholics like von Hügel and Dom Catholic Butler, of Anglo-Catholics like Evelyn Underhill, and 'scientific' studies of religion and mysticism like William James's *The Varieties of Religious Experience* (first published 1902). See Woodhead (2001 and 2011b) for more information.
9   Watts himself remarked that if he had remained a Christian he might have 'seemed more orthodox than Bishops James Pike [who participated in a televised séance] and John Robinson, let alone the "death of God" theologians' (1972: 229).
10   *Al-Salam*, the first Muslim newspaper to be published in Britain during the 1950s, often made appeals to the *umma* in an effort to organize local religious education and advocate the causes of other Muslim countries (Halliday 2010).
11   The Federation of Islamic Organisations in Europe (FIOE), for example, has redefined its strategic goal to highlight not only its effort to establish an effective Islamic presence in Europe but also to make it a welcome reality in European societies. Online. Available HTTP: www.euromuslim.com/en_Our_mission.aspx (accessed 19 March 2011). The Islamic Society of Britain (ISB), a key player in British Muslim activism, now articulates a civic mission of community development that 'bring[s] together the know-how of British Muslims for the benefit of all British people'. ISB's main projects over the past decade have included the annual nationwide Islam awareness week, the triennial family-orientated 'Living Islam' event which attracts a gathering of a few thousand British Muslims, and the Women's Weekends. This latter activity corresponds with an increasing emphasis on the role of women not only in ISB but also in organizations such as FIOE which has in recent years established a women's department and closely liaises with other Muslim women's organizations. ISB's Women's Weekend is highlighted as one of the three core activities in its 2006/2007 report. The weekend held under the motto 'Living Islam, Loving Humanity' emphasized the role of Muslim women in contributing to 'the wellbeing of humanity' which required of them public engagement with the media and the local authorities in Britain.
12   Online. Available HTTP: www.livingislam.org.uk/8-reasons-why/4-worship.html (accessed 14 March 2011).

Case study 3

The religiosity of young people growing up in poverty

Giselle Vincett and Elizabeth Olson[1]

Starting with the baby boomers (roughly, born between the end of the war and 1964), the subsequent generations of the post-war period are characterized as 'Generation X' and 'Generation Y'. Research is starting to shed light on the religious or secular commitments of Generation Y, and has pointed out that, of all the post-war generations, this is the one which is least likely to have direct experience of church. So far, however, research has concentrated on young people from middle-class backgrounds. This case study reports on findings from a research project funded by the AHRC/ESRC Religion and Society Programme and completed in 2011 which explored the religiosity – or secularity – of young people growing up in deprived areas of Glasgow and Manchester. It found that they made active use of a range of religious practices and resources, applied in the context of their own personal lives, rather than in orchestrated collective settings like churches or mosques.

Connor is a young man from East Manchester; he lives with his mother and four older brothers. All of Connor's brothers are gang members, though Connor claims he is not involved: 'It's not a good feeling [being in a gang]. [pause] It's not good for you.' However, his brothers' gang association limits Connor's movements around the city; he could not enter certain areas and be safe. Even staying in his own neighbourhood does not guarantee safety as gang members from elsewhere could 'just pop out of nowhere with a gun'. As Connor says, 'The only place like you can really … know that you're proper safe is at home.' Connor's knowledge of the precariousness of existence in his neighbourhood is chilling: 'My friend. He's dead now. He got shot in the head.'

For other young people, growing up in a similar neighbourhood in Glasgow generated close friendships and positive memories, but was also marked with a vigilance about whether or not it is safe to leave the flat when the 'junkies' are hanging around outside the front door. Zaheda was typical of many young people we spoke with in that she held together sharply conflicting feelings about her neighbourhood. Green spaces, such as parks, were especially problematic:

> [When I was a wee bit younger] the park is where I would always be – summer and winter – because I had a lot of friends there and stuff … Especially in the summer, it's nice to see so many people out and kids just running about and playing … it's kind of peaceful. [But] there are always people that can cause trouble as well, you know, young people that go around pure causing trouble – fighting, this and that, drinking in the park. So it depends.

How do these kinds of experiences shape young people's religiosity? There are few conceptual frameworks for understanding the ways that deprivation, religion and spirituality intersect, especially in the UK, and these categories are themselves contested. For example, there is little agreement as to what constitutes 'deprivation', and, like 'class', the term can quickly become a label coded with perceptions of worth and social value (Nayak 2006). But as the experiences above attest, it is as important to pay attention to the material conditions in religious and social contexts as it is to gender or ethnicity. Given the consistent increase in relative deprivation[2] and rising poverty in the UK since the 1980s and the most extreme conditions of inequality in Britain for a century (Dorling *et al.* 2007), these questions are of even more pressing concern.

Researching youth, religion and deprivation

We know substantially more about young people's religiosity than we did a decade ago, but there are still significant gaps in our understanding of precisely how young people influence, and are influenced by, broader trends in religious and social change. Large-scale studies on youth and religion have been conducted in the US (Smith and Denton 2005; Smith and Snell 2009) and Australia (Mason 2007), and have been matched in the UK (Francis and Robbins 2005; Savage *et al.* 2006; Collins-Mayo *et al.* 2010). However, research on youth religiosity and spirituality in the UK has focused largely on socially and economically included young people. The ways in which young people's contexts influence their religiosity or spirituality, and the ways in which deprivation might mediate experiences of religiosity and spirituality, are not clear, especially in the literature on youth and religion in the UK.

There is, nonetheless, good reason to suspect that social class would be an influential factor in young people's religious and spiritual practices and beliefs. Sociologists of religion have traditionally assumed that religious participation can be measured by religious institution attendance levels. However, such measures are often church-centric (Jewish women, for example, may not attend synagogue but their role in the *Shabbat* meal is central), prompting recent attention to alternative ways of religious participation, as discussed in the Introduction to this volume. But there has been little consideration of the way that such measures may be class-based, despite continuing acknowledgement that class and religion intersect in a multitude of ways. Pelling (1964) analysed low church attendance levels among the working class in nineteenth-century England, but emphasized that denomination and location made a difference. This link between class and active religious affiliation tends to be made in relation to 'white' Christianity, prompting Berger *et al.* to suggest that churchgoing in Europe is 'a middle-class activity' (Berger *et al.* 2008: 98). However, they point out that the 'non-practice of the working class is – and in some ways always has been – counter-balanced by [immigration]' (Berger *et al.* 2008: 99). Immigration is a complex influence on religion, and it is also the reason we might expect to find more vibrant forms of religiosity in economically deprived neighbourhoods, where migrant communities might be drawn to affordable housing and might subsequently establish a mosque, gurdwara or house church. Yet Fahmy writes that just 4 per cent of young people (aged 16–24) in areas of deprivation participate in a religious group or organization (Fahmy 2006: 364), though 14 per cent of those aged 18–24 use services provided by a place of worship (Fahmy 2006: 360).

When we designed a research project to examine how places of deprivation influence the spiritual and religious lives of young people, we thus began by acknowledging that we would be speaking with young people with a diverse set of religious experiences, with the majority having had little interaction with formal religious institutions. We were eager to avoid the patterns we saw in some other studies of young people, where too often anything other than traditional (adult) religion and spirituality is dismissed as 'fuzzy' belief. We also recognized that a focus on traditional structures or ideologies of religion may render socially deprived young people visible only as passive recipients of faith-based outreach or charity, despite evidence that young people in deprived settings do actively negotiate their own spirituality (Williams and Lindsey 2005).

We therefore started by asking about those spheres of human experience and practice that have traditionally been the domain of religion and spirituality; not simply to cover what religion and spirituality *do* in the everyday and in the extraordinary, but what they are *imagined* to represent. We became interested in themes of belonging and care, ethics and values, social and transitional rituals (new life, marriage, death), belief in and experience of the other-than-human or more-than-human (broadly defined), places of peace or evil, frameworks for understanding good and bad experiences or events, and hardship and sources of resilience or flourishing. We interviewed young people, neighbourhood elders, community service providers and faith leaders, and we conducted participant observation with detached[3] youth workers on the streets and at youth groups, centres or programmes. Over 100 interviews were conducted (plus less formal conversations in the field). In addition, two groups of young people engaged in a participatory film and photography programme, and produced videos and exhibitions of their work (see Olson *et al.* forthcoming).

The two neighbourhoods we focused upon are both located in large cities in the north of the UK: one in Scotland, in south Glasgow, the other in England, in East Manchester. These neighbourhoods are areas of long-term economic and social deprivation, compounded by the way that poor places tend to be clustered together, a situation which Glennerster *et al.* (1999: 14) refer to as poverty 'clumping'. Government measures of deprivation focus not simply on income or employment levels in an area, but on a range of indices from levels of car and home ownership to the proportion of children receiving free school meals to ease of access to services and various types of social and economic opportunities (Office for National Statistics 2010a). For us, it was important to acknowledge the material realities of entrenched economic inequality whilst allowing for young people's different opportunities for flourishing. Drawing on other poverty research (Lawson *et al.* 2010), we thus framed the research around 'poor places' rather than poor people in order to account for shared and divergent experiences of deprivation.

The importance of place

The two neighbourhoods where Connor and Zaheda grew up were built upon employment in industries which have largely disappeared over the past 30 years. Though never wealthy, they are areas with rich histories of community. In East Manchester, regeneration programmes bring benefits (gated back alleys, a new supermarket which will make shopping easier for those without cars, new facilities for schools and healthcare) but also instability as housing stock is torn down and people relocated until new housing is built. Young people from areas of deprivation struggle with issues of personal safety, from knife crime in south Glasgow to dangerous underground economies such as copper and lead 'stripping' from houses (falls are common). For complex reasons, the life expectancy of people living in the poorest areas of England is just 67 (Marmot *et al.* 2010: 38).[4] Rates of those claiming 'incapacity benefit' are also high in areas of deprivation, again for complex reasons, but driven in large part by the way that people with long-term illness or disability are allocated available – and affordable – social housing in economically deprived areas. As the Marmot

Review put it, 'people in poorer areas not only die sooner, but they will also spend more of their shorter lives with a disability' (Marmot *et al.* 2010: 17). Taken together, the lives of young people in areas of deprivation are often shaped by economic and social stresses, and young people are likely to have experienced various types of loss and instability that are less likely to be experienced by their middle-class peers.

Although church-attendance levels may traditionally have been lower in working-class areas, the built environment attests to the historical presence of multiple faith communities. Perhaps especially notable in East Manchester was the presence of many small nonconformist churches and missions. Since our chosen area in Glasgow has traditionally been a 'gateway' community for new immigrants, it is possible to trace that history through the built environment (churches built for Irish Catholics, a synagogue, mosques). Oral history from neighbourhood elders attests to the way faith communities provided services for, and structured the social life of, such neighbourhoods from Easter processions to hosting youth clubs and dances.

A walk around East Manchester now, however, quickly reveals the state of traditional religion in that neighbourhood: many churches and missions are gone, boarded up or in disrepair. Others have been taken over by African Pentecostal churches serving the recent wave of asylum seekers and refugees in the area (see Chapter 2), seemingly confirming the traditional pattern which Berger *et al.* (2008) describe earlier.[5] In Glasgow, two local mosques are vibrant and active (both located in former churches), and one church shares space with a Slovakian Roma church, representing the latest community to settle in the neighbourhood. But in the Church of Scotland and the Roman Catholic churches, numbers have declined and the majority of congregants now live outside the neighbourhood.

The built and oral histories of these areas point to the way that working-class areas have always tended to have a different relationship with the churches, different denominational affiliations, and perhaps also suggest different patterns of practice. Connor, for example, comes from an Irish-Catholic background, but says that he does not go to church. When asked if he believes in God, he replies (as if this is a really dumb question) 'yeah, yeah'. He also wears his rosary beads, not 'for fashion', but because they are 'good luck' – when he wears them he knows God will look out for him and keep him safe, so he makes sure to put them on every time he leaves the house. Connor also goes every Friday to his friend's grave to bless his rosary beads, pray and be with his friend, which he says feels 'relaxing, innit? You're praying with your friend, you're showing your respect.'

Death, loss and illness were subjects we did not need to bring up in our interviews; our young informants most often brought them up themselves and, yet, they very often claimed that they had never spoken of such things with anyone before. This kind of privatized 'crisis religiosity' has been noted among studies of middle-class young people, where it has been characterized as a 'make-do-and-mend' faith, an inadequate resource cobbled together in emergency from 'the cultural memory of Christianity in the absence of other religious and spiritual resources' (Collins-Mayo *et al.* 2010: 38). This is an interpretation which acknowledges some agency of young people in putting together their religiosity or spirituality, and Collins-Mayo *et al.* recognize that personal experience of death brings 'questions about the nature of God and the afterlife … into sharper focus' (2010: 42). Nevertheless, the fact that crisis, loss and instability are an almost constant feature of the lives of young people like Connor makes 'make-do-and-mend' an inadequate interpretation. Connor is quite explicit that he chooses to practise some forms of religiosity and not others and that his religiosity is based upon more than a vague cultural memory: 'I only believe in certain things. I don't … go to church or that … [But] *I know what to do.*'

Connor's privatized practice and belief in God were not unusual in our study of young people from areas of deprivation. Zaheda was raised Muslim and was drawn to Christianity after a difficult period in her life. Her faith in God is central to her wellbeing, but she attends several different churches and she says that she often finds the sacred when she is simply sitting outside a church. Zaheda's faith, like Connor's, is something that she thinks about often, but it exists largely outside the formal structures of any single denomination. Most of the young people we interviewed believed in God, though many told us that God was not to be found in their neighbourhoods. Jack said, 'religious people like to live better, healthier lives, so they won't want to move to like a trampy or scruffy area like [this]'. Young people also pointed out the social stigma of coming from an area of deprivation and the assumptions other people made about them because of where they lived. These assumptions can limit youth participation in certain spaces and can affect how young people engage with and frame everyday spaces, including sacred spaces. Our findings confirm Andrew Sayer's claim that whilst ethics and morals do not vary across social class, the perception is often different. This difference, Sayer writes, is partly because of 'moral boundary drawing' (2005: 952), such as the assumption that our young informants made that middle-class church attenders were 'better' than them. The tendency of sociologists of religion to 'measure' the ways in which people from working-class areas, and young people especially, do not fit the hegemonic norms of religious participation in faith institutions, and to label them non-religious or 'fuzzy', may further produce and reinforce people's alienation from the 'social bases of respect' (Sayer 2005: 954).

Despite Connor's high levels of vulnerability and instability, he retains a belief in God and an idealized sense of God as looking out for him and listening to his prayers. This construction of God as loving, personal and interventionist was common to most of our research participants, both Christian and Muslim. God was *supposed* to help young people negotiate the constraints and instability of their neighbourhoods, and provided an ideal model of relationship. However, the young people who were most vulnerable, whose lives were most characterized by general and persistent insecurity, and whose agency was most 'bounded' (MacDonald and Marsh 2001: 383; Leonard 2006) were also most likely to lose faith in God when 'he' did *not* live up to the ideal model. Zara's answer, for example, was not unusual when we asked 'When did you really find that you weren't believing [in Islam] any more?': 'When my Mum tried to commit suicide. And like – she's tried to do it twenty, thirty times … and I – I just thought, if there was a God, she wouldn't be like this, this stuff wouldn't happen to her, because she's a good woman.' For the minority of young people we interviewed who considered themselves atheists, there was little need to reconcile the presumed benevolence of God with their negative experiences. Yet even young people who did not believe in God expressed uncertainty about what happens after a person dies. Indeed, ghosts (frequently interpreted by young people as caring spirits of deceased friends or relatives) and 'guardian angels' were often mentioned in relation to sacred experiences or as evidence of the mystery of what happens when a person dies by both religious and non-religious young people. Many young people relayed an experience with a ghost or unseen 'spirit', with the majority of these encounters reassuring them that someone is looking out for them or a vulnerable loved one.

Day (2010) has pointed to what she calls 'practical belief' in the UK, a movement away from propositional or dogmatic belief. In relation to an earlier study of young Christians,[6] we argued that they create what we have termed 'performance' religiosity (Vincett *et al.* forthcoming), emphasizing everyday religious performances and places. To some extent, such characterizations would fit the religiosity we encountered among young people in areas of deprivation, but the bounded agency and mobility of young people in poorer areas limit the kinds of performances they can create and the places in which they can safely practise or express their beliefs. Indeed, if many young people in poorer areas sense that religious people are 'better' or of a different class from them, even crossing the boundary between the street and a church youth group requires a self-confidence and security that may not be available to them. And since many young people of all classes feel that religious beliefs cannot be discussed or admitted among peer groups, the boundaries around their religious performances become ever more fixed and unforgiving, especially, it seems, among young, white Christians. Privatized religious practices, however, do not necessarily translate into highly individualized (that is, purely self-focused) beliefs, as the fairly common conception of God outlined above indicates.

Returning to the question we posed at the start of this case study, we can make some general observations about how deprivation mediates religiosity and belief. It is significant that the type of God and religiosity which young people often articulated in our study (and which had also been expressed by some other young people from areas of deprivation in our previous study) placed a high emphasis on God as protector and friend, with angels popular for similar reasons. Churches and mosques can represent places of safety, including from police and other adults who make assumptions about young people. However, they can also be exclusionary and unwelcoming, particularly when they have a middle-class congregation which is perceived as having a negative view of young people in these neighbourhoods. Religious practices – which were common, even if hidden – often reinforced a sense of safety or peace, or connection to lost or vulnerable loved ones. Thus growing up in an area of deprivation mediates the ways that young people encounter religious institutions, and it influences the kinds of experiences that a young person is likely to have. Growing up in a poor place may not determine whether or not a young person believes in God, but these experiences lend shape to *how* young people like Connor or Zaheda construct their beliefs.

References

Berger, Peter, Grace Davie and Effie Fokas (2008). *Religious America, Secular Europe: A Theme and Variations.* Aldershot: Ashgate.

Collins-Mayo, Sylvie, Bob Mayo and Sally Nash (2010). *The Faith of Generation Y.* London: Church House.

Day, Abby (2010). 'Propositions and Performativity: Relocating Belief to the Social', *Culture and Religion*, 11/1: 9–30.

Dorling, Daniel, Jan Rigby, Ben Wheeler, Dimitris Ballas, Bethan Thomas, Eldin Fahmy, David Gordon and Ruth Lupton (2007). *Poverty, Wealth and Place in Britain, 1968–2005.* Bristol: Policy Press for the Joseph Rowntree Foundation.

Fahmy, Eldin (2006). 'Youth, Poverty and Social Exclusion', in David Gordon, Christina Pantazis and Ruth Levitas (eds), *Poverty and Social Exclusion in Britain*. Bristol: Policy Press, 347–372.

Francis, Leslie J. and Mandy Robbins (2005). *Urban Hope and Spiritual Health: The Adolescent Voice.* Peterborough: Epworth.

Glennerster, Howard, Ruth Lupton, Philip Noden and Anne Power (1999). *Poverty, Social Exclusion and Neighbourhood: Studying the Area Bases of Social Exclusion.* London: Centre for Analysis of Social Exclusion, London School of Economics.

Lawson, Victoria, Lucy Jarosz and Anne Bonds (2010). 'Articulations of Place, Poverty and Race: Dumping Grounds and Unseen Grounds in the Rural American Northwest', *Annals of the Association of American Geographers*, 100/3: 655–677.

Leonard, Madeleine (2006). 'Teens and Territory in Contested Spaces: Negotiating Sectarian Interfaces in Northern Ireland', *Children's Geographies*, 4/2: 225–238.

MacDonald, Rob and Jane Marsh (2001). 'Disconnected Youth?', *Journal of Youth Studies*, 4/4: 373–391.

Marmot, Michael, Tony Atkinson, John Bell, Carol Black, Patricia Broadfoot, Julia Cumberlege, Ian Diamond, Ian Gilmore, Chris Ham, Molly Meacher and Geoff Mulgan (2010). *Fair Society, Healthy Lives: The Marmot Review*. London: The Marmot Review.

Mason, Michael (2007). *The Spirit of Generation Y*. Melbourne: John Garratt.

Nayak, Anook (2006). 'Displaced Masculinities: Chavs, Youth and Class in the Post-industrial City', *Sociology*, 40/5: 813–831.

Office for National Statistics (2010a). 'Indices of Deprivation across the UK'. Online. Available HTTP: www.neighbourhood.statistics.gov.uk/dissemination/Info.do?page=analysisandguidance/analysisarticles/indices-of-deprivation.htm (accessed 16 February 2011).

Office for National Statistics (2010b). 'Life Expectancy'. Online. Available HTTP: www.statistics.gov.uk/cci/nugget.asp?id=168 (accessed 31 January 2011).

Olson, Elizabeth, Giselle Vincett, Peter Hopkins, Rachel Pain and Eduardo Serafin (forthcoming). 'Hanging Out and Hanging On: Researching Spirituality with and for Vulnerable Young People', in Linda Woodhead (ed.), *Innovative Methods in the Study of Religion*. Oxford: Oxford University Press.

Pelling, Henry (1964). 'Religion and the Nineteenth Century British Working Class', *Past and Present*, 27/1: 128–133.

Savage, Sara, Sylvie Collins-Mayo, Bob Mayo and Graham Cray (2006). *Making Sense of Generation Y: The World View of 15–25-year-olds*. London: Church House.

Sayer, Andrew (2005). 'Class, Moral Worth and Recognition', *Sociology*, 39/5: 947–963.

Smith, Christian and Melissa L. Denton (2005). *Soul Searching: The Religious and Spiritual Lives of American Teenagers*. New York, NY: Oxford University Press.

Smith, Christian and Patricia Snell (2009). *Souls in Transition: The Religious and Spiritual Lives of Emerging Adults*. New York, NY: Oxford University Press.

Vincett, Giselle, Elizabeth Olson, Peter Hopkins and Rachel Pain (forthcoming). 'Young People and Performance Christianity in Scotland', *Journal of Contemporary Religion*.

Williams, Nancy R. and Elizabeth Lindsey (2005). 'Spirituality and Religion in the Lives of Runaway and Homeless Youth: Coping with Adversity', *Journal of Religion and Spirituality in Social Work*, 24/4: 19–38.

Notes

1   This case study is based upon research for the AHRC/ESRC Religion and Society Programme funded large grant 'Marginalized Spiritualities' for which Elizabeth Olson was the Principal Investigator and Giselle Vincett was Research Fellow.

2   'Deprivation' in the West is usually framed in terms of 'relative deprivation', that is, although a person may be far better off materially than his or her counterpart in developing nations, he or she may be considerably disadvantaged in comparison to the average citizen in his or her country.

3   That is, youth work with deprived young people where they are, rather than just, for example, based in a centre.

4   England has the highest rates of life expectancy in the UK, while Scotland has the lowest (see Office for National Statistics 2010b).

5   The neighbourhood in which we worked in East Manchester had seen little immigration by non-Christian communities. This was not the case in the area we studied in south Glasgow which has a long history of religious and cultural diversity.

6   AHRC/ESRC Religion and Society funded small grant 'Relational Religious Identities: Exploring Contemporary Meanings of Religion among Scottish Christian Youth'.

6 Changing British ritualization

Douglas J. Davies

This chapter turns the spotlight on changes and continuities in the ritual life of Britain and the British   majorities as well as minorities. It suggests that rituals express and intensify cultural and personal values and identity and often implicate emotions. It considers both the historic Christian context of ritualization in Britain, and more recent developments in both personal and collective ritual. It notes the importance of 'political' rituals and rituals which reinforce identities (from Orange marches in Northern Ireland to the recent invention of tradition in Wootton Bassett), the role of religion in ritualizing national celebrations and tragedies, the growth of secular rites and rituals associated with new forms of spirituality, and even the ritual practices that now take place in relation to security in airports. Contextualizing these developments, the chapter shows how ritualization has come to be framed by a celebrity culture fostered by new forms of media with their increased opportunity of publicity.

Introduction

Ritual is a pattern of shared behaviour, repeated at appropriate times and places, that expresses some core convictions of a group. Some think of ritual as being like a language having a code that can be cracked to find the meaning, some others see it more as an end in itself, as something that satisfies us simply because we do it (Davies 2002: 111–145).[1] The Christian baptism of babies, for example, is an obvious 'ritual' often involving water, lighting candles, marking the newly named person with the sign of the cross and so on. But not everyone taking part is likely to give it the same 'meaning' or even be explicit about these things at all. Priests will have some knowledge of the long history of this rite through which a person joins the Christian world, while some relatives may think more in terms of simply 'doing the right thing' or wanting to express thanks for a safe delivery and healthy child. Still others join in to 'give support' and enjoy a party afterwards, an event that anthropologists would probably also describe as a ritual event. Sometimes, then, we are aware of taking part in 'a ritual' even though we may not be able to spell out all its potential significance, at other times we do things without even thinking of them as ritual performances. Birthdays, for example, are among the most widespread of rituals in contemporary life involving greetings cards, cakes, parties and the well-known singing of 'Happy Birthday to you', all marking kinship and friendship relationships focused on the identity of a single person. Yet, few would probably think of them as rituals. Both baptisms and birthdays offer good examples of core commitments coming to formal expression, not least in valuing individuals and wanting to wish them well, to bring good things to them and, in that sense, these are rituals of blessing.

Just as baptisms, birthdays and weddings, too, mark the identity of individuals, some rituals mark the identity of a whole community and reinforce its boundary against other groups. Within Great Britain, the Irish, Scots and Welsh all have ritual-like celebrations to spotlight their identity and these are often intensified in expatriate communities across the world. What is obvious from this is that 'ritual' is not simply a word belonging to formal religious traditions. It also underlies many contexts that bring and affirm identity or intensify our sense of commitment to our particular ways of life and, because of that, we should not expect 'ritual' to decrease in contexts of secularization. In many contemporary non-religious or secular weddings and funerals, for example, we find new ritual forms being developed by non-religious organizers, and even by individuals and their own family and friendship groups. Such invention of tradition is a mark of social change, human creativity and the deep fact of human nature as social nature.

Cultures seem to vary in their explicit focus on rituals. In some we find a heightened degree of interest in rituals, often for very distinctive historical reasons. And this is partly the case in Britain. Indeed, one of the best 'essays' on ritual and ritual changes in British religion is entitled 'Of Ceremonies, why some are abolished and some retained' and was first found in the Church of England's *First Prayer-Book of King Edward VI* of 1549, followed only by 'notes' on dress and ritual actions. It then remained for over 400 years as an accessible yet largely ignored text within the 1662 *Book of Common Prayer*.[2] Reflecting the delicate political and theological dynamics of the English Reformation it tells how 'the myndes of men bee so diverse' with some 'so addicted to their olde customes', and others 'bee so newe fangle that they woulde innouate all thyng' (The First Prayer Book of Edward VI 1549, see Text box 13).

TEXT BOX 13

'Of Ceremonies, why some are abolished and some retained' from the 1549 Book of Common Prayer

And whereas in this our tyme, the myndes of menne bee so diverse, that some thynke it a greate matter of conscience to departe from a peece of the leaste of theyr Ceremonies (they bee so addicted to their olde customes), and agayne on the other syde, some bee so newe fangle that they woulde innovate all thyng, and so doe despyse the olde that nothyng canne lyke them, but that is newe:

This clarity over diversity, addiction to custom and newfangled notions reflected the enormous complexity of England within the European Reformation and the world-changing centuries that followed. It is a firm reminder of Christian Europe's enduring preoccupation with practical ritual and abstract theologizing. These range from early Pagan conversion, the Iconoclastic controversies in Eastern Europe and Asia of the eighth to ninth centuries, the thirteenth century's theological analysis of the Mass and the Protestant Reformation, including its more extreme Puritan objection to ritual-symbolism, and even the very diversity of naming the 'same' ritual Mass, Eucharist, Holy Communion or Lord's Supper. Furthermore, within and beyond the churches, rites of royalty, military ceremonial, legal formality and the customs of colonized peoples would all gain enhanced attention through the Victorian emergence of anthropology as an academic venture. By the early twentieth century 'ritual' was set fair to become a field of social scientific study and would, later, also find some affinity with the liturgical studies of theologians.

More obvious sociological issues underlie this chapter on post-war, and particularly post-1960s, Britain. These include the shift from industrial to post-industrial and service-based society; the growth of diverse communities framed by explicit politics of multiculturalism; social-class realignments and economic betterment; gender-role politics; age-based cohorts; and the creation of a media-embedded celebrity culture fostered by processes of globalization-driven commerce, entertainment media, migration and holidays. Within religious worlds, other issues swarm into view including those of secularization, ecumenicity, fundamentalisms, interfaith activity, transformations in clerical training, and in relation to gender, sexuality and ordination. To avoid the paralysis this plethora of topics invites, this chapter has a theoretical orientation which pays particular attention to some emotional dynamics of ritual-related activities through the idiomatic themes of scepticism and excitement approached from a bio-cultural perspective that integrates emotions and social values (Hinton 1999). This makes it possible to consider how an emotional charge may be added to an idea to generate a 'value', and to suggest that when such values inform personal or group identity they function as 'beliefs' (Davies 2011: 13–37). Beliefs thus emerge as identity-conferring 'values' constituted by emotion-laden ideas, frequently shaped as destiny-framing narratives, and often allied with notions of supernatural entities.[3] Moreover, such beliefs are frequently ritualized, for example the concept of the family reveals an idea whose emotional charge transforms it into a core value for many and a belief for some; as such it frames identity, engenders a narrative base, and possesses ritual foci in life-cycle rites, Christmas and holidays.

Failure to appreciate the emotional excitement allied with core values and their ritual-symbolism hinders cross-group understanding.[4] The figure of Jesus, for example, is treasured by devoted Christians, respected by many, tolerated by others and used in swearing by yet more, all in a spectrum familiar to a single speech community but which may not apply to sacred figures in other communities, as with many Muslims and their attitude to Muhammad. The ritualized verbal respect paid to 'Muhammad', in its complement, 'Peace be upon him', or the literary ritualized respect evident when some Jews write of the deity as G-d, does not exist in wider British life. Similarly, attitudes to the Bible can carry fatal flaws if extrapolated to other sacred texts. By contrast, the relatively unknown figure of Guru Nanak has attracted but little negative interchange between Sikhs and others in Britain, replaced in one sense by the Sikh claim to wear the turban as part of their manifest identity whether in respect of crash helmets or work-uniforms. In recent decades the wearing of full-cover female dress by some Islamic traditions, and of a neck-cross by some Christians, has attracted similar affirmation and dispute over ritualized dress identity-values. These carry emotional charges sustained by cultural moods intensified by group convention and periodic ritual intensification. Many such ritualized behaviours serve well as vehicles for and boundary markers of distinctive identity when groups seek status in politically responsive contexts (see Chapter 1).[5]

Ritual, politics and identity

Ritual has frequently been influenced by political forces and used to stabilize or contest identities, not least in the post-war period. And this inevitably takes on special significance within a society possessing a relatively high-profile Church of England 'by law appointed' in England, and by the Presbyterians in Scotland. The disestablished Church in Wales, the

Catholic and other churches and Jewish groups, all maintain a recognized influence despite reductions in numerical attendance. The arrival of politically active groups of Islamic, Sikh, Hindu and Buddhist provenance alongside increased interaction among religious leaders has generated a degree of excitement within an elite ecumenical and interfaith stratum (see Case study 2). Indeed, many interfaith events assume their own ritual-like form of reciprocal respect, albeit with limited outcome among ordinary immigrant-rooted devotees whose intensified ritualizing of cultural practices helps sustain their identity in a new country. We will discuss some aspects of these groups now with further detail included towards the close of this chapter.

Two ritual-related issues arise here, one concerning religion and identity and the other authenticity. For some immigrants the traditions of their youth underlie the 'truthfulness' of adult identity, excited through ritual intensification in festivals, inspirational speakers, niche media, etc. However, generations born in Britain sometimes express a scepticism over bonding 'truth' to inherited customs, preferring to stress an authenticity of personal devotion and to their scriptures as 'purer' expressions of doctrinal truth. This echo of Cantwell Smith's distinction between 'cumulative tradition' and 'faith' within religious groups and individuals raises the wider theoretical question of authenticity and of what makes a 'real' Muslim, Christian or Sikh (Smith 1963). In connection with 'Islamic Fundamentalism', for example, many Muslims have spoken of the numerically small number of terrorists as not showing 'real' or 'genuine' Islam, just as some of those described as terrorists are likely to have defined themselves as among 'real' Muslims, ending their life as martyrs. In the apparently quite different world of the Church of England, many identify with that body and see themselves as Christians even though they attend church infrequently and may well be described as 'nominal' Christians by core attenders who self-define as 'committed' or 'real' Christians. The dynamics of this identity-mapping are profoundly significant as people variously utilize ritual-symbolic schemes for their own purpose of evaluating a meaningful life, even if frequent attendance gains most sociological attention.

The 'real' believer is, then, always an interesting phenomenon within religious identity-mapping, as is the notion of orthodoxy versus heresy in world history. Christianity's emergence from Judaism, the divisions between Eastern and Western Christendom, the Protestant Reformation and the numerous subsequent subdivisions of all these groups furnish classic cases easily replicated within Buddhism, Sikhism and Judaism. Scepticism and excitement inform all such divisions. Doubt over a traditional interpretation or the following of a particular leader combines with an excitement for a tradition's teachings and practices in the generation of revivals, renewals and schisms. It is not surprising that some younger Muslims and Sikhs, set in a social context of confusing multiculturalism, and with parents they deem to be 'religious' more by habit than conviction, should seek self-authentication in the pursuit of a 'purer' expression of their faith. In this they are no different from numbers of British Christian youth whose teenage identity formation involves a form of conversion to Christianity from a scepticism over their parents' 'conventional' religiosity of occasional practice. Such transformations of pre-existing identity often involve degrees of scepticism over pre-existing ritual habits and excitement over future religious possibilities, including creative deployment of tradition. The human proclivity for making moral as well as cognitive meaning finds a powerful catalyst in what is perceived as cold formality and a powerful trigger in what is glimpsed as hot creative truth. The very idea of a 'real believer' offers an attraction inherent in the notion of 'truth', one that is easily overlooked, for example, in what are often called rational choice theories of religious adherence.[6] Here, sociologically speaking, 'truth' means access to what is perceived as authentic identity, it carries an emotional charge constituted by hope. For the aroused sceptic truth becomes a beautiful goal in and of itself. This is something that Ernst Bloch fully understood in terms of the 'peace' offered to devotees, a peace that could, however, also lead on to an extinguishing of individuality under despotic leadership (Bloch 1986: 966).

One clear UK example of authenticity and identity, one echoing the English Reformation, was evident in the Northern Irish religious antipathy of Ulster Protestantism to the Republic of Ireland's essentially Catholic world (see Chapter 9). Notably, the Reverend Ian Paisley established his own denominational version of Protestant evangelicalism in Northern Ireland and combined his clerical role with that of a UK Member of Parliament (see Plate 1.4). His dogmatic anti-Catholicism would probably assert that 'ritual' – an idea associated with Roman Catholic error – was absent from his church culture while social scientists would certainly see in it dramatic exhibitions of ritualized religious-cultural affirmation of Protestantism, especially through the Orange Order. Originating in 1795 as an affirmation of Protestant religion and politics, this Order's contemporary street marches serve as a boundary-marking affirmation between geographical territories of Catholics and Protestants within Northern Ireland itself, areas often highly decorated with large-scale street painting.[7] The Marching Season brought with it raised levels of excitement, declaratory both of dominance and of repression, between populations, not least as bands played music redolent of old hostilities.

The rise of the media, especially television, throughout this period meant that such marches, as well as the results of bombings between these Christian political-religious populations and their terrorist wings, were rapidly seen throughout the UK. Such portrayals long fostered a sense of hopeless irritation over Northern Ireland and its religious conflicts. Entire generations of churchgoing people on the mainland became used to prayers 'for peace in Northern Ireland', while the deaths of soldiers as well as civilians underscored the need for it. The public funerals of those killed in what was long described as 'the Troubles', often with 'full military honours' – whether legal or illegal – provided their own ritual expression of religious-cultural conflict. In more recent times the formal repatriation of the dead, this time from warfare in Afghanistan, became markedly intensified in an invention of tradition in the Wiltshire town of Wootton Bassett. From 2007, former servicemen and women of the Royal British Legion, along with other local people and bereaved families, lined the town's main street as hearses brought the dead, coffins draped in Union Jacks, from the Royal Air Force base of Lyneham: church bells tolled appropriately (see Plate 2.10). This local ceremonial was recognized in an answering royal 'ritual' in the form of a Royal Charter given to the town in March 2011 despite the fact that from September 2011 the dead will arrive through RAF Brize Norton in Oxfordshire thus ending this particular event.

Ritual change within – and beyond – the churches

From these public ceremonial ritualizations of core values, we now turn to consider two cases of specific intra-ecclesial aspects of mixed excitement and scepticism, namely, the Charismatic Movement which intensifies certain biblical elements of faith and the Sea of Faith Network which appreciates doubt and a different kind of creativity of religious ideas. To these we will add a third case originating in the non-ecclesial arena of healthcare agencies and their interest in 'spirituality'.

Charismatic movement

The rise of the Christian Charismatic Movement from small beginnings in the late 1960s to a moderately dominant position by the 1990s roughly paralleled the burgeoning of youth culture, its music and movement, and the need for excitement among existing believers (see also Chapters 2 and 5). Both 'church' and 'world' sensed and shared in a widespread excitement with life and its opportunities, albeit framed by diverse values including the rush of optimistic capitalism under Prime Minister Margaret Thatcher along with the deeply sceptical moods following her defeat of the National Union of Mineworkers.

The Charismatic ethos of inspired congregational singing, prayer and sensed awareness of a divine power flourished in many parts of the world, offering its own form of globalization with an emphasis upon the power of the Holy Spirit to give individuals a sense of vigorous religious life, warmth in group membership through ritual forms of collective singing, praying, moving, swooning, speaking in tongues, receiving messages from God and being committed to ideas of divine healing. Private devotions often reflected such public ritualizing of spirit-power. To a degree, these influences changed the ritual pattern of established denominations whose members normally retained their seats or pews and did not stand or hold arms aloft in worship. Whilst sharing a collective mood of submission to spirit-power many also seemed lost in a private world with eyes shut and face uplifted. Such 'times of worship' sometimes occupy part of an otherwise standard form of denominational worship or may stand alone at other times. The interesting fact of this Charismatic 'movement' was that, whilst it includes a degree of scepticism over the full authenticity of established denominational patterns of faith, it remains within those traditions, unlike the innovative Pentecostal churches of the early twentieth century. The new process of mutual accommodation brought an emotional excitement into life, one that was followed by a variety of theological self-explanation. This might well have been due to the fact that the British Charismatic Movement was largely a middle- and not a working-class event, as was the case with the Pentecostal churches. Even the role of glossolalia was different in each case, with the working-class Pentecostals gaining a voice and status through this capacity for public utterance while the middle-class Charismatic, who often already possessed such a voice and status, gained from an emotional release and sense of friendship within a new community (Davies 1984a).

Although some forms of conservative evangelicalism, especially those influenced by Calvin-inspired forms of dogmatic theology, retained a ritual stance apart from the Charismatic influence, many Charismatic emotional tones influenced mainstream traditions, even affecting the ritual costume worn by religious leaders. From the 1980s it became increasingly popular for priests and ministers to wear artistically colourful garments; even the established custom of Anglican evangelicals wearing academic hood and scarf with their surplices often gave way to decorated stoles. It was now clear that, 'The Church of England does not attach any particular doctrinal significance to the diversities of vesture', itself a remarkable affirmation given the theological import previously informing Anglo-Catholic and evangelical parties within the church (*The Canons of the Church of England* 1969: 11, Canon B 8.5). This creativity in ritual clothing, aided by a consumerist response in companies providing such dress, was partially catalysed through the Church of England's ordination of women and the need to develop appropriate female-clothing catalogues.

Another feature of ecclesiastical ritualization lay in the increased popularity of the Eucharist. Though a long-committed feature of Anglo-Catholic and Catholic life, one also favoured by the Anglican Parish and People Movement of the post-war period, the liturgical reforms expressed in the Church of England's *Alternative Service Book* of 1980 and the *Common Worship* of 2000 provided many contemporary language variants of the *Book of Common Prayer*'s single Holy Communion service. Events such as Harvest Festival that would once have taken the form of Morning or Evening Prayer now became Eucharistic in the greatest Eucharist-shift in ritual that the English state church had ever seen. This may have been a response to a decrease in status of the clergy in society at large, one that encouraged them to affirm their status as the sole people with authority to conduct that rite, something not available to laity nor even to lay-officials.

Sea of Faith Network

This period of Charismatic growth, Eucharistic emphasis and women's ordination was overlapped by a theological movement of liberal theology. The 1960s had witnessed a series of new translations of the Bible, including the academically toned *New English Bible* (New Testament 1961, whole Bible 1970) and the Catholic *Jerusalem Bible* (1966), with *The Good News Bible* (1968) and *The Living Bible* (1969), as well as the interdenominational *Common Bible* (1973) being more popularly aimed. The *New Revised Standard Version* (1989) struck a note between these polarities. Numerous biblical sections were produced in dialect or local versions aimed at non-churched individuals, especially youngsters. Just as these new translations were aiming at bible-reading or potential bible-reading publics, so there emerged an interesting flourish in theological debate that spilled over from the academic world, not least due to the publicity afforded by television to people such as John Robinson. Robinson was a Cambridge clerical-don, who was made Suffragan Bishop of Woolwich despite some conservative opposition, and served from 1959 to 1969. Despite, or perhaps because of, his patrician background, he was part of an informal 'movement' seeking to bring an enlightened understanding of Christianity to working- and middle-class people. Though essentially a biblical scholar he ventured into more philosophical debate in his popularly aimed 1963 *Honest to God*. Its attempt to explain that one should not think of God in anthropomorphic ways or as being somewhere in heaven 'up there' was a version of the German-American theologian and existentialist theologian Paul Tillich who died in 1965, with further echoes of the German biblical textual-critic Rudolf Bultmann (1884–1976) and the socially involved theologian Dietrich Bonhoeffer (1906–1945). Robinson stirred a deep debate and his apparently unconventional religious ideas appear the more startling. Tillich had said that God did 'not exist'. That kind of sentence was shocking to many people, especially when repeated by a bishop. In context, Tillich and Robinson actually meant that God was not merely something which exists, but 'the ground of Being'. But the mass media were not given to offer such explanations, and many people saw this as playing with words. Nevertheless, Robinson's approach did touch a certain number of people who were unhappy with traditional ways of talking about God.[8]

This background brings us directly to the other significant Cambridge clerical-don and philosophical theologian Don Cupitt, whose 1984 television programme and book *The Sea of Faith* prompted a response from some people who felt that his philosophical interpretation answered their own sense of sceptical uncertainty over traditionalist forms of Christianity, whilst exciting their intrinsic interest in Christianity. Cupitt's 'Sea of Faith' idiom was taken directly from Matthew Arnold's poem 'Dover Beach' with its emotions of sadness, misery and melancholy in witnessing the outgoing tide of a 'Sea of Faith' that once had been 'at the full, and round earth's shore / Lay like the folds of a bright girdle furled' (Wain 1987: 166–167). Nevertheless, his enthusiasm promised an excitement of new possibilities of conceptualizing faith. This led to a conference in 1988 and to an ongoing series of conferences alongside regional and international Sea of Faith groups with their magazine *Sophia*.

Research conducted by the author and several postgraduate students, especially Dan Northam-Jones, on the Sea of Faith Network has revealed a collection of intelligent and highly educated individuals whose teenage and young adult excitement and active participation in Christianity, especially in the 1960s–1970s, slowly transformed into a continuing participation in local church rites. This was combined with scepticism over formal Christian beliefs, all alongside Network participation. The once-excited believers became excited sceptics, hence the success of the Sea of Faith as a Network and conference-organizing group, one feature of which lies in a positive engagement with creative arts as well as with intellectual debates over the nature of religion as a product of human imagination. When surveyed, many in this group not only agreed that the idea of God is a 'human-social construct' but that 'the Church misleads people' in its teachings.[9] The vast majority expressed no belief in an afterlife. What is interesting is how this 'non-realist' theology ran alongside a strong practical church, and ritual, involvement at the local level (some 62 per cent reporting participation on a weekly basis), plus a powerful interest in artistic, creative and often ritualized activities at the conferences.

Whereas at many denominational conferences the pre-breakfast timetable often includes a period of tradition-linked worship, the Sea of Faith event offers a variety of activities that might typically include a Pagan-style open-air event or some Tai Chi practice. The one recognizable 'traditional' format offered is that of a Quaker-style meeting, reflecting a disproportionate number of Quakers in the Network. This pre-breakfast timetable and numerous conference sessions encourage artistic creativity as a powerful resource informing and fostering the ongoing lives of Network members, and representing a ritual-like patterning of activity.

A great deal more could be said about such artistic creativity in the performative nature of numerous post-evangelical groups quite distinct from such Sea of Faith events. These include church-based services incorporating sound and light systems whose overall aim is that of excitement of sensory response to theologically suggestive stimuli. The Church of England has, in the post-2000 period, caught something of this emotive ritual-ideology in its espousal of 'Fresh Expressions', a programme fostering attitudinal and practical shifts in ritual and social events aimed at expressing essentially traditional theological ideas of salvation.

'Spirituality' and ethics

These Charismatic and Sea of Faith trends reflect 'in-house' and church-related concerns about the quality of life which is reflective of much wider social concern since the 1960s, and includes ideas about individual 'choice' and 'care'. These concerns are evident in the provisions available through the educational and national health services, the two major institutional processes through which the individual and family engage with 'society'. The implicit message behind the much vaunted political advocacy of 'choice' and 'care' is that one's quality of life can improve, a message that has long been carried in traditional Christian expression of salvation, divine grace and pastoral ministry, but now in relation to a sense of self-awareness and self-criticism.

In the ongoing secular shift underlying this period, understood sociologically as declining participation in the institutional churches and of those churches in the public sphere, there emerged a marginal variety of ritual activities reflecting a minority of individuals' engagement in self-fulfilment through self-directed 'choice' of potential 'care' options exemplified in 'new age' groups (see Chapter 4). Aimed at self-enhancement, individuals felt free of any single authority when selecting among available options in a 'non-aligned' spirituality (Wood 2007). Particularly after the 1980s, the concept of 'spirituality' began to develop a new life as its use was extended from a 'cultic milieu' and established Christian usage to describe the affect, emotional tone and quality of embodied values. 'Spirituality' was now rivalling the term 'religion', and was often either replacing it or used in close conjunction with it.

By the 1990s, 'spirituality' was developing a dynamic reference all of its own in the large-scale institution of the British National Health Service as a means of indicating a sensed quality of human existence tied to a sense of wellbeing. This take-up came to be something of a bridge between 'religious' and 'secular' categories. In this process 'religion' came to be identified all the more closely with the long-established world religions or varieties of Christian denominations, often reflected in the person of a hospital chaplain (see Plate 1.7). One bureaucratic ritual invention accompanying this change lay in the rise of ethics committees as a formal means of moderating behaviour within institutions, so much so that one can propose a formulaic description of the shift in life-framing dynamics as 'spirituality' plus 'ethics' replacing 'religion' (Davies 2011: 280–281). Traditional forms of religion embraced both of these functions whilst framing and enhancing them through acts of worship, leaving secular spirituality deciding how to express itself ritually.

So, in what might be seen as a 'new spirituality' allied with a 'new secularization', we find accounts of the depth, worth and quality of human experience, being driven by UK institutional processes of healthcare as they seek to deliver 'spirituality' to patients. The sheer size of the National Health Service (NHS), itself an enormous social innovation of post-war Britain, dwarfs the few engaged in 'new age' spirituality groups. While an obvious feature of this concern involves chaplaincies, it has increasingly extended to other healthcare staff, especially in hospitals. There has been a relatively clear sense of 'spirituality' as a wellbeing factor concerning religious-existential issues, but the issue of appropriate ritual has been less clear, often because of ward-management concerns over the ways families may want to relate to their sick, dying and dead relatives. When the NHS, through the National Council of Palliative Care, intensified its concern with this healthcare spirituality, that council created a subgroup in 2010 focused on Meaning, Faith and Belief, a title reflecting its constituency derived from cross-traditional religious groups as well as from the British Humanist Association and the National Secular Society. Spirituality was now a shared religious-secular concept in need of local ritual implementation.

Life-cycle spiritualities

One area in which such spirituality is being ritualized is in life-cycle rites of marriage and death. Two major ritual transformations that increased dramatically in elaboration from the 1960s were those of marriage and funerals. Earlier in our period, Register Office civic weddings were acknowledged to be 'simpler', the British expression of a minimum of formal ritual, but the turning decade of 2000–2010 witnessed a considerable increase in expenditure on weddings, both civic and ecclesial, with a dramatic opening up of possible venues for civic rites. Though the number of church weddings has decreased since the 1960s, a factor that could be seen to exemplify a degree of secularization, this has not resulted in any decrease of ritualization. Indeed, many new venues in hotels, castles and the like have opened as places for conducting legal weddings, with the cost and complexity of these events bespeaking a proclivity for formality and maintenance of 'custom' even though couples often want to give 'their event', their 'wonderful day', some distinctive, if not unique, feature. The very description of weddings as a bride's 'perfect day' can hardly be imagined apart from a well-planned and many-factored day of formality. Adding to the simplicity of etiquette books, themselves a form of ritual manual, has been the rise of wedding planners charging serious fees for managing larger weddings. Indeed, the cost of weddings has risen to quite considerable levels as the complexity of venue, ceremony and entertainment has increased. The post-2000 innovation of same-sex partnerships as 'civil partnerships' has added to ritual options. For a considerable minority, the role of church buildings, with their associated ritual resources, continues to be significant. Even before these expensive events, which cause some simply to live together as unmarried couples, people celebrate their relationship through more elaborate 'engagements' or flat or house-warming parties if and when they begin their domestic life together.

Another area fostering ritualized-secular outlooks became more obvious from the later 1960s through a major transformation in death rites in which cremation took over from burial as the dominant British mode of funeral. In 1960 some 35 per cent of the dead in British society were cremated, by 2010 that figure had doubled and stabilized to just over 70 per cent (Davies and Mates 2005: 433–456). The crematorium became the major innovation in ritual space of the twentieth century in Great Britain. Following traditional burial rites, clergy became the dominant officiants at crematorium rites, while the personal and family deposition of remains in places of their own choice became a hidden and unpublicized mass activity of the 1980–2010 period, an invention of tradition that marks a literal secularization of ritual, that is not conducted by religious officials. This is reflected in some late 1980s survey work which finds some 25 per cent of the public content at having non-clergy conduct funeral rites (Davies 1990: 18). This attitude was reflected in the increasing minority of rites that came to be conducted by secular representatives of the British Humanist Association and by 'self-professionalized' individuals allied with self-authenticating training agencies for funeral ritual.[10]

Gendered, political spiritualities

The period under consideration also witnessed another form of ritualization as issues of gender equality and sexual orientation became focused through church-related debates surrounding ordination, married clergy, female priests and homosexuality–heterosexuality. The Church of England ordained women priests in 1994 (see Plate 1.8) and by 2010 looked so likely to consecrate women bishops that the Pope created an Ordinariate, a kind of religious order for ex-Anglicans in which they could continue aspects of Anglican rites, much to the embarrassment of the Archbishop of Canterbury. This allowed for already married Anglican 'priests' to be ordained as Catholic priests. The use of ritual for ethical-religious politics by those with concerns with gender, sexuality, feminism and human rights thus came to be a most significant phenomenon in itself, whether in the ordination of women, civil partnerships between same-sex individuals or in denominational shift. All of this was set within wider social changes of lower rates and age of marriage, increased divorce rates, online dating schemes and an array of sexual practice available online in an electronic sexual age that left the Catholic Confessional largely empty.

Media and celebrity culture

Meanwhile, uncertain sexual identities and dramatic accounts of personal betrayal between partners flood the soap operas and celebrity magazines that set a backdrop for private lives. From 1960 to 2000 an astonishing growth, first in radio, television and film, and then in personal computers, the world wide web and increasingly complex cellphones, brought sophisticated levels of both sound and vision into the hands of millions. Some theoreticians took these transformations to be part of a post-modern shift in identity and social involvement, being quick to speak of the demise of widely shared and overarching ideological and theological narratives of life, leaving choice as the key task of individuals as they sought life-meaning. 'Religion' now appeared as an array of belief and ritual lifestyle choices selected by individuals to enhance individual senses of self. Because identity was not simply to be gained from active, face-to-face, participation in a community or congregation of others, but also from online contacts, it could adopt two or more forms in a 'second-life' online presentation of fictively imagined selves. Much sociological comment on such 'liquid' identities is, however, likely to have been exaggerated since most people's experience of others still lay within family, friendship or work-focused interpersonal relationships. Even so, individuals could easily identify themselves with celebrities as in Bob Geldof's 1985 'Feed the World' concert and the 1997 funeral of Diana, Princess of Wales. An underlying feature of all these cases lies in 'celebrated selves', a notion that sees existing status magnified through extensive media treatment. Far from thinking of these elements as anything to do with a post-modernity in which individual selves exist apart from grand narratives, they can easily be taken to express the opposite idea of individuals, friends and fans in a connectedness framed by the very idea of engaging with celebrity through a charisma of identity. Notions of celebrity 'royalty' easily partner established royalty in popular discourse and provide equal storyline copy.

Religion, too, enjoyed the interplay of media and celebrity with British churches employing public platforms to achieve social visibility, often punching above their actual significance in the process. Pope John XXIII, for example, was of great benefit to the Catholic Church as the media allowed his charismatic persona to reach beyond the crowds in St Peter's Square, not least in the Pope mobile. This in itself was almost a new religious symbol within the Catholic Church's liturgical repertoire (in practical terms it would enhance papal figures much more than the traditional triple tiara sold by Pope Paul VI as he became a much travelled and organizationally active church leader from 1963 to 1978). John Paul II was an ever media-visible and charismatic figure, kissing the ground of countries visited, and celebrating Mass in large popular gatherings. Whilst he witnessed the fall of the Berlin Wall, he was more than cautious over the Church of England's ordination of women to the priesthood in 1994. His death was, itself, a major media event as was the election of Cardinal Ratzinger as his successor whose visit to the United Kingdom in 2010 was an enormous media event (see Chapter 7 and Plates 1.4 and 1.5). By then, however, the Catholic world had changed through the cataclysmic accounts of child abuse, albeit among a minority of monks, nuns and priests, such that Catholic Ireland and many US dioceses lost ground that will probably never be recovered.

The rise of the world wide web (www) played its own part in allowing enormous individual comment on all these issues, permitting scepticism and excitement to flow apace through the mobilization of support groups. Individuals could as easily create a www-identity in terms of their real social self as of some fictitious self and engage in networks for many purposes. Here the web provided its own platform for ritualizing aspects of religion, with the existence of online churches as well as, for example, online memorializing of the dead. Not to be ignored is the possibility of terrorists creating a global presence at the press of a button.

Concurrently, the everyday life world was also becoming increasingly ritualized and secularized, as when Father's Day and even Grandparents' Day were created to echo Mother's Day, itself originally Mothering Sunday or the fourth Sunday in Lent. Other festivities that took increasingly schematized forms include the pre-marriage hen-parties for women and stag-parties for men. Again, with the growth in the number of British universities since the 1960s, and with increasing numbers of people attending them, hundreds of thousands of family members have experienced graduation ceremonies. In all of these the use of photography has added a celebrity-like tinge to events. In terms of major public gatherings it is the world of sport, notably football, that has become deeply ritualized in singing, chanting, distinctive clothing and their associated symbols, that has all become an implicit means of a public ritualization of values of club, local or national identity. The very ritual nature of such events has made it easy for these large-scale contexts to assume considerable power as ritual arenas when used, albeit for a few minutes, to mark a sporting celebrity's death. The interplay of sport spaces with traditional sacred spaces has also occurred in mutual validation as when Sir Bobby Robson, a recognized UK football 'legend' embedded in Newcastle United Football Club, had his memorial service in Durham Cathedral, with many football stars and some other celebrities in attendance. Tragedies allied with sport as in the Hillsborough disaster also evoked enormous ritualization of grief.

Multicultural dynamics

Another aspect of ritualization of British religion concerns architecture and dress, and involves minority religions supported by recent immigration, especially by those of Indian–Pakistani origin. Once established in family groups in particular parts of major towns, such communities slowly gained social and architectural visibility through dress and places of worship (see Chapter 3). With Sikhs, for example, a major feature of the 1960s and 1970s, was the establishment of gurdwaras as places both of worship and of community association. The emergence of Sikh families, with women and children, immediately involved them in education and medical facilities in a much more visible way than the lone male workers had been. The religious geography of England, in particular, now had a Sikh presence. Amongst the consequences of this was a renewed sense of distinctive individual and group identity. A legal case over Sikhs being allowed to wear turbans rather than crash helmets when riding motorcycles made the news (see Chapter 9), and schools now began to take an interest in Sikh religion. This was an interesting example of the reification of 'religion' as a kind of distillation of Sikh traditional beliefs and practices, much pervaded by Punjabi cultural assumptions. In some senses a traditional 'culture' was viewed as 'a religion'. The fact that Sikhs did have ritual buildings made it easy for 'indigenous' Christian Britons to equate them with churches, and the availability in Britain of 'Sunday' as an occasion for ritual practice led to a much more 'congregational' style 'church' than had existed in Punjab where anniversaries and festival days were the more common mode of engagement with gurdwara buildings and shrines. In a sense Sikhs became 'religionized'. And this mapping of new sets of communities (for Sikhs were internally divided along some enduring caste lines inaugurating their own gurdwaras, see the section on Sikhism in Chapter 3) was not entirely unlike aspects of Christian denominationalism. The association of Sikhs in particular parts of favoured towns, as in Southall in London, made this all the easier and provided a blueprint for other groups, especially Muslims, when they too increased in numbers. Issues of kinship and preferred marriage, and of chains of migration from particular areas in Punjab, both Sikh and Islamic, as well as from Bangladesh, Africa, India and the Middle East, ensured that cultural variants of Sikhism, Hinduism and Islam became embedded in Britain. At the same time, British politics advocated ideas of multiculturalism whilst academic interests in 'religion' fostered ideas of comparative religion, with Religious Studies becoming an identifiable discipline, not least through the charismatic influence of scholars such as Ninian Smart championing this discipline in a new centre at Lancaster University (see Plate 1.3). Trevor Ling, Geoffrey Parrinder, John Bowker, Ursula King and others also added considerable weight to pre-existing university interests in the History of Religion and in Theology.

But it was over the period 1990–2010 that Christianity's old identity sparring partner – Islam – magnified issues of multiculturalism and the political influence of another 'religion'. Here the explicitness of religious identity was reaffirmed, much as it had been between Catholic and Protestant identities during the English Reformation, and as had resurged in the 'Troubles' over Irish Nationalism versus British identity in Northern Ireland's strong Protestant communities. Martyrs to a cause had continued this sacrificial discourse between types of politicized Christianities and now a new power-politics, framing ritual action of jihad interpreted as a kind of holy war, came to the fore with Islam, highlighted through terrorist activity. And all of this was set against the political-religious scene of 'Western' aggressive warfare against Iraq and Afghanistan and support of Israel as a Jewish state, perceived by Muslims (and many others including some Jews) to be improperly hostile to Palestine and its Palestinian population. Now the word 'fundamentalism' became increasingly common in political discourse in reference to 'religion', making the reification of ritual-belief traditions into clear-cut 'religions' more conventional than ever, not simply because of terrorism and Islam, but also through an increasingly vocal and politically active strain of evangelical Christianity in the USA intensified through US presidential elections.

In terms of Islam, the impact of 'Islamic terrorism' was typified in the Lockerbie plane crash in Scotland in 1988, the destruction of New York's Twin Towers in 2001 – filmed and witnessed worldwide – and the suicide bomb attacks on London Transport in July 2005. Furthermore, the ongoing war in Afghanistan helped create an image of Islam far removed from the self-identity of the great majority of British Muslims. The notion of jihad gained a popular, non-Muslim, image as a negative holy war of terrorism by Muslim extremists against non-Muslims, its basic sense of striving or making an effort in pious self-development being almost entirely overshadowed. In complex turns of meaning, what appears as a search for truth by some becomes an occasion of fear or anxiety for others.

The very notion of suicide bombing has also generated a form of 'ritual' due to the way it is discussed as the act of a martyr. Here I refer to the outcome of terrorism involving millions of Britons who travel by air for business or holidays and who undergo what can easily be identified as a form of ritual examination at airports. This involves a verbal questioning concerning the packing of luggage and the possible intrusion of others into it, as well as the physical action of removing jackets, shoes and belts, and the passing of luggage and of the self through machines that seek out dangerous objects or substances. The diffuse yet insistent messages conveyed by these formalities are hard to disassociate from the specific cases of terrorist attack and its potential threat. The process is a kind of anti-religious rite. Associations from this shift of emphasis from the previous search of luggage for contraband goods that were personal to the passenger to a search for the means of death, attach to the full-cover dress of a minority of Islamic women and the wearing of full or part-beards by men. Here the theme of 'otherness' as opposed to welcomed familiarity is reinforced and probably underlies the questioning of a once-accepted political multiculturalism by Britain's

Prime Minister David Cameron in 2011 (see Chapter 1). Beards, for example, are not currently acceptable in much British public life; their partial covering of the face, and even more so the total covering of face and body in some female dress, accompanies the popular dislike of 'hoodies' (young men wearing hooded jackets) by many British adults. When combined with the emergence of minarets and 'Eastern' domes on the skyline of several larger British towns and cities, not to mention the use of Arabic, these various factors conduce a popular scepticism over the 'British' identity of 'immigrant' Muslims: a scepticism that easily involves anxiety and fear (see Chapter 5).

Here again the issue of religious ritual and the media should not be overlooked for the latter typically prefaces news reports with hundreds of men and youths prostrating themselves in unison and in the direction of Mecca, following a call to prayer in a language and voice-tonality not understood by the British at large. This form of ritual performance is highly telegenic and quite unlike, for example, the seldom-filmed Sikh's individual prostration or communal sitting in attention to the chanting of their sacred text in the gurdwara which accords more with the sense of ritual experienced in practically all mainstream Christian denominations. The unfamiliar unified Islamic prostration may easily breed an anxiety among a general public that associates such group behaviour more with 'mob' or 'crowd' action than with that of an ordered congregation: not to mention a potential induced sense of guilt that most Christians do not engage in their own form of worship as frequently as they might. Allied with this judgement, as illogical as it may seem, is the British opinion originating in the Reformation's repugnance towards public prayer conducted 'in a tongue not understanded of the people'.[11] The fact that post-Vatican II Roman Catholicism of the 1960s also turned from Latin to the use of English in the Mass reinforced this outlook.

While the symbolic complexity of personal appearance, language, dress, buildings and forms of worship is difficult to ascertain with any certainty, to ignore it is to miss an entire spectrum of emotional awareness and of the negative excitement of anxiety, fear or dislike of the 'other' echoing Britain's Christian history.[12] The mention of changing townscapes through the rise of Islamic minarets or Hindu or Sikh domes or symbols, and also of the changed use of a significant minority of Christian churches to non-ecclesial use, also marks a form of ritual transformation, for ritual is often deeply aligned with the space where it occurs: sacred place is almost always ritual space. The changed configuration of such places speaks its own message whether of 'secularization' when, as with many former Christian chapels in South Wales, they serve other 'secular' and commercial purposes, or whether adopted by other religions as their place of worship.

Conclusion

This chapter's broad view has argued for a sensitivity to elements of emotional dynamics within historical and recent ritual change within religion in Britain. From the Reformation to contemporary life-cycle rites or Eastern-influenced architecture, and within phenomena such as the Charismatic Movement and Sea of Faith Network, we encounter cultural innovations fostering individual and group identity, all entailing emotional dynamics of their own, and alluded to here through motifs of excitement and scepticism. What is obvious is that the human proclivity for making sense of life is ever adaptive, sometimes pursuing religious-political and sometimes psychological-philosophical pathways, with one contemporary direction being that of healthcare and wellbeing. While, in all of this, 'religion' and 'spirituality' shift in transient definition, the human adaptive proclivity for ritualizing its embodied engagement with itself, its customs and innovatory options remains an intriguing constant.

Key terms

Believers-real or nominal: Sometimes people distinguish between the intense sincerity of 'real' believers and others who belong to a particular tradition in name only.

Celebrated selves: A way of thinking about individuals known for being celebrities.

Charismatic Christians: Christians who place emphasis on the influence of the Holy Spirit in their lives, especially connected with 'gifts of the Spirit' such as speaking in tongues, also known as glossolalia.

Emotions: Certain strong and influential feelings such as fear or disgust that are often named and managed by each society in its own way. Sometimes distinguished from moods that are longer lasting and more pervasive.

English Reformation: The sixteenth-century period, much influenced by Protestant ideas in Europe, especially concerning the authority of the Bible and of the role of faith in salvation, when the Church of England, after separation from the Catholic Church and the Pope as its head, developed as a state church with the monarch as its earthly head.

Ordination of women: The Church of England has allowed women to become priests since 1992. The Catholic and Orthodox churches do not agree with this but most Protestant denominations do.

Sea of Faith Network: A network of people created after a 1984 TV series and books by Cambridge theologian Don Cupitt who view religion as a product of human imagination.

Further reading

Anderson, Allan (2004). *An Introduction to Pentecostalism: Global Charismatic Christianity*. Cambridge: Cambridge University Press. Shows the extent of Charismatic forms of Pentecostalism.

Cupitt, Don (2001). *Taking Leave of God*. London: SCM. An account of developing a religious outlook that leaves traditional perspectives behind.

Davies, Douglas J. (2011). *Emotion, Identity, and Religion: Hope, Reciprocity, and Otherness*. Oxford: Oxford University Press. Considers how emotions that help forge identity are selected and managed in religious traditions.

Rappaport, Roy (1997). *Ritual and Religion in the Making of Humanity*. Cambridge: Cambridge University Press. Probably the best social science book on ritual.

Ryrie, Alec (2003). *The Gospel and Henry VIII: Evangelicals in the Early English Reformation*. Cambridge: Cambridge University Press. Describes some of the ways Reformation ideas took shape in people's lives.

References

Bloch, Ernst (1986). *The Principle of Hope*, trans. Neville Plaice, Stephen Plaice and Paul Knight. First published in 1959. Oxford: Basil Blackwell.

Bruce, Steve (1999). *Choice and Religion: A Critique of Rational Choice Theory*. Oxford: Oxford University Press.

Davies, Douglas J. (1984a). 'The Charismatic Ethic and the Spirit of Postindustrialism', in David Martin and Peter Mullen (eds), *Strange Gifts*. Oxford: Basil Blackwell, 137–150.

Davies, Douglas J. (1984b). *Meaning and Salvation in Religious Studies*. Leiden: Brill.

Davies, Douglas J. (1990). *Cremation Today and Tomorrow*. Nottingham: Grove Books.

Davies, Douglas J. (2002). *Anthropology and Theology*. Oxford: Berg.

Davies, Douglas J. (2003). *An Introduction to Mormonism*. Cambridge: Cambridge University Press.

Davies, Douglas J. (2011). *Emotion, Identity, and Religion: Hope, Reciprocity, and Otherness*. Oxford: Oxford University Press.

Davies, Douglas J. and Lewis H. Mates (2005). *Encyclopedia of Cremation*. Aldershot: Ashgate.

Davies, Douglas J. and Daniel Northam-Jones (forthcoming). 'The Sea of Faith: Exemplifying Transformed Retention', in Elisabeth Arweck and Mathew Guest (eds), *Religion and Knowledge: Sociological Perspectives*. Aldershot: Ashgate.

Hinton, Alexander Laban (ed.) (1999). *Biocultural Approaches to the Emotions*. Cambridge: Cambridge University Press.

Moscovici, Serge (1993). *The Invention of Society*. Cambridge, MA: Polity.

Radford, Katy (2004). 'Protestant Women – Protesting Faith, Tangling Secular and Religious Identity in Northern Ireland', in Simon Coleman and Peter Collins (eds), *Religion, Identity and Change: Perspectives on Global Transformations*. Aldershot: Ashgate, 136–153.

Robinson, John (1963). *Honest to God*. London: SCM.

Smith, Warren Sylvester (ed.) (1967). *Shaw on Religion*. London: Constable.

Smith, Wilfred Cantwell (1963). *The Meaning and End of Religion*. New York, NY: Macmillan.

The Canons of the Church of England, Canons Ecclesiastical Promulgated by the Convocations of Canterbury and York in 1964 and 1969 (1969). London: SPCK.

The First Prayer Book of Edward VI (1549). Reprinted in *The Ancient and Modern Library of Theological Literature*, no date, no publisher given, 266–269.

Towler, Robert (1984). *The Need for Certainty*. London: Routledge and Kegan Paul.

Tylor, Edward Burnett (2010). *Primitive Culture, Volume 2*. First published in 1871. Cambridge: Cambridge University Press.

Wain, John (1987). *The Oxford Library of English Poetry*. London: Guild Publishing.

Wood, Matthew (2007). *Possession, Power, and the New Age: Ambiguities of Authority in Neoliberal Societies*. Aldershot: Ashgate.

Notes

1   See Tylor (2010: 328–400) for an important early account of 'Rites and ceremonies'.

2   In the 1552 Second Prayer Book of Edward VI it moved towards the front of the book, preceded by a Preface that also deals with change. The 1559 Prayer Book of Queen Elizabeth adds the Act of Uniformity before all other documents; this treated issues of uniform practice.

3   Serge Moscovici (1993) wisely contradicts the longstanding reading of Durkheim's approach to social facts that avoids psychological explanation.

4   See Davies (2003: 9–17) on excitement in Mormon life.

5   See Davies (1984b: 144–149) for 'rank-path syndrome' and British Sikhs.

6   See Bruce (1999) for critique of rational choice theory.

7   See Radford (2004: 136–151) for the role of women in Orange events.

8   Their scepticism was evident in Robert Towler's 1984 *The Need for Certainty*, a sociological analysis of all the letters sent to John Robinson in response to his publications.

9   Some 94 per cent of those surveyed agreed with 'social construct' and 98 per cent with the misleading factor (Davies and Northam-Jones, forthcoming).

10   Douglas Davies also supervised Hannah Rumble's studentship, in collaboration with the Arbory Trust and funded by the AHRC/ESRC Religion and Society Programme, 'British Woodland Burial: Its Theological, Ecological and Social Values', in which she found a small, but growing, trend for 'natural burial' in Britain.

11   Article Twenty-four of the Church of England's 1662 *Thirty-Nine Articles*. Created 'for the avoiding of diversities of opinions, and for the establishing of consent touching true religion'.

12   See Warren Sylvester Smith (1967: 148–171) for George Bernard Shaw's scathing essay on ritual.

Case study 4

Multi-faith spaces as symptoms and agents of change

Ralf Brand

Multi-faith spaces are the most distinctive form of religious architecture to develop in the post-war period. Future generations may view it as characteristic of the period. Yet it is a dilemma in stone: how can all faiths and none be accommodated in a single space? This case study, based on a research project in the AHRC/ESRC Religion and Society Programme[1] discusses various buildings and spaces which have been constructed in an attempt to answer that question. Most have arisen from grassroots initiatives rather than through central planning by government or a religious body. Many struggle with limited resources, and take their place within existing structures – shopping centres, airports, hospitals, universities, prisons, private companies and even football stadiums. What do they tell us about the religious and secular sensibilities of their times, and how are they being used and abused?

The 'problem' of multiculturalism is that of how people from different backgrounds live together in practical terms. Do they dwell together, or do they occupy different capsules? A recent consultation report on interfaith issues condensed this question – and the answer – into the slogan 'face to face and side by side' (Department for Communities and Local Government 2007; see Case study 2 in this volume on the Inter Faith Network). Multi-faith buildings and spaces (MFS) speak very directly to these issues – and religious (and secular) co-existence in particular (see Plate 3.9).

MFS are themselves beset by problems and dilemmas. One is how to create a genuinely inclusive space. The issue is signalled in the problem of naming. In some cases they are called Chapel, Prayer Room or Meditation Room; in others they are referred to as the Quiet Lounge, Room of Silence, Contemplation Space or Inter-faith Hub. Although the naming decision is not in all cases programmatic, the chosen name is often perceived as such. A focus-group session with the Manchester Humanist Society made this very clear: participants unanimously agreed that any reference to the word 'faith' or even 'prayer' in the title of such rooms would not make them welcoming to a humanist. Hence the frequent resort to the term 'Silent Room': silence is the ultimate attempt to offend no one. But then again, the adjective 'silent' indicates that the audible enactment of some religious ritual is considered inappropriate. The same applies to any olfactory evidence of certain rituals such as the burning of incense. So religious people may be offended.

It is thus not surprising that some cases go by extremely nondescript names. One is simply called 'The Room', and others are only indicated by a symbol – for example an abstract kneeling figure – or by a set of symbols, often a more or less comprehensive collection of religious symbols. It is therefore important to emphasize that the term 'Multi-Faith Space' was chosen simply for lack of a better term. So far, there does not seem to be a universally accepted and uncontested name for these types of spaces. There is, however, a differentiation many people make between multi-faith and interfaith where the former term implies a rather passive juxtaposition of different faiths and the latter a genuine encounter and collaboration between them.

The architecture of MFS is also revealing. What is the architectural language of shared spirituality? How do MFS connect physically to their secular context? What design criteria can be established to determine best-practice examples? In order to answer these questions we have documented more than 100 such spaces through photographs and measured drawings in the UK and overseas and we will continue to do so. Equally interesting is the question of the mutual shaping, even constitution, of the social and the material. Who are the typical actors (clients, municipalities, religious groups, architects, etc.) in the creation of MFS? And how do they affect those who use them? Does genuine religious mixing occur best in spaces perceived as sacred or in spaces that also allow and encourage mundane activities such as relaxation, cooking, eating and so on?

The architecture

The architectural and interior design of MFS is almost always fraught with massive challenges, sometimes controversies, around iconography, symbols, ornamentation, even orientation and colour schemes, because virtually everything carries some kind of meaning for one person/religion or another. This phenomenon, in combination with the attempt to avoid anything of offensive potential, leads very often not only to nondescript names but also to equally bland design solutions. In some sense, it is the *absent* artefact that is of particular importance in MFS and poses a radically new sort of problem for architecture as a design discipline.

One solution is to cram all possible symbols, literatures and religious paraphernalia into one and the same room. Though not common for MFS, the Plymouth Centre of Faiths and Cultural Diversity demonstrates this option. The model of no-offence is hereby eroded simply by equal offence to everyone, so to speak. The other strategy is to provide separate rooms for major religious groups, or at least to cluster kindred ones into the same room. For example, the 'Espace de Recueillement' at the Charles de Gaulle Airport in Paris consists of three separate rooms with a crescent, cross and star of David at the respective doors. The approach to separate religious groups is obviously more expensive due to the larger total floor space but allows much less bland design solutions.

The most common representative in the typology of MFS, however, is the single-room solution. Since space is almost always at a premium, most of them can be found at locations that are of lesser financial or commercial value within a building complex. This also explains why extremely few MFS have natural light. They are often placed in the inner parts of a building where no one would like to have an office or a retail space anyway. A relatively common feature of such windowless MFS is the use of back-lit stained glass, decorated with abstract motifs that keep with the principle of no-offence. Many resemble leaves or flames. Real candles are, despite a near universal acceptance of fire as a symbol for the spiritual, almost always banned for health and safety reasons. Careful attempts to display at least a minimal degree of aesthetic care can often be detected in the use of Macintosh-inspired, but IKEA-priced furniture. Financial pragmatics also translate into the almost ubiquitous use of suspended styrofoam ceilings and vinyl floors or anti-dirt carpet patterns.

What thwarts the consistent absence of all religious objects and symbols is the fact that the enactment of prayer sometimes requires the presence of certain infrastructures or utensils. Muslims, for example, need to know the direction towards Mecca, and this explains the near universal provision of a *qibla* – an arrow made of brass, wood, etched in metal, set into the floor, attached to the ceiling or simply hand-drawn on the wall. In some MFS, however, for example in Sofia Airport, one can find only a compass rose which serves the same purpose in a more secular guise. Muslims are also supposed to perform a ritual ablution before prayer and therefore appreciate the provision of washing facilities. In a number of cases, such *wudus* are available nearby, either in a separate room or incorporated in public toilets. Foot-dryers are even sometimes provided. Some interpretations of Islam also prefer a separation between male and female worshippers, which is only rarely implemented in the design of MFS.

Other religious artefacts are much more mobile and can be brought into an MFS and returned after use to a 'neutral' area such as a foyer. Prayer mats, holy books, rosaries, etc. fall into this category and are often provided in separate shelves, shelf-boards or plastic boxes. In some cases, even statues and tables are on wheels and can be moved in and out depending on the situation. Where no storage space is available, artefacts belonging to one religion only can sometimes be covered with a curtain, as in the case of a Jesus statue in the Trafford Centre shopping mall near Manchester. This hints at the perceived possibility that space can be contaminated by religious practices other than one's own. The removal of evidence of someone else's religious practice even goes so far as the deliberate design of 'air circulation to remove fragrances such as incense and sweetgrass so that the next users of the space have an odourless room' (Ota 2007) at the University of Toronto Multifaith Centre for Spiritual Study and Practices.

This MFS was designed by Moriyama and Teshima Architects and is thus a typical example of a relatively rare type: designed by professional architects and purpose-built with a nameable budget. Some companies even specialize in the design of such spaces. Of the MFS we have documented so far, about a dozen fit into this category.

MFS as symptoms

There are interesting historical precedents for MFS in places that were used by members of different faiths. Since the seventh century, for example, Muslims have been permitted to worship in the south transept of the Church of the Nativity in Bethlehem. Many examples of religious co-existence in concrete locations can also be found in India with its characteristic plurality, maybe even eclecticism, of spiritual and religious movements. Also quite common are shared churches and shrines for St George, who is honoured and revered by Christians and Muslims alike, in the Middle East and the Balkans. If not multi-faith, then at least multi-denominational, are also the so-called 'Simultankirchen' in Germany, the Alsace and Switzerland. More than 120 of them were or still are used by Catholics and Protestants, although rarely at the same time. In some cases, both denominations shared a bell tower but retained exclusive use of two separate naves built on either side of the tower. In all these cases, there was something going on at political, social or economic levels to which people responded, sometimes in very creative ways, with the creation of shared spaces. They can thus be seen as some kind of reaction or symptom, and we take it that contemporary MFS can and should be interpreted from the same angle.

There is early evidence that MFS in our modern sense are mainly a post-Second World War phenomenon. Some of the first ones were built as airport chapels in the USA as a response to increasing international air travel. Their number seems to have increased at hospitals in the UK during the late 1980s and early 1990s. MFS then gained additional prominence and were built at an accelerated rate in the post-9/11 world in which ideas around community cohesion and religious tolerance have made them more and more into public awareness and the policy arena.

Those critical of MFS might argue that their development is an attempt by an increasingly secular society to keep religion out of sight in public places. The assumed rationale here is, for example, to make sure Muslims perform their regular prayers behind closed doors rather than rolling out their prayer mats at an airport gate. In other discussions the suspicion was raised that MFS are a symptom of the opposite: a silent resacralization of the West, where people might not necessarily flock back to established religious institutions but create their own bespoke spirituality. Or maybe it is simply more economical to provide an in-house prayer room for an increasingly diverse workforce than to allow one's employees a prayer break at the nearest city mosque, temple or church. Similar rationales seem plausible for shopping malls where the risk of losing a customer if no MFS were provided might be too high. Hence looking at who initiates, pays and manages MFS is also important.

MFS as agents

Do MFS facilitate new understandings across religions or force them into awkward juxtaposition? To use Putnam's differentiation (2007), do MFS foster bridging or bonding social capital? The former would mean people from different groups have genuine encounters and build bridges. The latter could mean they build or reinforce 'tribal' identity within their homogeneous group, and in turn withdraw from anyone 'other' because otherness is uncomfortable. MFS, with their built-in exposure to the unknown, might thus even trigger the desire to articulate one's own faith more fervently.

Our informed hypothesis is that MFS rarely trigger genuine friendly encounters among their users. One likely reason for this is that the clear majority of MFS users seem to be Muslims performing one of their five daily prayers. And where people of different faiths use single-room MFS, the atmosphere is often one of awkward silence which only a few dare to break. After all, the word 'silence' in the name of many MFS indicates what is and what is not considered appropriate behaviour in them. However, it appears that in those multi-faith complexes where users of separate prayer rooms have a concrete opportunity to meet in a more secular shared setting (e.g. a cafeteria) some cross-religious conversations are more likely to occur. We also have evidence from several MFS that a well-managed and participatory-decision making process where representatives of, possibly many, faith groups can share their needs, preferences, hopes and concerns has the potential to nurture mutual understanding and trust. The Burnley and Pendle Faith Centre is one good example of such a process, but it is still an open question whether those who are willing to engage in such a process are already open-minded and tolerant.

Another working hypothesis yet to be tested is that the maintenance regime of MFS is as important as the design process for them to serve their intended purpose. The absence of any favouritism or discrimination towards any religion is a delicate balancing act. It is partially a question of design – but not only. The performative character of space is of at least equal importance. De facto usage is a self-reproducing phenomenon which requires careful maintenance, monitoring and accompaniment, sustaining the successful MFS's unstable equilibrium. Rigorous control against any rhetorical, symbolic or infrastructural dis-/advantage, however, can sometimes be an incarnation of a very mechanistic notion of justice and meaningless political correctness. But perhaps the superficial politeness of good-mannered people in MFS is the highest realistic ambition to be hoped for.

The effects of MFS on the relationship not only between religions but also between the religious and secular realms are of interest. A particularly striking case is rather deplorable. It concerns the prayer room in Ewood Park, home of the Blackburn Rovers Football Club – the only football ground in the Premier League to have an MFS. Its creation triggered an enormous controversy among the club's fans. They even created a Facebook group against it with a number of grossly offensive postings. Some of the less inflammatory ones claim that it has become a de facto mosque. The same allegation is rumoured around an MFS at Manchester Airport that is mainly used by taxi drivers and airport staff for worship. It was subject to a suspected arson attack on 11 September 2010. While the police investigation is still under way, it is clear that these two MFS are not the only ones that are perceived by sections of the UK population as a sign of an increasing 'Islamification' of British society; for those perceiving and fearful of such a trend the growing number of MFS is sometimes seen as the thin end of the wedge.

Conclusion

The evidence so far suggests that MFS as a relatively new type of space do not have massive impacts on the wider societal atmosphere in terms of community cohesion, religious toler-ance, multi-ethnic co-existence, etc. This is not to say that MFS are irrelevant for individual users – as many entries in visitor books and our interview findings indicate. The most immediate benefit of MFS is probably in hospitals where crises remind us, often quite brutally, of our shared human existence. The biggest difference they make as agents of some sort, however, is probably for their host institutions under the rubric of wellbeing, staff satisfaction and customer service. At the same time, most MFS are quite effective in keep-ing religious practices out of public sight in largely secular settings like airports. In all the above senses, MFS are absolutely symptomatic of our age characterized by a multi-ethnic society, a market economy, individualized religious practices, political correctness and equality legislation. The latter has no direct impact on the issue as there is no statutory right for an MFS in either public or work spaces. Accordingly, the genesis of MFS is mostly driven by local independent initiatives for a wide variety of reasons. But only a few of them seem to have found a way to cut, let alone untangle, the Gordian knot which is the chal-lenge to provide a spiritually meaningful space for all without offending anyone. Put the other way round: how to avoid offence to anyone without resorting to complete blandness which serves no one.

References

Department for Communities and Local Government (2007). *Face to Face and Side by Side: A Framework for Inter Faith Dialogue and Social Action*. London: Her Majesty's Stationery Office.

Ota, John (2007). 'Open Faith', *Canadian Architect*. Online. Available HTTP: www.canadian architect.com/issues/story.aspx?Aid=1000215570&PC=CA (accessed 12 January 2011, archived with WebCite at www.webcitation.org/5vdHZRpET).

Putnam, Robert D. (2007). 'E Pluribus Unum: Diversity and Community in the Twenty-first Century: The 2006 Johan Skytte Prize Lecture', *Scandinavian Political Studies*, 30/2: 137–174.

Note

1 The project 'Multi-Faith Spaces – Symptoms and Agents of Religious and Social Change' was carried out at the Manchester Architecture Research Centre (MARC) at the University of Manchester in collaboration with a colleague at the Liverpool School of Architecture. It was funded by the AHRC/ESRC Religion and Society Programme between 2009 and 2012. Principal Investigator: Ralph Brand, Co-Investigator Andrew Crompton, theological associate Terry Biddington, Research Associate Chris Hewson. For further information see www.manchester.ac.uk/mfs.

Images of religion and change in modern Britain

People

Plate 1.1 Mary Whitehouse (1910–2001) addressing a gathering in St Mary Woolnoth, London, for 'Women's World Day of Prayer' (1972). © Getty Images

Plate 1.2 Special Constable Harbans Singh Jabbal on duty at East Ham Police Station in London, the first British policeman to be allowed to wear a turban (January 1970). © Getty Images

Plate 1.3 Ninian Smart (1927–2001), Professor at Lancaster University, and a champion of religious studies in universities and schools. Courtesy of Lancaster University

Plate 1.4 Northern Irish politician and Presbyterian clergyman the Reverend Ian Paisley protests in Edinburgh against the visit of Pope Benedict XVI in September 2010. Paisley had previously protested against the visit of Pope John Paul II to the UK in 1982. © Press Association

Plate 1.5 Gay rights campaigner Peter Tatchell joins a demonstration against the Pope in London in September 2010. © Getty Images

Plate 1.6 Defending free speech against religious intolerance: Christopher Hitchens and Salman Rushdie at a festival organized by PEN, a charity which supports writers' freedom. Courtesy of Beowulf Sheehan

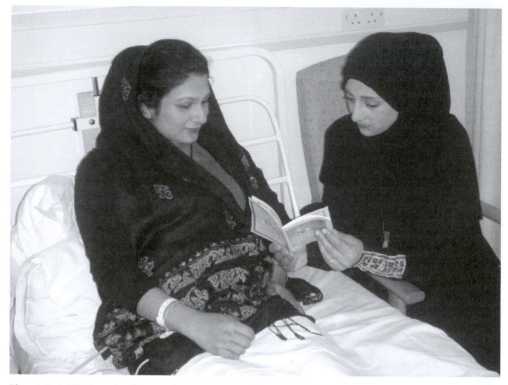

Plate 1.7 A Muslim chaplain working in an NHS hospital. Courtesy of Sophie Gilliat-Ray

Plate 1.8 Comedian and actress Dawn French joins female clergy from England and Wales in a campaign against poverty with Christian Aid in January 2005 in London. © Getty Images

Plate 1.9 Hare Krishnas publicize their faith on the streets. © Getty Images

Plate 1.10 Catholic/Protestant tension and violence have remained a feature of post-war life not only in Northern Ireland but in other parts of the UK. Here Celtic and Rangers fans confront one another at a football match in Glasgow. © Press Association

Events

Plate 2.3 British police officers remove a protestor demonstrating against nuclear deterrence and the arrival of US Tomahawk cruise missiles at Greenham Common Air Base, Berkshire (November 1983). © Getty Images

Plate 2.4 The Archbishop of Canterbury Robert Runcie (1921–2000) launches the *Faith in the City* report in 1985. Courtesy of Roger Hutchings

Plate 2.5 The 'Sermon on the Mound': Margaret Thatcher addresses the General Assembly of the Church of Scotland in May 1988. © The Scotsman Publications Ltd. Licensor www.scran.ac.uk

Plate 2.6 Sir Elton John sings 'Candle in the Wind' at the funeral of Diana, Princess of Wales, in Westminster Abbey (September 1997). © Getty Images

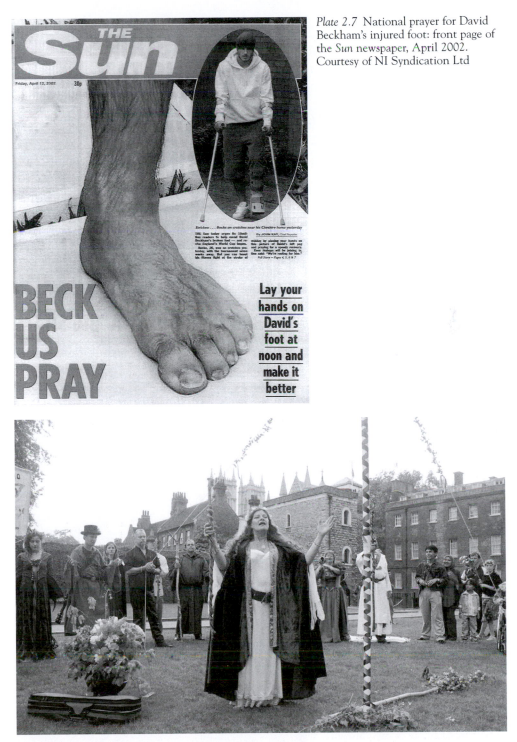

Plate 2.7 National prayer for David Beckham's injured foot: front page of the *Sun* newspaper, April 2002. Courtesy of NI Syndication Ltd

Plate 2.8 Druids representing multiple Druid orders take part in a Beltane (Mayday) ceremony to welcome spring in Abingdon Green, in sight of the Houses of Parliament and Westminster Abbey (2007). © Getty Images

Plate 2.9 Comedy writer Ariane Sherine, Professor Richard Dawkins and journalist Polly Toynbee launch the 'atheist bus' advertising campaign, which was also backed by the British Humanist Association (January 2009). © Getty Images

Plate 2.10 Mourners pay their respects as the coffins of soldiers who died serving in Afghanistan pass through the village of Wootton Bassett in Wiltshire (November 2009). © Press Association

Plate 2.11 Celebration at the 250th anniversary of the Board of Deputies of British Jews. Courtesy of The Board of Deputies of British Jews

Plate 3.1 The new Coventry Cathedral emerges by the ruins of the old, which had been bombed in the Second World War (May 1962). © Getty Images

Plate 3.2 Kingsway International Christian Centre, Walthamstow, London. The church was established in 1992 and now has one of the largest congregations in Britain. The majority of members are of West African origin. Courtesy of the Kingsway International Christian Centre

Plate 3.3 Covering over two acres, and taking 14 years to construct, the Shree Sanatan Hindu Mandir in Wembley finally opened in 2010. Courtesy of John Zavos

Plate 3.4 Wat Buddhapadipa, a Thai Buddhist temple in the affluent London suburb of Wimbledon.
© Getty Images

Plate 3.5 The practice of constructing 'roadside shrines' at the site of a fatal accident is one of a number of new popular ritual practices to emerge in the post-war period. © Press Association

Plate 3.6 Christmas lights in Oxford Street, London's busiest shopping street. © Press Association

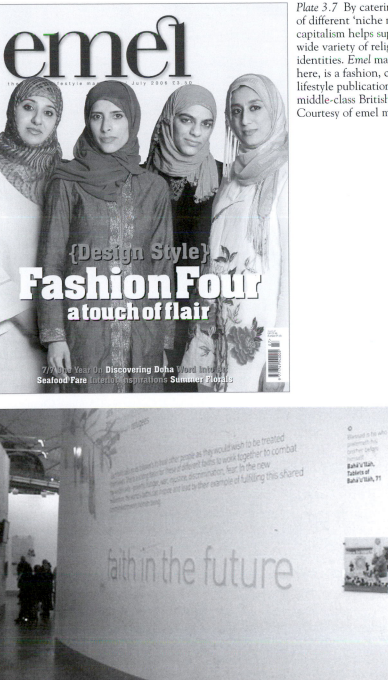

Plate 3.7 By catering to a wide range of different 'niche markets', consumer capitalism helps support and define a wide variety of religious and ethnic identities. *Emel* magazine, pictured here, is a fashion, comment and lifestyle publication targeted at a middle-class British Muslim audience. Courtesy of emel media ltd

Plate 3.8 The 'Faith Zone' in the Millennium Dome in London was one way in which the official Millennium celebrations attempted to give public space to religion. Courtesy of Sophie Gilliat-Ray

Plate 3.9 Multi-faith spaces are the most distinctive architectural form for religion spawned in the post-war period. This example is in Heathrow Airport, Terminal 4. Courtesy of Andrew Crompton

Part 2
Wider influences

7 The changing faces of media and religion

Kim Knott and Jolyon Mitchell

Having considered the changing forms of religion, Part 2 of the book broadens the focus to look at how religion has interacted with wider social arenas. It begins by looking at the changing relationship between media and religion since 1945, focusing on the overlapping fields of audience, protagonist, content and production. Although it concentrates on Britain, it necessarily makes international connections. Many factors, including rapid technological innovation, are shown to have affected the mediation of religion. Presenting findings from a project on the AHRC/ESRC Religion and Society Programme, it shows that media coverage of Christianity in Britain has grown less deferential and more irreverent, that representations of religion in the media have diversified rather than disappeared and that the BBC still plays a major role. Overall, the chapter shows the changing and growing importance of media for religion in the post-war period, and how the use of different media helps to shape different forms of religious organization, power, commitment and identity.

Introduction

Several of the images included in this volume are of widely recognizable faces. The digitization of pictures has contributed to a never-ending circulation of photographs, paintings and moving images. The result is that the faces of recent or current religious leaders (e.g. see Plate 1.4) can now circle the globe almost instantaneously and be preserved in pristine form on countless computers. These images can also be digitally remade and recreated (e.g. the face of 'Jesus' on the front of the *Radio Times*[1]) or replaced by other kinds of celebrity faces (e.g. Dawn French as the Vicar of Dibley, Plate 1.8, or Elton John singing in Westminster Abbey at Diana's funeral, Plate 2.6).

This highly plural, competitive and rapidly evolving communicative environment provides the background to this chapter. Its discussion is pertinent to many, if not all, of the chapters in this book. Understanding the role of different media is vital for any religious leader, scholar or citizen hoping to make sense of the changing religious landscape of Britain. To provide a comprehensive analysis, the full circle of communication is considered: the changing faces of producers, presenters, content and audiences.

The changing faces of audiences

Starting with the changing faces of audiences, it is clear that media audiences in the United Kingdom and beyond have undergone a number of radical transformations since 1945. In

the context of a radically changing communicative environment, four changes merit particular attention: how audiences have fragmented, identities have transformed, communities
have re-formed and distant suffering has been brought close.

Fragmenting audiences

Look at a photograph of a radio from the 1930s or 1940s, and see a family facing the wire-
less as they listen.[2] The children sit on the floor staring intently towards the talking box in
the corner of the room, while women and men cluster around the set. Often a middle-aged
man stands leaning on the radio with a pipe or drink in his hand. Other pictures show
engrossed listeners seated in rocking chairs or a comfy sofa: imagining a world beyond.
These are comfortable and peaceful scenes. Some pictures are clearly posed, while others
look more realistic, capturing early audience habits and the novelty of the experience.
There is intensity in the faces of these listeners. Half-smiles, open eyes and concentration
mark their physiognomies. It is as if they are projecting beliefs or authority onto the faceless
voice or tuneful music. From their faces it looks as if they are transposed into another state,
but nevertheless they are listening together.

In sharp contrast, images from the 1960s and 1970s depict listeners on their own holding a small transistor to their ear as they look out on the world. Other pictures show
individuals involved in washing, ironing or painting as they simultaneously listen alone to
the radio. Listeners no longer intently face the set with family or friends. The radio is no
longer the focal point of attention. Reduced in physical size it has been relegated to a
secondary activity, providing company, consolation or distraction alongside everyday
chores. More recently the sight of people commuting, walking or running with miniature
headphones in their ears has become ubiquitous in Britain and beyond. In the 1980s and
early 1990s these were commonly attached to a Sony Walkman, but now they are more
likely to be connected to an MP3 player or iPod. While many are listening to downloaded
music, others are absorbed in live radio or downloaded podcasts. They listen on their own,
inhabiting their own 'communication bubbles'. Communal experience has largely been
replaced by isolated listening, even if communal viewing of popular television programmes
or major sports events persists in some social settings, such as student residences or public
houses.

With the wide range of electronic communication now available, it is not uncommon
for families to be in the same physical space but inhabiting separate communicative
cocoons, in the words of Sherry Turkle: 'alone together' (Turkle 2011). Children can
remove themselves from their parents, and vice versa. Individuals who make up audiences
no longer face an electronic hearth together but instead become absorbed with their own
communicative devices. They face the screen alone. The result is that, even from within
the same family, different people can put different media to different uses. In Britain the
initial monopoly of the British Broadcasting Corporation (established in 1927 with
committed Christian Lord Reith as its Director General) and the BBC/ITV (Independent
Television) duopoly of the 1950s has given way to countless stations, channels and sites
vying for audiences' attention.

Digitization has contributed to exponentially increased choice for listeners, viewers and
surfers. If you have access to the net, choice is literally endless. The 'paradox of choice'
(Schwarz 2004) is that audiences can feel overwhelmed or simply resort to favourite channels, sites or programmes. The sheer diversity of choice now available through satellite and
cable has ensured that 'audiencehood is becoming an ever more multifaceted, fragmented,

and diversified repertoire of practices and experiences' (Ang 1994: 382). Some people do not opt into new media use or intentionally remove themselves from certain kinds of media consumption, believing 'media fasts' to be conducive to 'spiritual growth' (Cooper 2011), while others have limited access to new communication technologies because of economic constraints. These groupings contribute towards a highly fragmented media environment. Nevertheless, in spite of such fragmentation, audiences now have the resources to create their own 'mediascapes' (Appadurai 1996), while also observing global media events and producing their own content.

Forming identities

The transformation of communicative environments has facilitated the 'subjective turn' (Heelas and Woodhead 2005: 2–5) within religious experience. The opportunity for individuals to choose their own channels and to face the way they desire has significant implications for understanding the formation of religious identities. While some individuals draw on aspects of their religious practices and beliefs to define their own identities, other viewers also use television or film dramas such as *The X Files, Star Trek* and *Buffy the Vampire Slayer* to help them make sense of their own lives. Some teenagers appear to weave together their own religious experiences and backgrounds with stories found on television, in films or on the internet (Clark 2003). The vast range of choice combined with the 'pick and mix' quality of modern media technologies allows individuals to 'cut and paste' or 'mash together' from a wide range of media sources. These diverse resources can also facilitate the development of highly individualized and eclectic spiritualities. This contributes to an environment where it is possible for individuals to concentrate less on the external demands of a religious tradition and more on their own internal wellbeing or spiritual experiences. Equally, new media may become the means by which 'traditions' are disseminated anew and by which adherents of many different shades of belief contact and communicate with one another in a virtual space which is often made 'real' at annual or more frequent face-to-face gatherings, festivals, camps and so on.

How audiences actually use different media for religious or spiritual purposes has come under increased scrutiny in recent decades (e.g. Hoover and Clark 2002). In much the same way that there was a turn towards the audience in communication studies in the second half of the twentieth century, so there has been a similar shift among scholars analysing how audiences from different religious traditions actually create meaning around a range of media today (Horsfield *et al.* 2005). This includes considering the ways in which audiences develop practices of media consumption that ensure that they can resist, negotiate or play with the meanings of what they see or consume. For example, some viewers appear to have used certain programmes as 'a cultural reservoir of alternative visions', which allowed them to 'question traditional values and official interpretations' and thereby helped 'them to imagine alternative ways of living' (Thompson 1995: 178 after Lull 1991).

What was true of television in the late 1980s can be expanded to include other newer media today. As Stewart Hoover demonstrates in *Religion in the Media Age* 'media do provide a range of symbolic resources to contemporary "religious" and "spiritual" questing' (2006: 279). The symbolic resources that film, television and other media offer are often appropriated and recycled as people attempt to define their own identities, narrate their own life stories and understand the traditions and communities of interpretation to which they belong (Mitchell 2003: 339–340).

Reforming communities

New media are contributing to the formation of new kinds of virtual communities (Campbell 2005, 2010). As communication technologies continue to converge, viewers in affluent settings are increasingly able to use computer technologies to connect themselves with other members of the audience thousands of miles away. Websites, chat rooms and other digital media facilitate instantaneous conversations across the world around specific media events, popular films or religious news.

Thus while audiences in their domestic spaces can be separated by individualized communication technologies, they can also be brought together across thousands of miles through social networking sites such as Facebook, popular web blogs or the micro-communications of Twitter. These forms of media can bring individuals together as well as isolate or divide communicative communities, as it is possible now to remain interconnected with like-minded individuals and communities around the world, while ignoring those inhabiting different life worlds – even in one's own neighbourhood. In Britain it has almost become taken for granted that audiences can themselves interact with what they receive, making comments online, posting blogs and even re-editing original productions.

The tentacles of television, and more recently the internet, have spread all over the globe.[3] Television's early creators such as the Scot John Logie Baird (1888–1946) and the Russian Vladimir K. Zworykin (1889–1982) initiated a communicative process in the 1920s that has radically transformed the way in which humans learn about their planet, their histories and their neighbours. Through digitization the 'older' medium of television has combined with the 'newer' media of connected computers to bring even more distant faces and experiences into virtual connections. With the help of television, the internet, or both, it is now possible for a small child whose face looks out onto a housing estate in Liverpool to travel thousands of miles instantaneously to see different faces in a shantytown in Nairobi or in a *favela* in Buenos Aires without leaving their home. Digital media can take viewers far beyond the horizon, beneath the ocean and even to the edges of the known universe, where there are not yet faces to be seen or communities to be created.

Facing suffering

Before the invention of the telegraph in the earlier nineteenth century, audiences relied on far slower forms of communication. The fastest hooves and the largest sails determined the speed with which news about distant hardships was brought home. Letters from religious leaders pleading for assistance could take weeks or months to reach their destination. Now bearing witness to faraway heartbreak can be instantaneous and incessant. Viewers are regularly shown faces of distant suffering: the tired faces of earthquake victims in Haiti (2010), the terrified faces of those clutching fences in the wake of Pakistan's catastrophic floods (2010), the devastating testimony written on the faces of bystanders of another car bomb in Baghdad, can be revealed to a viewer safely ensconced in a thatched cottage in the Cotswolds (Mitchell 2007a).

Through the web audiences can now choose to reconsider faces or moments from history, watching again a global media event such as a president assassinated, a princess buried and a man taking one small step onto the moon. With only a few taps of an electronic mouse viewers can look again at the face of a screaming girl burnt by napalm running away naked from her burning village in Vietnam, at the hidden face of a lone student demonstrator halting a line of four tanks in Tiananmen Square, Beijing, or the faceless image of an airliner being flown into a skyscraper in Manhattan, New York. Audiences are exposed to these iconic images as they are repeated again and again on television, and recycled as pictures in newspapers and on the web. Audiences can now choose between sitting back and passively ignoring what they see, or sitting forward and interacting with what they observe. In one sense viewers are brought close to the other's face by what they see, but in another they are screened off and made distant as they cannot smell or touch the suffering face brought deceptively close. These virtual experiences highlight the tension between the individual living within their own media or spiritual worlds and the call of the other, which interrupts comfortable media consumption.

The changing faces of protagonists

Having considered how media audiences have changed since 1945, the next two sections consider first protagonists and then other aspects of content. This section focuses on religious figures and their ability to capitalize on diverse channels of communication to convey their message, as well as on how they have been represented by the media. The following section considers broader media portrayals of religion. As a result of the contemporary celebrity turn, as well as the drive to humanize religion rather than present it in the abstract, the figure of the religious leader will re-emerge in the third section, this time in the context of TV comedy.

Religion, communication and change

The mediation of the 'Other' and the communication of the divine message to a wider audience constitute the *raison d'être* for many religions. They take various forms, from the channelling of divine revelation and prophecy to the teaching of beliefs and values, as well as communicating with the divine through ritual. The act of communicating extends beyond the devout to outsiders too, either in their capacity as potential converts or as a wider public whose general curiosity and interest extend to religion as much as they do to other aspects of culture.

   With communication being at the heart of religion, it is not surprising that religious people have capitalized upon the opportunities provided as new media have developed (Campbell 2010). In Britain, from the earliest use of the printing press in the late fifteenth century to radio and television in the twentieth, and digital media in the twenty-first, Christians and, more recently, followers of other religions have seized the possibilities afforded by new technology. Since the nineteenth century, for example, evangelical Christians have found a variety of means of expressing and widely circulating their beliefs and views, from popular posters and handbills, to pamphlets, books of sermons, religious novels and autobiographies. In the period from 1945, Christian publications continued to be published, with some repeatedly reprinted. However, according to Callum Brown (2001, and in this volume Chapter 10), the 1960s marked a turning point – a 'discourse revolution' – after which the Christian underpinnings of British culture were much less in evidence, with the mainstream of popular culture becoming overtly secular.

   In the post-war period, though, there was still an appetite for popular Christian writing. Although better known for his children's fiction, particularly *The Chronicles of Narnia*, C. S. Lewis also wrote popular theological books. *Mere Christianity* (1952), one of the most widely read books by evangelical Christians, was based on a series of talks he gave on BBC Radio in the 1940s (Mitchell 1999) in which he explained the fundamentals of Christianity to a general audience. Another was John Stott's *Basic Christianity* (1958), which sought to answer questions about the identity of Christ and what He achieved, about what people need and how they should respond to Christ's teachings. Although originally published during 'a return to piety' when the Christian churches in Britain were experiencing what was to be a short-term period of growth (Brown 2001: 170), these books continued to be popular long after the 1950s, with both authors remaining on bestseller lists at the start of the new millennium.

Evangelical Christians continued to publish even in less inviting, more 'post-Christian' times such as the 1980s and 1990s (see Chapters 2 and 5 for more on evangelical Christianity in Britain). As ever, they sought to address pertinent issues from an evangelical perspective. The bishop and missionary Lesslie Newbigin, for example, tackled the challenging issue of the place of Christianity and the Bible in a context of social and religious diversity in *The Gospel in a Pluralist Society* (1989), and Phillip E. Johnson published *Darwin on Trial* (1993) in which he took on the scientific establishment with his account of intelligent design.

The role of these bestsellers, to bring the Christian gospel to a wider audience, has more recently been superseded by global electronic communications and the power of the internet, although some media-savvy evangelicals have found ways of converting the popularity of the old into new media formats. The American John Wimber's preaching on God's 'signs and wonders', from his widely read book *Power Evangelism* (1986), found new audiences in video format on GodTube (a Christian video-sharing website). C. S. Lewis did not go out of fashion either, with *Mere Christianity* available online for reading or downloading as an audio-book (Lewis). We know that such sermons and books – for that is what they remain, even if they are now in new formats – still hold considerable power for audiences because users are able to record their comments, often praising the medium as much as the message: 'God bless you for this convenient source,' wrote one user of the online version of *Mere Christianity*, with another suggesting it was much easier to listen to than to read.

Evangelicals in Britain as elsewhere continue to find dynamic, popular and often ingenious ways to share the Christian gospel. But the call to communicate a cherished message to a wider audience has also been pursued by ideological exponents of other persuasions. Liberal Christian and post-Christian sceptics such as John Robinson, *Honest to God* (1963), and Don Cupitt, *Taking Leave of God* (1980), and, later, confirmed atheists such as Richard Dawkins (see Plate 2.9), with *The God Delusion* (2006), and Christopher Hitchens (see Plate 1.6), with *God is Not Great: How Religion Poisons Everything* (2007), have succeeded in drawing huge audiences through their book sales. In the case of Dawkins and Hitchens, operating in a multimedia age, their willingness to embrace a variety of media formats has made it easy for an interested public to access their ideas. As atheists who are more at ease with a critique of religion than the expression of positive humanist or secular values, they can readily be found taking on formidable religious opponents and debating with them, whether online, on video or in newspapers and magazines.

The Richard Dawkins Foundation for Reason and Science, like many religious organizations, can be accessed through its website and various other new media, including RSS feeds, YouTube, Facebook and Twitter (richarddawkinsfoundation.org). As well as information about Dawkins's books, talks and other interventions, the site offers space for converts to atheism to express themselves, for the (non-religious) giving of aid, buying DVDs, books and other paraphernalia, and making donations to the Foundation. It is striking how many similar functions are fulfilled, to take just one example, on the website of Hope City Church (www.hopecitychurch.tv). The purpose here though is preaching, worship and prayer, and news about Christianity and the church, rather than atheist communication. Key personnel are featured on the site, in this case not the dominant male protagonist, but the husband and wife pastoral teams who serve their largely 18–30-year-old congregations.

These examples illustrate how religious and, more recently, atheist protagonists have utilized available means of communication to access British audiences. The means of communication have changed, with the printed medium – and, as will be seen later, radio and television – being the technologies of choice in the first half of the period, being joined (but not entirely surpassed) by digital media from the 1990s. But has the medium changed the message? A common Christian view in the 1970s, voiced succinctly by the critic Malcolm Muggeridge, was that the media – in particular, television – were bound to distort the message of religion: 'Even if you put the truth into it, it comes out a deception' (Green 1982: 177). Despite this negative view, as Heidi Campbell makes clear (2010), religious people have always been among the early adopters of new media, and indeed have adapted them to their own needs in accordance with their traditions, teachings and values.

Religious people are not, of course, always in control of the media portrayal of religion. Places of worship and preaching, books and other tracts, and religious websites all provide environments in which they are agents in the communication process. In the secular mass media, however, religious people are generally present by invitation, and in accordance with the mission, values, rhetoric and style of a particular medium and its producers. The remainder of this section and the next give examples of how religious actors – and religions in general – have been portrayed in the popular secular media, and to what extent such portrayals have changed. An awareness of ideological and other power differences, as well as the nature of media discourse and culture, is important for thinking about how religions and their people are represented. Although it will not be possible to address all the relevant issues in detail – for example religious and denominational diversity, gender, class, race and ethnicity, moderate and extremist voices, secularist and atheist as well as religious – it is important at least to have them in mind when thinking about the changing relationship of religion and media in Britain since the Second World War.

Changing voices

It would be a mistake to think that the mass media have necessarily been hostile to religions or unremittingly instrumentalist in their treatment of them. Public service broadcasters, for example, have made space for religious people to speak for themselves, albeit framed within a secular context. The 'talk show' and 'talking head' formats, in which an individual is invited either to converse with a host or to talk directly to an audience, remain classic mechanisms for allowing people to get their beliefs and views across, though subject to an editorial process that tempers content as well as presentation. Religious people have not infrequently been the subjects of these. David Frost, one of the most famous and prolific of television interviewers during the past half-century, often asked his guests about their religious beliefs. Many lay religious people as well as leaders were quizzed by Frost in his famous TV interviews including guests such as Catholic Cardinal Heenan and Cliff Richard. More recently, politically engaged religious leaders, such as Desmond Tutu and Muhammad Tahir-ul-Qadri, as well as outspoken atheists, have been given a voice in *Frost over the World*, on Al Jazeera television.

Using the 'talking heads' format, in 2007, a series of short, intimate films looking at different faiths in Britain (Buddhist, Muslim, Hindu, Catholic and Jewish) was commissioned by Channel 5 television (Bloom 2007). Originally shown on *Five News*, they offered vignettes by religious people of the impact of religion on family life. These films have now joined a plethora of video clips featuring religious speakers – both professional and home-made – on YouTube. YouTube has proved to be an ideal medium for the delivery of sermons, personal testimonies and witnessing, and for recording and sharing religious music, thus providing a new and widely accessible medium for traditional religious practices. These short films were by no means the first programmes to recognize Britain's increasing religious diversity. Broadcast coverage of world religions began in the late 1960s with a 'radiovision' educational series produced by Ralph Rolls. Combining Radio 4 programmes with integrated film strips, they introduced school audiences to religions through their artefacts, music, worship and texts.

Radio was the first mass medium to deliver religious voices to a national, then a global, audience. Perhaps the most well-known, and indeed controversial, religious talk slot in the period from 1945 has been *Thought for the Day* (Mitchell 1999: 107–143). Predominantly Christian, but with an increasing range of speakers from other religions, this three-minute slot now precedes the 8 o'clock morning news in BBC Radio 4's *Today* programme. Since it began, debate has raged about whether *Thought* should be broadened to include non-religious contributors, such as speakers from the British Humanist Association or the National Secular Society (Mitchell 1999; Clifford 2009, 2010). With religious and non-religious exponents lining up on both sides, the debate has led to formal complaints and appeals, as well as statements in the House of Lords, all of which have been countered by the BBC, with the status quo persisting. *Thought* has remained religious. Richard Dawkins was invited to record a 'thought' in February 2009, though it was broadcast outside the normal daily slot, and alternative non-religious 'thoughts' have been launched, for example, by the Humanist Society of Scotland, in conjunction with the British Humanist Association and *The Guardian*.

TEXT BOX 14

Thought for the Day

From its wartime beginnings as a comforting Anglican daily programme called *Lift Up Your Hearts*, broadcast by the BBC Home Service, it was superseded in 1965 by a less devotional five-minute reflection, and reduced again, in 1970, to a three-minute topical monologue from a faith perspective by one of a list of trusted broadcasters. The success of this format has led not only to the continuity of *Thought for the Day* on Radio 4, but to the spawning of other 'thoughts' on national and regional radio stations, generally religious, but sometimes including Humanist, New Age or atheist voices.

Representing an increasing diversity of religions over the years, its speakers have included a number of well-known voices whose tone, tolerance, gentle humour and topicality have shaped *Thought*: the 'Radio Rabbi' Lionel Blue; the broadcaster now priest, Angela Tilby; a former BBC head of religious broadcasting, Colin Morris; a Hindu Vaishnava teacher, Akhandadhi Das; the Sikh broadcaster and journalist Indarjit Singh; and Professor of Islamic Studies Mona Siddiqui. Since 2001, there have been some 80 speakers from six different religions, most of whom have been religious leaders, but including some academic theologians and media professionals who are themselves religious. Fewer than 20 have been women. In a study of 'thoughts' delivered from 2007 to 2009 (Clifford 2010), 78 per cent of 'thoughts' were delivered by Christians (more than half Anglican and a quarter Catholic), 8 per cent by Jews, 4 per cent by Muslims, 4 per cent by Sikhs, 3 per cent by Hindus and 2 per cent by Buddhists.

Religious faces in the media: diversification and backlash

If those invited to present their personal faith perspectives on radio and television have diversified since the Second World War, so indeed have media representations of people of faith (Mitchell and Gower forthcoming). Male clerics, often Anglican but sometimes Catholic, predominated in the early part of the period, but several lay Christian representatives emerged in the 1960s and early 1970s. Malcolm Muggeridge, Lord Longford and Mary Whitehouse (see Plate 1.1) became widely known outspoken critics of the 'permissive society', speaking out against pornography, the commercialization of sex and the moral breakdown of society. With cleaning up the media high on their agenda, they attracted attention not only in news, debates and discussions, but also from the comedy fringe where they became targets for mockery and caricature.

Key Christian leaders – the Archbishops of Canterbury and York, and the Pope, in particular – have been a constant focus of media attention throughout the period, with their views on social, political and ethical matters monitored. The issues have changed, from pornography and the depravity of youth in the 1960s, through contraception and women's roles in the 1980s, to assisted suicide, *shari'a* law and homosexuality in the new millennium. From time to time, the press – driven by a celebrity agenda (see previous chapter) – have exposed their biographies, personality quirks and daily routines. *The Times* printed sections of Archbishop of Canterbury Rowan Williams's autobiography in 2008. The two popes who visited Britain, John Paul II in 1982 and Benedict XVI in 2010, generated extensive media coverage.

In the press, particularly the tabloid newspapers, the culture of largely unquestioning respect for clergy was fractured as social attitudes towards religion changed. The deviant behaviour of clergy became more commonly exposed, though the portrayal of drunk and gambling vicars gave way from the 1990s to coverage of wholesale clerical child abuse, particularly within the Roman Catholic Church. Popular public interest has lain in uncovering hypocrisy and immorality among those who should know and act better, those – despite their own humanity – expected by an increasingly religiously indifferent society to uphold its moral standards and behavioural norms.

Set against such clerical figures were other faces, largely invisible in the popular media in the 1970s and 1980s, but by the late 2000s a regular feature in Britain's conservative newspapers (*The Telegraph*, *The Sun*, the *Daily Express*, the *Daily Star*). They were the faces of lay Christian women, whose faith convictions were presented as being at odds with liberal secular, politically correct attitudes to public behaviour: a nurse who prayed for her patient, an airport staff member who wore a cross to work and a school receptionist chastised by her school for raising the issue when her child was scolded for discussing her faith.[4] They constituted part of a wider conservative media discourse which linked what was seen as the persecution of Christianity with a secularist agenda that foregrounded equality and multiculturalism and, it was claimed, paved the way for the future Islamification of Britain. Such women became emblems in a political debate about the place of Christian identity and tradition in British public life. In the left-wing press, this debate was given a wholly different twist, with Christian organizations and leaders often presented as anti-egalitarian, homophobic and sexist, and as a brake on social change.

Although Britain's religious diversity was increasingly covered by the media from the 1990s, following the tragic events of 9/11 it was somewhat overshadowed by the extensive and repeated portrayal of Islamic extremism (commonly epitomized by references to terrorists and 'hate-preachers'). Media Islamophobia in Britain had been recognized in the 1990s, but certainly intensified after 2001 (Runnymede Trust 1997; Poole 2002; Moore *et al.* 2008; Allen 2010; Taira *et al.* forthcoming). As became clear in focus groups on religion and the media conducted in 2010,[5] many readers and viewers were aware of Islamophobia and of the over-reporting of Islamic extremists, but found it hard not to be swayed by it because they were offered so few positive stories (Taira *et al.* forthcoming). They recognized, though, that bad news stories attracted attention in a way that good news would not. 'The media does make things more scary,' one non-religious person said, with another clearly frustrated that Islam and extremism were always conflated in the press, and one Muslim fed up that the angriest of his co-religionists were always portrayed as if they represented the whole religion. A number of focus-group members – religious and non-religious – suggested that religious people in general were represented in the secular media as abnormal, different from the 'normal' mainstream, and marginalized for their faith.

Despite this focus on Muslims from 2001, other religious faces have increasingly become subjects of interest for television, from BBC's *The Long Search* in the 1970s, to *Everyman* in the 1980s and *Around the World in Eighty Faiths* in 2010. Diversity has even begun to find its way into popular entertainment, as performers such as Simon Amstell, Sacha Baron Cohen, Shazia Mirza and Omid Djalili, bring their comedic skills to bear on religious and ethnic issues. As with all new entrants to popular cultural representation, tokenism perhaps best describes the process whereby the occasional Muslim, Jew, Hindu or Sikh gains entry into a TV soap, sitcom (situational comedy) or drama.

The changing faces of content

Despite a degree of continuity, there can be no doubt that media audiences, protagonists and producers have changed significantly. In 1945, those consuming radio and print media and the voices broadcasting and reporting to them were very different from today's equivalents, in terms of class, religion, ethnicity and life experience. But what of the daily media fare to which listeners, viewers and readers are exposed: to what extent has that changed? Is there more or less religion in the media? How is it portrayed and represented? Do the media assist in fulfilling religious functions? And how do genres – such as entertainment and sport – contribute to the representation of religion?

The changing faces of religious broadcasting and narrowcasting

In the 1940s and 1950s, as Britain moved from war to peacetime, the BBC's approach to Christianity began to change from a protectionist stance to a more open, questioning one. The challenging religious discussion programme *Meeting Point*, first aired by the BBC in 1956, heralded this change. Some church leaders and lay Christians, including Mary Whitehouse, continued to resist change and stress the importance of the corporation in fostering moral guidance and understanding about Christianity (Noonan 2008: 66). Sundays remained the focus for religious broadcasting, though clerical advisors were insistent that religion on television should not be restricted, nor should it compete with actual church services (there was a real fear that the popularity of television could challenge religious participation and negatively affect moral standards). Debates and films, and occasionally hymn-singing broadcast from the studio, were the regular fare of the early Sunday evening 'closed period', though this changed with the advent of *Songs of Praise* in the 1960s.

TEXT BOX 15

Songs of Praise

From October 1961, *Songs of Praise*, a weekly outside-broadcast, was transmitted, becoming an immediate – and long-lasting – success. The winning musical format, of popular hymns sung by real congregations in churches and chapels all over Britain, and latterly beyond it, has changed over the decades as local Christians have become more directly involved in presenting their own faith stories and localities, and as the focus has shifted from single-denominational services, to ecumenical and, occasionally, interfaith gatherings (Barr *c*. 2006). The production team has responded to national and international crises and celebrations over the years, and the programme has remained the flagship of BBC TV's Sunday religious broadcasting (with a hymnbook, CD and DVD also available).

It has been joined, over the years, on both BBC and independent television, by worship and religious magazine programmes, such as *Stars on Sunday*, *This is the Day*, *Morning Worship*, *Highway*, *Praise Be*, *My Favourite Hymns*, *First Light* and *Sunday Morning*, and debates and documentaries, including *Meeting Point*, *Credo*, *Everyman*, *Heart of the Matter*, *The Heaven and Earth Show* and *The Big Questions*.

In her analysis of religious broadcasting in the UK, Rachel Viney (1999: 25) concluded that it was in broadly good health: different types of programmes featuring a variety of religious perspectives, transmitted at different times in the TV schedule, were available from different networks. She accepted, however, that religious broadcasting was subject to changing fortunes and to the 'enthusiasm and vision of those individuals responsible for [programme] commissioning' (Viney 1999: 25). By 2010, though the BBC's commitment had not declined significantly, the situation had changed, with ITV withdrawing its regular religious content, down from the 105 hours it delivered in 1998–1999. In addition to *Songs of Praise*, BBC TV's religion and ethics programmes included various series on world religions, Christianity and sacred music, and documentaries and debates on religion in public life, the case for God, atheism and British Muslims. BBC radio offered discussions on ethical choices, different beliefs and iconoclasm; BBC Asian Network added further diversity to the fare, by focusing on Ramadan and other festivals, and on devotional Islamic, Hindu and Sikh music. Channel 4 offered two major series on *The Bible: A History* and *Christianity: A History*, featured religious and non-religious celebrities such as Robert Beckford, Richard Dawkins and Colin Blakemore, and covered a variety of edgy religious topics such as the apocalypse, cults, religion and homosexuality, the unexplained, priests and paedophilia, the 'Turin shroud' and paganism.

In terms of variety and style, range of religions and ethical issues – despite the retreat of the independent provider, ITV – religious broadcasting was thriving on radio and TV.

Furthermore, new digital technologies enabled this astonishing array of programmes on religion to be available online to viewers beyond the initial point of delivery, through 'BBC iPlayer' and '4 on Demand'. At the same time, BBC and Channel 4 web pages on religion, ethics and belief supplemented programmes with additional public information, further demonstrating the capacity of digital technology to widen access and add value to old media rather than merely supplant them.

In the 1980s, clergy and broadcasters alike had expressed anxiety that the deregulation of television would mean the onset of a British form of 'televangelism' akin to the television ministries of Oral Roberts, Pat Robertson, Jerry Falwell and Morris Cerullo in the United States (Knott 1984; Fore 1987). Following the Broadcasting Act 1990, licences were available for independent cable or satellite companies which, although subject to consumer protection, were entitled to air religious views and to represent particular churches or other religious groups (Viney 1999: 11). In Britain, such 'narrowcasting' never became the force it had once been in the States, though the 'Christian Channel' (later 'Grace TV') operated in British media space in the 1990s, and the explicitly British-focused 'Christian TV' – begun by David and Jan Green in 2002 – provided a family-friendly platform for various Christian TV channels and radio stations.

The faces of sport, comedy and advertising: a barometer of changing representations of religion

Research on religion on television and in the newspapers, conducted at the University of Leeds in the early 1980s and repeated in 2008–2009 with funding from the AHRC/ESRC Religion and Society Programme (Knott 1984; Taira *et al.* forthcoming), showed clearly that the majority of references to Christianity and other religions and to 'common religion' (unorganized beliefs and practices which nevertheless refer to the supernatural) occurred not in programmes and articles explicitly focused on religion, but in other genres. In the newspapers, they featured in news stories, but also in editorials and comments – signalling the significance of popular debate about religious issues. Perhaps more surprisingly, they were often mentioned in the sports pages. These references were frequently but by no means exclusively to be found in the tabloids, and generally referred to common religion – especially to luck, gambling and magic – and also to religious cosmology. Footballers and their managers were attributed with divine status; hope for miracles and prayers for a good result were in evidence. Religion had a significant place in newspaper supplements too, particularly in relation to culture, travel, jobs and health.

Comparison between 1982–1983 and 2008–2009 showed that, on television, references to religion – whilst still generally in evidence in news and current affairs – had shifted from the more serious content of plays and films to the lighter genre of entertainment (Figure 7.1).

References to religion were found in abundance in murder mysteries, soaps and sitcoms. In the former, the traditional image of the village church often provided the backdrop for suspense, occult practices and unexplained events, with male, and increasingly female, clergy represented in all three types of programmes. By 2009, however, the most popular genre for religion references on TV was advertising. Adverts, despite representing only 6 per cent of available airtime, contained more than 30 per cent of all terrestrial TV references to religion, particularly to luck, the unexplained and magic, but also to life-cycle rites, prayer and meditation. Religious references contributed to idealizing commodities or their uses: by demonstrating that ordinary people could overcome or control everyday

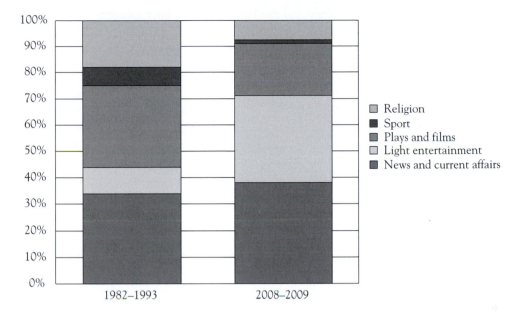

Figure 7.1 Religious references by TV programme genre

problems with the help of a new product, and often by connecting such problems to ideal or magical scenarios.

The presence of religion in the everyday language and images of popular media reflects its deep embeddedness in British culture – in metaphorical and literal references, in the landscape, and in norms and behaviours associated with hope, destiny, superstition and encounter with the unknown – even at a time when other statistical indicators signalled Christian decline and indifference.

Changing religious faces in comedy

The faces of British television comedy tell their own story of change across the period – not only of religious developments but also of the way in which programme makers have seen fit to represent religion in keeping with social and cultural expectations. In the immediate post-war period Christianity was rarely a laughing matter, with domestic and army life the key subjects for comedy, and with US imports bringing American living standards, celebrity and humour to British TV screens. As Brown (2001 and in this volume) has argued, the 1960s brought the challenge to Christianity of youth counter-cultures as well as women's changing lifestyles, the former heralding the growth of British satire in which religion, along with other aspects of class, establishment and tradition, was ripe for a laugh. Alan Bennett's 'Take a pew' spoof of the modern Anglican clergyman from BBC's *Beyond the Fringe* parodied conservative anxieties about society's moral decline. By the early 1970s, new as well as old religion was the butt of the satirist, with *Monty Python's Flying Circus* targeting new religious groups such as Scientology and the Family in 'Crackpot religions inc' (its 1979 film, *Monty Python's Life of Brian*, was later subject to accusations of blasphemy).

Sitcoms about the clergy charted changing attitudes, with BBC's *All Gas and Gaiters* (1966–1971), about the farcical antics of a Cathedral clerical team, and *Oh Brother* (1968–1970), about life in a monastery, assuming a degree of knowledge about church life that had all but disappeared by the time *The Vicar of Dibley* (BBC, 1994–2007) appeared on British TV screens (see Plate 1.8). This vicar, Revd Geraldine Granger, marked the entry of women into the Anglican priesthood and the emotions and attitudes surrounding their ordination. Set in an Oxfordshire village, and confirming many of the stereotypes of rural religious, social and cultural life, it is thought by many commentators to have helped Christians in Britain to accept women in priestly roles. Despite this, over the years it was aired, the number and range of references to Christian practice and theology declined, perhaps reflecting the growing illiteracy about religion in general and Christianity in particular among television viewers. In 2010 another BBC series focused on Anglican life was launched, this time in an urban setting. *Rev.* explored the challenges of inner-city life, the problems of church decline, and the indifference and, at times, antagonism of wider society.

The Church of England has not been the only subject of the TV sitcom format, however, with Irish Catholicism and rural Catholic clergy the focus of Channel 4's popular *Father Ted* (1995–1998), and with British Asian wit turned on religion as well as music, food and family life in the BBC's *Goodness Gracious Me* (1998–2001) and *The Kumars at No. 42* (2001–2006). Jewish families have also featured in this format, a recent example being Simon Amstell's *Grandma's House* for BBC 2 (2010). These shows were designed not only to reflect contemporary diversity but to appeal beyond niche ethnic and religious markets to a wider, more knowing, cosmopolitan audience. They exposed customs and traditions to the comedy imagination whilst taking seriously the ways in which British ethnic and religious communities were changing.

The changing faces and spaces of production and consumption

This fourth and final section considers the transformation of both media spaces and producers in several different contexts.

Changing spaces and places

This chapter began with descriptions of some of the earliest photographs of families listening together to the radio. There was a degree of novelty in what was shown. Few people now in the West would give a radio a second glance, even if they listen via a different delivery technology. In the UK by May 2009 'a third of adults (33 per cent) had listened to the radio online' which 'was up from 29 per cent a year previously and from 24 per cent six months before that'.[6] Even in these new contexts radio is not the only form of communication now largely taken for granted. Few visitors would be surprised to see a flat-screen television or personal computer in a neighbour's home. The ubiquity of electronic media means that it is now taken for granted. For example, consider television. It is part of the domestic landscape of suburban mansions and impoverished dwellings all over Britain and around the world.

Among more affluent households it is common to find television sets not only in the sitting room, but also in the kitchen and bedrooms. Viewers can now choose to watch even more easily what they like and, as mentioned earlier, when they like it through on-demand viewing technologies. Even in poorer urban settings it is extremely rare to discover local communities entirely free of television. Screens are now found in bars, shops, railway stations, aeroplanes and hospitals. Satellite dishes adorn the outside of many houses and blocks of flats around the UK. Wherever electricity is easily available television has become part of the urban wallpaper.

Computer screens, which can carry television programmes, are already beginning to supplement or even replace these forms of 'old media'. Nevertheless, television, like film before and the internet after, has attracted iconoclasts who wish to discard it, iconographers who wish to make use of it and interpreters who desire to see through it. While television's uses have fragmented and diversified around the globe, it can still attract huge global audiences to watch World Cup football matches, South American soap operas and Asian religious epics. John Paul II's funeral at the Vatican, in Rome, on 8 April 2005, was watched by as many as 2 billion people worldwide.

The coronation of Queen Elizabeth in 1953 is frequently described as a pivotal moment for the evolution of media in modern Britain (see Plate 2.1 and Chapter 2). It was certainly a turning point for television. An estimated 20 million people (over 50 per cent of the adult population) clustered around the limited number of televisions to watch the coronation service in Westminster Abbey. It was not long before television viewing had outstripped radio listening, with vast numbers of television sets purchased in Britain during the late 1950s and 1960s (Mitchell 1999: 48–49; Briggs 1995: 420–435). Scholars have since pointed to this as a seminal 'media event' (see Dayan and Katz 1992; Couldry 2003). The televising of the 1953 coronation provoked severe criticism from different religious groups. In Britain several religious and political leaders objected to the televising of this service, in particular the actual crowning in Westminster Abbey, arguing that it invaded and demeaned a sacred act. To temper these criticisms the moment in the service where the Queen was anointed on her head with oil was shielded from prying cameras by screens. By contrast Prince Charles and Diana's wedding in 1981, which attracted an estimated global audience of 750 million people, and Prince William and Kate Middleton's in 2011, which some journalists claimed attracted over 2 billion viewers, were broadcast live without any significant criticisms of television's invasion of a supposedly sacred space or act. The spaces the media cover, as well as those in which they are received and digested, have shifted.

Media exposure has made some faces and events more commonplace. Many institutions have lost their mystique as a result of allowing cameras behind the scenes. In *No Sense of Place* (1986) Joshua Meyrowitz argued that electronic media have transformed our social relationships: 'by revealing previously backstage areas to audiences, television has served as an instrument of demystification' (1986: 309). The result is that relations between woman and man, child and adult, political elite and average voter are transformed, blurred and potentially brought to a more equal level. Authority is questioned. As we saw earlier, it is also laughed at through the work of comedians. This applies not only to royalty but also to religious leaders. That which was hidden is being, if not shouted from the rooftops, at least electronically exposed: nowhere more so than with the repeated recent media exposure of priests involved in child abuse. The initial reticence regarding these stories partly reflects a lack of belief, knowledge and interest among the producers and editors. This was partly because of an initial refusal to face up to the rumours and criticisms circulating. The eventual coverage of clergy abuse illustrates a radical public transformation in how journalists, writers and producers tackled religious topics or leaders (Jenkins 1996). The popular deference of the 1930s–1950s, where the priest was depicted in popular culture as a saint or figure to be respected, gave way both to a satire revolution where the vicar's sermon was parodied and to a journalistic revolution where religious leaders could be called to account.

Changing creators

There is a widespread perception that radio and television producers in early post-war Britain were largely, though not exclusively, made up of a white male Oxbridge-educated elite. This was reflected in the kinds of programmes that were produced and celebrated. At least seven of the BBC's 1953 coronation lead commentators fell into this category, joined by one woman on the route.[7] With the growth of television, producers and directors found themselves working in increasingly well-paid and respected positions. In the 1970s and 1980s trainee schemes for the BBC became highly competitive attracting some of the 'brightest and best' graduates, but not necessarily Oxbridge educated. It is striking how the major history of the BBC's religious broadcasting between 1922 and 1956 (Wolfe 1984) reveals how the production and management were dominated by ordained men, among whom many were Anglican. They were initially encouraged to promote Reith's more muscular form of Christianity. In sharp contrast, in 2011 the BBC's Head of Religion and Ethics is a lay Muslim and his department is dominated by professional journalists and producers coming from many different religious or secular backgrounds. Likewise, independent production companies tackling religious subjects largely emerge from secular or independent settings. The BBC appears currently to be actively recruiting trainees from minority ethnic backgrounds. Producers, journalists and editors in the UK are now largely independent from institutional religion and therefore freer to be less deferential and more critical.

As already documented, the period from the 1990s has also witnessed a radical transformation in how information is communicated around both Britain and the globe. In 2010 out of a world population of well over 8.5 billion, nearly 2 billion people made use of the internet. This means that nearly 30 per cent of the world's population are sometimes able to access, through the internet, some of the billions of hypertext pages to be found on the world wide web. Between 2000 and 2010 there was an over 444 per cent increase in internet use. This growth has taken place all over the world, but especially in Africa (2,537 per cent increase), in the Middle East (1,825 per cent), in Latin America/Caribbean (1,032 per cent) and in Asia (621 per cent). These extraordinary statistics partly reflect the fact that these areas had comparatively few users in the early days of the internet. North America has the highest percentage per capita of internet use (77 per cent), with Australasia/Oceania (61 per cent) and Europe (58 per cent) being the other most 'connected' spaces in the world (Internet World Stats). In the United Kingdom over 82 per cent of the population have access to the internet, with over 51 million users, making Britain, after Germany, the most densely 'connected' country in Europe.[8]

The rapid growth, ever-expanding size and diversity of what is currently to be found on the web are hard to imagine. One study estimated that in 2003 the world wide web contained the equivalent of about 170 terabytes of information on its surface; which is equivalent in volume to 'seventeen times the size of the Library of Congress print collections' (How Much Information 2003). This is but a tip of the virtual iceberg, with the so-called 'deep web' or 'hidden web' 400 to 450 times larger, and constantly expanding. Unlike the rapidly expanding 'public web', popular search engines rarely touch this ever-increasing 'invisible web'. Individuals are now able to create their own pages in a matter of minutes. One of the results is the blurring between the role of the producer and the role of the audience, as audiences produce their own content.

From producing Religion-Online to Online-Religion

Given the huge and ever-increasing amount of material to be found on the internet, the 'network of networks', it is not surprising that many religious sites are sometimes overlooked. Just as in real life, there are multiple forms of religious and spiritual life to be found expressed on the web. A popular, and now much cited distinction, first made by Christopher Helland (2000), is between Religion-Online and Online-Religion. This helpful distinction can be drawn upon for understanding how the internet is actually used in the United Kingdom today. On the one hand, Religion-Online is where religious believers attempt to use their sites as a way of communicating both to their members and to potential converts. This is sometimes described as a one-to-many form of communication (Campbell 2005: 56). Examples of this would include sites set up by specific religious groups such as those emerging out of mosques in Bradford, New Age centres in Glastonbury and 'mega' or smaller evangelical churches in London. Among many different facilities, users are able to download sermons or lectures as podcasts from a countless number of different sources.

On the other hand, Online-Religion is where groups adapt their communicative practices in the wake of the new communication technologies which have ensured the flourishing of the internet. This is sometimes described as a many-to-many form of communication. Examples of this would include discussion groups, interactive 'prayer lists' or virtual religious services or spaces. It is now possible to enter into another world or inhabit a 'second life' where a temple, mosque, shrine or church is built not out of bricks and mortar but out of digital characters. In these contexts religious groups and individuals adapt their practices and even their identity in order to reside and to thrive in cyberspace. In other words, Online-Religion provides new ways of expressing and experiencing ancient and contemporary religious traditions which regularly transcend national boundaries.

In some settings the distinction between Online-Religion and Religion-Online is blurring. There is no evidence up to this point that participation in Religion-Online has led to the decline of active religious participation. Many traditions and religious groups have now recognized the inherently interactive form which use of the web regularly takes. Users are invited to participate, to explore and to respond. There are now thousands of examples of web blogs or web pages or Facebook groups which reveal the individual posters' own spiritual journey or existential questions. Recent studies demonstrate how cyberspace may not be so unusual a space as was sometimes predicted. Researchers are now investigating the everyday nature of internet use (Lövheim 2004; Mitchell and Marriage 2003). Surfing the internet, sending emails or visiting virtual worship or meditation spaces have become for many taken-for-granted practices in countries such as the UK where the internet is easily available.

Conclusion

While the precise influence of both 'old' and 'new' media upon religion in the UK is hard to discern, it is clear from this analysis of the changing faces of audiences, presenters, content and production and media content, that this part of the religious landscape in the UK has radically transformed since the Second World War. The BBC and other media organizations have themselves evolved and become increasingly open to providing a platform for a wide range of religious beliefs and practices, as well as non-religious views. This both reflects and contributes to the changing faces of religion in the UK.

It is important, however, to place this description of the demystification of both the churches and religious leaders by various media in a wider historical context. Consider, for example, the modern history of newspaper anti-clericalism. This was probably at its most virulent in the nineteenth century (Aston and Cragoe 2001) but abated a good deal in the early and middle years of the twentieth century. Anti-clericalism today is far harder to discern, being more fragmented and sporadic, complicated by the way in which different media often ignore religious perspectives, castigate leaders for their lack of 'moral leadership' or turn to them in times of national grief or commemoration. A good example of this highly ambiguous relationship between 'mainstream media' and religious leaders can be discerned by a comparison between how Pope John Paul II's visit to the UK in 1982 and Benedict XVI's visit in 2010 were covered (for more detail see Taira *et al.* forthcoming). In general terms, the historic nature of John Paul II's visit was widely celebrated before, during and after his visit. For some, here was a sign that the anti-Catholicism of post-Reformation Britain had, at last, largely evaporated. By contrast, Benedict XVI's visit attracted consider-able negative coverage before his arrival, partly because of the costs of hosting a state visit and partly because of his earlier pronouncements on contested ethical issues (see Plate 1.5). During and after the event, the Pope's 2010 visit largely attracted far more positive cover-age. Some claimed this was through skilful media management, while others suggested it was because the more humane face of his character was revealed close up.

The ambiguous relationship of different media towards religious leaders and belief is not a new phenomenon. What is new is for audiences to be able to navigate effortlessly from newspaper article via humanist blog to television clips of a papal Mass in Glasgow. There are endless other possibilities online, which allow a Londoner to travel in a few moments from the homepage of a rapidly growing Pentecostal church in Latin America via a virtual tour of a shattered Buddha statue in Afghanistan to photographs of a development project funded by Muslim Aid in Pakistan. Distraught faces following the attacks on a Coptic church in Cairo, a Catholic church in Baghdad or a Shi'ite mosque in Fallujah are only a few clicks away. There is now, more than ever before, a never-ending marketplace of images of religion and spiritualities. In some circles this has led to the questioning of beliefs that apparently promote violent action, or the demonization of other religious groups, while in others it has reinforced the move away from institutional religion towards more private forms of spirituality. For some people these changes are helping to create borderless, trans-national expressions of religion.

These transformations raise many significant issues, including: what kinds, if any, of new religious identities, new religious boundaries, new religious spaces or new religious authori-ties are being formed? How far does the exponential growth of new media use ensure that individuals in Britain now inhabit an interconnected and international religious landscape? What are the essential differences between an online-religion, meeting only in cyberspace, and a 'real-life' religion, which makes use of the internet to promote its everyday activities but still remains an actual physical community? What are the ethical, religious and theo-logical implications of these transformations? These are only a few of the issues that this chapter has raised. It is useful to be reminded that even though one of the most recent phenomena, the internet, is little more than 20 years old, the way that it is being used by both religious institutions and individuals is transforming the daily practices and expressions of religion not only in Britain but also around the world today.

Key terms

Islamophobia: The 'othering' of Islam and Muslims; in the case of the media, their persistent and pervasive negative portrayal in news and other genres.

Media: Some distinguish between primary media (e.g. speaking, singing), secondary media (e.g. writing, painting) and electronic media. This final category is commonly divided between 'old' media (e.g. television, radio and film) and 'new' media (e.g. computers, iPhones). With digitization and convergence of communication technologies these categories are blurring. The media is sometimes used as a collective singular noun (e.g. 'The media changes religion'), though it is more correctly used as a plural noun, reflecting the many different forms of media and individuals who produce and use different media.

Religion-Online/Online-Religion: 'Religion-Online' is where religious believers or religious institutions use their sites as a way of attempting to communicate about their beliefs and practices, often a one-to-many form of communication. 'Online-Religion' is where individuals or groups adapt their communicative practices in the wake of the new communication technologies, often a many-to-many form of communication. These practices are now commonly merging.

Representation: (In a media context) the act of representing people, things or events in words and images, and in accordance with media values, rhetoric and mission.

Further reading

Campbell, Heidi (2010). *When Religion Meets New Media*. London and New York, NY: Routledge. A discussion of how religions adopt and adapt new media for their own ends, with international examples.

Mitchell, Jolyon (2007). *Media Violence and Christian Ethics*. Cambridge: Cambridge University Press. Includes detailed discussion of how audiences remember, reframe and redescribe news about violence, as well as interact with film, advertising and new media.

Mitchell, Jolyon and Owen Gower (eds) (forthcoming). *Religion and the News*. Aldershot: Ashgate. Both academic and professional perspectives on the reporting of religion in the British news media.

Mitchell, Jolyon and Sophia Marriage (eds) (2003). *Mediating Religion: Conversations in Media, Religion and Culture*. London and New York, NY: T&T Clark. A collection of articles on media and religion with annotated bibliographies.

Poole, Elizabeth (2002). *Reporting Islam: Media Representations of British Muslims*. London: I. B. Tauris. An analysis of British newspaper portrayals of Islam.

Taira, Teemu, Elizabeth Poole and Kim Knott (forthcoming). 'Religion in the British Media Today', in Jolyon Mitchell and Owen Gower (eds), *Religion in the News*. Aldershot: Ashgate. A summary of research conducted in 2008–2010 on British media portrayals of religion.

Viney, Rachel (1999). 'Religious Broadcasting on UK Television: Policy, Public Perception and Programmes', *Cultural Trends*, 9/36: 1–28. An examination of religious broadcasting, policy and programming in the 1990s.

References

Allen, Chris (2010). *Islamophobia*. Farnham: Ashgate.

Ang, Ien (1994). 'Understanding Television Audiencehood', in Horace Newcomb (ed.), *Television: The Critical View*. 5th edition. Oxford: Oxford University Press, 367–386.

Appadurai, Arjun (1996). *Modernity at Large: Cultural Dimensions of Globalization*. Minneapolis, MN: University of Minnesota Press.

Aston, Nigel and Matthew Cragoe (eds) (2001). *Anticlericalism: From the Reformation to the First World War*. Stroud: Sutton Publishing.

Barr, Andrew (c. 2006). 'About *Songs of Praise* Past and Present', *BBC Online*. Online. Available HTTP: www.bbc.co.uk/songsofpraise/about.shtml (accessed 20 August 2010).

Bloom, Philip (2007). *Religion in Britain*. Online. Available HTTP: www.youtube.com/results?search_query=religion+britain&aq=f (accessed 10 December 2010).

Briggs, Asa (1995). *The History of Broadcasting in the United Kingdom. Volume IV: Sound and Vision 1945–55*. Oxford: Oxford University Press.

Brown, Callum G. (2001). *The Death of Christian Britain*. London and New York, NY: Routledge.

Campbell, Heidi (2005). *Exploring Religious Community Online: We are One in the Network*. New York, NY: Peter Lang.

Campbell, Heidi (2010). *When Religion Meets New Media*. London and New York, NY: Routledge.

Clark, Lynn Schofield (2003). *From Angels to Aliens: Teenagers, the Media and the Supernatural*. Oxford: Oxford University Press.

Clifford, Lizzie (2009). *Introduction to the 'Thought for the Day' Debate*, Ekklesia. Online. Available HTTP: www.ekklesia.co.uk/research/thought_for_the_day (accessed 2 January 2011).

Clifford, Lizzie (2010). *'Thought for the Day': Beyond the God-of-the-slots*, Ekklesia. Online. Available HTTP: www.ekklesia.co.uk/thought_for_the_day/main_report (accessed 2 January 2011).

Cooper, Thomas W. (2011). *Fast Media: Media Fast*. Boulder, CO: Gaeta Press.

Couldry, Nick (2003). *Media Rituals: A Critical Approach*. London and New York, NY: Routledge.

Cupitt, Don (1980). *Taking Leave of God*. London: SCM.

Dawkins, Richard (2006). *The God Delusion*. London: Bantam Press.

Dayan, Daniel and Eliyu Katz (1992). *Media Events: The Live Broadcasting of History*. Cambridge, MA: Harvard University Press.

Fore, William F. (1987). *Television and Religion: The Shaping of Faith, Values and Culture*. Minneapolis, MN: Augsburg Fortress.

Green, Jonathon (1982). *A Dictionary of Contemporary Quotations*. London: Pan.

Heelas, Paul and Linda Woodhead (2005). *The Spiritual Revolution: Why Religion is Giving Way to Spirituality*. Oxford: Blackwell.

Helland, Christopher (2000). 'Online-Religion/Religion-Online and Virtual Communities', in Jeffrey K. Hadden and Douglas E. Cowan (eds), *Religion on the Internet: Research Prospects and Promises*. New York, NY: JAI Press, 205–223.

Hitchens, Christopher (2007). *God is Not Great: How Religion Poisons Everything*. London: Atlantic Books.

Hoover, Stewart M. (2006) *Religion in the Media Age*. New York, NY: Routledge.

Hoover, Stewart M. and Lynn Schofield Clark (eds) (2002). *Practicing Religion in the Age of Media: Explorations in Media, Religion and Culture*. New York, NY: Columbia University Press.

Hope City Church. Online. Available HTTP: www.hopecitychurch.tv/ (accessed 2 January 2011).

Horsfield, Peter, Mary E. Hess and Adan M. Medrano (eds) (2005). *Belief in Media: Cultural Perspectives on Media and Christianity*. Aldershot: Ashgate.

How Much Information (2003). Online. Available HTTP: www2.sims.berkeley.edu/research/projects/how-much-info-2003/execsum.htm (accessed 2 January 2011).

Internet World Stats. Online. Available HTTP: www.internetworldstats.com/stats.htm (accessed 2 January 2011).

Jenkins, Philip (1996). *Pedophiles and Priests: Anatomy of a Contemporary Crisis*. New York, NY: Oxford University Press.

Johnson, Phillip E. (1993). *Darwin on Trial*. Downers Grove, IL: Inter-Varsity Press.

Knott, Kim (1984). *Media Portrayals of Religion and their Reception: Final Report*. Leeds: University of Leeds.

Lewis, C. S. (1952). *Mere Christianity*. London: Geoffrey Bles.

Lewis, C. S. 'Mere Christianity', *Truth According to Scripture*. Online. Available HTTP: www.truthaccordingtoscripture.com/documents/apologetics/mere-christianity/cs-lewis-mere-christianity-toc.php (accessed 28 December 2010).

Lövheim, Mia (2004). 'Young People, Religious Identity, and the Internet', in Lorne L. Dawson and Douglas E. Cowan (eds), *Religion Online: Finding Faith on the Internet*. New York, NY: Routledge, 59–73.

Lull, James (1991). *China Turned On: Television, Reform and Resistance*. London and New York, NY: Routledge.

Meyrowitz, Joshua (1986). *No Sense of Place: The Impact of Electronic Media on Social Behavior*. New York, NY: Oxford University Press.

Mitchell, Jolyon P. (1999). *Visually Speaking: Radio and the Renaissance of Preaching*. Edinburgh: T&T Clark.

Mitchell, Jolyon (2003). 'Emerging Conversations in the Study of Media, Religion and Culture', in Jolyon Mitchell and Sophia Marriage (eds), *Mediating Religion: Conversations in Media, Religion and Culture*. Edinburgh: Continuum/T&T Clark.

Mitchell, Jolyon (2005) 'Christianity and Television: Guest Editorial', *Studies in World Christianity*, 11/1: 1–8.

Mitchell, Jolyon (2007a). *Media Violence and Christian Ethics*. Cambridge: Cambridge University Press.

Mitchell, Jolyon (2007b). 'In Search of Online Religion', *Studies in World Christianity*, 13/3: 205–207.

Mitchell, Jolyon and Owen Gower (eds) (forthcoming). *Religion and the News*. Aldershot: Ashgate.

Mitchell, Jolyon and Sophia Marriage (eds) (2003). *Mediating Religion: Conversations in Media, Religion and Culture*. London and New York, NY: T&T Clark.

Moore, Kerry, Paul Mason and Justin Lewis (2008). *Images of Islam in the UK: The Representation of British Muslims in the National Print News Media 2000–2008*. Cardiff: Cardiff School of Journalism, Media and Cultural Studies.

Newbigin, Lesslie (1989). *The Gospel in a Pluralist Society*. Grand Rapids, MI: Eerdmans.

Noonan, Caitriona (2008). 'The Production of Religious Broadcasting: The Case of the BBC', unpublished PhD thesis, University of Glasgow.

Poole, Elizabeth (2002). *Reporting Islam: Media Representations of British Muslims*. London: I. B. Tauris.

Richard Dawkins Foundation for Reason and Science. Online. Available HTTP: http://richarddawkins.net/ (accessed 28 December 2010).

Robinson, John (1963). *Honest to God*. London: SCM.

Runnymede Trust (1997). *Islamophobia: A Challenge for Us All*. London: Runnymede Trust.

Schwarz, Barry (2004). *The Paradox of Choice*. New York, NY: Harper Perennial.

Stott, John (1958). *Basic Christianity*. Downers Grove, IL: Inter-Varsity Press.

Taira, Teemu, Elizabeth Poole and Kim Knott (forthcoming). 'Religion in the British Media Today', in Jolyon Mitchell and Owen Gower (eds), *Religion in the News*. Aldershot: Ashgate.

Thompson, John B. (1995). *The Media and Modernity: A Social Theory of the Media*. Cambridge: Polity.

Turkle, Sherry (2011). *Alone Together: Why We Expect More from Technology and More from Each Other*. New York, NY: Basic Books.

Viney, Rachel (1999). 'Religious Broadcasting on UK Television: Policy, Public Perception and Programmes', *Cultural Trends*, 9/36: 1–28.

Wimber, John (1986). *Power Evangelism*. San Francisco, CA: Harper Row.

Wolfe, Kenneth (1984). *The Churches and the British Broadcasting Corporation 1922–1956: The Politics of Broadcast Religion*. London: SCM.

Notes

1 Online. Available HTTP: http://news.bbc.co.uk/1/hi/entertainment/1243339.stm (accessed 1 January 2011).

2 See, for example, photograph by Philip Gendreau, 'Portrait of a family seated fireside listening to a radio', 1940s. Online. Available HTTP: www.corbisimages.com/Enlargement/BE067880.html (accessed 1 January 2011).

3 Elements of this section are developed from Mitchell (2005).

4 Disputes on these matters led to the following legal cases: *Chaplin v. Royal Devon and Exeter NHS Foundation Trust*, [2010] ET 1702886/2009, *Eweida v. British Airways Plc*, [2010] EWCA Civ 80 and *Cain v. Devon County Council*, [2009].

5 As part of the AHRC/ESRC Religion and Society funded project 'Media Portrayals of Religion and the Secular Sacred' discussed further later.
6 See OFCOM report on radio citing a RAJAR study. Online. Available HTTP: http://stakeholders.ofcom.org.uk/market-data-research/market-data/communications-market-reports/cmr09/keypoints/ (accessed 1 January 2011).
7 For more details see online. Available HTTP: http://news.bbc.co.uk/1/hi/programmes/bbc_parliament/2003023.stm (accessed 1 January 2011).
8 Elements of this section are developed from Mitchell (2007b).

Case study 5

Religion, youth cultures and popular music

Brendan Stuart and Christopher Partridge

This case study maps the relationship between youth cultures, popular music, religion and spirituality in post-war Britain. It brings to a focus several key themes explored elsewhere in the book, especially in Chapters 4 ('Alternative spiritualities') and 10 ('Cultural perspectives'). It examines how youth cultures – particularly those not associated with traditional forms of religion – have expressed and reflected changes in the expression of, and attitudes towards, religion from the collective youth cultures of the 1960s, through Generation X's more individualistic turn, to Generation Y's apparent disengagement.

As if to highlight the centrality of music to religion in British culture, David Martin has gone so far as to claim that the hymn is 'the central item in English religion' (1967: 88). As traditional forms of worship declined in post-war Britain, the relationship between religion and popular culture found new avenues for expression as successive, distinctive, self-determining youth cultures discovered, explored and invested in the development of religious understandings through the popular music cultures of their day. This extended the confluence of political radicalism and religion beyond the walls of the church articulated by prior generations of folk musicians, singers and visionaries (see Young 2010), and produced many of the continuities and discontinuities which frame contemporary religious beliefs and practices.

Music, drugs and the emergence of youth culture

Rejecting a post-war retrenchment of traditional forms of religious practice and codes of morality, created by 'a bohemian and "delinquent" minority' and fuelled by the relative affluence of the 1950s and 1960s (Davis 1990: 118), a newly emergent, independent youth culture, centred on skiffle and rock'n'roll music, provided an 'alternative discursive world' (Brown 2001: 174). Standing in opposition to the cultural, moral and religious mores of the day, it informed the nonconformist spiritual agendas of subsequent youth cultures, from the hippies, to punk rock, to rave culture (see Partridge 2006; St John 2009).

From its origins, it has not been difficult to identify the close relationship that exists between rock 'n' roll and religion and spirituality; many artists, from the early blues players onwards, owe an enormous debt to religious communities and their musical traditions. In particular, Pentecostal music and worship, with its ecstatic performative aspects, its beat-oriented music, its embodied exuberance and its creation of heightened emotional states has significantly influenced post-war popular music cultures. Many early artists, such as Elvis,

Johnny Cash (Sun Records), Marvin Gaye, Berry Gordy (Motown), Ray Charles (Atlantic Records, ABC Records), Sam Cooke (Specialty Records), were explicitly influenced by Pentecostal worship (Mosher 2008) and by particular religious performers, such as Sister Rosetta Tharpe (Decca). Many of these artists, of course, included gospel songs in their repertoires.

Rock 'n' roll accompanied the emergence of youth gaining collective societal recognition and relevance as a coherent social category. Youth groups prior to the Second World War, such as the Scouting Movement and Boys' Brigades, had tended largely to be linked with the church. In contrast, however, post-war youth culture was distinctly autonomous. By the 1960s access to technology increased and cultural products became increasingly oriented towards youth culture (see DeGroot 2008). The flourishing of 'pirate radio', 'the underground' and counter-cultural magazines began to shape the thinking of a new generation. Popular music became 'central to the signification of power' (Brown 2001: 178), from the emergence of politically informed songwriters such as Bob Dylan and Joan Baez to the mysticism and occultism of, for example, The Beatles' *Sgt. Pepper's Lonely Hearts Club Band* (Parlophone 1967) and The Rolling Stones' *Their Satanic Majesties Request* (Decca 1967).

Popular music witnessed a thematic shift from romance to occultism, existentialism and drug-induced mysticism in the 1960s (see Thompson 2008; DeGroot 2008). Greatly influenced by the use of LSD and cannabis, musicians took drugs to make music to take drugs to. By the end of the 1960s, the 'occulture' (Partridge 2005) of 'the underground' was becoming saturated with spiritual ideas from the East and a fascination with the subject matter of 'Gothic horror' and occult films and novels. Increasingly, these ideas were disseminated by the music industry in lyrics, performance, fashion and album art. Prominent examples include, again, The Beatles' *Sgt. Pepper's* album, the cover of The Incredible String Band's *5,000 Spirits or the Layers of an Onion* (Elektra 1967), and the music and the artwork of Black Sabbath's debut album, *Black Sabbath* (Vertigo 1970).

The baby boomers and Generation X

Collective purpose can be considered a defining theme of the 1960s 'baby boomer' generation, culturally and spiritually, as its members embedded the notion of 'youth as collective'. Behind the mantras of 'peace' and 'love', anti-war protests, anti-fascist politics, and human rights campaigns for racial and sexual equality were politically oriented sub-cultures united by music and style. Whilst, of course, members of youth sub-cultures were not all equally engaged, there existed a sense of collective responsibility. As traditional forms of religious and political affiliation lost support, alternative traditions became the focus of a 'generation of seekers' (Roof 1993). 'Seeking' became, paradoxically, simultaneously both an individual and a collective experience. Whilst 'the self' assumed greater spiritual importance, this change was happening across the generational culture, collectivity being sought and experienced in numerous religio-political spaces, from hippie 'love-ins' to alternative music festivals, and from experimental communes in Britain to ashrams and kibbutzim in India and Israel.

Coming of age in the mid-1970s, Generation X reframed religious practice and adherence in Britain. Instrumental to the explosion of punk (arguably the seminal youth cultural expression of opposition and independence) and 'new wave', which subsequently had a formative influence on the emergence of contemporary dub, techno, trance and rave (see Partridge 2006, 2010), this generation witnessed the hermeneutical shift 'from "public" event to "private" gnosis' (Sutcliffe 2003: 107) evident in much New Age spirituality. As if to confirm this turn to the self, punk nihilism insisted that the only person one could trust was oneself. With increased access to the means of musical production, Generation X witnessed the fragmentation of youth culture into multitudinous manifestations of individual expression, many questioning received codes of belief and behaviour. New spiritualities and systems of belief became as valid as traditions with long histories and complex theologies, often championed by popular musicians within particular musical cultures (see Cohen 1999). Whether the Satanism and occultism of black metal, the vampirism of Goth rock, the ambient spirituality inspired by New Age music or the Easternized psychedelia of psytrance, these developed and disseminated particular occultural ideas and themes; in turn leading to the emergence of distinct spiritual sub-cultures.

Festivals and travellers

Having modern roots in several large-scale events in the 1960s and early 1970s, notably Woodstock in the USA and the Isle of Wight, Glastonbury and Stonehenge Festivals in the UK, music festivals have emerged as the most socially significant spiritually oriented, counter-cultural 'happenings'. They present the principal visible indicator of the enduring vitality of popular music as a communal force. Seeking to retreat from a society perceived to be inhibited, materialist, violent and repressive, festivals have frequently become sites for counter-cultural experimentation and the search for authentic spirituality eclectically drawn from a range of discourses, including those of communal love and an indigenous esoteric relationship to the land.

Emerging partly as a protest against the commercialism and capitalism of large-scale festivals, the free festival in particular represented a microcosm of a new, utopian society. They were seeking to become what the anarchist thinker Hakim Bey (2003) has since termed a 'TAZ' (temporary autonomous zone), where members freely contribute to an economy based on mutual aid rather than money: 'The nature of a free festival is just that: freedom. You can do what you like, it doesn't matter how bizarre, as long as it doesn't impinge upon other people. No moralism. No prohibitions. Only the limits of common humanity, aware of our responsibility to each other and to the earth we all share' (Stone 1996: 185). Held for ten years between 1974 and 1984, Stonehenge is generally acknowledged to be the most important of the free festivals. A blend of music, counter-cultural politics and alternative spirituality, its location at the site of Britain's most famous prehistoric monument represents a meeting of the past and the present, a connection with pre-modern religion and culture. It was initiated by Phil Russell, described by his friend Jeremy Ratter as 'an English Shaman ... an animist ... involved in magical processes' (Stone 1996: 82), who wanted to 'claim back Stonehenge (a place he regarded as sacred to the people and stolen by the government) and make it a site for free festivals, free music, free space, free mind' (Rimbaud 1981: 7).

From the late 1970s, the 'New Age Travellers' became a central feature of the annual cycle of free festivals. As the free festival scene evolved, so groups of people travelled from one gathering to the next:

> By the end of the 1970s a regular summer circuit had been established. From May Hill at the beginning of May via the Horseshoe Pass, Stonehenge, Ashton Court, Ingleston Common, Cantlin Stone, Deeply Vale, Meigan Fair, and various sites in East Anglia, to the Psilocybin Fair in mid-Wales in September, it was possible to find a free festival ... almost every weekend.
>
> (Aitken 1990: 18)

Travelling this circuit, setting up festivals and, often, selling psychedelics along the way, was a band of hippies which became known as 'the Peace Convoy' because of its increasing involvement in anti-nuclear demonstrations. Moreover, they established 'a neo-medieval economy based around crafts, alternative medicine and entertainment: jugglers, acrobats, healers, food vendors, candle makers, clothes sellers, tattooists, piercers, jewellers, and drug peddlers' (Reynolds 1998: 136). Described by the then Home Secretary Douglas Hurd as 'medieval brigands', by the end of the 1980s, some, perhaps exaggerated, accounts calculated that the number of travellers had reached 40,000 (see Stone 1996: 153). Critical of their alternative lifestyles, the press soon dismissed them as 'New Age Travellers'. Having said that, the label is broadly accurate, in that, like the free festivals in which they had their genesis, they drew on many of the ideas and practices commonly associated with 'New Age' spirituality and the turn to the self. As Kevin Hetherington observed, not only were 'many of the forms of religiosity and therapy associated with the New Age' of interest to them, but there was 'some resonance between the Travellers' outlook and that of the wider New Age movement' (Hetherington 2000: 12). Indeed, there was, initially at least, much more than *some* resonance.

Meanwhile, on the beaches of Goa and then Ibiza, the confluence of Easternized psychedelic hippie culture and techno music produced a spiritually oriented, electronic dance culture. A new generation of musicians utilized developments in electronic instrumentation and production techniques, enhanced by the use of the drug MDMA (Ecstasy) to produce a definitive reaction to the punk and new wave rejection of the 'hippie' confluence of popular music and spirituality; punk nihilism gave way to renewed notions of 'feeling' and love. The eventual coming together of this new youth culture based around dance and the remnants of the New Age Travellers would lead to the events at the Castlemorton Common Festival (near Malvern in Worcestershire), an illegal free festival in 1992 at which up to 40,000 ravers and travellers partied for five days. The biggest free event since the demise of the Stonehenge Festival, it attracted significant media interest, which served to increase the numbers attending, making it too difficult for the police to shut down. There is little doubt that it served as a catalyst which led to the Criminal Justice and Public Order Act, a draconian piece of legislation introduced by Michael Howard in 1994, which effectively outlawed such events and suppressed alternative lifestyles. This, in turn, led to the reinvigoration of commercial music festivals which had suffered as a result of alcohol-, amphetamine- and urban-gang-fuelled crime and previous legislative tightening.

Youth culture in the 1980s and 1990s

The youth culture of the 1980s and 1990s was more cynical and politically disengaged than that of the 1960s. As Tom Beaudoin comments, 'much of my generation's antipathy to grand social movements comes from opposition to the idealism of the Baby Boomers in the 1960s' (1998: 10). As to why this might be, Davis highlights the economic deprivations of the 1980s recession, which contributed significantly to youth unemployment. That is to say, the economic climate was:

> too harsh to support the continuance of any large-scale positive cult of youth … At the same time youth sub-cultures and groupings have themselves become too fragmentary – and too commercial, too deviant or too alienated in image – to sustain the idea of youth as a ('progressive') class.

> (Davis 1990: 214)

Contributing to this fragmentation and decline were the actions of the authorities, such as the revoking of live music licences in the wake of punk events, the suppression of the 1980s counter-culture, violently culminating in the 'Battle of the Beanfield' in 1985 (effectively ending the summer free festival circuit), the Entertainments (Increased Penalties) Act 1990 and, following Castlemorton, The Criminal Justice and Public Order Act 1994 introduced in order to close down raves.

From the early 1990s, mainstream youth culture increasingly lacked innovative expression. The musical and cultural models of the past were reworked without establishing distinctively new positions, fulfilling collective spiritual expression in charity concerts rather than inspiring distinctively novel cultural gatherings. Again, one of the most important new genres to emerge in recent years, rap (and the related hip-hop), managed to migrate into other musical genres, but in so doing diminished its ability to convey a significant socio-spiritual message. Musical nonconformity increasingly represented a rejection of Generation X's emphasis on authenticity, and popular music markets became dominated by 'processed pop' acts (e.g. Spice Girls, Atomic Kitten, Boyzone) promoted as much for visual appearance as for talent and exhibiting little by way of creative innovation or socio-spiritual positioning. This period is likewise marked by the corporate appropriation of the symbols of religio-spiritual meaning and the packaging of both traditional and non-traditional belief practices into personal 'wellbeing' services.

Into the present

There is some evidence that 'Generation Y', defined by some as those born in the 1980s, exhibit little explicit spiritual interest, being focused on, argues Peter Brierley, 'happiness … achievable, primarily, through relationships with family and close friends, and the creative assumption of the resources of popular culture'. As for 'the lack of relevance of Christian faith to young people', this is, he observes, simply 'because they know hardly anything about it' (2006: 118). Indeed, as Alasdair Crockett and David Voas comment, 'for many young people, disconnected belief is giving way to no belief at all' (2005: 13; cf. Possamai 2005: 128) – but see the counter-evidence in Case study 3.

As for technological innovation and new social media, these present new opportunities for the location of the development of youth cultural expression and affiliation, providing opportunities for youths to express and experience themselves without the intercession and mediation of others (Chapter 7). By 2005, for example, downloads were included for the first time in the charts of music sales and the Arctic Monkeys became the first band to fully benefit from self-production, self-promotion and distribution via the internet, at one point outselling the combined remainder of the 'Top 40' album charts (BBC 2006). However, the development of this technology and youth interaction with it has, so far, made little significant impact on collective expressions of youth culture in Britain and it remains to be seen if and how this might translate into new, lasting expressions of religion.

Each generation of youth, Gordon Lynch (2006) argues, both sacralizes and draws its collective identity from the popular music of the time and attendant cultural forms and, although little work has been done to establish how audiences utilize popular music for their individual religious purposes, it remains clear that such utilization occurs. Music's centrality to youth cultures in the post-war period has seen the emergence of behaviours analogous to those in religion, the 'stars' of the day providing the liturgical soundtrack. Robin Sylvan places popular music at the heart of modern religious expression, locating in it the 'religious functions of community, meaning, and experience of the numinous' (Lynch 2006: 482; see also Sylvan 2002), whilst Johannes Eurich claims that 'within youth culture, pop music offers a wide area for the search to encounter the Absolute, meeting existence itself' (Eurich 2003: 58).

References

Aitken, Don (1990). '20 Years of Free Festivals in Britain', *Festival Eye*: 18–21.

BBC (2006). 'Arctic Monkeys Make Chart History', *BBC News Online*. Online. Available HTTP: http//news.bbc.co.uk/1/hi/entertainment/4660394.stm (accessed 3 April 2009).

Beaudoin, Tom (1998). *Virtual Faith: The Irreverent Spiritual Quest of Generation X*. New York, NY: Jossey-Bass.

Bey, Hakim (2003). *T.A.Z. The Temporary Autonomous Zone, Ontological Anarchy, Poetic Terrorism*. 2nd edition. Brooklyn, NY: Autonomedia.

Brierley, Peter (2006). *Pulling Out of the Nosedive: A Contemporary Picture of Churchgoing*. London: Christian Research.

Brown, Callum G. (2001). *The Death of Christian Britain: Understanding Secularisation 1800–2000*. London and New York, NY: Routledge.

Cohen, Sara (1999). 'Scenes', in Bruce Horner and Thom Swiss (eds), *Key Terms in Popular Music and Culture*. Oxford: Blackwell, 239–250.

Crockett, Alasdair and David Voas (2005). 'Religion in Britain: Neither Believing nor Belonging', *Sociology*, 39/1: 11–28.

Davis, John (1990). *Youth and the Condition of Britain: Images of Adolescent Conflict*. London: Athlone Press.

DeGroot, Gerard (2008). *The 60s Unplugged: A Kaleidoscopic History of a Disorderly Decade*. London: Macmillan.

Eurich, Johannes (2003). 'Sociological Aspects and Ritual Similarities in the Relationship between Pop Music and Religion', *International Review of the Aesthetics and Sociology of Music*, 34 /1: 57–70.

Hetherington, Kevin (2000). *New Age Travellers: Vanloads of Uproarious Humanity*. London: Cassell.

Lynch, Gordon (2006). 'The Role of Popular Music in the Construction of Alternative Spiritual Identities and Ideologies', *Journal for the Scientific Study of Religion*, 45/4: 481–488.

Martin, David (1967). *A Sociology of English Religion*. London: SCM.

Mosher, Craig (2008). 'Ecstatic Sounds: The Influence of Pentecostalism on Rock and Roll', *Popular Music and Society*, 31/1: 95–112.

Partridge, Christopher (2005). *The Re-Enchantment of the West*, 2 vols. London: T&T Clark International.

Partridge, Christopher (2006). 'The Spiritual and the Revolutionary: Alternative Spirituality, British Free Festivals and the Emergence of Rave Culture', *Culture and Religion*, 7/1: 41–60.

Partridge, Christopher (2010). *Dub in Babylon: Understanding the Evolution and Significance of Dub Reggae in Jamaica and Britain from King Tubby to Post-punk*. London: Equinox.

Possamai, Adam (2005). *In Search of New Age Spiritualities*. Aldershot: Ashgate.

Reynolds, Simon (1998). *Energy Flash: A Journey Through Rave Music and Dance Culture*. London: Picador.

Rimbaud, Penny (1981). 'The Last of the Hippies: A Hysterical Romance', in *A Series of Shock Slogans and Mindless Token Tantrums*. Booklet distributed with Crass, *Christ – The Album*. London: Crass Records/Rough Trade, 3–13.

Roof, Wade C. (1993). *A Generation of Seekers: The Spiritual Journeys of the Baby Boom Generation*. San Francisco, CA: HarperSanFrancisco.

St John, Graham (2009). *Technomad: Global Raving Countercultures*. London: Equinox.

Stone, Chris J. (1996). *Fierce Dancing: Adventures in the Underground*. London: Faber & Faber.

Sutcliffe, Steven J. (2003). *Children of the New Age*. London and New York, NY: Routledge.

Sylvan, Robin (2002). *Traces of the Spirit: The Religious Dimensions of Popular Music*. New York, NY: New York University Press.

Thompson, Gordon (2008). *Please Please Me: Sixties British Pop, Inside Out*. New York, NY: Oxford University Press.

Young, Rob (2010). *Electric Eden: Unearthing Britain's Visionary Music*. London: Faber & Faber.

8   Religion, welfare and education

Adam Dinham and Robert Jackson

Continuing this part of the book's theme of religious change in various social arenas, this chapter looks at religion in relation to welfare and educational provision. The Introduction highlighted the dominating influence of the welfare project in the post-war period. This chapter discusses its impact on religion's traditional roles in providing welfare, charity, philanthropy and education. Particularly in the immediate post-war period, the state took control of many of these functions. But religious providers remained important, despite talk of the 'privatization' of religion. After the late 1970s, as the ideal of an overarching welfare state gave way to the idea of a 'mixed economy' of provision, what started to be called 'faith-based services' came back into fashion. Yet they did so in different forms (not solely church-based), with new constraints, and in new relations to the state and the market.

Despite talk of 'privatization' and 'secularization' in post-war Britain, the residual resources of faith groups preserved them as public actors, even when the welfare state was at its greatest extent. As a 'market' ideology came to challenge a 'statist' one, it was possible to justify the continuing role of religion in both welfare and education in terms of a 'free market' in both spheres which makes the most of the financial and human 'capital' which 'faith-based providers' can supply. The effect has been to move welfare and education from partly or predominantly faith-based philanthropic enterprises before 1945, through a period of statism afterwards, and then from the 1980s back out to a plurality of providers again, which explicitly includes religious groups once more, though in a greater mix of 'competition'. This is not to say that faith-based provision ceased in the period after 1945 but that it was in some sense nationalized before being set back within a much more mixed context once again after 1979.

We explore these trajectories of change in this chapter, but there are two important caveats. First, religious change in the context of these processes should not be understood as inevitable. This is not a story of inexorable, impersonal and irreversible forces. Politics have been deliberate rather than incidental in debates and decisions about the public and social roles of religion. Schools policy *decided* to prefer non-confessional religious education (RE) in schools, though it reflected and consolidated changes that were also 'bottom up', as we shall see. Welfare policy *intended* to impose a control and command structure to address social need. And government *promoted* a multi-faith approach to social cohesion. These changes have been variously resisted and embraced. Second, the recent extension and reassertion of religious provision represent a shift from an emphasis on religion as 'belief' to religion as 'resource'. 'Faith', in policy parlance, becomes something which may (or may not) be useful and, moreover, 'usable' by the state and civil society.

Overall, this chapter suggests that what has happened over the post-war period has been the *deliberate* marginalization of religious socialization post-1945, especially from the late 1960s, resulting both from policy and from bottom-up changes, followed by the *accidental* re-emergence of religious social action in welfare and education after 1980. The resulting gap between thought and action accounts in large part for the poor quality of public debate about contemporary religion, which tends to ambivalence at best. As the chapter will conclude, it also means that many other aspects of religion, including beliefs and values, come to be treated as incidentals at best, or annoying encumbrances at worst.

Religion, welfare and change

Religious groups in Britain have been undergoing great change in relation to welfare since 1945. There is a long tradition of faith-based involvement in meeting 'welfare' needs, especially in urban and disadvantaged areas. John Wesley, the eighteenth-century revivalist, proclaimed that believers should not only 'earn all you can' and 'save all you can' but also 'give all you can' (Wesley 1771: 705–712). Religious or faith-based service provision is rooted in Victorian philanthropy, when society 'boasted millions of religious associations providing essential services and a moral training for citizenry' (Prochaska 2006: 2). The Victorians, in this view, 'believed that religion and the public good were inextricably linked' (Prochaska 2006: 3) and that 'charity could only be effectively exercised under the influence of sacred principle' (Prochaska 2006: 3). Bowpitt (2007: 2) notes that:

> While Florence Nightingale walked with her lamp in the hospitals of the Crimea, Ellen Ranyard's Bible nurses tramped the streets of London, giving comfort and medical help to the sick and dying in their own homes, inspired by the longing that none should leave this world without being prepared for the next.

He also comments that 'other areas of Christian philanthropy reflected the character of Victorian society and appear anachronistic to us now' (Bowpitt 2007: 2), for example the practice of 'district visiting' to all the inhabitants of a neighbourhood, the point of which was to show that no one was beyond the love of Christ.

The Victorian period has sometimes been seen as a golden age for faith-based (or more accurately, Christian and church-based) social action and welfare, involving among many other things '2,349 subsidiary associations to dispense the Bible' (Prochaska 2006: 17) at a time when 'myriad parish societies ... had membership numbers that varied from under ten to hundreds' (Prochaska 2006: 17–18). The role of the churches was widely seen as both legitimate and necessary. From a missiological point of view it was seen as the duty of people of faith to provide for need. Thus for Alexis de Tocqueville, Christianity was 'not an opiate, nor a morality of slaves but a religion of self-discipline and personal service that answered social and political needs' (in Prochaska 2006: 26). In his memoir on pauperism written in 1835 after a visit to England, de Tocqueville writes that one of the merits of Christianity is that it makes charity a divine virtue.

As has been well rehearsed in the social policy literature, and discussed in the Introduction to this volume, the extension of the franchise, the rise of a middle class and a growing awareness of grinding poverty culminated in the crucible of the war years in the 1940s in the emergence of a radically different approach to welfare. This shifted the emphasis from (voluntary) charity and philanthropy to (state) government. This was a period of statism which regarded welfare as far too important to leave to well-meaning amateurs –

including faith groups. It crystallized in the UK in the establishment of universal welfare after the Second World War – a strategic, nationalized commitment to intervention which incorporated and consolidated all sorts of 'welfare professionals' in the state's employ. These included doctors, nurses, midwives, district nurses and health visitors, dentists, social workers, teachers, probation workers and even (for a short time) community development workers. The idealism of universal welfare proved too strong an influence for a disparate non-governmental mix of service provision to elude. Practically every aspect of social service, from health, to employment, to family and community was incorporated in a hugely extended public policy arena – the very social contract which has been questioned since the debt crisis following 2008 which, though it emerged as a crisis of credit in private banks, was often recast as a public sector crisis caused by profligacy in spending on public services and welfare.

The nationalization of services in the 1940s also had an instant effect on their funding, since the welfare state encouraged the expectation that needs would be met without resort to charity. Philanthropy was recast as paternalistic, disempowering and unjust. The philanthropic approach was largely rejected and the Labour Party's critique displaced philanthropy with optimism that the state would eradicate social ills. Prochaska (2006) observes, nevertheless, that the welfare state, when it did come, inherited much of the Christian 'spirit' embodied in Victorian philanthropy, and cannot simply be read as the secularization of services which had hitherto been provided by faiths. Bowpitt (2007) cites the example of social work as a competitor to faith-based philanthropy well before 1948, arguing that social work as a secular humanist alternative was emerging from an ideological struggle for the heart of social welfare long before the advent of the welfare state. Statist welfare may have consolidated the decline of religious significance in welfare, but it does not mark the beginning of these processes. Neither does it mark the end of the involvement of faith in welfare.

A first wave of critique in the post-war period observed that the welfare settlement had failed to eradicate the 'five evils' and much of the blame was placed on an overemphasis on physical and material solutions embodied in huge new housing estates. To counter this, community-based policies were introduced which were rooted in neighbourhood and self-help – precisely the sorts of work faith-based providers had been so good at. In this period, community work came to be seen as 'a third method of social work intervention' (Younghusband 1959: 24) alongside group work and case work. Much of this new community work took place in local projects, many initiated by faith groups. This was in part a result of the Church of England's parish system which ensured that there were staff, buildings and resources in every area of the country. Concurrently, the Gulbenkian Report envisaged work in communities which is 'concerned with affecting the course of social change through the two processes of analysing social situations and forming relationships with different groups to bring about desirable change' (Younghusband 1968: 22). It identified three key values which were to prove significant: first, people matter, and policies and public administration should be judged by their effects on people; second, participation in decision-making about every aspect of life is of fundamental importance to human flourishing; third, work in communities should be concerned with the distribution of resources towards people who are socially disadvantaged. This provided a context with which faiths could identify in terms of an insistence on human worth and value and on structural critiques of society which refused to locate the causes of poverty and disadvantage with the people who suffered from its consequences. This was the first 'new space' for faith-based welfare after the welfare consensus. It proved short-lived. The structural socio-economic critiques endangered community-based approaches by being critical of government policy.

This came to a head in the Community Development Projects (CDPs) in the late 1960s and early 1970s. A report arising from one of the CDPs, called *Gilding the Ghetto*, was critical of government. Government subsequently (and quietly) closed the CDPs down, and the community approach to addressing welfare needs was over. This residue of faith-based provision was once again privatized.

But a second 'new space' has opened up since, in surprising ways. A shift in welfare to 'market led approaches in the 1980s and early 1990s' (Mayo 2000: 28) marked a conscious move towards provision of all sorts of services, not by government, but by voluntary sector agencies, regarded as cheaper, more efficient and more knowledgeable about local needs. While this was driven ideologically by monetarist economics which saw the welfare state as part of the problem, not the solution, it has been criticized for failing to achieve the hoped-for reduction in the role of the state. In practice it led to an increase in regulation of non-government services which placed a massive bureaucratic strain, both on providers and on the civil service which had to monitor them. In addition, the process of becoming a provider was usually based on contracts awarded on a competitive basis. This was criticized for making the winner the cheapest bidder rather than the best, and for introducing market competitive values and practices instead of collaborative ones which would better serve communities. Nevertheless, faith-based providers have consistently occupied the space this created, either by turning existing services in its direction or by introducing new ones. The faith-based contribution in Britain could, once again, not only be made but also acknowledged.

In recent years it has become fashionable for faith-based bodies to research and demonstrate their 'contribution' and this has often been put forward in economic terms. This has led the National Council for Voluntary Organisations (NCVO) to conclude that 'faith-based organizations are "a strong force" in the charitable sector, which encompasses a large range of social action projects and programmes' (National Council for Voluntary Organisations 2007: 15). Within this, many charities are engaged in religious activities, and NCVO's 2007 report states that at least one registered charity in seven is thus engaged. It is noted that: 'The total income of faith-based registered charities is estimated at £4.6 billion', though income appears to be unevenly spread across organizations so that 'those with an income of less than £200,000 account for 90 per cent of organizations but generate only 11 per cent of the total income' (National Council for Voluntary Organisations 2007: 16). This reflects the case that many faith-based organizations are very small, informal and heavily dependent on volunteers, though a few others are among some of the largest of all charities.

It is also noted that over half of faith-based charities aim to serve the general public, not just their own tradition, and two-fifths place a particular focus on children or young people (National Council for Voluntary Organisations 2007: 15). Grant-making for welfare projects is the majority area of activity (56 per cent of faith-based organizations) followed by welfare service provision (35 per cent) (National Council for Voluntary Organisations 2007: 15). This is supported in other research which shows that a significant amount of work across England focuses on children/young people and the elderly, although faith-based organizations are engaged in many other activities (see Dinham 2007: 9).

In each of the nine English regions there has been some sort of mapping of faith-based social welfare activity to identify what faith groups are doing. In some regions this has been extensive. Thus, *Beyond Belief?* (Southeast England Faith Forum 2004) claimed that there were at least two welfare projects for each faith centre in the South-East. *Faith in the East of England* (East of England Faiths Council and the University of Cambridge 2005) identified 180,000 beneficiaries of faith-based activity in the East. *Neighbourhood Renewal in London*

(Greater London Enterprise/London Churches Group 2002) identified 7,000 projects and 2,200 faith buildings in London. *Believing in the Region* (Regional Action West Midlands 2006) reported 80 per cent of faith groups delivering some kind of service to the wider community in the West Midlands. *Faith in England's Northwest* (Northwest Forum of Faiths 2003) showed faith communities to be running more than 5,000 social action projects and generating income of £69m–£94m per annum in the north-west. In Yorkshire and the Humber, *Count Us In* (Social and Economic Action Resources of Churches in Hull and District 2000) showed that in Hull 90 per cent of churches are involved in social action, and *Angels and Advocates* (Yorkshire and the Humber Churches Regional Commission 2002) reported that there were 6,500 social action projects in churches across Yorkshire and the Humber. *Faith in the North East* (Smith 2004) showed that there were more than 2,500 faith-based projects in the North-East. *Faith in Action* (Beattie *et al.* 2006) demonstrated that 165,000 people were supported by faith groups in the South-West by 4,762 activities. *Faith in Derbyshire* (Derby Diocesan Council for Social Responsibility 2006) claimed that, on average, churches ran nine community activities in the East Midlands.

While the evidence suggests that faith-based providers may be skilled and experienced at providing community-level, project-type interventions, the skills and capacities required to deliver larger-scale services as laid out in public sector contracts are of a different order. In many cases this means that faith-based organizations change shape in order to meet the new challenges and opportunities. They become recognizable 'brands' in their own right and are no longer understood primarily or popularly as 'faith-based'. Examples are of contracts run by organizations such as the YMCA (now 'Y') and the Salvation Army, whose 'social action' programmes are large but may have become dissociated from the faith base from which they started. Certainly their relationship with worshipping and fellowship communities is distended. Another example of much larger faith-based participation in the welfare sector is in housing (and provision for homelessness, as discussed in Case study 6). Housing associations are frequently faith-based, as in the example of the English Churches Housing Group, which is one of the country's largest housing associations providing homes for over 26,000 people.

There can be challenges, however, which reflect continuing attempts to protect the public realm as a secular space. An important obstacle is the mistrust of faith-based providers among funding bodies and a lack of knowledge and expertise on the parts both of the public sector and faiths at the local level (see Case study 6 on the prejudices faced by faith-based homelessness providers like the Salvation Army). For the public sector the lesson has been one of recognizing that faith groups have religious starting points and positions and sometimes their work in public spaces comes from that motivation. In other cases, faiths are motivated simply by a commitment to social justice and human fulfilment. In either case, the line between the social provision and the faith-based motivation for engagement may not be clear. This is a practical outworking of the division which secularism insists on between the public and the private.

Another pressure comes from the government's desire to encourage all the actors in the extended mixed economy, including faith groups, to develop financial self-sufficiency. Not only should the activities of welfare be taken on by organizations in civil society. So too should the costs, and the risks. This critique has gained traction since the 2008 debt crisis and government has been increasingly convinced of the need to reposition public services, not in a large public sector, but in a so-called 'Big Society'. Social enterprise and mutuality are the mechanisms by which governments in the UK would like to achieve this, and faith-based welfare activity is likely to evolve further in that direction in the coming years. The proposal is that the deconstruction of state welfare infrastructures will clear space for a wave of private and community-based social entrepreneurship, which is suppressed by current policy. It is arguable that many non-government actors, including faith groups, have been doing social enterprise for decades or even longer. An example is the Oxfam shops whose income supports wider community work in the developing world. But while many organizations might be doing social enterprise, according to some of the definitions of it, many more do not think of themselves in that way.

TEXT BOX 16

Shifting government approaches to welfare: from statism to big society

Tradition, community, family, faith, the space between the market and the state – this is the ground where our philosophy is planted.

From a speech by Prime Minister David Cameron to launch the 'Giving White Paper', in Milton Keynes, UK, 23 May 2011

The first principle is that … when the war is abolishing landmarks of every kind, [this] is the opportunity for using experience in a clear field. A revolutionary moment in the world's history is a time for revolutions, not for patching.

The second principle is that organisation of social insurance should be treated as one part only of a comprehensive policy of social progress. Social insurance fully developed may provide income security; it is an attack upon Want. But Want is one only of five giants on the road of reconstruction and in some ways the easiest to attack. The others are Disease, Ignorance, Squalor and Idleness.

The third principle is that social security must be achieved by co-operation between the State and the individual. The State should offer security for service and contribution. The State in organising security should not stifle incentive, opportunity, responsibility; in establishing a national minimum, it should leave room and encouragement for voluntary action by each individual to provide more than that minimum for himself and his family.

From The Beveridge Report, Presented to Parliament by Command of His Majesty, November 1942

A number of factors have coincided to drive an interest in social enterprise. Local authorities and other public sector bodies have passed on to new or pre-existing organizations areas of work they used to run themselves like social housing, leisure or social care, and much more of this will have to take place as their central government budgets are reduced by unprecedented amounts in the context of recession. Charities, including faith-based organizations, have to keep financially sustainable while many traditional sources of funding such as membership fees and almost all government grants become much harder to access. In the politics of meeting local needs a business or commercial approach has increasingly been perceived to be a more flexible and sustainable route to delivering multiple social benefits – members, staff and customers can all be beneficiaries in different ways.

It may be a challenging model for community-based faith groups, who make up the majority, at a number of levels. First, social enterprise requires a business ethos which may not be home territory for many faith groups whose interests often lie in questions wider than, and sometimes at odds with, accepted social hegemonies about capitalism, what makes people happy and how people should interrelate (for example, non-contractually). Profit generation, even where those profits are intended to be used for social 'goods', is a different kind of activity from that more usually engaged in by faith groups, even though there are examples of faith-based social enterprise stretching back over a long period.

The concern of many faith groups in relation to this is the invasion of their ethos and values by those of a business culture. Associated with this, too, is anxiety about the potential for separation from a core mission or set of activities. Another area of concern for faiths is the demands made by the need to 'professionalize' in market terms. Many faith-based activities are already working in highly professional ways and some have a long track record of doing so. But at the same time, the regulatory and monitoring regimes associated both with public sector contracting and with business in social enterprise and mutuals can be onerous.

The politics of the 'Big Society' also tends to look for big social actors. It sees in the Church of England the ability to lead the faith contribution. It has buildings, staff and volunteers in every neighbourhood, and political influence in Parliament. This may be a nostalgic view. As Chapter 2 reveals, things have changed for the national church. While reported affiliation holds up, attendance has steeply declined. Many parishes can no longer afford a full-time priest. Some have none at all. Churches often struggle to keep the roof on. Funds are committed to clergy pensions and the maintenance of ancient buildings. At the same time, the religious make-up of the UK has altered dramatically from the days when the churches were widely responsible for philanthropy. Religious plurality has become more embedded in the national psyche after decades of non-confessional RE (see later). In the new century a 'multi-faith society' found expression in government funding for multi-faith partnerships, and the resulting infrastructures of multi-faith bodies now reach out to ethnic and religious minorities which the Church of England struggles to reach.

So what sort of religious organizations will deliver welfare as the twenty-first century unfolds? They could go in either of two directions. In the market direction, they will emphasize competition, and large, established bodies may be most competitive, and power and resources will concentrate around them. In the community direction, they will emphasize collaboration and partnership. Local initiatives will emerge from the bottom up and reflect the interests of local people. Which prevails, and where, is still unclear. In welfare terms, what is likely to emerge is not so much the 'big society' as lots of very differently served small ones. Private providers may be well placed to deliver superstructures like hospitals or public transport; indeed, a small monopoly already do so in various private finance initiatives. Social services, such as meals on wheels, community transport, community centres and respite care, which are more locally based, and less visible, will depend upon less powerful 'big society' actors, especially volunteers.

In this context, welfare, and its faith-based providers, confronts a political sphere which both valorizes faith resources and yet gives practically no account of faith. Experience suggests that faith groups will continue to meet need, whatever the politics. It also suggests that faith itself may have a role for the first time since the Church of England's landmark challenge to church and nation, *Faith in the City* (Church of England 1985; see Introduction and Plate 2.4), in recalling people to the political dimensions of welfare. The welfare politics of the first half of the twenty-first century seem set for the first time to displace those of

1945, and religion is responding in a range of ways: from new forms of provision to critique and defence of the least powerful as huge shifts in power take place.

Religion, education and change

The post-war era has also been one of considerable change for religion as an educational provider, particularly in schools. Prior to the modern era the churches were, of course, the main educational bodies in Britain. State education was introduced in 1870, and this led to a gradual shrinkage of religion's role and place in the curriculum. This accelerated under the welfare state. But, as this section will show, the religious contribution was never fully 'privatized', and education in Britain has never been possible without the contribution of faith groups. Moreover, just as in relation to welfare, the new market emphasis since the 1980s has allowed 'faith' to become visible again, as well as generated considerable controversy about its right to do so.

From religious instruction to religious education

Modern RE in England evolved in its legal requirements and organizational arrangements after 1870. The process of structural evolution includes a radical change, namely the secularization of religious education in fully state-funded schools ('community schools'). Even though state funding for certain categories of religious school ('voluntary schools', now often called 'faith schools') was retained in the UK, the goal was no longer seen to be nurture in faith.[1]

Each step on this evolution in the post-war period reflects another twist in the tale of the struggle to manage a public religious inheritance alongside the assumption that public religion itself was dead. This has been playing out for decades, if not centuries. Religious groups have been involved since the nineteenth century in partnership with the state in the provision of schools and the curriculum subject of religious education (known then as religious instruction). Institutionally, in England, the Church of England still holds a privileged place as the established church, and it was a prime provider of mass education prior to 1870. However, religious education writing from the mid-1960s to the early 1970s began to take account of the increasing secularity and plurality of British society, notably Edwin Cox's book *Changing Aims in Religious Education* (1966) and Ninian Smart's *Secular Education and the Logic of Religion* (1968). Although there are differences in the argument of these writers, there was a general move (consistent with contemporary work in the philosophy of education and of religion) towards an epistemological justification of the place of RE in the curriculum. This was based not on religion's self-evident or publicly agreed truth, but on its role as a distinctive area of experience, 'form of knowledge' or 'realm of meaning'. At the same time, school-based RE shifted significantly from an emphasis on the teaching of Christian morality to teaching about 'world religions'. Many factors were involved. There was a 'bottom-up' disaffection with the state-funded school being used as an instrument for religious teaching (reflected in Cox's work and some local syllabuses since the late 1960s). Together with both the rise of a globally oriented Religious Studies in British universities (also influenced by Ninian Smart, see Plate 1.3) in the 1960s, and the broadening of the range of religions and religious groups within British society through immigration (see Chapter 3 and Cole 1972), this had a significant influence on the ethos and content of the school subject of RE. It brought a global dimension and an 'impartial' approach which was 'secular' rather than 'secularist'.

Smart's ideas were influential partly because they underpinned the Schools Council Secondary Project on Religious Education (established in 1969 and based at the University of Lancaster under Smart's direction) but also because they responded to the increasing dissatisfaction of many RE professionals with dogmatic approaches to their subject. *Religious Education in Secondary Schools*, the project's widely read working paper (Schools Council 1971), advocated the 'phenomenological' or undogmatic approach to RE. This approach saw the subject as developing an understanding of religions without promoting any particular religious stance, a process drawing on scholarly methods to generate empathy with those holding religious worldviews.

In general, phenomenologists of religion aimed to set aside or 'bracket out' their own presuppositions when attempting to understand another's faith and to study parallel phenomena in different religions in order to expose basic structures which give insight into the essence of 'religion'. The first of these aspects of phenomenology had very much more influence on religious educators than the second. The notion of an impartial study, with both teacher and pupil attempting to suspend their own presuppositions in empathizing with religious believers, was appealing to the many teachers who found theologically loaded approaches to RE distasteful.[2]

Certain political themes, coming to the fore at different periods, reflect these educational dimensions in wider society, as well as changing social policy towards areas such as community and 'race' relations, citizenship and community cohesion. The 1990s brought an interest in promoting democratic 'citizenship' in schools and welfare, which has influenced religious education (Jackson 2003), and led to a discourse of 'social inclusion' in place of 'welfare' (Lister with Campling 1997). Post-9/11, there has been an increase in attention to community cohesion, which is also having an impact on RE in schools (Department for Children, Schools and Families 2010). In these ways education, like welfare, has increasingly reflected supposedly secular public policy preoccupations in an increasingly diverse society, in which religious plurality is a key part, and in which religious actors participate.

Such changes in society have led to greater equality of treatment within education of different religious traditions, initially for the Roman Catholic and Jewish communities and more recently for other religious traditions, including Muslim, Sikh and Hindu communities. The combination of the intellectual shift towards religious studies, and the social change towards the recognition of religious diversity in Britain together made a powerful context for change. A 'citizenship' agenda – representing a trend in many European countries and in the Council of Europe – came to the fore in the 1990s (citizenship was introduced into the English secondary school national curriculum in 2002) and has made its own impact on RE.

The legal framework

The educational structures and arrangements that produce syllabuses for religious education in the fully state-funded schools in England and Wales have evolved from those of earlier times. In these schools in England and Wales, religious education aims to foster an understanding of Christianity and the other main religions represented in British society, and also to help pupils to form their own views and opinions on religious matters. In voluntary, mainly state-funded, faith-based schools (e.g. voluntary-aided schools), however, religious education continues to include religious formation or nurture.

The Education Act 1944 made mandatory the use, by fully state-funded schools, of Agreed Syllabuses for Religious Instruction. Each English Local Education Authority

(LEA) had to convene a Syllabus Conference consisting of four committees. Two of the four committees represented religious constituencies: the Church of England and 'other denominations'. In practice 'other denominations' meant 'other Protestant Christian denominations'.[3] It was not until the 1970s that some LEAs liberally interpreted the Act as allowing representatives of non-Christian religions on to the 'other denominations' panel.

Syllabuses for RE in community schools in England are drafted at local level by an Agreed Syllabus Conference (ASC) which includes four committees: representatives of teachers; the Church of England; other denominations and religions; and local politicians. ASCs can co-opt further members (for example humanists and members of minority religious groups represented in the locality). Thus the interests of professional educators, religious bodies and politicians come together at a local level in determining syllabus content. There is also a trend towards a national pattern for the subject (see later on the Non-statutory National Framework for Religious Education).

Changes to religious education brought about by the Education Reform Act 1988 have to be seen against the background of the introduction of a national curriculum, with compulsory core and foundation subjects. Mainly because of the local arrangements for religious education that already existed, RE was not included in the national curriculum. The Education Reform Act 1988 retained many features of the 1944 Act, but introduced changes which consolidated RE's place in the curriculum and acknowledged some recent developments in the subject. A significant change was the use of 'religious education' to replace the term 'religious instruction' with the latter's suggestion of deliberate transmission of religious beliefs. The subject now had to justify its aims and processes on general educational grounds. For the first time in law, representatives of faiths other than Christianity were 'officially' given a place on ASCs, on what used to be the 'other denominations' committee.

The Education Reform Act 1988 requires that any new Agreed Syllabus 'shall reflect the fact that religious traditions in Great Britain are in the main Christian, whilst taking account of the teaching and practices of the other principal religions represented in Great Britain' (UK Parliament 1988: Section 8.3). However, the Act specifically prohibits indoctrinatory teaching. Perhaps this implies some of the contested and muddled thinking which is reflected in wider public conversation about religion. Religious education both locates itself in an idea of secularity which leaves questions of religious truth open, while at the same time tacitly acknowledging the cultural legacy and inheritance of Christianity as significant in some way over and above other religious traditions and forms. This meant that new Agreed Syllabuses needed both to give proper attention to the study of Christianity and, regardless of their location in the country, to give attention to the other major religions represented in Britain. The Education Reform Act also sets religious education in the context of the whole curriculum of maintained schools which 'must be balanced and broadly based' and must promote 'the spiritual, moral, cultural, mental and physical development of pupils at the school and of society' (UK Parliament 1988: 1 (2) para 2). Again, references to spiritual dimensions raise a question about the extent and coherence of secularist assumptions and claims in education policy and practice. Here religious education, as well as being broad, balanced and open, should not simply be a study of religions but, like the rest of the curriculum, should relate to the experience of pupils in such a way that it contributes to their personal development.

National initiatives: the Model Syllabuses and the National Framework for Religious Education

In 1994, two Model Syllabuses were published by the School Curriculum and Assessment Authority (SCAA), including material on six religions in Britain (Christianity, Judaism, Islam, Hinduism, Buddhism and Sikhism) and produced in consultation with members of faith communities.[4] The two models (School Curriculum and Assessment Authority 1994a, 1994b) were non-statutory; they were for the use of ASCs, who could choose to ignore them or could edit or borrow from them. The model syllabuses used the terms 'learning about religion' and 'learning from religion' as the two attainment targets for religious education. This terminology has achieved wide circulation since the publication of the Model Syllabuses and is affirmed in the non-statutory National Framework (Qualifications and Curriculum Authority 2004) (see below).

TEXT BOX 17

The purposes of the National Framework

The national framework for religious education has four purposes, which mirror those of the National Curriculum.

1   To establish an entitlement. The national framework endorses an entitlement to learning in religious education for all pupils, irrespective of social background, culture, race, religion, gender, differences in ability and disabilities. This entitlement contributes to their developing knowledge, skills, understanding and attitudes. These are necessary for pupils' self-fulfilment and development as active and responsible citizens.

2   To establish standards. The national framework sets out expectations for learning and attainment that are explicit to pupils, parents, teachers, governors, employers and the public. It establishes standards for the performance of all pupils in religious education. These standards may be used to support assessment for learning. They may also be used to help pupils and teachers set targets for improvement and evaluate progress towards them.

3   To promote continuity and coherence. The national framework for religious education seeks to contribute to a coherent curriculum that promotes continuity. It helps the transition of pupils between schools and phases of education and can provide a foundation for further study and lifelong learning.

4   To promote public understanding. The national framework for religious education aims to increase public understanding of, and confidence in, the work of schools in religious education. It recognises the large extent to which the public is already involved with religious education, in the form of ASCs, SACREs [Standing Advisory Councils for Religious Education], LEAs [Local Education Authorities], governing bodies and the relevant religious and secular authorities and communities. It encourages those who are interested to participate in enriching the provision of religious education.

(Qualifications and Curriculum Authority 2004: 9)

Comment

The 'National Framework' was a non-statutory attempt to set *national* standards for religious education in England across a system in which syllabuses for state-funded schools are decided at local level.

Further work took place at national level in 2003–2004. The Department for Education and Skills commissioned the Qualifications and Curriculum Authority to produce a new national framework for religious education in consultation with faith communities and professional RE associations, for use by ASCs and others. The document (published in 2004), referred to hereafter as the National Framework, received the approval of all the professional associations and faith communities (Gates 2005a). It aims to clarify standards in religious education, promote high-quality teaching and learning, and recognize the important contribution of the subject to pupils' spiritual, moral, social and cultural development by supporting local SACREs (Standing Advisory Councils for Religious Education, see Key terms) and local ASCs (Qualifications and Curriculum Authority 2004).

The National Framework is intended to ensure that local syllabuses meet the needs of pupils, and to facilitate the development of more national support materials for RE. It is also intended to increase public understanding of religious education by providing clear guidance on what is covered in the subject. Like the Model Syllabuses, the National Framework lists Buddhism, Hinduism, Islam, Judaism and Sikhism as the principal religions that should be studied in addition to Christianity. The National Framework notes that 'It is important that ASCs and schools ensure that by the end of Key Stage 3 pupils (aged between 11 and 14) have encountered all of these five principal religions in sufficient depth' (Qualifications and Curriculum Authority 2004: 12). Christianity should be studied across the Key Stages. The National Framework also states that 'To ensure that all pupils' voices are heard and the religious education curriculum is broad and balanced, it is recommended that there are opportunities for all pupils to study other religious traditions such as the Bahá'í faith, Jainism and Zoroastrianism' and 'secular philosophies such as humanism' (Qualifications and Curriculum Authority 2004: 12).

The National Framework also explains how religious education can contribute to intercultural understanding and citizenship education. The structure of the National Framework closely follows that of national curriculum requirements.

Since the publication of the National Framework, the Religious Education Council of England and Wales, representing professional organizations and faith communities, lobbied for the development of a national strategy for the subject based on the National Framework. The strategy includes improving the quality of the religious education taught in maintained community schools and schools with a religious character (commonly known as faith schools). It also involves encouraging those responsible for RE in faith-based voluntary aided schools, academies and independent schools to consult and use the National Framework in planning their RE syllabuses, and encouraging schools generally to strengthen an inclusive approach to the subject, by developing links with faith communities in their local areas. Funding was provided by the Labour government of the time for extending and improving in-service training of teachers through the development of continuing professional development materials, and research was commissioned by the then Department for Children, Schools and Families (DCSF) on materials used to teach about world religions (Jackson *et al.* 2010).

State-funded religious schools

The existence of state-funded religious schools acknowledges institutionally an element of plurality in English education. It also represents the continuing historical legacy of religious provision in education. In 2011 there were 21,727 maintained schools in England of which 6,832 were faith-based schools of one type or another.

The close collaboration between church and state in education in England goes back to the Education Act 1870. The 'Dual System' of partnership between the state and the churches was developed further in the Education Act 1944. This distinguished different types of maintained (that is, state-funded) schools. County schools were entirely publicly funded and had no church-appointed governors. Voluntary schools, originally funded by religious bodies, went into voluntary partnership with the state.

Voluntary schools were of three types: Aided, Controlled and Special Agreement.[5] In Voluntary Controlled schools, the RE syllabus was provided by the LEA. Voluntary Aided schools (Church of England, Roman Catholic, some other Christian schools and, significantly, a few Jewish schools[6]) had a majority of governors appointed by the sponsoring religious body. Since 1988, Voluntary Aided schools, like all other maintained schools, have had to follow the national curriculum. However, they have continued to teach religious education and to have collective worship according to the religious tradition represented in the school using, in the case of the Church of England, for example, diocesan syllabuses. However, all the major religious traditions have acknowledged the importance of the National Framework for Religious Education in influencing their approach to religious education, and the survey and case studies from the DCSF research indicate that it is not uncommon for 'faith schools' to include some teaching about 'world religions' in their RE (Jackson *et al.* 2010).

Major changes have been brought about since 1997. In addition to the Labour government's stated aim of achieving fairness and good community relations, evidence (from Ofsted statistics) of higher attainment and a stronger sense of community in some religious schools contributed to a more pluralistic view of the state school system.

The School Standards and Framework Act 1998 introduced the concept of 'religious character' and modified the range of types of school receiving state funding (UK Parliament 1998). This provided four categories of school within the state system: Community (formerly County schools); Foundation; Voluntary Aided and Voluntary Controlled. All Community schools must use the local agreed syllabus as a basis for religious education and may not have a religious character. Schools within the other categories may have a 'religious character'. Most, but not all, Voluntary Aided and Voluntary Controlled schools and some Foundation schools have a religious character. All schools with a religious character can have collective worship that is distinctive of the religious body concerned. Only Voluntary Aided schools can have 'denominational' religious education. Voluntary Controlled and Foundation schools with a religious character have to use the local agreed syllabus, except in the case of schools where the majority of pupils' parents have specifically requested 'denominational' religious education. In effect, a wider range of religious schools was incorporated into the state system, partly for reasons of fairness and partly because such schools were recognized as potentially having certain qualities that might be more difficult to develop in some Community schools (Department for Children, Schools and Families 2007a).

In March 2000 the Labour government announced its intention to develop semi-independent Inner City Academies (later called Academies) catering for children of all abilities. As in relation to welfare, this was a move to a more 'mixed economy' of provision, and designed to improve 'choice' within the 'market'. Some of these are sponsored by church-related bodies. Some regard this as an example of government's confidence in the ability of religious bodies to make schools work in difficult social settings. Others criticize it for having a resource-driven aspect which instrumentalizes faith groups at the cost of diluting the supposedly secular public realm – the same criticism which has been made of 'using' faith to deliver welfare services. The Coalition government elected in 2010 pledged to expand the number of Academies, including primary Academies. At the time of writing Academies that do not have a religious character are required to use the local agreed syllabus for religious education.

Independent schools

Independent schools, which receive no state funding, may or may not have a religious character. There is great diversity within the independent school sector – from schools with ancient foundations, often religious foundations, although not necessarily now formally designated as having a 'religious character' – to small, financially struggling schools offering distinctive education.

The Department for Education and Skills contacted all independent schools in 2003 offering them the opportunity to apply to be designated as a school with religious character under the Designation of Schools Having a Religious Character (Independent Schools) (England) Order 2003. This Order extended the procedure undertaken with maintained schools following the publication of the School Standards and Framework Act 1998. By April 2004, 427 independent schools had been granted the designation of having a religious character.

Independent schools can make their own arrangements for teaching religious education. However, all independent schools are required to meet the Education (Independent School Standards) (England) Regulations 2003, regarding the spiritual, moral, social and cultural development of pupils. In order to meet this standard, the schools must promote principles which 'assist pupils to acquire an appreciation of and respect for their own and other cultures in a way that promotes tolerance and harmony between different cultural traditions.'

'Community cohesion'

The Introduction to this volume discusses the influence of the idea of social or community 'cohesion'. The 'duty to promote community cohesion' formed part of the Education and Inspections Act 2006 [21 (5)]. Since September 2007, there has been a requirement for schools to promote community cohesion, partly through curriculum subjects such as religious education and citizenship, and this requirement has influenced the development of some materials for use in religious education in schools. The non-statutory guidance on community cohesion requires that 'Every school – whatever its intake and wherever it is located – is responsible for educating children and young people who will live and work in a country which is diverse in terms of cultures, religions or beliefs, ethnicities and social backgrounds' (Department for Children, Schools and Families 2007b: 1).

The non-statutory guidance for religious education states that effective RE will promote community cohesion at each of four levels:

First, **the school community** – RE provides a positive context within which the diversity of cultures, beliefs and values within the school community can be celebrated and explored.

Second, **the community within which the school is located** – RE provides opportunities to investigate the patterns of diversity of religion and belief within the local area and it is an important context within which links can be forged with different religious and non-religious belief groups in the local community.

Third, **the UK community** – a major focus of RE is the study of the diversity of religion and belief which exists within the UK and how this diversity influences national life.

Fourth, **the global community** – RE involves the study of matters of global significance recognizing the diversity of religion and belief and its impact on world issues.

(Department for Children, Schools and Families 2010: 8)

Although the community cohesion advice is not directed towards independent schools, they are required to meet the standard of assisting their pupils to acquire an appreciation of and respect for their own and other cultures in a way that promotes tolerance and harmony between different cultural traditions. With the election of the Coalition government in May 2010, the language of community cohesion gave way in welfare contexts to that of 'economic integration' – the notion that being financially active (employed or self-employed) will do the job of cohesion. We must watch with interest what direction this takes in education too.

Quality of RE provision

The development of religious education in community schools in England, and also the provision of state-funded schools with a religious character, has been determined by the radical decoupling of Christian socialization from fully state-funded education. Although there has been some expansion of schools with a religious character, the great majority of state-funded schools continue to be community schools. Although voluntary-aided schools within the maintained sector may teach forms of religious education which promote a particular faith, there has been agreement that the National Framework is an important tool in facilitating forms of religious education that are outward looking and inclusive of learning about the main different religions represented in Britain. Although independent schools can make their own arrangements for religious education, they are required to promote principles which assist pupils to acquire an appreciation of and respect for their own and other cultures in a way that promotes tolerance and harmony between different cultural traditions. Religious education in all types of English schools is thus potentially an arena for learning about the different religions represented in the country and for dialogue between pupils from different religious and secular backgrounds.

However, the quality of RE teaching in English schools is mixed, especially in secondary schools. Recent Ofsted (the Office for Standards in Education, Children's Services and Skills, responsible for the inspection of schools) evidence shows that in primary schools where achievement was graded as 'satisfactory', weaknesses included a lack of knowledge and confidence among teachers to plan and teach high-quality RE lessons. In secondary schools the impact on RE of recent changes to the wider curriculum, particularly at Key Stage 3, was judged to be negative; moreover the quality of learning for short-course

General Certificates in Secondary Education in religious studies was often poor (Ofsted 2010). The Ofsted report shows much variability in the quantity and quality of support for RE provided to schools at the local level, with many schools having difficulty finding effective training provision. The report recommends a review to determine whether the statutory arrangements for the local determination of the RE curriculum should be revised. Other recent research evidence shows a need for the production of higher-quality materials on the various religions studied in RE that reflect high standards of scholarship and pedagogy (Jackson *et al.* 2010).

One success over the past ten years or so has been the improvement in pupils' attitudes towards RE. In most of the schools visited in collecting Ofsted evidence, pupils clearly understood the importance of learning about the diversity of religion and belief in contemporary society (Ofsted 2010). This finding is supported by research in English schools conducted as part of a European project (Ipgrave and McKenna 2008; McKenna *et al.* 2009).

Religion and the universities

Religious change can be understood through the experience of education in universities too. The oldest universities in Britain, Oxford and Cambridge, predate the Reformation, but these universities remained until fairly recently under the purview of the established church, and they remain to a certain degree tied to it, at least in terms of their cultural norms. Before the Victorian era the church's dominance over academic and community life inevitably meant the exclusion of Dissenters, Jews, Roman Catholics and those unable to subscribe to the Thirty-Nine Articles (Gilliat-Ray 1999: 22). Since these were the only two higher education institutions in England, very few people actually went to university. In the 1820s England only had a small number of university students: 1,000 compared to 4,250 in Scotland, in which four universities (St Andrews, Glasgow, Aberdeen and Edinburgh) were founded between 1400 and 1600. Compared to other European countries the system in England reformed very late (Rüegg 2004: 61–64; Graham 2005: 7–9). The establishment of University College London (UCL) in 1826 as Britain's third university was self-consciously secular and the institution is often known informally as 'the godless institution of Gower Street'.

Public pressure eventually led to the passing of two bills in 1852 and 1854 requiring reforms at Oxford and Cambridge, although only in 1871 were religious tests for entry finally abolished. At the same time, the university system in England expanded, driven by a combination of commercial interest and civic and nonconformist challenges to the established church. Together these changes opened higher education up to people for whom university had not been an option, and today no one is excluded, formally at least, from UK universities because of their religion or belief.

Through these and other processes, there has also been a secularization of higher education. In his reading of the history of the American university, Mark U. Edwards Jr (2008) links the secularization of higher education in America with the emergence of academic disciplinary communities which challenged dominant forms of Protestantism. As in welfare, there was a gradual 'professionalization'. Each discipline developed its own procedures and vocabularies for understanding its subject matter, and as they did so various alternatives to theological knowledge emerged, with these alternatives eventually becoming the norm. The sciences, the social sciences and then the humanities each 'declared their independence from religion'. But this had a side effect too. Challenges to Protestant dominance made possible the expression of other forms of faith – multiple strands of Christianity, Hinduism, Buddhism, Islam and many others.

School-based religious education has thus shifted significantly from an emphasis on the teaching of Christian doctrine and morality to teaching about 'world religions'. Similarly, there has been a shift, too, in university chaplaincy, for example, from parochial to pastoral ministry available to people of any faith and none, and in degree courses from Bachelor of Theology awards to Bachelor of Arts (and so on) and from study towards ordination to study of religions sociologically or as another humanities subject in the liberal arts tradition. There have been calls for 'culturally responsive' teaching that is sensitive to how learners might experience learning through the lens of their own cultural (and religious) experiences. Social scientific research in universities has also developed a strong appetite for a religion focus in recent years.

What this now means for universities is a facing up to the reality of the epistemological and foundational starting points they claim to reflect – whether secular or religious. To assert neutrality on religious matters is to imagine that it is possible somehow to rise above the fray, while in practice one person's neutrality is another's oppression. Universities – and school RE too – may be very well placed to inform a much better quality of public conversation after all, regardless of their own religious beliefs or those of individuals within them.

Debates and national variations

Since the 1960s, there has been a shift in fully state-funded schools and in higher education from religious nurture in Christianity to approaches emphasizing 'impartial' knowledge and understanding. In England, Wales and Scotland, change has also been strongly influenced by the increasing religious plurality of each nation, especially affected by the expansion of migration in the 1960s and 1970s which increased in particular the presence of Hinduism, Sikhism and Islam, and to a lesser extent Buddhism in British society (see Chapter 3). The influence of a globally aware academic religious studies has also been influential, but less so than changes in local demography which have determined the diverse composition of local ASCs and SACREs. More recent migrations have tended to accentuate the theological and cultural diversity of Christianity. The low presence of religions other than Christianity in Northern Ireland has meant that arguments for studying religious diversity have been heeded there less than in the other nations of the United Kingdom, although the aims of religious education in state schools, at least in policy terms, have changed (see Case study 7). More instrumental arguments for the study of religions – for contributing to good community relations, for producing well-informed and tolerant citizens, and for resisting violent extremism through the promotion of community cohesion – have also played their part at different times, and continue to do so.

There is continuing debate about what can be included in RE, and whether non-religious ethical philosophies like humanism should be. The British Humanist Association has taken a long interest in the debates about religious education. However, law determines that the content of religious education should be religions, and legal precedent defines humanism as not being a religion. Nevertheless, perhaps under the influence of human rights codes and wider European thinking about how to deal with teaching about religions and beliefs in schools, the National Framework (Qualifications and Curriculum Authority 2004) assumes that non-religious worldviews such as humanism should be studied as well as religious ones. Scotland has the closest to a 'synthetic' approach, with religious and moral education in primary schools, and religious, moral and philosophical studies as a pathway at standard grade in secondary schools. Arguments based on human rights principles, as embodied in the European Convention on Human Rights (see next chapter), for example, and on the inter-culturality of the European continent, rather than on the demography of particular nations, may well gain ground over time, and are likely to broaden the scope of the subject to incorporate the study of non-religious philosophies.

Each of the UK nations continues to support a system which includes state funding for some faith-based schools, which maintain a 'nurturing' form of religious education. The complexion of these faith schools reflects the religious history of each country, and the importance of different churches in each one. There are clear historical reasons why all this is so, but the debate about public funding for faith-based schools has grown and will continue, especially the argument over whether they erode or enhance community cohesion.

Conclusions

Both welfare and education have shifted since 1945 in ways which reflect the changing relationship between religion and society. There has been a shift from an emphasis on the role of religious beliefs themselves to the role of *religions* in a pluralized society. Religion is now seen in education as a variable to be examined and understood. In welfare, religious groups are recognized for the instrumental role they play in delivery of services and cohesion. It is their public activity which is in focus, not the interior life of faith itself, nor the religious reasons or goals which motivate it. These shifts contribute to an anxiety about religious extremism and violence, and the tension between them makes of faith communities both heroes and villains. At the same time, since the 1980s the mixing of secular and religious concerns has been played out in a 'mixed economy' which recognizes diversity of both service users and providers. Anyone who can show they have something to offer can participate in this mix. It requires being outward-looking and a readiness to work in partnership, whether in provision of schools, welfare services or 'community' more generally.

The main resisters to change have tended to be those wishing to maintain the status quo for one reason or another (sometimes political, sometimes theological, sometimes both) and whose interests are not served by change. This has happened in both directions, and many faith communities have reported resistance on the grounds that government policy seeks to 'instrumentalize' them as deliverers of welfare services or community cohesion on the cheap, and with all sorts of strings attached. Other forces militating against change are economic and structural. Policy changes tend not to be well implemented because the necessary resources have often not been channelled into the continuing professional development of teachers, welfare professionals and a struggling grass-roots voluntary sector, while ambitious objectives for religious education are difficult to attain in a heavily crowded curriculum. In particular, the topics of religious education in schools and state-funded religious schools continue to be the subject of heated debate (see Flint 2009; Jackson 2004).

It should be noted that there is a good deal of European and international discussion of the place of religion in public education in recent years which is likely to have a growing influence on national debates in the UK. For example, the Council of Europe, which has 47 member states, supports the study of religions and beliefs in public education as part of a broad inter-cultural education (Council of Europe 2008; Jackson 2009). Similarly the Organization for Security and Co-operation in Europe, with 56 participant states, advocates a form of education about religions and beliefs grounded in the human rights principle of freedom of religion or belief, but adapted to the social contexts of particular countries

(Organization for Security and Co-operation in Europe 2007). The Higher Education Funding Council for England (HEFCE) has also funded action research to develop better religious literacy in universities in pursuit of a better quality of conversation about religion in wider society.[7] These wider debates about the place of religion are reflected too in welfare terms, where a large programme of research on 'welfare and values in Europe' (WaVE, funded by the European Commission) has also taken the debate forward, and the place of religious faith in a wide range of public spheres has been increasingly debated. The Faith-Based Initiative in the USA has also focused attention on the public role of religion. Its place in both education and welfare thus unsettles public discourse and challenges assumptions about the 'secularity' of the public realm while greater religious diversity presents policy with the challenge of how to address it.

But while there are similarities in the processes mobilizing change in each sphere, there are differences too. The traditional involvement in welfare by religious communities, which was historically central to the voluntaristic structure and culture of British (Christian) pluralism, may have served to hold off some of the secularizing tendencies of the public sphere, despite professionalization and market forces. Indeed, the recent (re)turn to 'faith communities' to deliver welfare under state programmes strengthened their hand once again. Their role in public delivery of welfare services grew as ideas like the 'Big Society' entered the political lexicon and made new spaces for faith-based actors to take their place alongside any other actors with resources to contribute. In the case of education, however, the cumulative effect of changes in educational policy towards religious education in schools has been to remove the process of Christian socialization from state-funded community schools, even though it remains in the growing number of mainly state-funded voluntary-aided schools.

In these contexts, the continuing participation of religious groups and individuals unsettles questions which had been thought to be settled. What this chapter shows is that religion never disappeared, though it was profoundly challenged and changed by both secularizing and pluralizing forces in the post-war period. The spheres of welfare and education reveal that the public realm is not after all the post-religious space which had been imagined, and that Britain is neither simply secular nor simply religious but complexly both.

Key terms

Agreed syllabus: A local syllabus for religious education produced by a conference within a local authority in England or Wales consisting of committees representing the Church of England (in England only), other denominations and religions, the local authority and representatives of teachers. Agreed syllabuses are used in Community (formerly County) schools and in Voluntary-Controlled schools.

Civil society: 'Civil society' is usually defined to refer to the level of governance between the state and the governed (Cohen and Arato 1992). It is located in organizations such as non-governmental organizations (NGOs), charities, foundations and professional associations which exercise influence and help shape the formal layers of governance.

Community cohesion: Coined in the Cantle Report (2001) to describe the effect desired by public policy-makers of building up networks of trust and reciprocity in local areas. The key aim is to avoid the 'parallel lives' which Cantle identified.

Gulbenkian Report: Originating in a study group by the Gulbenkian Foundation in 1966 (the first report appeared in 1968) to look at the nature and future of community work in the

UK. This was intended to be focused around training but inevitably spread its net much wider to structural critiques.

Maintained schools: In the UK, schools under the control of local councils (local authorities in England and Wales and the Department of Education in Northern Ireland). In England and Wales, maintained schools include voluntary schools, some of which (voluntary-aided schools) are partially funded by religious bodies. Maintained schools do not include academies, a minority of secondary schools in England funded directly by central government but having semi-independent status.

Phenomenological: An approach to the study of religions requiring the setting aside of the researcher's presuppositions, and empathy with the position of the insider. The approach also requires the capacity to intuit common themes or categories across religions.

Primary schools: In the UK, normally schools for children below the age of 11. They are usually divided into an infant and a junior section.

SACRE: The abbreviation for Standing Advisory Council for Religious Education. In England and Wales SACREs have a consultative and advisory function within local authorities in relation to religious education. Their composition mirrors that of Agreed Syllabus Conferences (ASCs).

Secondary schools: In the UK, usually schools for young people aged 11 to 18.

Statism: An approach to government which introduces planned interventions at a national level through economic and social policy to try to shape the experiences and lives of citizens; to be contrasted with privatization, laissez-faire and free-market approaches which stress the 'rolling back of the state'.

Voluntary schools: These are mainly state-funded schools in England and Wales which have a religious character. In voluntary-aided schools, religious bodies pay a modest contribution towards buildings and maintenance, while the state pays the rest, plus staff salaries. Voluntary-controlled schools are completely funded by the state, but still have a religious character.

Further reading

Chapman, Rachael (2009). 'Faith and the Voluntary Sector in Urban Governance: Distinctive yet Similar?', in Adam Dinham, Richard Furbey and Vivien Lowndes (eds), *Faith in the Public Realm*. Bristol: Policy Press, 203–222. Explores divergences and continuities in the relationship between Third Sector welfare providers and faith-based ones, to consider the distinctiveness of faith-based services.

Dinham Adam (2009). 'Faiths and the Provision of Services', Chapter 6 of his book *Faiths, Public Policy and Civil Society: Problems, Policies, Controversies*. London: Palgrave Macmillan. Critically examines research and data about the role played by faith communities in the mixed economy of welfare.

Jackson, Robert (2003). 'Should the State Fund Faith-based Schools? A Review of the Arguments', *British Journal of Religious Education*, 25/2: 89–102. A discussion of the main arguments for and against state funding of schools with a religious character in the context of England and Wales.

Jackson, Robert, Siebren Miedema, Wolfram Weisse and Jean-Paul Willaime (eds) (2007). *Religion and Education in Europe: Developments, Contexts and Debates*. Münster: Waxmann. Includes a chapter by Robert Jackson and Kevin O'Grady on the religious education system in England and Wales, as well as parallel chapters on seven other European countries and discussions of generic European issues concerning religion and education.

Kuyk, Elza, Roger Jensen, David W. Lankshear, Elisabeth Leoh Manna and Peter Schreiner (2007). *Religious Education in Europe*. Oslo: IKO & ICCS. Short articles on different systems of religious education in Europe, including Scotland and Northern Ireland.
Prochaska, Frank (2006). *Christianity and Social Service in Modern Britain: The Disinherited Spirit*. New York, NY: Oxford University Press. Locates contemporary welfare in the context of the legacy and continuity of Christian provision prior to the welfare state.

References

Barnes, L. Philip (2009). *Religious Education: Taking Religious Difference Seriously, Impact No. 17*. London: Philosophy of Education Society of Great Britain.
Beattie, Alistair, Clare Mortimore and Heather Pencavel (2006). *Faith in Action: A Survey of Social and Community Action by Faith Groups in the South West of England*. Bristol: Faithnetsouthwest.
Bowpitt, Graham (2007). 'Stemming the Tide: Welfare, Mission and the Churches' Response to Secular Modernity in Britain, 1850–1950', paper presented to the Faiths and Civil Society seminar, Anglia Ruskin University, February.
Cantle, Ted (2001). *Community Cohesion: A Report of the Independent Review Team*. London: Her Majesty's Stationery Office.
Church of England. Commission on Urban Priority Areas (1985). *Faith in the City: A Call for Action by Church and Nation*. London: Church House.
Cohen, Jean and Andrew Arato (1992). *Civil Society and Political Theory*. Cambridge, MA and London: MIT Press.
Cole, W. Owen (1972). *Religion in the Multifaith School*. Yorkshire: Yorkshire Committee for Community Relations.
Council of Europe (2008). *Recommendation CM/Rec(2008)12 of the Committee of Ministers to Member States on the Dimension of Religions and Non-religious Convictions within Intercultural Education*. Online. Available HTTP: https://wcd.coe.int//ViewDoc.jsp?Ref=CM/Rec(2008)12&Language=lanEnglish&Ver=original&BackColorInternet=DBDCF2&BackColorIntranet=FDC864&BackColorLogged=FDC864 (accessed 24 December 2010).
Cox, Edwin (1966). *Changing Aims in Religious Education*. London: Routledge.
Department for Children, Schools and Families (2007a). *Faith in the System: The Role of Schools with a Religious Character in English Education and Society*. London: Department for Children, Schools and Families.
Department for Children, Schools and Families (2007b). *Guidance on the Duty to Promote Community Cohesion*. London: Department for Children, Schools and Families.
Department for Children, Schools and Families (2010). *Religious Education in English Schools: Non-statutory Guidance 2010*. London: Department for Children, Schools and Families.
Derby Diocesan Council for Social Responsibility (2006). *Faith in Derbyshire: Working Towards a Better Derbyshire*, May.
Dinham, Adam (2007). *Priceless, Unmeasurable: Faith-Based Community Development in 21st Century England*. London: Faith-based Regeneration Network.
East of England Faiths Council and the University of Cambridge (2005). *Faith in the East of England: A Research Study on the Vital Role Played by Faith Communities in the Social, Economic and Spiritual Life of a Region*, July.
Edwards, Mark U., Jr (2008). 'Why Faculty Find it Difficult to Talk about Religion', in Douglas Jacobsen and Rhonda Hustedt Jacobsen (eds), *The American University in a Postsecular Age*. Oxford: Oxford University Press, 81–98.
Flint, John (2009). 'Faith Based Schools: Instituting Parallel Lives?', in Adam Dinham, Richard Furbey and Vivien Lowndes (eds), *Faith in the Public Realm*. Bristol: Policy Press, 163–182.
Gates, Brian (2005a). 'Editorial', *British Journal of Religious Education*, 27/2: 99–102.
Gates, Brian (2005b). 'Faith Schools and Colleges of Education since 1800', in Roy Gardner, Josephine Cairns and Denis Lawton (eds), *Faith Schools: Consensus or Conflict?* London: RoutledgeFalmer, 14–35.

Gilliat-Ray, Sophie (1999). *Religion in Higher Education: The Politics of the Multifaith Campus*. Aldershot: Ashgate.

Graham, Gordon (2005). *The Institution of Intellectual Values: Realism and Idealism in Higher Education*. Exeter: Imprint Academic.

Greater London Enterprise (GLE)/London Churches Group (LCG) (2002). *Neighbourhood Renewal in London: The Role of Faith Communities*. London: LCG for Social Action/GLE.

Grimmitt, Michael H. (ed.) (2000). *Pedagogies of Religious Education: Case Studies in the Research and Development of Good Pedagogic Practice in RE*. Great Wakering: McCrimmons.

Ipgrave, Julia and Ursula McKenna (2008). 'Diverse Experiences and Common Vision: English Students' Perspectives on Religion and Religious Education', in Thorsten Knauth, Dan-Paul Jozsa, Gerdien Bertram-Troost and Julia Ipgrave (eds), *Encountering Religious Pluralism in School and Society: A Qualitative Study of Teenage Perspectives in Europe*, Religious Diversity and Education in Europe Series. Münster: Waxmann, 133–147.

Ipgrave, Julia, Robert Jackson and Kevin O'Grady (2009). *Religious Education Through a Community of Practice: Action Research and the Interpretive Approach*. Münster: Waxmann.

Jackson, Robert (1997). *Religious Education: An Interpretive Approach*. London: Hodder and Stoughton.

Jackson, Robert (ed.) (2003). *International Perspectives on Citizenship, Education and Religious Diversity*. London: RoutledgeFalmer.

Jackson, Robert (2004). *Rethinking Religious Education and Plurality: Issues in Diversity and Pedagogy*. London: RoutledgeFalmer.

Jackson, Robert (2009). 'The Council of Europe and Education about Religious Diversity', *British Journal of Religious Education*, 31/2: 85–90.

Jackson, Robert, Julia Ipgrave, Mary Hayward, Paul Hopkins, Nigel Fancourt, Mandy Robbins, Leslie J. Francis and Ursula McKenna (2010). *Materials used to Teach about World Religions in Schools in England*. London: Department for Children, Schools and Families.

Lister, Ruth with Jo Campling (1997). *Citizenship: Feminist Perspectives*. Basingstoke: Macmillan.

McKenna, Ursula, Sean Neill and Robert Jackson (2009). 'Personal Worldviews, Dialogue and Tolerance: Students' Views on Religious Education in England', in Pille Valk, Gerdien Bertram-Troost, Markus Friederici and Céline Beraud (eds), *Teenagers' Perspectives on the Role of Religion in their Lives, Schools and Societies: A European Quantitative Study*. Münster: Waxmann, 49–70.

Mayo, Marjorie (2000). *Cultures, Communities, Identities: Cultural Strategies for Participation and Empowerment*. Basingstoke: Palgrave Macmillan.

National Council for Voluntary Organisations (2007). *Faith and Voluntary Action: An Overview of Current Evidence and Debates*. London: National Council for Voluntary Organisations.

Northwest Forum of Faiths (2003). *Faith in England's Northwest: The Contribution Made by Faith Communities to Civil Society in the Region*, November.

Ofsted (2010). *Transforming Religious Education: Religious Education in Schools 2006–09*. Manchester: Ofsted.

Organization for Security and Co-operation in Europe (2007). *Toledo Guiding Principles on Teaching about Religions and Beliefs in Public Schools*. Warsaw: Organization for Security and Co-operation in Europe (Office for Democratic Institutions and Human Rights). Online. Available HTTP: www.osce.org/item/28314.html (accessed 24 December 2010).

Prochaska, Frank (2006). *Christianity and Social Service in Modern Britain: The Disinherited Spirit*. New York, NY: Oxford University Press.

Qualifications and Curriculum Authority (2004). *Religious Education: The Non-Statutory National Framework*. London: Qualifications and Curriculum Authority.

Regional Action West Midlands (2006). *Believing in the Region: A Baseline Study of Faith Bodies across the West Midlands*, May.

Rüegg, Walter (2004). *A History of the University in Europe. Volume III: Universities in the Nineteenth and Early Twentieth Centuries*. New York, NY: Cambridge University Press.

School Curriculum and Assessment Authority (1994a). *Model Syllabuses for Religious Education: Model 1: Living Faiths Today*. London: School Curriculum and Assessment Authority.

School Curriculum and Assessment Authority (1994b). *Model Syllabuses for Religious Education: Model 2: Questions and Teaching*. London: School Curriculum and Assessment Authority.

Schools Council (1971). *Religious Education in Secondary Schools, Schools Council Working Paper 36*. London: Evans/Methuen.

Smart, Ninian (1968). *Secular Education and the Logic of Religion*. London: Faber.

Smith, Kath (2004). *Faith in the North East: Social Action by Faith Communities in the Region*, September. North East Churches Regional Commission.

Social and Economic Action Resources of Churches in Hull and District (2000). *Count Us In*.

Southeast England Faith Forum (2004). *Beyond Belief?: Faith at Work in the Community*, March.

UK Parliament (1988). *Education Reform Act 1988*. London: Her Majesty's Stationery Office.

UK Parliament (1998). *School Standards and Framework Act*. London: Department for Education and Employment.

Wesley, John (1771). *Sermons on Several Occasions, Volume 1*. London (no publisher given).

Yorkshire and the Humber Churches Regional Commission (2002). *Angels and Advocates*, November. Church Social Action in Yorkshire and the Humber.

Younghusband, Eileen L. (1959). *Report of the Working Party on Social Workers in the Local Authority Health and Welfare Services*. London: Her Majesty's Stationery Office.

Younghusband, Eileen L. (1968). *Community Work and Social Change: Report of a Study Group on Training Set Up by the Calouste Gulbenkian Foundation*. London and Harlow: Longmans.

Notes

1   Fully state-funded schools that do not have a religious character, since 1998, have been called community schools (formerly, county schools). Voluntary schools are schools, funded wholly or partially by the state, that retain a connection with their founding religious group.

2   A recent attack on phenomenology, assuming that it has propagated a liberal Christian approach to religious education in which all religions are regarded as basically the same (Barnes 2009) misses the point that few educators were interested in the theological aspects of phenomenology and greatly overestimates its long-term influence. A recent set of 20 case studies in schools shows a variety of approaches – including textual, philosophical and experiential – to be in widespread use in English schools (Jackson *et al.* 2010), while other pedagogical approaches have been developed by educators and researchers and are in use via teacher training and professional development programmes (e.g. Grimmitt 2000; Ipgrave *et al.* 2009; Jackson 1997).

3   In Wales, there are three committees, the Church of England being part of the committee that includes faith group representation.

4   Humanism was not included on the grounds that there had been an earlier court ruling (not in the context of RE) that it was not a religion. Many SACREs and AS conferences have co-opted humanist members or have ensured a humanist presence on the committee including representatives of teachers.

5   Special Agreement schools had curriculum arrangements close to those of Aided schools.

6   There were some Jewish schools with public grants even before 1870 (Gates 2005b).

7   Also AHRC/ESRC Religion and Society Programme funded large grant 'Young People's Attitudes to Religious Diversity' with research in secondary schools led by Robert Jackson.

Case study 6

The role of faith-based organizations in service provision for homeless people

Sarah Johnsen

The provision of services to homeless people and other vulnerable groups is one of the longest-standing means by which faith communities have sought to contribute to the welfare of society, and Faith-based Organizations (FBOs) continue to be key players in the homeless sector. Yet some 'secular' agencies – including local authorities – remain suspicious of this faith-based provision. They often assume that it comes 'with strings attached', imagine that it may not be as professional as secular provision and fear that it may discriminate against certain groups. The AHRC/ESRC Religion and Society-funded project which informs this case study[1] found little support for this view: indeed, it concluded that secular provision is more likely to attach conditions to the support offered. Above all, however, the study sheds light on the sheer diversity of contemporary provision in the UK, and the blurred boundaries between the religious and secular in practice, including within the faith sector itself.

Detailed case studies were conducted in London and Manchester, involving interviews and focus groups with over 100 managers, frontline workers and homeless service users in secular and faith-based projects. These were complemented by interviews with representatives of central government and national bodies, together with a review of existing literature and service databases. A range of faith groups were involved, including: Christian, Hare Krishna, Hindu, Muslim and Sikh.

The study highlights the sheer diversity of homelessness provision in the early twenty-first century. The majority of FBOs grew out of faith-based initiatives (most commonly soup runs or emergency night shelters), but they have followed very different developmental trajectories. Today, services that continue to provide only basic food, shelter, clothing and/or 'hospitality', such as soup kitchens and traditional dormitory-style winter shelters, are predominantly run by FBOs. These tend to be small, staffed by volunteers and resourced almost exclusively by charitable sources. In contrast, specialist services such as high-support hostels and some day centres are provided by a mix of faith-based and secular agencies. These offer a much wider range of services, typically employ paid and professionally trained staff, and derive a significant proportion of their funding from statutory sources. Of the services provided by FBOs, specialist projects are dominated by Christian organizations (with many different denominational associations), while a wider range of religious groups are represented in the provision of the basic services such as soup runs. Further, and contrary to what is often assumed, most faith-based projects are staffed by a mix of people with faith, of no faith and/or from a range of different religious backgrounds.

Significantly, in light of ongoing debates about 'secularization', faith-based providers have also evolved in terms of their degree of 'coupling' to religion, that is, in the degree of influence faith has on their public identity, ethos and day-to-day practice. A small proportion remain strongly linked with a faith community (often a church or congregational partnership), are resourced almost exclusively by that community and will actively utilize opportunities to share their faith with service users – via scriptural teaching and informal discussion, for example. Others, however, are now faith-based 'in name only', with their faith origins barely evident in palimpsest. A number of former FBOs now self-identify as 'secular' and are publicly rebranding (by removing religious referents from their title and mission statement, for example) to disassociate themselves from formalized religion. Adding further complexity to their corporate identities, the 'public face' that service providers present to the outside world is rarely static. It is very common for FBOs, together with some secular projects that grew out of faith initiatives, to emphasize or de-emphasize their project's faith affiliation or history according to their audience: 'playing it up' when seeking support from faith communities and 'playing it down' when applying for public funding.

Faith was found to be integral to the motivations underpinning FBO provision. The belief, shared by many religious traditions, that adherents should actively combat social injustice and care for vulnerable members of society, is central. The visibility and practice of faith in project programmes has, however, declined significantly in recent years. Some of the FBOs had once required service users to participate in religious practices, such as attend worship services, but such requirements had been discontinued in all but one (atypical) project. Such a shift in approach results, in part, from commissioning bodies' restrictions on overt expressions of religion, but also reflects a wish on the part of FBOs to avoid appearing unwelcoming to people from other faith backgrounds or of no faith. Service users had mixed views about this declining visibility of faith in FBO projects: some approved strongly, believing there to be 'no place' for religion in such services (particularly those financed by public money); others were adamant that FBOs should not feel obliged, or be pressured, to conceal their beliefs if faith is what motivates them to provide what they do.

Given the factors mentioned above, many homeless people reported finding it very difficult to discern any tangible or systematic difference between faith-based and secular services; indeed many found it very difficult to tell whether projects they used regularly had a faith affiliation at all. This finding, together with the strong parallels in value bases underpinning faith-based and secular provision and mix of belief systems among staff in both, suggests that care should be taken to avoid exaggerating the uniqueness of faith-based provision. That said, most faith-based projects do offer a 'spiritual' element – such as access to pastoral care, prayer and/or scriptural teaching – which is highly valued by some service users. Both secular and faith-based providers acknowledged the value of supporting homeless people in developing their sense of meaning, identity and purpose – including following their faith (whatever it may be) and connecting with relevant places of worship where they expressed a desire to do so. The study thus highlighted tensions between the homeless sector's increasing promotion of 'holistic' therapeutic approaches, and widespread public sensitivities surrounding links between spirituality and 'organized religion'. Secular agencies feel ill-equipped in this sphere; and staff in both faith-based and secular projects uncertain how (or whether) to raise such issues with their clients given the lack of defined boundaries regarding what is 'acceptable' in projects supported by public money. Many staff worry that discussing spirituality may leave them vulnerable to charges of proselytism. These concerns are particularly acute given recent high-profile cases wherein staff in public institutions (e.g. the National Health Service) had had contracts terminated after discussing religion with clients (see Chapter 7).

When asked about their service preferences, most homeless people were indifferent with respect to the faith or secular affiliation of homelessness services, as long as two conditions applied: first, that service receipt was not contingent on participation in religious practices (which they very rarely were – see earlier); and second, that providers respected their right to desist from conversations about faith should they so wish (which virtually all did). Indeed, with regard to the second 'condition', only a very small minority of service users reported that they had ever been subjected to unwelcome proselytism ('bible bashing') by a faith-based service, and then never in a publicly funded project. This is significant in light of the central government's acknowledgement that local authorities are often 'squeamish' about supporting FBOs, given their concern that public funds might be used to propagate religion. Such nervousness, it seems, is unfounded, in the homeless sector at least. Similarly, widespread (albeit rarely publicly articulated) fears that FBOs might discriminate against particular groups were also shown to have little foundation in practice, as no FBO (or secular provider) excluded potential service users on grounds of ethnicity, sexuality or religious belief.

There is widespread consensus among service providers and commissioners that FBOs had 'further to travel' than their secular counterparts to achieve necessary quality standards under government-funding streams, most notably 'Supporting People'. This differential has however diminished, and in many instances been eliminated, due to increased monitoring and accountability associated with such funding. There was widespread formal and informal joint working between FBOs, secular providers and local authorities, but little evidence of formal partnerships between FBOs associated with different religious traditions.

The nature of relationships between FBOs and local authorities is to a large degree determined by their degree of 'fit' with government directives. These have become increasingly interventionist in recent years, characterized as they are by greater expectations that homeless people utilize available services, with more severe consequences if they fail to 'engage'. The key axis differentiating homelessness projects is in fact not so much whether they are faith-based or secular, but rather their stance on expectations of service users and the conditionality of service receipt. These stances fall along a continuum. At one end, there are firmly 'non-interventionist' approaches which have an open-door policy, ask few (if any) questions of service users and hold no expectation that they should alter their lifestyle. At the other end, there are highly 'interventionist' approaches which assertively encourage service users to desist from damaging behaviours (e.g. drug or alcohol abuse) and make positive lifestyle changes, sometimes making service receipt contingent upon commitment to defined support plans in so doing. The interventionist end of this spectrum is dominated by secular agencies, and while FBOs can be found right along the continuum, they are clustered towards the non-interventionist end. This finding is interesting in light of the fact that FBOs have historically been, and sometimes still are, labelled 'paternalistic', given common assumptions that they will push for behaviour change. In fact, FBOs typically eschew coercive or enforcement approaches, while secular agencies tend to be more sympathetic towards the 'rehabilitative' measures promoted by central government.

Against this backdrop, several providers supported by public funding (including both faith-based and secular organizations) reported experiencing a decline in their ability to challenge government directives that they considered to conflict with their ethos. They are, consequently, becoming more reliant on agencies that operate independently of state funding to act as advocates for their clientele. With some exceptions, the vast majority of such agencies are faith-based, and typically small organizations staffed predominantly by volunteers. Some commentators are thus concerned that the task of campaigning is falling on the shoulders of those agencies and individuals least equipped to advocate on behalf of some of the most vulnerable members of society.

Attempts to foster debate regarding this and other issues affecting the sector are often impeded by miscommunication between faith-based and secular agencies. Commonalities in ethos are often obscured by major differences in the language employed to convey the values underpinning different approaches. Moreover, providers' and commissioners' lack of 'religious literacy', particularly unfamiliarity with religious terms and precepts, sometimes leads to misunderstanding or mistrust of FBO motives. Equally, 'policy illiteracy' on the part of some charitably funded FBOs can contribute to miscommunication with other providers or local authorities.

To conclude, FBOs have been profoundly influential in the development and evolution of Britain's homelessness services, and they will almost certainly continue to be key players in the sector in the future. Faith communities offer a vast repository of financial and material resources, combined with intense commitment to improving the circumstances of disadvantaged people. The ethos of many FBOs does nevertheless depart significantly from the rehabilitative approaches endorsed by government in recent years. Given their investment in the sector, faith communities will not be mere 'fair-weather friends' to those attempting to combat homelessness; nor, however, will they necessarily be the most comfortable of companions if the increasingly interventionist tone in homelessness policy continues.

Note

1 The ARHC/ESRC Religion and Society Programme small grant 'The Difference that "Faith" Makes' led by Sarah Johnsen.

9 Religion, politics and law

Gladys Ganiel and Peter Jones

> This chapter explores in depth the historical and contemporary intertwining of religion, politics and legislation in Britain, bringing to bear a particular focus on issues, events and trends already introduced in previous chapters, including Chapter 1 on conflicts and controversies. It discusses relations between religion, politics and law in the whole of the United Kingdom, including Northern Ireland. Although the latter is considered separately, in order to highlight some of the distinct features of its religio-political history in the post-war period, the use of the frame of 'civil religion' throughout the chapter helps to highlight common themes and linkages.

Britain, like all European countries, has a past in which religion and politics have been closely intertwined. Indeed, for much of that past, it would have made little sense to conceive religion and politics as separable subjects. Peter Berger's (1990) image of a 'sacred canopy' uniting spiritual, social and political life seems an apt description of Britain's past. In the modern age, as the Introduction to this volume explains, we have become used to a sharper separation between religious and political institutions and to thinking about and conducting politics independently of religion. Yet Britain, again like all European countries, has a religious legacy that still bears upon its political life. In all four regions of the United Kingdom – England, Scotland, Wales and Northern Ireland – sacred canopies have shaded first into 'civil religions' (see over), and then to even more religiously diverse societies. These developments prompted significant changes in the governance of religion by the British state. By 'governance' we mean the way that the state enacts laws to manage, restrict or promote the role and rights of religious actors in the public sphere.

This chapter begins by discussing the still important public role of religion, then analysing how the governance of religion (in terms of legislation) has changed in response to pluralism in England, Scotland and Wales, and ethno-religious conflict in Northern Ireland, and moving on to analyse changes in the ways religious actors participate in politics. Because of the particularities of its ethno-religious conflict, the final part of the chapter is devoted to Northern Ireland. But the chapter shows that, in *all* parts of the UK, religious and political actors and institutions remain deeply engaged with each other, so much so that it is simply misleading to conceive of the UK as a straightforwardly secular state.

Religion, politics and law in England, Scotland and Wales

The public role of religion: establishment and civil religion

For significant periods of their histories, some form of Protestantism served as a 'civil religion' in England, Scotland and Wales (as well as in Northern Ireland, see final section). Civil religions blur the boundaries between religion and politics. Their 'god' is identified with the 'civil unit' itself, and their reverence is directed accordingly. Thus they infuse a people, group, nation or state with a semi-sacred quality, which in turn affects 'identity', including how people see themselves religiously and politically. The nineteenth-century Scottish missionary explorer David Livingstone, who saw it as his calling to take both Christianity and commerce to the African continent, could be seen as embodying a brand of Protestant civil religion. The idea that a nation or people has a 'manifest destiny', a 'sacred calling', or is 'chosen' by God, is typical of civil religions.

Civil religions do not require an official link between church and state, but in regions where there are 'established' churches – that is, churches which have a close constitutional link with the state which makes their religion the 'official' religion in the territory – civil religions can draw on the symbolic power of their relationships with the state. Today there are only remnants of widespread allegiance to Protestant civil religions in England, Scotland and Wales, and religious establishment was abolished in Ireland in 1871 and in Wales in 1920. The Church of Scotland is an 'established church' in that it is formally recognized in law as Scotland's national church, but its institutions are separate from those of the state. This is not the case in England, where the Church of England remains an 'established' church. The principal ways in which the Church of England is linked to the British state are through its Supreme Governor the monarch, government involvement in senior church appointments, parliamentary oversight of some of the church's activities and the presence of its bishops in the House of Lords. Since 1974, Parliament no longer exercises control over the doctrine and worship of the Church of England and, for the most part, Parliament now leaves the church to order its own affairs. However, the Church's Commissioners, who manage its finances, are answerable to Parliament. Unlike many other established churches in Europe, the Church of England is funded by its own resources. It receives some indirect state support through state funding of Anglican chaplaincies and church schools, and support for some of its historical buildings, but other religious organizations are also beneficiaries of these forms of support, albeit on a smaller scale.

The most 'political' feature of establishment is the right of bishops of the Church of England to sit, ex officio, in Parliament. With the exception of the Manx Tynwald, the UK Parliament is unique in Europe in making formal provision for religious representation (Morris 2009: 45). Forty-two bishops and archbishops of the church are eligible to sit in the House of Lords, though since 1847 only 26 may sit at any one time. In reality, bishops attend in significant numbers only infrequently and rarely make a critical difference to votes of the House (Bown 1994). Moreover, they now accept that in their parliamentary role they should represent Christianity, and perhaps even religious faith generally, rather than only Anglicanism narrowly understood. There is no formal provision for the representation of other churches or faiths in the House of Lords, although the life peerage system has been used to appoint people who can serve as de facto representatives of other faiths.

For a modern, religiously plural, liberal democratic society, the establishment of the Church of England is clearly anomalous, and perhaps establishment in its Scottish form is too. That said, the issue of establishment in relation to the Church of Scotland is not 'political' in the way that it is for the Church of England, and the Church of Scotland is sometimes held up as a model for a reformed Church of England (e.g. McLean and Linsley 2004).Yet in recent decades calls for disestablishment have been more muted and infrequent than they were during the nineteenth century, for several reasons. One is that the Church of England now largely governs its own affairs. Another is that establishment has become a largely symbolic matter and does not significantly disadvantage other denominations or faiths. A third is that for many people establishment now matters as a form of public recognition of religious faith. Whereas in the past different denominations of Christianity have seen one another as rivals and demands for disestablishment have come primarily from Protestant Dissenters, Christians and members of other faiths now frequently see secularism (rejection of religious faith) as their common enemy. Disestablishment is now more likely to be seen by other denominations and faiths as a triumph for secularism rather than a blow for religious equality (Modood 1994).

It is possible that some remnants of attachment to civil religion also preserve establishment in England. As discussed in Chapter 6 on ritual change, when major national celebrations and mourning take place the Church of England remains the 'master of ceremonies'. Whether at the coronation (see Plate 2.1), the royal weddings or the funeral of Diana Princess of Wales, it is the Church of England which hosts and orchestrates the rituals and collective emotions of the British people (and of members of the Commonwealth who still feel some allegiance to Britain). Here we also see a slippage between an 'English' civil religion and a 'British' one. The tension between a sense of 'British' identity and identity focused around being English, Welsh, Scottish or Irish is a theme of what follows.

The transition to a multi-faith society

As much of this volume shows, post-war Britain has changed from a largely mono-faith (Christian, chiefly Protestant) to a multi-faith society. Judaism has had a presence in Britain for centuries, long enough for it to have secured a settled place for itself in British life. There have also long been people in Britain subscribing to other non-Christian faiths, such as Buddhism. But it was only with post-war migration that non-Christian faiths were represented in sufficient numbers to change the religious and political landscape in Britain.

Many migrants, especially those from South Asia, brought new religions to the country. Although their overall numbers remain relatively small (see Introduction and Chapter 3), in absolute and in political terms they constitute a significant new religious presence in Britain, particularly in certain areas of the country. In whatever terms these populations thought of their own identities, politicians and policy-makers – and many academics – initially conceived them in terms of race. Widespread acceptance of the idea of multiculturalism modified that narrowly racial perspective, but it was only during the 1990s that policy-makers began to think of religion as a more significant identifier. This was partly because of the insistence on faith identities by the new British citizens themselves (Modood 2009). Inevitably, race, culture and religion remain closely entangled as features of people's different identities in Britain and as foci for public policy.

Why should the *religious* allegiances of these new populations be of concern to public policy? In large part, the answer is that the established arrangements of British society were not attuned to them. Arrangements that had worked reasonably well for a society whose members were either Christians of various sorts or adherents of no religion were not similarly suited to other faiths. Think, for example, of the structure of the working week in Britain and the timing of national holidays, or of the difficulties faced by a Sikh who sought employment with a bus company whose uniform included a peaked cap, or of a Muslim woman who sought employment with a department store whose uniform required her to expose her legs. Thus, public and private action has been required, either nationally or locally, to adjust procedures, practices and requirements to mitigate the disadvantages religious minorities incur because of their faith. That process of adjustment has itself given rise to debates about how comprehensive it should be: should the goal be complete equality, or should Britain's Christian inheritance retain a special status so that some asymmetry between Christianity and other faiths remains acceptable? And what becomes of church establishment, of the old civil religious sensibilities, and of 'Britishness' when new religions are admitted into the picture?

One issue that illustrates this process of adjustment is faith schools (see Chapter 8). Britain already had state-aided Anglican, Roman Catholic and Jewish schools before mass immigration. Understandably, many Muslims insisted there should also be state-aided Muslim schools. For several years governments resisted their demands, partly because of fears of the social consequences of reinforcing the separation of the Muslim community through education and partly because of misgivings over the kind of education Muslim schools might provide. However, given the existence of other state-funded faith schools, it was plainly inequitable to deny the same facilities to Muslims, and in 1998 the first two voluntary-aided (see Key terms in Chapter 8 for definition) Muslim schools were opened. Further impetus was given to faith schools by Tony Blair's government, though less to placate the demands of the faithful, or Blair's own religious convictions, than to improve choice and the educational attainment of schools. In fact, in 2010 publicly funded faith schools included only 11 Muslim, four Sikh schools and one Hindu school, compared with nearly 5,000 Church of England and over 2,000 Roman Catholic schools. Nevertheless, the association in the public mind of faith schools with non-Christian faiths, especially Islam, has served to sharpen debate about their potential divisiveness (critics often point to the divided school system in Northern Ireland as an example of how this can reinforce social and political division). In addition, faith schools, more than any other measure, have evoked protests against the use of public funds to promote and sustain religious faith. On the other hand, faith schools remain popular with parents.

Law, accommodation and discrimination

The issue of accommodating non-Christian minorities did not arise only with post-war immigration. Britain previously had measures accommodating the Jewish community. For example, under the old Sunday Trading laws, Jewish shopkeepers who closed their shops on Saturdays were allowed to open them and trade as normal on Sundays. Jews were also given exemption from animal welfare legislation, so that they could slaughter animals according to the rites of Judaism. However, the issue of accommodation became much more pressing and controversial with the increasing presence of other non-Christian faiths.

One of its earliest manifestations arose in 1972 when legislation was passed requiring motorcyclists to wear crash helmets. That created difficulties for turban-wearing Sikhs. When the issue was tested in the European Court, the law was held not to contravene Sikhs' right to freedom of religion. Nevertheless, in 1976, the government amended the legislation to exempt biking Sikhs from the requirement to wear a crash helmet provided they wore a turban. Subsequent legislation prohibiting the carrying of knives in public also exempted Sikhs who wished to carry the *kirpan* as their religion requires. Muslims, like Jews, enjoy an exemption that enables them to practise ritual slaughter.

Apart from these occasional exemptions and with the exception of Northern Ireland, there was until 2003 no general provision in law for dealing with disadvantages that people might encounter because of the requirements of their faith. The Race Relations Act 1976 prohibited discrimination on racial grounds in employment. The Act defined 'racial grounds' with reference to 'colour, race, nationality, or ethnic or national origins'. The courts decided that both Jews[1] and Sikhs[2] constituted ethnic groups, who therefore gained the protection of the Act. But they also ruled that, while a common religion might contribute to a group's ethnicity, possession of a common religion alone was not enough to render a group 'racial' or 'ethnic' for purposes of the Act. Hence, groups such as Muslims and Rastafarians fell outside its compass. However, because of the different social circumstances of Northern Ireland, religious rather than racial discrimination in the workplace was prohibited there by the Fair Employment Act 1976.

One other legal source to which an aggrieved religious adherent might turn is Article 9 of the European Convention on Human Rights (ECHR), which gives everyone 'the right to freedom of thought, conscience and religion' (see Text box 18). In cases relating to employment, however, the courts have interpreted the Article rather ungenerously. Broadly, their position has been that, if an employee encounters a conflict between his religious convictions and an employment practice, that conflict does not breach the employee's rights, since the employee need not have taken up that employment in the first instance and has the option of leaving and seeking alternative employment (Vickers 2008: 86–94; Ahdar and Leigh 2005: 165–168).

TEXT BOX 18

The European Convention on Human Rights

Article 9

9.1 Everyone has the right to freedom of thought, conscience and religion; this right includes freedom to change his religion or belief, and freedom, either alone or in community with others and in public or private, to manifest his religion or belief, in worship, teaching, practice and observance.

9.2 Freedom to manifest one's religion or beliefs shall be subject only to such limitations as are prescribed by law and are necessary in a democratic society in the interests of public safety, for the protection of public order, health or morals, or the protection of the rights and freedoms of others.

Comment

The European Court of Human Rights treats the freedom to *hold* a belief as absolute, but the freedom to *manifest* a belief as conditional, given the 'limitations' specified in the second clause of Article 9. The 1998 Human Rights Act incorporated the ECHR into British law, so that individuals were able to seek remedy for breaches of the Convention in the British courts. Previously, they could seek remedy only through the Strasbourg court system.

Provision for adverse treatment of people by virtue of their religious beliefs changed radically in 2003. Spurred by an EU Directive on discrimination in employment, Parliament adopted the Employment Equality (Religion or Belief) Regulations 2003. The Regulations made it an offence to discriminate, directly or indirectly, in employment on grounds of religion or belief. Direct religious discrimination consists in discriminating for religious reasons – for example, refusing to appoint someone to a post because she is a Muslim. Indirect religious discrimination arises when an employer has a provision, criterion or practices, which disadvantages the members of a particular religion (relative to those who adhere to a different or to no religion), even though that disadvantage may be unintended. For example, if an employer requires his employees to be clean-shaven, he discriminates indirectly against male Sikhs, unless he can show that that requirement is 'a proportionate means to a legitimate aim' (e.g. because his production process requires strict standards of hygiene that are incompatible with beards). The Regulations also outlawed harassment and victimization in employment for reasons of religion or belief. The Equality Act 2006 extended the same principles to the provision of goods and services.

Both of these measures have now been superseded by the Equality Act 2010, which applies to England and Wales and in almost all respects to Scotland, but in almost none to Northern Ireland, since equal opportunities and discrimination are 'transferred matters' under the Northern Ireland Act 1998. The Act designates 'religion or belief' as one of a number of 'protected characteristics' which also include age, disability, race, sex and sexual orientation. Its primary purpose was to harmonize legislation dealing with different forms of discrimination and, for the most part, the substance of the rules governing religion or belief remain as they had been in the 2003 Employment Equality Regulations and the 2006 Equality Act.

Efforts to prohibit religious discrimination have created difficulties as well as benefits for religious adherents, since religious organizations often want to discriminate on religious grounds, in, for example, employment and the use they allow others to make of their premises. The law relating to employment has allowed 'exemptions' to discrimination law in order for account to be taken of a person's religious beliefs where that is a genuine occupational qualification, as it would be for a priest or imam. It also allows account to be taken of religion in the appointment of teachers, and in the admission of pupils, to faith schools. Similarly discrimination in the provision of goods and services is permitted where it is genuinely necessary for a religious organization to comply with its purpose. However, this is an area of law where there is scope for different judgments on how generously the domain of permitted discrimination should be understood.

Another problematic area has been clashes between different sorts of protected characteristics. The law has granted organized religions exemptions to discriminate on grounds of sex, sexual orientation and gender reassignment, but only insofar as that discrimination is a genuine and proportionate requirement of the religion's doctrines. The 2010 Act provided that civil partnerships can be registered on religious premises (formerly that was prohibited), but obliged no religious organization to host civil partnerships against its wishes. In other areas, however, the claims of religion have been subordinated to those of other characteristics. For example, as Chapter 1 documents in more detail, in 2007 the government decided that Catholic adoption agencies that refused to place children with gay or lesbian people should cease to be publicly funded, and in 2010 the Charity Commission denied such agencies charitable status.[3] In one high-profile legal case, a Christian registrar lost her job because she was unwilling to officiate at civil partnerships; in another, a Christian employee of the charity Relate, who refused to give sex therapy to same-sex couples, was judged to have been lawfully dismissed.[4] As these cases illustrate, in the new millennium Christians have come to figure as prominently in actions for discrimination as adherents of other faiths.

Law and freedom of expression

How far should freedom of expression be curbed to protect religious belief and religious sensibilities? For centuries blasphemy was a common-law offence in England but, until the 1970s, there had been no public prosecution for blasphemy since 1922 (and none in Scotland since 1843) and it was widely supposed that the offence of blasphemy was obsolete. That supposition was corrected by a successful private prosecution for blasphemy brought by the campaigner Mary Whitehouse (see Plate 1.1) against the publisher and editor of *Gay News* for publishing a poem, 'The Love that Dares to Speak its Name', by James Kirkup (see Chapter 1 for more discussion). The case sparked debate about whether freedom of expression should be curtailed to protect religious beliefs. A majority report of the Law Commission recommended in 1985 that the offence of blasphemy should be abolished but, for the rest of the twentieth century, this was an issue that governments studiously avoided. In a multi-faith context, the common-law offence of blasphemy was inequitable in that it applied only to Christianity and, arguably, only to Anglicanism, but there was sharp division over whether that inequity should be removed by abolishing the offence or by extending its protection to other faiths.

As we have seen in Chapter 1, the *Gay News* case was a little local difficulty compared with the international storm that followed the publication of Salman Rushdie's novel *The Satanic Verses* in 1988. This episode illustrated how it had become impossible to contain fundamental issues concerning religious faith within national boundaries. The Rushdie Affair did much to create and foster a sense that the values of Islam and the West were fundamentally in conflict (Malik 2009). As Chapter 1 also documents, since the Affair, several other episodes have raised the same basic issue if in less dramatic form. For example, many Christians found Monty Python's film *Life of Brian*, Martin Scorsese's film *The Last Temptation of Christ* and, more recently, *Jerry Springer the Opera* similarly objectionable.

With the onset of the new millennium, Tony Blair's government created a new offence of incitement to religious hatred rather than reforming the existing law of blasphemy. The offence was not entirely new in that incitement to hatred, including religious hatred, had been an offence in Northern Ireland since 1970. The prospect of the law seriously curtailing people's freedom to criticize and debate religious beliefs made the government's proposals deeply controversial, both inside and outside Parliament. Some religious groups favoured the proposed legislation, but others joined with secular groups in opposing it as unacceptably restricting people's freedom to propagate and criticize beliefs. The government's principal defence – that criticism of beliefs would be unaffected since the bill would protect believers rather than beliefs – was unconvincing (see Barendt 2011).

There was also much confusion about quite what the bill would proscribe; some Muslims believed it would enable the banning of Rushdie's *Satanic Verses*, while government ministers insisted that it would not. After several abortive attempts, the government secured passage of its Racial and Religious Hatred Bill in 2006, but only after it had been effectively neutered by amendments passed in the House of Lords. Parliament abolished the English common-law offence of blasphemy in 2008; its abolition did not extend to Scotland, but there is doubt whether blasphemy survives as an offence in Scotland anyway. Blasphemy remains a common-law offence in Northern Ireland.

How far free expression should be curtailed for the sake of religious belief is not an issue that will be settled by these or any other legal measures. In part this is because, in a global age, it is an issue that transcends national boundaries. But it is also because it is an issue for which a society's public culture on what constitutes acceptable treatment of religious subjects is likely to matter more than the letter of its law.

Religious differences, security and social cohesion

The development of Britain into an increasingly ethnically diverse society has been punctuated by periodic outbreaks of violence, such as the riots in Brixton and Toxteth in 1981. For many people, these disturbances reinforced the case for multiculturalism: recognition and respect for people's cultural differences were essential to their feeling full members of a society and were anyway a basic requirement of justice. Other voices worried about the divisive consequences of policies that stressed difference rather than commonality, exacerbated in part by disturbances in some towns in the north of England in 2001, particularly Oldham, Burnley and Bradford, and concerns about the 'parallel lives' lived by effectively segregated communities (Cantle 2001). Worries about social cohesion became much greater after the attack on the Twin Towers in New York on 11 September 2001, and still greater after the suicide bombings in London on 7 July 2005, which killed 52 people as well as the four bombers, and the failed attempt two weeks later to mimic those bombings. The later attack on Glasgow Airport and the uncovering of other terrorist plots have sustained concern about Islamic radicals in Britain.

The government was particularly struck by the fact that the 7/7 bombings were carried out not by 'foreigners' but by four British Muslims, three of whom had been born in Britain and one who had been in the country since he was aged five. While the 7/7 bombings seem to have been prompted in part by the 'War on Terror', particularly the Iraq War, that was a connection the government was reluctant to concede. Rather, it saw 7/7 as a symptom of the failure to integrate young Muslims into British society and that led to its switching its policy emphasis from encouraging difference to promoting social cohesion. Social cohesion became a particular concern of the Department for Communities and Local Government, which was created in 2006, and which set up a Race, Cohesion and Faiths Directorate and disbursed funds to Faith Groups to promote community integration. At the same time, the government adopted a policy designated 'Preventing Violent Extremism', which channelled resources to Muslim communities designed to enable them to identify and to redirect young Muslims who were susceptible to what had become known in policy circles as 'radicalization'. Efforts to detect terrorist activity and to counteract the 'radicalization' involved the government in a difficult balancing act. On the one hand these efforts inevitably focused on the Muslim community; on the other hand, they risked alienating and stigmatizing that community, whose co-operation was essential to the execution of the government's policy. The Prevent strategy is now thought by many to have been poorly designed and to have had little success (Thomas 2010). Moreover, in seeking to encourage 'moderate' Islam and to counter 'extremism', the government has sought to influence the content of Muslims' beliefs, a use of political power that would normally be found quite improper in a liberal society (see Norman 2008).

In contrast to this drift away from a policy of multiculturalism towards one of 'integration' or even 'assimilation' to an ideal standard – or even a new imagined civil religion – of 'Britishness', there has been widespread concern that the diverse character of Britain's population should be reflected in the membership of its public institutions, such as Parliament, local authorities, the judiciary and the police. This is partly for reasons of social cohesion. This concern is most commonly spoken of in terms of ethnicity but, in many instances, that now equates with faith. For instance, particular attention has been paid to the number of Muslim members of the House of Commons (four in 2005 and eight in 2010, both proportionate under-representations). That is generally thought to matter because it symbolizes the inclusion of members of that faith in the public life of British society.

Religion and party politics

Britain's transition from a mono- to a multi-faith society has also resulted in changes in the ways people from all religious backgrounds interact with government and in the public sphere, whether that is through party politics or religious 'cause' groups.

Religion has greatly diminished as an influence upon people's political loyalties. There has remained an association between membership of the Church of England and support for the Conservative Party, and between Catholicism and dissenting Protestantism and support for the Labour and Liberal Parties. In Scotland there has been an association between membership of the Church of Scotland and support for the Conservative Party, though this has diminished as the Conservative vote in Scotland has declined. There has been a particularly close association between Catholicism and Labour voting in Scotland.

These associations can be explained in considerable measure by the class-based nature of support for political parties and the different class compositions of different religious denominations. However, there is some evidence that religion has continued to exert an independent influence upon people's political loyalties and voting patterns (Kotler-Berkowitz 2001; Seawright 2000). In large part, that influence seems to be a legacy of past divisions and conflicts (e.g. Catholic hostility to the Conservative Party over the issue of Irish Home Rule) which has been transmitted by parents' influence upon the voting patterns of their children (Butler and Stokes 1974: 155–166; Denver 2003: 56–59). But, with increasing partisan dealignment (people's decreasing propensity to align themselves with a single political party) and the rise of 'issue voting', religious belief and belonging may also exert a non-historical influence on people's voting behaviour (Steven 2010: 36–42).

Religious faith and political activity

The story of how religious organizations and individuals motivated by faith have mobilized on political issues in post-war Britain is extremely complex. In part, that is because it encompasses so many different actors. Churches and other organizations formally representing particular faiths regularly make known their positions on social and political issues, both to governments and to the public. But so too do innumerable groups who are avowedly religious in motivation and purpose but who are either ecumenical or independent of any particular church or denomination, such as Christian Aid, the Christian Institute, and the Lesbian and Gay Christian Movement. To these we must add the multitude of groups who do not present themselves as religious in character or purpose (even when they were founded by faith groups), but to whom people motivated by faith make significant contributions, such as Barnardo's, Oxfam, CND, Amnesty International and Greenpeace (see Chapter 8 and Case study 6). In recent years several religious think tanks concerned with public policy issues have emerged, such as Ekklesia, Theos and the Quilliam Foundation.

From a government's point of view, and perhaps from the public's point of view, churches and religious organizations have a stronger entitlement to be listened to on some issues than on others. On matters that directly affect them as organizations or that have an immediate religious relevance, government departments typically consult them as interested parties. Beyond that, churches are often treated as having a special status in relation to 'moral issues', a term used to describe issues such as contraception, abortion, euthanasia, embryo research, sexuality, and issues relating to marriage and divorce. On issues of this sort, Members of Parliament (MPs) are commonly, though not invariably, allowed a free vote – a vote free from the usual discipline imposed by the party whips. MPs can then vote according to their consciences, including their religious convictions. The evidence shows that, even on conscience issues, party membership remains the strongest predictor of how MPs will vote, but religion has also been significant (Hibbing and Marsh 1987; Pattie *et al.* 1998).

As the next chapter documents in more detail, the decade most associated with the liberalization of law on 'moral issues' is the 1960s. Homosexual conduct was decriminalized by the Sexual Offences Act 1967 and in the same year abortion, under certain specified circumstances, was legalized. The Divorce Reform Act 1969 replaced the concept of 'matrimonial offence' with that of 'irretrievable breakdown' as ground for divorce. The 1960s also saw the abolition of theatre censorship, the relaxation of cinema censorship, and a more relaxed policy on the content of television and radio programmes. These changes and the move to a 'permissive society' (that phrase was generally used pejoratively) provoked a strong negative reaction from conservative Christians.

The highly public campaigner Mary Whitehouse (Plate 1.1), established the National Viewers' and Listeners' Association, which aimed to 'clean up' television. She was also a leading figure in the predominantly evangelical Festival of Light, which aimed to halt moral decline and which later became Christian Action Research and Education (CARE). The Society for the Protection of the Unborn Child (SPUC) was established in the 1960s to oppose and secure the repeal of the Abortion Act 1967. However, more liberal responses were also well represented among Christians. Theologians, clergy and laity were themselves caught up in the changing attitudes of the 1960s (McLeod 2007; Parsons 1994a: 242–263). The Church of England gave qualified approval to the legalization of abortion and, accepting that not all sins should be crimes, supported the decriminalization of homosexual acts (Willett 2009). It also played a significant role in changing the grounds for divorce (McLeod 2007: 223–226).

Most of these issues remained live after the 1960s. There have, for example, been repeated efforts to tighten up the law on abortion, efforts in which Catholic and evangelical Christians have been prominent. In addition, other highly controversial issues have come to fore, such as euthanasia and stem cell research. Bishops voted (unusually) as a bloc to help to defeat a bill introduced in the House of Lords that would have permitted assisted dying. The Labour government's proposal to whip its MPs on its Human Fertilisation and Embryology Bill, enacted in 2008, met with strong protests from its Catholic MPs, including some government ministers. Eventually the government allowed its MPs to vote freely on three crucial aspects of the bill, while whipping them on the remainder (Steven 2010: 109–114). The Catholic Church has been particularly vocal on issues of abortion and embryology. Partly because of its more sharply defined doctrinal position on these issues, but also because of the different place it occupies in British society, the Catholic Church has been a much more strident critic than have either of the established churches (Steven 2010: 114–120). The rise of feminism and the women's movement and the gay liberation movement have also been tremendously influential on public policy and both have proved great sources of controversy and division for churches, not only in relation to public policy but also with respect to their own constitutions and doctrines.

In general, openly partisan interventions by churches, especially the established church, would be frowned upon. Churches and religious bodies have also to be cognizant of the diverse political loyalties of their own members. However, churches have sometimes taken sides. We saw in the Introduction to this volume that, in the immediate post-war period, churches worked with the government in actively shaping the welfare state. During the 1980s, by contrast, churches became pitted against the strongly market-oriented

Conservative government of Margaret Thatcher. In part the tension between churches and the government arose in relation to a series of policy issues and episodes. These included the government's policies on poverty, unemployment and community care, the poll tax, the miners' strike, and triumphalism following the Falklands War. But it also arose over the general values driving government policy, which its critics perceived as encouraging greed, selfishness, excessive individualism and neglect of society's duty to provide for its less fortunate members. As we have seen, the most celebrated instance of this tension was the report *Faith in the City*, issued by the Archbishop of Canterbury's Commission on Urban Priority Areas, which was highly critical of the government's policy and which one cabinet minister dismissed as Marxist (Church of England 1985, see Plate 2.4). Criticism of the general direction of government policy was also voiced by the Church of Scotland and the Methodist and Catholic churches.

Margaret Thatcher responded by claiming biblical support for her values, as did many other supporters of her government, including the Conservative Party Chairman, John Selwyn Gummer, and the head of Mrs Thatcher's No. 10 think tank, Brian Griffiths, both (then) prominent lay Anglicans. Some prominent members of the Jewish community, including the Chief Rabbi, also supported her values (see the Introduction to this volume). The other form of response the churches' intervention evoked from government supporters was that their pronouncements on economic and social policy were ill-informed and politically naïve, and that their increasing preoccupation with political issues represented a sacrifice of their core religious purpose to secular enthusiasms.

Unusually fractious as the Thatcher era was, it illustrates another feature of the relation between religion and politics in Britain. Arguments about the implications of religious belief for public policy very often take place *within* churches and religious organizations rather than only between them and external actors. During most of the period under consideration here, the clergy's political centre of gravity has been to the left of most of their laity. One commentator has described the average Church of England service as a *Guardian* reader preaching to *Telegraph* readers (Durham 1997: 220). However, rather than following a simple split between an active clergy and a passive laity, political divisions have often been most pronounced between competing activist minorities, radical and conservative, which include both clergy and laity (see Parsons 1994b: 145–146; Medhurst and Moyser 1988, and Chapters 1 and 2 in this volume).

How much impact does this activity have upon governments? That question is not easily answered, but on issues such as social, economic and foreign policy, churches and religious organizations function as 'cause groups' and cause groups generally have less leverage with governments than interest groups. The government does not usually need their co-operation for the formulation or implementation of policy and, unlike interest groups such as business organizations, trade unions and professional associations like the British Medical Association, they are not normally in a position to make life difficult for a government. That is not to say that religious groups are wasting their time, but any influence they exert usually has to be by way of their ability to persuade politicians or the public of the merits of their case. For example, Christian opinion, especially that of Archbishop Ramsey and the Anglican episcopate, seems to have been significant in securing a parliamentary majority for the abolition of the death penalty (Medhurst and Moyser 1988: 314; McLeod 2007: 222–223). The campaigns led by Mary Whitehouse in support of the passage of the Child Protection Bill (dealing with child pornography) and the Video Recordings Bill (restricting the sale and rent of 'video nasties') proved highly successful in securing their enactment in 1978 and 1984 respectively, though partly because of a supportive media and an absence of parliamentary opposition (McCarthy and Moodie 1981; Marsh *et al.* 1986). For the most part, on general issues of public policy, religious organizations have to settle for being one voice among many.

The devolution of political authority to Scotland and Wales and the development of the European Union (EU) have created new sites of political power that religious organizations have to address. Though the churches' support for devolution in both jurisdictions varied, they now have more accessible sites of political power to deal with. Churches also have chosen to ensure their voices are heard at the European level and have done so, in part, by cooperating with one another across national and denominational boundaries (Hill 2009; Leustean and Madeley 2009). In Northern Ireland, most religiously based political activism is focused on the devolved Assembly and local government.

Northern Ireland: a law unto itself?

The preceding discussion has already highlighted Northern Ireland's legislative distinctiveness within the UK. For people living in England, Scotland or Wales, Northern Ireland has often been considered a place apart – a law unto itself due to its high levels of religious commitment, sharp religio-political divisions, troubled past and its present precarious peace.

With the Belfast/Good Friday Agreement of 1998, the region emerged from nearly four decades of violence. The causes of the Northern Ireland conflict are complex (Ruane and Todd 1996). One of the main contentions is the constitutional status of the region itself – an issue that has been central in UK politics for most of the period since 1886. At that time the entire island of Ireland was part of the UK, but most Irish Catholics (and a few Protestants) were agitating for a 'home rule' parliament based in Dublin. This was opposed by most Protestants living in the north-east of Ireland, who campaigned under the slogan 'home rule is Rome rule' (that is, their loyalty was to 'Protestant' Britain, and they did not want to be subject to the rule of the Roman Catholic Church). The Dublin-based Easter Rising of 1916 marked the start of the Irish War for Independence, a result of which was the partition of the island in 1921, with six counties in the province of Ulster remaining within the UK (in the 'union').

Today, Irish 'nationalists' (who live in Northern Ireland as well as in the Irish Republic in the south) still want what they refer to as the 'six counties' to be a part of a 'united' Republic of Ireland. 'Unionists' prefer to remain part of the UK. Nationalists usually hail from a Catholic background and unionists usually identify with Protestantism. Throughout the early twentieth century, the British Conservative Party identified highly with unionists, and the Ulster Unionist Party, which was elected to the British Parliament, could at times tip the balance of power at Westminster. This is no longer the case, and many unionists feel that British parties (especially since Labour under Tony Blair) are more sympathetic to the nationalist cause.

Up until the late 1990s, there was an 'academic consensus', even in relation to Northern Ireland, that religion was no more than an 'ethnic marker' (McGarry and O'Leary 1995; Hayes and McAllister 1999). Especially in the past decade, there has been a shift in this way of thinking, as analysts have begun to tease out the ways religion has contributed to division and conflict, as well as to peacemaking and the peace process. The concept of 'civil religion' is one way to take better account of the role of religion.

Civil religion in Northern Ireland

Northern Ireland has much higher rates of church attendance and levels of traditional religious belief than the rest of the UK (Mitchell 2004, 2006). It has not had an official state church since the middle of the nineteenth century, when the Anglican Church of Ireland was the established church. Much of Northern Ireland's history has been marked by the presence of two powerful and competing civil religions: Protestantism and Catholicism (Demerath 2001; Elliott 2009). Civil religion can function in benign, community-building ways. But in the case of a divided society like Northern Ireland, civil religions may prompt people to define themselves over and against the 'other.' People then construct 'common-sense' understandings of the other that justify violence or division.

A civil religion approach pushes beyond the idea that religion is simply an ethnic marker. In her wider body of work on religion and politics in Northern Ireland, Claire Mitchell has not often used the term civil religion. But she captures what we mean by civil religion in her analysis of a process in which 'religion in Northern Ireland continues to inform identities, provide values, organise activities and help structure social life' (2004: 250). Civil religion is a 'thick' rather than 'thin' concept, providing resources for people to give real meaning to their identities.

Protestant civil religion

The political assumptions and social mores of most unionists have been infused with a Reformed, Presbyterian, Calvinist-informed brand of evangelicalism, which had its roots in the seventeenth-century 'covenanting' traditions of Scotland and in the evangelical revivals of the 1740s and 1850s–1860s (Ganiel 2008; Mitchel 2003; Brewer with Higgins 1998). The 'covenant' denotes the idea that God made a deal with Protestants to bless them if they promoted Protestant principles in government. Protestants thought of themselves as a 'chosen people' who had been 'called' from Scotland and England to bring the gospel to the 'pagan' Catholics of Ireland. Accordingly, the province of Ulster was their 'promised land'. Thus Protestant migration to Ireland could be interpreted as fulfilment of their God-given destiny rather than a colonial land-grab. Since Protestants eventually established overwhelming economic, political and social privilege within what is now Northern Ireland, these religious ideas were reinforced by real-world power.

Though not always articulated so explicitly or crudely, these ideas formed the basis of what Wright (1973) called a 'Protestant ideology'. Coupled with that was fear of the political agenda of the Catholic Church. Protestants believed that in a united Ireland – which they assumed would be in thrall to the Catholic Church – they would be discriminated against. Further, Protestants thought it right to extol aspects of Protestantism in public life, such as the praise of Protestant liberty, a high regard for the Bible, and Sabbatarianism. Protestantism was also promoted in the symbols of the Orange Order (Kaufmann 2007; Bryan 2000; Jarman 1997). The banners carried at Orange parades often feature images such as open Bibles, church buildings, crosses, Martin Luther or John Wesley.

During the Troubles (the term used to describe the most recent period of conflict in Ireland, generally dated from the late 1960s to the 1998 Belfast/Good Friday Agreement), many regarded the Reverend Ian Paisley (see Plate 1.4) as embodying an extreme evangelical form of Protestant civil religion (Moloney 2008; Southern 2005; Mitchel 2003; Brewer with Higgins 1998; Cooke 1996). Paisley is a unique figure in modern Europe, having started both his own church (the Free Presbyterian Church in 1951) and his own political party (the Democratic Unionist Party, DUP, in 1971). Steve Bruce (1986, 2007) explains the popularity of 'Paisleyism' in terms of Paisley's ability to appeal to the evangelical core of Protestant ethnic identity.

Catholic civil religion

Unlike Protestant civil religion during the era of unionist-dominated governance (1921–1972), Catholic civil religion in Northern Ireland was not embedded in the symbols and practices of public life. Rather, it was centred on communal practice. Fionnuala O'Connor (1993) has described Catholics in Northern Ireland as 'in search of a state'. For a considerable period of time, she says that Catholics found identity and belonging in the church (O'Connor 1993: 274). This was in contrast to Catholicism in the independent Irish Republic, where church and nation were bound together in a nationalistic form of civil religion, in which the 'holy' Irish nation fulfilled a God-given vocation not only to remain faithful itself, but to spread Catholicism throughout the world by means of an 'Irish diaspora', which included many monks, nuns and priests.

Catholic civil religion throughout Ireland was reinforced by high levels of religious practice, including Mass-going and popular devotion to saints and the Virgin Mary. In Catholic West Belfast, statues of the Virgin Mary still adorn roundabouts and other public spaces. Ideologically, Catholic civil religion emphasized ideas such as the blood sacrifice, martyrdom and victimhood (Elliott 2009; Ganiel and Dixon 2008; Mitchell 2006). The idea of blood sacrifice can be found in the writings of Pádraig Pearse, one of the leaders of the Easter Rising, who likened Ireland to Christ and said that the nation would never be free from British rule unless young men were willing to die for it. The hunger strikes of 1981, in which ten prisoners died, can be seen in part as drawing on wider Catholic traditions of martyrdom and blood sacrifice. To this day, depictions of hunger strikers on nationalist murals incorporate Christological themes, such as quotes from the gospels: 'Greater love hath no man than this, than he lays down his life for his friends', or 'blessed are they who hunger for justice'. Finally, Catholic civil religion is permeated by a sense of victimhood, with Catholics depicted as meek, Christ-like victims at the mercy of ruthless Protestants and a brutal British state. Marianne Elliott (2009) has argued that this sense of victimhood has had at times a paralysing effect on Irish Catholics, marked by an unhealthy deference to the Catholic Church and political parties such as Sinn Féin (a deference which some blame for the long-term and widespread failure to prevent child abuse carried out by a minority of monks and priests in Ireland, and only fully exposed in the twenty-first century).

Religion and slow change

Religion continues to structure social life through educational and residential segregation. The vast majority of children in Northern Ireland are educated in single-faith schools: state-supported Catholic schools and state schools (which are de facto Protestant schools) (see Case study 7). Although there have been some efforts to cross boundaries through the Education for Mutual Understanding programme, the small integrated education movement and specialist 'cross community' ventures for children, many people do not meet someone from the other community until they enter university or the workforce. The churches express little will to challenge segregated education. Further, housing has become more segregated since the Belfast Agreement, with people choosing to live in mono-religious communities due to security concerns or convenience. There are now more 'peace walls' separating Catholic and Protestant communities than there were during the Troubles (Shirlow and Murtagh 2006).

That said, the Troubles prompted some Northern Irish Christians to reflect on the religious aspects of the conflict (Brewer *et al.* 2011). This has contributed to the development of a small but committed ecumenical movement, and major revisions to Protestant identities. There is less evidence of revisions of Catholic identities, although some credit the Catholic charismatic revivals beginning in the 1970s with softening Catholic perceptions of Protestants (Ganiel 2010a). The development of ecumenism and changes within evangelicalism are important because they demonstrate that people can and do actively change their religious identities in ways that promote peace-building and reconciliation.

Ecumenism

The word ecumenism is derived from the Greek *oikoumene,* which means 'the whole inhabited earth'. It is generally used to describe efforts to promote unity and co-operation among Christian denominations, although recently some have argued that it should include 'non-Christian' religions (McMaster 2008, and see Case studies 1 and 2). Ecumenism gained momentum in Ireland after the Second Vatican Council (1962–1965). Among church leadership, Catholic–Protestant relations had begun to thaw before the outbreak of the Troubles. But early in the Troubles, ecumenism was unpopular, particularly among Protestants (Taggart 2004). Paisley got his start as an anti-ecumenical preacher. Neither was ecumenism easy within Catholicism, as the founder of the Irish School of Ecumenics, Fr Michael Hurley, faced considerable opposition from the Archbishop of Dublin when he tried to establish the school in 1970 (Wells 2010: 111–118). Many early ecumenical activities consisted of clergy study groups and then expanded to prayer and worship services, study groups and other events including lay people (McMahon 2009). Lay people collaborated with clergy to start ecumenical communities such as Corrymeela, the Christian Renewal Centre and the Columbanus Community; or inter-church groups like the Clonard Monastery–Fitzroy Presbyterian Fellowship in Belfast, or regional church forums (Wells 2010; Power 2007; Brewer 2003). They have been an important part of a wider cross-community 'civil society' movement (Brewer 2010). There were also efforts to promote ecumenical education, including the work of the Irish School of Ecumenics, now part of Trinity College in Dublin and Belfast (Hurley 2007), and that school's Moving Beyond Sectarianism project. Moving Beyond Sectarianism engaged people at the grassroots through workshops and resulted in the publication of a major book (Liechty and Clegg 2001).

But Power (2007) has concluded that ecumenism has become dominated by a 'community relations' agenda, and its educative and theological aspects have been ignored. This argument has been supported by surveys conducted by the Irish School of Ecumenics, which found that lay people and faith leaders in Ireland tend to think of ecumenism in civic as well as religious terms (Ganiel 2009a, 2009b, 2010b).

Ecumenism, then, provided an alternative religious identity that either transcended Catholic–Protestant divisions, or, more commonly, allowed people to hold multiple religious identities simultaneously, that is, someone might identify as both a Catholic and an ecumenical Christian.

Evangelicalism

From the mid-1980s an evangelical reform movement gathered pace. Those involved sought to change aspects of Protestant identity, such as emphases on the covenant, chosen people and promised land (Ganiel 2008; Mitchel 2003). The most prominent expression of this movement was the socio-political action group Evangelical Contribution on Northern

Ireland (ECONI), which surfaced in 1985 to critique Paisley's religiously themed rallies against the Anglo-Irish Agreement. ECONI consciously subverted the traditional Protestant slogan 'For God and Ulster', arguing that this was an idolatrous equation of God's people with the people of a particular place. They replaced it with 'For God and His Glory Alone' (ECONI 1988).

ECONI disseminated its ideas through Bible studies, conferences, training courses, publications and a periodical, *Lion and Lamb*. The group was remarkably successful in creating a media profile and acquiring funding up until the early 2000s (Ganiel 2008). Indeed, the funding of ECONI is similar to current government attempts to encourage 'moderate' Islam and to counter 'extremism'. A publication by ECONI, *Fields of Vision: Faith and Identity in Protestant Ireland* (Thomson 2002), is emblematic of ECONI's critique of Protestant identity and civil religion. ECONI developed an alternative Christian identity, drawing on Anabaptist ideas about the separation of church and state, the celebration of religious pluralism and a conception of church as a model community (Ganiel 2008).

Researchers have now begun to uncover further evidence that evangelicals were not as blindly allied to Paisleyism as had been previously supposed (Mitchell and Ganiel 2011; Ganiel 2008; Mitchell and Todd 2007; Jordan 2001). Ganiel's research revealed that some people's involvement with ECONI or the Evangelical Alliance had prompted them to rethink their Protestant identities and to distance themselves from Paisleyism (Ganiel 2008). Others described different routes to a moderation or transformation of their Protestant identities, including travel abroad, experiences at university, or personal reading and reflection (Mitchell and Ganiel 2011).

Northern Irish Catholicism has not produced groups akin to ECONI, but Wells (2010) has argued that the Irish School of Ecumenics – while not a Catholic organization – has played a similar role in engaging Catholics. In addition, increased immigration, though not on as large a scale as in England, Scotland or Wales, has made for even greater religious and ethnic diversity, thus somewhat blurring a simple Protestant/Catholic division.

Religion and recent political activity

Especially since the Belfast Agreement, there has been a restructuring of Northern Ireland's political institutions and civil society. There is now a devolved Assembly, elected by proportional representation, which requires power-sharing. British policy has favoured the development of a 'community relations' agenda, including establishing the Community Relations Council (CRC), rewarding civil society groups that do 'cross-community' work with funding and safeguarding equality between different groups.

The CRC is an independent company and registered charity, set up in 1990 to promote better relations between Catholics and Protestants. The CRC is the main gatekeeper for funding for civil society groups in Northern Ireland. But in order for churches or other religious groups to receive CRC support, they must demonstrate a commitment to cross-community work. So, CRC funds work like a 'carrot' to entice groups to cross religious boundaries, with considerable effectiveness. However, this policy has generated resentment on the part of 'traditional' evangelical organizations like the Caleb Foundation, Evangelical Protestant Society and the Independent Orange Order, which cannot meet cross-community requirements (Ganiel 2006, 2008).

In a further legal-political intervention into religion, Section 75 of the Northern Ireland Act 1998 promotes equality of opportunity within public authorities. The groups named in Section 75 are persons of different religious belief, political opinion, racial group, age, marital status or sexual orientation; men and women; persons with disability and persons with-out; and persons with dependants and persons without. Section 75 has provoked consternation among traditional evangelicals, who see it as promoting homosexuality and protecting the rights of everyone *except* evangelicals. While such policies have not elimi-nated sectarianism, they have helped to create a context in which interaction – rather than division – has some financial rewards and legal backing.

Despite these changes, Northern Ireland's political parties remain divided along ethno-religious lines. There are two main political parties within each communal block: the Democratic Unionist Party (DUP) and the Ulster Unionist Party (UUP) within unionism; and Sinn Féin and the Social Democratic and Labour Party (SDLP) within nationalism. The DUP, founded by Ian Paisley, and Sinn Féin, once considered the political wing of the Irish Republican Army (IRA), have historically been considered the more 'extreme' parties. Prior to the Belfast Agreement, the UUP and the SDLP were the larger parties within the two blocks, but since the Agreement the DUP and Sinn Féin have overtaken their rivals. Some argue that the Belfast Agreement's consociational structures reward extreme parties, and others claim that the DUP and Sinn Féin have moderated their positions (Wilson 2010; Wilford and Wilson 2006). After multiple suspensions of the Assembly, unionists and nationalists now share power at every level of government.

Churches and religious organizations' relationships with political parties have changed since the Belfast Agreement. Most significant are the changes in the way evangelical organ-izations interact with the DUP. Among the 33 members of the DUP elected to the Assembly in 2003, 17 belonged to the Free Presbyterian Church (Southern 2005: 129). Given that there are only about 12,000 Free Presbyterians in Northern Ireland, this means that Paisley's small church wields a disproportionate amount of power within the party. But since the DUP has become the largest party, it has had to make compromises that have rankled with its traditional evangelical grassroots – including sharing power with the 'terrorists' of Sinn Féin and upholding legislation that protects the rights of homosexuals. Such compromises were probably behind Paisley being pushed out as Moderator of his church in 2008.

Traditional evangelical organizations have realized that they can no longer influence DUP policy to the extent that they might have in the past. Similar to 'cause' groups in other parts of the UK, they now focus their energies on 'moral' issues, such as abortion and homo-sexuality. For example, Iris Robinson, the wife of DUP leader Peter Robinson, declared on BBC Radio Ulster in 2008 that homosexuality was an 'abomination' and Nelson McCausland, the Minister for Culture, Arts and Leisure, in 2010 tried to force the Ulster Museum to feature creationism. The party remains mindful that it cannot alienate its evan-gelical base. When Peter Robinson lost his Westminster seat in the May 2010 elections, it was thought that a significant part of the evangelical base had voted against him due to his wife's 'immoral' behaviour in having a sexual affair with a 19-year-old man, and his family's 'immoral' relationships with property developers.

There has also been some political activism by Catholics, but it has not taken the form of interest groups like the Evangelical Protestant Society, that is, there are no comparable Catholic groups attempting to influence the policies of Sinn Féin or the SDLP. Rather, during the Troubles, Redemptorist priests at Clonard Monastery in Belfast played a key role as mediators, first between the SDLP and Sinn Féin, and later between these parties and government officials (Wells 2010). This was at a time when the British and Irish govern-ments officially declared it unacceptable to talk with the 'terrorists' of Sinn Féin. Outside Northern Ireland, a significant Irish-American diaspora has been engaged with the peace process. While that involved covertly funding the IRA, other engagement was more benign, such as the activities of Irish-American Chuck Feeney's Atlantic Philanthropies or the US–Ireland Alliance (O'Clery 2007). It is difficult to disentangle to what extent the activism of the Irish diaspora has been motivated by religious, humanitarian and/or political concerns.

The British government seems to regard the churches (at least some churches) as potential partners in addressing outstanding issues related to Northern Ireland's troubled past. In 2007, Northern Ireland Secretary Peter Hain appointed a Consultative Group on the Past (CGP), whose remit was to liaise with people throughout Northern Ireland and submit proposals on dealing with the past. The group included several 'religious' appointees, including the chairs: former Anglican Archbishop Lord Robin Eames and former Catholic priest Denis Bradley. Other appointees included Presbyterian minister Lesley Carroll and David Porter of ECONI. CGP's recommendations, including a legacy commission and reconciliation forum, have been shelved and it is unclear if any will be implemented. The group's 2009 report explicitly called on the churches to make a unique contribution to dealing with the past (Ganiel 2010c; Consultative Group on the Past 2009). In a quite calculating way, people acting on behalf of the British state have favoured some religious actors over others in an attempt to foster good community relations and peace-building.

Conclusion

As 'sacred canopies' have given way to 'civil religions', and then to religiously diverse societies in all parts of the UK, the state has used legislation to manage the relationships between itself and a wider range of religious (and secular) actors. This process is complex, and reflects contemporary concerns about human rights, the protection of minorities and the sometimes violent consequences of religious division. Churches and other religious organizations have also been active players in this process, in some cases undergoing changes in their own religious identities, taking up 'moral' causes in the public sphere, or working for social justice or peace. Clearly, the UK is not simply a secular state where religion is relegated to the private sphere. Questions about how to strike a balance between respecting difference and promoting harmony between all religious groups will continue to vex policy-makers and religious people themselves for the foreseeable future. And conflicts between those who still cherish remnants of the 'civil religions' associated with the four nations of the UK, as well as with those who favour a new, more secular civil 'religion' of 'Britishness', are likely to continue.

Key terms

Calvinist, Presbyterian, Reformed (Protestant): Religious ideas and practices inspired by the French theologian John Calvin (1509–1564), who is considered a founder of Presbyterian or Reformed expressions of Protestant Christianity. Calvinism stresses the sovereignty of God in all things and the importance of Christians living in accordance with the teachings of the Bible, in alliance with the Protestant Reformation's (c. 1517–1648) emphasis on *sola scriptura* (by scripture alone). Key ideas of Calvinism include the total depravity of humankind, unconditional election (those whom God has chosen or elected to be saved will be saved), limited atonement (only those chosen by God will be saved, others will go to hell as a result of their sin), irresistible grace (the chosen will be unable to resist God's calling to salvation) and perseverance of the saints.

Civil religion: When a religion infuses a society, so much so that the 'god' of that religion is identified with the 'civil unit' itself. Civil religions provide a people, group, nation or state with a semi-sacred quality, which in turn affects 'identity', including how people see themselves religiously and politically.

House of Lords: The House of Lords is the upper chamber of the British Parliament. During the past 100 years, its powers have declined relative to those of the elected lower chamber, the House of Commons. For most of its history, membership of the upper chamber was confined to 'Lords Temporal', aristocrats who held hereditary peerages, and 'Lords Spiritual', bishops of the Church of England. In 1958 a system for appointing 'Life Peers' was introduced. Life peers are men and women appointed to the House, on the recommendation of the Prime Minister, but who do not receive hereditary titles. Hereditary membership of the House of Lords was abolished in 1999, although some 'hereditaries' were allowed to remain as 'working peers'. Further reform of the House is likely. If it becomes a wholly elected chamber, Church of England bishops will cease to be members. If it becomes a wholly or partly appointed chamber, bishops may remain, but almost certainly in reduced numbers and probably accompanied by the representatives of other faiths.

Party whip: The 'whips' are party officials who try to ensure that MPs toe their party's line in parliamentary votes. The term also describes the instructions issued by those officials. Occasionally, especially on 'conscience issues', parties do not impose a whip so that their MPs have a 'free vote'.

Sectarianism: Discrimination or hatred against (or between) people or groups because of their religious affiliation. Sectarianism can become systemic and deeply embedded in some societies, reflected not only in overt violence or bigotry but also in everyday patterns of prejudice such as avoidance of people from different religions and/or strained relationships between people of different religions.

The Troubles: A period of political violence, concentrated mainly in Northern Ireland but including violent incidents in Great Britain, the Republic of Ireland and parts of Europe, between the late 1960s and the Belfast/Good Friday Agreement of 1998. Conflicting parties disagreed about the constitutional status of Northern Ireland (whether it should be part of the United Kingdom or the Republic of Ireland) and the degree of economic, social and political inequality between Catholic nationalists and Protestant unionists in Northern Ireland. Actors in the violence included state forces such as the British Army and paramilitary groups such as the nationalist/republican Irish Republican Army and the unionist/loyalist Ulster Volunteer Force, among others. More than 3,500 died during the violence.

Further reading

Brewer, John D., Gareth Higgins and Francis Teeney (2011). *Religion, Civil Society and Peace in Northern Ireland*. Oxford: Oxford University Press. Critically examines the achievements of the churches and Christian peace-builders during the Northern Ireland peace process, while offering insights into the limitations of their contributions.

Mitchell, Claire (2006). *Religion, Identity and Politics in Northern Ireland: Boundaries of Belonging and Belief*. Aldershot: Ashgate. Analyses how Catholicism and Protestantism inform oppositional communal identities, contributing to division and affecting politics in Northern Ireland.

Morris, Robert M. (ed.) (2009). *Church and State in 21st Century Britain: The Future of Church Establishment*. Basingstoke: Palgrave Macmillan. Explains how church and state remain connected in Britain and explores the issues surrounding that connection.

Sandberg, Russell (2011). *Law and Religion*. Cambridge: Cambridge University Press. A comprehensive, accessible and expertly informed survey of law relating to religion in Britain.

Steven, Martin H. M. (2010). *Christianity and Party Politics: Keeping the Faith*. London: Routledge. Examines the influence of Christianity on contemporary British politics.

Weller, Paul (2008). *Religious Diversity in the UK: Contours and Issues*. London: Continuum. Portrays religious diversity in Britain, including its impact on governance and on law relating to religious discrimination and freedom of expression.

References

Ahdar, Rex and Ian Leigh (2005). *Religious Freedom in the Liberal State*. Oxford: Oxford University Press.

Barendt, Eric (2011). 'Religious Hatred Laws: Protecting Groups or Beliefs?', *Res Publica*, 17/1: 43–53.

Berger, Peter (1990). *The Sacred Canopy: Elements of a Sociological Theory of Religion*. New York, NY: Anchor Books.

Bown, Francis (1994). 'Influencing the House of Lords: The Role of the Lords Spiritual 1979–1987', *Political Studies*, 42/1: 105–119.

Brewer, John D. (2003). *C. Wright Mills and the Ending of Violence*. London: Palgrave Macmillan.

Brewer, John D. (2010). *Peace Processes: A Sociological Approach*. Cambridge: Polity Press.

Brewer, John D. with Gareth Higgins (1998). *Anti-Catholicism in Northern Ireland 1600–1998: The Mote and the Beam*. London: Palgrave Macmillan.

Brewer, John D., Gareth Higgins and Francis Teeney (2011). *Religion, Civil Society and Peace in Northern Ireland*. Oxford: Oxford University Press.

Bruce, Steve (1986). *God Save Ulster! The Religion and Politics of Paisleyism*. Oxford: Clarendon Press.

Bruce, Steve (2007). *Paisley: Religion and Politics in Northern Ireland*. Oxford: Oxford University Press.

Bryan, Dominic (2000). *Orange Parades: The Politics of Ritual, Tradition and Control*. London: Pluto Press.

Butler, David and Donald Stokes (1974). *Political Change in Britain*. London: Macmillan.

Cantle, Ted (2001). *Community Cohesion: A Report of the Independent Review Team*. London: Her Majesty's Stationery Office.

Church of England. Commission on Urban Priority Areas (1985). *Faith in the City: A Call for Action by Church and Nation*. London: Church House.

Consultative Group on the Past (2009). *Report of the Consultative Group on the Past*. Online. Available HTTP: www.consultationonthepast.org/?cat=52 (accessed 2 January 2011).

Cooke, Dennis (1996). *Persecuting Zeal: A Portrait of Ian Paisley*. Dingle: Brandon.

Demerath, N. Jay, III (2001). *Crossing the Gods: World Religions and Worldly Politics*. New Brunswick, NJ: Rutgers University Press.

Denver, David (2003). *Elections and Voters in Britain*. Basingstoke: Palgrave Macmillan.

Durham, Martin (1997). '"God Wants Us to Be in a Different Party": Religion and Politics in Britain Today', *Parliamentary Affairs*, 50/2: 212–222.

ECONI (1988). *For God and His Glory Alone*. Belfast: Evangelical Contribution on Northern Ireland.

Elliott, Marianne (2009). *When God Took Sides: Religion and Identity in Ireland – Unfinished History*. Oxford: Oxford University Press.

Ganiel, Gladys (2006). 'Ulster Says Maybe: The Restructuring of Evangelical Politics in Northern Ireland', *Irish Political Studies*, 21/2: 137–155.

Ganiel, Gladys (2008). *Evangelicalism and Conflict in Northern Ireland*. New York, NY: Palgrave Macmillan.

Ganiel, Gladys (2009a). '21st Century Faith: Results of the Survey of Clergy, Pastors, Ministers and Faith Leaders'. Online. Available HTTP: www.ecumenics.ie/wp-content/uploads/Clergy-Survey-Report.pdf (accessed 2 January 2011).

Ganiel, Gladys (2009b). '21st Century Faith: Results of the Survey of Laypeople in the Republic of Ireland and Northern Ireland'. Online. Available HTTP: www.ecumenics.ie/wp-content/uploads/Lay-Survey-Report.pdf (accessed 2 January 2011).

Ganiel, Gladys (2010a). 'Visions of Faith: Case Study of the Holy Cross Monastery, Northern Ireland', paper presented at workshop *Visioning 21st Century Ecumenism*, Trinity College Dublin, December.

Ganiel, Gladys (2010b). 'Visioning 21st Century Ecumenism: The View from the Pulpits, the View from the Pews', *Doctrine and Life*, 60/5: 31–46.

Ganiel, Gladys (2010c). 'Surveying Religion's Public Role: Perspectives on Reconciliation, Diversity and Ecumenism in Northern Ireland', *Shared Space*, 9: 53–68. Online. Available HTTP: www.community-relations.org.uk/fs/doc/chapter-42.pdf (accessed 2 January 2011).

Ganiel, Gladys and Paul Dixon (2008). 'Religion in Northern Ireland: Rethinking Fundamentalism and the Possibilities for Conflict Transformation', *Journal of Peace Research*, 45/3: 421–438.

Hayes, Bernadette and Ian McAllister (1999). 'Ethnonationalism, Public Opinion and the Good Friday Agreement', in Joseph Ruane and Jennifer Todd (eds), *After the Good Friday Agreement: Analysing Political Change in Northern Ireland*. Dublin: University College Dublin Press, 30–48.

Hibbing, J. R. and David Marsh (1987). 'Accounting for the Voting Patterns of British MPs on Free Votes', *Legislative Studies Quarterly*, 12/2: 275–298.

Hill, Mark (2009). 'Voices in the Wilderness: The Established Church of England and the European Union', *Religion, State and Society*, 37/1: 167–180.

Hurley, Michael (ed.) (2007). *The Irish School of Ecumenics 1970–2007*. Dublin: Columba Press.

Jarman, Neil (1997). *Material Conflicts: Parades and Visual Displays in Northern Ireland*. Oxford: Berg Publishers.

Jordan, Glenn (2001). *Not of this World? Evangelical Protestants in Northern Ireland*. Belfast: Blackstaff.

Kaufmann, Eric (2007). *The Orange Order: A Contemporary Northern Irish History*. Oxford: Oxford University Press.

Kotler-Berkowitz, Laurence A. (2001). 'Religion and Voting Behaviour in Great Britain: A Reassessment', *British Journal of Political Science*, 31/3: 523–554.

Leustean, Lucian N. and John T. S. Madeley (2009). 'Religion, Politics and Law in the European Union: An Introduction', *Religion, State and Society*, 37/1–2: 3–18.

Liechty, Joseph and Cecelia Clegg (2001). *Moving Beyond Sectarianism: Religion, Conflict and Reconciliation in Northern Ireland*. Dublin: Columba Press.

McCarthy, M. A. and R. A. Moodie (1981). 'Parliament and Pornography: The 1978 Child Protection Act', *Parliamentary Affairs*, 34/1: 47–62.

McGarry, John and Brendan O'Leary (1995). *Explaining Northern Ireland*. Oxford: Blackwell.

McLean, Iain and Benjamin Linsley (2004). *The Church of England and the State: Reforming Establishment for a Multi-Faith Britain*. London: New Politics Network.

McLeod, Hugh (2007). *The Religious Crisis of the 1960s*. Oxford: Oxford University Press.

McMahon, Andrew (2009). 'A Force for Good: The Contribution of the South Down Ecumenical Study Group to Reconciliation, 1968–1978', unpublished MPhil dissertation, the Irish School of Ecumenics, Trinity College Dublin at Belfast.

McMaster, Johnston (2008). 'What on Earth is Ecumenism?', *Irish School of Ecumenics' Church Fora Newsletter*, 3: 2. Online. Available HTTP: www.tcd.ie/ise/assets/pdf/Newsletter-Spring-2008.pdf (accessed 2 January 2011).

Malik, Kenan (2009). *From Fatwa to Jihad: The Rushdie Affair and its Legacy*. London: Atlantic Books.

Marsh, Dave, Peter Gowin and Mervyn Read (1986). 'Private Members' Bills and Moral Panic: The Case of the Video-Recordings Bill', *Parliamentary Affairs*, 39/2: 179–196.

Medhurst, Kenneth and George Moyser (1988). *Church and Politics in a Secular Age*. Oxford: Clarendon Press.

Mitchel, Patrick (2003). *Evangelicalism and National Identity in Ulster 1921–1998*. Oxford: Oxford University Press.

Mitchell, Claire (2004). 'Is Northern Ireland Abnormal? An Extension of the Sociological Debate on Religion in Modern Britain', *Sociology*, 38/2: 237–254.

Mitchell, Claire (2006). *Religion, Identity and Politics in Northern Ireland: Boundaries of Belonging and Belief*. Aldershot: Ashgate.

Mitchell, Claire and Gladys Ganiel (2011). *Evangelical Journeys: Choice and Change in a Northern Irish Religious Subculture*. Dublin: UCD Press.

Mitchell, Claire and Jennifer Todd (2007). 'Between the Devil and the Deep Blue Sea: Nationality, Power and Symbolic Trade-offs among Evangelical Protestants in Northern Ireland', *Nations and Nationalism*, 13/4: 637–655.

Modood, Tariq (1994). 'Establishment, Multiculturalism and British Citizenship', *Political Quarterly*, 65/1: 53–73.

Modood, Tariq (2009). 'Ethnicity and Religion', in *The Oxford Handbook of British Politics*. Oxford: Oxford University Press, 484–499.

Moloney, Ed (2008). *Paisley: From Demagogue to Democrat?* Dublin: Poolbeg Press.

Morris, Robert M. (ed.) (2009). *Church and State in 21st Century Britain: The Future of Church Establishment*. Basingstoke: Palgrave Macmillan.

Norman, E. R. (2008). 'Notes on *Church and State: A Mapping Exercise*', in Robert M. Morris (ed.), *Church and State: Some Reflections on Church Establishment in England*. London: Constitution Unit, UCL, 9–13.

O'Clery, Conor (2007). *The Billionaire Who Wasn't: How Chuck Feeney Secretly Made and Gave Away a Fortune*. New York, NY: PublicAffairs.

O'Connor, Fionnuala (1993). *In Search of a State: Catholics in Northern Ireland*. Belfast: Blackstaff.

Parsons, Gerald (1994a). 'Between Law and Licence: Christianity, Morality and "Permissiveness"', in Gerald Parsons (ed.), *The Growth of Religious Diversity: Britain from 1945. Volume II: Controversies*. London: Routledge, 231–266.

Parsons, Gerald (1994b). 'From Consensus to Confrontation: Religion and Politics in Britain since 1945', in Gerald Parsons (ed.), *The Growth of Religious Diversity: Britain from 1945. Volume II: Controversies*. London: Routledge, 123–159.

Pattie, Charles, Ron Johnston and Mark Stuart (1998). 'Voting without Party?', in Philip Cowley (ed.), *Conscience and Parliament*. London: Frank Cass, 146–176.

Power, Maria (2007). *From Ecumenism to Community Relations: Inter Church Relationships in Northern Ireland 1980–1999*. Dublin: Irish Academic Press.

Ruane, Joseph and Jennifer Todd (1996). *Dynamics of Conflict in Northern Ireland: Power, Conflict and Emancipation*. Cambridge: Cambridge University Press.

Seawright, David (2000). 'A Confessional Cleavage Resurrected? The Denominational Vote in Britain', in David Broughton and Hans-Martien Ten Napel (eds), *Religion and Mass Electoral Behaviour in Europe*. London: Routledge, 44–60.

Shirlow, Peter and Brendan Murtagh (2006). *Belfast: Segregation, Violence and the City*. London: Pluto Press.

Southern, Neil (2005). 'Ian Paisley and Evangelical Democratic Unionists: An Analysis of the Role of Evangelical Protestantism within the Democratic Unionist Party', *Irish Political Studies*, 20/2: 127–145.

Steven, Martin H. M. (2010). *Christianity and Party Politics: Keeping the Faith*. London: Routledge.

Taggart, Norman W. (2004). *Conflict, Controversy and Co-operation: The Irish Council of Churches and the Troubles 1968–1972*. Dublin: Columba Press.

Thomas, Paul (2010). 'Failed and Friendless: The UK's "Preventing Violent Extremism" Programme', *British Journal of Politics and International Relations*, 12/3: 442–458.

Thomson, Alwyn (2002). *Fields of Vision: Faith and Identity in Protestant Ireland*. Belfast: Evangelical Contribution on Northern Ireland.

Vickers, Lucy (2008). *Religious Freedom, Religious Discrimination and the Workplace*. Oxford: Hart.

Wells, Ronald (2010). *Hope and Reconciliation in Northern Ireland: The Role of Faith Based Organizations*. Dublin: Liffey Press.

Wilford, Rick and Robin Wilson (2006). *The Trouble with Northern Ireland: The Belfast Agreement and Democratic Governance*. Dublin: New Island Books.

Willett, Graham (2009). 'The Church of England and the Origins of Homosexual Law Reform', *Journal of Religious History*, 33/4, 418–434.

Wilson, Robin (2010). *The Northern Ireland Experience of Conflict and Agreement: A Model for Export?* Manchester: Manchester University Press.

Wright, Frank (1973). 'Protestant Ideology and Politics in Ulster', *European Journal of Sociology*, 14/2: 212–280.

Notes

1   *Seide v. Gillette Industries Ltd*, [1980] IRLR 427.
2   *Mandla v. Dowell Lee*, [1983] 2 AC 548.
3   *Catholic Care (Diocese of Leeds) v. Charity Commission for England and Wales*, [2011] CA/2010/0007.
4   *Ladele v. London Borough of Islington*, [2008] UKEAT 0453_08_1912; [2009] EWCA Civ 1357. *McFarlane v. Relate Avon Ltd*, [2009] UKEAT 0106_09_3011; [2010] EWCA Civ 771.

Case study 7

Religion, human rights law and 'opting out' of religious education

Alison Mawhinney, Ulrike Niens, Norman Richardson and Yuko Chiba

Several chapters in this volume mention that religion in Britain is increasingly regulated by law (see, for example, Chapters 1 and 9, which discuss some recent controversial legal cases). The following case study reflects on one facet of this development, namely the operation of human rights law in relation to religious education. In particular, it reports on research carried out in Northern Ireland and funded by the AHRC/ESRC Religion and Society Programme to examine the effectiveness of the opt-out clause as a means of protecting the 'right to freedom of thought, conscience and religion'.[1] International human rights law and domestic law rely on this opt-out mechanism to protect religious liberty when doctrinal religion is taught in schools.

Northern Ireland is a particularly interesting case because of its relatively high level of Christian participation (Francis *et al.* 2006), its history of sectarian violence and dispute between the majority Protestant and minority Catholic communities (see Chapter 9 and Muldoon *et al.* 2007), and its growing number of non-Christians, both religious and non-religious (Jarman 2005). This profile, combined with a school system which has been shaped by the past and which largely assumes that pupils will be either Catholic or Protestant, raises particular challenges for the religious freedom of individuals. In this context, it was interesting to see whether the right to 'opt out' of education was able to protect such freedom, and whether this international protection is effective in regulating a particular national situation.

Tensions around the religious education (RE) curriculum, school ethos, and peer and teacher acceptance

The public education system in Northern Ireland is divided between Catholic Maintained schools, State Controlled (de facto Protestant) schools and Integrated schools. There are very few private schools in Northern Ireland, and no faith schools serving religions other than Christianity. The Religious Education Core Syllabus, which is statutory for all schools, is drawn up exclusively by the four largest Christian denominations in Northern Ireland and is predominantly Christian in content (Department of Education 2007; Richardson 2010). The 2007 Revised RE Core Syllabus includes world religions other than Christianity only at Key Stage 3 (ages 11–14) and omits any reference to alternative non-religious life stances.

A consistent finding from the study was that people of minority religion and belief expressed significant dissatisfaction with the content of RE and with the way it is taught. Some of the parents and pupils interviewed appeared to have learned to tolerate this situation and to try to make the best of it and have made positive choices about how they participate in RE; in a few cases our respondents noted good practice of which they very much approved. Almost all, however, expressed a desire for an approach to RE that is broadly based rather than narrowly focused on Christianity; one that is non-doctrinal, non-confessional, open and inclusive in tone and style and committed to the development of critical thought.

Pupils felt that their religious beliefs were being respected when their RE teachers demonstrated an interest in and awareness of the pupils' various beliefs. Even presenting Christian beliefs as one way of thinking rather than the norm could facilitate a sense of inclusion for minority belief pupils. Where interviewees did not see teachers paying this attention to their 'otherness' in faith, they expressed feelings of being tolerated rather than respected. It was important for teachers to strike a balance between attentiveness to pupils' different beliefs, whilst not singling them out. Pupils appreciated being given the flexibility to decide whether or not they wished to participate.

Respondents wanted more emphasis on teaching a range of world religions and other life stances (for example, humanism) and greater balance in the discussion of morality from a range of perspectives instead of the implication of Christian superiority. Some community representatives mentioned their involvement with schools in teaching world religions, but felt that this should be covered more formally in the curriculum. It appears that at present schools which attempt to teach a more inclusive range of topics and approaches than those prescribed in the statutory syllabus inevitably and heavily rely on the resources of voluntary organizations and minority faith communities, resources which may be difficult or impossible for schools in rural areas to access.

Particular concerns were expressed about the limitations of public examination syllabuses (in particular, the General Certificate of Secondary Education (GCSE) examination, taken at age 16) and the ways in which topics and modules were chosen at this level. The training and deployment of RE teachers were also a cause for concern, especially with regard to teachers' awareness of religions and beliefs other than Christianity and their capacity for inclusive classroom practice.

Overall, respondents' schools varied considerably in relation to the prominence of religion in their ethos and everyday life, ranging from a strong influence of Christianity to it having little importance. School assemblies were generally seen as compulsory and influenced by Christianity. Some interviewees said they enjoyed them because of their moral aspects; others found them 'funny' or boring. Some interviewees felt that it would have been impossible to opt out of assemblies. None of the respondents appeared to feel particularly uncomfortable during prayer in assembly,[2] and most said they tried to show respect, although some reported occasional pressure from teachers to join the prayer in assembly, to which they objected.

Generally, the research indicated that most respondents felt their faith was respected by school staff and while this was mainly attributed to teachers' attitudes, the question was also raised if this was (partly) due to potential retributions against staff if they were seen to discriminate against pupils on religious grounds. If schools paid attention to pupils' different backgrounds, for example, by celebrating their religious festivals and by accommodating their dietary needs, respondents praised their responsiveness to religious diversity. Where such accommodation was not offered by the school, some pupils reported not feeling sufficiently confident to request it and, unless they felt very strongly about it, resigned themselves to the situation.

Relationships between pupils of different religions within the school community were mostly regarded as unproblematic although a small number of interviewees reported instances of verbal and/or physical bullying which highlighted the intertwined nature of religious and racial prejudice. All interviewees reported having friends within their school who were not members of their respective religious communities, and saw these friendships as unaffected by religion. However, discussions about religion only entered some of these friendships, while they were seen as irrelevant or too sensitive in others. Younger interviewees were more affected by their desire to fit in with their peers and not to stand out.

Generally, the research revealed that a broad approach to the RE curriculum and school ethos which takes account of other religions and belief systems, as well as a more diverse student population, including pupils from religious and/or cultural minority communities, was by no means the norm. However, where it existed, even in part, it was associated with reduced tensions between pupils' own beliefs and the majority beliefs within the school.

Tensions around the experience of opting out

Given that all schools in Northern Ireland tend to exhibit a Christian ethos to a greater or lesser extent, minority belief individuals have no choice but to attend a Christian school. They then are faced with the decision of whether to participate in RE classes and activities. As noted above, some do. However, the Christianity-focused curriculum and the manner in which it is taught forces others to exercise their right to opt out.

The research suggests that reaching this decision can be a challenging process for students and parents. It is not one that is taken lightly and often it is reached only after children have been attending RE classes and have felt increasingly uncomfortable with the lesson content. Both parents and students reported a concern that opting out in a school and societal environment that is heavily Christian will stigmatize the child and cause relationship problems within the school with peers and teachers.

The actual process of exercising the right to opt out proved to be a tense one at times. While a number of ethnic religious minorities reported that schools had made them aware of the right to opt out, the majority of parents stated that the school did not inform them of this right, either in the school literature or through the school website or other formal communication. In some cases, teachers reacted in an emotional and negative way when parents raised the question of opt outs, and parents were not always provided with accurate information and advice. For humanist and non-belief parents, there was a sense that opting out because you were non-religious was more difficult than opting out because you belonged to another (non-Christian) religion.

Once students have been opted out, most felt supported by their peers, some of whom, they thought, were 'jealous' and would have liked to opt out of RE too. For some the decision to opt out changed their relationships with teachers whom they felt now treated them differently. A parent whose son opted out noted that it made them feel as if they were 'somehow disruptive' and 'causing trouble' for the school. Furthermore, this parent stated that the process did not value the child or their beliefs and was detrimental to the self-esteem of a child.

Opt outs have to be requested by parents. While the research revealed tension between families and school authorities around the issue of opt outs, it did not indicate any conflicts between young people and parents in relation to opt-out decisions. In fact, opt-out decisions appeared often to have been left to the young people or were discussed with them. There was clear support from both parents and students that the students themselves should be legally allowed to exercise the right to opt out at a given age. For young people this was often seen to be around the age of 13 to 15 years; for parents the age range was typically 14 to 16 years. Even where it was felt that the right should always remain a parental one, it was suggested that students should be more formally involved in the decision-making process as well as in discussions around the kind of alternative provision that should be offered during the opting-out period.[3]

Conclusion

The way in which young people experience school life substantially influences their sense of self and their sense of belonging to the school and to the wider community. This research highlights how RE in schools tends to reflect majority beliefs, and how this can lead to a sense of exclusion for minority belief students, undermine their relationship with the school community, and ultimately negatively impact on the way they view their own beliefs and their community's place in the wider society. From a human rights perspective, the right to opt out of religious education – a right mandated by international human rights law to protect religious freedom in schools – is therefore of great importance. It means that students and their parents from a minority belief background – whether religious or secular – are able to choose *not* to participate in a religious educational system which is inappropriate for them.

As this case study shows, some parents and children avail themselves of this right. However, more striking were the many additional factors which complicate what appears at first sight to be a simple legal procedure. For one thing, school policies and procedures relating to opt-out rights are often not clear, and opting out is not advertised or encouraged. In addition, if students do opt out, there is rarely any meaningful alternative provision. Moreover, opting out takes place in a social setting and not in a vacuum. There are many countervailing pressures to opting out including peer inclusion and parental or community pressure.

The research clearly highlights the challenges experienced by an increasingly diverse student population whose beliefs do not easily fit into the existing institutional structures of a Christian-dominated society. The research revealed that tensions were particularly brought to the fore where the RE curriculum was seen to be taught in a doctrinal/confessional way with little value attributed to other religions and beliefs. This experience was compounded for young people attending schools where staff and pupils had little experience of those from outside the majority belief communities. As such, tensions emerged between human rights legal requirements, which consider the right to opt out a sufficient means to protect the right to freedom of religion, and the implementation of these in schools, which were sometimes seen as insufficient to protect the beliefs of minority belief individuals.

While Northern Ireland may be considered a unique political context based on its past and present circumstances, it provides a highly relevant case study in demonstrating tension between individual rights and group belongings of various kinds. Such tensions are by no means confined to this particular case. Human rights remain an important national and international instrument for upholding individuals' freedom of belief and conscience, but in practice their outworking takes place in the complicated circumstances of everyday social belongings, structures and pressures. Even if parents and pupils have a 'right' to opt out of RE, they may not be in a position to exercise it, and the cost of exercising that right may be too high. There is also a tension between the right to opt out of unsuitable RE provision (which may serve to protect the status quo), and a drive to improve provision so that no one feels they have to opt out. Such dilemmas occur wherever there are minorities who do not share the beliefs of the majority.

References

Department of Education (2007). *Core Syllabus for Religious Education*. Bangor: Department of Education

Francis, Lesley J., Mandy Robbins, L. Philip Barnes and Christopher A. Lewis (2006). 'Sixth Form Religion in Northern Ireland: The Protestant Profile 1968–1998', *British Journal of Religious Education*, 28/1: 3–18.

Jarman, Neil (2005). *Changing Patterns and Future Planning: Migration and Northern Ireland*. Belfast: Institute for Conflict Research.

Mawhinney, Alison, Ulrike Niens, Norman Richardson and Yuko Chiba (2010). *Opting Out of Religious Education: The Views of Young People from Minority Belief Backgrounds*. Belfast: Queen's University Belfast.

Muldoon, Orla T., Karen Trew, Jennifer Todd, Nathalie Rougier and Katrina McLaughlin (2007). 'Religious and National Identity after the Belfast Good Friday Agreement', *Political Psychology*, 28/1: 89–103.

Richardson, Norman (2010). 'Division, Diversity and Vision – Religious Education and Community Cohesion in Northern Ireland', in Michael Grimmitt (ed.), *Religious Education and Social and Community Cohesion*. Great Wakering: McCrimmons, 215–231.

Notes

1   This research was funded by the AHRC/ESRC Religion and Society Programme. See Mawhinney *et al.* (2010).

2   This is a regular, formal gathering of all the school, often held at the start of the day to impart information and commonly featuring religious content.

3   The lack of tension in the findings between parents and children may be partly due to the research design. Parental consent was required for young people's participation in the research and all participants were recruited through community networks. The sampling strategy may therefore have precluded parents and pupils who adhered to different beliefs or who did experience tensions in relation to opt-out decisions from coming forward.

Part 3

Theoretical perspectives

10 Cultural perspectives

Callum Brown and Gordon Lynch

Having reviewed changing forms of religion, and religion's changing interactions with wider social arenas, this final part of the book considers theoretical perspectives put forward to explain these changes. One important way of explaining religious change in post-war Britain is in relation to wider cultural changes. This chapter argues that there was a major shift in post-war Britain from a dominant Christian culture associated with traditional views of gender, sexuality and the body to a new, more diverse cultural context in which far fewer people identified with this moral framework. This shift involves the clearer emergence of 'non-religion' in British society, the consolidation of conservative religious sub-cultures, and the growing importance of new forms of circulation and negotiation of the meanings and place of religion. Whilst these trends are unlikely to be reversed in coming decades, it is much harder to predict what the implications will be for social life and public institutions in Britain.

Introduction

This chapter offers a cultural account of the changing significance of religion, and the emergence of new forms of non-religion, in post-war British society. This involves not only attending to the significance of different aspects of cultural life in Britain, but practising a particular approach to academic enquiry which involves not just thinking about culture (as an object of study), but thinking through culture (as a theoretical approach) to make sense of social life. Before saying more about religion, non-religion and post-war Britain, it is important to explain what is meant here by a cultural approach to the study of religion and what constitutes 'explanation' in this form of academic work.

First, then, what is 'culture'? The British cultural theorist Raymond Williams argued that culture could be understood as a 'structure of feeling' (Williams and Orrom 1954; Williams 1961), a way of experiencing and making sense of the world, through which we create and interpret material objects, conduct social relations and perform meaningful actions. Whilst the nature and social significance of 'culture' continue to be argued over across a range of academic disciplines,[1] Williams's phrase identifies two elements that are important for any substantial theory of culture. First, culture is the structure *through which* we experience, make sense of and 'feel' our social worlds. In this sense, we never simply experience the world 'as it is', but filtered through the cultural frames and meanings available to us in our particular situation. Second, culture is a *structure*. The meanings of culture are not simply the creation of our individual imaginations. They have a wider social existence that precedes specific thoughts, feelings and actions and which is consciously and unconsciously reproduced through people's everyday, or specialized and ritualized, actions.[2] Furthermore, these cultural structures are not universal or timeless, but are both linked to particular institutions, places and societies, and are historically contingent, that is, they change over time as a result of specific historical actions and events.

Whilst theories of culture have become more differentiated over the past 30 years, these basic ideas inform a common 'cultural turn' that has become increasingly important across a range of disciplines in the latter part of the twentieth century (Bonnell and Hunt 1999), and which forms the basis of the disciplinary approaches within which we work as authors, namely cultural history (Brown) and cultural sociology (Lynch).[3] Within this broader cultural turn there has been an important shift away from seeing culture (as Marx did in his later work) as something that is simply the ideological expression of 'real' social structures and interests (namely class and economic relations), or which functions simply to maintain social hierarchies (Bourdieu 1984) or to help the effective operation of social systems (Parsons 1949). Such an understanding of culture as 'a gearbox, not an engine' of social life (Alexander 2003: 18), has been increasingly challenged by approaches which see cultural structures as having the power to shape social life. This has led to cultural explanations of social life that seek to move beyond thinking about human action simply in terms of material relationships or the strategic pursuit of political or economic goals in which culture is seen only as a tool used in the quest for 'profit, power, prestige or ideological control' (Alexander 2003: 20). Instead, this approach focuses on how cultural structures make society possible by providing the meaningful 'inside' of social life.

Cultural structures are never isolated, free-floating ideas or meaning systems, however. They are always connected to specific social institutions, spaces, bodies, relationships and practices through which they are reproduced, and, at times, challenged or transformed; at the same time, they are closely interlinked to individuals' experiences, helping to shape and be shaped by the everyday self we each present to the world. To develop a cultural explanation of social life therefore means attending to the ways in which cultural structures are bound up with processes of social stability, conflict and change as these unfold in particular times and places, and to consider how they are enveloped in the diversity and limits to diversity of each person's life. This means accounting for the ways in which cultural meanings, social structures and individual and collective social agents interact to bring about particular patterns in social life.

In offering a cultural explanation of religious change in Britain since 1945, this chapter will therefore examine the ways in which cultural structures – such as the way in which people perform gender and sexuality, the social values they express, the ways they raise their children, the ways in which they imagine opposing cultural forces, and the ways in which they do and do not talk about 'religion' – are bound up with a significant period of religious change. The argument developed here is that these cultural structures are not simply expressions of some other, supposedly 'more fundamental' causes of religious change (as suggested, for example, in some versions of the secularization thesis, see Chapters 11 and 12). Rather, the shifting meanings of the body, moral responsibility, sexuality and 'religion' itself, bound up with changing social institutions, economic conditions and public media, form an integral part of any adequate explanatory narrative of religious change in post-war Britain.

This chapter presents evidence to show that, in the decades after 1945, there was a weakening of a normative Christian culture in Britain. This is not to suggest that before then it was commonplace for people in Britain to adhere consistently to all core tenets of Christian morality and dogma or to attend church services on a regular basis (although more people did before 1945 than do in contemporary Britain today). Rather, ways of feeling about gender, the body and sexuality that were bound up with a particular form of Christian culture began to change through social and cultural transformations following the Second World War, with radical implications for traditional religious beliefs, practices and institutions. Our argument can therefore be read in relation to Chapter 2, which places a greater emphasis on religious continuity in post-war Britain. In contrast, this chapter suggests that in the wake of the decline of a *dominant* Christian culture, a new cultural context has emerged involving the emergence of cultural forms of 'non-religion', the consolidation of new religious sub-cultures and the circulation of new cultural constructions of 'religion'.

This is not to suggest that all forms of Christianity in the post-war period were inherently conservative. As McLeod (2007) points out, leading figures in the church were actively involved in supporting more liberal legislation on issues ranging from the death penalty to divorce, homosexuality and abortion, and Christian ethicists have adopted diverse perspectives on these major changes in post-war society. Rather, there was a particular kind of widely shared cultural framework, or 'sacred canopy', in early post-war Britain which fused Christian symbols with conservative moral sentiments and assumptions about gender, the body and sexuality. This framework cannot be understood simplistically as encapsulating all views held by all Christians in the period. Yet, it was the fragmentation of this widely shared framework, associated with people's weakening identification with the churches, that created the new cultural conditions described later in the chapter.

The narrative developed here is by no means the only one offered by historians of the post-war period. McLeod considers most of the issues raised here, but he argues ultimately that whilst the religious crisis of the 1960s was 'a rupture as profound as that brought about by the Reformation' (McLeod 2007: 1), it was a crisis to a great extent internal to Christianity in which liberal Christians, with the assistance of 'pragmatic' leaders, gained an ascendancy. This led in the decades that ensued, he argues, to the advancement of liberal values in government and society, including the advance of pluralism, which had the effect of turning the 'Christian country' into a 'civilized society'. Thus McLeod's narrative tends to prioritize the role of Christian liberal reform in tackling racism, homophobia and restrictive religious laws. This differs from the emphasis given here, which is upon the role of the people in fomenting a vast cultural change driven by a desire for individualism and autonomy from authority – and especially a desire for freedom from others' control of their bodies.

The cultural landscape of post-war Britain

Religion and social conformity in the early post-war period

The decade and a half following the end of the Second World War seemed in some ways to establish Britain on a new footing. A political consensus emerged to eliminate poverty, unemployment, ill health, bad housing and poor education through the establishment of the welfare state (as laid out in the Beveridge Report of 1942, see Chapter 8). Meanwhile, even the Conservatives agreed to create a managed economy through the nationalization of many industries ranging from transport to coal. A brave new world of advanced technology seemed imminent in the 1950s, with the completion of the national electricity grid, nuclear power stations and the arrival of national television.

But behind the material change, there was cultural stasis. Old values were reasserted in the return to the pre-war status quo; women's place was reconstituted in culture to be in the home and procreation, in fostering respectability and the spread of suburban cosiness in their utility clothes and utility furniture. From government policy to advertisements for kitchen appliances, women were encouraged to forsake new economic roles to enable returning menfolk to find work and fulfilment in the workplace. Meanwhile, children became the repositories for the older generation's values, raised in an atmosphere of intense conformity. It was the generation of 'conservative and respectable ordinariness': 'The ordinariness of manners, or please-and-thank-you'd politeness, of being a nice girl, who went to the Brownies and Guides, and for whom the competitions in the annual Produce Association show provided one of the most exciting occasions of the year' (Walkerdine 1985: 65). Made through the rhetoric of the 'juvenile delinquent' to fear the establishment's terror of deviancy, the young were trained in the benevolent greyness of short trousers and school uniforms to savour the special treat of rationed sweets and to expect little more.

Individuality and self-expression were difficult in this cultural and religious context. Signs of incipient change can with hindsight be pinpointed: the street gangs, the teddy boys, the fostering of rock 'n' roll from 1955 onwards and the rise of skiffle music and town hall dance culture in the late 1950s (see Case study 5). But these were limited and fenced-off cultural developments. They were widely criticized by the press and local authorities, by churchmen and politicians, and there was very limited penetration of youth culture into the media of the age. Television rarely showed popular music shows (the first all-music show being *Oh Boy!* on Independent Television from 1958), and vinyl records were still limited in sales until record players became accessible to the young in the early 1960s. Making music was still difficult; skiffle began in 1957 because British bands could not afford drum kits and made rhythm instead on washboards and wooden boxes. Affluence was constrained by the export drive, poor availability of goods and limited credit, whilst state control of electric technology, censorship of theatre and of books, and poor sexual knowledge constrained individuality. Free expression was culturally constructed as deviant, and even judicially construed as criminal.

This attempt in the 1950s to perfect a Victorian culture of repressed emotions and obedience to 'betters' interacted with the forging of a conservative religiosity. Religious conformity was at its height between 1945 and 1960; whilst church attendance for older age groups slipped (especially men's), the young became more than usually enthusiastic patrons of churches, church coffee bars and Billy Graham's crusade to London and Glasgow in 1954 and 1955 (which attracted more than 4 million attendances). In 1947, 44 per cent of men and 56 per cent of women claimed to be churchgoers, though only a quarter of them weekly; whilst in 1950–1951, 42 per cent of under-18s claimed to attend church or Sunday School at least once a month (Brown 2006: 183–184). In this decade, 58 per cent of parents claimed to teach their children to say prayers. Even if their parents were backsliding churchgoers, Christianity was hard for children to shake off. It represented the spirit of the age.

Religious individuality was difficult. Those who expressed divergence from the Christian norm were chased as deviants. In 1955, Margaret Knight of the University of Aberdeen was pursued relentlessly by the press and letter writers when she gave two talks on the BBC Home Service making the argument for humanism and more open religious education for children. Her atheism was bad enough, but it was her gender that compounded it. The *Sunday Graphic* newspaper carried a front-page headline: 'The Unholy Mrs Knight', and proclaimed beside a picture of this lecturer in Psychology: 'Don't let this woman fool you. She looks – doesn't she? – just like a typical housewife: cool, comfortable, harmless. But Mrs Margaret Knight is a menace. A dangerous woman. Make no mistake about that.'[4] Those who sought a new spirituality were treated in exactly the same way. Sheena Govan, born to a missionary, sought 'the god within', and in 1957 was hailed by her husband as 'a world teacher': 'God in his infinite love and mercy for mankind has at the eleventh hour sent

Sheena to save the world. She is a Redeemer in the form of a woman.' The press hounded Govan, calling her and her followers 'the Nameless Ones'. Pilloried as a freak, she eventually camped on land beside an RAF base in Scotland, grew giant vegetables and founded the Findhorn Community which, by 2000, some claimed as the world's largest residential centre for New Age religions. In the context of the mid-century, experimental religion was the object of tabloid exposé, derision and condemnation; by century's end it was accepted as a large part of the zeitgeist (Sutcliffe 2010, see also Chapter 3).

The shock of the new: cultural change from the 1960s

The world of deference, conformity and respectability came to a stuttering halt between 1960 and 1975. In these 15 years, a complex revolt of ideas, cultural forms, youth and sexuality overtook much of the Western world, a process nowhere more deep and affecting than in mainland Britain. The sixties cultural revolution has been characterized in various ways – the expressive revolution, a religious crisis fomented by liberal Christians who had been pursuing conservative theology for decades, and as either a real or a mythical sexual revolution (Martin 1981; McLeod 2007; Cook 2004). Another way to approach it is as a revolt centred on the body.

The sexual revolution burst upon the sense of wellbeing of the conservative British establishment. First, deference was struck down in the media – satire and comedy from *Beyond the Fringe* (1961) to the arrival of the anarchic *Monty Python* (1969) and their lampooning of royalty, churches and the military in almost equal measure. Then, the churches were especially aghast at what seemed to be a sudden rise of sexual promiscuity, characterized during the hippie era of 1965–1968 by displays of nudity, sexualized behaviour, new fashions (notably the mini-skirt, hot pants and, for men, long hair) and growth in recreational drugtaking – a series of changes in which young single women played a key role in relation to both sex and religion (Brown 2011). By 1970, the churches had both the gay and women's liberation movements to contend with, shaking the doctrines of most churches on both counts. The loss of inhibition, the rebuff of moral authority and the rejection of a normative Christian culture were startling and frightening to many.

During this 'liberal hour', both Conservative and Labour governments seemed to many church people to be complicit: decriminalizing gambling (1960), suicide (1961 England and Wales), abortion (1967 mainland Britain), homosexuality (1967 England and Wales); ending censorship of theatre (1968) and liberalizing divorce (1969 England and Wales). Through the British Medical Association, the oral contraceptive pill was initially limited to married women (1961), then offered to single women (1968). The government then made contraceptive advice free (1968) and contraceptives themselves free on the National Health Service in 1974 (Latham 1999). Premarital sex grew between 1964 and 1974/1975 from only 15 per cent of 16- and 17-year-old girls to 58 per cent, with a modest rise from 40 to 52 per cent among boys (Lewis and Kiernan 1996). Family formation started to change dramatically. Births outside marriage rose in England and Wales from 4.9 per cent in 1958 to 9.1 per cent in 1975 and on to 40.6 per cent by 2002 (Brown 2006: 32). With relaxation of parental control, the number of people marrying first boomed to 17.3 per 1,000 population in 1972 (the highest since records began in the 1840s except for the years 1936–1942 and 1945–1948) but then – as cohabitation, singlehood, single parenthood and later marriage became more widely accepted – commenced a sustained collapse to 13.1 in 1990 and 9.5 in 2001 (the lowest ever recorded). With similar trends in Scotland and Northern Ireland, a demographic revolution was set in train from the 1960s which still shows no sign of ending.

TEXT BOX 19

Statistics of religious change

Since the Second World War ended in 1945, there has been massive change in levels of religious adherence and practice. This can be measured in religious demographics. Church attendance and formal church adherence fell significantly. Table 10.1 below shows the level of decline in communicants in the Church of England and the Church of Scotland to have been very high. The peak year in 1956 marked a post-war high for these religious indicators, but then the figures fell dramatically from the 1960s and keep falling for the rest of the century. The fall in the proportion of babies being baptized in the Church of England was even more dramatic – with a fall from 60 to 20 per cent in less than 50 years.

Table 10.1 Churches' strength (1956–2000)

	1956		1970		1995	
	Number	*% age of population*	*Number*	*% age of population*	*Number*	*% age of population*
Church of England Easter communicants	2,348,000	5.2	1,814,000	3.7	1,264,900	2.5
Church of Scotland communicants	1,319,574	25.8	1,154,211	22.1	698,552	13.7

	1956	1970	2000
Church of England baptisms as percentage of all births	60.2%	46.6%	19.8%
Proportion of marriages in England and Wales religiously solemnized	72% (1957)	60.5%	36.3%

Sources: Data in Callum G. Brown's running datasets, calculated from figures in Currie *et al.* 1977: 223–234; *Church of England Yearbook* and Census of population; *Registrar General (Scotland), Annual Reports*; *Church of England Yearbook, 2000; Church Statistics 2002*, Table 17. Online. Available HTTP: www.gro.gov.uk (accessed 1 April 2005).

There was growing pressure for other types of change. One was for freedom of activity on Sundays. This was previously controlled in England and Wales by a complex legislative framework which restricted selling on Sundays (no meat or haircuts specifically). In Scotland there was little legislative restriction (except on opening of pubs and cinemas), but enormous religious pressure that, by and large, was accepted by the population and closed all leisure activities on Sundays (including sport) and even children's play parks. The greatest change came initially in Scotland which, though more famous for Sabbath dourness, lacked laws to stop supermarkets starting to open on Sundays in the late 1960s and 1970s. This was followed by the development of Sunday sport and the opening of public houses from 1976. In England, change to the laws was resisted both by the churches and by trade unions which sought to protect members from a lengthening working week. However, in 1994 the law was relaxed, with shops being permitted to open on Sundays, and only large stores prevented from trading for more than six hours.[5]

Where once there was a certainty in a Christian formulation of social mores, there grew from the 1960s to the 2010s an unstoppable cascade of change which rolled back this consensus. The change to Britain was at root a cultural one. Quite fixed notions of the social morality of the nation had previously been generally accepted: sexual relations were acceptable when hetero- and within marriage (or, with mild disapproval, between engaged couples immediately prior to betrothal); family respectability was constructed around a principal male breadwinner, with the desirability that women should generally not work; and complex social signs of respectability (involving clean doorsteps, washed milk bottles and stern sexual correctness) were demanded. This was supported by formalized notions of femininity and masculinity – such as the undesirability of men looking after babies (or even pushing prams), and of women not playing anything but a narrow range of 'ladylike' sports, and wearing 'respectable' hats and skirts. This world involved a vast lexicon of supposedly fixed certainties about the universal nature of gender, Christian supremacy over other religions, and racial issues (though the latter were subject to great change in church circles from the 1910s to the 1950s).

One mark of the fixed certainties was the prevalence of blackmail, which almost wholly focused on sexual misdemeanours and deviations from the 'norm' and the hypocrisy of those keen to preserve family, political or professional reputation. Born in its modern form in the nineteenth century, it reached a peak in the 1920s and 1930s, but revived in the 1950s especially with the blackmail of British homosexuals; in a survey in the 1950s, 13 per cent of gay men claimed to have been blackmailed. But with the sexual revolution, decriminalization of homosexuality, the decline of hypocrisy and the dissipation of a fixed sexual respectability, blackmail fell appreciably in the 1960s and 1970s. Sexual hypocrisy was a product of religious culture; the decline of the one marked the decline of the other (McLaren 2002: 105–143, 222–238).[6]

The trends set in train from the 1960s also involved a cascade of change to Christian outlooks on profound moral issues. One key example is that of suicide and assisting suicide. Both law and public opinion seemed down to the 1960s quite hostile to suicide, seeing it as the product only of a person 'while the balance of their mind was disturbed'. With the decriminalization of attempted suicide in 1961 in England and Wales (unlike in Scotland where it was never an offence in itself, though generally fell under the hold-all rubric of a breach of the peace), it is difficult to know in detail what public attitudes were. Certainly from that point, there has been evidence of public attitudes considerably at variance with orthodox church teachings. There have been consistently high poll figures in favour of assisted suicide. NOP polls gave 69 per cent in favour in 1976 and 79 per cent in 1993, whilst the British Social Attitudes Survey gave 75 per cent in 1984, 82 per cent in 1994 and 82 per cent in 2009 (including 71 per cent of 'religious' respondents).[7]

From the 1990s, public sympathy for assisted suicide grew more open and politicized, and allowed organizations like Dignity in Dying (formerly the Euthanasia Society) to enjoy considerable support from politicians and celebrities and the prospect of legislative change. The result has been growing public sympathy for those who travel to Zurich in Switzerland to use the services of Dignitas (a group assisting terminally ill and disabled people to die) – both those who take their own lives and those who accompany and assist others in their journey there. A House of Lords ruling in the case of Diane Purdy (who wished to protect her husband from possible prosecution should she decide to follow this course) resulted in the Director of Public Prosecutions indicating that prosecutions would not occur in bone fide cases.[8] More than any, this issue is symbolic of the gulf which has opened between ecclesiastical and public opinion. Though individual clergy have, no mainstream church has approved, or looks likely to approve, suicide and its assisting, and the gulf will only become more significant as changed legislation becomes more likely.

Assisted suicide is one of a number of issues exemplifying growing public desire in modern Britain for autonomy over the human body. It joins sexual activity and sexuality as basic freedoms that have become regarded in the late twentieth and early twenty-first centuries as human rights. There is a wide acceptance of the diversity of human action which should be respected as an individual's choice and not delimited by either laws or ecclesiastically endorsed social pressures. Notwithstanding that these new views envelop many Christians and persons of other faiths, and in some regards there has been significant support from liberal Christians in support of legislative changes,[9] the liberalization of the moral framework of British society between the 1960s and the 2010s is one that has decentred Christian understandings, and, more broadly, *all* religious understandings as authoritative guides for policy on behaviour. And it is not just attitudes to the body that are affected. The rise of the environmental and green movement which began also in the 1960s has begat a suite of new moral positions (concerning conservation of nature, the reduced consumption of goods, packaging and energy, and reuse and recycling of waste) which do not mesh with a traditional religious outlook. Respect for body and for planet are two touchstones of modern moral culture, and even if churches are now often in support of these, religious authority is no longer accepted as a reliable guide to what is acceptable in personal conduct.

So the ecclesiastical crisis of the late twentieth century reveals a wider cultural change. The two have been inseparable, and the direction of travel seemingly irreversible.

Three consequences of the loss of a normative Christian culture

The remainder of the chapter explores three implications of the loss of normative Christian culture: the emergence of a culture of 'no religion' among a very large part of the population, the development of religious sub-cultures, and the circulation of 'religion' through media and culture.

The rise of 'non-religion'

The way in which a space for 'no religion' emerged in post-war Britain is complex. The difficulty of explanation is compounded by the lack of familiarity social science has with the concept of 'no religion', and the tendency to apply ready clichés and philosophical tags – like the term atheism or, sometimes, agnosticism, unbelievers or non-believers. In recent years, the term 'new atheism' has been applied, centred on a very small number of popular writers (Richard Dawkins, Christopher Hitchens and from the USA Sam Harris). But the drift from religion has been a major demographic phenomenon in Britain since the 1960s, and the commitments, causes and the backgrounds of those involved are multifaceted.

The varieties of non-belief have a long history in Britain, emerging within Christian traditions like Unitarianism (which has historically included an agnostic and even atheist tendency, notable in the case of Thomas Aikenhead, a 20-year-old student who was the last person in Britain to be executed for blasphemy at Edinburgh in 1697) and spreading into wholly areligious movements. Atheism and secularism emerged as important elements of the eighteenth-century Enlightenment (seen in the ideas of David Hume and the legacy of the French Revolution respectively), and developed in the nineteenth and early twentieth centuries into a small but dedicated freethinking movement fighting for freedom of conscience, birth control and other moral reforms (Royle 1974, 1980; Budd 1977; Nash 1999). Yet the freethinking movement remained small even in the middle and later decades of the twentieth century when alienation from the Christian churches grew on a very significant scale. In this way, the rise of no religion cannot be seen as a consequence of the movement, but of wider trends in society.

From the evidence of interviews in Britain by Callum Brown carried out in 2009–2010, there is huge diversity in the causes and timing of individuals' turn against religion. Amongst older men like Nigel Bruce, who served as a tank commander in the Second World War, the battlefield was the venue for his change: 'And then of course came the attack, when we attacked from Normandy to Caen with pretty disastrous results really, and a number of my friends were killed and I saw the padre came into action, you know, and blessed them all. This was a terrible time and this made me feel that there wasn't a God, there couldn't be a God. This was absolutely ridiculous, and here we God lovers being killed by other God lovers, it made no sense at all.' Joan Gibson from Edinburgh found a combination of things led her in the 1970s from being a Christian married to a Church of Scotland minister to being a humanist:

> I mean I had all these sort of marital personal problems and my father had died of cancer of the oesophagus which had been horrible and I think I was just realising that, you know, religion didn't have any answers.

A very significant proportion, perhaps as many as a third, of those interviewed trace their drift from Christianity to childhood. Kirsten Bulmer, born in 1975, recalled:

> I remember being deeply sceptical as a child and I've always been should I say anti-religious, organised religion. I've always been sceptical, even would say cynical about it as a child. I remember thinking 'what's this about, this isn't right, how can this how can this be, how can people, how can men assume that they have understood the message?' To me it was obvious it was entirely manmade as a child.

For Dr Harish Mehra, a leading figure of the Asian Rationalist Society based in Birmingham, his college studies led him to challenge religious knowledge:

> I started questioning my own thinking and my own concept of religion … I start reading some of the works of Buddha, because Buddha never believed in any God at all at the time and his philosophy is very based on rationality … I read a lot of books on Marxism, particularly the literature from Russia, which was translated quite extensively in all the languages of India and in Punjabi. I read a lot of work by Maxim Gorki for example, his famous novel 'Mother' … And then people like Bertrand Russell actually influenced me, *Why I am not a Christian*, so that sort of stuff. I started reading. Voltaire and other people, that strengthened my views … Also I think being a student of science, because in my B.Sc. I had subjects like botany and zoology, so evolutionary theory of Darwin also actually helped me in that.

Increasingly, though, for younger people born since the 1960s, a position of 'non-religion' became not so much a conscious choice, but the default position for the growing numbers of children who did not receive any strong religious formation from within their families or schools.

One way of approaching this is to think of the decline of organized religion in Britain since the 1960s as a series of drifts, overlapping in nature, and often starting earlier. There has been the decline of weekly churchgoing (underway from at last the 1870s, but accelerated especially from the 1960s, and now at a low point of around 6.5 per cent of the population). There has been the decline of church adherence (membership or affiliation), which started very slowly from around 1905 and then accelerated again from the 1960s, and stands today at around 20 per cent of the population. There has been the decline of observance of the religious *rites de passage*, notably marriage (very slowly since 1900, much faster from the 1960s), baptism (which peaked in the 1920s but which started a very sharp fall from the mid-1950s) and funerals (which until the 1990s seemed to have shown little appreciable decline in popularity or change in form in response to secular pressures, but now religious funerals are showing signs of slow diminution in popularity to perhaps 85 or 95 per cent of funerals). There has been the decline of belief in God, heaven, hell and other indicators of religion which seem to have fallen more gradually since the 1970s. This has been accompanied by decline in personal religious activity, notably prayer, baptism and religious marriage. Lastly, there has been the decline of identification with either a church or a religion; this is a longer-term process that began in a small way in the 1960s but which has rapidly accelerated in the 1990s and into the new millennium.

This last process – the renouncing of religious identification – may come to be seen as the most important process yet in cultural secularization. So much of the earlier processes have tended to be passive ones – starting with adults straying from religious habits but often enforcing them among children (by sending them to Sunday school or church day schools), but leading through a second stage of unthinking alienation from church habits (when a next generation had no knowledge or experience of going to church except for 'hatches, matches and dispatches'). Within such processes as declining churchgoing, adherence, baptism or religious marriage, there was usually a sustained identification with religion – often as a 'default position' that many people adopted when asked their religion on entering the armed forces, hospital or employment. In England, the default was 'Church of England', in Scotland 'the Church of Scotland' or, more generically, 'Christian'.[10] This default position has been in decline since the 1990s, and this is a most important, and perhaps the ultimate, trend of de-Christianization.

The timing of this trend to 'no religion' is more difficult to follow for Britain than for many other countries; this is largely due to the absence of state censuses of religion before 2001. We do know, though, that the level of people declaring themselves to be of 'no religion' prior to the 1960s was extremely low. In 1942, only 0.06 per cent of men and women in the British Army professed to being atheist (Snape 2005: 146). In 2001, the figure for no religion in the United Kingdom population was 15.4 per cent. But there is evidence of dramatic change since 2001. The Scottish Household Survey, asking the same 2001 Census question among its panel of 12,000 people, has shown the percentage shoot up from 30 per cent in 2002 to 40 per cent in 2008.[11] Using a less stringent question than the Census ('Do you regard yourself as belonging to any particular religion?), the British Household Survey found that those of 'no religion' made up 31 per cent of the British adult population as a whole in 1983, rising to 40 per cent in 1995 and to 46 per cent in 2006.[12]

Differences in formulation of the 2001 Census make complete comparison problematic, but there was notable variation in levels of 'no religion' returns within the UK. In England the figure was 14.6 per cent, in Wales 18.5 per cent, in Scotland (with different answers offered) 27.5 per cent and in Northern Ireland (with Scottish-style answers offered) approximately 1 per cent. The figure in Northern Ireland is even lower than in the Republic of Ireland; here the figure in 1960 was 0.04 per cent, then rose steadily to 0.26 per cent in 1971, 3.35 per cent in 2002 and 4.45 per cent in 2006.[13] However, with the exception of Northern Ireland, and despite the variation between the other constituents, it seems likely that the direction and pace of change are very similar in England, Wales, Scotland and Ireland.

The demographic character of the people of no religion worldwide shows that in the 1950s they were overwhelmingly male; since then they have been becoming significantly more female. In England and Wales in 2001, those classifying themselves as 'no religion' tended to be less female (43.6 per cent) than in the population as a whole (51.3 per cent); they tended to be younger, with 40.5 per cent under 25 years of age (compared to 31.1 per cent in the general population), and had a higher proportion in higher managerial and professional occupations (8.9 per cent) than the general population (6.1 per cent). Marginally more were students (4.9 per cent) than in the general population (3.4 per cent), and significantly fewer were outright home owners (14.6 per cent) than was general (24.2 per cent).[14] Similar trends were observable in Scotland, though the proportion female at 47.6 per cent was interestingly higher than in England and Wales.[15] No religionists are overwhelmingly white in ethnic background with a lower percentage from black and Asian groups than in the population as a whole.

Amongst the people of no religion there is no single credo. A minority classify themselves as one of – or more often a combination of – atheists (non-believers in God), agnostics (those who either doubt the existence of God, or who proclaim it as the most scientific position), humanists (who believe in a dominant and guiding humanity), freethinkers (who oppose the intellectual strictures of organized religion), secularists (who emphasize the need to separate civic society and government from religious control) and 'brights' (who celebrate scientific rationality and emphasize the natural world in ultimate philosophical justification). Some join organizations dedicated to these traditions (such as the British Humanist Association, the Humanist Society of Scotland, the Rationalist Association and the National Secular Society). Increasing numbers are being married or having funerals conducted by celebrants from some of these organizations: the most advanced area is in Scotland where, alone in the UK, the Humanist Society of Scotland (HSS) was in 2005 granted power to conduct 'legal' weddings. In 2009, the 73 celebrants of the HSS conducted 1,544 weddings, more than all churches except the Roman Catholic (1,788) and the Church of Scotland (6,143).[16]

Amongst those of no religion, there are a variety of positions adopted on philosophical issues; about a third express an interest in 'spirituality', and many have taken inspiration from Eastern and native people's religions like Buddhism, or partake of alternative therapies and medicines. On the other hand, those with a background in science and engineering have a strong attachment to scientific principles, and tend to reject alternative medicine and spiritualities. The cultural spread of processes of individualization mean that, like many people identifying as religious, those of 'no religion' tend to have a high regard for the importance of the autonomy and authenticity of the self. In practice, however, significant sources of meaning and value in their lives tend to be mediated through personal relationships with partners, family and friends.

Such significant relations extend beyond the immediate social world of the living, with some people of 'no religion' still experiencing a significant sense of attachment to, and even interaction with, loved ones who are deceased and who might be thought of in terms of ghosts or angels – a phenomenon which Abby Day (2009) has referred to as the 'secular social supernatural'. However, it is important to note that, in interview, those who subscribe to spiritual humanism emphasize their non-belief in an afterlife or a god; they distance themselves from religion and interventionist other beings. Whilst having little or no involvement with traditional religious rituals, people of 'no religion' may engage instead with broader public rituals – often performed through the media – which provide opportunities for collective emotional experience or identification with particular images or stories of the sacred. The media coverage of the public mourning and funeral of Diana, Princess of Wales (see Plate 2.6), the public reception of the returning coffins of British soldiers killed in Afghanistan at Wootton Bassett (see Plate 2.10 and Chapter 6), or news coverage of humanitarian disasters and subsequent appeals and relief efforts, all provide examples of such sacred symbols and rituals beyond institutional religion (see Lynch forthcoming; Pantti and Sumiala 2009).

The diversity of the character of those in Britain who are of no religion extends to the causes of their turning against organized religion. In Scotland, unlike England and Wales, the 2001 Census asked people in what religious tradition they were raised. This showed 58 per cent of those of no religion to say that they were raised in no religion, suggesting they were second- or even third-generation 'no religion'. A further 25 per cent were raised in the Church of Scotland, whilst only 6.2 per cent were raised in the Roman Catholic Church (which accounts for 15.9 per cent of Scots), and only 0.3 per cent were raised in a non-Christian religion (which accounts for 1.9 per cent of the people). This implies that it is the main Protestant churches of Scotland that have been the source of no religionists, haemorrhaging people who identify with religion in the late twentieth century. The default national Church of Scotland has been losing the most people – a fact confirmed for the early twenty-first century by the results of the Scottish Household Survey which showed a decline in Church of Scotland identifiers from 42.4 per cent in 2002 to 30.0 per cent in 2008.[17]

Thus the people of no religion should not be regarded as a homogeneous group. They are extremely diverse in their outlook, philosophical positions and priorities. Through their individual routes they are driving Britain from a Christian culture in the mid-twentieth century towards what remains a complex and rather unstable current situation, but one in which little apparently remains of a normative religiosity. In this context, it is also important to acknowledge that whilst those of 'no religion' have become a larger and more distinctive group in post-war Britain (particularly in younger age cohorts), the process of dis-identification with religion across society is not always quick or clear-cut. As David Voas has put it, 'people stop becoming religious more quickly than they start being wholly secular' (Voas 2009: 165), leading to the phenomenon which Voas describes as 'fuzzy fidelity': a notional attachment to religion which is underpinned by a fundamentally secular orientation. Such 'fuzzy fidelity' may, though, give way to increasingly clear forms of 'non-religion' in coming decades (Voas 2009).

The consolidation of conservative religious sub-cultures

If one implication of the loss of a normative Christian culture has been the emergence of a diverse group of people identifying as being of 'no religion', a related development has been the consolidation of religious sub-cultures within existing religious traditions. The concept of 'sub-culture' originated within the Birmingham school of cultural studies, in which it was used primarily to refer to the popular cultural movements and practices of working-class young men which were interpreted by the Birmingham school as forms of resistance to dominant, conservative and capitalist meanings and values (Hall and Jefferson 1976; Hebdige 1979). Whilst this particular neo-Marxist understanding of sub-culture has been subject to extensive critique (Muggleton 2000; Bennett and Kahn-Harris 2004), it can still be useful to understand sub-cultures in terms of structures of feeling which define a cultural way of being in opposition to an imagined cultural mainstream which is profoundly differ-ent from, and usually hostile to, that sub-culture (Thornton 1995; Smith 2002).

In referring to 'religious sub-cultures', then, the suggestion is not that whole religious traditions can be thought about as sub-cultures or that all religious activity can be under-stood as sub-cultural. The reference is rather to the consolidation of conservative religious sub-cultures, defined more clearly in opposition to liberal changes in Britain since the 1960s, which imagine themselves to be marginalized and opposed by a dominant liberal, secular culture. This clearly does not include the progressive strands across religious tradi-tions which have largely embraced or encouraged more open, liberal and egalitarian societies (Lynch 2007), or indeed the more common religious attempts to strike a pragmatic approach to new social realities. But these consolidated conservative religious sub-cultures have acquired a significance sometimes greater than their numbers of supporters by gener-ating conflicts within religious institutions (e.g. over issues of gay sexuality in the Church of England), by generating particular kinds of religious activism and protest in public life, and by contributing to wider public perceptions of religion. All of these influences are linked to the fact that such religious sub-cultures often draw media attention because their oppositional stances can be attractive to news media which frame contemporary issues in terms of polarization and conflict (see Chapter 7).

Roots of these emergent religious sub-cultures can be seen in conservative religious reac-tions to the greater liberalization of attitudes towards the body, gender and sexuality in the 1960s and 1970s. In the United States, conservative Christian reaction against the 1960s counter-culture, and more culturally liberal media, led to the emergence in the 1970s of the Moral Majority and the new Christian Right, that was to become an increasingly influen-tial force in American culture and politics from the 1980s (Wuthnow 1988). In Britain, high-profile conservative religious protests against new, more liberal cultural attitudes were led by Mary Whitehouse (see Plate 1.1), Cliff Richard, Lord Longford and Malcolm Muggeridge, leading to the Festival of Light demonstrations of 1971 which culminated in a major rally in Trafalgar Square attended by around 10,000 people.

As the new, more liberal understandings of the body, gender and sexuality became more widespread, and the normative Christian culture weakened, so conservative religious oppo-sition became increasingly constructed as a sub-cultural, or counter-cultural, reaction to an imagined, dominant secular and liberal culture that was actively hostile to religion. This sub-cultural perspective became increasingly widespread among evangelical Christians, whose worship songs from the 1980s increasingly represented followers of Christ as an army or stronghold against a culture of unbelief (Ward 1996). It was reflected in formal Catholic denunciations of the mores of secular, liberal views of society, and exemplified in the claim of the Archbishop of Westminster, Cardinal Cormac Murphy O'Connor, in 2001 that Christianity had been 'almost vanquished' as a source of moral guidance in the dominant, secular culture of Britain. For many British Muslims, this sense of opposition to a dominant secular order became powerfully focused around the publication of Salman Rushdie's novel *The Satanic Verses* in 1988. Muslim protests over the representation of the Prophet Muhammad in the book drew strong reactions from those who sought to defend their own secular, liberal commitment to freedom of speech and artistic expression (see Chapter 1 for more detail on the controversy). This sense of Muslim communities living within a hostile, secular culture drew further strength after 9/11, as British Muslims increasingly found themselves addressed by public and policy concerns over security, 'radicalization' and violent extremism.

Over the past 20 years, three points have emerged as recurrent foci of religious sub-cultural tension with an imagined dominant secular order and also served to mobilize sub-cultural religious networks and activism. First, conservative religious views of the body, gender and sexuality appear to be increasingly in conflict with a secular, liberal acceptance of premarital sex, same-sex relations, gender equality and a woman's right to choose to terminate her pregnancy. In reality, this liberal consensus has not been as widespread as suggested by some religious accounts. British media, committed to reflecting the diversity of their audience, may have been giving greater representation of different sexual lifestyles – with the soap opera *EastEnders* broadcasting the first kiss between two male characters on primetime British television in 1987. But more conservative social attitudes have also been present, reflected in the Conservative government's introduction of Section 28 of the Local Government Act 1988 which prohibited the promotion of homosexuality in school and college classes, and which was only repealed with some difficulty by the Labour government in 2003. The progressive extension of equalities and anti-discrimination legislation in relation to gender and sexual orientation has, however, brought a new focus for conservative religious objections to the imposition of secular, liberal values, illustrated by the case of Lillian Ladele, an evangelical Christian, who lost an appeal against religious discrimination in 2009, having refused to conduct same-sex civil partnerships as part of her job as a registrar with Islington Council (see Chapters 1 and 9).

A second site of conflict with secular culture has been in relation to issues of religious dress, and in particular the wearing of religious dress in the workplace or in other public roles. This has often focused around the wearing of the hijab, niqab or burqa by Muslim women, such as the case of Aishah Azmi, who was dismissed from her post as a classroom assistant in 2006[18] after refusing to work without wearing the niqab, or the decision by Imperial College London to ban the wearing of the niqab in its buildings in 2005. But conflicts have also emerged over forms of Christian dress. In 2007, the High Court ruled in support of a school's decision not to suspend its dress code on jewellery to allow one of its pupils, Lydia Playfoot, to wear a ring symbolizing her Christian commitment to sexual abstinence before marriage. There was also national media attention given, the previous year, to the decision by British Airways to suspend one of its employees, Nadia Eweida, who refused to remove a crucifix whilst at work.

A third point of tension between religious sub-cultures and their secular other has concerned issues of freedom of speech. Conservative religious objections to obscenity and blasphemy in the media became increasingly well organized through the 1960s, with the creation of the National Viewers' and Listeners' Association under the leadership of Mary Whitehouse in 1965. But the protests following the publication of *The Satanic Verses* provided an example of spectacular protests against specific publications or broadcasts. This was to be replicated with the protests led by Sikhs in response to the play *Behzti* at the Birmingham Repertory Theatre in 2004, Christian protests following the BBC broadcast of *Jerry Springer the Opera* in 2005 and the global demonstrations following the publication of the Danish cartoons of the Prophet Muhammad later in the same year (see Chapter 1 for more details).

Whilst these cases may be sporadic, subject to media fashions and often directly involving only small numbers of people, they nevertheless form the basis of narratives of religious opposition to a newly dominant and hostile secular culture that circulate through religious sermons, books, songs and websites.[19] As the numbers of people actively involved in religious organizations continue to fall as a percentage of the wider population, younger religious adherents show signs of more consistent commitment to core religious beliefs and practices (Lambert 2004), in which narratives of being marginalized and silenced by an imagined mainstream secular culture form an increasing part of their sense of religious identity. For younger adherents, maintaining a sub-cultural religious identity and lifestyle may involve not only a sense of marginalization from the secular mainstream, but an immersion in a cultural world that reproduces and legitimates their religious commitments and relationships.

The emergence of new technologies of design and production in the 1980s made it increasingly possible for manufacturers to make limited production runs of goods that were marketed to appeal to different 'niche' forms of lifestyle. In this wider context, new forms of religious branding developed, in which various products (including clothing, books and music) became associated with different styles of faith as well as, in many cases, celebrity figures within specific religious sub-cultures (Einstein 2008; Hendershot 2004; Schofield Clark 2007). The development of digital media has provided renewed opportunities for the production, distribution and consumption of religious sub-cultural materials such as websites, video and audio downloads, and other electronic means of distribution, which allow sub-cultural religious content and services to be produced, marketed and circulated at relatively low cost. The viability of particular forms of religious sub-cultural product may have previously been limited by the scope of national markets (hence the limited potential for a professional, contemporary Christian music scene in the UK compared to the USA; Ward 2005). Now, however, digital media accelerate the transnational flow of religious sub-cultural products and services, making niche sub-cultural scenes (e.g. Christian heavy metal; Moberg 2009) more commercially viable by opening them up to a global market.

The symbolic status of maintaining minority religious positions in a dominant, secular culture, together with new technologies of production and consumption that allow the circulation of religious sub-cultural goods and services, suggests that religious sub-cultures are likely to remain an important part of the religious landscape of Britain for the foreseeable future. Such sub-cultures may be significant, not only in generating conflictual interactions with real or imagined secular forces, but in challenging traditional religious institutions and authorities that are perceived as being too accommodating to the liberal, moral ethos of secular society.

The cultural circulation and negotiation of 'religion'

A final implication of the loss of a normative Christian culture, and associated popular involvement with traditional Christian organizations and rituals, is that the category of 'religion' (and symbols and practices traditionally thought of as 'religious') becomes increasingly detached from traditional institutional structures and circulates through culture in new, and at times unpredictable, ways (Beckford 2003). As fewer people engage directly with traditional religious institutions, so public media have increasingly become a primary context through which people encounter, learn and communicate about 'religion'. Stig Hjarvard (2008) has described this process in terms of the 'mediatization of religion'. By this he means both that the media become an increasingly important site for public engagement with religion, and that, at the same time, religion is reshaped according to the particular logics of the media through which it circulates (whether the sound-bite culture or polarized debates encouraged by news media, or the genre conventions of different forms of popular entertainment media). Whilst Hjarvard's theory of the mediatization of religion does not fit all societies equally well, it does provide a useful framework for thinking about the implications of media as a key site for public engagement with religion in Britain (see also Chapter 7 on religion and the media).

A useful element of Hjarvard's theory is his argument that the mediatization of religion encourages the spread of 'banal religion', by which he means the circulation of images of religious symbols and practices in ways that form a backdrop for everyday life without necessarily forming an important part of people's identities or their understanding of the world. Popular entertainment in Britain – from *The Da Vinci Code*, to the *Harry Potter* and *Twilight* series of books and films or even sitcoms like *The Vicar of Dibley* or *Rev.* – allow representations of religion and the supernatural to continue to circulate widely through contemporary culture. Indeed, as Chapter 7 shows, one of the striking features of contemporary British media is that there continues to be the same amount of coverage given to religion compared to the early 1980s, despite the ongoing weakening of a normative Christian culture. The loss of a normative Christian culture does not, therefore, mean that religion and the supernatural entirely drop out of the repertoire of widely used cultural meanings, although the lack of engagement with traditional religious institutions does lead to a loss of more detailed memory of religious tradition (Hervieu-Leger 2000). Rather the cultural category of 'religion', and its associated symbols and practices, continue to circulate through popular media in ways which are less likely to be received reverently but more likely to form an unthought-about backdrop of cultural meanings or, at times, a resource for defining oneself against (e.g. 'I'm not intolerant, like those religious fundamentalists …', see Lövheim 2007).

Alongside the circulation of religion through public media, the weakening of a normative Christian culture and popular disengagement from traditional religious institutions, present new challenges for other public institutions. Since the acceptance at the Reformation of the Church of England as the established church of England and Wales, and the passing of the Act of Toleration in 1689 and the Catholic Relief Act 1829, public life in England proceeded on the assumption that Anglicanism provided the central religious identity and institutional structure for the state, with toleration for other Christian denominations and other religious faiths being extended from this centre. In Wales, the Church of England was disestablished in 1920, and the resulting episcopal Church in Wales became a minority denomination among many. In Scotland, toleration took longer to be established, and the dominant Presbyterianism was more divided than the English Anglican tradition from 1733 to 1929; yet the Church of Scotland was effectively disestablished in 1925–1930, and since then it has been forced to share its self-proclaimed status as 'the national church' with the Roman Catholic Church. In Northern Ireland, there never was an established church, but Protestantism collectively until the commencement of the 1997 peace process dominated the organs of the civil state (see Chapter 9).

Despite different country histories within the UK, it remains true that, outside Northern Ireland, there has been a loss of a normative Christian culture and a loss of its associations with the Anglican Church or the Church of Scotland. In place of default denominations of national identity, new challenges arise in contemporary Britain for how 'religion' is thought about in public life, as well as the role of religion in relation to public cultural institutions. In this context, a cultural discourse of 'faith communities' is increasingly used by public organizations, including the government, which constructs Christianity as one faith community among many others (despite the fact that the monarch remains the 'supreme governor' of the Church of England, and 26 Anglican bishops continue to sit in the House of Lords).

The process of constructing religious traditions and organizations as 'faith communities' can be understood as part of a cultural frame that seeks to include religious diversity in public life, whilst at the same time not privileging any particular tradition over another. These processes of defining what is, and is not, included, in relation to the cultural category of religion are under continual negotiation. Atheism and humanism are now taught more widely in religious education in British schools (though humanist organizations claim exclusion by some headteachers and local authorities). Similarly, the Equality and Human Rights Commission has a duty to uphold protection against discrimination on the basis of 'religion or belief', where belief is understood in terms of 'philosophical beliefs, such as humanism, which are considered to be similar to religion'.[20] Such processes are not neutral attempts to define a stable phenomenon of 'religion'. Rather they are cultural processes of 'meaning making' in which the meaning of religion, and related terms such as belief or spirituality, continue to be reworked in ways that often unwittingly replicate or subvert more established historical meanings and uses.

The ongoing negotiation of the cultural meanings and place of 'religion' also creates new challenges for public cultural institutions in Britain. Cultural institutions, such as publicly funded museums, may be familiar with a remit of reaching out to communities (including minority faith communities) who are not regular users of their services, as part of a public commitment to social inclusion. More complicated questions arise, though, in relation to the religious or secular nature of such public cultural institutions. Are museums secular spaces in which visitors are to be trained into particular secular, enlightenment ways of understanding local and world cultures, or can they be religious or post-secular spaces in which the religious meanings of objects can be understood and even experienced in some way? Similar uncertainties arise in the context of public educational institutions. As Chapter 8 discusses, one of the remnants of a normative Christian culture in English and Welsh schools is the legal requirement to maintain a daily act of collective worship. In practice, most schools other than faith schools either interpret this requirement very broadly or largely ignore it. But in coming decades, it seems unlikely that schools will be able to continue to avoid difficult questions about what place 'religion' has in the educational process, and whether requirements such as the act of collective worship are viable in pluralist societies in which growing numbers of people have no attachment to religious traditions or institutions. How 'religion' will be constructed and negotiated across different public institutions therefore remains an open and uncertain process, and may arrive at unstable resolutions.

Taken together these three implications of the loss of a normative Christian culture may seem contradictory. We have clear evidence of the emergence of 'non-religion' as a growing part of cultural life in twenty-first-century Britain, alongside the persistence and renewal of religious sub-cultures, and the continued circulation of categories and representations of 'religion' through different public institutions. Yet these developments are all deeply intertwined. It is precisely through the loss of a normative Christian culture and popular disengagement with the churches, that a sense of a hostile, secular mainstream has become more potent for conservative religious sub-cultures. Moreover, as Chapters 4 and 5 discuss, at the same time progressive religious movements which favour individualized spirituality over institutionalized religion continue to emerge and grow, and to embrace liberal values of institutional freedom, personal liberty and religious toleration (see also Lynch 2007). As a sense of a common Christian culture and heritage continues to weaken, so new and pressing questions emerge about whether Britain is indeed, or should be, a secular culture, and what the meaning and position of 'religion' should be in relation to contemporary cultural life. Increasing popular disengagement with traditional Christian structures and sources of meaning has therefore encouraged new forms of minority religious imagination, community and practice. It has also generated new and complex conflicts over the status of the religious and the secular in British cultural life which are increasingly negotiated through public media rather than traditional religious institutions.

Paradoxically this means that as growing numbers of people live their lives with little reference to traditional religious structures of feeling, and as religious symbols and practices circulate most commonly as 'banal religion' through popular media, body tattooing or jewellery, so 'religion' does not disappear from the British cultural landscape. It can in fact be a more conscious focus of cultural anxiety and uncertainty, as well as, for a minority of people, a strong organizing centre for their lives. There is nothing to suggest that any of these processes – the growth of non-religion, the circulation of banal religion, the vitality of minority religious sub-cultures, or the contestation of the place of religion in British cultural life – will be reversed. But the implications of these processes for the kind of social lives and institutions that emerge in Britain through the coming century is much harder to predict.

Conclusion: cultural explanation and religious change in post-war Britain

This chapter presents a narrative about the loss of a normative Christian culture in Britain since 1945, and discusses some of the key implications arising as a consequence of this. In conclusion, two broader points can be drawn out from this discussion concerning the nature of cultural explanations of processes of religious change.

First, cultural meanings, for example concerning the body, gender, sexuality or the meaning of 'religion', are not straightforward *causes* of social change. Rather cultural meanings that shape social life are themselves influenced by social structures and processes, as well as the impulses of individuals increasingly feeling empowered since the 1960s to reject ecclesiastical and Christian-dominated discipline of behaviour. In the case of the narrative that we have presented above, for example, it is clear that changing meanings of sexuality and gender, driven by awakening freedoms and personal desires, led growing numbers of people away from the structures of feeling nurtured by a traditional, normative Christian culture in Britain. But the changing meanings of sexuality and gender did not occur simply at an abstract or symbolic level, but in conjunction with choices that people made. These included women rejecting the constraints of traditional gender roles, new technologies (e.g. the contraceptive pill) or other cultural practices (e.g. new styles of popular music), as well as wider changes in social and economic conditions (e.g. the expansion of higher education). Cultural change therefore takes place through a complex interplay of cultural meanings, historical contexts, social, political and economic conditions, and the choices that people make as social actors. Explaining the changing religious landscape of Britain after 1945 therefore involves recognizing the importance of changing structures of feeling in the process of popular disengagement from traditional Christian practices and institutions. However, it also involves recognizing how these changes were bound up with factors such as rising affluence, new media and technologies, the emergence of the women's movement, the expansion of educational opportunities and new possibilities for lifestyle choice.

Second, and following on from this, cultural explanations of religious change are therefore always, to a lesser or greater extent, contextually specific. Some sociological theories of religious change – most notably the secularization thesis – have sought to develop a model of religious change associated with broadly observable features of modernization which can be widely generalized across a range of developed societies (as explored in the next chapter). It is certainly true that modernization and globalization have typically brought particular changes to many societies across the world, including mass migration, the extension of transnational institutions and markets (and the accompanying expansion of neoliberalism), the growing cultural importance of public and social media, and new global popular cultural scenes. Some of the trends we have discussed in relation to Britain in this chapter are also broadly observable in other national contexts. But because changing cultural meanings are always embedded in wider social, economic and political processes which play out differently according to the national context being studied, cultural explanations of religious change can never easily be developed into theories that provide generalizable predictions about religious change across a wide range of societies.

Secularization may still be an important descriptor of religious change, but it does not need to be taken to be the 'thesis' or 'theory' of the same name – it simply names the varied processes of declining social significance of religion in individual nations, regions, cultural groups, and even individuals. What this chapter offers is both an invitation for further refinement of cultural explanations of religious change in post-war Britain, and a particular model of cultural and religious change which could be used as a point of comparison with societies of other times and places.

Key terms

Conservative religion: Religious movements and ideologies which emphasize an authentic expression of religious tradition over its modern reinterpretation tend to hold conservative social positions regarding gender, sexuality and individual autonomy, and engage in various forms of religious and political activism often oriented towards demonstrating the truth of their core convictions.

Cultural turn: A movement across a range of academic disciplines in the humanities and social sciences that treats culture as a key concept through which social life can be analysed.

Culture: Structures of meaning through which people experience their interior and embodied lives, their social worlds and their physical environments.

Liberal religion: Religious movements and ideologies which see religious tradition as needing to be reinterpreted in line with modern knowledge and standards of critical thinking, support liberal values of freedom, diversity and equality, and tend to engage with broader issues of social justice.

Mediatization: The process by which particular aspects of social life are increasingly performed through public and social media, which in turn changes those aspects of social life in particular ways.

Non-religion: The position of non-identification with any religion, typically in Britain of those previously of a Christian heritage, and including those with agnostic, atheist, secularist or freethinking outlooks.

Presbyterian: System of church government popular in Scottish and Northern Irish Protestantism, in which a form of democratic election by communicant members of ministers and lay elders obtains in congregations, district presbyteries and national general assemblies, and in which no permanent leaders are usually countenanced, leading to annual election of 'moderators' (see also p. 316).

Sub-culture: Cultural practices, resources and structures of feeling which are experienced by participants as existing in a critical relationship to a dominant and often hostile cultural mainstream.

Further reading

Alexander, Jeffrey C. (2003). *The Meanings of Social Life: A Cultural Sociology*. New York, NY: Oxford University Press. This is a key text that sets out the theory and methodology of one of the most influential approaches within cultural sociology.

Brown, Callum G. (2009). *The Death of Christian Britain*. 2nd edition. London: Routledge. This argues for the strength of Christian culture until the 1950s, followed by its sudden collapse in the 1960s, using a gendered analysis.

Lynch, Gordon (2009). 'Religion, Media and Cultures of Everyday Life', in John Hinnells (ed.), *The Routledge Companion to the Study of Religion*. 2nd edition. London: Routledge, 543–557. This chapter provides an overview of a growing academic literature on religion, media and popular culture and identifies important ways in which this can help us to make sense of contemporary religious change.

Lynch, Gordon (forthcoming). *The Sacred in the Modern World: A Cultural Sociological Approach*. Oxford: Oxford University Press. This book explores how the sacred takes broader and more complex cultural forms than suggested by conventional distinctions between the religious and the secular, exploring, for example, the sacralization of the care of children and the role of news media as a key site for engaging contemporary forms of the sacred.

McLeod, Hugh (2007). *The Religious Crisis of the 1960s*. Oxford: Oxford University Press. This argues that the religious crisis in England, Europe, North America and Australia was one generated by liberal Christians' involvement in creating a modern pluralist society.

References

Alexander, Jeffrey C. (ed.) (1988). *Durkheimian Sociology: Cultural Studies*. Cambridge: Cambridge University Press.

Alexander, Jeffrey C. (2003). *The Meanings of Social Life: A Cultural Sociology*. New York, NY: Oxford University Press.

Beckford, James (2003). *Social Theory and Religion*. Cambridge: Cambridge University Press.

Bennett, Andy and Keith Kahn-Harris (eds) (2004). *After Subculture: Critical Studies in Contemporary Youth Culture*. Basingstoke: Palgrave Macmillan.

Biersack, Aletta and Lynn Hunt (eds) (1989). *The New Cultural History*. Berkeley, CA: University of California Press.

Bonnell, Victoria and Lynn Hunt (1999). *Beyond the Cultural Turn: New Directions in the Study of Society and Culture*. Berkeley, CA: University of California Press.

Bourdieu, Pierre (1984). *Distinction: A Social Critique of the Judgment of Taste*. London: Routledge and Kegan Paul.

Brown, Callum G. (2005). *Postmodernism for Historians*. London: Pearson Longman.

Brown, Callum G. (2006). *Religion and Society in Twentieth-Century Britain*. London: Longman Pearson.

Brown, Callum G. (2011). 'Sex, Religion and the Single Woman c.1950–1975: The Importance of a "Short" Sexual Revolution to the English Religious Crisis of the Sixties', *Twentieth Century British History*, 22/2: 189–215.

Budd, Susan (1977). *Varieties of Unbelief: Atheists and Agnostics in English Society 1850–1960*. London: Heinemann.

Clark, Schofield Lynn (ed.) (2007). *Religion, Media and the Marketplace*. New Brunswick, NJ: Rutgers University Press.

Cook, Hera (2004). *The Long Sexual Revolution: English Women, Sex, and Contraception 1800–1975*. Oxford: Oxford University Press.

Currie, Robert, Alan Gilbert and Lee Horsley (1977). *Churches and Churchgoers: Patterns of Church Growth in the British Isles since 1700*. Oxford: Clarendon Press.

Day, Abby (2009). 'Believing in Belonging: An Ethnography of Young People's Constructions of Belief', *Culture and Religion*, 10/3: 263–278.

Einstein, Mara (2008). *Brands of Faith: Marketing Religion in a Commercial Age*. London: Routledge.

Eley, Geoffrey (1995). 'What is Cultural History?', *New German Critique*, 65: 19–36.

Gross, Neil (2005). 'Jeffrey Alexander's Too Strong Program?', *Newsletter of the Sociology of Culture Section of the American Sociological Association*, 19/2: 6–8.

Hall, Stuart and Tony Jefferson (1976). *Resistance Through Rituals: Youth Subcultures in Post-War Britain*. Birmingham: University of Birmingham Press.

Hebdige, Dick (1979). *Subculture: The Meaning of Style*. London: Routledge.

Hendershot, Heather (2004). *Shaking the World for Jesus: Media and Conservative Evangelical Culture*. Chicago, IL: University of Chicago Press.

Hervieu-Leger, Daniele (2000). *Religion as a Chain of Memory*. Cambridge: Polity.

Hjarvard, Stig (2008). 'The Mediatization of Religion: A Theory of the Media as Agents of Religious Change', *Northern Lights*, 6/1: 9–26.

Inglis, David, Andrew Blaikie and Robin Wagner-Pacifici (2007). 'Sociology, Culture and the 21st Century', *Cultural Sociology*, 1/1: 5–22.

Knight, Margaret (1954). *Morals Without Religion and Other Essays*. London: Dennis Dobson.

Lambert, Yves (2004). 'A Turning Point in Religious Evolution in Europe', *Journal of Contemporary Religion*, 19/1: 29–45.

Latham, M. (1999). 'Emergency Contraception: Why the Law Should Make it Available "Over the Counter"', *New Law Journal* (12 March), 149/6879: 366–367. Online. Available HTTP: www.prochoiceforum.org.uk/ri3.php (accessed 23 May 2010).

Lewis, Jane and Kathleen Kiernan (1996). 'The Boundaries Between Marriage, Nonmarriage, and Parenthood: Changes in Behavior and Policy in Postwar Britain', *Journal of Family History*, 21/3: 372–387.

Lövheim, Mia (2007). 'Virtually Boundless? Youth Negotiating Tradition in Cyberspace', in Nancy Ammerman (ed.), *Everyday Religion: Observing Modern Religious Lives*. New York, NY: Oxford University Press, 83–101.

Lynch, Gordon (2007). *The New Spirituality: An Introduction to Progressive Belief in the Twenty-First Century*. London: I. B. Tauris.

Lynch, Gordon (forthcoming). *The Sacred in the Modern World: A Cultural Sociological Approach*. Oxford: Oxford University Press.

McLaren, Angus (2002). *Sexual Blackmail: A Modern History*. Cambridge, MA: Harvard University Press.

McLeod, Hugh (2007). *The Religious Crisis of the 1960s*. Oxford: Oxford University Press.

Martin, Bernice (1981). *A Sociology of Contemporary Cultural Change*. Oxford: Basil Blackwell.

Moberg, Marcus (2009). *Faster for the Master: Exploring Issues of Religious Expression and Alternative Christian Identity within the Finnish Christian Metal Scene*. Abo: Abo Akademi University Press.

Muggleton, David (2000). *Inside Subculture: The Postmodern Meaning of Style*. Oxford: Berg.

Nash, David (1999). *Blasphemy in Modern Britain 1789 to the Present*. Aldershot: Ashgate.

Pantti, Mervi and Johana Sumiala (2009). 'Til Death do us Join: Mourning Rituals and the Sacred Centre of Society', *Media, Culture and Society*, 31/1: 119–135.

Parsons, Talcott (1949). *The Structure of Social Action, Volume 1*. New York, NY: Free Press.

Royle, Edward (1974). *Victorian Infidels: The Origins of the British Secularist Movement 1791–1866*. Manchester: Manchester University Press.

Royle, Edward (1980). *Radicals, Secularists and Republicans: Popular Freethought in Britain 1866–1915*. Manchester: Manchester University Press.

Smith, Christian (2002). *Christian America? What Evangelicals Really Want*. Berkeley, CA: University of California Press.

Snape, Michael (2005). *God and the British Soldier: Religion and the British Army in the First and Second World Wars.* London: Routledge.

Spilman, Lynn (2005). 'Is the "Strong Program" Strong Enough?', *Newsletter of the Sociology of Culture Section of the American Sociological Association*, 19/2: 4–6.

Sutcliffe, Steven (2010). 'After "The Religion of My Fathers": The Quest for Composure in the "Post-Presbyterian" Self', in Lynn Abrams and Callum G. Brown (eds), *A History of Everyday Life in Twentieth-century Scotland*. Edinburgh: Edinburgh University Press, 181–205.

Tehrani, Dabir (2010). 'Growth of Humanism in Scotland', *Humanitie*, 3/2: 16–17.

Thornton, Sarah (1995). *Club Cultures: Music, Media and Subcultural Capital*. Cambridge: Polity.

Voas, David (2009). 'The Rise and Fall of Fuzzy Fidelity in Europe', *European Sociological Review*, 25/2: 155–168.

Walkerdine, Valerie (1985). 'Dreams from an Ordinary Childhood', in Liz Heron (ed.), *Truth, Dare or Promise*. London: Virago, 63–77.

Ward, Pete (1996). *Growing Up Evangelical: Youthwork and the Making of a Subculture*. London: SPCK.

Ward, Pete (2005). *Selling Worship: How What We Sing Has Changed the Church*. Milton Keynes: Authentic Media.

Williams, Raymond (1961). *The Long Revolution*. Harmondsworth: Penguin.

Williams, Raymond and Michael Orrom (1954). *Preface to Film*. London: Film Drama Limited.

Wuthnow, Robert (1988). *The Restructuring of American Religion: Society and Faith since World War II*. Princeton, NJ: Princeton University Press.

Notes

1   See e.g. Alexander (2003); Spilman (2005); Gross (2005).

2   The extent to which such structures are open to being changed through the conscious, or unintended, actions of individuals and groups is an important theoretical debate concerning human agency, historical contingency, culture and social change. The extent to which these cultural structures are constructed through local interactions or are persistent and deeply embedded in particular forms of subjectivity, practice or social institution is also an important debate. For example, the differing forms of macro-analysis of culture structures offered by Foucault and Alexander can be contrasted with localized theories of meaning-making in symbolic interactionism and ethnomethodology.

3   For more detailed discussions of cultural history, see Biersack and Hunt (1989); Eley (1995); and Brown (2005), and of cultural sociology, see Alexander (1988, 2003); Inglis *et al.* (2007).

4   *Sunday Graphic*, 9 January 1954, facsimile appearing on dust jacket of Knight (1954).

5   The Sunday Trading Act 1994 repealed the Shops Act 1950 which had consolidated a variety of measures from earlier decades. This had closed butchers and hairdressers and prohibited the selling of everything except items on a list – including intoxicating liquors, meals except fish and chips, newly cooked provisions, sweets, ice cream, flowers, tobacco and newspapers.

6   Elsewhere, McLaren (2002) has said that blackmail lost its zing due to 'changes in public attitudes, and declining hypocrisy and, then, in the 1960s and 1970s, changes in the law'. Online: Available HTTP: http://timesofindia.indiatimes.com/world/rest-of-world/Sex-lies-and-the-art-of-blackmail-/articleshow/5109628.cms (accessed 24 May 2010).

7   Data cited by Ben Goldacre on Bad Science website. Online. Available HTTPs: www.badscience.net/2008/12/public-opinion-has-moved-sharply-in-favour-of-assisted-suicide-according-to-a-poll-for-the-sunday-times/; and www.dignityindying.org.uk/news/general/n231-new-survey-shows-overwhelming-support-for-assisted-dying.html (accessed 5 June 2011).

8   Online. Available HTTP: www.cps.gov.uk/news/press_releases/144_09/ (accessed 23 May 2010).

9   In relation to homosexual law reform in England and Wales, see McLeod (2007: 41–45).

10 When an individual responded with 'don't know' or even 'no religion', there are many stories of administrators in hospitals and the armed forces entering 'Church of England' or 'Church of Scotland' on the forms.

11 Figures from Scottish Household Survey, quoted in Tehrani (2010: 16).

12 BHS data given online. Available HTTP: www.britsocat.com/BodySecure.aspx?control= BritsocatMarginalsandvar=RELIGIONandSurveyID=221 (accessed 1 July 2010).

13 Irish Censuses 1926–1991, online at www.cso.ie/census_26 etc. (accessed 27 November 2009); Census 2006, vol. 13 Religion. Online. Available HTTP: http://beyond2020.cso.ie/census/ ReportFolders/ReportFolders.aspx (accessed 30 November 2009); for 2002: http://beyond2020.cso.ie/Census/TableViewer/tableView.aspx (accessed 30 November 2009).

14 Data calculated from figures at ONS, 2001 Census, England and Wales, Theme Table T53. Online. Available HTTP: www.statistics.gov.uk (accessed 16 July 2010).

15 Data calculated from GRO, 2001 Census, Scotland, Theme table T25. Online. Available HTTP: www.gro-scotland.gov.uk (accessed 16 July 2010).

16 Data online. Available HTTP: www.gro-scotland.gov.uk/statistics/publications-and-data/vital-events/ref-tables-2009/marriages.html (accessed 18 August 2010).

17 Data from Scottish Household Survey, supplied by R. Stewart.

18 *Azmi v. Kirkless Metropolitan Council* [2007] UKEAT 00009 07 30003.

19 We are grateful to Anna Strhan for this insight, drawing on her work on Conservative Evangelicalism in Britain.

20 See the Equality and Human Rights Commission's website. Online. Available HTTP: www.equalityhumanrights.com/advice-and-guidance/your-rights/religion-and-belief/what-is-a-belief/ (accessed 5 June 2011).

11 Social perspectives

Elisabeth Arweck and James A. Beckford

This chapter discusses social factors which help to explain religious change in post-war Britain. Social perspectives focus attention on patterns in human life and the factors that shape them. The discussion begins by explaining what a social approach involves and by showing how the meanings attributed to religion in Britain are socially constructed and reproduced. The chapter then considers how religious change is associated with changes in social context and analyses a range of theoretical perspectives which can explain the social dimensions of religious change in Britain (even though some of these theories are at variance with others). It also discusses various theories of secularization as well as criticisms and alternative perspectives. It considers how a range of social changes in post-war Britain have interacted with religion, including changing identities, gender relations, educational processes, forms of media, global interconnections and shifting organizational forms.

Nature and importance of social perspectives of religion

Why is it important to investigate the social dimensions of religion? The short answer is that religion is simply interesting for the intriguing ways in which it is intertwined with social and cultural life. This purely intellectual interest in the social aspects of religion is good enough for many people – but not for those who wish to study these aspects in order to criticize, challenge or eliminate religion's social influence. Their answer to the question of why they investigate the social aspects of religion is longer because their interests are both intellectual *and* practical. This is equally true of people who wish to gain a better understanding of the social aspects of religion in order to promote and extend its influence in society or those who wish to promote good relations. But perhaps the longest answer to the question about reasons for being interested in social perspectives on religion comes from people who take up the challenge of trying to make sense of religion against the background of high-level social and cultural changes. For them, what is interesting is how well religion can be fitted into the grand narratives about social change such as modernization, decolonization, globalization, post-modernization, secularization, the commodification of popular culture or the diffusion of neoliberal programmes of governmentality. And they also want to know how far religion acts as a driving force for social change in, for example, campaigns to abolish slavery, capital punishment and the debts loaded on to the world's poorest countries.

There are many different ways of explaining what social perspectives are, but they all agree that religious beliefs, experiences, emotions, practices and forms of organization have social dimensions. Continuity and change in religion simply cannot be understood without looking at them from social points of view. This means considering religion in Britain from the angle of 'the social' or the patterned ways in which the lives of human beings are lived through social roles, relationships, groups, communities, organizations, neighbourhoods, institutions, tribes, nations, states and global networks. Adopting a social perspective also means taking account of the frameworks of shared ideas, identities, meanings, languages and values with which countless generations of human beings have tried to make sense of their experiences and situations. Above all, social perspectives focus our attention on patterns in human life and in the factors that shape it.

A perspective is only one point of view among others. However, gaining a perspective on a subject really means being able to appreciate how different points of view can be aligned in order to achieve a better, more rounded understanding of the subject in question. Therefore, although social perspectives can make an important contribution to the understanding of religion, they are far from providing the entire picture.

The importance of social perspectives can be illustrated with four examples of how they bring particular aspects of religious change in Britain since 1945 into focus. Each example picks out a few social aspects of one of the most visible features of religion in public places, namely, attendance at churches, mosques, synagogues, temples, gurdwaras and other places of worship.

First, they are all locations for *collective* gatherings that bring participants together for shared activities which express shared beliefs and emotions in forms that vary across time and space. Second, social perspectives can throw light on the social *characteristics* of the participants in collective religious activities – in terms of such factors as age, sex, sexual orientation, marital status, number of children, ethnicity, social class, level of education, cultural interests, political preferences and moral values. Consideration of these characteristics helps to show how far participants in particular religious groups are similar to, or different from, each other. Third, social perspectives are essential to understanding how religious ideas and activities are *organized and reproduced* across time and space. For example, the ways of joining, being members of, or merely identifying with, religious communities or organizations provide vital clues as to how religious ideas and practices are reproduced over time. Analysis of forms of leadership and other authority relations can also reveal a lot about the capacity of religious organizations to grow or shrink and to be influential or marginal to the life of the societies in which they operate. An understanding of the alliances, encounters and conflicts between religious organizations is also indispensable to an appreciation of religious history. Finally, *communication* is a social process at the heart of religions and clearly at work in places of worship. It involves the creation, exchange and circulation of all kinds of ideas, information, teachings, attitudes, codes, moods and feelings – to say nothing of material resources – among people associated with religious traditions, communities and organizations. And it is centrally concerned with the processes of social interaction through which human beings learn about – and, in some cases, change or reject – religious beliefs, practices, moral codes and worldviews. Hence the notion of being socialized into a religious tradition or group.

These four examples can only hint at the rich variety of things that social perspectives can bring to light about religion and religious change in Britain since the end of the Second World War. They will be developed at greater length as the chapter unfolds and discussed under the umbrella of overarching theoretical ideas about the social aspects of religion. These ideas are high-level generalizations about the social factors that are at work in relation to religion as both cause and effect of social change. Social factors not only generate, shape, transform, regulate or suppress religion, but they are also, in their turn, influenced by religion. Inevitably, then, change is central to theoretical ideas about religion in its social contexts.

However, at this point, it is important to emphasize that social perspectives are deliberate abstractions from the complexity of religion. This means that they artificially simplify things in order to make analysis easier and more fruitful. They bring certain things into clear focus such as social roles, interactions, settings, characteristics, forms of organization, processes and structures. But there are many alternative perspectives on religion – psychological, political, theological and so on – which give precedence to different aspects of religion.

What counts as religion and religious change from a social perspective?

So far, the words 'religion' and 'religious' have been used without paying close attention to their meaning. It is not helpful to impose a strict or narrow definition which runs the risk of favouring any particular religious or theological tradition(s). Instead, it is more helpful to work with an approach which recognizes that concepts of religion are bound to be contentious and contextual and which also regards the definition of religion as an ongoing social process. Definitions are not given in the nature of the world: they are constantly constructed, promoted, defended and criticized. In other words, the changing definition of religion is, itself, a prime topic for investigation from the viewpoint of social perspectives on religion, both in the past and in the present.

Disputes about the definition of religion come to the fore in administrative and legal settings where questions about what counts as religion have to be formally resolved. This applies especially to cases in which allegations of unfair discrimination lead to arguments about the distinction between religion, culture and ethnicity. These arguments also arise when groups try to claim benefits – such as tax-free status or eligibility to provide salaried chaplains in prisons or hospitals, or privileges – such as teaching a particular religion in school – that are available only to recognized religious groups. In other words, social perspectives focus on the processes whereby meanings of religion are somehow given effect in social life and the extent to which religion is an agent in (power) relations between institutions and interest groups. In this sense, they become 'operative' definitions that come to appear 'natural' and taken for granted.

If the meanings widely attributed to religion are varied and contested, part of the reason is that what counts as religion, however it is defined, undergoes change. For example, there can be pressure to accept that new, would-be religious ideas or practices are 'really' religious and should, therefore, be treated as similar to much more established ones. But there can also be pressure to resist the acceptance of new developments in religion, especially if they are considered to lead to radical changes in behaviour and views of the world, to have an impact on the status quo or to lend legitimation to particular groups. In short, discussion of religious change is inseparable from discussion of what counts as religion. This is particularly clear in disputes about the tendency for growing numbers of Muslim women in Europe to adopt forms of dress such as the hijab, jilbab or burqa. But arguments rage around the question of how far these forms of dress are 'really' matters of religious, ethnic, national or cultural identity. Some parties to these disputes clearly believe that it is somehow possible to isolate religion from ethnicity, nationality and culture.

This means that changes in the social construction of religion have to be seen against the backdrop of broader changes taking place in Britain as it emerged from the Second World War. Many of these changes are discussed in the Introduction to this volume and the chapters following it. No list of such changes could possibly be exhaustive, but Text box 20 summarizes some of the most significant dimensions of social change and continuity in the period, beginning with material conditions.

TEXT BOX 20

Significant changes in Britain since 1945

- The process of repairing bomb damage and clearing slums boosted the expansion of new inner-city and suburban housing estates.
- The proportion of women in employment outside the home continued a trend that had begun at the time of the First World War.
- The birth rate rose more abruptly.
- The post-war economy began to be affected by stiffer competition from other parts of the world.
- The central institutions of the welfare state took over most of the responsibility for childcare, schools, healthcare, public housing, state pensions and social welfare.
- Trade union membership and power continued to assume greater significance in employment relations and politics.

The changes listed in Text box 20 were not necessarily matched or mirrored by corresponding changes in the structure of local government or national politics. Moreover, differences in the distribution of wealth, property and life chances between the principal social classes, regions and nations of the UK remained sharp. And voluntary associations, especially for young people, continued to attract large percentages of various age groups in all four nations of the UK.

Against the backdrop of these broad patterns of change and continuity in post-war Britain, this chapter focuses specifically on three aspects of religion as a social phenomenon. The first is the social patterning of religious belief and practice. The second deals with the social factors that shaped religion. And the third investigates theoretical ideas that seek to account for these patterns.

Social patterns of belief and practice

Social scientific studies of religious belief and practice were neither numerous nor probing in the aftermath of the Second World War in Britain. Nevertheless, the social anthropologists, sociologists and journalists who conducted investigations in the early post-war period (Mass Observation 1947; Gorer 1955; Wickham 1957; Pickering 1957; Ward 1961; Highet 1964) were able to confirm that Judaism and Christianity had very few competitor religions; that subscription to the central beliefs of these two religious traditions remained widespread; that about one-third of children attended Sunday Schools; that about 15 per cent of the population claimed to attend churches on a weekly basis, and as many as 50 per cent on an occasional basis. They also found that most rituals marking birth, marriage and death still took place under the auspices of religious organizations; that men retained most of the leadership positions in religious organizations; and that the mainstream Christian churches and denominations occupied a place of respect in public life and were often closely associated with cultural, civic, leisure and sporting activities. Support for the 'crusades' run in British cities in the 1950s by the evangelical American preacher the Reverend Billy Graham (Target 1968, and in this volume see the Introduction, Chapters 2, 5 and 10), was congruent with a mood of moral conservatism that prevailed until the mid-1960s (Brown 2006, 2009; McLeod 2007). This pattern of continuity and stability in the social aspects of British religion began to show at least six signs of change in the following decades (see summary in Text box 21).

The first indication that the post-war configuration in the social patterns of religion was starting to fragment came in the late 1950s. The bonds that had tied families to particular parishes and places of worship became more fragile under pressure from new geographical mobility, longer periods of formal education, exposure to television programmes and employment for women. As a result, the rates of participation in worship services, religious rites of passage, Sunday Schools and religiously based youth groups began to decline slowly at first, but with an accelerating pace throughout the 1960s and 1970s (McLeod 2007). The levels of reported belief in the central teachings of the main branches of Christianity and Judaism eventually followed the same downward trend, while interest grew among a small minority in a wide variety of alternative religious and spiritual practices. Support for atheism increased only slightly, but more and more people associated themselves with agnostic and humanist outlooks. Yet, as we shall see later, all these changing patterns of religious belief, identification and practice varied by social class, sex, age, ethnicity and region.

A second piece of evidence to suggest that the social patterns of religion were undergoing major change in Britain came in the 1960s with the expanding number of immigrants (mostly male to begin with) from Britain's shrinking empire and the growing number of newly independent countries in the Commonwealth (see Introduction and Chapter 3 for more detail). Many immigrants from the Caribbean region identified with Pentecostal and Adventist branches of Protestantism as well as with Anglicanism and Hinduism. Immigrants from South Asia at this period were much more likely to be Muslims, Sikhs or Hindus and their number swelled in the 1970s with the arrival of their co-religionists who had been expelled from Uganda. As a result, the religious 'complexion' of many cities where these migrants settled has been transformed not only by the sheer diversity of faiths on display, but also by the attempts to promote multi-faith activities and interfaith understanding (see Case study 2 on the Inter Faith Network). Mainstream Christian and Jewish traditions have also been affected by the ideas, practices, rituals and forms of sociability that immigrants have introduced into Britain.

This relatively rapid increase in Britain's religious diversity since the 1960s has led to numerous adjustments in such things as the content of religious education curricula in schools (see Chapter 8); the provision of chaplaincy services in hospitals, prisons, universities and military institutions; and the authorization of methods of slaughtering animals for food in accordance with Islamic and Jewish codes. Following the riots in northern cities in 2001, the al-Qaida-inspired attacks in the USA in September that year and in Madrid in 2004 and London in 2005, issues of national security, community cohesion and relations between faith communities have also come to dominate government policy in relation to Britain's 2 million Muslims.

A third sign of religious change in post-war Britain was the growing popularity of relatively conservative forms of Christianity. Evangelical currents had run through many churches and denominations since the eighteenth century, but the closing decades of the twentieth century saw the development, albeit on a modest scale, of new social expressions of evangelicalism. The emphasis on having a personal relationship with Christ and in some cases the experience of being 'born again', believing in the truth of the Bible and following strict codes of personal morality, started to flourish in the 1960s in a wide variety of groups such as house churches, 'restorationist' groups and student societies. In addition, some of these groups adopted elements of Pentecostal and Charismatic beliefs in the continuing power of the Holy Spirit to transform individual and collective lives, to heal illness, to send prophecies and to inspire prosperity.

Some conservative evangelical groups broke away from larger churches and established themselves as independent entities. Others have always operated as alternative currents within mainstream churches. In recent decades the most spectacular growth has been among three different kinds of religious enterprises. One kind attracts mainly members of African diasporic communities of, for example, Ghanaians or Nigerians living in Britain's largest cities (Wood 2006). The second kind is associated with transnational evangelical enterprises such as the Universal Church of the Kingdom of God, which is a Brazilian movement with branches in many parts of the world (Freston 2001). The third kind is the Alpha Course, a vehicle for introducing newcomers to a conservative evangelical form of Christianity that operates within and across a variety of churches (Hunt 2004).

From a sociological perspective, these evangelical and Pentecostal groupings display three distinctive characteristics. First, they cultivate intense forms of voluntary commitment. The groups tend to be 'high-demand' or 'strict' in terms of the social and intellectual requirements that they place on members. A second and closely related aspect of conservative evangelical groups is the strong authority of the leaders. Combining the roles of pastor, prophet, teacher and healer they are usually in a position to shape what the members of the group think and do. Their influence over the members' private lives can be powerful and they are not often subject to any form of accountability above the level of the local congregation. A third social characteristic of conservative evangelical groups today is their public engagement with selected issues of politics and morality. They can combine a strong sense of their separateness from 'the world' with a powerful sense of their obligation to transform it by means of political action in campaigns about, for example, abortion, pornography, crime and the perceived legal discrimination against Christians (see Chapters 2, 5, 6 and 7 for more on evangelical Christianity).

A fourth, and less well-studied social aspect of religious change in Britain, concerns the expressions of religion that have emerged by way of the internet. Although virtual religion is an important aspect of the changing face of religion in Britain, it is clearly transnational – if not global – in reach. Some of the virtual networks have British origins and may even contain a majority of British participants, but it makes no sense to think of them as confined to this country (Bunt 2003, 2009). Similarly, it is unwise to consider all of these networks as completely new media or forums for religion: in many cases they are extensions or outgrowths of pre-existing religious organizations. Indeed, many of the major religious organizations in Britain now have their own websites, user lists and blogs. Some are also represented on social networking sites. As Chapter 7 explains, these forms of virtual communication amount to 'religion online' rather than 'online religion' in the sense of a 'cyber religion' that has no existence beyond the internet (Helland 2000). One of the internet's effects has been to complicate the struggles for control over doctrine, liturgy, loyalty and resources in some religious organizations.

One of the prime reasons why the control that religious organizations tried to exercise over their teachings, members and practices started to become more difficult in the latter half of the twentieth century was the growth of competition from the promoters of 'spirituality' – a fifth aspect of change. As 'brand loyalty' to mainstream churches and other formal religious organizations began to decline in the 1960s, and as the high-demand groups drew themselves increasingly apart from the rest of society, a cultural and economic 'space' opened up for interest in the production and consumption of spirituality. As Chapter 4 shows, this took many different forms, ranging from the highly individualistic human potential movement to more collective inspirations for environmentalism and alternative healing practices. But they all tended to share such common convictions as the need to cultivate balance and harmony in the self as an ongoing project in life, to be suspicious of external sources of authority, to resist the separation of mind and body, and to appreciate the interconnectedness of all life. These features of spirituality surfaced in myriad activities and small businesses ranging from aromatherapies and paganism to Tai Chi (Heelas and Woodhead 2005). From a social perspective, it is important to note that the 'vehicles' of these forms of spirituality were a mixture of social networks, leading authors, bookshops, seminars, workshops, websites, healing practices and massage centres. And there was heavy overlap between networks of spiritual seekers and activists in movements for peace, environmentalism, human rights, vegetarianism and feminism.

Concern with spirituality has also been growing in recent decades in the National Health Service where links are often made between ideas of 'spiritual development' and health (Walter 1997; and the Introduction and Chapter 6 in this volume). Healthcare chaplains are nowadays considered the professional agents of spirituality as well as of religion. Spirituality is also bound up with the market and consumer capitalism. Heelas (2008: 185) argues that 'inner-life spirituality' can serve as a bulwark against the worst excesses of capitalism, whereas Carrette and King (2005: 22) criticize the assimilation of spirituality into aspects of 'the market-driven economy of corporate capitalism'.

The final location for change (and continuity) in the social patterning of religion in Britain is schools (see Chapter 8 for more detail). The legal requirements for state-maintained schools in England and Wales to deliver religious education (RE) and to hold daily acts of collective worship have undergone several modifications since the Education Act 1944 (Jackson 2000). However, some major shifts have occurred both within this general framework and independently of it. First, not only is the RE curriculum increasingly shaped by a national framework for all state-maintained schools except those which are voluntary-aided, but the content has also come to pay much more attention to the diversity of faiths represented in the UK as well as to the growing significance of interfaith activities and the promotion of community cohesion. These changes have been contentious in some places. Second, the 'dual system' of education, which has enabled schools owned or managed by Anglican, Catholic, Methodist and Jewish organizations to be funded by the British state since the late nineteenth century, has slowly been expanded to include a small number of Hindu, Sikh and Muslim schools. Such faith schools now constitute about one-third of all primary and secondary maintained schools. Third, there is considerable continuity between the policies of New Labour governments beginning in 1997 and those of the Conservative–Liberal Democrat coalition government that took office in May 2010 for increasing the number of 'faith schools' in the maintained sector of education. This is in keeping with New Labour policies for promoting 'partnership' between the British state and faith communities.

TEXT BOX 21

Six key indicators of religious change in post-war Britain

1 Declining rates of participation in worship services, religious rites of passage, Sunday schools and religiously-based youth groups since the late 1950s.
2 Commonwealth immigration since the 1960s.
3 The flourishing of relatively conservative forms of Christianity from the 1960s.
4 The emergence of virtual religious expression and networks.
5 The growth of 'spirituality'.
6 Religion's shifting place in schools.

Despite the six indicators of changing belief and practice in post-war Britain shown in Text box 21, it would be a mistake to believe that the period since 1945 has seen nothing but change in religion. Continuity is also a feature of religion in Britain, although it tends to attract less attention. For example, the Church of England remains established in law and therefore closely related to the state (see Chapter 2). It also continues to offer its religious, educational, community and welfare services to all the residents of England (see Chapter 8). In this sense, it sees itself as functioning vicariously like a public utility on behalf of the nation (Davie 2007a), although the notion of 'vicarious religion' has come in for criticism (Bruce and Voas 2010).

More importantly, all the mainstream Christian churches continue to provide extensive facilities and services in relation to the civic life of local communities, social welfare, education, youth work and so on (Davis *et al.* 2008). The latter claim that their research records 'a veritable empire of civil society founded, funded, sustained and maintained by Christian congregations, churches and believers' (Davis *et al.* 2008: 27). At the same time, as Douglas Davies shows in Chapter 6, deep-seated folk beliefs and informal theologies continue to survive in varying degrees of proximity to popular beliefs and practices which some dismiss as 'magic' and 'superstition'.

Social factors and religious change

The social factors which shape religious change relate to the characteristics of those who participate in religious activities. These include, among others, age, sex, sexual orientation, gender, ethnicity (which relates to migration), social class, level of education, geographical location (urban/rural) and generation (which relates to migration in terms of first or second generation). Some of these factors are given or socially attributed (e.g. ethnicity, disability), while others may be chosen (e.g. geographical location) and/or may be subject to change over individuals' lifetimes (e.g. socio-economic status, immigration).

Factors are interrelated and are usually combined into different clusters. This allows for particular profiles to be identified and mapped so that changes over time can be traced or particular theories tested. For example, whether some social factors are more relevant in particular processes than others. However, it is important to emphasize again that there is a reciprocal relation between social factors and religion: the factors shape and transform religion while also being shaped and transformed *by* religion. Of course, social factors also relate to the individual and thus refer to the micro-level of social life. However, when applied to groups or communities or institutions, they provide information which goes beyond the individual level, thus allowing for generalizations on the meso- and macro-levels (see also Mills 1959).

Both qualitative and quantitative research methods explore the relevance of social factors in the populations they are concerned with. Most research operates with a standard repertoire of social factors: a set of standardized 'indices' or variables which are primarily used in quantitative research. Thus, indices of religious vitality, such as statistics of church membership, church attendance, levels of belief, etc., are correlated with indices which measure social factors, usually including a number of the factors cited above (e.g. gender, age). This produces datasets that allow for comparison over time. Thus, in the case of post-war Britain, they provide a broad historical picture of trends, showing, for example, the weakening of the positive correlation between indices of religious commitment and higher education, the partial weakening of the positive correlation between religious activity and being female or the maintenance of the positive correlation between religious commitment and older age cohorts.

The complex relationship between social factors and religious change

While it is useful to bring together empirical findings from research correlating social factors with indices of religious vitality, the underlying problem for sociological analysis is to identify what plausibly explains both the correlations and the changes in them, as neither meanings nor explanations are self-evident. For example, does the weakening of the positive correlation between high levels of education and religious commitment mean that higher education in itself now, unlike in the past, erodes commitment – and, if so, what is it about higher education that has changed? Alternatively, does it reflect the fact that among people with higher education some are more hostile to religion than the average? Similarly, the weakening of the positive correlation between religious commitment and being female might be explained by the hypothesis about post-1960s feminism destroying the 'culture of female piety' (Brown 2006), or by the more materially based account of the effects of technological change, women's employment, the expansion of leisure activities and the virtual collapse of religious socialization after the 1960s (McLeod 2007). Or could it be explained by something else that has as yet not been considered?

In a period of rapid social change, such as the past few decades, there is a further complication: the very social factors social scientists are attempting to isolate as variables are mutually implicated in a way that often alters the meaning of the social facts they are trying to capture under the indices labelled 'social factors'. The apparently straightforward, factual example of the age distribution of the population illustrates this point. There has been a shift to an ageing population after the post-war population surge, which is coupled with radically increased life expectancy. It has altered both the nature of the different stages of life (e.g. 'sixty is the new forty') and the inter-generational dynamic. Added to this is the tendency, particularly among the professional classes, for women to postpone childbirth, which calls the nature and age range of a 'generational cohort' into question. This matters when social scientists look at the relation between religion and age. The nature of the social implications of age for a range of choices and behaviour comes into play and makes straight comparisons across time potentially misleading. For example, the dip in religious activity in the 25–45 age group and a minor surge in the 45+ cohort has been explained by heavy family commitments at the weekend in two-earner families with dependent children. Yet it could also be the case that these commitments are no less onerous for the 45+ cohort today, who either still have dependent children – if they had them late – or often find themselves caring for elderly parents when their own children leave home. This older cohort then still does not find time for church, although the apparently parallel cohort in the previous 'generation' did.

The situation is even more complicated for 'social class'. The structures of employment have radically changed with the collapse of heavy industry, the shrinking of the manufacturing sector and the rise of the service sector, with a large base of low-paid, insecure jobs that typically go to women, and a big expansion in retail, services and finance. The clerical worker of the 1950s is effectively obsolete. Although the category C1 in which she or he would have been put is still there, it covers mainly service-sector workers whose work and non-work experiences and identities are not comparable with the C1 class experience of the past. Thus apparent continuity in the index hides radical mutation.

The unionized category of the 'working class' has declined significantly, with its former heartlands in mining and manufacturing having become 'rust belts' with high levels of un- or under-employment. Class as 'tribal identity' has given way to fragmented divisions based on consumer choices and the notion of being 'upwardly mobile'. Even though this may obscure what Marxists would identify as continuing structural inequalities, especially since the income and wealth gap between top and bottom has increased, status differences are now experienced through consumer and status-based symbols of identity and self-definition. Therefore, correlations between 'social class' and other social factors, including religion, need to be treated with great care, and also viewed in the light of individuals' or groups' own understanding of their social class status (see also McCloud 2007, and Case study 3 in this volume which examines youth, religion and deprivation).

The example of class suggests that tribal identities are under pressure in the globalized and mobile post-war world, which becomes visible in relation to once solid 'factors' like 'ethnicity' or the category of the 'religious group'. The practices of boundary maintenance vary between successive generations in migrant as well as citizen ethnic/religious minorities (e.g. third-generation Muslims are more religious than second-generation). Localized and national patterns of religious diversity become important in this context, especially in respect of endogamy and exogamy. As the committed religious constituency shrinks in size, it encounters more difficulty in maintaining its boundaries. This difficulty is associated with increased rates of marrying out, the interaction of siblings with non-religious (or other ethnic) family members and the strengthening of boundaries around religious/ethnic sectors, especially in response to government policies (Voas 2007) – the latter essentialize religions and ethnic categories and thus cut across groups of committed religionists and make life difficult for them. However, although intermarriage affects boundary maintenance (Voas 2009), those who marry out commonly distance themselves from their ethnic/religious traditions *before* they get married (Arweck and Nesbitt 2010). This suggests that intermarriage itself does not erode boundaries, but rather reflects their erosion. Further, 'ethnicity' and 'religion' as social factors need to be qualified in relation to children who grow up in mixed-faith families, as they tend to cite hyphenated identities (e.g. British-Indian, Christian-Sikh), indicating a sense of belonging to both parental traditions and embracing their dual heritage as a distinct identity (Arweck and Nesbitt 2010). On the other hand, the comparison of family size among religious and non-religious population sectors has led to the argument that the religiously committed 'out-breed' the secular sector, thus partly compensating for the above.

All these examples show how difficult it is in practice to isolate (and identify/define) 'social factors' and to hold comparisons steady over time. Therefore, social scientists can only make sociological sense of research into religion and social change if they use what the historians of religious (and other social) change tell them (even if their explanations are taken as hypotheses to be considered). The same is true of theories of social change that seek to pinpoint the causal role in social change of some particular factor, such as globalization, rational choice, etc. (usually involving a cluster of factors rather than one), reflecting underlying assumptions of change (functionalist, conflict, cyclical). Sociological analyses will only capture part of the picture because its complexities defy simple linear accounting. Social scientific research will miss the mark or risk reductionist theories, if it does not recognize that the 'social factors' used to account for change are themselves involved in shaping and being reshaped by that change in a way that leaves datasets open to contested interpretation.

The social contexts, forms and effects of religious change

Social perspectives on religious change in Britain are concerned not only with the social factors that shape it, but also with other dimensions of change and continuity. They include social contexts, forms and effects.

Contexts

Taking the social *contexts* of religious change into account means examining the extent to which Britain's major social institutions have influenced changes in religion and vice versa. Starting with the economy, changes in such aspects as levels of affluence, standards of living, disposable income, contributions of money and voluntary work to religious groups, their ownership of property and their financial stability have all influenced the opportunities for religions to flourish or perish. These changes are also related to shifts in global economic conditions, including the regulations governing the circulation of currencies and capital between countries. In addition, changes in taxation law, charity law and immigration law can have implications for religious organizations, especially if their professionals are predominantly recruited from overseas. In return, religions contribute directly and indirectly to Britain's economy by, for example, maintaining sacred buildings that attract large numbers of tourists or visitors; making buildings available to host public ceremonies, meetings and concerts; generating contributions to charitable appeals; and providing extensive services to the community, educational and welfare sectors.

As Chapter 9 explains, politics, public policy and the law form another cluster of social institutions that have either promoted or constrained religious activities in Britain. At the highest level, there are constitutional arrangements that favour the Church of England and the Church of Scotland while continuing to disbar Catholics from the monarchy. Campaigns to disestablish the Church of England have waxed and waned since 1945, but no government has given priority to this question. Meanwhile, successive governments since 1979 have strengthened the involvement of religious interests in the state system of school-level education. At the same time, various acts of legislation have introduced legal protection against unfair discrimination on the grounds of religion and against religiously aggravated criminal offences (see Chapter 1). Yet, political and legal remedies have not succeeded in entirely eradicating conflict and violence from Northern Ireland where the deepest social and political divide still draws symbolic support from the labels 'Protestant' and 'Catholic' (see Chapter 9).

As Chapter 7 documents, the media, in their print, broadcast and electronic forms, are part of the social context of religious change which has grown considerably more important since 1945. Long-running Christian and Jewish publications are now joined by those from all the other major faith communities in Britain. Terrestrial, satellite and cable broadcasts of religious programmes have expanded slowly since the 1980s, benefiting from partial relaxation of controls over the ownership and content of religious broadcasts and advertising, but the rise of online outlets for religion has been much more rapid and pervasive. Online religion also sidesteps most of the British legislation governing broadcasts, thereby creating overlapping networks that cross national borders. The role of social networking could become particularly important in the reproduction of religions and religious socialization.

Finally, hospitals, higher education institutions, military establishments, prisons, airports, emergency service bases and large shopping centres have all become locations where formal support for religious identities and activities is provided by voluntary or salaried chaplains. Chaplaincies have expanded in recent decades as attendance at regular services of worship has declined in many churches and synagogues. The provision of these non-parochial forms of ministry has also given opportunities to Hindus, Muslims and Sikhs, among others, to participate in publicly funded chaplaincy on their own terms (see Plate 1.7). As a result, chaplaincies have become a major site of interfaith and, in some cases, multi-faith activities. This thereby reflects not only the growth of religious diversity in Britain since the 1960s, but also the willingness of public authorities to accommodate this diversity – albeit within the limits of what are considered 'acceptable' partners in chaplaincy – and the increased assertiveness of religious communities in requesting representation in these various domains.

Social forms

Social perspectives of religious change also focus, second, on the *social forms* in which religion is expressed. In 1945 the religious landscape of Britain was dominated by mainstream Christian churches, denominations and smaller sectarian groups, such as Jehovah's Witnesses, Elim Pentecostals and Seventh-day Adventists. All these organizations are still in place in the twenty-first century, but the distinction between churches and sects is no longer so clear cut. Many of the churches and denominations have shrunk in terms of their numbers and influence, while the sects have continued to grow steadily and to shake off their earlier reputation for being attractive only to deprived or disprivileged people. At the same time, new generations of religious movements, or 'cults', and a wide variety of spiritual currents have mobilized unknown numbers of mostly young people. These mobilizations, which probably peaked in the 1980s, introduced ideas and practices from many of the world's faith traditions, sometimes combining them in hybrid or syncretic forms. And the currents of New Age spirituality which have grown in popularity in Britain are distinctive for the commercial forms in which many of them have been marketed for consumption by individuals who do not necessarily have a strong sense of identification with the producers. Alongside them are growing numbers of organizations representing, for example, Baha'is, Buddhists, Hindus, Jains, Muslims and Sikhs. Some of them take the form of committees for running temples, mosques and seminaries; others are registered as charities with the aim of promoting particular religions; yet others are adopting congregational forms of organization which also have their own agencies for delivering welfare and educational services for the benefit of their members. Most of them not only operate on the national level, but form part of international networks of related organizations.

Forms of religious leadership in Britain have also diversified since 1945. Most of the leading positions are still occupied by men, but in recent decades the number of women exercising senior authority in, for example, the Church of Scotland, the Methodist Church, the Salvation Army, the Free Churches Group and Charismatic fellowships has increased. However, there is still controversy about how far women can rise in the respective hierarchies. And the rise of religious groups intended for lesbian, gay, bisexual and transgender followers has expanded the opportunities for women leaders. In relation to Catholic, Hindu, Muslim and Sikh organizations, however, formal leadership remains in the hands of men and is indistinguishable from the ritual, educational and pastoral roles of priests and imams.

Effects

Finally, social perspectives try to bring into focus the changing *consequences* of religions for their practitioners and the wider society, although questions about the direction of causation are notoriously difficult to answer in this area. Indeed, evidence of well-documented changes brought about in Britain by religion since 1945 are in short supply. Nevertheless, it is clear that interest has been growing in recent decades in, for example, the benefits claimed for religion in terms of its practitioners' good physical and mental health and well being, longevity, robustness of marriage, extent of friendship networks, positive attitudes towards citizenship and work, volunteering, community engagement and happiness. And interest is increasing among employers' organizations in the place of spirituality in the workplace. Moreover, religious themes have recently acquired a higher profile in popular novels, films and music. More contentiously, the claims advanced for religion's capacity to prevent prisoners from reoffending on release are celebrated in some quarters and derided in others. Indeed, all these claims about the changing effects of religion on the lives of individuals and communities are subject to strong reservations because it is notoriously difficult to isolate the effects of religion from all other, cross-cutting and mutually interacting factors. This is partly why the range of theoretical perspectives or frameworks which seek to capture various factors and explain how they fit together is so wide.

Theoretical perspectives

Theoretical perspectives are frameworks of ideas that claim to make general sense of social life. They are abstract ways of explaining patterns of social relations, interactions, organizations, processes and so on. In this sense, theoretical perspectives serve as useful landmarks or signposts in the social landscape – pointing towards what they highlight as the most important features from different theoretical positions. In other words, theoretical perspectives sensitize us to the impact of certain factors, or clusters of factors, on the ways in which social life is organized and experienced.

At the same time, theoretical perspectives are 'big ideas' that can blind us to alternative views. They can divert our attention away from features of social life that are not considered important from their point of view. They can prevent us from taking account of things that become significant when looked at from different theoretical positions. Indeed, there is competition and conflict between theoretical perspectives when they offer incompatible or contradictory explanations.

Some theoretical perspectives convey highly methodical sets of interrelated assumptions about the world, from which predictions can be derived and tested against empirical reality. This type of perspective is found widely in the natural sciences, but is less influential in the social sciences. It is more common for philosophers, historians and social scientists to operate with relatively loose sets of ideas which purport to explain social phenomena in distinctive ways. This often involves the telling and retelling of narratives which try to explain how and why events unfolded and situations developed in the way that they did.

Some of the most influential theoretical narratives about religious change emerged from the writings of Karl Marx, Friedrich Engels, Emile Durkheim and Max Weber in the late nineteenth and early twentieth centuries (Beckford 1989; Collins 2007). Their narratives about, respectively, capitalist society, industrial society and modern society tried to capture the social and cultural forces that had swept away many forms of society in which religion had been dominant. For Marx and Engels, religion was an ideological illusion which might be comforting, but which invariably served the interests of the ruling classes in any social formation. They expected that 'the opium of the people' would no longer be necessary if exploitative capitalism could be replaced by communism. In contrast, Durkheim considered that religion, in the sense of the 'sacred', fulfilled indispensable functions by sacralizing, in symbols and rituals, the social forces that held societies together. Nevertheless, he expected that industrial societies would increasingly regard the individual rather than the whole society as the most appropriate location of the sacred. Max Weber went even further by arguing that processes of modern rationalization would undermine the plausibility of many religious views of the world whilst leaving open the possibility that forms of religious charisma could still disrupt the predominantly demystified, rationalized and bureaucratized forms of modern life.

As far as religious change in modern Britain is concerned, theoretical ideas tend to cluster around a few general themes, some of which are direct descendants of Marxian, Durkheimian and Weberian outlooks. The most prominent perspective depicts post-war religious change as first and foremost a matter of decline. Explanations for this decline centre on processes of *secularization*, although, as Chapters 10 and 12 show, there are many different – but interrelated – ways of interpreting these processes. Some interpretations give priority to narratives of long-term intellectual transformation of religious ideas into scientific and rational modes of thought which may be difficult to reconcile with religious outlooks. Others focus on processes of differentiation between major social institutions with the result that religion gradually loses its capacity to bind the whole of society together by symbolic means. Yet another variant on the theme of secularization attributes it to the declining authority of community-based religious organizations to reproduce and regulate the religious thoughts and feelings of individuals.

Post-war changes in patterns of employment, gender relations, education, leisure, family structure, urbanization and personal morality have also been said to weaken identification with religious organizations. A more radical interpretation is that this amounts to 'The end of Christianity as a means by which men and women, as individuals, construct their identities and the sense of "self"' (Brown 2009: 2). Moreover, as other chapters in this book have shown (e.g. Chapters 4, 5, 6 and 10), the changing fabric of British society has encouraged the growth of values and ideals of individualism, subjectivity and authenticity which are not easily compatible with the collective rhythms and disciplines of organized religions, but which may be conducive to new forms of spirituality (Heelas and Woodhead 2005).

These varied accounts of secularization have given rise, in turn, to six important criticisms and new theoretical developments which attempt to grasp the distinctiveness of religious change in Britain.

Religious vitality

First, there is a set of arguments about achieving a more *balanced* account of religious change and continuity. They acknowledge some of the evidence about declining rates of identification with mainstream religious organizations, but they also insist that this is far from being the whole story (Martin 1978, 2005; Davie 2007b). They draw attention to many of the topics discussed in Chapters 2, 5, 6 and 9, namely, the persistence of popular religion, everyday religion, civil religion and 'vicarious religion' whilst stressing the rising popularity of subjective spiritualities and charismatic expressions of Christianity. These arguments also point to evidence that is analysed in Chapters 1 and 3 about the organized expressions of the Hindu, Muslim and Sikh faith traditions, among others, which are continuing to gain strength in Britain.

The nature of modernity

Second, various theoretical arguments have centred on the place of religion in societies that no longer appear to be straightforwardly capitalist, industrial or modern. 'Post-industrial' societies, for example, were thought to release workers from the constraints of long working weeks and lives, thereby allowing them more opportunities to develop their cultural, spiritual or religious interests. The next theoretical idea was about 'post-modern' conditions which might have relaxed the control exercised by hierarchical religious organizations over their members' beliefs, feelings and actions (Lyon 2000). This might then have fostered more hybrid, playful and ironic expressions of religion as well as a concern for moral certitude (Bauman 1992), especially in connection with religion online and online religion.

In comparison, the space envisaged for religion in 'high-modern' societies was expected to be restricted to expressions of 'repressed' feelings as, for example, in fundamentalisms (Giddens 1991). But the intriguing notion of 'multiple modernities' opens up the possibility that there could be a variety of routes to a range of different ways of being modern (Eisenstadt 2000). This allows for a conceptual distinction between processes of modernization and the idea that the decline of religion is necessary. Finally, 'ultramodernity', in the sense of a radicalized modernity, is believed to involve going beyond secularization into an age characterized by heightened reflexivity and individualization (Willaime 2006). This would supposedly herald the rediscovery of religion as a cultural resource for reinstilling human values into work, politics and family life and for holding off the bleakness and moral vacuity of the secularized world.

Deprivatization

The claim about the capacity of religion to resupply values to spheres of life that had allegedly been stripped of meaning except the need to be efficient and profitable is closely related to a third theoretical development, namely, the idea that religion had re-emerged in the *public sphere* of various societies towards the end of the twentieth century. The main trigger for this renewed interest in politics and religion was the prominent role played by the Catholic Church and some Protestant churches in civil society organizations that had helped to establish democratic regimes in Spain and Brazil in the 1980s and to bring about the downfall of Communist regimes in Central and Eastern Europe after 1989 (Casanova 1994). In the case of Britain, however, there have been two widely different strands of thinking about religion in the public sphere.

On the one hand, the Church of England's 1984 report on *Faith in the City* (Church of England 1985) was highly critical of the (then) Conservative government's neoliberal policy of reducing the state's role in providing social welfare (see Plate 2.4). The church took a 'prophetic' stance of criticism towards Mrs Thatcher's Conservative government. This drew public attention to the continuing potential of religious organizations to act as critics of government. On the other hand, the New Labour governments that were in office between 1997 and 2010 not only actively sought out faith groups as 'partners' in a mixed welfare economy, but also invested heavily in schemes to increase the number and variety of 'faith schools' within the state sector of education (see Chapter 8). These two contrasting theoretical developments suggested that secularization, far from effacing religion from the British public sphere, had been superseded by a resurgence of religion.

Globalization

Fourth, the renewed interest in religion as a force in Britain's public sphere from the late 1990s onwards also owes part of its plausibility to theoretical ideas about *globalization* and 'glocalization' (Robertson 1992). And, while disputes about the meaning and significance of these terms have been numerous, they undoubtedly fit into a high-level theoretical perspective which is capable of throwing interesting light on religious change in recent decades. In a nutshell, this perspective highlights both the processes which make the world a smaller place and the implications of time–space compression for social and cultural life. As far as religious change is concerned, globalization and glocalization – the mutual adaptations between the global and the local – are thought to have boosted and accelerated numerous developments. They include such things as a rising degree of standardization among religious ideas and practices in some faith traditions; an emerging emphasis on 'humanity', human rights and the risks to the global environment as a focus for religions in all regions of the world; and the emergence of transnational religious movements that have virtually globe-wide diffusion without necessarily being managed from any single centre. They also include the centrality of the internet and electronic communications to religious communication; the acceleration of religious controversies and disputes as a result of global communications media; and the spread of similar legal and constitutional instruments for protecting the freedom of religion in many, but not all, countries.

Theoretical ideas about globalization and glocalization are notoriously difficult to specify and test, but globe-wide movements such as the Universal Church of the Kingdom of God, which originated in Brazil, but came to Britain via southern Africa, have been growing since the 1990s (Freston 2001). Many of the new forms of spirituality that have been gaining followers for even longer draw on cultural resources from many different regions of the world (Beckford 2004). In addition, Britain now has legal protections for the freedom of religion which share much in common with United Nations and European conventions. And the internet has helped to link religious groups in Britain, like most other countries, into genuinely global networks of groups, some of which have no existence other than online (see Chapter 7). Indeed, global communications may also generate religious responses to heightened anxiety about perceived threats to global security and order emanating from climate change, epidemics and terrorism (Robertson 2007).

Gender

Fifth, it may be true that the sociology of religion lacks a theory of religion and gender (Woodhead 2007: 567), but many explanations of religious change in post-war Britain attribute great importance to shifts in gendered inequalities of opportunity and power, especially in their intersections with social class and ethnicity. This includes changes in religious ideas of gender differences as well as in norms regulating gender relations, sexualities and sexual identities. An emerging theoretical perspective on gender, and on women in particular, has therefore helped to explain the rapid decline in the fortunes of many Christian churches that began in the mid-1960s (Brown 2009). Key factors include the persisting attractions to some women of conservative evangelical forms of Christianity (Aune 2008), the generational differences in Muslim women's identification with Islam (Jacobson 1998), the controversies surrounding the ordination and promotion of women priests in the Church of England and the numerical dominance of women in New Age spiritualities and among women who 'fuse' Christianity with other spiritualities (Woodhead 2007, 2008; Vincett 2008).

Rational choice

Finally, it is worth noting that a theoretical perspective which has become increasingly influential in the USA and elsewhere since the 1980s has failed to stimulate much research on religious change in Britain: Rational Choice Theory or Subjective Rationality (Stark and Bainbridge 1987; Young 1997). This perspective is based on assumptions about the rational aspects of faith at the level of individual 'consumers' of religion and about the rationality displayed by the religious organizations that compete with each other in the religious marketplace. It makes testable predictions about such issues as the overall vitality of religion in national and international markets and the probability that 'high-demand' religious organizations will thrive more than liberal ones in the competition for members and resources. A common theme in the many different applications of the rational choice perspective is that the level of religious activity in any country tends to be higher when the level of state regulation of religion is lower. Thus, the persistence of national churches in England and Scotland might be thought to explain the low level of participation in formal religion in these countries, relative to that of the USA, on the grounds that their religious markets were inefficient because the established churches stifled competition and enjoyed unfair advantages over their competitors.

But there are at least two major objections to this reasoning. One is that the established churches can actually use their privileges to promote the interests of all bona fide religions in, for example, healthcare, military and prison chaplaincies. The other is that the British 'market' is so clearly divided between different faith communities that it makes no sense to expect that competition for members could ever be intense between them. There is no evidence of significant 'switching' between religions in a single market. Competition exists only at the margins. In short, the rational choice perspective has not proved very useful in explaining post-war religious change in Britain so far, but it will probably continue to be influential in the USA.

Conclusion

Social perspectives on religious change in Britain are indispensable and challenging. They focus on the ways in which a wide range of social factors, processes and forms of organization help to shape religious change and are, in turn, affected by it.

This two-way dynamic is evident throughout this chapter. It began with debates about the definition of religion in public life. Changes and continuity in the patterning of religious belief and practice were then shown to have a social basis. And the interplay between religious change and social factors such as age, generation, gender, sexual orientation, social class and ethnicity emerged as a pivotal topic. At the same time, social perspectives clearly included the political and legal contexts that affect religious change as well as the changing forms of religious organizations and the wider effects of religious change on British society.

The final part of the chapter explored some of the theoretical ideas which influence research into religious change in post-war Britain. For a long time, the dominant ideas were about secularization – the claim that levels of religious belief, identification, practice and influence in social life were in long-term decline as a result of processes such as rationalization, modernization, differentiation and privatization. But critical reactions against theoretical ideas of secularization have been gathering momentum in recent years. The range of critical arguments continues to grow, but the most significant departures from the previously dominant versions of secularization theory include the following: vitality remains a feature of the religious landscape in Britain; modernization can take various forms and does not necessarily exclude religion; privatized religion is increasingly balanced by expressions of religion in the public domain; globalization has boosted religion in some places; challenges to the gendered distribution of power in religious organizations have stimulated new forms of spirituality; and, from a rational choice perspective, relatively unregulated religious 'markets' can generate competitiveness and vitality in religions.

Empirical research is beginning to show how far these theoretical ideas have succeeded in dislodging some of the previously taken-for-granted assumptions about the inevitability of secularization in post-war Britain. The results are mixed. On the one hand, robust empirical indicators of declining rates of subscription to central Christian beliefs and rates of participation in, and identification with, Christian organizations appear to defy interpretation in terms of any of the new theoretical ideas. Moreover, interest in the varied phenomena of atheism, non-belief, humanism and secularism has flourished among intellectual commentators on religion – albeit with less enthusiasm among the British public. On the other hand, signs of religious, or, more likely, spiritual, vitality are undeniable in some conservative Christian fellowships, among Hindus, Muslims and Sikhs, in the context of New Age, pagan and alternative spiritualities, in the growing popularity of state-maintained schools with a faith-based ethos and in connection with the rise of faith-based organizations offering welfare, health and community services.

In short, arguments about these big theoretical ideas have not been resolved, but they will continue for the foreseeable future to emphasize the importance of social perspectives of religious change. Nevertheless, it is equally important to bear in mind that social perspectives cannot tell the whole story: they need to be complemented by psychological, historical, theological, philosophical and other perspectives. Indeed, some critics allege that social perspectives unfairly reduce religion to its trivial or transient features, thereby excluding the claims to ultimate truth, beauty and power that religions supposedly embody. This amounts to an accusation that the social dimension is superficial. An even more serious accusation is that studies which adopt social perspectives on religion run the risk of actually denying the reality or truth of religion by implying that religion represents nothing but the social and is merely an epiphenomenon of social life, not an independent realm of reality in itself.

These objections to the use of social perspectives in studying religious change are important and challenging, but none of them is fatal to the limited project of trying to understand the dynamic interplay between social factors and the place of religion in social life. Nor does it mean that philosophical and theological approaches to studying religion are any less interesting just because social factors may be irrelevant to them. The fact is that the well-rounded study of religion, in Britain and around the world, must surely take account of all these different approaches, including the tensions and conflicts between them.

Key terms

Cults: A term often used interchangeably with 'New Religious Movements' (see below). Religious groups which tend to be controversial for attracting intense loyalty outside the boundaries, or on the fringes, of mainstream religious traditions.

Endogamy: The institutional practice of marriage between people from the same social or cultural categories.

Ethnicity: The identity and culture shared by people who claim descent from common ancestors.

Exogamy: The institutional practice of marriage between people from different social or cultural categories.

Micro-, meso- and macro-level: The hierarchy of relative levels at which social life can be analysed. The focus of micro-level analysis is on individuals, events or small groups; the meso-level focuses on conditions, processes or activities occurring at an intermediate level; and the macro-level focuses on conditions, processes and activities occurring at the level of entire organizations, institutions or societies.

New Religious Movements (NRMS): Mobilizations of people and resources in pursuit of religious ideas that are relatively new and marginal to those of mainstream religious traditions. Also referred to as 'cults' (see above).

Qualitative methods: Procedures and techniques for collecting and analysing information about the meanings and values that pervade social and cultural life, generally involving ethnographic enquiry (interview and participant observation).

Quantitative methods: Procedures and techniques for collecting (often by questionnaire) and analysing information expressed in the form of numbers.

Social construction: The idea that the meanings attributed to religion are forged, in part, by social interactions and processes.

Social factors: Indicators of the extent to which religion is shaped by, and in turn helps to shape, the social characteristics of individuals, processes and situations.

Social perspectives: Ways of looking at religion in terms of its mutual relations with patterns of social life, structures, organizations, cultures and processes.

Theoretical perspectives: Frameworks of ideas that claim to explain or interpret religion.

Further reading

Arweck, Elisabeth (2005). *Researching New Religious Movements: Constructions and Controversies.* London: Routledge. A 'reception study' which addresses how the emergence of New Religious Movements has been understood and responded to by the interested parties, including a close examination of the intellectual repertoire of the sociology of religion as applied to the understanding of this phenomenon.

Beckford, James A. (2003). *Social Theory and Religion.* Cambridge: Cambridge University Press. A critical examination of how social theorists have tended to construct and interpret religion.

Collins, Randall (2007). 'The Classical Tradition in Sociology of Religion', in James A. Beckford and N. Jay Demerath III (eds), *The SAGE Handbook of the Sociology of Religion.* London: Sage, 19–38. An account of how the first generation of sociologists shaped social scientific thinking about religion.

Davie, Grace (2007). *The Sociology of Religion.* London: Sage. A survey of contemporary sociology of religion which sets out the key questions and interrogates the discipline's agenda.

Weller, Paul (2008). *Religious Diversity in the UK: Contours and Issues*. London: Continuum. An analysis of religious diversity in the UK and of public policy responses towards its growth.

References

Arweck, Elisabeth and Eleanor Nesbitt (2010). 'Plurality at Close Quarters: Mixed-Faith Families in the UK', *Journal of Religion in Europe*, 3/1: 155–182.

Aune, Kristin (2008). 'Evangelical Christianity and Women's Changing Lives', *European Journal of Women's Studies*, 15/3: 277–294.

Bauman, Zygmunt (1992). *Intimations of Postmodernity*. London: Routledge.

Beckford, James A. (ed.) (1989). *Religion and Advanced Industrial Society*. London: Unwin-Hyman.

Beckford, James A. (2004). 'New Religious Movements and Globalization', in Phillip Lucas and Thomas Robbins (eds), *New Religious Movements in the 21st Century*. New York, NY: Routledge: 253–263.

Brown, Callum G. (2006). *Religion and Society in Twentieth-Century Britain*. London: Longman.

Brown, Callum G. (2009). *The Death of Christian Britain*. 2nd edition. London: Routledge.

Bruce, Steve and David Voas (2010). 'Vicarious Religion: An Examination and Critique', *Journal of Contemporary Religion*, 25/2: 243–259.

Bunt, Gary (2003). *Islam in the Digital Age: E-Jihad, Online Fatwas and Cyber Islamic Environments*. London: Pluto Press.

Bunt, Gary (2009). *iMuslims: Rewiring the House of Islam*. London: Hurst.

Carrette, Jeremy and Richard King (2005). *Selling Spirituality*. London: Routledge.

Casanova, José (1994). *Public Religions in the Modern World*. Chicago, IL: University of Chicago Press.

Church of England. Commission on Urban Priority Areas (1985). *Faith in the City: A Call for Action by Church and Nation*. London: Church House.

Collins, Randall (2007). 'The Classical Tradition in Sociology of Religion', in James A. Beckford and N. Jay Demerath III (eds), *The SAGE Handbook of the Sociology of Religion*. London: Sage, 19–38.

Davie, Grace (2007a). 'Vicarious Religion: A Methodological Challenge', in Nancy T. Ammerman (ed.), *Everyday Religion: Observing Modern Religious Lives*. New York, NY: Oxford University Press, 21–35.

Davie, Grace (2007b). *The Sociology of Religion*. London: Sage.

Davis, Francis, Elizabeth Paulhus and Andrew Bradstock (2008). *Moral, But No Compass: Government, Church and the Future of Welfare*. Chelmsford: Matthew James Publishing.

Eisenstadt, Shmuel (2000). 'Multiple Modernities', *Daedalus*, 129/1: 1–30.

Freston, Paul (2001). 'The Transnationalisation of Brazilian Pentecostalism: The Universal Church of the Kingdom of God', in André Corten and Ruth Marshall-Fratani (eds), *Between Babel and Pentecost*. Bloomington, IN: University of Indiana Press, 196–215.

Giddens, Anthony (1991). *Modernity and Self-Identity*. Cambridge: Polity Press.

Gorer, Geoffrey (1955). *Exploring English Character*. London: Cresset Press.

Heelas, Paul (2008). *Spiritualities of Life: New Age Romanticism and Consumptive Capitalism*. Oxford: Blackwell.

Heelas, Paul and Linda Woodhead (2005). *The Spiritual Revolution: Why Religion is Giving Way to Spirituality*. Oxford: Blackwell.

Helland, Christopher (2000). 'Online-religion/Religion-online and Virtual Communities', in Jeffrey K. Hadden and Douglas E. Cowan (eds), *Religion on the Internet*. New York, NY: JAI Press, 205–223.

Highet, John (1964). 'A Review of Scottish Socio-religious Literature', *Social Compass*, 11/3: 21–24.

Hunt, Stephen (2004). *The Alpha Initiative: Evangelism in a Post-Christian Age*. Aldershot: Ashgate.

Jackson, Robert (2000). 'Law, Politics and Religious Education in England and Wales', in Mal Leicester, Celia Modgil and Sohan Modgil (eds), *Spiritual and Religious Education*. London: Routledge, 86–99.

Jacobson, Jessica (1998). *Islam in Transition: Religion and Identity among British Pakistani Youth*. London: Routledge.

Lyon, David (2000). *Jesus in Disneyland: Religion in Postmodern Times*. Cambridge: Polity.

McCloud, Sean (2007). *Divine Hierarchies: Class in American Religion and Religious Studies*. Chapel Hill, NC: The University of North Carolina Press.

McLeod, Hugh (2007). *The Religious Crisis of the 1960s*. Oxford: Oxford University Press.

Martin, David (1978). *A General Theory of Secularization*. Oxford: Blackwell.

Martin, David (2005). *On Secularization: Towards a Revised General Theory*. Aldershot: Ashgate.

Mass Observation (1947). *Puzzled People: A Study of Popular Attitudes to Religion, Ethics, Progress and Politics in a London Borough*. London: Victor Gollancz.

Mills, C. Wright (1959). *The Sociological Imagination*. New York, NY: Oxford University Press.

Pickering, William S. F. (1957). 'The Place of Religion in the Social Structure of Two English Towns', unpublished PhD thesis, University of London.

Robertson, Roland (1992). *Globalization: Social Theory and Global Culture*. London: Sage.

Robertson, Roland (2007). 'Global Millennialism: A Postmortem on Secularization', in Peter Beyer and Lori Beaman (eds), *Religion, Globalization, and Culture*. Leiden: Brill, 9–34.

Stark, Rodney and William Sims Bainbridge (1987). *A Theory of Religion*. New York, NY: Peter Lang.

Target, George W. (1968). *Evangelism, Inc.* London: Allen Lane, the Penguin Press.

Vincett, Giselle (2008). 'The Fusers: New Forms of Spiritualized Christianity', in Kristin Aune, Sonya Sharma and Giselle Vincett (eds), *Women and Religion in the West: Challenging Secularization*. Aldershot: Ashgate, 133–146.

Voas, David (2007). 'The Continuing Secular Transition', in Detlef Pollak and Daniel Olson (eds), *The Role of Religion in Modern Societies*. London: Routledge, 25–48.

Voas, David (2009). 'The Maintenance and Transformation of Ethnicity: Evidence on Mixed Partnerships in Britain', *Journal of Ethnic and Migration Studies*, 35/9: 1497–1513.

Walter, Tony (1997). 'The Ideology and Organization of Spiritual Care: Three Approaches', *Palliative Medicine*, 11/1: 21–30.

Ward, Conor K. (1961). *Priests and People: A Study in the Sociology of Religion*. Liverpool: Liverpool University Press.

Wickham, Eric R. (1957). *Church and People in an Industrial City*. London: Lutterworth.

Willaime, Jean-Paul (2006). 'Religion in Ultramodernity', in James A. Beckford and John Walliss (eds), *Theorising Religion: Classical and Contemporary Debates*. Aldershot: Ashgate, 77–89.

Wood, Matthew (2006). 'Breaching Bleaching: Integrating Studies of "Race" and Ethnicity with the Sociology of Religion', in James A. Beckford and John Walliss (eds), *Theorising Religion: Classical and Contemporary Debates*. Aldershot: Ashgate, 237–250.

Woodhead, Linda (2007). 'Gender Differences in Religious Practice and Significance', in James A. Beckford and N. Jay Demerath III (eds), *The SAGE Handbook of the Sociology of Religion*. London: Sage, 566–586.

Woodhead, Linda (2008). '"Because I'm Worth it": Religion and Women's Changing Lives in the West', in Kristin Aune, Sonya Sharma and Giselle Vincett (eds), *Women and Religion in the West: Challenging Secularization*. Aldershot: Ashgate, 147–164.

Young, Lawrence A. (ed.) (1997). *Rational Choice Theory and Religion*. New York, NY: Routledge.

12 The religious and the secular

David Martin with Rebecca Catto

It is a recurring theme of this book that, in the modern context, the religious cannot be understood apart from the secular. This chapter closes the book with an extended reflection on that theme. It begins by reflecting on the 'standard model' of secularization (and its recent rival theories of 'desecularization'). Here the 'religious' and the 'secular' are mutually constituted terms. In some versions of secularization, the religious is the superstitious and the secular the rational and scientific; in some the religious has to do with violent conflict and the secular with peaceful debate; in some the religious is repressive and the secular liberating. The chapter then complicates the story by showing how the religious–secular binary intersects with that of the sacred and profane, as well as with the Christian contrast between faith and the world. In its second part, it relates these observations to the history of modern Britain. The effect of this historical and sociological exploration of the religious and the secular is to destabilize the terms. It is no longer possible to employ them as neutral and unencumbered once their complicated genesis and entanglement with various modern projects are taken seriously.

Sociology destabilizes the obvious, including the categories of the religious and the secular and what we think obvious about secularity (the condition of being secular), secularization (the process of becoming secular) and secularism (the ideology promoting secularization), even in modern Britain. Concepts in sociology are not thing-like entities with settled boundaries. They are historical constructs, bundles of different elements with shifting contours.

We cannot fully understand categories like 'religious' and 'secular' without understanding how they have been shaped historically, by their origins in Christianity and by the way they were construed in early modernity with the advent of the nation state. Talal Asad (1993, 2003) suggests that the way we conceptualize religious and secular in our multicultural society has its roots in Christianity and in the early modern colonial encounter, while William Cavanaugh (2009) suggests it was part of the emerging ideology of the nation state. We must make a historical detour in order to understand how the concepts came into being in their current form.

Destabilization does not end there, however, because there is a further contrast between *sacred* and *profane* cutting across the *religious* and the *secular*. Mostly we focus on Durkheim's understanding of the sacred as the majestic aura of the Social, for example, in ancient and early modern forms of sacred monarchy. But then we treat the sacred as also encompassing the sense of the majestic and inviolable in Nature, in the inner sanctum of the self or soul, and in non-negotiable principles and ultimate concerns. It should be obvious, if we look for example at the arts, that sacred and profane are mixed as well as contrasting categories.

Only once this work is done will it be possible to address what can be called 'the standard model of the secular and secularization' and to see it as part of the unfolding history of Christianity and Christendom, rather than a simple description of its demise. Given the title of this volume, it is natural that the chapter should bring the British – and English, Scottish, Irish, Welsh – aspects of this topic into sharpest relief, whilst situating them in a larger frame.

Rival versions of the obvious

We can begin by taking the most common contemporary form of the religious/secular contrast for granted, and setting this standard model of secularization against a rival version of the 'obvious truth'. The standard model is 'standard' because in Britain and in culturally affiliated societies in Western Europe the argument for a linear movement in identification, belief and practice, from the relatively 'religious' to the rather 'secular' looks compelling. Of course, the patterns of secularization vary in different countries depending on their particular histories, and on whether they are wholly Catholic or Protestant or straddle the Catholic/Protestant border. France is very different from Britain on account of a long conflict between a monopolistic Catholic Church and militant *laïcité* (Martin 1978). Yet the direction of travel is similar (McLeod and Ustorf 2003). The standard model expects the influence of religion in the public realm to decline with 'modernity' until it is no more than a private idiosyncrasy.

Yet comparisons across cultures in modern contexts like the USA and Singapore, and maybe Russia too, complicate the story. These complications, including cases where the story appears to spool back, may jeopardize the standard model, and even encourage some observers to put forward a desecularization thesis. The rival model offers a second reading in a global perspective and regards Western Europe as 'exceptional' (Berger 1999; Berger *et al.* 2008). So, depending on which version you believe, either *God is Dead* (Bruce 2002), or *God is Back* (Micklethwait and Wooldridge 2009).

The rival model posits a resurgence of religion in the public realm as well as in religious identification, belief and practice. It cites the decline of secular nationalism since the late 1970s in Turkey, Iran, India and Israel, and notes that religion played a major role in the collapse of the Soviet Empire, signalled by the election of a Polish Pope in 1979. Orthodoxy is back in the public realm of the Russian Federation and Ukraine, the American Religious Right emerged in the late 1970s and Pentecostalism has rapidly expanded in the 'two-thirds world': hence the label 'post-secular' alongside the label 'post-modern'. In Britain the combination of Islamic resurgence with an American liberal imperialism, in part resting on a conservative evangelical electoral base, has revived a popular view of religion as potentially violent, and made it easy to label varied and ambiguous developments 'fundamentalist'.

None of this worries proponents of the standard model of secularization. Even if we *talk* more about religion, the decline of belief, practice and identification continues, religious people remain concentrated in the older generation and religion has decreasing influence on voting. If 'vicarious religion' or dormant Christianity is still influential – in Britain believing but not actively belonging to a church, or in Scandinavia belonging without believing – that is said to be transitional on the way to full secularity because it is dependent on the active religious minority (Davie 2008; Voas 2007).

The standard model can also deal with the supposed return of religion in the public sphere. The reversals suffered by secular nationalism and secular politics derive from the mobilization of religious masses in Islamic lands and India; fundamentalism in the USA and worldwide is interpreted as a *reaction* to the advance of secularization; in Eastern Europe religion revives when powered by nationalism and rarely recovers the influence it had even a century ago. It can be pointed out that in Britain and Western Europe the mobilization of groups not hitherto heard from, for example through the nonconformist churches once influential in the aspiring working and lower middle classes, and the Catholic Irish, eventually subsided. The empty nonconformist chapels of Wales presage the future of the Christian global revivals. To the extent that Western European conditions are replicated, such as greater equality and the removal of the immediate pressures of survival by the welfare state, as well as individualization and the loosening of all communal bonds, secularization can be predicted to take its course (Norris and Inglehart 2004). What happens in the Balkans has no implications for Western Europe, where micro-nationalisms have mostly shed their religious colouring. The association of religion with the early manifestations of Scottish, Welsh, Ulster and Catholic Irish national consciousness, like the parallel movements in France and Spain, has given way to secular politics.

Those with reservations about both the obvious truth of this standard model of secularization *and* the idea that God is back in the public realm might supplement the debate by pointing to the *continuing* public presence of religion in countries like Britain and Germany – and America for that matter – ever since 1945. European integration owed much to religious influences. For example, the creation of Christian Democratic parties through co-operation between the Vatican, the USA and Protestant lobbies, and the United Nations was a characteristic Anglo-American Liberal Protestant project (Leustean and Madeley 2009). Little has altered recently beyond the political effects of the Muslim migration to Britain and Europe and the admission to the European Union of ethno-religious countries like Poland, Slovakia and Romania. A Christian migration to Britain and Europe hardly signals religious resurgence.

TEXT BOX 22

The New Atheists

The New Atheists are not new if you know the history of the National Secular Society (founded 1866) or The Rationalist Press Association (founded 1899). Nor is the deployment of the authority attributed to science to make incautious pronouncements elsewhere a novelty.

New Atheists promote the inevitable triumph of universal testable truth over the multitudinous delusions of quarrelling faiths and believe these delusions have morally evil consequences, notably in promoting violence. Their excoriating moral vocabulary is perhaps surprising in view of their implicit restriction of truth to empirical and logical propositions. Their indifference to scientific understandings of social phenomena is also surprising – for example, the vast outbreaks of violence not necessarily tied to religion (economic, political, ideological, nationalist, the dynamic of realpolitik and alliances). One way to solve the empirical problem of violence and religion is to define *all* fanaticism as religious and have done with complexity. New Atheists often maintain that religion is a 'hard-wired' infantile delusion *and* demand that people

> freely shake it off. No account seems to be taken of the ease with which 'genetic programmes' are turned on or off by such cultural variables as generation, class and national history, for example in the former East Germany and the Czech Republic, with no functional equivalent of religion to replace it.

Different emphases in the rival models

These rival positions are not simply opposed readings of the evidence, one focused on Western Europe, the other focused globally. They understand the key features of religion differently, privileging some aspects above others. The standard model, for example, derives some of its plausibility from religion understood as mis-cognition or superstition, and as a futile appeal to the causal intervention of supernatural agencies. On this account, religion belongs to the vast corpus of failed science and mythic speculation. This approach omits much of religion, including, for example, most of the Christian repertoire: the sources and resources of being and goodness; presence and absence; incarnation, transformation, trans-figuration and transcendence; faith, hope, peace, love, communion, celebration and the gift relationship; sacrificial death and resurrection; renewal, rebirth, repentance, reconciliation, judgement and forgiveness. Yet mis-cognition plays a sufficiently important role in the stan-dard model and in the assumptions of the New Atheists to merit further comment, before looking at other differences of emphasis.

All human beings believe *beyond* the evidence, but superstition means to believe *against* the evidence. Treating religion as fundamentally superstition underpins a narrative based on science as tested and testable knowledge steadily dispersing religious delusions. Truth-loving scientists face down obscurantist believers and even suffer secular martyrdoms, like Galileo and Bruno. This narrative, which is mythical in its own way, has been subjected to rigorous historical criticism, especially concerning what happened in Britain in the wake of Spencerian and Darwinian theories of evolution, but few doubt that there has been a shift towards naturalistic explanations. From the Lisbon earthquake of 1756 to contemporary floods, tsunamis and earthquakes, the notion that natural phenomena reflect 'acts of God' by way of either favour or judgement has lost credibility. What Paul Hazard labelled the 'crisis in European consciousness' from 1680 to 1715 provides one plausible starting point for this master narrative (Hazard 1953). To call it plausible is not to say it has pride of place among sociologists as the main driver of secularization. Rather, it feeds into a somewhat more plausible master narrative of the advance of technical rationality, or rationalization, in part charting the *indirect* impact of science. It also feeds into a much more dubious master narrative still influential in contemporary Britain based on the march of reason at the expense of religious irrationality and emotionality.

In the social realm there has been a less dramatic shift in understanding towards an unsta-ble combination of the divine will (invoked in both world wars), the consequences of our moral choices, and the social dynamics, causes and contingent events that limit our options and defy prediction. The blood sacrifices demanded by the nation state and the revolution-ary party, often in collusion, in the two world wars and in the Holocaust, had paradoxical consequences. There has been an understandable loss of faith in an optimistic Liberal Protestantism and Progress, but traditional faith is also unpalatable because it reminds people of the abyss of evil. So it is not surprising when British religious leaders are still asked: 'Where was God in Beslan or on 9/11?' Perhaps a God who manipulates events is still around.

The standard model embraces two other presuppositions alongside the march of reason. One is the closely related 'modern' shift from what is imagined as the veiled rhetorical colouring provided by religion to the more detailed and empirically based proposals of politics; the other a much more distantly related shift from dependence to individual autonomy and all the options of personal choice. The growth of individual autonomy and the 'turn to the self' trails a different genealogy from the growth of reason, because it has tangled roots in Christianity itself as well as the various Enlightenments and Romanticism, but it can provide an ancillary presupposition for proponents of the standard model (Taylor 1989).

The alternative model of desecularization trails different assumptions. One of these adopts the idea that groups with an emerging self-consciousness mobilize behind religious banners. If politics fails they may revert to religion. There is no unilateral movement to secular politics. Religion can be bound in with the politics of identity, as it is in India, and stay that way. Once you abandon the idea that religion stands on a preordained downward slope, a space opens up for alternative modes of modernity, some religious and some not (see also Chapter 11 for discussion of modernity).

The alternative model also holds that individuals and communities in a contingent and threatening world seek meaning and purpose. Religion makes sense, even good sense, because it allays perennial anxieties and because social nature abhors a moral and/or a religious vacuum. For the alternative model there must be something sacred thrown up on the screen to display the 'credits' and ideals of the community. In modern Britain this causes anxiety, because the British (or English) 'civil religion' (see Chapter 9) was a contingent union of selected aspects of Christianity, neighbourliness, proverbial wisdom, Stoic courage, and loyalty to country, realm and polity. There is another very loosely related supposition proposed by the American sociologist of religion Rodney Stark, attributing religious apathy to lazy monopolies and lack of vigorous competition (Stark and Finke 2000). Yet Britain has had competition for centuries, which throws the weight of explanation for apathy onto the effects of perceived social establishment and subsequent downward spirals.

Early Christian sources of destabilization

We begin destabilization in earnest by reviewing how Christianity anticipated the religious/secular distinction with the contrast between 'faith' and 'world'. According to Max Weber and Karl Jaspers, religion underwent a crucial mutation about two and half millennia ago by way of an increasing reserve about 'the world' understood as a realm of oppressive violence, power, wealth and sensuality (Weber 1946; Jaspers 1953). Hebrew prophets made semi-successful attempts to secularize the world by rejecting the sacredness of Nature and of Monarchy, and sought to purify religion of ideas of ritual pollution by focusing on doing justly, practising mercy, and loving both God and neighbour (Berger 1967). Christianity increased the tension by rejecting 'the world' of 'the powers' and the wealthy and powerful, as well as the idea of an elect nation in a Promised Land, and the emphasis on sexual reproduction in Genesis. All these concepts were spiritualized in the notion of a living temple realized wherever two or three faithful came together in the body of Christ, and in the idea of a universal New Jerusalem 'above, the mother of us all' (St Paul). The family of procreation became a peaceable fraternity of disciples, later realized in the orders and rules of monasticism and experiments in egalitarian groups or communal living; and ritual pollution gave way to inner purity and sincere obedience to the will of God, so that his kingdom 'come on earth as it is in heaven'.

The contrast of *faith* and *world* complicates our ideas of *religious* and *secular*. And there are reversions, because even though Hebraism secularized the social world of sacred political power and the world of sacred Nature, both returned when Christianity entered the inspirited world of ancient classical religion. Though Christianity converted Jerusalem and the Promised Land into the spiritual goals of our earthly pilgrimage, the sacred returned as Christianity was established in power and threw a protecting veil round the sacred person of the emperor. Rome (or Babylon), once a blood-soaked whore, became a sacred Christian city.

Complications multiply. Christianity anticipates a kingdom that lies in wait, as well as being immanent 'within us' and in the sacraments, here in this *secular* world. This kingdom seeks to overcome the persistent, resistant secular and *worldly* realities of oppressive power, wealth and violence. Christianity drives wedges into resistant secular realities through movements like monasticism, the urban friars, the Magisterial and Radical Reformation and evangelicalism, and inserts subversive subtexts and images, as well as throwing seeds over the wall of the institutional church that fructify anonymously and in combination with seeds from many other sources.

And yet Christianity also conforms to the realities of the world, taking on many of the characteristics of the types of society in which it is incarnated. For example, an evangelical 'spiritual capitalism' still with us today (Hilton 1986). It devises settled rules of engagement between faith and world, the City of God and the City of Man.[1] As for the resistant, persistent secular realities, they achieve a scientific articulation quite late in Christian history through the exposure of the dynamics of power by Machiavelli, of wealth by Adam Smith and political economy, and of survival in Nature and Society alike by Spencer, Darwin, Nietzsche and Freud.

Early modern sources of 'religion'

We now turn to the close link in Britain and early modern Europe between the genesis of our contemporary concepts of the religious and the secular, and the migration of the sacred to sacred monarchy and the 'secular' state (a theme discussed in the Introduction to this book, in relation to the welfare state). The scare quotes around the secular remind us that the state takes on some of the characteristics of the sacred, especially in its modes of justification (*vox populi vox Dei* – the voice of the people – the voice of God), in its ceremonies, its resort to violence and demand for sacrifice.

We return to Cavanaugh (2009) and Asad (1993, 2003). Cavanaugh questions the timeless and transcultural construction of the category of religion, and explores how 'religion' was constructed in early modern Europe according to specific configurations of political power. The religious/secular distinction, like the faith/world distinction, prescribes rules of engagement between the two realms, notably the subordination of religion to the secular state, and even the privatization of religion. The proper role of religion is now to throw a protecting veil over current dispositions of power and wealth.

For Cavanaugh the construction of the religious/secular distinction, and of religion as *specifically* prone to violence, is a founding myth of the liberal state. According to this myth, other societies outside 'the West' have not yet learned to remove the dangerous, divisive and irrational potential of religion from the political sphere, which according to Jürgen Habermas is a space where peaceful conversations can take place based on shared rational criteria (Habermas 2008). But in fact the transfer of power from international church to national state predated the division of Europe into Catholics and Protestants and was a cause, among many, of the violence of the so-called wars of religion, and – with the substitution of treason for heresy – established the ideal of killing and dying for one's country.

'Religion' is a modern word. In medieval times *religio* was simply a mode of devotion and it distinguished clergy in orders (religious) from secular diocesan clergy. Cavanaugh underlines the emergence of two features privileged in the course of the construction of a supposedly universal category of religion: religion as doctrinal proposition and as interior private impulse (see the related analysis by Riis and Woodhead 2010). Calvinism shifts from saving knowledge of election to doctrinal assent, and new conceptions of religion facilitated state dominance by distinguishing inward religion from the political and bodily disciplines of the state.

Asad emphasizes the importance in this development of the European encounter with other imperial systems in Russia, Turkey, China and India as that morphed into the colonial encounter. Colonialism generated two self-serving discoveries, first that other peoples lacked 'religion', and second that their religion could be compared with European religion, though lacking some essential features. This is how Hinduism emerged as a religion and Buddhism as an inward and pacifist religion that might appeal to gentle English people and attract Immanuel Kant, as though it were not as implicated in violence as any other religion or secular ideology (Jerryson and Juergensmeyer 2010). Later, religion was extended along Durkheimian and functionalist lines to include political religion, political Messianism and civil religion, but that is a story too far for our purposes here (Toscano 2010).

The British example

From sacred monarchy to sacred nation

Henry VIII provides a pivotal example from English history of the Renaissance idea of the 'Godly Prince'. In Henry, the centuries-old conflict and collusion of Pope, kings, free cities and Holy Roman Emperor collapsed into a single figure, armed with all the insignia of sacred monarchy. His image engrossed the potency of generational and dynastic continuity, of power and wealth, and of the central sinews of state violence and power. His legacy remains in the form of a more or less autonomous nation and an established if fragile national church. He was first challenged in the name of a supranational Catholic Church by Thomas More and others. The violent suppression of this challenge defined *Roman* Catholicism for centuries as an alien power, associated first with rival nations, like France and Spain, and then with Ireland.

Sacred monarchy was also challenged by Protestants who cherished faith and conscience above conformity and who towards the end of the sixteenth century anticipated the American separation of church and state by asserting the 'free exercise' of religion. Choice may well have been thrown into stark relief by the way successive monarchs made different religious choices according to a principle finally articulated for much of Europe in 1648 by the Treaty of Westphalia. Recusant Catholics and Protestants alike suffered as martyrs for conscience, thereby establishing the supremacy of conscience and conscientious choice in British culture. How this existential autonomy relates historically to the autonomy of individual reason is too tangled a tale to be told here.

The example of Henry VIII was eventually repeated all over Europe, but absolute monarchy came to an end in England in 1689. An increasingly limited monarchy emerged and nationalist sentiment also acquired a comparatively modest hue. The cumulative disruptions and vertiginous shifts of religion under different monarchs and under Protector Cromwell between the 1530s and 1660s probably weakened forever the hold of the established church and slaked the thirst for Puritanism and violent revolution. The checks on monarchical power extended by the constitutional settlement of 1688/1689 were accompanied by a shift towards the sacred character of Parliament, and ensured the English Enlightenment was partly Christian and quite moderate. The English Enlightenment was affiliated with moderate Enlightenments in Scotland, Holland, Switzerland, Germany and North America rather than the increasingly radical Enlightenment in France (Sorkin 2008). The French Enlightenment remained the more influential worldwide, at least among intellectual elites, until finally overtaken by the Anglo-American Enlightenment in the mid-twentieth century (Himmelfarb 2005).

A moderate enlightenment and a weakened established church with a space available for religious Dissent, including Unitarianism, and some free exercise, facilitated the rise of Methodism and further inhibited violent revolution. The increasingly limited monarchy of what became a United Kingdom in 1707 went through various phases, one under Victoria where it was associated with Empire, and another when what had been an Anglican institution became first a generalized Protestant institution and then an institution promising to protect people of all faiths.

The failure fully to establish a sacred monarchy is on all fours with other partial failures and partial realizations in Britain. For example, the failure of industrialism fully to establish its social presence in the world's first industrial country. No principle is driven through to a logical conclusion in social, intellectual, artistic or architectural terms. Even in Scotland there has been no Durkheim or Weber to articulate logically our situation and there have been few signs of the kind of intelligentsia found in France and Germany. The presence of industrial society, for example, is realized architecturally in the classical (and later Gothic) civic centres and mills and canals of Liverpool, Manchester, Leeds and Bradford in industrial northern England, but in London it reaches no farther than the great stations and the warehouses of the port, and the Kensington complex around the Albert Hall (along with the Crystal Palace).

This stalled realization is symptomatic. The established church achieved only a shadowy dominance, the Free churches had their final moment in the sun rather late in the day with the Liberal government of 1906, but then faded and partly collapsed into (or re-emerged inside) the established church, and the movement to re-Catholicize the country and the established church eventually stalled. The English Enlightenment was modest and so too were English Romanticism and modernism. Our modernism conspicuously included poets who articulated an orthodox Christianity, like Eliot and Auden. The pattern of partial realizations ensures that contemporary British politicians seek to occupy the middle ground.

Consider only the architectural dispositions reflecting the modest realization of sacred monarchy in Britain and its continuous overlap with the modest realization of sacred nationhood. Even the Baroque splendours of Blenheim fail to match the palaces of Central Europe. Plans to create great processional ways for London have always collapsed, and there have been no great reorganizations of the city to compare with the cityscapes or royal complexes of Paris, Washington, Vienna, St Petersburg, Berlin (and Potsdam) and the Escorial, let alone their Renaissance prototype in Rome. Chelsea military hospital is not Les Invalides, perhaps because Britain has not been a military nation with a citizen army, but a naval power. The great architectural complex is downriver at the Royal Naval College, Greenwich. Even the avenues of historical and contemporary protest, for example Trafalgar Square, Parliament Square and the Embankment, complementing the processional ways, do not allow the great eruptions facilitated by the boulevards and clear spaces of Washington, Paris and St Petersburg. These great cities excite our admiration because they represent the unimpeded spaces of Enlightenment. Yet Enlightenment, like Christianity and science, has compromised its universal human promise and ideals of perpetual peace to cohabit with absolutism, racism, political messianism, imperialism and the militarization of society presaged by the *levée en masse* (Kidd 2006).

Thus the rather crabbed principles of limited monarchy and constitutional representation in the 1689 Bill of Rights have resulted in implicit understandings and partial realizations, compared with the more explicitly Enlightened declarations of America and France. The most grandiose expressions of monarchy in Britain came with the reinvention of tradition in the late nineteenth and early twentieth centuries in a context of Empire, and its greatest realizations were in the durbars of India and Lutyens's Delhi. Maybe religious buoyancy has some relation to imperial confidence. The history of Empire is written all over church walls and the end of Empire corresponds to an evacuation of sacred space and the end of an idea of England at the heart of Empire with St Paul's as its parish church. What was left in that space was a curious relic of the great period when things were 'made in England', including the rules of sport, above all football. Englishness today expresses itself mainly on the football fields and terraces.

Christian legitimation and subversion

Christianity both legitimated sacred monarchy and sacred nation and subverted them. We need first to canvass the Christian subversion, which may well have found early expression in the Peasants' Revolt of 1381. The subversion was particularly marked in the Radical Reformation as distinct from the Magisterial Reformation of Luther, Calvin and Cranmer. Apart from one or two abortive attempts to set up Christ's kingdom on earth by violence, the Radical Reformation either founded segregated geographical communities or created sects with strong boundaries, and these embodied egalitarian experiments in family structure and forms of communal property. As the boundaries of such groups weakened, the experiments they encapsulated seeped into society at large and generated reform movements in education, industrial organization and penology, as well as promoting anti-slavery and peace movements (Stark 2001).

A genealogy can be traced of radical reform issuing from the impulses of the Radical Reformation and mingling with evangelical charitable impulses, the anti-imperial sentiments of Exeter Hall, utopian thinking and secular projects for the rational and utilitarian reorganization of society. This genealogy extends through all the experiments in creating 'Heavens Below': Heavenly Cities, and New Jerusalems, up to Bourneville, Saltaire and the Quaker Ebenezer Howard's Garden Cities for Tomorrow, and even the creation of New Towns after the Second World War (Hunt 2004 and Introduction to this volume). William Blake exercised a seminal influence here, and radical reform derives in part from the secularization of Christianity implied by the prayer for the kingdom to come on earth as it is in heaven. The examples of John Ruskin and William Morris, the former a Christian, the latter emerging from Christian influences, show how seminal ideas blow over the walls of the institutional church and combine with other seminal materials until it is impossible to attribute them to a single distinctive source (Hughes 2007). Prophetic figures draw on a deep well of Christian reserve about wealth and the love of money. They create an ethos that permeates the cultural and political atmosphere and in particular helps build up a critique of the domination of the ethos of Utility. Of course, the Radical Reformation represents only one subversive genealogy. Pugin's Catholic critique of the 'cold' spirit of classicism is one major expression of Romanticism. The tradition of Catholic social teaching from the 1890s onwards has expanded that Romantic critique and actually underpins contemporary theories of the Big Society (see Chapter 8).

The Catholic critique of inordinate wealth, which exercised increasing influence in the earlier years of the twentieth century, not only reflects the primitive Christian reserve about riches, but picks up on the complex linkage between Calvinism and early capitalism proposed by Max Weber in his *The Protestant Ethic and the Spirit of Capitalism* (Weber 1958). This relates to an internal secularization of Christianity based on the sacred currency of money as embodied in the great commercial cities of early modernity beginning with Florence and Venice, moving to Bruges, Antwerp and Amsterdam before achieving successive incarnations still with us in London and New York (Spufford 2006). Perhaps this is where the secularizing influence of the Jewish faith makes a particular impact, especially when allied to Calvinism in seventeenth-century Amsterdam, London and New Amsterdam, later to become New York in 1664. In Britain, Jews migrating from Europe have provided an intellectual articulation of One Nation Conservatism and of capitalism from Disraeli to Keith Joseph and Oliver Letwin, and have promoted a left-wing or centre-left politics from Laski to Mandelson and the Millibands. Perhaps a case could be made for a Jewish contribution to secularization in Britain comparable to that in France and the United States.

In England, Scotland, Ireland and Wales, men and women have fought for 'king and country' as though they were necessarily packaged together, and have linked classical notions about dying *pro patria* with Christian sentiments about 'laying down your life for your friends'. Contingent packages create auras of necessary association. In France Catholicism appeared linked by necessity to the old monarchical regime, so that an attack on the monarch became an attack on the church. The seemingly necessary links between collapsing elites, regimes, social orders and Christianity have generated critiques and tensions, particularly in Catholic countries, throughout Europe. Nevertheless the links are contingent, and in modern Britain, as elsewhere in Europe outside the ethno-religious cultures, one can trace a loosening of the ties that bind the various elements together. The creation of the General Synod and provisions for Anglican self-government signalled this loosening in England, and the Second Vatican Council coded it for Europe as a whole. In the USA, by contrast, the links were broken long ago with the separation of church and state. In Europe and in the USA alike, 'civil religion' moved into the vacant space, sometimes associated with a generalized Christianity reformulated as Judaeo-Christianity for the sake of inclusiveness. Civil religion does not call together its own version of a Vatican Council.

In England, liturgical change has coded the momentous historic shifts from papal allegiance to the national monarch and the nation, and this was followed in the 1960s by the demotion of the monarch in favour of the church community and its representatives. The loosening of hierarchy and deference has been coded in the reorganization of liturgical space in order to promote communitarian participation, and there are visible analogues in the reorganization of educational, legal and museum space. Yet, as Chapter 2 reminds us, in times of national peril, mourning and celebration, above all when it comes to the idea of the supreme sacrifice, the sacred canopy returns, especially on Remembrance Day and contemporary ceremonies for the Fallen (see also Chapter 6 on changing religious rituals and practices).

The Christian churches, especially since the mid-century, increasingly resemble transnational voluntary associations. During the two World Wars there was an invocation of Britain, and its constituent nations, which included imagery of landscape, and the churches in a landscape, that still has some drawing power. Yet even between the World Wars there was a shift from a national church ready to provide militant rhetorical support for warfare in 1914 to one that in the Second World War provided emotional solace for the combatants

(Snape 2010). The kind of intense identification with the national cause that you find in some French Catholics, such as Péguy, or in the Republican ferocity of Clemenceau, is comparatively rare in Britain, perhaps in part because the country was not invaded and devastated. The Unknown Warrior rests in Westminster Abbey, not in some British equivalent of the Arc de Triomphe.

Social differentiation and the second confessional phase

In Britain there is a disjunction between developments in the intelligentsia, and processes of differentiation partially separating law and education from ecclesiastical and theological aegis and giving rise to denominational sub-cultures from the mid-nineteenth century to the mid-twentieth. The lively sub-cultures of this period, with their ancillary organizations, described by Stephen Yeo in Reading and Simon Green in industrial Yorkshire, constituted what has been labelled the second confessional phase (Blashke 2002; Yeo 1976; Green 1996, 2010). In spite of a shift, for example, to secular education, signalled by the founding of Birkbeck College and University College in London and later a national system of education, as discussed in Chapter 8, the church maintained a major presence in education and socialization through religious instruction and assemblies, training colleges and Sunday Schools, as well as in nonconformist foundations like Birmingham University and Anglican foundations like King's College London.

All this weakened in the 1930s and broke down in the 1960s, and from the 1960s onwards the diminishing and ageing religious sector became just one symptom of slackening social bonds in the areas of political identification and participation, class identity and national identity (McLeod 2007, and Chapter 10 in this volume). In Durkheimian perspective this diminution in the majesty of the Social might be traceable in the easier acceptance of family break-up and homosexuality and the rejection of punitive (or judgemental) social and criminal sanctions, in particular capital and corporal punishment (Davies 2004). The collapse of deference towards the social sacred as represented by Parliament has been signalled by a declining respect for politicians, much accelerated by the exposure in 2009 of the venality of Members of Parliament when claiming expenses, modest though it was by the standards of some European countries. Jean-Paul Willaime has drawn attention to the 'secularization of politics' and the way religious belief is ceasing to be political as it shrugs off the constraint that the sacral model had exercised over all possible representations of society, making collective governance more difficult to exercise (Willaime 2009: 33).

The ambiguous legacy of Romanticism

English Romanticism from about 1800 on was ambiguous with regard to religion. The early Romantics protesting against mechanism and the reduction of colour to 'measurement and line' were not obviously less religious or even less Christian than late eighteenth-century aristocratic sceptics like Horace Walpole, creator of the Gothick mansion at Strawberry Hill, or libertines like Francis Dashwood, creator of the classical Mausoleum at West Wycombe. There is no obvious decline from 1750 to 1850, in spite of the role played by the Enlightenment and the French Revolution in telling the secularization story. The examples of Wordsworth and Coleridge, who returned to Christianity, and in Germany of the painter Caspar David Friedrich, the poet Novalis and the theologian Schleiermacher, underline the religious ambiguity of Romanticism, as does the association of Romanticism with the revival of Catholicism and medievalism.

Yet the individualization embodied in the notion of genius, and the sanctification of Nature and natural impulse, had different implications, and from about 1870 or 1880, one can trace multiple secular movements, political and artistic. In the arts in the 1890s there was an aesthetic movement for which art and creativity were accorded sacred status. Elite attitudes ambivalent about or hostile to religion shifted down the social scale, first with the political radicalism of the 1930s and finally with an anarchist and expressivist radicalism in the 1960s. This influenced a rapidly expanding youth culture and pop culture and was hostile to *all* institutional forms and long-term commitments. A new anti-establishment establishment took over elite institutions like the BBC and the upper echelons of teaching. At the same time a bureaucratic rationalization overtook the universities and created a crisis in the Humanities. Christian clergy and secular clerisy *alike* experienced a threat to their sacred vocation from the market and the spirit of utility. The threat affects all the caring professions and can easily undermine what Paul Halmos called *The Faith of the Counsellors* (Halmos 1965).

Secular sacreds

The words 'faith' and 'sacred' insinuate a further destabilization of the conventional religious/secular divide, now in the context of contemporary spirituality. The distinction between what is sacred, understood as what is pure, special, non-negotiable and of ultimate concern, and what is impure and negotiable, creates a cross-border category with many dimensions, and one that may lie dormant until a *casus belli*, often with legal implications, stimulates an eruption (Knott 2010). As Chapter 1 has shown, the twin affairs of *The Satanic Verses* and the Danish cartoons created sites of contestation between two versions of the sacred – a cherished text and a cherished non-negotiable right to free speech – a contestation made the more complex because the right to free speech was historically located in Milton's classic expression of the Protestant conscience in his *Areopagitica*. Archbishop Rowan Williams's suggestion that some partial recognition be extended to shari'a law exposed the contradiction between liberal demands for the universal application of rights expressed in law, especially women's rights, and liberal respect for the cultural norms of the Other, including the religious Other. Sometimes the problem is not the relativism identified by Pope Benedict but passionate moral intensity (Ratzinger and Pera 2006).

The cross-border category of the sacred encompasses topographical sites, animals – including issues relating to hunting and modes of slaughter – persons, phenomena, events and experiences, and the distinction between natural and unnatural acts. The horror of paedophilia as an 'unspeakable evil' is articulated both by Catholics, who experience the violation of childhood innocence by priests as a shameful humiliation, and by others who have no religious commitment whatever. Moreover this site of contestation is made the more complex because it brings into play a violation of the Christian category of innocent victim, and of the Catholic category of natural law. Natural law, and with it the category of unnatural acts, has been largely abandoned, thereby ranging Liberal Protestants, Catholics *and* the non-religious against secular and religious conservatives, but not when it comes to paedophilia. Perhaps there are other cross-border instances of the sacred that draw on a reservoir of Christianity. These include the invocation by politicians of compassion, including care for neighbours and the vulnerable, and going the extra mile, as well as the rejection of 'unbridled' greed, even though the sanctity of the moral law may be redescribed as 'unacceptable' as in 'the unacceptable face of capitalism', or being 'out of order', or 'socially useless activities'.

Spirituality as a mutation of memory

Some observers see religion, especially spirituality, as a (threatened) chain of memory undergoing constant recomposition and mutation (Davie 2000). Of course, there has always been space for non-institutional religion, for example, Protestant choral societies and north-ern and Welsh choirs singing Handel's *Messiah*. Practical and moral Christians have long fed off the Protestant objection to clerical mediation and dismissed ritual as mumbo jumbo, and they still claim one can be as Christian as pious 'hypocrites' who go to church. But contemporary spirituality is rather different, even though from the nineteenth century onward the search for 'real' religion has been largely powered by objections to the coldness, even the rationalism, of institutional Christianity (Kippenberg 2002, and see Chapter 5 this volume).

From Anglo-Saxon and Norman times until now churches have included pagan imagery and there has been a continuous current of superstition and spiritual agency inside and outside churches, even allowing for the cleansing activities of the Puritans. Angels were once fixed to lofty interiors of churches as intimations of heaven: now they fly freely on the spiritual ether, often to comfort parents mourning dead offspring. As we see in Chapter 4, contemporary paganism now emerges in its own right, part of a trend traceable from Brazil to Estonia. When it comes to re-enchantment we need to discriminate between occult prac-tices, Wicca, spiritualism, meditation, reverence for nature and/or creation, the holistic and therapeutic milieu, Gnosticism, and classical Christian or Eastern mysticism.

One powerful contemporary mutation finds expression in the non-institutional spiritu-ality of the mystical group, forcing us to ask how far spirituality extends Christianity or signals its repudiation. One major expression of contemporary spirituality can be located in the intermittent coming together of like-minded people for protest about ecological depre-dation and global warming, and the ideological genealogies of this activity are very varied. The proliferation of non-governmental organizations like Christian Aid and Amnesty International signals the rise of pressure groups based on values rather than interests. However, many of these draw on Christian initiatives and motivations and arguably continue the Victorian tradition of Christian philanthropy. The Campaign for Nuclear Disarmament was an obvious case of a middle-class movement combining Christian and non-Christian motivations, and embracing a secular eschatology.

Maybe spirituality is the Western version of the explosion of Pentecostalism in the two-thirds world, but without any need for long-term institutional commitment. Insofar as it achieves institutional form, the Charismatic Movement does so among middle-class people seeking moral guidance and discipline for threatened family structures as well as finding a refuge from the stresses of professional life where they can let go and express themselves in company with others, as well as enjoy mutual support.

Conclusion

This chapter began by discussing the 'standard model' of the religious and the secular and the narratives of secularization or 'desecularization' which it supports. It then complicated and destabilized this standard model by discussing alternative understandings and historical outworkings of the religious and the secular, as well as the associated pairings between sacred and profane, and faith and world. These serve to complicate the standard picture of religious decline and secular enlightenment in modern times, and to situate it as part of the history it claims to interpret, rather than an impartial perspective upon it.

In order to explain the background of the 'standard model' and its contemporary plausibility, this chapter has traced the way in which, in Britain, the state, the nation and the law have been partly divested of their sacred aura. These changes have intersected with Christianity's loss of its cultural monopoly as Britain has become more religiously diverse. In dealing with this postcolonial situation, the state has increasingly seen itself as the 'secular' arbiter in the 'religious' field rather than as part of a unified constitutional and cultural nexus of monarchy, church and Parliament. It has relied on the law to adjudicate the status of religious groups, wavering between a notion of them as 'faith communities' and as bodies of belief, and between seeing them as hindrances to and resources for 'social cohesion'.

We have seen that the paradoxes written into the Christian repertoire include a reserve towards 'the world' of power and wealth as well as a divine imprimatur bestowed on authority and productive work. They include other intersecting axes: 'inwardness' as opposed to rule-governed habit, and purity of intention as opposed to rituals focused on tangible icons. Then there is the axis of our Nature and its transformation. Insofar as the world of Nature is an arena of sex and violence, Christianity seeks to transform it, but it also accepts the actual and potential goodness of the created order. All these axes have profound consequences for contemporary faith in Britain, and our conventional categories of the religious and the secular. The 'secular' turns out to be a version of the 'religious' which draws out themes inherent, above all, in Christian tradition.

So inwardness and the suspicion of mediated authority were both accentuated by Protestantism, and have migrated into a strong sense of existential autonomy and authenticity. They are expressed in emphases on transparency and sincerity that threaten to undermine the viability of political, religious and educational institutions alike. The suspicion of tangible icons of beneficence and of prophylactic spiritual power, such as flourish in Eastern and Southern Europe, still retains its hold on institutional religion, and even affects Catholicism following the purifications endorsed by Vatican II. Though tangible icons have found some acceptance in contemporary Christianity, for example in the lighting of candles, the modes of protection have mostly migrated elsewhere, and are particularly luxuriant in the rituals surrounding death. Here we move uneasily between 'spiritual' categories and scientific or pseudo-scientific categories. Anthropologists distinguish between the imagistic and the doctrinal, and maintain that the latter leads to boredom. Therein lies, maybe, the decline of the sermon, the political speech, the lecture and even articulate speech.

Similar changes have affected the disciplines of the self. These have a long and profound history in Christianity from the desert fathers to Puritanism, evangelicalism and of the Counter-Reformation. They have been partly revived in the churches, for example in retreats and pilgrimages, but they mostly flourish elsewhere as techniques of 'wellness', 'wellbeing' and 'human flourishing'. When it comes to our social and human nature, traditional Christianity identifies a powerful resistance to the good, not only with respect to sex and violence but also to all forms of pride and concupiscence, a resistance curiously echoed in socio-biology and genetics. The vocabulary of the cross, of sacrifice and sin is located here, often incidentally allied with Stoic ideas of service, self-control and duty.

Though Liberal Protestantism plays down sin it re-emerges in chronic forms of free-floating guilt and the cult of apology, just as the divine victim re-emerges in the cult of victimhood. About sex, contemporary society is chronically ambivalent. About violence, however, Christian reservations, carried forward by the Radical Reformation, supplemented by other seminal ideas, some of Eastern provenance, have found expression in vegetarianism, the abolition of corporal and capital punishment, and a general suspicion of the disciplines and the hierarchy associated with the police and the military. The contradictions evident about sex are echoed in a demand for control of the unruly alongside approbation for 'letting it all hang out'.

What finally of the world of Nature? Contemporary attitudes reach back to early Romanticism, if not earlier. Wordsworth used the Christian category of 'the world' to complain that 'the world is too much with us ... getting and spending we lay waste our powers' and this finds an echo in 'post-materialism'. For Christianity the world is good, but marred, and the sacraments are colonies of 'the Kingdom', signifying and embodying its potential redemption. The Harvest Festival as a typical 'sacrament' of the Romantic era was an early intimation of a care for the natural productivity of the earth. Now the idea of sacrament floats freely in a world of 'spiritual' signifiers that includes the sanctification of the whole world of Nature, its fruits, its resources and its teeming life forms. The theologian Albert Schweitzer coined the phrase 'reverence for life' to summarize Christianity. Paradoxically in Britain, this has become a quasi-universal sentiment as much outside the church as within it.

The minority religions in Britain today have their own different histories of tension and collusion with 'the world', whereby what is here divided into the religious and the secular is configured in all sorts of different ways, and may simply be the way people live. The 'secular' world of Britain, which they have to inhabit and negotiate, is a continuing deposit of the cultural history of Christendom.

Key terms

Civil religion: When a society becomes sacred, or a religion infuses a society to such an extent that the religion inheres in the 'civil unit' itself; a people, group, nation or state imbued with a semi-sacred quality; a 'chosen people'.

Durkheim: Émile Durkheim (1858–1917), French sociologist who argued that religion is where a society holds up an ideal of itself and worships itself; the sacred is 'Society'.

Evangelicalism: A pan-denominational movement within Protestantism (with roots in the Reformation, but which has flourished in the twentieth and twenty-first centuries) which emphasizes the authority of the Bible, a commitment to personal conversion and sharing the gospel.

Exeter Hall: A purpose-built building for mainly religious meetings on the Strand in London, completed in 1831 and demolished in 1970; particularly associated with meetings of Protestant groups and societies, often with philanthropic and reforming aims, e.g. anti-slavery.

Levée en masse: Mass conscription to a national army (as in the French Revolutionary Wars).

Magisterial Reformation: A general term which includes the various strands of the sixteenth-century Protestant Reformation which achieved greatest power and which were less politically radical than those of the 'Radical Reformation', most notably Lutheranism and Calvinism (also called Presbyterianism).

Radical Reformation: A general term which refers to a wide variety of religious reform movements of the Protestant Reformation (starting in the sixteenth century) which were more radical in their politics (more critical of the status quo, and often more egalitarian) than the movements of the 'Magisterial Reformation'. For example, Anabaptists and Quakers.

Recusant: In the history of England and Wales, the 'recusants' were those who remained faithful to the Catholic Church after the English Reformation and refused to attend services of the Church of England.

Sacred: A category which can refer to 'Society' (e.g. a sacred monarchy), or to sacred Nature, or to varied 'special' phenomena (practices, texts, sites, etc.), or non-negotiable principles.

Secularism: Ideologies advocating secularization.

Secularity: The condition of being secular.

Secularization: The movement from religious to secular.

Urban friars: Christian movements of the later medieval period which were associated with the growing cities of Europe, and which advocated a radical form of discipleship and imitation of Christ, including poverty – e.g. the Franciscans. They were absorbed into the Catholic Church.

Voluntarism: Situations where you choose your religion rather than belonging to it automatically by birth.

Westphalian Settlement: The Treaty of Westphalia (1648) finalized the reverse situation to voluntarism, still largely present today, where there is a majority religion acquired by birth in a particular territory.

NB The chapter assumes a typology: a *church* (a large group, often related to power and territory); a *denomination* (a free church with a tradition of conversion, e.g. Methodism, the Evangelical Revival); a *sect* (a bounded, tight community, often encapsulating radical counter-cultural principles, e.g. the Quakers in the Radical Reformation).

Further reading

Beckford, James A. and N. Jay Demerath III (eds) (2007). *The SAGE Handbook of the Sociology of Religion*. London: Sage. An important sourcebook, especially chapters on 'Civil religion' (Chapter 13), 'Secularization' (Chapter 3), 'Cross-national European comparisons' (Chapter 22) and 'Assessing modernities' (Chapter 2).

Martin, David (2005). *On Secularization: Towards a Revised General Theory*. Aldershot: Ashgate. Picks up on the author's *General Theory* with overviews of the debate on secularization in the Introduction, Chapters 1 and 9, and of religion in Europe in Chapters 3–8.

McLeod, Hugh (ed.) (2006). *The Cambridge History of Christianity: World Christianities c.1914–c.2000*. Cambridge: Cambridge University Press. Important sourcebook, especially introductory and concluding chapters and Chapter 36 by Hugh McLeod, comparing Christianity at the beginning and end of the twentieth century.

Molendijk, Arie L., Justin Beaumont and Christoph Jedan (eds) (2010). *Exploring the Postsecular: The Religious, the Political and the Urban*. Leiden and Boston: Brill. Important source, particularly Parts 1 and 2 raising all the issues of exploring the field and conceptualizing the post-secular.

Taylor, Charles (2007). *A Secular Age*. Cambridge, MA: Harvard University Press. Brings together the author's work from the classic book on *The Sources of the Self* to the present, and compares the worldview of 1500 with 'the immanent frame' of 2000. Chapter 15 offers major clues.

References

Asad, Talal (1993). *Genealogies of Religion: Discipline and Reasons of Power in Christianity and Islam*. Baltimore, MD: Johns Hopkins University Press.

Asad, Talal (2003). *Formations of the Secular: Christianity, Islam, Modernity*. Stanford, CA: Stanford University Press.

Berger, Peter L. (1967). *The Sacred Canopy: Elements of a Sociological Theory of Religion*. New York, NY: Doubleday.

Berger, Peter L. (1999). 'The Desecularization of the World: A Global Overview', in Peter L. Berger (ed.), *The Desecularization of the World: Resurgent Religion and World Politics*. Grand Rapids, MI: Eerdmans, 1–18.

Berger, Peter, Grace Davie and Effie Fokas (2008). *Religious America, Secular Europe? A Theme and Variations*. Aldershot: Ashgate.

Blashke, Otto (ed.) (2002). *Konfessionen in Konflikt: Deutschland zwischen 1800–1970. Ein Zweiter Konfessionelles Zeitalter*. Göttingen: Göttingen University Press.

Bruce, Steve (2002). *God is Dead: Secularization in the West*. Oxford and Malden, MA: Blackwell.

Cavanaugh, William (2009). *The Myth of Religious Violence: Secular Ideology and the Roots of Modern Conflict*. Oxford: Oxford University Press.

Davie, Grace (2000). *Religion in Modern Europe: A Memory Mutates*. Oxford: Oxford University Press.

Davie, Grace (2007). 'From Believing without Belonging to Vicarious Religion', in Detlef Pollak and Daniel Olson (eds), *The Role of Religion in Modern Societies*. London: Routledge, 165–176.

Davies, Christie (2004). *The Strange Death of Moral Britain*. London: Transaction.

Green, S. J. D. (1996). *Religion in the Age of Decline: Organisation and Experience in Industrial Yorkshire, 1870–1920*. Cambridge: Cambridge University Press.

Green, S. J. D. (2010). *The Passing of Protestant England: Secularisation and Social Change, c.1920–1960*. Cambridge: Cambridge University Press.

Habermas, Jürgen (2008). *Between Naturalism and Religion: Philosophical Essays*. Cambridge: Polity.

Halmos, Paul (1965). *The Faith of the Counsellors*. London: Constable.

Hazard, Paul (1953). *The European Mind, 1680–1715*. London: Hall and Carter.

Hilton, Boyd (1986). *The Age of Atonement: Influence of Evangelicalism on Social Thought, 1795–1865*. Oxford: Oxford University Press.

Himmelfarb, Gertrude (2005). *The Roads to Modernity: The British, French and American Enlightenments*. New York, NY: Vintage.

Hughes, John (2007). *The End of Work: Theological Critiques of Capitalism*. Oxford: Blackwell.

Hunt, Tristram (2004). *Building Jerusalem: The Rise and Fall of the Victorian City*. London: Weidenfeld and Nicolson.

Jaspers, Karl (1953). *The Origin and Goal of History*, trans. Michael Bullock. New Haven, CT: Yale University Press.

Jerryson, Michael and Mark Juergensmeyer (eds) (2010). *Buddhist Warfare*. Oxford: Oxford University Press.

Kidd, Colin (2006). *The Forging of Races: Race and Scripture in the Protestant Atlantic World, 1600–2000*. Cambridge: Cambridge University Press.

Kippenberg, Hans (2002). *Discovering Religious History in the Modern Age*. Princeton, NJ: Princeton University Press.

Knott, Kim (2010). 'Theoretical and Methodological Resources for Breaking Open the Secular and Exploring the Boundary between Religion and Non-religion', *Historia Religionum*, 2: 115–134.

Leustean, Lucian N. and John T. S. Madeley (2009). 'Religion, Politics and the Law in the European Union: An Introduction', *Religion, State and Society*, 37/1–2: 3–18.

McLeod, Hugh (2007). *The Religious Crisis of the 1960s*. Oxford: Oxford University Press.

McLeod, Hugh and Werner Usdorf (eds) (2003). *The Decline of Christendom in Western Europe, 1750–2000*. Cambridge: Cambridge University Press.

Martin, David (1978). *A General Theory of Secularization*. Oxford: Blackwell.

Micklethwait, John and Adrian Wooldridge (2009). *God is Back: How the Global Rise of Faith is Changing the World*. London: Penguin.

Norris, Pippa and Ronald Inglehart (2004). *Sacred or Secular: Religion and Politics Worldwide*. Cambridge: Cambridge University Press.

Ratzinger, Joseph and Marcello Pera (2006). *Without Roots: The West, Relativism, Christianity, Islam*. New York, NY: Basic Books.

Riis, Ole and Linda Woodhead (2010). *A Sociology of Religious Emotion*. Oxford: Oxford University Press.

Snape, Michael (2010). 'War, Religion and Revival: The United States, British and Canadian Armies during the Second World War', in Callum G. Brown and Michael Snape (eds), *Secularisation in the Christian World*. Farnham: Ashgate, 135–158.

Sorkin, David (2008). *The Religious Enlightenment: Protestants, Jews and Catholics from London to Vienna*. Princeton, NJ: Princeton University Press.

Spufford, Peter (2006). 'From Antwerp and Amsterdam to London', *De Economist*, 154: 143–175.

Stark, Rodney (2001). *One True God: Historical Consequences of Monotheism*. Princeton, NJ and Oxford: Princeton University Press.

Stark, Rodney and Roger Finke (2000). *Acts of Faith: Explaining the Human Side of Religion*. Berkeley, CA: University of California Press.

Taylor, Charles (1989). *Sources of the Self: The Making of the Modern Identity*. Cambridge: Cambridge University Press.

Toscano, Alberto (2010). *Fanaticism: On the Uses of an Idea*. London and New York, NY: Verso.

Voas, David (2007). 'The Continuing Secular Transition', in Detlef Pollak and Daniel Olson (eds), *The Role of Religion in Modern Societies*. London and New York, NY: Routledge, 25–48.

Weber, Max (1946). 'Religious Rejections of the World and their Direction', in *From Max Weber: Essays in Sociology*, edited and translated by H. H. Gerth and C. Wright Mills. Oxford: Oxford University Press, 323–358.

Weber, Max (1958). *The Protestant Ethic and the Spirit of Capitalism*, trans. Talcott Parsons. New York, NY: Scribner.

Willaime, Jean-Paul (2009). 'European Integration, *Laïcité* and Religion', *Religion, State and Society*, 27:1/2: 23–35.

Yeo, Stephen (1976). *Religion and Voluntary Organisations in Crisis*. London: Croom Helm.

Note

1   From Augustine to Marsilio and Dante, and (in England) from William of Ockham to T. S. Eliot by way of Hooker, Fox, Locke, Coleridge, Newman, Ruskin and Maurice.

Index